Necessity and Proportionality in International Peace and Security Law

This is not an official publication of the United States Military Academy, Department of the Army, or Department of Defense. The views expressed in this volume represent the authors' personal views and do not necessarily reflect those of the Department of Defense, the United States Army, the United States Military Academy, or any other department or agency of the United States government. The analysis presented stems from their academic research of publicly available sources, not from protected operational information.

The Lieber Studies is one of the two flagship publications of the Lieber Institute for Law and Land Warfare. It is designed to provide scholars, practitioners, and students with in-depth and critical analysis of the most challenging legal issues related to warfare in the 21st Century. Established by the Department of Law of the United States Military Academy at West Point, the mission of the Lieber Institute is to foster a deeper understanding of the complex and evolving relationship between law and land warfare in order to educate and empower current and future combat leaders. It does so through global academic engagement and advanced interdisciplinary research. As such, it lies at the crossroads of scholarship and practice by bringing together scholars, military officers, government legal advisors, and members of civil society from around the world to collaboratively examine the role and application of the law of armed conflict in current and future armed conflicts, as well as that of other regimes of international law in situations threatening international peace and security.

Lieber Institute for Law and Land Warfare
The Lieber Studies

VOLUME 5

Necessity and Proportionality in International Peace and Security Law

---

General Editor

PROFESSOR MICHAEL N. SCHMITT

Managing Editors

COLONEL SHANE R. REEVES

LIEUTENANT COLONEL WINSTON S. WILLIAMS

DR. SASHA RADIN

Volume Editors

PROFESSOR CLAUS KREß

MAJOR ROBERT LAWLESS

OXFORD
UNIVERSITY PRESS

OXFORD
UNIVERSITY PRESS

Oxford University Press is a department of the University of Oxford. It furthers the University's objective of excellence in research, scholarship, and education by publishing worldwide. Oxford is a registered trade mark of Oxford University Press in the UK and certain other countries.

Published in the United States of America by Oxford University Press
198 Madison Avenue, New York, NY 10016, United States of America.

Library of Congress Cataloging-in-Publication Data

Names: Kress, Claus, editor. | Lawless, Robert (Lawyer), editor. | Lieber Institute for Law and Land Warfare (United States Military Academy), sponsoring body.
Title: Necessity and proportionality in international peace and security law / volume editors, Professor Claus Kress, Major Robert Lawless.
Description: New York, NY : Oxford University Press, 2021 | Series: The Lieber studies; volume 5 | Includes bibliographical references and index.
Identifiers: LCCN 2020014821 (print) | LCCN 2020014822 (ebook) | ISBN 9780197537374 (hardback) | ISBN 9780197537398 (epub) | ISBN 9780197537404 (online) | ISBN 9780197537381 (updf)
Subjects: LCSH: Intervention (International law) | Necessity (International law) | Propostionality in law.
Classification: LCC KZ6368 .N43 2020 (print) | LCC KZ6368 (ebook) | DDC 341.5—dc23
LC record available at https://lccn.loc.gov/2020014821
LC ebook record available at https://lccn.loc.gov/2020014822

9 8 7 6 5 4 3 2

Printed by Integrated Books International, United States of America

Note to Readers
This publication is designed to provide accurate and authoritative information in regard to the subject matter covered. It is based upon sources believed to be accurate and reliable and is intended to be current as of the time it was written. It is sold with the understanding that the publisher is not engaged in rendering legal, accounting, or other professional services. If legal advice or other expert assistance is required, the services of a competent professional person should be sought. Also, to confirm that the information has not been affected or changed by recent developments, traditional legal research techniques should be used, including checking primary sources where appropriate.

(Based on the Declaration of Principles jointly adopted by a Committee of the American Bar Association and a Committee of Publishers and Associations.)

CONTENTS

FOREWORD

MILITARY NECESSITY AND PROPORTIONALITY IN INTERNATIONAL PEACE AND SECURITY LAW

The legal obligation of any professional military to wage war in a just and lawful manner remains unquestioned. This commitment includes constraints both in the decision whether to use military force (the *jus ad bellum*) as well as in the conduct of hostilities during armed conflict (the law of armed conflict or *jus in bello*), the combination of which this volume refers to as International Peace and Security Law.

Adherence to these legal regimes remains a bedrock value of professional militaries. Yet each regime's rules are regularly challenged. In particular, in the law of armed conflict context, proponents of increased requirements—often in the form of further restrictions—argue that such requirements will better protect innocent civilians. And in some cases, they may. But ever more legal restraint leads to inherent tension in the system. As every combat-tested leader knows, the enduring reality in armed conflict is an unquestioned necessity for operational flexibility and clarity in fundamental legal requirements. Furthermore, professional militaries operate under the fundamental principle that law of armed conflict restraints apply regardless of the willingness of an opponent to abide by those same restraints. This bedrock principle, coupled with the *jus ad bellum* notion that in war there are both just and unjust parties, may undermine the thesis that the uncritical piling on of the law of armed conflict restraints necessarily leads to less costly war. Battle-tested soldiers with moral clarity understand these concerns. But this is not enough, because differences in the understanding between militaries and the societies they serve over the scope of the fundamentals of the law governing military force are at best risky. At its worst, however well-intentioned, confusion further burdens those in the greatest immediate risk of physical danger with a corresponding risk of long-term legal jeopardy to the continued and proper functioning of the legal order.

Rapid, exponential advances in technology, or even new techniques in the asymmetric employment of simpler, long-standing technology, routinely create new challenges to the law's scope, meaning, and application. Even with such changes, *lex lata* remains the coin of the realm. Visionary senses of *lex ferenda* are often well received by the body politic. However gallant the intent, foundational legal principles must remain inviolate. Attempting to reframe the moral or ethical application of International Peace and Security Law may undermine the decision-making space of commanders, reduces their flexibility, and, as an unintended consequence, limits the options they have to lawfully, effectively, and quickly eliminate an opposing force and hopefully set conditions favorable to a return to law and order.

In the context of the law of armed conflict, Francis Lieber's General Orders No. 100 and the World War II–era *Hostage Case* reiterated the first of two realities this book addresses: military necessity permits a belligerent, subject to the law of armed conflict, to apply *any* amount and kind of force to compel the complete submission of the enemy with the least possible expenditure of time, life, and money.[1] The second reality is equally brutal in that the restraint imposed by the principle of proportionality requires combatants to refrain from attacks in which the expected loss or injury to civilians and damage to civilian objects incidental to such attacks would be excessive in relation to the contract and direct military advantage expected to be gained. Yet, injury—even death—and damage—even great damage—are not only not prohibited but expected. In the *jus ad bellum* context, the principles of necessity and proportionality play a crucial limiting role when a state considers using military force in accordance with the U.N. Charter.

The continuing dialogue about the nature and content of International Peace and Security Law owes much of its impassioned advocacy to this confluence of the long-standing clarity that results in well-trained practice and the desire to always do more and do better. In the discussion, practitioners must listen; advocates must too. This volume from the Lieber Institute for Law and Land Warfare builds upon a robust body of previous works and critically addresses the challenges professional armies already face in the conduct of hostilities. These essays, reflecting the experiences of military practitioners and intellectual thought of noteworthy scholars, help frame the discussion necessary to arm our nation's and the allies and partners alongside whom we fight, with the clearest possible understanding of what the law requires. That clarity informs the training that, in the moment, allows those uniquely tasked with the lawful application of lethal violence, to get it right. From our nation's earliest days, and through even our darkest hours, advisors like Francis Lieber ensured leaders like Abraham Lincoln made clear our shared commitment to established legal standards in warfare. The commitment endures. This dialogue must inform it.

Brigadier General Joseph B. Berger III
Commander and Commandant
The Judge Advocate General's Legal Center and School

1. United States v. List (The Hostage Case), Case No. 7 (Feb. 19, 1948), *reprinted in* 11 Trials of War Criminals Before the Nuremberg Military Tribunals Under Control Council Law No. 10, at 757, 1253 (1950); *see also* Dep't of the Army, FM 27–10, The Law of Land Warfare ¶ 3(a), at 1–7 (1956).

CONTRIBUTORS

Brigadier General Joseph B. Berger III is the Commander and Commandant of the U.S. Army Judge Advocate General's Legal Center and School.

Adam Brown is an Associate Professor of Psychology at the New School for Social Research, a clinical psychologist, Director of the Trauma and Global Mental Health Lab, and an Adjunct Assistant Professor at New York University School of Medicine.

Geoffrey S. Corn is the Vinson & Elkins Professor of Law at South Texas College of Law.

Elisabeth Günnewig is a Judge in the District Court in Aachen, Germany.

Sarah Knuckey is an Associate Clinical Professor of Law, Director of the Human Rights Clinic, and Co-Director of the Human Rights Institute at Columbia Law School.

Claus Kreß is Professor of Public International Law and Criminal Law. He is Director of the Institute for International Peace and Security Law and Chair for German and International Criminal Law at the University of Cologne.

Dino Kritsiotis is a Professor of Public International Law at the University of Nottingham.

Masahiro Kurosaki is an Associate Professor of International Law and the Director of the Study of Law, Security, and Military Operations at the National Defence Academy of the Japanese Ministry of Defence.

Major Robert Lawless is a Judge Advocate in the U.S. Army Judge Advocate General's Corps.

Eliav Lieblich is an Associate Professor at Tel-Aviv University.

Audrey McCalley is a public health professional who graduated from Columbia University. She specialized in the intersection of the social and medical sciences as well as sustainability issues.

Jeff McMahan is the White's Professor of Moral Philosophy at the University of Oxford.

Rebecca Mignot-Mahdavi is a PhD candidate in Law at the European University Institute.

Alex Moorehead is a Human Rights Officer at the U.N. Office of the High Commissioner for Human Rights.

Stefan Oeter is a Professor of German and Comparative Law and Public International Law at the University of Hamburg.

Jens David Ohlin is a Vice Dean and Professor of Law at Cornell Law School.

Sasha Radin is Director of Research and Publications at the Lieber Institute for Law and Land Warfare.

Colonel Shane Reeves is Professor and Head of the Department of Law at the U.S. Military Academy. He is also Co-Director of the Lieber Institute for Law and Land Warfare.

Tom Ruys is a Professor of International Law at Ghent University.

Michael Schmitt is the Distinguished Lieber Scholar at the U.S. Military Academy. He is also Professor of Public International Law at the University of Reading, Strauss Center Distinguished Scholar and Visiting Professor of Law at the University of Texas, and Professor Emeritus at the U.S. Naval War College.

Larissa van den Herik is the Vice Dean and a Professor of Public International Law at Leiden University.

Wolff Heintschel von Heinegg is Chair of Public Law at European University Viadrina.

Sean Watts is Professor and Co-Director of the Lieber Institute for Law and Land Warfare.

Lieutenant Colonel Winston S. Williams is an Academy Professor in the Department of Law at the U.S. Military Academy.

INTRODUCTION

Necessity and proportionality occupy a firm place in the international law governing the use of force by states. Perhaps most importantly for practical purposes, the exercise of the right of self-defense, as recognized in Article 51 of the U.N. Charter, is subject to the requirements of necessity and proportionality, as the International Court of Justice determined in the *Nicaragua* case.[1] Necessity and proportionality are also firmly anchored in the international law governing armed conflicts. In its Nuclear Weapons Advisory Opinion, the International Court of Justice even referred to one articulation of the idea of necessity, that directed against the causing of unnecessary suffering, as one of two "cardinal principles" of this body of law.[2] However, beyond statement in such general terms, the realms of uncertainty and controversy soon begin. It is far from clear, for example, how to distinguish with precision between necessity and proportionality in the international law on self-defense and, in immediate connection herewith, what it means precisely to say that forcible action taken in the exercise of self-defense must be proportionate. It is all the less clear what legal significance, if any, necessity and proportionality possess in other contexts of the international law governing the use of force.

Moving to the international law governing armed conflicts, the picture does not change fundamentally. Regarding necessity, that notion traditionally being referred to as "military necessity" in this specific legal context, the fact that the law, explicitly or implicitly, refers to it at various places and in the form of different formulations presents a first challenge. As far as military necessity is concerned, the broad consensus on its foundational and thus overarching character goes hand in hand with an apparent lack of a shared understanding about the principle's basic function and its possible significance in the interpretation of specific conduct rules. While in that respect there would seem to be a fairly robust

1. Military and Paramilitary Activities in and Against Nicaragua (Nicar. v. U.S.), Judgment, 1986 I.C.J. Rep. 14, ¶ 176 (June 27).

2. Legality of the Threat or Use of Nuclear Weapons, Advisory Opinion, 1996 I.C.J. 226, ¶ 78 (July 8).

Introduction In: *Necessity and Proportionality in International Peace and Security Law.* Edited by: Professor Claus Kreß and Captain Robert Lawless, Oxford University Press (2021). © Oxford University Press. DOI: 10.1093/oso/9780197537374.003.0001.

consensus concerning the principle of proportionality under *jus in bello*, it is striking that the high frequency of that principle's invocation by political actors on the international plane correlates with an enormous difficulty experienced by international lawyers in the application of the principle to concrete sets of facts. The legal complexity gets even more significant if an attempt is made to carefully delineate between *jus ad bellum* and *jus in bello* considerations of proportionality.

Against this background, I considered it worthwhile to use the honorable invitation to serve as the 2018 Francis Lieber scholar to make necessity and proportionality in international peace and security law the topic of the Lieber Institute's 2018 annual workshop. Fortunately, a considerable number of highly distinguished experts followed Major Robert Lawless's and my invitation to West Point where, while enjoying the prestigious academy's usual hospitality and its excellent conference infrastructure, we held an intensive and most productive three-day workshop in October 2018. The presentations and their discussion at that occasion have laid the ground for what has become this book. We have sought a few further contributions, which we thought would nicely complement those emerging from the workshop.

The volume opens with two chapters of an overarching nature: Jeff McMahan introduces the international lawyer to the state of the discussion in international ethics and more specifically to how the concepts of necessity and proportionality are understood in this scholarly discipline. In including this chapter, we do not take a position on the status of a moral argument, if any, in construing the content of an existing rule of international law. But we suggest that at least any proper legal policy reflection about how best to articulate necessity and proportionality as principles of international peace and security law should take into account the discussion on those principles in international ethics. The fact that McMahan identifies important divergences between morality and law when it comes to the subject matter of this book should therefore give the international lawyer reason to pause. Eliav Lieblich then makes the case that the *jus ad bellum* principle of proportionality applies throughout the armed conflict. The question is not new, but it had not received an analysis of such depth and circumspection as that contained in Lieblich's chapter. From that basis, Lieblich takes up the further challenge to spell out in more concrete terms than it is usually done how the principles of *jus ad bellum* and *jus in bello* proportionality apply concurrently during hostilities. In his view, it is possible to apply those two proportionality principles concurrently and yet to respect their functional separation, the latter being necessary because the *jus ad bellum* requires a legality judgment as regards the recourse to force as such while the conduct of hostilities is governed by the *jus in bello* principle of belligerent equality.

Geoffrey S. Corn then cautions against emphasizing the distinctiveness of necessity and proportionality as requirements for a lawful exercise of the right of self-defense. In his view, it is preferable to conceptualize *jus ad bellum* proportionality as an integral component of the overall necessity of forcible action taken in self-defense. Such an overall necessity requirement would include necessity as the trigger for the lawful recourse to defensive force and necessity governing the scope and duration of such forcible action. This latter component of an overall necessity requirement, in Corn's view, best articulates the proper meaning of *jus ad bellum* proportionality. While Corn's approach to *jus ad bellum* proportionality may initially seem provocative to some, it may in fact far better capture the often so-called functional understanding of that requirement, as it was prominently articulated by International Law Commission's Articles on State Responsibility Special Rapporteur Roberto Ago[3] than an emphasis on the distinctiveness of necessity and proportionality as requirements for the lawful exercise of the right of self-defense under international law. Corn makes it explicit that his position is incompatible with an often so-called quantitative understanding of *jus ad bellum* proportionality, which includes a balancing of (anticipated) harm, and he engages in a detailed criticism of the latter view. One of Corn's considerations is that the quantitative approach is conducive to a conflation between *jus ad bellum* and *jus in bello* proportionality, among which, so the argument runs, the latter principle may claim the exclusive competence for a balancing of (anticipated) harm. In this respect and also as regards the question of a concurrent application of *jus ad bellum* and *jus in bello* proportionality, I would encourage reading the chapters by Lieblich and Corn in close comparison.

Jens David Ohlin and Rebecca Mignot-Mahdavi discuss the requirement of *ad bellum* proportionality in connection with forcible cross-border state action in response to or in anticipation of non-state violence. Ohlin begins by presenting an innovative rationale for justifying the infringement upon the non-state actor's host state's territorial sovereignty entailed in a forcible state response to a non-state armed attack. He then suggests that a unique proportionality standard should govern such state action in view of the fact that the normative status of the host state is stronger than that of a state that has itself committed an armed attack. Mignot-Mahdavi shows in considerable empirical detail to what extent the more recent use of armed drones by several Western states has given rise to the invocation of the right of self-defense in instances where the violent threat emanates from allegedly dangerous individuals rather than from aggressive non-state organizations. In Mignot-Mahdavi's view, such an individualization of the right of self-defense entails a veritable chain of problematic consequences including, not least, a significant diminishing of the restraining function of the requirement of *jus ad bellum* proportionality.

Tom Ruys's chapter moves the discussion beyond self-defense into the realm of forcible action within a state. He discusses the question whether, as a matter of *lex ferenda*, an additional *jus ad bellum* layer is needed to restrain the internal government use of force against rebels. In that context, Ruys takes up the question occasionally asked in the literature whether it is possible for a state government under the *lex lata* to escalate a situation of internal tension to the level of a

3. Robert Ago, Int'l L. Comm'n, Addendum to the Eighth Report on State Responsibility, ¶¶ 119–21, U.N. Doc. A/CN.4/318/ADD.5-7 (Feb. 29, 1980, June 10, 1980, & June 19, 1980), *reprinted in* [1980] 2 (pt. 1) Y.B. Int'l L. Comm'n 13, 68–70 (1980).

non-international armed conflict in order to move from the law enforcement paradigm, which is governed by a rigorous human rights necessity standard, to the more permissive conduct of hostilities paradigm. In that context, Ruys observes that the existence of the conflict classification requirement of a sufficiently organized non-state party is beyond the government's control. This leads him to make the intriguing suggestion that the twin requirements of intensity and organization, and specifically the latter one, to a certain extent operate as an implicit proportionality barrier preventing the government from unduly moving from the law enforcement to the conduct of hostilities paradigm in dealing with a violent internal opposition. Ruys then turns the direction of inquiry around and asks, as it has been done in the more recent literature, whether the right of an individual under domestic legal orders to exercise self-defense under strict conditions of necessity and proportionality might get supplemented, as a matter of *lex ferenda*, by an international legal right of armed resistance by a civilian population subject to an attack by its government rising to the level of a crime against humanity or genocide. In that context, Ruys devotes closer attention than was done before to the question what formidable challenge it poses to give necessity and proportionality their proper place in circumscribing such a novel right to armed resistance.

The volume's coverage of questions pertaining to *jus ad bellum* necessity and proportionality concludes with Larissa van den Herik's exploration of how the relevant discourse could be enhanced through the widening and deepening of Security Council reporting requirements, the starting point for this analysis in the *lex lata* obviously being the reporting requirement in Article 51 of the U.N. Charter. Van den Herik's chapter presents an inspiring argument for interpreting the latter requirement so that it acquires a content that is meaningful in practice. She further inquires about extending the reporting requirement into the realm of instances of the use of force which have traditionally been referred to as "interventions by invitation." Van den Herik also submits concrete proposals for the creation of an institutional environment which would enable a richer discourse among states, including third states, on the legality of the use of force in the international relations including not least considerations of necessity and proportionality.

From here the volume moves to the international law governing armed conflicts. In the first two chapters of this segment, Dino Kritsiotis and Major Robert Lawless deal with the notion (and various articulations) of military necessity at a conceptual level. Kritsiotis invites the reader for a promenade through history in order to prepare his conceptual analysis. The reader may enjoy reading the beginning of his essay as a bridge between the volume's parcour through *jus ad bellum* and *jus in bello* as Kritsiotis sets in with the development of the *jus ad bellum* in the first half of the nineteenth century and shows how necessity then became increasingly understood to be a legal requirement for the exercise of the right of self-defense, a requirement ultimately subject to an objective application by a third party. This legal evolution, Kritsiotis posits, constitutes an important part of the legal background against which the Lieber Code made its important contribution to anchoring the principle of military necessity in the *jus in bello*.

And on the closer inspection to which Kritsiotis proceeds, the Lieber Code, as under the burning glass, foreshadows the complexity of the principle. This complexity unfolds in the various articulations that the principle of military necessity has come to receive in numerous international treaties on the *jus in bello* adopted subsequent to the Lieber Code. As he peruses the rich sequence of references to the principle of military necessity as from the 1863 Lieber Code through to the 2005 International Committee of the Red Cross's Study on Customary International Humanitarian Law, Kritsiotis ponders on the linguistic nuances and wonders what precisely is meant by *epitheta* such as "imperative," "unavoidable," or "absolute" and whether they have perhaps led to a hierarchy of necessities in the *jus in bello*. While Kritsiotis carefully avoids any rush to easy conclusions with respects to these finesses, he emphasizes the sharp contrast between the core of the *jus in bello* principle of military necessity and what the U.S. Military Tribunal in *United States v. List*,[4] with an emphatically critical direction, referred to as the "German theory of expediency and military necessity," that is "a kind of resolutory condition implied in all the particular prescriptions of the law of war." The existence of this sharp contrast is confirmed in Lawless's thought-provoking chapter at the heart of which lies a thorough study of the very function of the *jus in bello* principle of military necessity. After careful theoretical analysis of categories such as "authority," "right," "permission," "justification," "privilege," "liberty," "prohibition," "limitation," as well as "perceptual principle" and "conceptual interest," and after careful perusal of official doctrinal expositions of the principle, Lawless recommends a change of direction. In his carefully explained view, military necessity, as currently stated in reflection of formulations in the Lieber Code and the *List* case, appears as being part of the applicable law governing the conduct of armed conflicts, but without providing service members with any useful guidance. Lawless opines that those officers on the ground would be better served if official doctrine conceived of military necessity, instead of as a "perceptual principle" as an "overarching conceptual interest" that recognizes what the conditions of the enemy and the political objectives demand military forces act on to be successful and if the same doctrine would view the international law of armed conflicts as reflecting the limitations that states have agreed to notwithstanding these demands. In his own words, "(a)ny attempt to distill military necessity in a regulatory form will be fleeting at best and at worst will be fool's errand."

With Wolff Heintschel von Heinegg's and Stefan Oeter's chapters, the emphasis shifts to *jus in bello* proportionality. In looking more closely at this principle, both authors, however, also shed light on those considerations of necessity, which are intimately related to the proportionality analysis. In the case of Heintschel von Heinegg's chapter, it constitutes even the main ambition to lay out an "integrated approach" which embraces considerations of military necessity and proportionality

4. United States v. List (The Hostage Case), Case. No. 7 (Feb. 19, 1948), *reprinted in* 11 Trials of War Criminals Before the Nuremberg Military Tribunals Under Control Council Law No. 10, at 757 (1950).

in the targeting process to which the author refers as the "targeting cycle." Oeter reminds the reader of the structural reasons for the difficulty to apply the principle of *jus in bello* proportionality in practice: He emphasizes the need never to lose sight of the fact that the principle is to be applied from an ex ante perspective and that on the battlefield such a perspective is likely to entail a significant degree of uncertainty and risk. Rather than aspiring to perfection, he suggests relying on the development of professional ethics in order to work against the danger of serious misjudgment. Both authors also look at the way current international criminal law deals with *jus in bello* necessity and proportionality, and they both stress the limitations of the criminal sanction if compared with the reach of the underlying conduct rules. In their view, this is due not only to international criminal law's stringent mental standard which goes beyond a requirement of due diligence, but it also follows from the fact that the relevant war crime definition would not seem to cover violations of what Heintschel von Heinegg might call the necessity pillar of an integrated approach to lawful targeting. I leave it to the reader to judge whether both authors also agree on their assessment of international criminal law as a matter of legal policy.

The following two chapters remain within the territory of *jus in bello* proportionality, but both choose a specific focus. Sarah Knuckey, Alex Moorehead, Audrey McCalley, and Adam Brown have devoted their innovative contribution to the question whether mental harm including, in particular, post-traumatic stress disorder should figure within the anticipated civilian harm to be balanced against the anticipated military advantage. The authors begin by providing the reader with an overview of how international law and the law of armed conflicts more generally deals with the issue of mental health. They then look at the still nascent scholarly discussion of mental harm and the *jus in bello* proportionality principle and also, relying on the specific disciplinary expertise included in their author's group, at the state of public health, psychology, and neuroscience research on post-traumatic stress disorder. This latter part of the chapter provides an international law readership with an impressive amount of precious scientific knowledge, which would otherwise be far more difficult to gather. The authors then look at the available scientific data, and they ask, in the context of *jus in bello* proportionality, whether and to what extent the occurrence of post-traumatic stress disorder among civilians (the question of which civilians should count is also given special attention) can be reasonably anticipated in the targeting process. The authors formulate their conclusions with great prudence. But they do suggest that despite the important challenge of feasibly operationalizing anticipated civilian mental harm, the state of relevant scientific research has advanced up to a point where such harm should, in principle, be taken into account as a matter of law. Looking at the *jus in bello* proportionality test in the context of the potential use of "fully autonomous" weapons, Masahiro Kurosaki turns his mind to another cutting-edge facet of the topic. Kurosaki suggests that what he calls the current "human centered paradigm" should not be considered the only means to ensure adherence to the foundational principles underlying the international law of armed conflicts and that it has not been persuasively explained why the principle of human dignity should make it a taboo to introduce a computer-centered approach which satisfies a more stringent *jus in bello* proportionality standard. Such an approach, he emphasizes, would not do away with the role of humans. It would, however, redefine their role and focus, for example, on their involvement in the establishment and application of a quality assurance mechanism for standardized, auditable algorithms through an independent international certification body. This may sound rather provocative, but that is not a reason to reject debating it. Kurosaki's chapter rather calls for a reconsideration of the strength of the argument against the use of "fully autonomous" weapons based on the principle of human dignity, and it makes one wonder what the envisaged computer-centered more stringent reformulation of the *jus in bello* proportionality test could look like in detail.

The volume's final chapter widens the scope of inquiry beyond the *jus ad bellum* and the *jus in bello*: Elisabeth Günnewig reaches out to a possible *jus post bellum* and asks whether proportionality could be among the guiding principles of such a body of international law. More specifically, she inquires whether the duty to repair arising from a violation of the prohibition of the use of force in the international relations might be mitigated through considerations of *jus post bellum* proportionality. Based on a careful analysis of state practice and general principles, she concludes that the unique *post bellum* demand to consolidate a fragile peace may require tempering the victim state's right to full reparation by reference to considerations of proportionality. Such considerations would operate as a *lex specialis* within the meaning of Article 55 of the International Law Commission's Draft Articles on State Responsibility.

Necessity and proportionality in the law of international peace and security is too vast a topic to be comprehensively covered in one single book. But together with my co-editor Major Robert Lawless and the other authors, I entertain the hope that this volume will contribute to a deeper understanding of those two fundamentally important concepts and to a healthy evolution of their role with this body of law.

May I conclude by extending my warmest thanks to Robert who, apart from contributing an outstanding chapter, was a wonderful teammate in preparing this volume, my old and trusted friend Professor Michael Schmitt not only for his illuminating contributions to our workshop but also for his unfailing support during all phases of the project, our fantastic West Point hosts for providing us with excellent working conditions, and Oxford University Press's professionals for ensuring, in their usual efficiency and kindness, a smooth path to publication.

PART ONE

An Encounter of International Law with Morality

1

Necessity and Proportionality in Morality and Law

JEFF MCMAHAN*

I. INTRODUCTION

If an act would harm someone, there is a moral presumption against doing it. For the act to be permissible, there must be a justification for the harm it would cause. There are various types of moral justification for harming someone. Several of these are based on what the person has done. Most people believe, for example, that by culpably engaging in wrongdoing, a person can deserve to be harmed. If this is so, there can be a *desert justification* for harming that person. Or, if one person is responsible for making it unavoidable that someone will be harmed, there may be a *liability justification* for harming that person as a means or side effect of preventing an innocent or nonresponsible person from being harmed instead. Finally, there may be a *consent justification* for harming a person who has freely and rationally consented to be harmed as a means or side effect of the achievement of some good aim.

There are other types of justification for harming a person that may apply independently of what that person has done. The most important of these applies when harming a person is necessary to prevent a greater harm. In the least controversial case of this sort, it can be permissible to harm a person when that is

* White's Professor of Moral Philosophy, University of Oxford. This chapter provides a condensed explanation, intended primarily for legal theorists, of various claims about proportionality that I have defended in other publications that would normally be seen only by philosophers. Although there is a substantial amount of new material here, my main aim has been to collect together a unified set of views about proportionality that would otherwise remain scattered throughout a number of mainly philosophical publications. References to these publications are provided in the notes.

Jeff McMahan, *Necessity and Proportionality in Morality and Law* In: *Necessity and Proportionality in International Peace and Security Law*. Edited by: Professor Claus Kreß and Captain Robert Lawless, Oxford University Press (2021).
 DOI: 10.1093/oso/9780197537374.003.0002.

necessary to prevent that same person from suffering a greater harm. Certain forms of consequentialism also imply that it is permissible to harm a person when that is necessary to prevent a greater harm to *another* person or persons, even if the harm prevented is only slightly greater. The more common view, however, is that there is a moral constraint against harming people that is stronger than any corresponding constraint against allowing people to suffer equivalent harm. Thus, for there to be a justification for harming an innocent person as a necessary means or unavoidable side effect of preventing greater harm to others, the harm prevented must be *substantially* greater than that inflicted. Only then is the constraint overridden. In moral philosophy, this form of justification is often referred to as a *lesser-evil justification*.

Sources of justification for harming people that are rather more controversial include duties derived from authoritative commands, permissions to give some degree of priority to one's own interests over those of others, and permissions or duties to give some degree of priority to the interests of those to whom one is specially related. Although I will briefly discuss the last two of these forms of justification in section VI, I will be primarily concerned with liability justifications, lesser-evil justifications, and, for purposes of comparison, desert justifications.

All justifications for harming people are subject to certain constraints. One of the two most important of these constraints is proportionality. With the exception of the consequentialist justification, which is explicitly constrained in its own formulation (the harm prevented must be greater than that caused), all the forms of justification for harming that I have cited are subject to a proportionality constraint. Much of this chapter will be concerned with explaining the nature of these different proportionality constraints and the ways in which they differ from one another.

But before I distinguish and elucidate these forms of proportionality, I should note a potential source of confusion, which is that there is a type of justification that shares the same label with a type of constraint: "necessity." In criminal law, a person who has harmed another person may be charged with a criminal offense but not be convicted if he has one of two defenses against the charge: an excuse or a justification. If the person can show that, in harming the other person, she acted in the only way possible to prevent a greater harm, she may be deemed to have acted with legal justification and will not be convicted. The particular form of justification or, in common-law terminology, "affirmative defense" that rebuts the charge against her is referred to as a "necessity defense," or necessity justification.

In criminal law, in other words, a person may have a necessity justification for an act that would otherwise be criminal *if* the consequences of her action have been better than those that would have ensued had she not done the act. A necessity justification in law thus has the form of a lesser-evil justification, except that it may in principle apply even when the difference in the possible consequences is slight; so in this respect it is relevantly like the consequentialist form of justification.

Similarly, in the law of armed conflict, there can be a justification of *military necessity* for harming innocent civilians as an unavoidable side effect of an attack on a military target. This too is a form of justification that in moral philosophy might be called a lesser-evil justification.[1]

These forms of justification in domestic and international law bear the label "necessity." But that is also the label of the second of the two most important *constraints* on moral justifications for harming people. This constraint, which is often called the *requirement of necessity*, is quite complicated and difficult to state with both clarity and precision. A familiar, though crude, statement is that one must not cause more harm than is necessary to achieve one's aim. There are, in effect, two such necessity constraints in the law of armed conflict. One is that one must not cause more harm to civilians than is necessary to achieve one's military goals. The other is that it is prohibited to employ means of fighting that cause "unnecessary suffering" or "superfluous injury" to enemy combatants—that is, to cause more harm to enemy combatants than is necessary to achieve one's military aim. These are both clear instances of what I call a *necessity constraint*.

Surprisingly, however, the requirement not to cause unnecessary suffering or injury is often referred to in writings on international law as a matter of *proportionality*. Judith Gardam, for example, observes that "the relevance of proportionality to the assessment of weapons is borne out by the fact that many articulations of the test of superfluous injury or unnecessary suffering use this term."[2] But the use of the word in this way by some legal writers does not show that the tests for unnecessary suffering and superfluous injury are matters of proportionality. Indeed, it might show only that these writers use the word "proportionality" in a confusing way. Gardam cites as an instance of "the proportionality equation" the claim of another legal theorist that "the crucial question is whether other weapons or methods of warfare available at the time would have achieved the same military goal as effectively while causing less suffering or injury."[3] Yet this question is about whether the use of some weapon or method of warfare and all the suffering and injury it would cause are *necessary* for the achievement of the military goal, not about whether the goal is sufficiently important to justify the suffering and injury.

Gardam also cites a passage from the ICRC commentary on antipersonnel mines, which says that it is a "basic rule" of international humanitarian law that "it is prohibited to use weapons which cause unnecessary suffering. Therefore, the

1. The principle of military necessity is regarded by some legal theorists as a matter of *in bello* proportionality. I suspect that this is because they assume that, when an act of war is necessary for a certain military advantage that outweighs the harm to civilians, the act is proportionate and therefore justified. But, while this overall judgment may be correct, a claim of military necessity is best analyzed as a claim that there is a lesser-evil justification for harming innocent civilians, which presupposes that the harms inflicted satisfy both the necessity and proportionality constraints. More on these matters in subsequent sections.

2. Judith Gardam, Necessity, Proportionality and the Use of Force by States 69 (2004). She also remarks that "commentators constantly use the word 'proportionate' in relation to the regulation of weapons to protect combatants." *Id.* at 15 n.37.

3. *Id.* (quoting Christopher Greenwood, Command and the Laws of Armed Conflict 24 (1993)).

use of weapons whose damaging effects are disproportionate to their military purpose is prohibited."[4] But, again, it is not that the bad effects are disproportionate in relation to the military purpose but that they are unnecessary for the achievement of that purpose. Suppose, for example, that unless one combatant fighting for unjust goals (an "unjust combatant") is not incapacitated, he will launch a weapon that will kill 1,000 combatants fighting for just goals ("just combatants"). The just combatants have a choice between two weapons, each of which would be wholly effective in incapacitating the unjust combatant. One would inflict an injury from which he would soon recover, while the other would inflict a disability that would cause chronic pain for the rest of his life. The second weapon is ruled out because it would cause unnecessary suffering. The suffering would be unnecessary because the military aim could be equally well achieved by the use of the other, less damaging weapon. The second weapon is clearly *not* ruled out because its "damaging effects are disproportionate to their military purpose"; for causing a single unjust attacker to have a painful disability is not a disproportionately bad effect in relation to the purpose of preventing him from killing 1,000 morally innocent just combatants.

These uses of the term "proportionality" are, I believe, a potential source of confusion. There is no general understanding of the concept of proportionality with which I am familiar that can coherently encompass a requirement not to cause suffering solely on the ground that it is unnecessary. In international law, for example, Article 51(5)(b) of the 1977 First Additional Protocol to the Geneva Conventions (Additional Protocol I) is widely recognized as a statement of the proportionality constraint on acts of war. And in international criminal law, there is a similar statement in Article 8(2)(b)(iv) of the Rome Statute.[5] These statements of the proportionality constraint are quite different in form and substance from rules, such as Article 8(2)(b)(xx) of the Rome Statute, that prohibit the infliction of unnecessary suffering and superfluous injury.

Principles that prohibit the infliction of unnecessary suffering or superfluous injury are principles of *jus in bello*. But there seems to be a similar tendency in the law of *jus ad bellum* to conflate principles of proportionality with principles of necessity. There is general agreement that "the exercise of the right of self-defence under international law is governed by principles of necessity and proportionality" and that the source of these principles in the law of *jus ad bellum* is the 1837 *Caroline* incident.[6] Gardam, for example, comments that the understandings of necessity and proportionality in the exchanges between Daniel Webster and

4. *Id.* (quoting INT'L COMM. OF THE RED CROSS, ANTI-PERSONNEL LANDMINES—FRIEND OR FOE?: A STUDY OF THE MILITARY USE AND EFFECTIVENESS OF ANTI-PERSONNEL MINES 24 (Mar. 1, 1996)).

5. Each is quoted in section V *infra*.

6. Claus Kreß, *The International Court of Justice and the "Principle of Non-Use of Force," in* THE OXFORD HANDBOOK OF THE USE OF FORCE IN INTERNATIONAL LAW 586 (Marc Weller ed., 2017).

Lord Ashburton on that occasion now "represent the position under the United Nations Charter system."[7] Yet the relevant passages in that correspondence, including those cited as references to proportionality, are concerned more with matters of necessity. Gardam, for example, cites as an "allegation of disproportionate conduct" Webster's statement that the claim that there was "[a] necessity for all this [the British military action], the Government of the United States cannot believe existed." To Webster's skepticism, Ashburton responded that the British chose their means "for the express purpose of preventing injury to persons or property" and that "the time of night was purposely selected as most likely to ensure the execution with the least loss of life."[8] These claims rebut an accusation that the British action was unnecessary, not that it was disproportionate. Much of the subsequent legal discussion supposedly concerned with proportionality in the resort to force has similarly been concerned with whether the resort to force, or the resort to a particular level of force, is necessary.

Even in constitutional law, "proportionality" is sometimes used to refer to a requirement of necessity. Thomas Hurka has called my attention to the fact that the Canadian Charter of Rights and Freedoms has an interpretive provision that explains when legislation that infringes a Charter right may nonetheless be constitutional. The conditions cited closely parallel the conditions of *jus ad bellum* in just war theory. Legislation must have a "pressing objective" (that is, a just cause), be rationally connected to that objective (hope of success), involve minimal impairment of Charter rights (necessity), and not have costs that exceed its benefits (proportionality). The standard terminology refers to the last three conditions together as the "proportionality" test and to the last condition on its own as "proportionate effects." This has led some legal scholars to argue that the last condition is redundant, as proportionality is covered by the first two of the three. But, as Hurka observes, it clearly is not.[9]

There have, however, been clearly expressed concerns with proportionality in the law of *jus ad bellum*. In 1980, for example, Roberto Ago, Special Rapporteur of the International Law Commission, distinguished between proportionality in reprisals and proportionality in self-defense when he wrote that the resort to force in self-defense "may well have to assume dimensions disproportionate to those of the attack suffered. What matters in this respect is the result to be achieved by the 'defensive' action."[10] *Ad bellum* proportionality also seemed to be clearly recognized by the International Court of Justice when it wrote in 2005 that "the Court cannot fail to observe . . . that the taking of airports and towns many

7. Gardam, *supra* note 2, at 40.

8. *Id.*

9. This is based on personal communication. My thanks to Hurka for citing this instance of the conflation of proportionality with necessity in another area of the law.

10. Kreß, *supra* note 6, at 587 (quoting Roberto Ago, Addendum to the 8th Report on State Responsibility, *reprinted in* [1980] 2 (pt. 1) Y.B. Int'l L. Comm'n 69 (1980)). I return briefly to proportionality in reprisals in section VI *infra*.

hundreds of kilometres from Uganda's border would not seem proportionate to the series of transborder attacks it claimed had given rise to the right of self-defence, nor to be necessary to that end."[11]

These are hopeful developments. There are conditions in which a just cause cannot be pursued without causing harms to innocent people that would be disproportionate in relation to the importance of the cause. Wars involving the use of weapons of mass destruction, such as nuclear weapons, or likely to escalate to the use of such weapons, are likely to be disproportionate in this sense. It is imperative that the law should have the resources to condemn such wars even when they are necessary for the achievement of a just and important cause.

In this chapter, I will distinguish carefully between the constraints of necessity and proportionality and will classify constraints that forbid the infliction of harm on the ground that it is ineffective or unnecessarily harmful as *necessity* constraints. The necessity and proportionality constraints are conceptually and morally distinct, and we should avoid terminology that conflates them.

A necessity *constraint* is also quite different from a necessity *justification*. They are of course related, in that necessity justifications are always subject to a necessity constraint. But a necessity constraint, like a proportionality constraint, applies to virtually all forms of justification for harming. The conspicuous exception is a desert justification, since giving a person what she deserves is an end in itself; hence desert justifications apply even when giving a person what she deserves is not instrumental to, or necessary for, any good effects. Thus, there cannot be a necessity constraint on a pure desert justification.

II. HOW THE PROPORTIONALITY CONSTRAINT DIFFERS FROM THE NECESSITY CONSTRAINT

Despite the way the labels are often used in international law, the constraints of proportionality and necessity impose different requirements because they are based on different comparisons. To determine whether an act of harming satisfies the necessity constraint one must compare the act's expected consequences with those of *alternative means* of achieving the *same* goal or end. Only if an act of harming is the morally best means of achieving a just aim—taking into account the probability of success, the expected cost to the agent, the expected harm to others as a side effect, and the expected harm to the threatener—can it satisfy the necessity constraint. I will not attempt to elucidate these complexities here.[12]

11. *Id.* (quoting Armed Activities on the Territory of the Congo (Dem. Rep. Congo v. Uganda), Judgment, 2005 I.C.J. Rep. 168, ¶ 147 (Dec. 19)). The final clause in this quotation shows that the Court has taken care to distinguish proportionality from necessity. Kreß's article contains an illuminating general discussion of the ICJ's attention to proportionality in its case law.

12. For discussion, *see* Seth Lazar, *Necessity in Self-Defense and War*, 40 PHIL. & PUB. AFF. 3 (2012); Jeff McMahan, *The Limits of Self-Defense*, *in* THE ETHICS OF SELF-DEFENSE 185 (Christian Coons & Michael Weber eds., 2016).

To determine whether an act of harming is proportionate, one does not compare its effects with those of alternative possible acts. One instead compares the act's good effects (generally, the prevention of harms, protection of rights, etc.) with its bad effects (generally, the infliction of harms, infringement of rights, etc.). If the bad effects would outweigh or be excessive in relation to the good, the act is disproportionate and therefore impermissible.

This claim is, however, deceptively simple. Suppose we want to know not only what the consequences of person *P*'s doing act *A* would be but also how to evaluate those consequences as good or bad. We must determine what would happen were *P* to do *A* *and* what would happen were *P* *not* to do *A* and then compare the two sets of possible consequences. Only then can we know whether *P*'s doing *A* would be *better* or *worse*, and by how much, than *P*'s not doing *A*. But *P* cannot *not do A* without doing something else, even if it is only to remain entirely motionless. So, the question arises which of the courses of action that *P* might undertake instead of doing *A* is the one with which one should compare *P*'s doing *A* in order to assess the good and bad effects of doing *A*.

There has been considerable discussion of this issue in the literature on proportionality in self-defense and war.[13] Particularly in the literature on war, various proposals have been defended that specify the alternative with which a state's resort to war should be compared in the assessment of *ad bellum* proportionality. These include what the state would have done, or been most likely to do, if it had not gone to war, what it would have been most likely to do among its permissible alternatives, and whatever it might have done among its permissible alternatives that would have produced the least good consequences.[14] All these suggestions are vulnerable to what seem to be decisive objections.[15] Until recently I thought that it might be sufficient to say that the assessment of proportionality requires only a comparison between the bad effects that an act or policy would cause and those that it would prevent, the latter being those bad effects that would occur were the agent to do nothing to prevent them. But recent work by Ben Bronner has convinced me that rather technical problems in understanding "counterfactual conditionals," such as problems of causal overdetermination and preemption, show that there is unlikely to be any general formula for identifying the precise alternative to which a war or act of war must be compared to determine whether it would be proportionate. According to Bronner, the harm that an act or policy would prevent "*is* picked out by some

13. *See, e.g.*, Jeff McMahan & Robert McKim, *The Just War and the Gulf War*, 23 CAN. J. PHIL. 501, 507–10 (1993); David Mellow, *Counterfactuals and the Proportionality Criterion*, 20 ETHICS & INT'L AFF. 439 (2006); Thomas Hurka, *Proportionality and Necessity*, *in* WAR: ESSAYS IN POLITICAL PHILOSOPHY 127, 130 (Larry May ed., 2008).

14. The last of these is suggested by Hurka. *See* Hurka, *supra* note 13.

15. Jeff McMahan, *Proportionate Defense*, *in* WEIGHING LIVES IN WAR 131, 132–34 (Jens Ohlin, Larry May, & Claire Finkelstein eds., 2017).

counterfactual or other," but "different counterfactuals are relevant in different cases."[16]

I will not pursue this problem further here except to note that the assessment of whether an act by some agent would be proportionate does not take into account good or bad effects that the agent might cause, or good or bad effects that she might prevent, were she to do some other act. Such "opportunity costs" and "opportunity benefits" may well be relevant to the moral evaluation of her act, but they are not relevant to whether it would be proportionate.

Nor are they relevant to whether her act satisfies the necessity constraint, which is concerned with alternative means of achieving the *same* end that the act is intended to achieve, such as the prevention of a particular harm. Opportunity costs and benefits are concerned with *alternative ends* one might pursue. Again, doing an act as a means of achieving a certain good end might well be wrong if one could, at no more cost to oneself or others, instead achieve a *different* and much better end by doing some other act. But, I know of no discussion in traditional just war theory of the idea that it could be wrong to go to war because of the war's opportunity costs.[17]

The claim that an act intended to achieve one end cannot be judged *unnecessary* because of the possibility of instead achieving a *different end* requires qualification. Just war theorists have sometimes claimed that an act of war intended to destroy one military target is ruled out as unnecessary if combatants could instead destroy a *different* but equally important target at lesser cost in harm to civilians as a side effect.[18] If the destruction of the one target is understood as a different end from the destruction of the other, this claim conflicts with my understanding of the comparisons required in the assessment of necessity. But there is no serious conflict given that the destruction of each target, while in one sense an end, is also a means of achieving the ultimate end, which is the achievement of the just cause for war. A choice of this sort thus raises two issues of necessity: first, for each target one must determine what the morally best means of destroying it is; then, assuming that it is not possible, or perhaps not desirable, to destroy both, one must compare the best way of destroying one with the best way of destroying the other to determine which of the two is the morally better means of contributing to the achievement of the just cause. The act of war that is the morally best means of

16. Ben Bronner, The Modal Fog of War (unpublished). This paper is a component of Bronner's PhD dissertation (Rutgers University).

17. For discussion, *see* Peter Singer, *Bystanders to Poverty*, *in* ETHICS AND HUMANITY: THEMES FROM THE PHILOSOPHY OF JONATHAN GLOVER 185 (N. Ann Davis, Richard Keshen, & Jeff McMahan eds., 2010); Jeff McMahan, *Humanitarian Intervention, Consent, and Proportionality*, *in* ETHICS AND HUMANITY, *supra*, at 44.

18. *Cf.* Protocol Additional to the Geneva Conventions of 12 August 1949, and Relating to the Protection of Victims of International Armed Conflict (Protocol I) art. 57(3), June 8, 1977, 1125 U.N.T.S. 3 [hereinafter AP I] ("When a choice is possible between several military objectives for obtaining a similar military advantage, the objective to be selected shall be that the attack on which may be expected to cause the least danger to civilian lives and to civilian objects.").

destroying the target whose destruction is the morally better means of advancing the just cause is the act that satisfies the necessity constraint.

III. PROPORTIONALITY IN DEFENSE AND PROPORTIONALITY IN PUNISHMENT: LIABILITY AND DESERT

Even before there were any formal legal systems, it was possible for one person's harming of another to be disproportionate. The legal concept of proportionality thus derives from the more general moral concept, which is logically prior. In law, "proportionality" has various meanings. In constitutional law, for example, it refers to a relation between the social benefit of limiting the scope of the protection afforded by a constitutional right and the social harm occasioned by the restriction of the right. This is quite different from the meaning of proportionality in criminal punishment, which is in turn different from various other forms of proportionality in the law, such as proportionality in private defense, in law enforcement through police action, and in war or armed conflict. Similarly, there are different notions or forms of proportionality in moral theory that must be carefully distinguished. Although my primary concern in this chapter is with proportionality in defensive harming, it will be helpful to elucidate that notion by contrasting it with proportionality in the morality of punishment.

Some philosophers believe that punishment is justified only if, and because, it protects innocent people from wrongful harm through defense (restraining dangerous offenders) or deterrence.[19] According to this view, an offender's desert is irrelevant to the justification for punishing him. Although I think this view is probably correct as a matter of morality, it is uncommon in legal thinking, and I will not discuss it here. According to the more common, retributivist view, even though social defense and deterrence of wrongdoing are welcome and often intended effects of punishment, punishment is justified only when an offender *deserves* to be punished. Although retributivists believe that desert is not only necessary but also sufficient for punishment to be justified, there are other theorists who believe that, although desert is a necessary condition of justified punishment, its effect is only "negative," in that it merely negates a constraint against harming and is not itself a reason for harming.[20] On this view, desert is necessary but not always sufficient for state punishment to be justified. This view of desert is, however, inconsistent with the common view of *positive* desert. If, for example, a person deserves our gratitude, or deserves a benefit, it is commonly accepted that that

19. *See, e.g.*, Daniel Farrell, *The Justification of General Deterrence*, 94 PHIL. REV. 367 (1985); PHILLIP MONTAGUE, PUNISHMENT AS SOCIETAL DEFENSE (1995); VICTOR TADROS, THE ENDS OF HARM (2011).

20. The most prominent recent exponent of this view is H.L.A. Hart. *See* H.L.A. HART, *Prolegomena to the Principles of Punishment*, *in* PUNISHMENT AND RESPONSIBILITY: ESSAYS IN THE PHILOSOPHY OF LAW 1 (2nd ed. 2008).

alone is a justification for our expressing gratitude or providing the benefit. No further good effects are required. If this is true of positive desert, it seems it should be true of negative desert as well.

Suppose that the justification for punishment is purely retributive, so that proportionality in punishment is a constraint on a desert justification. On this view, punishment is proportionate only to the extent that it is deserved. Proportionality in punishment is a relation between the harm inflicted on a wrongdoer and the gravity of his past wrongdoing, which itself is a function of the degree to which his action was wrong or morally objectionable and the degree of his culpability in doing it. These latter two considerations determine how much harm the wrongdoer deserves. An instance of punishment is thus disproportionate if the harm it inflicts exceeds that which the offender deserves. Although it is rarely invoked, there is another way in which punishment might be disproportionate—namely, by failing to inflict *as much* harm as the offender deserves.[21] If this is indeed a form of disproportionality, then punishment is proportionate only if the harm it inflicts is neither greater nor less than that which the offender deserves, taking into account the unavoidable imprecision in judgments of desert.

Desert is not an important moral justification for attacking people in war. Indeed, some moral philosophers argue that it is never an acceptable justification for military action in war.[22] The main moral justification for harming and killing people in war is instead what I have referred to as a liability justification. This is also the main moral justification for harming and killing people in individual self-defense and defense of others ("other-defense"). This form of justification is subject to certain constraints, of which proportionality is one.

Desert justifications and liability justifications are related in that both typically appeal to the idea that the person who may justifiably be harmed has forfeited the right not to be harmed in certain ways. Yet a person who forfeits her right not be harmed may either deserve to be harmed without being liable to be harmed or she may be liable to be harmed without deserving to be harmed. Or she may both deserve to be harmed and be liable to be harmed. If so, she may be liable to suffer more harm than she deserves or she may deserve more harm than she is liable to suffer.

Desert justifications and liability justifications are also similar in that the bases of desert and the bases of liability—or at least those bases of liability that consist in facts about the agent (the "agential conditions" of liability)—are much the same. Just as an offender's beliefs, motives, and intentions are relevant to the determination of his desert and the severity of the punishment he might deserve, so a threatener's beliefs, motives, and intentions are also relevant to the amount of defensive harm to which he might be liable.

21. For discussion, though without reference to the notion of proportionality, *see* Shelly Kagan, The Geometry of Desert (2012).

22. Jeff McMahan, *Aggression and Punishment*, *in* War: Philosophical Perspectives 67 (Larry May ed., 2008).

Yet liability differs from desert in various ways. First, whereas one can deserve to be harmed even when it is possible for no one to suffer further harm, one can be liable to be harmed only when harm is unavoidable, such as when a threatener will harm a victim unless the victim or a third party harms the threatener. Liability is a matter of justice in the distribution of harm when *some* harm is unavoidable. It thus constitutes a *justification* for harming (albeit a defeasible one) and not just the lowering of a barrier to the permissibility of harming; for if the person who is liable to be harmed is not harmed, someone else will be harmed instead. That is, harming a person who is liable to that harm always prevents harm to someone who is not liable to it. Liability is thus always instrumental.

Retributive or purely punitive harming is, by contrast, not instrumental. That a person deserves to be harmed is generally regarded, at least among philosophers who believe in desert, as a sufficient justification for punishment in the absence of special reasons not to inflict it. Although further effects, such as defense, deterrence, or the reform of the wrongdoer are often sought through punishment, they are generally not thought necessary for the infliction of *deserved* punishment to be morally justified.

A second difference between liability and desert is that liability is sometimes a comparative matter, whereas desert is not. According to the view of liability that I have defended, the moral basis of liability to defensive harm is moral responsibility for a threat of wrongful harm, and the amount of harm to which a person may be liable varies, when other things are equal, with the degree of the person's responsibility.[23] Suppose that two people, *A* and *B*, both bear responsibility for the fact that someone will suffer a harm that cannot be divided—that is, it must all be suffered by only one person. If *A* bears greater responsibility than *B*, then *A* is liable to suffer the harm and *B* is not, though *B* would have been had *A* been less responsible than *B*. Yet if both are culpably responsible and culpability grounds desert, what *B* deserves is unaffected by *A*'s greater culpability, and the total harm they together deserve may be greater or less than that to which one of them is liable.

A third and closely related difference is that liability is sensitive to circumstantial conditions in ways that desert is not. Suppose that a wrongdoer culpably attempts to kill an innocent person in a way that is certain to fail. That he causes no harm is arguably irrelevant to his desert; but that he will cause no harm does exempt him from liability to be harmed. (Not all philosophers accept this last claim. Some believe that at least certain forms of culpability can make a person liable to be harmed as a means or side effect of averting a threat for which that person is in no way responsible. This view narrows the gap between desert and liability but does not close it, assuming that liability is always instrumental whereas desert is not.[24])

23. *See, e.g.*, Jeff McMahan, Killing in War ch. 4 (2009).

24. *See* Tadros, *supra* note 19, at 186–96; Lars Christie, Harming One to Save Another (unpublished PhD thesis, University of Oslo, 2015); Matthew Oliver, Liability and Culpability (unpublished DPhil thesis, University of Oxford, 2018). The arguments in these and other texts have convinced me that causal responsibility for a threat is not a necessary condition of liability to be

A fourth and final difference is conceptual. It is a conceptual truth that desert of punitive harm requires or presupposes culpability, but there is no corresponding conceptual truth about the conditions of liability. Although some philosophers argue that culpability is indeed a necessary condition of liability, their claim is substantive rather than conceptual, as is the claim, which I accept, that morally responsible agency is a necessary condition of liability.

Both desert justifications and liability justifications are retrospective in certain ways. Although the constraints on desert justifications, such as those concerned with side effects, can be prospective in character, desert itself is arguably determined entirely by what a person has done in the past. Similarly, what one has done in the past is often relevant to one's liability in the present. This is most obvious when one is morally liable to the harm involved in having to compensate the victim of one's earlier harmful action.

One may also be liable to be harmed in defense of another on the basis of action done entirely in the past. In one of the familiar examples involving runaway trolleys, a trolley will hit and kill five innocent people unless a person is toppled off a bridge into its path, in which case the trolley will be stopped when it hits and kills her. Most people believe it is impermissible to kill this person as a means of saving the five. But their intuition changes if we stipulate that she has maliciously set the trolley in motion and stationed herself on the bridge to get a good view of her intended victims being killed. In these circumstances, it is permissible to kill her as a means of saving the five, not because she deserves to be killed but because justice demands that she be the one to be killed when it is her own voluntary, wrongful action that has made it unavoidable that someone will be killed. Although she now poses no threat, killing her is necessary to prevent her from killing the five through action she did in the past.

IV. WIDE PROPORTIONALITY, NARROW PROPORTIONALITY, AND PROPORTIONALITY IN THE AGGREGATE

I have argued that, given the common assumption that justified punishment must be *deserved*, proportionality in punishment is quite different from proportionality in defense. This claim is, however, an oversimplification. Both justified punishment and justified defense are subject to more than one proportionality constraint. Although this is seldom recognized, justified punishment is constrained by two distinct proportionality requirements. And justified defensive harming is, I believe, constrained by three.

Punishment is governed by two proportionality constraints because the harms it inflicts must satisfy two distinct forms of justification. There is first the proportionality constraint on the desert justification: the harm intentionally inflicted on

harmed as a means or side effect of averting the threat. Yet no one, to my knowledge, has provided a plausible account of the limits of liability in the absence of causal responsibility.

the offender must be proportionate in relation to his desert. But the infliction of punishment often harms people other than the offender. If, for example, one of the states in the United States executes a middle-aged man, he may have parents, a wife, and children who love him and who will all suffer great and lasting harm because of what is done to him. These harms are side effects of the punishment. While the law may ignore them, morality does not. For an instance of punishment to be morally justified, all things considered, there must be a justification for the harms it causes to people other than the offender. Because these people normally bear no responsibility for the offender's wrongdoing, the justification for harming them cannot be a desert justification or a liability justification. It must instead be a lesser-evil justification. That is, for the act of punishment to be justified, the harms it inflicts on innocent people as a side effect must be substantially outweighed by whatever is achieved by punishing the offender (such as giving him what he deserves, preventing him from causing further harm, and preserving deterrence).

The specification of what constitutes the lesser evil in the circumstances is a matter of proportionality. This form of proportionality governs acts of causing people harm or allowing people to be harmed when those people neither deserve nor are liable to suffer that harm. It is often referred to as "wide proportionality," as it applies to a wide range of harms—namely, those for which there is neither a desert justification, a liability justification, nor a consent justification. A harm inflicted on an innocent person that exceeds what can be justified as the lesser evil is disproportionate in the wide sense.

The standard that determines what constitutes the lesser evil, and thus how much harm is proportionate in the wide sense, varies with certain factors. These include whether the person harmed by an act is also the beneficiary of that act or whether the beneficiary is instead a different person, whether the good effect of the harmful act is the prevention of a harm or the conferral of a benefit, whether the harm is inflicted as an intended means or as an unintended side effect, whether the harm inflicted is all suffered by one innocent person or is divided and dispersed among many innocent people, and so on. Whereas it might, for example, be proportionate to inflict a harm of a certain magnitude on a person as a *side effect* of preventing that *same* person from suffering an only slightly greater *harm*, it might nevertheless be disproportionate in the wide sense to inflict the same harm on that same person as a *means* of conferring even a vastly greater *benefit* on a *different* person.

Wide proportionality contrasts with "narrow proportionality," which governs a narrower range of harms—namely, those for which there is either a desert justification, a liability justification, or a consent justification. A harm inflicted on a person that exceeds the harm he deserves, to which he is liable, or to which he has consented is disproportionate in the narrow sense.

Harms that the victim deserves, is liable to suffer, or has consented to suffer, and which are thus proportionate in the narrow sense, do not wrong the victim or infringe the victim's rights; for both desert and liability involve the forfeiture of certain rights not to be harmed, and consent constitutes the waiving of those rights. By contrast, harms inflicted on the innocent that are justified as the lesser evil, and are thus proportionate in wide sense, often do infringe the rights of the victims. Although the infringement is permissible, so that the right is overridden rather than violated, the victim may nevertheless be owed compensation. Yet not all harms that are justifiably inflicted on the innocent as the lesser evil involve the infringement of a right. Even though the parents of an offender who is severely but justly punished may, for example, be grievously harmed by what is done to their child, they may have no moral right not to be harmed in that way and thus may have no right to compensation. Although there is a moral reason not to inflict this harm on the parents, so that the harm weighs in the assessment of whether the punishment is proportionate in the wide sense, the reason not to inflict it is not as strong as it would be in a case in which the infliction of the same amount of harm would violate the victims' rights.

Suppose that an act of self-defense by a victim against a threatener is disproportionate in the narrow sense, in that the harm it inflicts on the threatener exceeds that to which he is liable. This does not entail that the act is impermissible; for the harm that the victim inflicts on the threatener beyond that to which the threatener is liable may be differently justified—for example, as the lesser evil. This may be easier to appreciate if we consider a related example. Suppose that what is necessary for the successful defense of the victim is the infliction of a certain harm on the threatener to which the threatener is liable (and which is therefore proportionate in the narrow sense) *and* the infliction of a further harm on an innocent bystander, either as a means or as a side effect. It is possible that there is both a liability justification for the harming of the threatener and a lesser-evil justification for the harming of the bystander, so that the defensive action is overall justified. If this is so, it should also be permissible to inflict both harms on the threatener if that would be equally effective.[25] In both cases, the harm beyond that to which the threatener is liable would be inflicted on someone who is not liable to it, but there would be a lesser-evil justification for the infliction of this further harm. In the case in which the additional harm would be inflicted on the threatener, this harm would be disproportionate in the narrow sense but proportionate in the wide sense, just as it would be proportionate in the wide sense if it were inflicted on the bystander instead.

Although the infliction of harms that are disproportionate in the narrow sense may be permissible all things considered, the infliction of harms that are disproportionate in the wide sense is always impermissible. Lesser-evil justifications are justifications of last resort. One appeals to them only when no other form of justification applies. If, for example, there is a liability justification for harming a person, the claim that harming that person would be the lesser evil is otiose. Thus,

25. For discussion of this form of "combined justification," *see* McMahan, *Proportionate Defense*, *supra* note 15, at 136–38. A complication would arise if the additional harm to *T* would be intended as a means, whereas the equivalent harm to *B* would be inflicted only as a side effect. For more extensive discussion of combined justifications and certain challenges to them, *see* Jeff McMahan, *Liability, Proportionality, and the Number of Aggressors*, *in* THE ETHICS OF WAR: ESSAYS 3, 18–24 (Saba Bazargan-Forward & Samuel C. Rickless eds., 2016).

when the harming of an innocent person cannot be justified even as the lesser evil, it cannot be justified at all.

In both morality and law, proportionality in individual self-defense and defense of others is primarily narrow proportionality. This is because acts of individual self—and other-defense seldom cause serious harms to innocent people as a side effect. Wide proportionality is therefore rarely a serious issue in these cases. But it is, of course, a very serious issue in war. In traditional just war theory, both the *ad bellum* and *in bello* proportionality constraints are wide proportionality constraints only. Neither in the resort to war nor in the conduct of war is there a proportionality constraint on the harming of enemy combatants—though the *in bello necessity* constraint applies to both harm to noncombatants and harm to combatants. (This is true in the law of armed conflict as well, as I indicated in the discussion of the prohibition of weapons that cause unnecessary suffering or superfluous injury.[26])

Proportionality in the law of war is arguably even more limited in scope. Not only is there no *ad bellum* or *in bello* narrow proportionality constraint—that is, there is no proportionality constraint on the harming of combatants—but also the references to *ad bellum* proportionality are usually, as we saw, about necessity rather than proportionality.[27] There has been comparatively little legal discussion of whether a state's resort to force in self-defense can be in violation of the law on the ground that the harm this would cause to civilians would be excessive in relation to the importance of the defensive action.

Recently developed variants of "revisionist" just war theory tend, by contrast, to recognize a rich range of proportionality constraints. Like traditional just war theory and the law, they of course recognize an *in bello* wide proportionality constraint. They also, like traditional just war theory, recognize an *ad bellum* wide proportionality constraint—that is, they recognize that a war as a whole could be disproportionate because of the harms it would cause to people who are not liable to those harms. But many revisionist just war theorists also argue that there is an *in bello* narrow proportionality constraint, according to which an act of war may inflict harms on enemy combatants—particularly unjust combatants—that are disproportionate in relation to their good effects. This is denied by both traditional just war theory and the law.

There is, moreover, one further type of proportionality constraint that is still under-recognized even in revisionist just war theory. We can appreciate the necessity of recognizing this further constraint by considering what the other proportionality constraints fail to take into account. Both *ad bellum* and *in bello* wide proportionality take into account the *number* of innocent victims who are harmed. If other things are equal, the more people who are harmed by an act of war who are not liable to the harms inflicted on them, the more seriously disproportionate the act of war is, in the wide sense. But because narrow proportionality is a

26. *See supra* pp. 11–14.

27. *See supra* pp. 11–14.

constraint on a liability justification and liability justifications apply to individuals one by one, an act of war cannot be disproportionate in the *narrow* sense on the ground that it harms *too many* people. But both wars as wholes and individual acts of war can be disproportionate because the number of combatants—even unjust combatants—they would kill would be excessive in relation to the good effects they would produce. I call this form of proportionality "proportionality in the aggregate."[28]

V. *JUS IN BELLO* WIDE PROPORTIONALITY

I believe the revisionist just war theorists are right to claim that war is morally constrained by various requirements of proportionality. These do not include a requirement of *ad bellum* narrow proportionality; for it is true almost by definition that if there is a just cause for war, some substantial proportion of the unjust combatants must be individually liable to be killed in its pursuit. It is therefore impossible in practice that a war with a just cause could be impermissible on the ground that it would unavoidably inflict harms on individual unjust combatants that would exceed the harms to which they are liable. There is, however, a constraint of proportionality in the aggregate that applies to the killing even of unjust combatants. There are both *ad bellum* and *in bello* versions of this constraint, and the *ad bellum* version could in principle rule out the resort to war, or the continuation of war, simply because the *number* of unjust combatants who would have to be killed is disproportionate in relation to the importance of the just cause. For example, even though I believe the Falkland Islands belong to Britain, I think the Falklands War would have been clearly disproportionate if it had been necessary to kill 100,000 Argentine combatants to preserve British sovereignty.

Both traditional and revisionist just war theory agree, moreover, that there is an *ad bellum* requirement of wide proportionality. For the resort to or continuation of war to be morally justified, the achievement of the just cause must be sufficiently important to outweigh the harm to innocent people that the war would cause. Traditional just war theory and revisionist just war theory are also largely in agreement about what good effects can weigh against and potentially offset the harms that a war would inflict on innocent people. These good effects consist mainly in those that are constitutive of the achievement of the just cause for war. But other good effects that might be brought about either intentionally in the course of the war or as side effects may also weigh against and potentially offset harms to the innocent that the war would cause.

In the morality of *jus in bello*, there is more scope for a requirement of narrow proportionality. There can be occasions in war when attacking and, in particular, killing unjust combatants is disproportionate. These include occasions when attacking them would make only a negligible contribution to the achievement of the just cause (for example, when they are soon to be demobilized and replaced

28. *See* McMahan, *Liability, Proportionality, and the Number of Aggressors*, *supra* note 25.

by other soldiers) or when the unjust combatants bear little or no responsibility for the threat they pose, as may be true of some child soldiers. (This second basis of disproportionality presupposes that whether a person is liable to be harmed, as well as the amount of harm to which he can be liable, depend on whether and to what degree he is responsible for his action.) These same considerations can, moreover, contribute to making large-scale attacks on unjust combatants disproportionate in the aggregate.

The most important form of proportionality in war, though, is of course *in bello* wide proportionality. And on this matter, the traditional and revisionist just war theories are in deep disagreement, with the law of armed conflict firmly aligned with traditional just war theory. A core tenet of the traditional theory of the just war is the "moral equality of combatants"—the view that combatants all have the same permissions, rights, and liabilities irrespective of whether their cause is just.[29] And just as this doctrine is at the core of the traditional moral theory of *jus in bello*, so what might be called the "legal equality of combatants" is at the core of the law of armed conflict. According to these doctrines, combatants who fight for unjust aims are neither morally nor legally guilty of wrongdoing provided they obey the rules governing the conduct of war—that is, the rules of *jus in bello*—among which is a requirement of wide proportionality. Both traditional just war theorists and international lawyers have, moreover, insisted that it must be possible for unjust combatants to fight in obedience to the *in bello* rules without in general incurring a burden greater than that which conformity with the rules imposes on just combatants. Unjust combatants must, in other words, be able to obey the rules without exposing themselves to systematic military disadvantages vis-à-vis their adversaries.

The reason for this insistence is, I believe, that both legal and moral theorists have thought it essential that both law and morality should impose *effective* constraints on those who fight in unjust wars. These theorists have thought that if law and morality both say to unjust combatants that, because their aims are unjust, virtually every act of war in which they engage is impermissible, the response of the unjust combatants may be simply to turn a deaf ear to the voices of both law and morality. Even if unjust combatants recognize, or suspect, that the aims for which they have been ordered to fight are unjust, they may nevertheless continue to fight for fear of the social and domestic legal sanctions they would suffer for refusing to continue. If they believed that their every harmful act in continuing to fight would be both illegal and immoral, they might feel effectively unconstrained. If everything they might do other than refuse to fight would be wrong, they might think—though in my view mistakenly—that there are no good reasons other than those of self-interest to do one wrong act rather than another. Many legal and moral theorists have therefore insisted on saying to unjust combatants that, while it is permissible for them to fight, there are various types of belligerent action that

29. The classic statement and defense of this view in the modern literature is Michael Walzer, Just and Unjust Wars 34–37 (1977).

are legally and morally impermissible. And the use of force that is disproportionate in the wide sense is one of these. These legal and moral theorists have thus insisted that the *in bello* requirement of wide proportionality must apply symmetrically to the action of both just and unjust combatants.

It is natural to suppose that, when just combatants are considering whether some act of war they might do would be proportionate, they should reason about the individual act of war in the same way that they should reason about whether the war as a whole would be proportionate. That is, they should weigh the harms that the act would cause to people who are not liable to those harms against the probable contribution that the act would make to the achievement of the just cause, together with any other good effects the act might have that are capable of morally offsetting the harms. According to this understanding, whether the war as a whole is proportionate in the wide sense is an aggregative function of the extent to which each of the many acts of war that together constitute the war is or is not proportionate in the wide sense. In the simplest cases, if every act of war is disproportionate in this sense, then the war as a whole must be disproportionate, and if every act of war is proportionate, then the war as a whole must be proportionate.[30] This is because the good and bad effects that determine whether the war as a whole is proportionate are just the sum totals of the good and bad effects of the individual acts of war that together constitute the war.

This understanding of *in bello* wide proportionality cannot, however, be accepted by those legal and moral theorists who insist that the requirements of *jus in bello* be in general satisfiable by unjust combatants at no greater cost in military effectiveness than that incurred by just combatants in their obedience to the same requirements. This is of course because unjust combatants have no just cause to weigh against the harms their acts of war inflict on those who are not liable to those harms. According to these theorists, there must be a type of good effect that just and unjust combatants are equally capable of producing through military action that can weigh against the harms that military action often causes to innocent people as a side effect. The effect they have settled on is "military advantage."

In both international law and international criminal law, the determination of *in bello* proportionality requires the weighing of harms to civilians against military advantage. Although it confusingly describes the following type of act as "indiscriminate" rather than "disproportionate," Additional Protocol I prohibits "an attack which may be expected to cause incidental loss of civilian life, injury to civilians, damage to civilian objects, or a combination thereof, which would be excessive in relation to the concrete and direct military advantage anticipated."[31] Similarly, the Rome Statute includes in its list of war crimes "intentionally

30. There are complexities here that arise from the Non-Identity Problem, a notorious problem in population ethics that was discovered by Derek Parfit. These complexities are illuminatingly discussed by Patrick Tomlin in two important but as-yet-unpublished papers: "The Impure Non-Identity Problem" and "Proportionality in War and Fallacies of Composition."

31. AP I, *supra* note 18, art. 51(5)(b).

launching an attack in the knowledge that such attack will cause incidental loss of life or injury to civilians or damage to civilian objects or widespread, long-term and severe damage to the natural environment which would be clearly excessive in relation to the concrete and direct overall military advantage anticipated."[32]

One can perhaps make sense of these statements of the *in bello* proportionality requirement by designing—or stipulating—two finite, cardinal scales, one that measures harm to civilians and another that measures military advantage. These two scales would be isomorphic, in that there would be a one-to-one correspondence between the points on each. For every point on one scale, in other words, there would be a precisely corresponding point on the other. An act of war that is expected to cause an amount of harm to civilians at a particular point on the scale that measures harm would then be proportionate only if it is also expected to yield a degree of military advantage at a point that is some distance higher up the scale that measures advantage. It might then be a matter of dispute whether an act of war would be proportionate if the military advantage it is expected to provide were only one point higher than the harm to civilians it is expected to cause, or whether the military advantage would have to exceed the harm by some greater number of points.

One serious objection to this way of understanding *in bello* proportionality is that it assumes that the value of some amount or degree of military advantage as measured on the scale is the same in all wars. This has to be the case if the value of a unit of military advantage is not to vary with the moral importance of the goals of the war. And the moral importance of the goals of the war cannot affect *in bello* proportionality without systematically favoring just combatants over unjust combatants. But if the measure of military advantage is not sensitive to the importance of the goals of the war, then harms to innocent people that are disproportionate when very little is at stake in the war must also be disproportionate when much is at stake.[33] Suppose, for example, that an act of war would have been disproportionate in the Falklands War if it would have provided a military advantage that would have increased the probability of victory by the British by 1 percent but would also have caused a certain amount of harm to innocent people. On the view of proportionality I have sketched, an act of war that would have increased the probability of victory by the Allies in the Second World War by 1 percent would also have been disproportionate if it would have caused the same amount of harm to innocent people. This, however, is clearly mistaken.

The decisive objection to this understanding of proportionality is that it is morally arbitrary—indeed, morally incoherent. Proportionality is an element of a *justification* for harming people. An act that harms innocent people is proportionate, and therefore justifiable, only if the harm it causes is *offset*. And harms can be offset only by good effects, such as the prevention of other harms. Yet military

32. Rome Statute of the International Criminal Court art. 8(2)(b)(iv), July 17, 1998, 2187 U.N.T.S. 90.

33. *See* Thomas Hurka, *Proportionality in the Morality of War*, 33 PHIL. PUB. AFF. 34 (2005).

advantage is in itself not a good effect. In itself it has no value. Its value is only instrumental—that is, it is valuable only to the extent that what it is *advantageous for* is valuable. Only if the military advantage provided by an act of war increases the probability that combatants will achieve aims that are impartially good is the advantage valuable and capable of offsetting harms caused by that same act of war.

The understanding of proportionality that weighs bad effects against military advantage may thus be morally coherent in its application to an act of war by just combatants, provided that the act's military advantage is understood as a proxy for the contribution the act makes to the achievement of the just cause. But it makes no sense to suppose that when military advantage produces effects that are impartially bad, such as facilitating the achievement of aims that are unjust, it could nevertheless offset the infliction of harms, including injury and death, on innocent people. Bad effects cannot be offset and thereby justified by other bad effects.

Here is another way of making the same point. Recall that the justification for killing innocent civilians in war must be a lesser-evil justification. Wide proportionality is a constraint on such a justification. It specifies how much harm an act may cause as the lesser evil in relation to the harm it prevents. But an act that has the bad side effect of harming innocent civilians cannot be justified as the lesser evil on the ground that, by producing military advantage for unjust combatants, it also facilitates the achievement of other impartially bad effects. (Effects that are impartially good or bad contrast with those that are merely "relatively" good or bad. Military advantage for the Nazis is, for example, relatively good for the Nazis but impartially bad. Only effects that are impartially good or bad count in the assessment of proportionality.)

Another, though less serious, objection to weighing the harms to civilians caused by acts of war against military advantage only is that some acts of war, such as those classified under the heading of "non-kinetic targeting," are not military in nature. Some forms of cyberwarfare, for example, are harmful to civilians and must thus satisfy a wide proportionality requirement. They may, for example, be intended to cause economic disruption or to induce false beliefs about political matters among members of the civilian population. But in such instances they neither produce nor are intended to produce a military advantage because they are not directed at objects that "by their nature, location, purpose or use make an effective contribution to military action and whose total or partial destruction, capture or neutralization, in the circumstances ruling at the time, offers a definite military advantage."[34] It seems, therefore, that either the current legal principle of proportionality is defective in failing to apply in a range of cases to which it ought to apply or it implies that all instances of non-kinetic targeting that harm civilians but do not produce a military advantage are disproportionate because they have no effects that can offset the harms they cause to civilians.

34. AP I, *supra* note 18, art. 52(2).

The case for retaining the understanding of *in bello* proportionality currently found in international law and international criminal law depends on two claims: that it is the best of the possible understandings that are symmetrical between just and unjust combatants and that the adoption of an asymmetrical understanding would have dire consequences. Suppose that, as I and other revisionist just war theorists claim, *in bello* wide proportionality is, as a matter of morality, highly asymmetrical in its application, because acts of war by unjust combatants can only rarely have impartially good effects that are sufficient to offset both their impartially bad side effects *and* their impartially bad *intended* effects. Most acts of war by unjust combatants are therefore disproportionate in the wide sense and thus impermissible. It is, in short, not possible to fight in an unjust war without continually violating the morally correct principle of *in bello* wide proportionality, which demands that the harms that an act of war inflicts on innocent people be outweighed by its impartially good effects, such as the contribution it makes to the achievement of a just cause.[35]

Acknowledgment of these claims by the law would, it is often claimed, have bad effects for at least two reasons. First, by repudiating the symmetrical principle that weighs harms to innocent civilians against military advantage only, the law would deprive unjust combatants of a standard of proportionality that they believe these combatants can satisfy and would thereby forfeit one important way of motivating these combatants to exercise restraint in the conduct of war. Second, it would bring the law under pressure to acknowledge that fighting in a war with unjust aims is criminal, as one cannot fight in such a war without violating the *in bello* principle of wide proportionality—violations of which, I have claimed, can never be morally permissible. But if mere participation in an unjust war were criminalized, the law would be committed, at least in principle, to punishing unjust combatants simply for attacking just combatants, at least whenever such attacks would harm civilians as a side effect and thus violate the wide proportionality constraint.

Let us consider these two claims in turn. The first assumes that the current legal understanding of proportionality actually has a restraining effect on unjust combatants. It might be supposed to have this effect in either or both of two ways. First, combatants might believe that it would be morally wrong to seek military advantage in ways that would cause excessive harm to civilians as a side effect. They might then be morally motivated to avoid acting in this way. Second, they might be deterred from violating the principle of proportionality by the threat of legal punishment.

I suspect that the current symmetrical principle of proportionality does sometimes motivate unjust combatants to exercise restraint for moral reasons. An unjust combatant might well believe, for example, that killing 100 enemy civilians

35. It is also not possible, according to revisionist theorists, to fight in an unjust war without continually violating the morally correct *jus in bello* principles of discrimination and necessity, though I will not attempt to explain this here.

as a side effect would be disproportionate in relation to the military advantage to be gained from the destruction of a single tank, and he might be motivated by that belief to refrain from destroying the tank. His mistake would be to suppose that there is some degree of military advantage for his side that *could* offset and justify the killing of 100 civilians. (He would also be mistaken to suppose that the destruction of the tank would be proportionate if the only side effect would be the infliction of a slight bruise on a civilian.)

The relevant question is therefore empirical—namely, what the effect on such a combatant's attitudes and motivation would be if the law were to impose the morally coherent requirement that the harms an act of war causes to civilians be proportionate in relation to the act's impartially good effects, including, of course, its contribution to the achievement of a just cause. One possibility is that, like many or most unjust combatants, he would believe that he was in fact a just combatant and would thus, if he were morally motivated, attempt to weigh the harms his act would cause against the imagined impartial good effects he might expect it would have.[36] In that case, the law would be inducing restraint, perhaps more effectively than it could by urging him to weigh the harms against expected military advantage—for the latter would, after all, require him to be thinking incoherently.

The other possibility is that he correctly believes himself to be an unjust combatant. In that case, he should understand the morally correct principle of *in bello* proportionality to imply that his destroying the tank, or indeed virtually any other military target whose destruction would unavoidably cause harm to civilians, would be disproportionate to a higher degree, and in a more fundamental way, than he might imagine it to be if he were weighing the harm to civilians against military advantage. If we continue to assume that he is morally motivated, he will then be more strongly motivated to refrain from acting than he would be if he accepted the current legal standard of *in bello* proportionality.

Consider next the issue of enforcement. This is to a considerable degree independent of the content of the proportionality principle. The current legal principle could be made reasonably precise and then be enforced on the basis of the isomorphic scales I sketched earlier that would measure harm and military advantage. And the morally correct principle could be enforced as well. Up to the present, however, there have been no serious prosecutions in either international law or international criminal law for violations of the proportionality principles stated in Additional Protocol I[37] and the Rome Statute.[38] At present, therefore, there is no credible threat to punish combatants, just or unjust, for violations of *in bello* proportionality. It is thus unlikely that the current morally incoherent principle has any significant effect in restraining unjust combatants by means of deterrence.

36. He might imagine that it would have good effects that it would not have or that what are in fact bad effects would instead be good. This will be addressed later in this section.

37. *See supra* note 31.

38. *See supra* note 32.

It would of course be desirable to have a legal principle of *in bello* proportionality that could be enforced in a way that would motivate combatants, including unjust combatants, to exercise restraint in the conduct of war. But revisionist just war theorists must concede that, whatever its precise terms might be, the morally correct principle of *in bello* wide proportionality, which weighs the harms an act of war would cause to innocent people against the act's impartially good effects, is singularly ill suited to impartial legal enforcement against both just and unjust combatants. The problem is not enforcement against just combatants. It is rather that any attempt to enforce the correct principle against unjust combatants would be likely to have very bad consequences overall. This is because virtually the only acts of war by unjust combatants that could satisfy this proportionality requirement are those that would prevent just combatants from causing wrongful harms while pursuing their just aims by impermissible means. Other acts of war by unjust combatants—particularly those intended as means to the achievement of unjust goals—are, as I noted, highly unlikely to have impartially good effects that are sufficient to outweigh their intended and unintended impartially bad effects. Most acts of war by unjust combatants will therefore be in violation of the correct principle of wide proportionality. Because of this, effective enforcement would require trying and punishing most of the combatants who fight for unjust aims in unjust wars.

Punishing acts of war by unjust combatants that harm innocent people as a side effect but have few or no offsetting good effects would in practice be tantamount to punishing unjust combatants simply for fighting in an unjust war. This would be objectionable for a variety of reasons. It would, for example, require the law to distinguish between just and unjust wars, or between wars with impartially good aims and wars with impartially bad aims. Because no area of law can ever simply restate the principles of morality that govern the area of life covered by that law, the relevant moral distinctions are unlikely to coincide with the distinction between legal and illegal wars. This is because the correct moral principles of *jus ad bellum*, if we could discover them, are likely to be both complex and subtle, whereas law must be comparatively simple to be able induce us, with our many cognitive, moral, and motivational infirmities, to act in morally acceptable ways. And to be able to punish soldiers without injustice, the law would also have to provide some public guidance about which wars were unjust, both before they were initiated and as they progressed, as their aims and moral status would be susceptible to change.

It is certainly possible and desirable that, particularly through the creation of new international institutions, the law of war can be brought into much closer congruence with morality. But in the near term it is unrealistic, for the reasons just stated, to suppose that the law could appropriately punish combatants on the basis of its judgments about which wars are just and which are unjust.

But suppose for the sake of argument that the law could overcome the obstacles to identifying which wars are unjust and communicating this information to soldiers. Many other problems would remain. If, at the end of a war, one state was judged to have fought unjustly, it would certainly be unwilling to submit all or most of the members of its military who had fought in the war to trial by a court, even an international court. Perhaps a further war would have to be fought to compel it to do so. But suppose that it would somehow be possible to put a large number of ordinary soldiers who had fought in an unjust war on trial. Even if all of them had engaged in acts of war that killed or injured innocent people, most of them would be to some degree excused for having done so as a result of duress, nonculpable ignorance, and other mitigating considerations. If these considerations were taken into account, few of these erstwhile unjust combatants would deserve more than a very mild form of punishment, the prospect of which would do little to deter them or others from obeying an order to fight in an unjust war.

It would, moreover, be prohibitively time consuming and costly for a court to examine the claimed excuses of a very large number of soldiers. There are at least three alternatives. One would be to assume for convenience that all the former unjust combatants had substantial excuses. That, however, would decisively undermine the deterrent effect of the threatened punishment. A second option would be to have full trials though only for some small proportion of the former unjust combatants, perhaps selected by lottery. But if the proportion tried were relatively small, which it would have to be to avoid overburdening the courts, the deterrent effect would again be lost. The third option would be to hold all the unjust combatants strictly liable by declining to take their claimed excuses into account. This, however, would not only be profoundly unjust but could also have a significant bad effect. While threatening all unjust combatants with relatively harsh punishment would help to deter combatants from participating in unjust wars, in cases in which the deterrent effect was insufficient to prevent an unjust war from being fought, the threat of severe *post bellum* punishment could then deter unjust combatants from surrendering when they would otherwise do so. They might prefer to continue to fight in the hope that victory would shield them from punishment than to surrender and face the prospect of severe punishment. If so, their unjust war would be unnecessarily prolonged, thereby increasing the harms that they would inflict on innocent people.

A further possibility might be to make violations of *in bello* proportionality illegal but not criminal—that is, not punishable. Although that would involve abandoning the aim of deterring violations, it would bring the authority of the law to bear in strengthening the moral motivation that combatants might have to avoid causing disproportionate harm to innocent people. This, however, would abandon too much. Somehow the law ought to be able to punish genuine violations of wide proportionality by just combatants—for example, the killing of hundreds of children as a foreseen side effect of destroying a single enemy tank.

It would, however, be absurd if the law could punish, and thereby deter, violations of *in bello* proportionality only by just combatants, allowing unjust combatants to go unpunished and undeterred. There is therefore reason to explore other possible ways of understanding *in bello* proportionality—ways that might not be fully correct morally but that would not be altogether incoherent and would enable the law to deter both just and unjust combatants from conducting certain military operations that would cause extensive harm to innocent people as a side effect. One might try, in particular, to identify a different way from that found in current law of understanding *in bello* wide proportionality that is symmetrical between just and unjust combatants, in the sense of being satisfiable by each at roughly equal cost in overall military effectiveness.

In previous work, I have developed and discussed two such proposals. I will briefly rehearse those discussions here to indicate why neither proposal is acceptable.

What we seek is a principle of *in bello* wide proportionality that weighs the harms that acts of war would cause to innocent people against good effects that can be expected to be produced in roughly equal measure by acts of war by just and unjust combatants alike. Only a principle of this sort is well suited to being effectively enforced as a means of motivating both just and unjust combatants to exercise restraint in the conduct of war.

One suggestion is that the good effects of an act of war that can weigh against harms to innocent people be restricted to preventions of harm that are the immediate causal consequences of the act.[39] Suppose, for example, that a missile launcher is located next to a civilian home (perhaps intentionally, to exploit any scruples that enemy combatants might have about killing the inhabitants as a side effect of destroying the launcher). Suppose further that unless it is destroyed, the launcher will be used to kill a certain number of enemy combatants and noncombatants. But if the combatants who would be the targets of the missile destroy the missile launcher in self-defense, they will kill the civilians in the adjacent home. According to this first suggested understanding of *in bello* proportionality, if the prevention of the killings of the combatants and noncombatants by the missile launcher is sufficient to outweigh the killing of the innocent civilians in the home, the destruction of the launcher would be proportionate. If the saving of the immediate potential victims of the launcher is insufficient to outweigh the killing of the inhabitants, the attack would be disproportionate. These claims concern the weighing of harms caused against harms averted and are neutral between just and unjust combatants—that is, they make no reference to whether the combatants who might destroy the launcher are just combatants or unjust combatants. Whether the destruction of the launcher would contribute to the achievement of a just cause is irrelevant to whether destroying it would be proportionate.

Although this proposal may seem promising, there are, I believe, at least two decisive objections to it. First, many acts of war by just combatants have three features: they make it more likely that the just cause will ultimately be achieved, they cause harm to innocent people as a side effect, and they have no immediate good effects, such as the prevention of harm. It is clear, I think, that acts of this sort can be permissible; therefore they can be proportionate. But they cannot be

39. This is a slightly different and, I think, better version of a view I previously sketched and then criticized. *See* Jeff McMahan, *War Crimes and Immoral Action in War*, *in* The Constitution of Criminal Law 151, 181–82 (R.A. Duff, Lindsay Farmer, S.E. Marshall, Massimo Renzo, & Victor Tadros eds., 2013).

proportionate according to this first suggested understanding of *in bello* wide proportionality because they have no immediate good effects that can offset the harms they immediately inflict on innocent people.[40]

The second, equally decisive objection is that this understanding's apparent neutrality between just and unjust combatants is an illusion. Consider again the case in which, if combatants destroy a missile launcher, they will prevent themselves and some nearby civilians from being killed but will also, as a side effect, kill the civilians in the house that is adjacent to the launcher. According to the proposed understanding of proportionality, the prevention of harms to the combatants is an immediate causal consequence of the act of war and thus weighs against and can offset the harms to the innocent people in their home. As a matter of morality, however, this is true only if the prevention of harm to the combatants is an impartially good effect. But if the combatants are unjust combatants, preventing them from being harmed by just combatants is not an impartially good effect; it is an impartially bad effect, as it enables the unjust combatants to continue both to pursue the unjust aims of their war and to threaten the lives of just combatants and of civilians on the just side. The saving of the unjust combatants' lives is of course a relative good for the unjust combatants themselves, but effects that are relatively good but impartially bad cannot offset other impartially bad effects of an act of war in the assessment of proportionality.

The other way of understanding the *in bello* proportionality requirement so that it could be satisfied by just and unjust combatants alike stipulates that the harms that an act of war would cause to innocent people be weighed against whatever impartially good effects the combatants might *most reasonably believe* the act will have.[41] Early in the Iraq War, for example, American soldiers might reasonably have believed that their acts of war would have the impartially good effect of preventing the Ba'athist regime from being able to use weapons of mass destruction against regional enemies or from supplying those weapons to terrorists for use against the United States. They might then have weighed the harms their acts would cause to innocent civilians against likely prevention of harms to innocent people that might have been caused by Iraq's weapons of mass destruction. They could then reasonably have judged their action to be proportionate even though there were in fact no weapons of mass destruction.

This way of understanding proportionality seems to apply equally to just and unjust combatants. In the example, the possible implication of the view that acts of war by American forces were proportionate does not depend on the claim that the American war in Iraq was just, either in its early phases or overall. It depends

40. For elaboration, *see id.*

41. An alternative version weighs the bad effects against whatever good effects the combatants actually believe the act would have. This is less plausible because it allows that an act can be proportionate because of the agent's unreasonable beliefs. It is also less serviceable because it makes proportionality vary from combatant to combatant, as they may have different beliefs. I will therefore not consider it here.

only on what it could have been reasonable to believe about the effects of the American action, which is compatible with the war's actually being unjust.

One objection to this proposal is that it makes proportionality depend on what it might be reasonable for combatants to believe in the circumstances rather than on the facts. But in practice this is unavoidable whenever anyone attempts to determine whether an act will be—or, indeed, was—proportionate. This is presumably why Additional Protocol I explicitly requires the weighing of bad effects that an act of war is "expected" to cause against the act's "anticipated" good effects.[42]

While this second proposal has some plausibility when applied to cases, such as that of the American war in Iraq, in which combatants may have reasonable, though false, *empirical* beliefs about the impartial good effects of their acts of war, it has no plausibility when applied to acts of war that could be thought to have impartially good effects only on the basis of mistaken *moral* beliefs. Suppose, for example, that a group of people were to go to war with the sole aim of exterminating another race of people whom they believe ought not to exist—not because they believe the existence of this race is harmful in some way but just because they believe the members of the race are unworthy of existence. There is no way that such a belief could be reasonable, and, more importantly, no way that the supposed impartial goodness of exterminating some number of these people could be measured for the sake of comparison. Thus, if some act of war would both kill a certain number of the members of the race but also harm some innocent people of another race as a side effect, it is unintelligible to suppose that the latter harms could be weighed against or offset by the supposed good of the killings.

My argument in this section leaves the law in a quandary. The proportionality principle as stated in Additional Protocol I and the Rome Statute provides only the illusion of guidance to unjust combatants, as the effects it weighs against the harms their acts of war cause to innocent people are incapable of offsetting and thereby justifying those harms, except in rare instances in which the military advantage gained consists in preventing just combatants from causing wrongful harms by acting impermissibly (assuming that simply preventing wrongdoing by just combatants actually comes within the scope of the notion of "military advantage"). There is, in my view, no sense in which acts of war by unjust combatants can be proportionate when the only aims they advance are unjust and they also cause harm to innocent people as a side effect.

It may be that legal theorists have failed to notice the moral incoherence of the current legal understanding of the requirement of proportionality because

42. *See supra* note 31. It is curious, and perhaps unwarranted, that the drafters of the Rome Statute decided to insist on weighing the bad effects that an act of war "will have" against its "anticipated" good effects. There are other differences between the statements in the two documents, but I will ignore them here and treat the two statements as if they were the same. On the differences between the protections afforded to civilians in international humanitarian law and in international criminal law, *see* Adil Haque, *Protecting and Respecting Civilians: Correcting the Substantive Defects of the Rome Statute*, 14 NEW CRIM. L. REV. 519 (2011). For the main discussion of proportionality, *see id.* at 541–48.

the courts have never really been called upon to enforce it against violations by ordinary soldiers. If the courts were to begin to enforce this requirement against allegations of violations by unjust combatants, it would become very difficult for them to conceal the moral arbitrariness of weighing harms inflicted on innocent civilians against military advantage.

Eventually the law may have to concede that unjust combatants cannot fight in ways that are proportionate and thus, insofar as proportionality is a condition of moral permissibility, cannot fight permissibly when their acts harm innocent civilians as a side effect. We would then have to choose between acknowledging that the law of armed conflict permits the widespread violation of the correct moral principles of *jus in bello* and making participation in unjust wars illegal. I suspect that the latter is the better of these two options. In declaring that those who fight and kill as a means of achieving unjust aims act illegally, the law would not be committed to declaring as well that their action is also criminal, or punishable. One might hope that declaring most of the acts of war by unjust combatants illegal without threatening to punish them for those acts would be at least as effective in moderating their behavior as what the law does at present, which is to declare some of their acts disproportionate, at least by implication, without credibly threatening to punish them for those acts.

VI. PROPORTIONALITY IN ACTS OF WAR BY JUST COMBATANTS

As I noted at the beginning of this chapter, proportionality is a constraint on a justification for causing harm. It should therefore not be surprising that most acts of war by unjust combatants cannot satisfy the morally correct *in bello* proportionality requirement, for there is simply no moral justification for these acts that might be constrained by a proportionality requirement. One might say of these acts either that the harms they inflict on innocent people as side effects are disproportionate because they are not offset and outweighed by other effects that are impartially good, or one might say that in these cases the issue of proportionality simply does not arise, as the acts are already impermissible because they lack even a presumptive moral justification.

There are, however, clearly proportionality constraints that apply to acts of war by just combatants, when those acts support the achievement of just aims. In these cases, the morally correct understanding of *in bello* wide proportionality and the current legal understanding may be closely aligned in their judgments, assuming that military advantage from an act of war by just combatants is a contribution to, or increases the probability of, the achievement of a just cause. There is, however, potential for divergence insofar as the morally correct principle allows that impartially good effects produced by an act of war that are not elements of the achievement of a just cause and are unrelated to military advantage may nevertheless weigh against and offset at least some of the bad effects of that act of war. But we can ignore this here and simply assume, in this section, that the correct moral principle and the current legal principles coincide. It should become evident that this is an innocuous assumption for the purposes of this section.

One concern that is frequently expressed in assessments of the proportionality of acts of war by just combatants is that the bad and good effects are often very different in kind and thus difficult to compare. How, for example, does one weigh the deaths of hundreds of innocent people against some increase in the probability of preserving certain political freedoms for a much greater number of different people? There are no simple answers to questions of this sort. The relevant comparisons are highly imprecise and the questions may have no determinate answers. This is not to say, of course, that the protection or promotion of values that are impossible to measure or compare with precision cannot count in the assessment of proportionality. Many, though not all, such values do count, and many, though fewer, are capable of offsetting and thereby justifying the killing of innocent civilians as a side effect. And some can provide the basis of a just cause for war.[43] But there are also cases in which the impartially good effects of an act of war consist in the prevention of the same types of bad effect that the act would inflict on innocent people as a side effect. In these cases, the good and bad effects may be reasonably precisely comparable. These cases, therefore, are particularly well suited to explaining how the *in bello* proportionality requirement applies in practice to acts of war by just combatants.

This phenomenon is, I believe, well illustrated by most of the military operations conducted by Israeli forces in the invasions of Gaza in 2008–2009 and 2014. In both those wars, Israel's main aim was to prevent rockets and terrorist fighters from Gaza from killing ordinary Israeli citizens. I will assume that this aim was a just cause for war in each instance.[44] Certainly the prevention of the killing of innocent people is an impartially good effect. But acts of war by Israeli combatants that were intended to destroy missile launchers and tunnels from Gaza into Israel killed many ordinary Palestinian citizens of Gaza as a side effect.[45] These good and bad effects—preventing killings of ordinary Israelis and killing ordinary Palestinians—are readily comparable.

Before I explain the considerations that I believe are relevant to determining whether acts of war by Israeli combatants in Gaza were proportionate, it is worth digressing briefly to note a mistake about proportionality that was often made in discussions of both Gaza wars. The Israeli invasions were sometimes condemned as disproportionate on the ground that the number of Palestinian civilians who were killed greatly exceeded the number of Israeli civilians who had previously been killed by rockets fired from Gaza. But the number of Israeli civilians who had been killed in the past was irrelevant to whether the killings of Palestinian

43. On which good and bad effects may count, and which do not, *see* Hurka, *supra* note 33, at 39–50; McMahan, *Proportionate Defense*, *supra* note 15, at 148–54.

44. I will also put aside doubts about whether these wars satisfied the *ad bellum* requirement of necessity. For a brief, parenthetical discussion, *see* Jeff McMahan, *Proportionality and Necessity in* Jus in Bello, *in* The Oxford Handbook of the Ethics of War 418, 428 (Helen Frowe & Seth Lazar eds., 2017).

45. I will set aside the possibility that some of the killings were intended.

civilians in the Gaza wars were proportionate, except insofar as the previous killings furnished evidence of the attackers' intentions for the future and their military capabilities.

One might think that the previous killings of Israelis were relevant to whether the later killings of Palestinians were proportionate if one thought that the justification for the killings of Palestinians was that they were *reprisals*. In law, a reprisal is a use of force intended to compel an adversary to halt or repair some breach of international law. It is an act of retaliatory harming intended to deter an adversary from engaging in further harmful action. It is meant to work by implicitly threatening further reprisals in response to further provocations. Proportionality in reprisals is thought to be a relation between the harm one has suffered and the harm one inflicts. Thus, in the International Criminal Tribunal for the Former Yugoslavia, the Trial Chamber offered an account of proportionality in reprisals when it ruled that "reprisals must not be excessive compared to the precedent unlawful act of warfare."[46]

I am assuming, however, that the Israeli attacks that killed Palestinian civilians were not reprisals. I am assuming that the harms to civilians were side effects rather than intended effects and, in particular, were not intended to convey implicit threats of further killings of civilians. If these assumptions are wrong and the killings of civilians were intended, at least in some cases, to deter Hamas militants from continuing to try to kill Israeli civilians, then the killings were wrong, and illegal, because they violated the requirement of discrimination.[47] On this alternative assumption, the killings of civilians were acts of terrorism, as are all reprisals that intentionally harm innocent people as a means of coercing or intimidating others.[48]

But on the assumption that the killings of Palestinian civilians were unintended consequences of military attacks intended to defend ordinary Israeli civilians, whether they were proportionate depends entirely on the comparison between the harms inflicted on the Palestinian civilians and the harms that the Israeli attacks prevented Hamas militants from inflicting on innocent Israelis in the future. In previous writings I have stated this point in more general terms by claiming that proportionality in defense is entirely *prospective*.[49]

The relevant question, therefore, is how many innocent Palestinians it could be permissible for Israeli combatants to kill as a side effect of preventing the

46. Prosecutor v. Kupresic, Case No. IT-95-16-T, Judgment, ¶ 535 (International Criminal Tribunal for the Former Yugoslavia, Jan. 14, 2000).

47. *See* AP I, *supra* note 18, arts. 48, 51(2); *see also id.* art. 51(6).

48. *See id.* art. 51(2).

49. Discussions with Aidan Penn and Todd Karhu have convinced me that this is an overstatement and that harms that one has inflicted in the past can affect the amount of harm to which one is liable now for defensive purposes—that is, that past harms can be relevant to narrow proportionality. But, as the type of case in which past harms can affect liability is unlikely to arise in war, I will ignore this complication here.

wrongful killing by Hamas of a fixed number of innocent Israeli civilians.[50] The most illuminating way to think about this question, I believe, is to consider a range of common beliefs about the permissibility of the infliction of harms as a side effect of otherwise permissible acts of self- and other-defense. Suppose, for example, that an innocent victim is about to be killed by a fully culpable threatener. Although the victim is unable to defend herself, a third party is able to defend her at no cost to herself by killing the threatener. Assume that killing the threatener is both necessary and proportionate in the narrow sense. If these were all the facts, I believe that the third party would have a duty to defend the victim by killing the threatener. But suppose further that, in killing the threatener, the third party would unavoidably kill an innocent bystander as a side effect and that the harm to the bystander in being killed would be roughly the same as the harm to the victim in being killed. When this detail is added, I believe that it is clear that the third party must allow the victim to be killed. This is because there is a moral asymmetry between killing innocent people and allowing innocent people to die or be killed. And the third party's choice is between killing an innocent person and allowing an innocent person to be killed.

Only if the harm caused to innocent people by the third party's intervention would be substantially less than the harm to innocent people that the intervention would prevent would the intervention be justifiable as the lesser evil, thereby overriding the constraint against killing the innocent, even as a side effect. Some philosophers have argued, however, that there is a possible justification for self-defense that does not apply to third-party defense of others. This is that each individual has, at least in certain contexts, an "agent-relative permission" to give some degree of priority to her own interests over the equivalent interests of others. Some philosophers have thought, for example, that an innocent person can have an agent-relative permission to kill a person who will otherwise kill her even though the threatener is in no way morally responsible for the threat and thus has not made herself liable to be killed.[51] The victim can, in other words, have an agent-relative permission to kill the nonresponsible threatener in self-defense even though there is neither a liability justification nor a lesser-evil justification for the defensive killing. Other philosophers have thought that there can be an agent-relative permission not only to kill a nonresponsible threatener in self-defense but also to kill an innocent person as an unavoidable side effect of action that is necessary to save one's own life. If this is right, it might be that, although the third party is not permitted to kill the bystander as a side effect of defending the victim's life, the victim would be permitted to do so if she could.

50. For further discussion of some of the claims in the remainder of this section, as well as further comments on the Gaza war of 2014, *see* McMahan, *Proportionality and Necessity in* Jus in Bello, *supra* note 44.

51. Jonathan Quong, *Killing in Self-Defense*, 119 Ethics 507 (2009); Jonathan Quong, *Agent-Relative Prerogatives to Do Harm*, 10 Crim. L. & Phil. 815 (2016).

My own view is that people are permitted to give some degree of priority to their own interests over the interests of others, though normally only when their doing so is not opposed by a moral constraint, such as the constraint against killing an innocent person. Thus, for example, I believe that a person is permitted to save her own life rather than save the lives of two strangers when she cannot do both, but that she is not permitted either to kill a nonresponsible threatener in self-defense or to kill an innocent person as a side effect of saving her own life—assuming that other things are equal.[52]

Even those who argue that there is an agent-relative permission to kill an innocent person either as a means or side effect of the defense of one's own life recognize that there is a proportionality constraint on this form of justification. Some accept that, although it can be permissible, for example, to kill one innocent person as a side effect of saving one's own life, it is not permissible to kill two. Others accept that it can be permissible to kill two. Few believe that it can be permissible to kill three.

One important question for those who believe that there can be an agent-relative permission to kill an innocent person is whether that permission can be transferred by the agent to a third party. I believe that, if there were such a permission, it would be genuinely *agent*-relative and could not be transferred. Suppose, for example, that I have an agent-relative permission to kill an innocent bystander as a side effect of defending my own life. And suppose I also have a paid bodyguard who has a professional duty to defend my life. A situation arises in which an aggressor threatens my life, but I am unable to defend myself. My bodyguard can defend me but will unavoidably kill an innocent bystander as a side effect if he does so. It is clear, however, that an ordinary passerby is not permitted to kill the bystander as a side effect of defending my life, even if I ask her to do so (that is, even if I try to transfer my agent-relative permission to her). If that is right, then I also cannot make it permissible for my bodyguard to kill the innocent bystander merely by paying him to do it.

There is another possible justification for killing an innocent bystander as a side effect of the defense of a single person. Perhaps surprisingly, this justification—if in fact there is such a justification—applies only to other-defense and not to self-defense. It derives from the fact that special relations between people can be the source of special duties. A parent's special relation to her child, for example, gives her special duties to that child. It may well be that the special relation gives the parent not only special duties but also special permissions that even the child himself does not have. Suppose, for example, that a young adult has no agent-relative permission to kill an innocent bystander as a side effect of defending his own life. The young adult's parent might nevertheless have a special permission (a

52. For arguments against the view that there can be an agent-relative permission to kill innocent people, *see* Helen Frowe, Defensive Killing 54–63 (2014). For arguments that it is generally impermissible to kill a nonresponsible threatener in self-defense, *see* Jeff McMahan, *Nonresponsible Killers*, 15 J. Moral Phil. 651 (2018).

"special relations permission"), grounded in the moral significance of the parental relation, to defend her child's life even if in doing so she will unavoidably kill an innocent bystander as a side effect.

In my view, the claim that it can be permissible to kill an innocent bystander as a side effect of saving the life of someone to whom one is importantly specially related is more plausible than the claim that there is an agent-relative permission to kill an innocent person as side effect of saving one's own life. This is simply because special relations are *morally* significant in ways that simple self-interest is not. Hence, if it were true that there are both agent-relative permissions and special relations permissions, I think that the amount of harm it could be permissible to inflict on innocent bystanders as a side effect of defending the life of someone to whom one is importantly specially related would be greater than the amount that it could be permissible to inflict as a side effect of defending one's own life.

In endeavoring to understand, in cases such as the Israeli invasions of Gaza, how much harm it can be proportionate to inflict on innocent people as a side effect of preventing terrorists or unjust combatants from unjustifiably harming or killing other innocent people, we must first achieve an understanding of the matters of moral theory I have just mentioned. We must determine, among other things:

1. whether there really is a moral asymmetry between killing innocent people and allowing innocent people to die that establishes a presumption or constraint against killing one innocent bystander as a side effect of saving a different innocent person;
2. if there is such an asymmetry, how strong it is;
3. whether people have an agent-relative permission to give some degree of priority to their own lives and interests over those of others;
4. if there is such a permission, how strong it is, and in particular how many innocent people it can make it permissible to kill as a side effect of self-defense of one's life;
5. whether such a permission can be transferred to a third party, such as combatants who have a duty to defend their fellow citizens or others, or both;
6. whether there can be a special relations permission to kill an innocent person as a side effect of defending the life of someone to whom one is importantly specially related;
7. if there can be such a permission, how many innocent people it can make it permissible to kill as a side effect of saving people to whom one is specially related;
8. also if there can be such a permission, whether the relations between just combatants and the innocent people they have a duty to defend are sufficiently important to make it permissible for a combatant to kill an innocent person as a side effect of saving the life of someone he has a duty to defend; and

9. if so, how many innocent people it can be permissible for him to kill as a side effect of saving a single person he has a duty to defend.

Although I have indicated what my tentative views about some of these matters are, I will not defend those views here. But simply showing what the relevant considerations are enables us to understand the work in moral theory that must be done before we can reach a sound understanding of how the action of just combatants in war is morally constrained by wide proportionality. It also helps us to understand what the range of potentially defensible views is. We can again illustrate this with the case of Israel's invasions of Gaza.

Consider first the most restrictive range of potentially defensible assumptions about the relevant issues. Suppose, that is, that

1. there is a strong moral asymmetry between killing innocent people and allowing innocent people to die or be killed;
2. there is no agent-relative permission to kill an innocent or nonresponsible person in self-defense; and
3. there is no special relations permission to kill an innocent or nonresponsible person in defense of someone to whom one is specially related.

On these assumptions, it was not proportionate for Israeli combatants to kill even one innocent Palestinian civilian as a side effect of preventing the killing of one innocent Israeli civilian. Indeed, depending on how strong the asymmetry is between killing an innocent person and allowing an innocent person to be killed, it might have been proportionate for Israeli combatants to kill one innocent Palestinian as a side effect only if they would thereby have prevented the killing of some larger number of Israeli civilians—for example, four, five, or even more. It is perhaps revealing that, in discussions of trolley cases,[53] now familiar well beyond academic philosophy, it is usually assumed to be permissible to kill one innocent person as a side effect of saving other innocent people only if the number of people saved is five or more.

Next consider the most permissive range of potentially defensible assumptions. These are that

1. there is either no moral asymmetry between killing innocent people and allowing innocent people to be killed or only a weak asymmetry of that sort;
2. people have a strong agent-relative permission to give priority to their own interests and lives over those of other innocent people;
3. this agent-relative permission is transferrable to third parties;
4. people have strong special relations permissions to give priority to the interests or lives of those to whom they are importantly specially related over the interests and lives of other innocent people;

53. *See supra* p. 14.

5. the ways in which just combatants are specially related to those whom they have a duty to defend—such as co-citizenship, contractual relations, and so on—are sufficiently important to ground strong special relations permissions to harm or kill innocent people as a side effect of fulfilling their duties of defense; and
6. agent-relative permissions and special relations permissions are additive—that is, each applies separately so that the number of innocent people one has a special relations permission to kill is simply added to the number one has an agent-relative permission to kill.

On these assumptions, an innocent Israeli citizen's agent-relative permission might make it proportionate for her to kill as many as three innocent Palestinians as a side effect of defending her own life. Because her agent-relative permission transfers to Israeli combatants whose duty it is to defend her, they too are permitted to kill as many as three Palestinian civilians as a side effect of defending her. These combatants are also specially related to her in a way that permits them to give her priority over Palestinian civilians for that reason as well. The combatants might, for example, have a special relations permission to kill two or three Palestinian civilians as a side effect of preventing her from being killed. Assuming that these two sources of special permissions are additive, it can be proportionate for Israeli combatants to kill five or six innocent Palestinian civilians as a side effect of defending the life of a single innocent Israeli civilian.

These different sets of assumptions, which constitute the range of reasonable views about the relevant considerations, yield the range of possibly defensible views about harms that it can be proportionate in the wide sense for just combatants to inflict on innocent civilians as a side effect in war. On the most restrictive assumptions, it can be proportionate for just combatants to kill one innocent civilian as a side effect only if their action saves at least five innocent civilians on their own side. On the most permissive assumptions, it can be proportionate for just combatants to kill as many as five or six innocent civilians on the opposing side as a side effect of saving only one innocent civilian on their own side.

Which view within the range is correct depends on which of the different views about the relevant issues of moral theory are correct. As always, arcane matters of moral theory turn out to be essential to understanding the morality of war.

VII. CONCLUSION

In the previous sections, I have sought to provide constructive guidance for both just war theorists and theorists of the law of armed conflict in the practical application of the *in bello* principle of wide proportionality to the conduct of just combatants.

My aim in section V, however, was critical: to show that in most actual cases, this same principle either condemns as disproportionate, or disclaims as eligible for evaluation as proportionate or disproportionate, virtually all acts of war by unjust combatants. This verdict will be unaffected by whatever we determine to be true about the issues in moral theory discussed in section VI. The challenge posed in section V should be profoundly worrying for legal theorists. I have been unable to find a reassuring response to it. Perhaps I have overlooked some obvious solution—or some unobvious solution. I hope, in any case, that theorists of the law of armed conflict will take the challenge seriously.

PART TWO

Considerations of Overarching Significance

On the Continuous and Concurrent Application of *Ad Bellum* and *In Bello* Proportionality

ELIAV LIEBLICH*

I. INTRODUCTION

The principle of proportionality in international law exists both in the law regulating the resort to force—or *jus ad bellum*—and the law that governs how wars are fought, or *jus in bello*. In both spheres of law, proportionality seeks to constrain force in relation to a certain lawful objective. Few would dispute that this is common to proportionality on both levels. Yet, beyond this simple understanding, few other aspects relating to the interaction between *ad bellum* and *in bello* proportionality are clear.

This chapter addresses two distinct yet interrelated aspects of the interaction between proportionality on both levels of international law. The first is, broadly speaking, temporal, and concerns the question whether, or the extent to which, *jus ad bellum* proportionality applies throughout an armed conflict, alongside proportionality under *jus in bello*. The second is substantive, and relates to the manner in which both levels of proportionality interact, assuming that they indeed apply concurrently.

Concerning the temporal question, one view—which we may call the *static approach*—posits that there are at least some cases in which *ad bellum* proportionality ceases to apply after the initial judgment on the resort to force. On the opposing view, *ad bellum* proportionality applies continuously throughout the

* Associate Professor, Tel-Aviv University's Buchmann Faculty of Law. This research was supported by the Israel Science Foundation (grant no. 1787/17). I would like to thank Shani Rozenzweig for her excellent research assistance, and the participants at the Lieber Institute's Annual Workshop, U.S. Military Academy, West Point, October 2018.

Eliav Lieblich, *On the Continuous and Concurrent Application of* Ad Bellum *and* In Bello *Proportionality* In: *Necessity and Proportionality in International Peace and Security Law.* Edited by: Professor Claus Kreß and Captain Robert Lawless, Oxford University Press (2021). © Oxford University Press. DOI: 10.1093/oso/9780197537374.003.0003.

conflict. This view can be called the *continuous application* approach. In this chapter, I revisit the debate on this question, as best represented by the position of Yoram Dinstein, on the one hand, and Christopher Greenwood, on the other. While both views reflect the thought of two of the foremost international lawyers in the field, the debate between them remains undertheorized. I seek to offer a fresh take on this debate, by exploring the underlying normative assumptions of these positions. Doing so, I defend the continuous application view, on the basis of legal policy considerations and recent advances in just war theory.

This is worthwhile, I think, although the vast majority of legal commentators reject the static approach. This is because, I suspect, the static approach guides states more than is openly admitted.[1] Indeed, whether the static or continuous approach is adopted has immense practical ramifications, in particular in long and intractable conflicts. Consider the current situation between Iran, Israel, and Syria. As reported, in recent years, Israel has attacked targets in Syria dozens of times.[2] Because there are usually several weeks between such exchanges—if not months—it is perfectly possible, in operational terms, to view them as separate incidents. In legal terms, the question is whether each hostile exchange in situations such as Syria must be subject to a new *jus ad bellum* analysis requiring a new *ad bellum* necessity and proportionality assessment, or rather, once a certain threshold is crossed—for instance, a full-scale war erupted in the distant past—only *jus in bello* proportionality remains relevant.

The second, substantive aspect addressed in this chapter assumes that *jus ad bellum* indeed applies continuously throughout the conflict and then considers the manner in which it might apply *concurrently* with *in bello* proportionality. Here, a host of complex questions arise. Are the same state organs obliged to consider both levels of proportionality? Do *ad bellum* proportionality considerations

1. So much so, that Yishai Beer argues critically that by not applying throughout the conflict, the principle of proportionality under *jus ad bellum* enables a Clausewitzian model of total war. As a solution, Beer argues that this should be corrected through the application of *jus in bello* necessity. Yishai Beer, *Military Strategy: The Blind Spot of International Humanitarian Law*, 8 Harv. Nat'l Sec. J. 333, 355–58 (2017). For a wider presentation of the argument, *see* Yishai Beer, Military Professionalism and Humanitarian Law: The Struggle to Reduce the Hazards of War (2018); *cf.* Brian J. Egan, *International Law, Legal Diplomacy, and the Counter-ISIL Campaign*, Just Security (Apr. 4, 2016), https://www.justsecurity.org/wp-content/uploads/2016/04/Egan-ASIL-speech.pdf ("In the view of the United States, once a State has lawfully resorted to force in self-defense against a particular armed group following an actual or imminent armed attack by that group, it is not necessary as a matter of international law to reassess whether an armed attack is imminent prior to every subsequent action taken against that group, provided that hostilities have not ended").

2. Some of these attacks targeted alleged weapon shipments to Hizbullah in Lebanon, while more recently, Iranian or pro-Iranian forces that support the Assad regime. When Syrian anti-aircraft forces respond, Israel attacks these targets also. For an updating overview, *see* Int'l Crisis Grp., Golan Heights and South/West Syria, Int'l Crisis Grp.: Flashpoint, https://www.crisisgroup.org/trigger-list/iran-us-trigger-list/flashpoints/golan-heights (last updated Oct. 1, 2019).

inform *in bello* assessments? Is the *ad bellum* proportionality assessment affected by the aggregation of harms and benefits that figure in *in bello* proportionality analyses? How does concurrent application relate to the principle of equal application of international humanitarian law (IHL)? More generally, should there be conflation between the two levels?

When attempting to answer these questions, it quickly becomes apparent that in order to understand concurrent application, we must first commit ourselves to a certain understanding of *jus ad bellum* proportionality. This, however, is tricky. While there is a general consensus on the contents of *in bello* proportionality—namely, that it comprises an ex ante comparison between the anticipated military advantage accrued by an attack and the expected incidental civilian harm it would inflict[3]—there is significant disagreement on the content of *jus ad bellum* proportionality. International lawyers have sometimes understood proportionality under *jus ad bellum* as a quantitative comparison between force and counterforce, sometimes as a comparison between the harms and benefits accrued by the resort to force, but mostly, as a means-ends test, which assesses whether the scope of the forcible response was required in order to halt and repel an armed attack and, perhaps, imminent counterattacks.[4] Each one of these understandings gives rise to specific difficulties in concurrent application. This chapter, thus, discusses these difficulties under the different approaches to *ad bellum* proportionality.

Furthermore, once concurrent application is recognized, there is a strong pull to conflate *ad bellum* and *in bello* proportionality. Conflation, in this context, might mean several things. Either that the leeway allowed in *in bello* proportionality is somehow affected by justness *ad bellum* (which challenges the idea of belligerent equality); or that the *ad bellum* proportionality assessment is affected by the results of *in bello* proportionality decisions; or, that the application of both tests is somehow similar in any other manner. As this chapter argues, while there is significant overlap between the underpinning normative rationales on both levels of proportionality, concurrent application should not mean conflation. This is because there is no convincing alternative to the pragmatic idea of belligerent equality, and the other types of conflation are impracticable. *Functionally*, therefore, the spheres should remain separate.

Section II revisits the debate on the static and continuous approach to *jus ad bellum* proportionality. Section III inquires into the possible underlying rationales for the static approach and makes the case that those are indefensible. In this part, for the sake of analysis, I hold constant the understanding of *ad bellum* proportionality as a means-ends test, as it is usually understood by lawyers. In section

3. For a recent summary and discussion of key issues, *see* INT'L COMM. OF THE RED CROSS, INTERNATIONAL EXPERT MEETING: THE PRINCIPLE OF PROPORTIONALITY IN THE RULES GOVERNING THE CONDUCT OF HOSTILITIES UNDER INTERNATIONAL HUMANITARIAN LAW (Laurent Gisel ed., 2018).

4. For a discussion of the positions on the latter issue, *see* David Kretzmer, *The Inherent Right to Self-Defence and Proportionality in* Jus ad Bellum, 24 EUR. J. INT'L L. 235, 264–66 (2013).

IV, I assume that *ad bellum* proportionality indeed applies continuously and then move to discuss the challenges that arise when applied *concurrently* with *in bello* proportionality. Here, I break down the possible understandings of *ad bellum* proportionality in order to uncover the possible interactions between the levels of proportionality in each one. All in all, this section argues that in general, a functional separation between the levels of analysis should be maintained.

II. REVISITING THE STATIC AND CONTINUOUS APPROACHES TO *JUS AD BELLUM* PROPORTIONALITY

The static approach is rather simple. On this view, once a just cause is established for a resort to force (in law, mainly, an armed attack),[5] and a certain level of confrontation begins or is reached, *jus ad bellum* is no longer relevant. Rather, we now move to the realm of *jus in bello*, in which we analyze the legality of each attack, but no longer the legality of the operation as a whole. In other words, if, in point in time *t1*, a resort to force was proportionate, then in point *t2*, we do not have to question *again* whether the ongoing operation is proportionate.

In contemporary international law, the foremost proponent of this approach is Yoram Dinstein. Most recently, Dinstein repeated this view in the 2017 edition of his seminal textbook *War, Aggression and Self-Defence*. There, Dinstein distinguishes between three levels of lawful resorts to force in response to an armed attack. The first being an immediate "on-the-spot reaction" to a small-scale armed attack, and the second, a "defensive armed reprisal," which in Dinstein's (controversial) view can take place after an attack is over. Both of these responses are measures *short of war*. The third type of resort to force is "war," which is defined as a "comprehensive," all-encompassing use of force rather than a limited reaction.[6]

The upshot of this distinction is that the three levels of force are regulated by different proportionality standards. When measures "short of war" are involved, proportionality requires a quantitative comparison between the "quantum of force and counter-force used," and an effects-based analysis of "casualties and damage sustained." As Dinstein concedes, such a comparison can only be drawn ex post.[7] Yet, this type of proportionality is "unsuited" for a full-scale *war* of self-defense. Once war takes place, the defender can fight until the end—destroying the enemy's army in its entirety—regardless of proportionality considerations of the type mentioned previously.[8] In case of war, therefore, proportionality is different: it is

5. When I say "just cause" in this chapter I mean a just defensive cause under international law. In ethics (and sometimes in law), some argue for other just causes, such as humanitarian intervention. *See generally* Helen Frowe, The Ethics of War and Peace: An Introduction ch. 3 (2015).

6. Yoram Dinstein, War, Aggression and Self-Defence 13–16 (6th ed. 2017).

7. *Id.* at 282.

8. *Id.* at 282–83.

only assessed at the *inception* of war. Thus, the proportionality calculus concerns only the nature of the armed attack, that is, whether it amounted to war, or at least, to an attack of "critical character."[9] Proportionality, on this view, becomes a threshold question, asking only whether the gravity of the armed attack justifies a full-scale war in response. In this sense, the distinction is at once constraining and permissive: constraining, since it only permits "war" in extreme situations; permissive, since once that threshold is satisfied, *ad bellum* considerations no longer apply.[10] Since on this view proportionality applies differently in cases of "war," I call it the *war exceptionalist* approach.

This particular view of war and proportionality interrelates with two other characteristics of the static approach. One concerns the unchanging nature of aggressor-defender relations. Because proportionality is a threshold assessed only at war's inception, a war of self-defense remains legal throughout, regardless of its twist and turns.[11] In the same vein, in war the aims of the belligerent can be "ratcheted up" in the course of the hostilities, regardless of the initial aims of the war.[12] Even if the aggressor indicates that it is willing to stop the aggression, there is no "moral or legal" duty to stop when there is a war of self-defense.[13] On this view, therefore, aggressor-defender relations are fixed. I call this approach the *fixed just cause* approach.

The other related characteristic concerns the importance attributed to the formal *ending* of a state of war. Because *jus ad* bellum—including proportionality—is not assessed continually, there cannot be factual grounds that might *require* that a war be concluded (short of total victory). This is because the assessment whether any such factual grounds exist must necessitate *some* form of ongoing *jus ad bellum* analysis. War, therefore, can only be concluded upon *decision*; which is to say that as long as a formal state of war exists—even for decades—the initial defender can continue to use force, even if hostilities are suspended. Here lies one of the most important aspects of the static approach: when separate hostile acts take place within the duration of a formally existing war—such as, perhaps, between Israel and Syria—they are not assessed as "stand-alone armed conflicts" that require a separate *jus ad bellum* analysis.[14] Since this approach sees the formal existence of

9. *Id.* at 283.

10. It is possible to reconcile the static approach with *ad bellum* proportionality by arguing that it *presumes* that when an armed attack is especially grave, war will be required to counter the threat. I thank Mike Schmitt for making this point. Yet, if this was so, the static approach would not be phrased in such absolute terms, namely, as discussed later, that there is no moral or legal duty to stop a war of self-defense even when the aggressor surrenders.

11. Dinstein, *supra* note 6, at 280.

12. *Id.* at 286–87.

13. *Id.* at 284–85.

14. Applying this approach, Dinstein argues that the 2003 Iraq War would be lawful because Iraq remained the aggressor since the invasion of Kuwait in 1990, and the war did not end formally since. Dinstein, *supra* note 6, at 281. Similarly, Israel did not have to offer a separate

war as a justification for resort to force, we may call it the *formal justification* approach. In sum, the static approach comprises three interrelating positions: *war exceptionalism*, *fixed just cause*, and *formal justification*. I will return to analyze and criticize the assumptions undergirding these positions later on. But before that, a few words on the continuous approach.

Most commentators reject the static approach in favor of some form of a continuous approach.[15] According to this view, perhaps best represented by Christopher Greenwood, the static approach is an adaptation of the pre-U.N. Charter distinction between peace and war as disconnected legal spheres, in which modern *jus ad bellum* would only serve to regulate the transition between war and peace but cease to apply once the threshold is crossed.[16] But because the formal distinction between peace and war lost much of its importance throughout the years, *jus ad bellum* can no longer be contained to the mere resort to force, but "regulates the

justification for its 1981 attack on a nuclear reactor in Iraq, or for its 2007 attack on a nuclear reactor in Syria, since the countries remained in the state of war for decades. *Id.* at 227. For an analysis of this view concerning Israel, *see* Dino Kritsiotis, *Topographies of Force*, *in* International Law and Armed Conflict: Exploring the Faultlines 29, 37–40 (Michael N. Schmitt & Jelena Pejic eds., 2007). Presumably, this approach could justify Israel's recent attacks in Syria since the eruption of the Syrian civil war.

15. *See* Christopher Greenwood, *The Relationship between* Ius ad Bellum *and* Ius in Bello, 9 Rev. Int'l Stud. 221 (1983). Similarly, Gardam argues that proportionality "remains relevant throughout the conflict" and cannot be dispensed with at the initial decision to resort to force. Each choice of target must involve the consideration whether these attacks are "sufficiently related" to the justified end of self-defense. Judith Gail Gardam, *Proportionality and Force in International Law*, 87 Am. J. Int'l L. 391, 404 (1993); *see also* Francoise J. Hampson, *Belligerent Reprisals and the 1977 Protocols to the Geneva Conventions of 1949*, 37 Int'l & Comp. L.Q. 818, 821, 836 (1988); Raphaël van Steenberghe, *Proportionality Under* Jus ad Bellum *and* Jus in Bello: *Clarifying their Relationship*, 45 Isr. L. Rev. 107, 113 (2012) ("They [*ad bellum* and *in bello* proportionality] simultaneously govern the conduct of hostilities while also serving as a restraint upon such activity. . . . [P]roportionality under jus ad bellum also has a role to play as a restraint upon the conduct, as opposed to the initiation, of hostilities."); Julian M. Lehmann, *All Necessary Means to Protect Civilians: What the Intervention in Libya Says about the Relationship between the* Jus in Bello *and the* Jus ad Bellum, 17 J. Conflict & Sec. L. 117, 129 (2012); Robert D. Sloane, *The Cost of Conflation: Preserving the Dualism of* Jus ad Bellum *and* Jus in Bello *in the Contemporary Law of War*, 34 Yale J. Int'l L. 47, 67–68 (2009); Avril McDonald, *Declarations of War and Belligerent Parties: International Law Governing Hostilities between States and Transnational Terrorist Networks*, 54 Neth. Int'l L. Rev. 279, 294 (2007); Jasmine Moussa, *Can* Jus ad Bellum *Override* Jus in Bello? *Reaffirming the Separation of the Two Bodies of Law*, 90 Int'l Rev. Red Cross 872, 963, 968 (2008); Mary Ellen O'Connell, *Combatants and the Combat Zone*, 43 U. Rich. L. Rev. 845, 861–62 (2009); *cf.* Eyal Benvenisti, *Rethinking the Divide between* Jus ad Bellum *and* Jus in Bello *in Warfare Against Nonstate Actors*, 34 Yale J. Int'l L. 541, 543–47 (2009). *But see* Michael Bothe, *Terrorism and the Legality of Pre-emptive Force*, Eur. J. Int'l L. 227, 234–36 (2003) (seemingly accepting that *ad bellum* applies only in the beginning of hostilities, but rejects the formal justification view).

16. Greenwood, *supra* note 15, at 221.

use of force as a whole." Ergo, once hostilities begin, it is necessary to consider both *jus ad bellum* and *jus in bello*.[17]

The continuous approach also rejects *war exceptionalism*. Since modern *jus ad bellum* contains no references to "war" but rather to "force," proportionality must be a unitary concept for all uses of force, and accordingly, nothing suggests that *jus ad bellum* ceases to apply once "war" erupts. Accordingly, *fixed just cause* is also rejected: in *all uses of force*, legality does not remain fixed in the outbreak of the hostilities, but all "measures involving the use of force, throughout the conflict, [must be] reasonable, proportionate acts of self-defense." If the initially justified response ceases to be so, the original defender itself violates *jus ad bellum*.[18] Of course, a continuous, functional analysis of a defensive response must also reject the *formal justification* approach.[19]

To Greenwood, therefore, "an initiative that would significantly widen the conflict," geographically or otherwise, would be disproportionate even if the initial resort to force was lawful. Yet, he inserts a significant caveat, which pushes his view closer to that of the static approach. As Greenwood concedes, continuous application must be applied "reasonably," and as the conflict broadens, so do the range of permitted measures of self-defense. In a total war such as World War II, for instance, it would be "unlikely that the continuing application of the *jus ad bellum* would have any real significance."[20] It seems, therefore, that his version of the continuous approach shares an intuition with the static approach, that as a practical matter, the role of *ad bellum* proportionality diminishes as a conflict intensifies.

Both the static and continuous approaches remain undertheorized, in that mostly the legal literature does not elaborate on their possible justifications.[21] In the following section, I revisit the static and continuous approaches. In particular, I probe the assumptions that seem to be behind the static approach and expose their weaknesses. To paraphrase Koskenniemi, I seek to uncover "what it takes to

17. *Id.* at 222.

18. *Id.* at 223–24.

19. *See generally* Christopher Greenwood, *The Concept of War in Modern International Law*, 36 Int'l & Comp. L.Q. 283 (1987).

20. Greenwood, *supra* note 15, at 223. Robert Sloane makes a comparable observation that "realistically, in any sustained conflict, the effect of *ad bellum* proportionality as a genuine constraint on force will diminish as the objectives of that force multiply and expand." Sloane, *supra* note 15, at 67–68.

21. David Luban views this as a hallmark of the difference between legal and moral discussions on the laws of war: "[a] feature of the law of war that makes it essentially different from just war theory is that its rules and standards must be detachable from the reasoning that justifies them. Lawyers going forward use the 'holding' or 'rule' of a precedent, not the *ratio decidendi*." David Luban, *Just War Theory and the Laws of War as Nonidentical Twins*, 31 Ethics & Int'l Affairs 433, 437 (2017).

believe" that the static approach is good, which would then allow us to challenge these beliefs.[22]

III. THE CASE FOR CONTINUOUS APPLICATION OF *JUS AD BELLUM* PROPORTIONALITY

A. War Exceptionalism

What do we have to believe in to find *war exceptionalism* desirable? Clearly, we must believe that there is a fundamental difference between violence short of war and "war," one that would justify a different proportionality standard. There are two strands of arguments that can support such a view. One posits that war is *normatively* distinctive from other human activities, and accordingly, it is not susceptible to the same moral limitations as other forms of violence. Therefore, it should not be subject to similar legal limitations. Another can be broadly defined as *realist*: because of the special dynamics of war, it would be impossible to subject war to the same rules of other types of violence, proportionality among them. I will discuss the latter assumption when I address *fixed just cause*, in the next subsection. Here, I will address the normative approach undergirding war exceptionalism.

1. War Exceptionalism in Law

Before doing so, however, it should be stressed that it is difficult to find support in modern international law for war exceptionalism. As is frequently pointed out in the literature, the treatment of "war" as a separate category of violence is almost completely absent from the text of modern treaties, the rulings of the International Court of Justice (ICJ), and the practice of states.[23] War exceptionalism, conversely, is embedded in pre–U.N. Charter understandings of international law.

Prior to the U.N. Charter, as is well known, there was no prohibition on the use of force but only a distinction between legal spheres of "peace" and "war." Beyond some procedural limitations, and assuming no specific treaty between them, states could move between these spheres freely, if they were willing to suffer the legal and political consequences that war entailed.[24] Under this assumption, a legal differentiation between levels of force made perfect sense: it was meant to circumscribe the types of coercive measures that could be employed in peacetime, without bringing about the legal relations of war.[25] In a world where, on the

22. Martti Koskenniemi, *What Is Critical Research in International Law? Celebrating Structuralism*, 29 Leid. J. Int'l L. 727, 730 (2016).

23. For a doctrinal analysis, *see* Kritsiotis, *supra* note 14, at 40–45.

24. Eliav Lieblich, International Law and Civil Wars: Intervention and Consent 74 (2013).

25. 2 Lassa Oppenheim, International Law: A Treatise ¶ 27 (1912); *see also* Arnold D. McNair, *The Legal Meaning of War, and the Relation of War to Reprisals*, 11 Transactions Grotius Soc'y 29 (1925).

one hand, a clear legal difference between peace and war was maintained and, on the other, war was not legally prohibited, there was logic in regulating measures short of war differently. Indeed, because war was not prohibited, it made no sense to subject it to *ad bellum* constraints, and if forcible reprisals must be somehow distinguished from war, they *must* be constrained somehow. Accordingly, compulsive means short of war had to be *proportionate* "to the wrong done," while war was not.[26]

In the contemporary international system, however, the broader term "force" was purposefully placed in the U.N. Charter precisely to avoid the perplexities, technicalities, and abuse of war as a legal term.[27] This development is also reflected by the practice of states, where the legal use of the term "war"—contra its ever expanding political use—has been practically abandoned.[28] This trend was mirrored in contemporary *jus in bello*, which applies in "armed conflicts," regardless of whether these amount to "war," whether formally or in terms of scope.[29] Indeed, even in the law of naval warfare—one of the most conservative spheres of international law—in which, historically, "war" was a necessary condition for wide-ranging powers to limit neutral commerce,[30] the term "war" has been abandoned in favor of the functional term of "armed conflict."[31] Where peace and war are no longer determinative legal categories, and all nondefensive force is prohibited—whether "short of war" or "war"—there is no legal basis for the application of different standards to uses of force.

2. War Exceptionalism in Just War Theory

Would such a distinction be desirable? The question here, I think, is whether human activity in "war" is normatively different from any other. If war is somehow morally different from lesser acts of violence, there can be a preliminary argument on why it should be subject to different *legal* standards. The intuition that war

26. Oppenheim, *supra* note 25, ¶ 39. Indeed, Oppenheim distinguished between "compulsive means" that do not alter the otherwise peaceful relations between states, and war. While compulsive means, such as reprisals, were limited by nature, belligerents could apply "any amount" of force during war. Similarly, while compulsive means short of war must end once the target state agrees to settle the difference, in war the belligerents were not required to stop fighting when the other party indicated it is willing to do so. *Id.* ¶ 27.

27. *See* Christine Gray, International Law and the Use of Force 9 (2018); Greenwood, *supra* note 19, at 287. Namely, the use of the term "war" in the 1928 Kellogg Briand Pact incentivized states to deny the existence of war as a mean to circumvent their obligations. *See* Philip Marshall Brown, *Undeclared Wars*, 33 Am. J. Int'l L. 538, 540 (1939).

28. Kritsiotis, *supra* note 14, at 31–34, 45–47.

29. *See, e.g.*, Geneva Convention Relative to the Treatment of Prisoners of War arts. 2, 3, Aug. 12, 1949, 75 U.N.T.S. 135 [hereinafter GC III]; Kritsiotis, *supra* note 14, at 35–36.

30. Lieblich, *supra* note 24, at 81.

31. *See* Int'l Inst. of Humanitarian L., San Remo Manual on International Law Applicable to Armed Conflicts at Sea (Louise Doswald-Beck ed., 1995).

is morally distinctive is shared by many. In contemporary thought, it is best reflected in Michael Walzer's argument in his seminal *Just and Unjust Wars*. Walzer famously argued that states bear unique moral standing, which, in turn, spawns the special gravity of aggression against them, and that all combatants are morally equal, which justifies reciprocal killing in war.[32] Indeed, both the notion of killing to defend a political entity, and of moral equality in killing, can only be understood as relating to the uniqueness of the condition of war: simply put, we have no comparable permissions in any other form of human activity. Yet, much recent literature on the morality of war—commonly referred to as *revisionist* just war theory—challenges the idea that war is normatively different from other forms of violence.[33] To revisionists, a war is merely a collective form of violence undertaken by a large group of people, and as such, it cannot be subject to different moral standards that should guide any individual action.[34] If this is true, war must be held to the same moral standards that apply to individual self-defense ("reductive individualism")—including standards of proportionality.[35] Revisionism, which gained much ground in recent years, would reject outright the normative significance of war for the purpose of a different standard of proportionality.

Interestingly, however, the static approach makes a claim that is both more nuanced and more difficult: it differentiates not between individual and collective forms of violence but between *different forms of collective violence* (measures "short of war" and "war"). This distinction, too, relates to current debates in just war theory. In recent writings, Walzer called for the development of a theory of *jus ad vim*—a theory of just use of force short-of-war, which will be more permissive than traditional *jus ad bellum*.[36] To Walzer, "measures short of war" should be subject to laxer rules than full-scale wars, because the former do not have war's "unpredictable and often catastrophic consequences." Accordingly, for instance, while preventive war might be unjust, preventive measures of containment, such as the enforcement of no-fly zones, may be sometimes permitted.[37] Some writers

32. MICHAEL WALZER, JUST AND UNJUST WARS: A MORAL ARGUMENT WITH HISTORICAL ILLUSTRATIONS 127–28 (1992).

33. *See* Seth Lazar, *Introduction to the Debate*, *in* THE MORALITY OF DEFENSIVE WAR 1 (Cécile Fabre & Seth Lazar eds., 2014).

34. Most notably, *see* JEFF MCMAHAN, KILLING IN WAR 81–82 (2009).

35. *See, e.g.*, HELEN FROWE, DEFENSIVE KILLING 1–3 (2014).

36. WALZER, *supra* note 32, at xv. In a sense, *jus ad vim* inserts some form of *expectabilism* into decisions on the resort to force, because it claims the epistemic threshold for force should be lower when the overall expected risk from the force is low. On expectabilism in comparable contexts, *see* ADIL AHMAD HAQUE, LAW AND MORALITY AT WAR 114 (2017). As Haque shows, expectabilism is a problematic measure for decisions that involve killing, because it ignores the deontic threshold of certainty required in order to conclude that someone is liable to killing. *Id.* at 116–17.

37. WALZER, *supra* note 32, at xiv.

have embraced the idea of *jus ad vim* as a distinct moral category in contemporary conflicts, subject to the requirement that measures short of war be assessed by an additional criterion of probability of escalation.[38] Yet leading thinkers have—convincingly, I think—rejected the separate normative category *jus ad vim*, mainly because existing *jus ad bellum* can quite easily encompass minor uses of force and the risks they generate. *Jus ad vim*, therefore, seems redundant in ethical terms,[39] and in legal terms it seems that such a category, if introduced into law, would only serve to destabilize the prohibition on the use of force.

Whatever the case may be, *jus ad vim* could not help us justify the idea of war exceptionalism as presented here. Note that *jus ad vim* proposes that the threshold for measures short of war should be more permissive than war. War exceptionalism, however, posits the opposite: while measures short of war would be subject to an ongoing proportionality analysis, war would only be assessed at its inception. It would seem that if there were indeed grounds to distinguish between forms of proportionality in accordance with the scope of defensive force, these would point to the opposite conclusion: it is war, because of its disastrous consequences, that should be more tightly regulated—not only in its inception but also throughout.

B. Fixed Just Cause

Recall, that the static approach assumes that the just defensive cause is fixed at the inception of the conflict. In other words, the aggressor-defender relations remain constant. Moreover, echoing Oppenheim, the static approach does not merely base its claim on positive law but also argues that there are no *moral* grounds to stop a war when the initial cause has been satisfied (or where the aggressor seeks surrender).[40] It seems that to defend the *fixed just cause* approach, we must adopt either of several positions. One possible argument would be that defenders cannot become aggressors, because they are not responsible for the war. In other words, they have not willingly put themselves in the situation, and therefore cannot be blamed for its consequences. Another explanation could be that the defender, even after securing the just cause, remains just, since it now fulfills the role of a just punisher. A third possible defense is broadly realist: that there is something in the dynamics of war the prevents us from being able to assess the continuing existence of just cause, and therefore of proportionality under international law, throughout the conflict. Are these explanations convincing?

38. *See* Daniel Brunstetter & Megan Braun, *From* Jus ad Bellum *to* Jus ad Vim: *Recalibrating Our Understanding of the Moral Use of Force*, 27 Ethics & Int'l Aff. 87 (2013).

39. Helen Frowe, *On the Redundancy of* Jus ad Vim: *A Response to Daniel Brunstetter and Megan Braun*, 30 Ethics & Int'l Aff. 117 (2016).

40. Dinstein, *supra* note 6, at 284–85; Oppenheim, *supra* note 25, § 66.

1. Fixed Aggressor-Defender Relations

First, are aggressor-defender relations frozen merely because of the former's initial culpability? Quite clearly, this view fails on either traditional or revisionist accounts of just war. Walzer's domestic analogy, which famously equates the rights of states on the international plain to those of individuals in domestic society,[41] makes it clear that just as an individual loses her claim to self-defense when using excessive force against an attacker, a state that uses force beyond its just cause (whatever its precise definition) is no longer exercising its right to self-defense but is using aggressive force. On this view, just as the criteria governing self-defense between individuals under criminal law would never allow extending self-defense beyond what is required to counter a threat, so should be the relations between states.[42] This notion rests on sound pedigree. As already found in Vattel, if a just party refuses an offer of "just satisfaction" from the aggressor, the "balance of justice" turns and the initial war has "no longer any foundation."[43]

As aforementioned, newer, revisionist accounts of just war reject the domestic analogy of states as individuals and break down war to an iterated sequence of violent human interactions, subject to the same morality applicable in regular human life. On these accounts, when a state reacts beyond what is needed to halt and repel a life threatening attack, its agents kill people without sufficient justification, even if these people are combatants.[44] As Helen Frowe points out, "One may not continue to fight a war after its just cause has been secured—not least because in the absence of just cause, no offensive can be militarily necessary for securing the just cause, and thus any fighting is impermissible."[45] It is clear, therefore, that we cannot argue simultaneously that only defensive force is permitted *and* that defensive force can be limitless.

41. Walzer, *supra* note 32, at 58.

42. *Cf.* Uwe Steinhoff, *Just Cause and the Continuous Application of* Jus ad Bellum, *in* The Cambridge Handbook of the Just War 80, 92–93 (Larry May ed., 2018).

43. Emer de Vattel, The Law of Nations bk. III, ch. III, § 36 (Béla Kapossy & Richard Whatmore eds., 2008).

44. *See, e.g.*, McMahan, *supra* note 34, ch. 1; Tom Dannenbaum, *Why Have We Criminalized Aggressive War?*, 126 Yale L.J. 1242 (2017); *see also* Alejandro Chehtman, *Revisionist Just War Theory and the Concept of War Crimes*, 31 Leiden J. Int'l L. 171 (2018).

45. Frowe, *supra* note 39, at 120. It is worthwhile to point out that recent writings in just war theory discuss whether there are normatively distinctive considerations for the *termination* of war, as opposed to the inception of war. Interestingly, David Rodin argues that the decision to terminate war poses distinctive moral problems that don't exist at war's outset, and therefore the decision to end war is subject to a different set of moral standards, which he calls *jus terminatio*. As Rodin argues, for instance, the "risk of defeat" is an additional potential harm that emerges and that sometimes, there can be a moral justification to continue an overall unjust war. *See* David Rodin, *The War Trap: Dilemmas of* Jus Terminatio, 125 Ethics 674, 677 (2015). But nowhere does he argue that once there is no just cause, war can simply be continued on account of the initial existence of just cause, as is suggested in the fixed just cause approach. *Cf.* Steinhoff,

2. War as Punishment

On a charitable reading, it could be that the underlying argument for *fixed just cause* says something else: just cause should be fixed at the inception of the conflict because any action beyond its achievement is not an unjust use of force, but rather a just punishment against the aggressor. Of course, in order to explore this possibility, we have to decide on the ends of punishment itself, whether these are based on pure retributivism or on deterrence. While it seems to me that retributivism is a much weaker justification for acts that involve killing in war,[46] it is not needed to decide between the two here, because, I think, *both* cannot justify the idea of fixed just cause.

It must be conceded that the idea of war as punishment has deep roots in the just war tradition.[47] In the Augustinian and Thomist tradition, war can be undertaken to "avenge injuries"[48] against those that "deserve to be attacked."[49] In Grotius, as in Vattel, offensive war can be undertaken to punish a nation.[50] The idea of "war as punishment" can be found even in the twentieth century, in the writing of legal positivists such as Kelsen,[51] and in contemporary just war theory, in Walzer's domestic analogy.[52] Nonetheless, even within this tradition, the notion of *fixed just cause* would be unacceptable. This is because any understanding of punishment which does not collapse into "vengeful rage" cannot entail the right to "fight until the end." Rather, it is bound in its scope to its own ends.[53] To Augustine, for instance, the final aim of war can only be peace, and therefore, presumably, punishment that goes beyond this goal would be unjust.[54] In Vattel's view, the understanding of punishment is intrinsically woven with the right to security—and thereby of self-defense—and not to unlimited vengeance.[55] Walzer,

supra note 42, at 92–97 (arguing that just cause should be analyzed throughout the war, and not only in its inception, and that contra Rodin, that no separate category of *jus terminatio* is needed).

46. *See* Victor Tadros, *Punitive Wars, in* How We Fight: Ethics in War 18, 18–19 (Helen Frowe & Gerald Lang eds., 2014).

47. *See generally* David Luban, *War as Punishment*, 39 Phil. & Pub. Aff. 299 (2012).

48. Augustine, *Quest. In Heptateuchum, VI, 10a, in* The Catholic Tradition of the Law of Nations 74 (John Eppstein, 1935).

49. Aquinas, *Summa: Secunda Secundae, Question XL (de Bello), in* The Catholic Tradition, *supra* note 48, at 84.

50. For a summary of these sources and others, *see* Luban, *supra* note 47, at 305–12.

51. Hans Kelsen, Pure Theory of Law 322 (2d ed. 1967).

52. Walzer, *supra* note 32, at 62.

53. Luban, *supra* note 47, at 323 ("[R]etribution demands proportionality, and vengeful rage cannot provide it.").

54. Augustine, *Ad Bonifacium, 189, VI, in* The Catholic Tradition, *supra* note 48, at 78.

55. Vattel, *supra* note 43, ¶ 41.

too, analyzed the idea of war as punishment in preventive terms.[56] Notably, even those that phrase punishment as pure retribution emphasize that it should be proportionate to the crime.[57] It follows that even if one accepts the controversial view that war can be punitive, this would require an ongoing analysis, during war, whether the goals of punishment have been achieved. If we were retributivists, we would have to ask, has our retribution gone beyond the harm that we suffered? If we are focused on deterrence, we would have to inquire in real time whether we have already achieved that purpose and therefore cannot go any further. In sum, not even the notion of punitive war can justify the idea of fixed just cause.

In any case, contemporary international law—in its unequivocal rejection of the practice of forcible reprisals[58]—has explicitly ruled out punishment as a lawful justification for war, whether for retributivist—or deterrence-based reasons. Now, if it is unlawful to resort to forcible reprisals when there is no self-defense claim at all, it should also not be lawful to do so if there was an initial self-defense claim that is no longer valid. Law's position makes sense. Modern commentators convincingly point out the problematic aspects of war as punishment.[59] David Luban, for instance, illuminates several such problems. Mainly, that the defender is a "biased judge," and therefore likely to act excessively out of vengeance, and that war "punishes the wrong people" by harming individuals who are not responsible for their state's conduct.[60] Relatedly, revisionist just war philosophers would be quick to point out that war as punishment, in any form, entails the killing of combatants who are not liable to be killed, because the war is no longer one of self-defense, and therefore, they no longer threaten anyone, at least not imminently. This would be obvious concerning retributive war but also concerning wars of deterrence, which essentially use these combatants as means.[61]

In sum, it is impossible to defend punitive wars in positive law and hard to do so morally. However, even if it were possible, the idea of fixed just cause would not be vindicated because even war as punishment is judged in light of its own ends.

3. The Limitlessness of War

The last defense of fixed just cause—and the one, I suspect, from which it originates—relates to the Clausewitzian notion of total (or absolute) war. On this view, assessing proportionality during war should be different—and is perhaps

56. Walzer, *supra* note 32, at 63.

57. Luban, *supra* note 47, at 322.

58. *See, e.g.*, G.A. Res. 2625 (XXV), Declaration on Principles of International Law Concerning Friendly Relations and Co-Operation Among States in Accordance with the Charter of the U.N. (Oct. 24, 1970) ("States have a duty to refrain from acts of reprisal involving the use of force.").

59. *See generally* Tadros, *supra* note 46.

60. Luban, *supra* note 47, at 305.

61. For a discussion, compare Tadros, *supra* note 46, at 30–35.

altogether impossible—because as opposed to one-off limited acts of force, "war," as comprehensive force, *cannot* be restricted to its initial cause. As Clausewitz famously argued, limitlessness is an essential characteristic of war, since it is based on "reciprocal action" that necessarily leads to continuous escalation.[62] In international law, the echo of this approach is markedly found in Oppenheim, to which the resort to war defied regulation in general and a fortiori proportionality limitations. To Oppenheim, while war begins for certain ends, these change as the war progresses. These follow the "alteration or modification of circumstances" created during the war itself.[63] Now, if the ends of war are not restricted to the initial just cause and are subject to constant alteration, assessing proportionality throughout the conflict resembles aiming at a moving target.

Yet, to concede the essential limitlessness of war requires us, I think, to give up both the moral and legal project of *jus ad bellum*. Clausewitz, by way of understatement, was no just war philosopher, and his negation of the mere possibility for moderation in war barely needs repeating.[64] Oppenheim, in the tradition of early twentieth-century international lawyers, held at once the competing beliefs that limitations on resort to war between equal sovereigns *cannot* be imposed by law, and yet—for reasons never fully explained—that law can still regulate the *way* war is fought.[65] Yet the fixed just cause approach seems even less consistent in that, contra Oppenheim, it assumes that law can indeed regulate the resort to force by sovereigns—indeed, it accepts, as a baseline, the prohibition on the use of force and also the application of proportionality when measures short of war are undertaken—but installs, on top, considerations that seem to negate the ability of law to govern force to begin with.

Still, even those thinking within the just war tradition must concede that the escalatory dynamics of war make it *practically difficult* to assess whether an action goes beyond the just cause (ergo means-end disproportionate) along the time continuum. If something is exceptionally difficult to do, perhaps law—as the province of the practical—should not require it. Ongoing means-ends proportionality assessments are difficult in war because of the problem of counter-responses, which may extend the just cause or generate new just causes throughout the hostilities. Assume that aggressor state *A* launches an armed attack against defending state *V*. *V* responds in a means-ends proportional manner, in order to halt and repel

62. *See* Walzer, *supra* note 32, at 23–24 (citing Clausewitz); Beer, *supra* note 1, at 126.

63. Oppenheim, *supra* note 25, ¶ 66.

64. *See* Martin van Creveld, *The Clausewitzian Universe and the Law of War*, 26 J. Contemp. Hist. 403, 404 (1991). *But see* Daniel Statman, *Ending War Short of Victory? A Contractarian View of* Jus Ex Bello, 125 Ethics 720, 726–29 (2015) (arguing that the Clausewitzian view can be defended morally). It should be stressed that Clausewitz himself was well aware that in practice most wars are limited, which seems to be in tension with the notion that war is essentially limitless. *See* Terence M. Holmes, *The Clausewitzian Fallacy of Absolute War*, 40 J. Strategic Stud. 1039 (2017).

65. Oppenheim, *supra* note 25, ¶ 53.

the attack. However, each defensive act by *V* is met with a forcible response by *A* (counter-response) on top of the initial armed attack. Such counter-responses can be either "defensive" (in the tactical, not normative sense)—meaning, aimed to curtail the specific defensive attack—or "offensive," by widening the scope of the initial attack.[66] In analytical terms, because "there is no self-defense against self-defense," each counter-response by *A* might provide justification for a further defensive response by *V* against that counter-response. To add to this complexity, note that many believe that *jus ad bellum* proportionality permits not only to halt and repel the attack but also to preempt further imminent counter-responses.[67] These attempts of preemption, in turn, prompt counter-responses themselves, and so on and so forth.

A case in point is the clash between Israel, Syria, and Iran, which took place on February 10, 2018. The episode began when Israel intercepted an allegedly armed Iranian drone in its airspace, launched from Syria.[68] Immediately after, Israel attacked—perhaps to preempt further drone incursions—a Syrian airbase near Palmyra, from which the drone was launched. In response, Syrian air defenses downed an Israeli F-16. This, in turn, prompted Israel to destroy three Syrian air-defense batteries and several other Syrian and Iranian targets.[69] Assuming that the drone incursion merited a reaction of self-defense, how should proportionality be assessed? How should it take into account counter-responses? A simple answer is that it was unlawful for Israel to attack the Palmyra airbase after repelling the attack by downing the drone. If that is the case, Syria was justified in its defensive reaction against the Israeli Air Force, and, accordingly, Israel's attack on Syrian air defenses was not. But what if we see the armed drone as a weapon launched from a platform in Palmyra? If this is the case, then arguably, Israel's attack on the platform was a lawful preemption. That would render the Syrian air-defense response unlawful. Now, the question is the permitted scope of defensive action against Syrian air defenses. Arguably, it would be only permitted for Israel to attack the battery that launched the successful missile; but then, other batteries can be used to curtail that attack, and therefore preemptive attacks against them can be

66. Defensive counter-responses are especially problematic, since they may prompt the defender to respond even if this is not necessary in order to achieve any significant just cause. Consider, for instance, anti-aircraft fire which engages aircrafts on their return home, or an artillery barrage launched by the adversary just before a ceasefire begins. Since both parties seek to "fire the last shot," this dynamic can lead to elongation of conflict even if the just cause has been achieved.

67. *See* Terry Gill, *When Does Self-Defence End?*, *in* The Oxford Handbook on the Use of Force in International Law 737, 744 (Marc Weller ed., 2015).

68. Isabel Kershner, *Iranian Drone Launched from Syria Was Armed, Israel Says*, N.Y. Times (Apr. 14, 2018), https://www.nytimes.com/2018/04/14/world/middleeast/syria-iran-israel-drone.html.

69. Isabel Kershner et al., *Israel Strikes Iran in Syria and Loses a Jet*, N.Y. Times (Feb. 10, 2018), https://www.nytimes.com/2018/02/10/world/middleeast/israel-iran-syria.html.

justified. This, potentially, can continue *ad infinitum*. Now think of a full-scale war in which hundreds of such scenarios take place simultaneously. We see how the problem of counter-responses, along with the problem of preemption, can make it incredibly problematic to assess proportionality along the time continuum.

How can an ongoing proportionality assessment deal with the problem of counter-responses? One possible solution is to draw from the idea that there is a minimum threshold for an "armed attack."[70] Let us break down the February 2018 clash into a slightly altered simplified scenario:

(a) State *A* launches an armed drone against state *V*;
(b) *V*'s air force attacks the drone platform and destroys it;
(c) *A* fires an anti-aircraft missile which misses;
(d) *V* attacks *A*'s anti-aircraft battery.

On this view, if counter-response (c) would have not been considered an independent armed attack in itself, *V* would have not been justified to do (d) and would have to leave it at that. This approach, however, while granting some conceptual clarity, should be rejected. First, the content of "armed attack" threshold is controversial and vague to begin with[71] and is especially difficult to apply during active hostilities. Second, while this approach might work in a simple sequence of responses and counter-response, it would quickly fragmentize and become inapplicable in more complex exchanges. It could bring about absurd results, according to which a single shot during an armed exchange cannot be responded to, since it does not itself rise to a level of an armed attack.

Another possible approach would require—as much as possible—to break down the dynamics of the fighting in order to spot the point in time in which the just cause has been achieved *and* stopping the defensive action will also halt the aggressor's counter-responses. One plausible way to do so is to ask, throughout the conflict, the following questions:

1. Has the initial just cause been achieved (for example, by the armed attack being preempted, or halted and repelled)?
2. If so, are offensive counter-attacks continuing (for example, new incursion attempts by the aggressor)? If yes, the just cause is renewed.
3. Are defensive counter-attacks continuing (for example, anti-aircraft fire, retaliatory artillery, or attacks against defending forces that entered the aggressor's territory)?
4. If so, are they likely to end if the defensive action ends, or are they likely to continue regardless (thereby becoming offensive counter-attacks producing

70. On the threshold for an "armed attack," *see* Tom Ruys, "Armed Attack" and Article 51 of the U.N. Charter: Evolutions in Customary Law and Practice 139–58 (2010).

71. Monica Hakimi & Jacob Katz Cogan, *The Two Codes on the Use of Force*, 27 Eur. J. Int'l L. 257, 269–73 (2016).

new just causes)? If they are likely to end, it becomes unnecessary to respond to further defensive counter-responses.

In our simplified scenario above, question 4 would come into play between steps (c) and (d). Here, (c) is a defensive counter-attack. Deciding whether to undertake attack (d)—and possibly escalating the situation further—requires consideration whether *A* would continue with (effective) attempts to down *V*'s aircrafts, should *V* refrain from attacking the anti-aircraft battery. If not, attack (d) would be unnecessary. Note that question 4 is where the political echelon is the most competent to make the decision. Figuring out whether the adversary will stop if you stop is one of the most fundamental diplomatic questions during war.

In sum, while the problem of escalation makes it difficult to assess proportionality throughout an armed conflict, this is not conceptually impossible and also not entirely impracticable, at least not to an extent that justifies adoption of the idea of fixed just cause as part of positive law.

C. A Formal State of War as Justification

The last pillar of the static approach, the *formal justification* view, is especially problematic. I have already noted the diminished importance of formal war in modern international law. Moreover, in terms of legal coherence, it seems strained to argue that, on the one hand, a formal declaration of war alone cannot merit an armed response (because it is not an armed attack) but, on the other hand, a continuing formal state of war can alone justify resuming hostilities even if these have completely ceased.

1. The "Active Belligerency" Standard

It is unsurprising, thus, that the idea of formal justification has not been accepted in positive international law. Already in the 1950s, Egypt claimed a right to exercise maritime belligerent rights against vessels passing in the Suez Canal, on account of its ongoing formal state of war with Israel.[72] This view was rejected by the U.N. Security Council.[73] Tellingly, Resolution 95 of 1951 held that the armistice regime between the parties, which existed by then for two and half years, was of "permanent character" and that "neither party can reasonably assert that it is actively a belligerent."[74] The emphasis on "active belligerency" stresses that any justification to use force must rely on functional, rather than formal, criteria. Furthermore, the Council noted that, "in the prevailing circumstances," the Egyptian interference in maritime commerce could not "be justified on the ground that it is necessary

72. Greenwood, *supra* note 19, at 287.

73. *Id.* at 287–88.

74. S.C. Res. 95 (Sept. 1, 1951).

for self-defence."[75] This is a clear statement that even in a formal state of war, when no active belligerency is present, a separate analysis of *jus ad bellum*—including of proportionality—would be required. Indeed, as Michael Bothe points out, it has been the consistent practice of the Security Council, throughout the decades, to judge separate attacks undertaken within the context of a formally existing war as requiring a renewed *jus ad bellum* analysis. As he argues, the valid test is whether there was "a continuous armed conflict" since the inception of the hostilities. If not, a new *jus ad bellum* analysis would be required.[76]

The "continuous armed conflict" standard, however, might cause confusion. Indeed, when analyzing *jus ad bellum* continuously, we must be careful not to replace the standards of *ad bellum* necessity and proportionality with the *jus in bello* rules governing the end of application of IHL. It is generally accepted that IHL continues to apply until the "general close of military operations."[77] But this is a factual, not a normative test. IHL does not grant justification to resort to force, which can only be found in *jus ad bellum*; rather, it only identifies situations of armed conflict.[78] Accordingly, the aggressor cannot rely on the fact that IHL applies in its relations with the defender as a justification for further force. Similarly, the defender cannot maintain that its acts are lawful only because the initial aggressor continues fighting—and thus, IHL applies—even after the just cause has been satisfied.

2. The Epistemic Role of a Formal State of War

Assuming it is accepted that an ongoing formal state of war cannot release the defender from a new *ad bellum* analysis, the question remains whether it has any meaning for the purpose of resort to force. When states remain in a state of war after hostilities die down, this implies that the parties see each other as enemies, which is to say—borrowing from Carl Schmitt—that they openly acknowledge "the ever present possibility of combat" between them.[79] A possibility of combat, however, does not grant states the right to self-defense under international law. But to the extent that international law recognizes anticipatory self-defense against an imminent attack, the open acknowledgment of the possibility of combat can be evidence for aggressive intentions, when other factual circumstances are

75. *Id.*

76. Bothe, *supra* note 15, at 235–36. It should be noted, that Bothe's position raises difficulties, because on the one hand, he accepts the static approach in the sense that *jus ad bellum* does *not* apply throughout the conflict, but on the other, he requires the existence of ongoing hostilities for the continuing lawfulness of defensive actions. It is clear that in essence he uses the notion of ongoing hostilities as a substitute for the continuous application of *jus ad bellum*, which pushes him closer to the continuous approach.

77. *See, e.g.*, GC III, *supra* note 29, art. 5.

78. Haque, *supra* note 36, at 26; Eliav Lieblich, *Internal Jus ad Bellum*, 67 Hastings L.J. 687, 735–36 (2016).

79. Carl Schmitt, The Concept of the Political 37 (1932).

present.[80] Of course, the determination that such circumstances exist requires a fact-intensive analysis. For instance, if the French Army would conduct massive maneuvers near the Swiss border, a Swiss argument for imminent self-defense would probably be rejected. But if this happens in a border where a state of war exists—for instance, between the Koreas—aggressive military posturing could be interpreted differently.

Nonetheless, even in this limited epistemic role, the importance of the existence of a formal state of war should not be overstated. Quite possibly, a formal state of war can play a political or symbolic role only, in particular when hostilities have been absent for many years.[81] This is particularly so when the parties have signed an armistice or a ceasefire, in which they terminate hostilities until the conclusion of "peace," without formally abolishing the state of war between them.[82]

The takeaway for the ongoing proportionality analysis is that even when a formal state of war exists, proportionality would be assessed functionally, against a new emerging threat, and not against a general statement on the possibility of combat. The latter, in some circumstances, can serve an epistemic function, but no more.

IV. THE CHALLENGES OF CONCURRENT APPLICATION OF *AD BELLUM* AND *IN BELLO* PROPORTIONALITY AND THE CASE FOR A FUNCTIONAL SEPARATION

Having established that *ad bellum* proportionality should apply continuously during an armed conflict, the question is *how* it should apply concurrently with *jus in bello*. The answer, of course, depends on the content of *ad bellum*

80. *Cf.* Greenwood, *supra* note 15, at 225.

81. For instance, Israel and Iraq remained in a state of war since 1949, with hostilities subsiding for decades. *See id.*

82. *See, e.g.*, the 1974 Israel-Syria Separation of Forces Agreement of 1974, Separation of Forces Agreement, Syria-Isr., May 31, 1974, https://avalon.law.yale.edu/20th_century/pal04.asp, establishing a ceasefire in which, on the one hand, the parties would "refrain from all military actions against each other, from the time of the signing of the document," *id.* ¶ A, while, on the other, it was emphasized that the agreement was not a peace agreement, *id.* ¶ H. The 1953 Korean War Armistice Agreement also aimed to "insure a complete cessation of hostilities and of all acts of armed force in Korea until a final peaceful settlement is achieved." Agreement Between the Commander-in-Chief, United Nations Command, on the One Hand, and the Supreme Commander of the Korean People's Army and the Commander of the Chinese People's Volunteers, on the Other Hand, Concerning a Military Armistice in Korea pmbl., ¶ 12, July 27, 1953. I set aside here the formal distinctions that might be between cease-fires, truces, and armistices. *See, e.g.*, Sydney D. Bailey, *Cease-Fires, Truces and Armistices in the Practice of the UN Security Council*, 71 Am. J. Int'l L. 461 (1977). Another interesting question, which I will not touch upon here, concerns whether an aggressor can invoke the right of self-defense against attacks across armistice lines. *See*, in this context, Oscar Schachter, *The Right of States to Use Armed Force*, 82 Mich. L. Rev. 1620, 1627–28 (1983–1984).

proportionality. On the *jus in bello* level, the content of proportionality is doctrinally undisputed: an attack would be proportionate if it "may be expected to cause incidental loss of civilian life, injury to civilians, damage to civilian objects, or a combination thereof which would be excessive in relation to the concrete and direct military advantage anticipated."[83] While the interpretation of the different components of the test—and even more so its application—are fraught with difficulties,[84] it is clear that *in bello* proportionality requires a (slightly distorted) harm-benefit analysis, in which a concrete and direct military advantage is weighed against civilian loss (and I will detail later what makes it distorted and how this affects concurrent application).

The contents of the relevant test for *jus ad bellum* proportionality are less clear.[85] Beyond the general agreement that *ad bellum* proportionality serves to constrain the permissible scope of forcible self-defense against an armed attack,[86] the meaning of the term under international law remains contested. As David Kretzmer observes, some understand proportionality as a quantitative test, in which the scope of the response is measured against the scope of the attack ("tit for tat").[87] Most, however, understand proportionality as a means-end test, in which the scope of the response is measured against the achievement of the defensive aim.[88] On this view, if, as is the case in international law, the only lawful cause for unilateral force is the occurrence of an "armed attack," a forcible response would be proportionate if it does not exceed what is required to halt and repel the attack. Granted, there is some debate on whether, in judging the response, some leeway should be given to the defender in order to avert additional imminent, or perhaps reasonably foreseeable threats.[89] Yet, it is reasonably well established that anything beyond would be a prohibited form of punishment through war or reprisal.[90]

83. Protocol Additional to the Geneva Conventions of 12 August 1949, and Relation to the Protection of Victims of International Armed Conflicts (Protocol I) art. 51(5)(b), 8 June 1977, 1125 U.N.T.S. 3. [hereinafter AP I].

84. Kretzmer, *supra* note 4, at 236–37.

85. *See* Dapo Akande & Thomas Liefländer, *Clarifying Necessity, Imminence and Proportionality in the Law of Self-Defense*, 107 Am. J. Int'l L. 564, 566–68 (2013).

86. Military and Paramilitary Activities in and Against Nicaragua (Nicar. v. U.S.), Judgment, 1986 I.C.J. 14, ¶¶ 176, 194 (June 27).

87. *See, e.g.*, Oil Platforms Case (Iran v. U.S.), Judgment, 2003 I.C.J. 161, ¶ 77 (Nov. 6).

88. Kretzmer, *supra* note 4, at 237; *see also* Andreas Zimmermann, *The Second Lebanon War:* Jus ad Bellum, Jus in Bello *and the Issue of Proportionality*, *in* 11 Max Planck Y.B. U.N. Law 99, 122–23 (Armin von Bogdandy & Rüdiger Wolfrum eds., 2007).

89. On the reasonably foreseeable standard, *see* Kretzmer, *supra* note 4, at 265, 270; Michael N. Schmitt, Counter-Terrorism and the Use of Force in International Law 19 (2002).

90. *See supra* section III.B.2.

To philosophers, this would be odd. In just war theory, proportionality is taken to mean something entirely different: first, whether the threat is of such gravity that it justifies a forcible response to begin with and, on top of that, a universal harm-benefit inquiry of whether the benefits from the resort to force would outweigh its costs.[91] What most lawyers refer to as proportionality, to philosophers is subsumed in other conditions for just war, chiefly the notions of *necessity* or of just cause: when defensive force exceeds what is needed to achieve the just cause, there is no just cause for this additional force, which becomes therefore unjust. By employing a harm-benefit analysis, the philosophical account of *ad bellum* proportionality is closer—but, as we shall see, by no means similar—to *in bello* proportionality under international law than to the mainstream view of the *legal* test of *ad bellum* proportionality. Yet, some international lawyers—among them, unsurprisingly, those writing in the just war tradition—argue that the harm-benefit view of proportionality does, or at least should, play a role also in the *law* on the use of force.[92] In any case, it is clear that as much as the tests for *ad bellum* and *in bello* proportionality are drawn closer, so, on the one hand, it is easier to think of their concurrent application; but on the other, it becomes difficult to decide whether they should remain somehow distinct and to maintain the *ad bellum-in bello* distinction.

In this section, beyond a few words, I will not attempt to offer a sustained defense of one standard of *ad bellum* proportionality over the other. Rather, I set out to highlight key dilemmas of concurrent application that arise in each one. While many of these dilemmas are unique to each standard, three preliminary challenges permeate concurrent application across the board.

The first concerns the extent to which the general separation of *jus ad bellum* and *jus in bello* is maintained, even when both levels of proportionality apply concurrently. While the mainstream of international lawyers urge to maintain this separation,[93] this notion has been under attack by philosophers, who in the

91. *See generally* Henry Shue, *Last Resort and Proportionality*, *in* The Oxford Handbook of Ethics of War 260 (Seth Lazar & Helen Frowe eds., 2018).

92. Adil Ahmad Haque, *Necessity and Proportionality in International Law*, *in* The Cambridge Handbook of the Just War, *supra* note 42, at 255, 259–61; van Steenberghe, *supra* note 15, at 113; *see also* Exec. Comm., Int'l L. Ass'n, Final Report on Aggression and the Use of Force 12 (2018) ("[T]he proportionality assessment should weigh the relative interests against each other, thereby assessing whether the harmful effects of the force taken in self-defence are outweighed by achieving the legitimate aims.").

93. *See, e.g.*, AP I, *supra* note 83, pmbl. ("Expressing [the] conviction that nothing in this Protocol or in the Geneva Conventions of 12 August 1949 can be construed as legitimizing or authorizing any act of aggression or any other use of force inconsistent with the Charter of the United Nations, [and] [r]eaffirming further that the provisions of the Geneva Conventions of 12 August 1949 and of this Protocol must be fully applied in all circumstances to all persons who are protected by those instruments, without any adverse distinction based on the nature or origin of the armed conflict or on the causes espoused by or attributed to the Parties to the conflict. . . ."); Adam Roberts, *The Equal Application of the Laws of War: A Principle Under Pressure*, 90 Int'l Rev. Red Cross 931 (2008); Sloane, *supra* note 15, at 103–108; Keiichiro

context of proportionality, argue that incidental harm *in bello* cannot be justified when inflicted by an unjust party on the *ad bellum* level.[94] Of course, if one argues for some conflation between these spheres, this might affect the concurrent application between *ad bellum* and *in bello* proportionality. Here, in general, I do not challenge the idea of belligerent equality, but rather demonstrate how some forms of concurrent application might complicate it.

The second challenge relates to the level of decision-making in which proportionality assessment takes place. A common intuition is that international law demands that *ad bellum* assessments would be conducted by leaders, looking at the conflict as a whole, while *in bello* assessments would be done mainly in the field and in relation to specific attacks.[95] To the extent this is the case, the question arises whether concurrent application would require leaders to make *in bello* assessments or—more controversially—whether soldiers would be required (or even permitted) to make *ad bellum* assessments. To be clear: while every moral agent is under the obligation to consider all relevant moral reasons, it is doubtful whether law requires the same thing.[96]

The third common challenge is temporal. While *in bello* proportionality is quite explicit in its ex ante application (with some caveats discussed later), it seems—although this is also debatable—that *ad bellum* proportionality applies more dynamically on the time continuum and includes also an ex post assessment. These three challenges will rise time and again in our analysis.

Okimoto, *The Cumulative Requirements of* Jus ad Bellum *and* Jus in Bello *in the Context of Self-Defense*, 11 Chin. J. Int'l L. 59 (2012). Some lawyers argue, conversely, that at least in some cases, a degree of conflation is warranted, or at least happens de facto. *See* Benvenisti, *supra* note 15. For an analysis of the debate, *see* J.H.H. Weiler & Abby Deshman, *Far Be It from Thee to Slay the Righteous with the Wicked: An Historical and Historiographical Sketch of the Bellicose Debate Concerning the Distinction between* Jus ad Bellum *and* Jus in Bello, 24 Eur. J. Int'l L. 25 (2013); Sloane, *supra* note 15, at 54–55 (arguing that conflation happens as a matter of politics and legitimacy).

94. Although, tellingly, most contemporary philosophers accept the separation in positive law as a pragmatic concession. *See* McMahan, *supra* note 34, at 24 (arguing that if one has not just cause *ad bellum*, one cannot act proportionally *in bello*). *But see* Jeff McMahan, *The Ethics of Killing in War*, 114 Ethics 693, 730 (2004) (pointing out that as a matter of pragmatics, positive law should maintain this separation). Some philosophers adopt this position for nonpragmatic reasons. *See* Yitzhak Benbaji, *The War Convention and the Moral Division of Labour*, 59 Phil. Q. 593 (2009).

95. Greenwood, *supra* note 15, at 231; van Steenberghe, *supra* note 15, at 115; Judith Gardam, Necessity, Proportionality and the Use of Force by States 21 (2004).

96. *But see* Benbaji, *supra* note 94, at 613–14 (disputing that morality requires soldiers to consider justness of cause, as part of the *in bello/ad bellum* distinction). Moreover, not that the Crime of Aggression as defined in the Rome Statute, includes a "leadership clause," which limits its application to persons "in a position effectively to exercise control over or to direct the political or military action of a State." Rome Statute of the International Criminal Court arts. 1, 8bis(1), July 17, 1998, 2187 U.N.T.S. 90. This means that at least for the purpose of criminal liability, *ad bellum* assessments are required only from senior leaders.

A. Concurrent Application and the Quantitative Test for *Ad Bellum* Proportionality

Let us assume that *ad bellum* proportionality is a quantitative test, comparing the scope of force employed by the attacker and the defender. At the outset, this test is questionable, because it imports to *jus ad bellum* proportionality—which is concerned with self-defense—thought associated with punishment and reprisal, generally alien to the logic of defense.[97] The quantitative approach is therefore not really defensive at all. Indeed, it could be both too permissive and too restrictive in relation to the just defensive cause.[98]

Beyond this problem, there is another reason why the quantitative test should be set aside when discussing concurrent application of *ad bellum* and *in bello* proportionality. It seems that the only way to salvage this approach as relevant to self-defense is if we view it as a proxy for the *other* two versions of the proportionality standard. If we adopt a means-ends test—which assesses proportionality in relation to the fulfillment of the defensive cause—the quantitative test might establish a presumption against a defender that uses significantly more force than the attacker, requiring the former to explain why such a quantum of force was needed to repel the attack. If, conversely, we adopt a harm-benefit approach, the quantitative test can be a measure to compare the harm caused by the armed attack and the harmed caused by the defender. Because on both approaches to proportionality the quantitative test is at best only derivative, we do not have to discuss it independently.

B. Concurrent Application and the Halt-and-Repel Test

Recall, the halt-and-repel test for *ad bellum* proportionality holds that a defensive response would only be lawful to the extent that it serves to counter the armed attack and, perhaps, further imminent counterattacks. On its face, this notion of *ad bellum* proportionality seems disconnected from *in bello* proportionality, since it says nothing of collateral damage to civilians; it only considers whether the response was reasonably necessary, in functional terms, to counter the threat.[99] In this sense, the more natural connection is between the halt-and-repel test and the

97. This is why we can find the root of the quantitative test in relation to force in the standards governing reprisals. *See* OPPENHEIM, *supra* note 25, ¶ 39; *cf.* Kretzmer, *supra* note 4, at 238.

98. To see this, assume that state *A* attacks state *V* with a single rocket launcher, which launches dozens of rockets in a rapid sequence. A quantitative test would allow *V* to launch a counterattack equivalent in its scope to that of dozens of rockets, while for the strict purpose of *V*'s self-defense, it would be sufficient to take out the launcher with a single missile. In this sense, the quantitative test is too permissive. Conversely, assume *A* is attacking *V* with a well-entrenched mortar. To take it out, *V* must use several bunker-busting bombs. A strictly quantitative approach might prohibit such a response.

99. *See, e.g.*, Moussa, *supra* note 15, at 968.

notion of *necessity* under IHL.[100] Yet, upon closer consideration, the two levels of proportionality—even under the halt-and-repel test—can interrelate. *Jus in bello* proportionality balances a "concrete and direct military advantage" in relation to civilian harm. To the extent that what is needed to halt and repel the attack somehow figures in our understanding of "concrete and direct military advantage," then, arguably, *jus ad bellum* considerations would affect the *in bello* proportionality analysis.

It is tempting, therefore, to argue that the halt-and-repel test should inform specific decisions concerning *in bello* proportionality.[101] On this view, a concrete and direct military advantage will include not only the generic harm caused to the adversary's armed forces or other tactical advantages, but would be judged in light of the attack's contribution to the defensive cause. This view can cut both ways: possibly, if its contribution to the defensive cause is positive, this benefit will be added on top of military advantage reaped by the attack. If, conversely, it does not contribute to the defensive cause, the military advantage would be diminished, even if the tactical harm to the adversary's forces is significant. In my view, there are three strong reasons to reject this view. One relates to legal policy, another relates to the ethics of decision-making in uncertainty, and the third concerns the nature of *in bello* proportionality as a norm of lesser evil.

First, the black letter law of *in bello* proportionality refers only to a "concrete and direct military advantage" as a valid counterbalance against incidental harm to civilians, and not to political or grand-strategic goals of the war or its lawful causes.[102] Accordingly, the authoritative commentaries on Additional Protocol I posit that "military advantage can only consist in ground gained and in annihilating or weakening the enemy armed forces."[103] Janina Dill has likewise

100. The principle of necessity under IHL states that "the only legitimate object which States should endeavour to accomplish during war is to weaken the military forces of the enemy; [and] [t]hat for this purpose it is sufficient to disable the greatest possible number of men. . . ." Declaration Renouncing the Use, in Time of War, of Explosive Projectiles Under 400 Grammes Weight pmbl., Dec. 11, 1868, *reprinted in* The Laws of Armed Conflicts: A Collection of Conventions, Resolutions, and Other Documents 91 (Dietrich Schindler & Jiri Toman eds., 4th ed. 2004). Although this principle was understood as providing a blanket permission to target combatants and military objectives, some recent scholarship emphasizes the limiting aspect of necessity. Gabriella Blum, *The Dispensable Lives of Soldiers*, 2 J. Legal Analysis 115 (2010); Ryan Goodman, *The Power to Kill or Capture Enemy Combatants*, 24 Eur. J. Int'l L. 819 (2013). Taken to an extreme, one can argue that attacks that are not necessary to halt and repel the attack *ad bellum* are also not necessary *in bello*. I will not explore this notion here.

101. *Cf.* Lehmann, *supra* note 15, at 129–30.

102. Of course, the military advantage is commonly understood in relation to the "attack as a whole"; but this is in the tactical sense rather than in relation to the war as a whole. *See* Eliav Lieblich with Owen Alterman, Transnational Asymmetric Armed Conflict under International Humanitarian Law: Key Contemporary Challenges 127–31 (2015).

103. Int'l Comm. of the Red Cross, Commentary on the Additional Protocols of 8 June 1977 to the Geneva Conventions of 12 August 1949 ¶ 2218 (Yves Sandos et al. eds., 1987).

argued that the military advantage, under *jus in bello*, can relate to military advantages "that appeal to [the] concept of generic military victory only, rather than directly to the political or moral reasons for which [belligerents] are ultimately fighting."[104] The most convincing argument for this capping of the valid military advantage, in my view, is one of legal policy: considering the non-ideal reality of warfare and the imperfect nature of belligerents, as the military advantage becomes wider and vaguer, so is the potential of abuse. If the military advantage of each attack could be understood in reference to the goals of the entire campaign, it would be quite easy to inflate the advantage of a single attack in a way that would justify massive collateral damage. This is especially true in asymmetric conflicts, in which the notion of *ad bellum* victory is vague to begin with.[105] It seems that in light of this risk, any legal interrelation between the valid military advantage *in bello* and *ad bellum* consideration is likely to cause more harm than good overall, even, if in some cases, it would limit attacks.

A second reason why the just defensive cause should not enter the *in bello* proportionality calculation relates to the causal proximity between any specific attack and the overall goal of halting and repelling the attack. A concrete and direct military advantage would be presumably close causally and temporally to the attack and thus can be said to be of high epistemic certainty. Conversely, the overall aim to halt and repel an armed attack would be in the vast majority of cases much further down the road from one specific attack. In the ethics of decision-making in uncertainty, uncertain benefits in the future, involving assumptions about intervening agents, should receive less weight when judged in relation to harm inflicted here and now.[106] This rings particularly true when this harm involves (incidentally) killing and maiming of people. Note, in addition, that on the tactical levels of command, such decisions would suffer from even more uncertainty, as field commanders do not have the tools to assess the grand picture of the conflict. Accordingly, the contributions of a single attack to the general *ad bellum* goals should not receive significant weight, in the vast majority of cases. It therefore makes sense that law would prohibit their consideration altogether.

The third difficulty in importing into the notion of military advantage the overall cause of war relates to the resulting complication of the idea of equal application of *jus in bello*. Usually, when concurrent application is assessed, it is discussed from the point of view of the defender. The discussion assumes the existence of a just defensive cause, and then questions the relation between the former and the military advantage under *jus in bello* proportionality.[107] The problem, however, is

104. Janina Dill, Legitimate Targets? Social Construction, International Law and U.S. Bombing 107 (2015).

105. *See generally* Gabriella Blum, *The Fog of Victory*, 24 Eur. J. Int'l L. 391 (2013).

106. *See* David Rodin, *The Myth of National Self-Defence*, *in* The Morality of Defensive War, *supra* note 33, at 64, 81.

107. *See* Greenwood, *supra* note 15, at 230–31.

that owing to the principle of belligerent equality, *in bello* proportionality under international law is quite distorted: it applies not only to the defender but also to the aggressor.[108] In other words, the aggressor's military advantages can cause "proportional" collateral damage under IHL, even when the overall cause is unjust. Such incidental killings will not give rise to state responsibility as such, nor would they be considered war crimes, *although* they are caused in the pursuit of an aggressive cause. In this sense, *jus in bello* proportionality is a norm of lesser evil, not of ideal morality.

Under these circumstances, adjusting the military advantage in *in bello* proportionality in light of the overall cause is fraught with difficulties. It would require, perhaps, to apply different understandings of the military advantage to the just and unjust party. On this view, the defender's military advantage could be enhanced if it contributes to the just cause, while the value of the aggressor's military advantage would diminish. But this, of course, undermines the idea of belligerent equality to the core. Alternatively, in order to maintain belligerent equality, it would be needed to judge the unjust party's military advantage by reference to its unjust cause, which does not seem to promote any meaningful value at all.

It therefore seems that under the halt-and-repel test for *ad bellum* proportionality, concurrent application should not result in the intermixing between the cause of the war and the notion of military advantage in *jus in bello* proportionality. Rather, it should mean that the defending state must assess whether in any given moment, its military operations reasonably contribute to the achievement of the defensive cause. Naturally, such assessment can only be expected from those capable of viewing the big picture and deciding on the general course of the campaign, meaning it cannot—and should not—be a field-level decision.

C. Concurrent Application and the Harm-Benefit Test

The issue becomes more complicated if *ad bellum* proportionality under international law is to be understood in a closer manner to proportionality as understood in the just war tradition. On this view, law would require subjecting the decision to resort to defensive force to a harm-benefit analysis, rather than only to a means-end analysis. Of course, to examine the interactions between both levels of proportionality under this assumption, we must first determine what harms and benefits are ideally included in the *ad bellum* proportionality in the just war tradition, and then which harms and benefits can be realistically included in law. This determination is beyond the scope of this chapter, and I will only address it preliminarily.

1. Wide and Narrow Harm-Benefit, Sunk Harms, and Impartiality

Being a universalist notion, the *ad bellum* harm-benefit analysis under the just war tradition is not morally egoistic, meaning proportionality is not judged only

108. *See id.*

in relation to the defender's interests. It must also take account of harm to others. Beyond this basic understanding, many other aspects of harm-benefit proportionality are contested. In terms of benefits, on one influential account, *ad bellum* proportionality would include all benefits to the defender and third parties reaped from and relating to achieving the just cause.[109] In terms of harms, it would include harms to the defender, its civilians and combatants; but also harms to the aggressor (or at least to the aggressor's nonliable elements[110]); and harms to third parties.[111] Within this analysis, arguably, uncertain benefits and harms and those involving intervening agents should be discounted in relation to certain and immediate benefits and harms;[112] and perhaps, the prospects of the success of the defensive action should also figure as an overall consideration.[113] The application of this form of proportionality is excruciatingly difficult. If we adopt the notion of continuous application, it requires an initial judgment before resorting to force, and then, ongoing adjustments of the weight given to the benefits and harms as these become more or less certain and closer, while taking into account new unforeseen considerations.

It can be argued at this point, that this understanding of *ad bellum* proportionality is too normatively indeterminate and epistemically difficult to be made a part of positive law and that, therefore, it should be relegated to the sphere of public discourse and moral critique.[114] Furthermore, the indeterminacy of this standard breeds problems reminiscent of those that occur if we widen the notion of "military advantage" in proportionality *in bello*. Including universal benefits in *ad bellum* proportionality—even those related to the achievement of the just cause—can be used to inflate the benefits of responding to an armed attack. Putative and ambiguous benefits such as "deterrence," "maintaining the international rule of

109. Thomas Hurka, *Proportionality in the Morality of War*, 33 PHIL. & PUB. AFF. 34, 39–44 (2005). Some may claim that proportionality can include in this context only the benefit of achieving the just cause. Without exhausting this question, I tend to disagree. While only the just cause can provide permission to resort to force, I do not see why some benefits must be excluded from the universal proportionality assessment *once such just cause exists*. For an overview of this debate, *see* FROWE, *supra* note 5, at 69–72.

110. MCMAHAN, *supra* note 34, at 26–27.

111. Hurka, *supra* note 109, at 45–51; *cf.* Shue, *supra* note 91, at 263–71 (suggesting at least five types of evils that should be considered in the *ad bellum* proportionality analysis: wrongful harm to civilians on both sides; wrongful harm to combatants on both sides; possible defeat of the just side and its consequences; environmental harm; additional unpredictable evils the possibility of which should be considered).

112. *Cf.* Rodin, *supra* note 106, at 81.

113. *Cf.* Daniel Statman, *On the Success Condition for Legitimate Self-Defense*, 118 ETHICS 659 (2008).

114. *Cf.* DAVID RODIN, WAR AND SELF-DEFENSE 115 (2002).

law," or quickening the demise of a dictator can always be used to empty the test of real content.

Perhaps for these reasons, some offer a simplified version of the harm-benefit test in international law, in which what would be included in the assessment would be mainly harm to life and limb prevented by the defensive force versus harm to life and limb it causes (as opposed to the *wide* test discussed previously, we can call this the *narrow* harm-benefit test).[115] While this test is much more workable, it seems that all versions of harm-benefit *ad bellum* proportionality require to overcome two more challenges: one is conceptual, and the other is political.

Conceptually, all versions of continuous harm-benefit proportionality require an ongoing assessment of accumulating harms and benefits. Indeed, this is the only way to understand the common view that *ad bellum* proportionality looks at a conflict "as a whole." Some, however, doubt whether continuous assessment of harm-benefit proportionality is rationally possible, because it is unclear how to account for harm accumulated as the conflict progresses.[116] Jeff McMahan identifies two broad views on the question of accumulation. The "quota view" requires an initial assessment of proportionality, and then a continuous assessment of whether the accumulated harms, during the conflict, have exceeded the benefit of achieving the just cause (and perhaps, it should be added, new emerging just causes).[117] The other view, which McMahan largely endorses, is the "prospective view." On this view, past harms are sunk costs—sunk harms, if you will—and as such are largely irrelevant to ongoing proportionality assessments, which should be forward-looking.[118] In other words, the accumulation of past harms in war is simply another manifestation of the famous sunk cost fallacy.[119] This would mean, for instance, that in a sequence of attacks, harm caused by attack *1* cannot prospectively affect the morality of attack *2*, if the latter is justified in itself.

As McMahan concedes, the prospective view might be understood as permitting "the indefinite continuation of war and the infliction of an indefinite amount of harm beyond the initially recognized maximum."[120] He also acknowledges that

115. As Haque puts it, "[T]he best combination of the 'instrumental' [means-end] and 'balancing' [harm-benefit] approaches [to *ad bellum* proportionality] may be that harm inflicted on enemy military forces must be no greater than necessary to prevent or repel their armed attack, but that harm inflicted on civilians must be outweighed by the harm that the armed attack would inflict if not prevented." Haque, *supra* note 92, at 261.

116. Jeff McMahan, *Proportionality and Time*, 125 Ethics 696 (2015).

117. *Id.* at 701–703.

118. *Id.* at 703–705. Importantly, to McMahan, "[c]laims about past attacks and their casualties were . . . relevant, but only to the extent that they were predictive of the future," meaning that past harm can only serve as *evidence* for the assessment of future harms. *Id.* at 697.

119. *See* Richard Thaler, *Toward a Positive Theory of Consumer Choice*, 1 J. Econ. Behav. & Org. 39, 47–50 (1980).

120. McMahan, *supra* note 116, at 707.

leaders—knowing that sunk harms would not count into the overall proportionality of the conflict—might ex ante plan wars that would exceed what would be initially considered proportionate.[121] But to me, the main problem with the exclusion of sunk harms is moral vertigo: if this view is accepted, the external observer cannot find any solid ground for an assessment of war. In this context, Moellendorf makes the commonsensical objection that the prospective view robs proportionality "of much of its important critical force, for it renders incomprehensible the claim that a war is disproportionate because of its cumulative cost."[122]

Those that argue that harm-benefit *ad bellum* proportionality should be introduced into law, must take a position on the problem of accumulation. As a preliminary argument, it would seem that the prospective view, if adopted in law, is prone to abuse. Not only would it facilitate the elongation of conflict because repeated failures would not "add up," so to speak, it also might lead parties to become reckless about harm, because they would perceive themselves as having a clean slate to continue the war after each instance of harm. Furthermore, while the prospective account has some merit if we adopt the narrow view of harm-benefit (weighing lives), positive international law assesses defensive actions also in relation to the defense of territorial integrity and political independence.[123] It is one thing to justify repeated harmful attempts to defend life, but it is another thing altogether to do so in order to prevent harms that do not constitute a threat to life. Last, Moellendorf's appeal to proportionality's "important critical force" is especially true in law, both because of its appeal to common sense and because accumulation of harm might be the only external proxy lawyers have to make a harm-benefit assessment.

Yet, even if the issue of sunk harms accumulation is resolved, it seems that the main challenge facing the incorporation of any kind of harm-benefit analysis into positive law would be political. Indeed, such an incorporation would have a dramatic meaning in international relations.[124] Recall that the means-end proportionality test assumes as a given that if an armed attack occurs and diplomatic means are unavailable, self-defense is *always* lawful. Any harm-benefit proportionality analysis, if adopted in law, would entail that in some cases, self-defense would be legally prohibited, even if a significant armed attack would take place.[125] While this approach could be morally virtuous, it is doubtful whether

121. *Id.* at 708.

122. Darrel Moellendorf, *Two Doctrines of* Jus ex Bello, 125 ETHICS 653, 663, 667–68 (2015). For a helpful summary of these positions, *see* Janina Dill, *Ending Wars: The* Jus ad Bellum *Principles Suspended, Repeated, or Adjusted?*, 125 ETHICS 627, 628–29 (2015).

123. *See* Greenwood, *supra* note 15, at 223.

124. Although, as some commentators point out, there are some dicta in international jurisprudence that imply a harms-benefit understanding of proportionality as a matter of positive law. Haque, *supra* note 92, at 259; Akande & Liefländer, *supra* note 85, at 567.

125. Interestingly, it is possible to imagine a rare case that even under widely accepted positive law, a state would be prohibited to act in self-defense, but under *jus in bello*. This might

states would accept, in the foreseeable future, such restrictions as a matter of positive law, or if any state ever refrained from responding to an armed attack because of the results of a universal harm-benefit analysis. This is probably because such a standard would require states to exercise a degree of impartiality in matters to which state constituencies afford utmost importance, especially in our world of increasing nationalism.[126]

2. The Interaction between *Ad Bellum* and *In Bello* Harm-Benefit Analysis

Setting these challenges aside, how could harm-benefit proportionality, continuously applied, interact with *in bello* proportionality? Can both notions inform each other? On its face, there is more potential for interaction here than, say, with the halt-and-repel test, because *in bello* proportionality is a form of a harm-benefit test itself. In my view, however, there still is a strong case for an analytical (and operational) separation between proportionality on both levels. Indeed, if we adopt the *wide* approach to *ad bellum* proportionality, the latter differs significantly from *in bello* proportionality under positive international law. Recall, that while the benefits envisioned in *ad bellum* proportionality are universal goods, *in bello* proportionality refers to an egoistic good, namely, the concrete and direct military advantage, even that of an aggressor.[127] Indeed, even on part of the defender, some military advantages might promote the greater good, while others would not. These advantages would figure in *in bello* but not *ad bellum* proportionality. Conversely, some attacks might bring about, in addition to the military advantage, goods that are not strictly military, which might be captured by *ad bellum* but not *in bello* proportionality.

be the case where any possible attack would cause excessive harm *in bello*, which would therefore prevent the state from responding. These scenarios seem to be more plausible in an era of small-scale operations such as targeted killings. However, the vast majority of cases would not conform to this scenario, since states would virtually always have alternatives means and methods of attack—the only question is whether they would be willing to risk their own troops by adopting an alternative mode of operation.

126. A fair counterargument is that if this is so, how can we expect a state to act impartially when assessing proportionality *in bello*, as law already requires? Quite possibly, the answer is that it is more realistic to expect that a state refrain from a specific attack—and consider other targets, or means or methods of attack—rather than to refrain from responding altogether.

127. In this sense, *jus in bello* proportionality is a hybrid normative construct. On one hand, it harks back to the Catholic doctrine of double-effect, by tolerating incidental harm when inflicted in the achievement of a greater cause. For an overview, *see* Alison McIntyre, *Doctrine of Double Effect*, *in* The Stanford Encyclopedia of Philosophy (Edward N. Zalta ed., 2019), https://plato.stanford.edu/archives/spr2019/entries/double-effect. But on the other hand, as opposed to the doctrine of double-effect, positive *in bello* proportionality does not pit incidental harm against a greater good, but refers to the amoral concept of military advantage. This divergence is owed to the pragmatic principle of belligerent equality.

On the harm side, while *ad bellum* proportionality would require the consideration of universal harms, *in bello* proportionality refers only to "incidental loss of civilian life, injury to civilians, damage to civilian objects, or a combination thereof." This excludes—even on broad interpretations—harms to the defender or harms to the aggressor and to third parties.

The takeaway is that it would be impossible to simply add up all the military advantages and civilian harms accrued throughout the conflict and then conclude whether the response, at any given moment, is *ad bellum* proportionate. While this comparison might be an important element of the assessment, it would not exhaust it. An additional level of assessment would be required.[128] Since this type of an assessment could not be possibly expected from field-level commanders, this supports the conclusion that concurrent application, even if one adopts the harm-benefit approach, still requires separation in practice.[129]

This separation would remain true, I think, even if we adopt the *narrow* harm-benefit proportionality test. Consider the following table, representing a simplified example of a short operation comprising four independent attacks ("Operation Quadruple"), aimed against an adversary's missile bases.

Attack No.	**Military Advantage (lives saved)**	**Civilian Harm (lives incidentally taken)**
1	100	2
2	10	5
3	4	2
4	2	3
Aggregate Harm-Benefit	**116**	**12**

Assume that attacks *2* through *4* are disproportionate, both ex ante—and therefore in violation of *jus in bello* proportionality—and ex post, when looking at their actual consequences. Assume, conversely, that attack *1* is clearly proportionate in both respects. If we take seriously that *jus ad bellum* proportionality looks at a conflict "as a whole," Operation Quadruple is *ad bellum* proportionate although the vast majority of its attacks are *in bello* disproportionate. Yet, clearly, and to the extent that the attacks are independent, this does not mean that prior to attacks *2*, *3*, and *4*, military commanders are allowed more leeway in proportionality, because of the advantages accrued in attack *1*. Again, the case is made that even if *ad bellum* and *in bello* harm-benefit standards apply concurrently, the analysis in practice must remain separate.[130]

128. Shue, *supra* note 91, at 271–72.

129. *Cf. id.* at 273.

130. Although, a case can be made that previous harms can affect *in bello* assessments in later attacks, since patterns of harm can affect what "may be expected" by reasonable commanders prior to the attack. *See, e.g.*, U.N. Hum. Rts. Council, Report of the Detailed Findings of the

Yet, it seems, that while *in bello* decision-making should remain separate from *ad bellum* harm-benefit analysis, the opposite isn't completely true: the expected decisions of field commanders *in bello* should form part of the *ad bellum* harm-benefit analysis. When anticipating the overall harm-benefit, before and during Operation Quadruple, high-level commanders and leaders should consider the results of previous or prospective *in bello* decisions in the field. In this sense, there would be some overlap between the levels of assessment.[131]

To sum up this point, even if we adopt a (wide or narrow) view of harm-benefit *ad bellum* proportionality, it makes sense to keep this analysis separated from *in bello* proportionality, although there is conceptual overlap.

D. Concurrent Application and *In Bello/Ad Bellum* Normative Spillover

The last question on concurrent application addressed here arises whether we adopt the halt-and-repel or harm-benefit standard. The issue is whether there is, or should be, a "normative spillover" between violations of proportionality *in bello* and proportionality *ad bellum*, meaning whether violations of the former are necessarily violations of the latter. It seems that the mainstream view opposes such spillover, arguing that a forcible response can indeed be disproportionate under *jus in bello*, but remain proportionate *ad bellum*.[132] Yet, some prominent commentators support this idea. To Greenwood, for instance, "an act which contravened the *jus in bello* could not be a reasonable and proportionate measure of self-defence. In that sense, the rules of the *jus in bello* give detailed expression to one of the principles of the *jus ad bellum*."[133] Similarly, Gardam argues that "[v]iolations of the jus in bello, including disproportionate attacks, are also unjustifiable as measures of self-defense under the jus ad bellum."[134]

What would the spillover theory mean under the different understandings of *ad bellum* proportionality? Suppose we adopt a means-end approach (halt and repel). Saying that a disproportionate attack *in bello* would also be *ad bellum* disproportionate, under this assumption, seems incommensurate. This is because an attack can cause disproportionate harm to civilians but still be within the confines of what is operationally required to halt and repel an attack. In such a case, it is

Independent Commission of Inquiry Established Pursuant to Human Rights Council Resolution S-21/1, ¶ 385, U.N. Doc. A/HRC/29/CRP.4 (June 24, 2015) (suggesting that previous harm in similar circumstances might affect the perception of the reasonable commander later on).

131. *Cf.* Enzo Cannizzaro, *Contextualizing Proportionality:* Jus ad Bellum *and* Jus in Bello *in the Lebanese War*, 88 Int'l Rev. Red Cross 779, 791–92 (2006).

132. Moussa, *supra* note 15, at 968, 977–78; van Steenberghe, *supra* note 15, at 116–17; Okimoto, *supra* note 93, at 58–59, 66–67.

133. Greenwood, *supra* note 15, at 231.

134. Gardam, *supra* note 15, at 392.

analytically difficult to draw from the unlawfulness of the action on one level, unlawfulness on the other. To see this, think of a police officer who can prevent a murderer from imminently killing someone, but only at the cost of killing the murderer and incidentally killing five bystanders. Should the officer do so, we would say that she acted unlawfully because of the disproportionate harm she caused to the bystanders. But we cannot deduce from this conclusion that the killing of the murderer was *itself* unlawful.[135]

Therefore, only if we adopt a harm-benefit approach to *ad bellum* proportionality can we make sense of an argument that violations of proportionality *in bello* are necessarily also disproportionate *ad bellum*. In this context, some of the proponents of the spillover theory cite, in support, the ICJ's dicta in the *Nuclear Weapons* advisory opinion, holding that "use of force that is proportionate under the law of self-defence, must, in order to be lawful, also meet the requirements of the law applicable in armed conflicts, which comprise in particular the principles and rules of humanitarian law."[136] Some view this ruling as providing for an "interlinkage between *jus ad bellum* and *jus in bello*."[137]

The *Nuclear Weapons* case, however, is a shaky support for normative spillover. First of all, note that the Court referred to use of force which was *ad bellum* "proportionate," and held that to be lawful, this use of force must also abide by IHL. Meaning, it was already assumed that the use of force was *ad bellum* proportionate *independently* from considerations of IHL, but that, rightly so, in order to be lawful *overall*, that use of force must *also* abide by IHL. In other words, for a particularly use of force to be entirely lawful, it must fulfill two cumulative requirements: be undertaken in the context of an *ad bellum* lawful use of force *and* be legal under IHL. This does not mean, however, that violation of one of the requirements necessarily affects the other.

Furthermore, and crucially, the *Nuclear Weapons* opinion, if at all, opened the door for extreme separation of the spheres. Famously—and controversially—it held that it could not "conclude definitively whether the threat or use of nuclear weapons would be lawful or unlawful in an extreme circumstance of self-defence, in which the very survival of a State would be at stake."[138] This caveat implies that

135. Rather, the *in bello* mirror image of *ad bellum* means-end proportionality can be found, perhaps, in the IHL principles of necessity and distinction. Distinction means that only military objectives and combatants can be intentionally attacked. Necessity is closely related and provides that the only legitimate purpose of attacks is weakening the enemy's military. Indeed, a violation of these principles—for instance, intentionally attacking civilians—could also be phrased as a violation of *ad bellum* means-end proportionality, since intentionally attacking protected civilians is never a defensive action to begin with. Now, since this chapter is about concurrent application of proportionality—not of necessity or distinction—I set this possibility aside.

136. Legality of the Threat or Use of Nuclear Weapons, Advisory Opinion, 1996 I.C.J. 226, ¶ 42 (July 8); *see also* Zimmermann, *supra* note 88, at 124 (citing this case).

137. Zimmermann, *supra* note 88, at 124; *cf.* Haque, *supra* note 92, at 259–60.

138. *Legality of the Threat or Use of Nuclear Weapons*, *supra* note 136, ¶ 105.

in extreme circumstances, in the eyes of the Court, even clear violations of IHL might not affect the legality of an attack *ad bellum*.[139]

Last, there are conceptual problems in adopting the spillover theory. Assume that in a defensive campaign a state conducts 50 attacks, and of them only one is *in bello* disproportionate. Are we now to conclude that the entire defensive campaign was *ad bellum* disproportionate? This seems awkward: a state is not generally perceived to be in violation of *jus ad bellum* only because one or several of its soldiers committed war crimes. Rather, the state incurs state responsibility for that violation of *jus in bello*. In terms of criminal liability, those authorizing the attack, although perhaps guilty of a war crime of disproportionate attack,[140] would not be guilty of the crime of aggression.[141] It seems that we cannot apply the spillover theory without breaking down the campaign to a multitude of *ad bellum* assessments, pertaining to each specific attack. But that would run counter to the idea that *ad bellum* proportionality is assessed in toto. It is unclear, therefore, what is added to the analysis by normative spillover, beyond muddling the existing legal concepts. While a single attack, to be lawful overall, must be *in bello* proportionate *and* undertaken in the context of a defensive campaign, it seems that there is not much valued added if we argue that a single *in bello* disproportionate attack is also *ad bellum* disproportionate.

V. CONCLUSION

The relationship between *ad bellum* and *in bello* proportionality is a sticky problem, not least because so much about these standards is contested. This chapter sought to clarify two aspects of the question: whether *ad bellum* proportionality continues to apply after the outbreak of an armed conflict (continuous application), and assuming that it does, what are the problems that arise when the two standards apply together (concurrent application).

Concerning the first question, I defended the view that there are no convincing grounds to argue that *ad bellum* proportionality ceases to apply after a conflict erupts (the static view). This is because the normative assumptions of static view—war exceptionalism, fixed just cause, and formal justification—are unconvincing. Concerning the second question, at the end of the day, this chapter offers a defense of the *functional* separation between the spheres. Indeed, *ad bellum* and *in bello* proportionality may overlap morally and conceptually. However, unless we are willing to forgo the principle of belligerent equality, or require field commanders to take into account political and grand-strategic considerations when planning an attack, it makes sense to keep them operationally—and legally—separate.

139. For these and other conundrums in the *Nuclear Weapons* Advisory Opinion, *see* Claus Kreß, *The International Court of Justice and the Law of Armed Conflicts*, *in* The Development of International Law by the International Court of Justice 263 (Christian J. Tams & James Sloan eds., 2013).

140. Rome Statute of the International Criminal Court, *supra* note 96, art. 8(2)(b)(iv).

141. *Id.* art. 8bis.

PART THREE

The International Law Governing the Use of Force

3

The Essential Link between Proportionality and Necessity in the Exercise of Self-Defense

GEOFFREY S. CORN*

I. INTRODUCTION

It is said that necessity is the mother of invention, and for good reason.[1] Necessity arises in response to an urgent problem, often a problem that cannot be addressed through "normal" solutions. As a result, necessity justifies measures that deviate from the normal problem-solving modus operandi. This necessity-based deviation norm is reflected in the legal concept of necessity.[2] In its legal form, necessity

* Vinson & Elkins Professor of Law, South Texas College of Law Houston; Lieutenant Colonel, U.S. Army (Retired), and formerly Special Assistant for Law of War Matters and Chief of the Law of War Branch, Office of the Judge Advocate General, U.S. Army; Chief of International Law for U.S. Army Europe; Professor of International and National Security Law at the U.S. Army Judge Advocate General's School. A special note of thanks to my research assistants, Second Lieutenant Steven Arango, U.S. Marine Corps, J.D., University of Alabama, 2019, and Carson Walker, South Texas College of Law Houston Class of 2020.

1. Jared Diamond, *Best Invention; Invention Is the Mother of Necessity*, N.Y. Times (Apr. 18, 1999), https://www.nytimes.com/1999/04/18/magazine/best-invention-invention-is-the-mother-of-necessity.html ("Our widespread misunderstanding of inventors as setting out to solve society's problems causes us to say that necessity is the mother of invention.").

2. *Necessity Defense*, Cornell L. Sch. Legal Info. Inst. (Aug. 15, 2018, 1:27 PM), https://www.law.cornell.edu/wex/necessity_defense ("Defense to liability for unlawful activity where the conduct cannot be avoided and one is justified in the particular conduct because it will prevent the occurrence of a harm that is more serious. In tort law, there are two different categories of the necessity defense that can be employed: public necessity and private necessity.").

Geoffrey S. Corn, *The Essential Link between Proportionality and Necessity in the Exercise of Self-Defense* In: *Necessity and Proportionality in International Peace and Security Law.* Edited by: Professor Claus Kreß and Captain Robert Lawless, Oxford University Press (2021). © Oxford University Press. DOI: 10.1093/oso/9780197537374.003.0004.

provides legal justification[3] for action that is normally prohibited when it is reasonably assessed that normal legal modalities are insufficient to protect a legally recognized interest.[4]

The legal concept of necessity is central to the notion of self-defense,[5] a specific application of the legal principle of "general" necessity that applies to situations involving response to an act or imminent threat of unlawful violence.[6] In such situations, the right of self-defense justifies the use of "self-help" measures that would otherwise be legally prohibited, precisely because those measures are objectively "necessary."[7] This theory of legal justification plays a critical role not only in the domestic context but also in regulating use of force by states.[8] In both contexts, necessity provides the foundation for treating such self-help measures as legally justified. In short, a state's inherent right to protect itself from an actual or imminent unlawful armed attack begins with a reasonable assessment that the conditions indicating necessity exist. But because necessity is the foundation of legal justification, the right to take self-help measures also terminates once the threat is reduced and the victim of the attack is no longer able to claim a reasonable basis for the duration or scope of the self-defense operation.[9]

3. "[N]ecessity identifies the overarching concept of legal justification." *See* Thomas Morawetz, *Reconstructing the Criminal Defenses: The Significance of Justification*, 77 J. CRIM. L. & CRIMINOLOGY 277, 294 (1986); *Necessity Defense, supra* note 2.

4. *See Necessity Defense, supra* note 2.

5. Boaz Sangero, *Heller's Self-Defense*, 13 NEW CRIM. L. REV. 449, 466 (2010) ("As we have seen above, the rationale of self-defense dictates several conditions, central among them the requirements of necessity and proportionality.").

6. *Id.*

7. *Id.* at 457 ("However, it is still possible, at least for the purposes of the present article, to summarize briefly the basic requirements of self-defense as follows: the attack that is defended against must be an *unlawful attack by a culpable aggressor who is responsible for his attack.* The two most important requirements that are essential for the use of defensive force to be considered justifiable are *necessity* and *proportionality.*").

8. *Id.*; Michael N. Schmitt, *Military Necessity and Humanity in International Humanitarian Law: Preserving the Delicate Balance*, 50 VA. J. INT'L L. 795, 796 (2010) [hereinafter Schmitt, *Preserving the Delicate Balance*]; *see also* Major Robert W. Gehring, *Defense Against Insurgents on the High Seas: The Lyla Express and Johnny Express*, 27 JAG JOURNAL 317, 338 (1973) ("Necessity and proportionality are the two central elements which must be present for the permissible use of coercion in self-defense under international law.").

9. Sangero, *supra* note 5, at 457. As Dr. Claus Kreß explains,

> In the Nicaragua case, the ICJ rejected the necessity of the use of force by the US because the "major offensive of the armed opposition against the Government of El Salvador had been completely repulsed, and the actions of the opposition considerably reduced in consequence." "Thus," the Court continued, "it was possible to eliminate the danger to the Salvadorian Government without the United States embarking on activities in and against Nicaragua." In this passage, the Court alluded to the temporal aspect of the necessity

Self-defense in both the domestic and international domain is often defined by focusing on requisite elements, specifically the elements of necessity and proportionality. These two elements are often characterized as distinct requirements of self-defense.[10] However, because the concept of necessity in the general sense *is* the foundation of any legal justification, there may be value in conceptualizing what is normally characterized as the "necessity" element as something more precise: the self-help trigger. Indeed, when addressed as a self-defense element, necessity is really the element that is understood to trigger the self-help response. Once triggered, the focus then shifts to the proportionality element of the justification. When conceptualized in these terms, both the self-help response trigger and proportionality help define when a state's resort to self-defense is objectively necessary in the broadest sense of the term and therefore legally justified. In other words, it may be beneficial to view proportionality as an element of overall self-help necessity, meaning that even when a self-help response is justified the scope of the response may be so out of proportion to the triggering threat that the action can no longer be deemed necessary. While compliance with both elements is essential for a valid invocation of self-defense, this chapter proposes a potential benefit in treating them as elements of the validity of the *overall* necessity of action in self-defense.

This conceptualization may contribute to greater clarity related to implementing and assessing the validity of state self-defense. First, it will mitigate the risk of conflation between proportionality as it relates to a state's overall decision to employ force (the *ad bellum* variant) and proportionality as it relates to protecting civilians and civilian property during the conduct of hostilities (the *in bello* variant). As explained later, this conflation undermines the logic of proportionality in each distinct conflict regulation context.[11] Furthermore, conceptualizing *ad bellum*

> requirement and its formulation may be read to suggest that forcible measures of self-defence are no longer necessary when the armed attack has ended.

Claus Kreß, *The International Court of Justice and the Principle of Non-Use of Force*, *in* THE OXFORD HANDBOOK OF THE USE OF FORCE IN INTERNATIONAL LAW 588 (Marc Weller ed., 2015) (citation omitted); *see also* Michael K. Murphy, *Achieving Economic Security with Swords as Ploughshares: The Modern Use of Force to Combat Environmental Degradation*, 39 VA. J. INT'L L. 1181, 1204 (1999) ("[T]he customary and inherent right of self-defense which remains for states to utilize in situations of grave danger, including protecting themselves from massive environmental danger."). Necessity is equally central to the application of the self-defense doctrine in the domestic criminal context. Indeed, a number of scholars have contrasted these two distinct contexts of self-defense doctrines. *See, e.g.*, Jens David Ohlin, *The Doctrine of Legitimate Defense*, 91 INT'L L. STUD. 119, 123–24 (2015); Gina Heathcote, *Article 51 Self-Defense as a Narrative: Spectators and Heroes in International Law*, 12 TEX. WESLEYAN L. REV. 131, 139 (2005).

10. *Id.*

11. Robert D. Sloane, *The Cost of Conflation: Preserving the Dualism of* Jus Ad Bellum *and* Jus in Bello *in the Contemporary Law of War*, 34 YALE J. INT'L L. 47, 47–81 (2009) [hereinafter Sloane, *The Cost of Conflation*] ("The dualism of *jus ad bellum* and *jus in bello* is at the heart of all that is most problematic in the moral reality of war.").

proportionality as a component of the overall assessment of self-defense justification better aligns that assessment with the strategic decision-making process.

By focusing on the strategic nature of the decision to resort to a self-help use of force, *ad bellum* proportionality assessments will gravitate toward the overall strategic objective of the military mission.[12] This will mitigate the temptation to focus on *in bello* proportionality considerations as a touchstone of compliance with *ad bellum* obligations. More specifically, treating proportionality as nested within the ultimate strategic self-help justification may offset the distorting and increasingly common tendency to assess *ad bellum* proportionality by comparing the extent of *operational* combat effects between the two parties to the resulting armed conflict.[13] While, as explained later, some harm/effects balancing may be a legitimate aspect of assessing strategic proportionality, this does not justify a "tit-for-tat" approach to the assessment.

Second, analyzing proportionality as a component of overall self-defense necessity may contribute to more effective assessments of *ad bellum* compliance by focusing that assessment on the *overall* scope of the self-defense military action as opposed to disaggregated operational components.[14] This is because proportionality at the *ad bellum* level should be understood to dictate a rational alignment between the threat triggering a self-defense response and the strategic scope of a self-defense military operation. In contrast, the *operational* objective must be to defeat enemy forces as rapidly and efficiently as possible.[15] Accordingly, *ad bellum* proportionality frames the strategic

12. Ziv Bohrer & Mark Osiel, *Proportionality in Military Force at War's Multiple Levels: Averting Civilian Casualties vs. Safeguarding Soldiers*, 46 VAND. J. TRANSNAT'L L. 747, 752, 769 (2013) ("The first is *jus ad bellum* proportionality, governing the decision to resort to force in the first instance and determining what overall measure of force will be consistent with the goal of national self-defense. Second is *jus in bello* proportionality, regulating operational and tactical conduct during an armed conflict. . . . Decisions about *ad bellum* proportionality concern strategic issues, however, and are made by high-ranking officials, for they are the only people authorized to establish those comprehensive goals.").

13. *Id.* at 771 ("Because *in bello* proportionality governs war in its tactical and operational respects, the military advantage must be concrete and direct, in this way delimited in scope.").

14. *Id.* at 752 ("Part II assesses current international law, which distinguishes between two forms of proportionality. The first *is jus ad bellum* proportionality, governing the decision to resort to force in the first instance and determining what overall measure of force will be consistent with the goal of national self-defense. Second is *jus in bello* proportionality, regulating operational and tactical conduct during an armed conflict.").

15. *See* Michael N. Schmitt, *"Below the Threshold" Cyber Operations: The Countermeasures Response Option and International Law*, 54 VA. J. INT'L L. 697, 723–26 (2014) [hereinafter Schmitt, *"Below the Threshold" Cyber Operations*]; Michael N. Schmitt, *"Change Direction" 2006: Israeli Operations in Lebanon and the International Law of Self-Defense*, 29 MICH. J. INT'L L. 127, 153–55 (2008) [hereinafter Schmitt, *"Change Direction" 2006*] (*In bello* proportionality "prohibits an attack which may be expected to cause incidental loss of civilian life, injury to civilians, damage to civilian objects, or a combination thereof, which would be excessive in relation to the concrete and direct military advantage anticipated. It considers the consequences of individual or related operations, not the scope of a response to an armed attack.").

scope of a self-defense military operation, but does not qualify operational and tactical execution.[16] In other words, while this proportionality obligation does require alignment of the strategic objective with operational scope, this is not analogous to an ongoing *operational* constraint.[17] Viewing the obligation as a component of the overall legal determination that self-defense is justified will contribute to preserving the strategic focus of compliance.[18]

Section II of this chapter provides an overview of how necessity provides the foundation for any legal justification based on a claim of self-defense and how this necessity foundation is integrated into the self-defense provision of the U.N. Charter. Section III then summarizes the treatment of *ad bellum* proportionality in international legal discourse. Section IV then addresses why proportionality is central to the assessment of self-defense justification. Section V addresses the potential value of conceptualizing necessity and proportionality as integrated requirements for any valid claim of self-defense. The chapter will conclude in section VI.

II. THE ESSENTIAL LINK BETWEEN PROPORTIONALITY AND NECESSITY IN THE EXERCISE OF SELF-DEFENSE: THE CHAPTER'S MAIN THESIS IN OUTLINE

International law justifies state resort to measures in self-defense—measures that would otherwise be unlawful—based on the imperative necessity of self-protection or protection of others.[19] This indicates that the concept of "necessity" really has a dual meaning. The notion of "general" necessity provides the overall justification for measures that would normally be prohibited. However, as an element for assessing the validity of self-defense, it focuses more directly on whether an unlawful threat necessitates, or triggers, resort to those measures.[20]

16. "The first is *jus ad bellum* proportionality, governing the decision what overall measure of force will be consistent with the goal of national self-defense. Second is *jus in bello* proportionality, regulating operational and tactical conduct during an armed conflict." *See* Bohrer & Osiel, *supra* note 12, at 752.

17. Jeff McMahan, *Proportionate Defense*, 23 J. TRANSNAT'L L. & POL'Y 1, 23 (2014) ("But it would be a mistake to conflate proportionality in reprisal with proportionality in defense. The aim of defensive violence is the physical prevention of harm by a threatener. Proportionality in defense is therefore essentially prospective."); John Yoo, *International Law and the War in Iraq*, 97 AM. J. INT'L L. 563, 567 (2003) [hereinafter Yoo, *International Law and the War in Iraq*].

18. Bohrer & Osiel, *supra* note 12, at 769 ("Decisions about *ad bellum* proportionality concern strategic issues, however, and are made by high-ranking officials, for they are the only people authorized to establish those comprehensive goals.").

19. Michele Cotton, *The Necessity Defense and the Moral Limits of Law*, 18 NEW CRIM. L. REV. 35, 37 (2015) ("Both necessity and self-defense involve the situation where a person has committed an otherwise unlawful act as a means of protecting herself from an immediate threat.").

20. Madison Fair, *Dare Defend: Standing for Stand Your Ground*, 38 LAW & PSYCHOL. REV. 153, 159 (2014) ("The justification for requiring a duty to retreat posits that, as long as there is a safe

Article 2(4) of the U.N. Charter establishes that "all Members shall refrain in their international relations from the threat or use of force against the territorial integrity or political independence of any state, or in any other manner inconsistent with the Purposes of the United Nations."[21] This provision of the Charter, which is included under the heading of "[P]urposes and Principles of the United Nations," reflects this presumptive prohibition against the threat or use of force by states. However, situations of necessity rebut this presumption, indicating that necessity is the essential requirement to justify resort to self-help violence.[22] This relationship between the presumptive prohibition against such measures and the necessity-based rebuttal of this prohibition is central to the contemporary international legal framework for the exercise of individual and collective state self-defense.[23] Accordingly, actions in self-defense are justified only in situations of objectively valid necessity.[24] Absent such necessity, international law permits no deviation from the presumptive prohibition and thus demands peaceful resolution of disputes.[25]

The standard for rebutting the presumptive illegality of a resort to force by states to protect their interests is articulated in Article 51 of the Charter.[26] Article 51 recognizes state self-defense as an "inherent" right, indicating that all states are

escape available to the person who is attacked, the necessity to kill does not exist, and necessity is required to justify homicide as self-defense.").

21. *Id.*; U.N. Charter art. 2, ¶ 4.

22. "Nearly all of us agree, for example, that (genuine and not putative) cases of self-defense describe circumstances in which persons are permitted to commit the presumptive wrong of deliberately killing another." *See* Douglas Husak, *The Costs to Criminal Theory of Supposing That Intentions Are Irrelevant to Permissibility*, 3 CRIM. L. & PHIL. 51, 66 (2009).

23. Amos N. Guiora, *Self-Defense from the Wild West to 9/11: Who, What, When*, 41 CORNELL INT'L L.J. 631, 649 (2008) ("Self-defense—whether personal or state—is a universal concept; however, this article analyzes the concept from an American perspective.").

24. Yoram Dinstein, *The Gulf War: 1990–2004 (and Still Counting)*, 81 INT'L L. STUD. 337, 345 (2006) ("Having said all that, it is the considered opinion of the present writer that the right to self-defense can be invoked in response to an armed attack as soon as it becomes evident to the victim State (on the basis of hard intelligence available at the time) that the attack is in progress."); Thomas K. Plofchan Jr., *Article 51: Limits on Self-Defense?*, 13 MICH. J. INT'L L. 336, 354 (1992).

25. Louise Arimatsu, *The Law of State Responsibility in Relation to Border Crossings: An Ignored Legal Paradigm*, 89 INT'L L. STUD. 21, 24 (2013) ("The negotiating history of the Charter reveals that Article 2(4) was 'intended to be a comprehensive prohibition on the use of force by one State against the other' and, as the text makes clear, the provision was only concerned with inter-State uses of force. The Charter recognizes two exceptions to this prohibition: enforcement actions as provided under Articles 39, 41 and 42; and the right of individual and collective self-defense, codified in Article 51. . . . Article 51, on the other hand, has traditionally been regarded as an inter-State right that could be invoked only in the event of 'an armed attack' by another State.").

26. Michael N. Schmitt, *21st Century Conflict: Can the Law Survive?*, 8 MELB. J. INT'L L. 443, 448 (2007) ("The most fundamental right of a state is to defend itself from attack. Article 51 of the

legally justified in employing self-help measures in response to unlawful armed attacks. However, this right arises only in response to the genuine necessity resulting from a failure of international law to protect against unlawful aggression in the form of an armed attack.[27] Indeed, Article 51 indicates a textual limit on the right: measures taken in individual or collective self-defense are justified only until the U.N. Security Council effectively assumes responsibility for restoring the *status quo ante* of international peace and security.[28] This qualification reflects the underlying foundation of genuine necessity for any invocation of this legal justification for self-help measures otherwise prohibited by the Charter.[29] These two aspects of Article 51—the recognition that the Charter in no way altered the inherent right of self-defense, coupled with a textual qualification on the scope of that right—are in no way incompatible.[30] Instead, this reflects the fundamental necessity foundation for invocation and exercise of the right.[31] In this sense, the Article 2(4)/Article 51 relationship reflects the logic of all legal justifications: only when the situation produces genuine necessity to resort to self-help use of force in response to an actual or imminent threat of unlawful violence—itself a deviation from the presumptive prohibition against the use of force—will the self-defense justification arise.[32]

Charter of the United Nations codifies this customary international law norm."); David Turns, *The "War on Terror" Through British and International Humanitarian Law Eyes: Comparative Perspectives on Selected Legal Issues*, 10 N.Y. City L. Rev. 435, 477 (2007); Major William G. Schmidt, *The Protection of Victims of International Armed Conflicts: Protocol I Additional to the Geneva Conventions*, 24 A.F. L. Rev. 189, 236 (1984).

27. Ryan Schildkraut, *Where There Are Good Arms, There Must Be Good Laws: An Empirical Assessment of Customary International Law Regarding Preemptive Force*, 16 Minn. J. Int'l L. 193, 232 n.59 (2007) ("[S]tating reference to 'inherent right' in Article 51 indicates 'an existing right, independent of the Charter and not the subject of an express grant.'").

28. *Id.*

29. Plofchan, *supra* note 24, at 340 ("The textual argument against this position, it seems to me, is very strong. Article 51 is, as we all know, not an affirmative grant of a right of self-defense but a statement of the situations in which the exercise of an 'inherent right' is not precluded by the Charter. But those situations are subject to a limit of time. They endure only 'until the Security Council has taken the measures necessary to maintain international peace and security.'").

30. Dinstein, *supra* note 24, at 345 ("Having said all that, it is the considered opinion of the present writer that the right to self-defense can be invoked in response to an armed attack as soon as it becomes evident to the victim State (on the basis of hard intelligence available at the time) that the attack is in progress."); Plofchan, *supra* note 24, at 354.

31. Dinstein, *supra* note 24, at 345; Plofchan, *supra* note 24, at 341 ("As was pointed out above, Article 51 allows for self-defense action until the Security Council takes action.").

32. Plofchan, *supra* note 24, at 366 ("This requirement of necessity for actions justified as self-defense was given legitimacy in the passage of the final resolution on the crisis.").

Therefore, legitimate invocation of the inherent right of self-defense is today conditioned on satisfying two essential principles or elements.[33] Necessity is commonly identified as the first principle, for it provides the prima facie self-help justification.[34] This requisite necessity arises only in response to a threat to a state's security that is considered sufficient within the meaning of international law to justify an armed self-help response: an actual or imminent armed attack which leaves the target state with no other means of protection than the use of defensive force.[35]

But the necessity required for a valid invocation of self-defense extends well beyond the prima facie state assessment that it is the victim of an actual or imminent

33. Eustace Chikere Azubuike, *Probing the Scope of Self Defense in International Law*, 17 ANN. SURV. INT'L & COMP. L. 129, 162 (2011) ("The conditions of necessity and proportionality are the core factors taken into consideration in the determination of the lawfulness or genuineness of a state's claim to the exercise of the right of self defense.").

34. *Id.*

35. Colonel Gary P. Corn, *Cyber National Security: Navigating Gray Zone Challenges in and Through Cyberspace*, *in* COMPLEX BATTLESPACES: THE LAW OF ARMED CONFLICT AND THE DYNAMICS OF MODERN WARFARE 345 (2019) ("While some of these cyber operations have been conducted as part of on-going armed conflicts, the vast majority have taken place in the so-called 'Gray Zone'—the far more uncertain space between war and peace. Alternatively described as gray-zone challenges or gray-zone conflicts, these activities are more accurately understood as actions that are coercive and aggressive in nature and rise above normal, everyday peacetime geo-political competition, 'but that [are] deliberately designed to remain below the threshold of conventional military conflict and open interstate war.' Although these activities are not limited to any single domain or modality, cyberspace offers fertile terrain for gray-zone confrontation."); YORAM DINSTEIN, WAR, AGGRESSION, AND SELF-DEFENCE, 199, 205 (6th ed. 2017) ("The text of Article 51 hinges on the expression 'armed attack'. This is the threshold requirement: recourse to self-defence is not vindicated by any violation of international law which falls short of an armed attack."); Major Jason F. Keen, *Conventional Military Force as a Response to Cyber Capabilities: On Sending Packets and Receiving Missiles*, 73 A.F. L. REV. 111, 144 (2015) ("In the Congo case, the ICJ declined to definitively say that the killing or capture of 200 Ugandans by paramilitaries was enough to exceed the armed attack threshold. In the Nicaragua case, it distinguished between armed attacks and 'mere frontier incident[s],' where apparently there some lesser, acceptable amount of shooting and killing occurred. In the Oil Platforms case, the Court decided that a missile strike, gunboat attacks, and minelaying, assuming proper attribution, would still not rise to the level of 'armed attack.' Given these actual examples from the ICJ, it is hard to imagine an incident stemming from a cyber-only capability that will result in an outcome tantamount to the gravest of attacks occurring when compared to bombardments, invasions, blockades, and military occupations."); Tyler B. Musselman, *Skirmishing for Information: The Flaws of the International Legal System as Evidenced by the Russian-Georgian Conflict of 2008*, 19 TRANSNAT'L L. & CONTEMP. PROBS. 317, 339 (2010) ("The ICJ has previously stated that an armed attack must rise to the same level of 'sending by or on behalf of a State of armed bands, groups, irregulars or mercenaries, which carry out acts of armed force against another State of such gravity as to amount to . . . an actual armed attack conducted by regular forces.'").

armed attack;[36] the right of self-defense arises with necessity, and ends when no longer necessary.[37] This simply reflects the basic notion that an unlawful armed attack justifies only those measures genuinely necessary in response to it.[38] This limitation on self-defense use of force also means that employing measures that go beyond what is necessary to achieve the self-protection goal are unjustified and therefore unlawful.[39]

The reasoning behind this self-defense limitation, which is commonly addressed in terms of *ad bellum* proportionality, is one of strategic scope: that law allows the victim state to employ force to protect itself but go no further; to use necessary force "without unnecessarily escalating the hostilities."[40] Importantly, and as will be further developed later, this necessity-based proportionality limitation does not require that the means employed to *operationally* implement the *strategic* self-defense objective be proportional *to the operational capabilities* of the enemy.[41] As Professor Michael Schmitt notes, proportionality requires that "the use of force be reasonable in intensity, duration, and magnitude, based on all the facts known to the commander at the time, to decisively counter the hostile act or hostile intent and to ensure the continued safety of U.S. forces."[42] However, Schmitt also

36. Sheng Li, *When Does Internet Denial Trigger the Right of Armed Self-Defense?*, 38 Yale J. Int'l L. 179, 208 (2013) ("The functional element requires the scope of force used to be proportional to the object of self-defense, and limits the use of armed force to the goal of successful restoration of the status quo ante.").

37. United States v. Peterson, 483 F.2d 1222, 1229 (D.C. Cir. 1973), *cert. denied*, 414 U.S. 1007 (1973) ("But '[t]he law of self-defense is a law of necessity;' the right of self-defense arises only when the necessity begins, and equally ends with the necessity; and never must the necessity be greater than when the force employed defensively is deadly.").

38. Schmitt, *"Below the Threshold" Cyber Operations*, *supra* note 15, at 723–26 ("Proportionality in the law of self-defense equally limits a State's defensive measures to those that are required to defeat the armed attack, even if they fall short of the intensity of the armed attack that precipitated them."); Li, *supra* note 36, at 206 ("The principle of necessity dictates that legitimate self-defense is permissible only when a state exhausts alternatives to the use of force.").

39. John F. Murphy, *Afghanistan: Hard Choices and the Future of International Law*, 85 Int'l L. Stud. 79, 86 (2009) ("Arguably, while it was permissible for Enduring Freedom to eliminate the military capacity of the Taliban and al Qaeda, in order to prevent a future attack by them, '[e]liminating the whole government structure created by the Taliban, as a war aim, was beyond necessary self-defense' and therefore a disproportionate use of force.").

40. *Id.* at 765.

41. Michael N. Schmitt, *Clipped Wings: Effective and Legal No-Fly Zone Rules of Engagement*, 20 Loy. L.A. Int'l & Comp. L.J. 727, 764 (1998) [hereinafter Schmitt, *Clipped Wings*] ("Many laymen interpret the requirement as 'proportional' to the force used against them. By this interpretation, one could not respond to small arms ground fire with bombs or use a missile to down a helicopter that has employed machine guns against an aircraft. This is clearly not the proper reading. The right to use self-defense is designed to protect without unnecessarily escalating the hostilities; it is not a rule designed to ensure a 'fair fight' on a level playing field.").

42. *Id.*

explains that *ad bellum* proportionality should not be construed to "ensure a fair fight."[43] On the contrary, the permissible operational scope of such military action must be to bring about the prompt submission of the enemy in the most efficient manner possible.[44] In other words, once a self-defense action is initiated, the *ad bellum* proportionality principle functions to limit "a State's defensive measures to those that are required to defeat the armed attack . . ."[45] as a whole, and not to limit the operational scope of the military action assessed as necessary to produce this strategic end-state.

Accordingly, proportionality is best understood as the principle that is intended to ensure alignment between the strategic justification for military action in self-defense and the nature of the threat necessitating such action. In contrast, *ad bellum* necessity is widely understood as *triggering* the right to self-defense, while *ad bellum* proportionality defining the justifiable *scope* of a self-defense action.[46] Indeed, because proportionality relates to the scope of such an operation as opposed to the trigger, it is understandable why it is frequently treated as distinct from the necessity element. But if scope is understood as linked to overall justification, then proportionality may be better conceptualized as a component of necessity. Such conceptualization should ensure that not only the resort to force but also the nature and scope of that use of force is truly necessary to respond to the threat and therefore legally justified.

III. *AD BELLUM* PROPORTIONALITY AS A LIMITATION DISTINCT FROM *AD BELLUM* NECESSITY: THE PREVAILING VIEW IN INTERNATIONAL LEGAL DISCOURSE

The International Court of Justice (ICJ) analyzed the requirements for a valid state invocation of self-defense in its 1986 opinion in *Military and Paramilitary Activities in and against Nicaragua*,[47] concluding that any such invocation must comply with both necessity and proportionality. The Court's analysis was subsequently reinforced in the Advisory Opinion on the *Legality of the Threat or Use of Nuclear Weapons*, in which the Court noted that "[t]he submission of the exercise

43. *Id.* at 764–65.

44. *Id.*

45. Schmitt, *"Below the Threshold" Cyber Operations*, *supra* note 15, at 724.

46. Kimberly Kessler Ferzan, *Defending Imminence: From Battered Women to Iraq*, 46 Ariz. L. Rev. 213, 222 (2004) ("Both domestic and international law require that the self-defensive force be necessary. This necessity component has two parts: the actor may only act when necessary and to the extent necessary. The latter requirement is one of proportionality.").

47. Military and Paramilitary Activities in and Against Nicaragua (Nicar. v. U.S.), Judgment, 1986 I.C.J. Rep. 14 (June 27).

of the right of self-defence to the conditions of necessity *and* proportionality is a rule of customary international law."[48] Subsequent decisions by the ICJ have confirmed that proportionality is an essential requirement for a valid invocation of self-defense and also that it is generally viewed as distinct from the necessity requirement.[49]

According to the *United States Department of Defense Law of War Manual*, proportionality requires that "the State's means in resorting to force be proportionate to its just cause in using force, such as the threat that the State seeks to address."[50] This definition reflects the generally accepted understanding of *ad bellum* proportionality and is also reflected in the 2018 *Final Report on Aggression and the Use of Force* adopted by the International Law Association (*ILA Report*).[51]

These sources reflect a broader consensus that proportionality is an essential element of self-defense.[52] But they also indicate that this element is normally viewed as distinct from the equally essential necessity element when assessing the authority to invoke that inherent right.[53] For example, as the *ILA Report* notes, "The application of both necessity and proportionality presupposes that the measures

48. Legality of the Threat or Use of Nuclear Weapons, Advisory Opinion, 1996 I.C.J. 226, 257 (July 8) (emphasis added).

49. For a comprehensive overview of ICJ jurisprudence related to the use of force, *see* Kreß, *supra* note 9; *see also* Armed Activities on the Territory of the Congo (Dem. Rep. Congo v. Uganda), Judgment, 2005 I.C.J. Rep. 168, ¶ 147, at 223 (Dec. 19) ("Equally, since the preconditions for the exercise of self-defence do not exist in the circumstances of the present case, the Court has no need to enquire whether such an entitlement to self-defence was in fact exercised in circumstances of necessity and in a manner that was proportionate."); Legal Consequences of the Construction of a Wall in the Occupied Palestinian Territory, Advisory Opinion, 2004 I.C.J. Rep. 136, ¶ 142, at 195 (July 9) ("In conclusion, the Court considers that Israel cannot rely on a right of self-defence or on a state of necessity in order to preclude the wrongfulness of the construction of the wall resulting from the considerations mentioned in paragraphs 122 and 137 above. The Court accordingly finds that the construction of the wall, and its associated régime, are contrary to international law.").

50. Office of the Gen. Counsel, U.S. Dep't of Def., Department of Defense Law of War Manual ¶ 2.1.2.3 (June 2015, updated Dec. 2016) [hereinafter DoD Law of War Manual].

51. Exec. Comm., Int'l L. Ass'n, Final Report on Aggression and the Use of Force 11–12 (2018), http://www.ila-hq.org/images/ILA/DraftReports/DraftReport_UseOfForce.pdf [hereinafter Use of Force Report] (stating that the proportionality assessment does not necessarily balance the proportionality between the measures taken in self-defense in response to the preceding armed attack; rather, it should assess whether force taken in self-defense results in harm that outweigh the legitimate aim that such force is trying to achieve).

52. *See* Kreß, *supra* note 9; *see also* DoD Law of War Manual, *supra* note 50; Legality of the Threat or Use of Nuclear Weapons, Advisory Opinion, 1996 I.C.J. 226, ¶ 41 (July 8); Am. L. Inst., 1 Restatement of the Law Third, The Foreign Relations Law of the United States § 431 (1987).

53. *Id.*

are being taken for a legitimate end."[54] This same report also reinforces the conclusion that the *ad bellum* proportionality requirement is intended to align the scope and duration of self-help military action with the triggering justification, noting that

> [t]he principle of proportionality is additional to and separate from necessity. Proportionality is a formula requiring the balancing of two elements against each other. It might be said that the measures taken in self-defence must be proportionate to the armed attack which preceded them. However, such a pure "equivalence of scale" approach to proportionality is incorrect: the preferred position is that the measures be balanced in light of the aims of the self-defence. As examined above, the legitimate aims in this context are to halt any ongoing attack and prevent the continuation of further attacks. Accordingly, the proportionality assessment should weigh the relative interests against each other, thereby assessing whether the harmful effects of the force taken in self-defence are outweighed by achieving the legitimate aims.[55]

Beyond that statement, the report unfortunately provides little in terms of defining *how* proportionality is to be assessed. The *U.S. DOD Law of War Manual* provides a similar definition, although it more accurately links the proportionality of a self-defense action to the strategic objective of neutralizing the overall threat necessitating the military response:

> Proportionality involves a weighing of the contemplated actions with the justification for taking action. For example, the proportionality of the measures taken in self-defense is to be judged according to the nature of the threat being addressed. Force may be used in self-defense, but only to the extent that it is required to repel the armed attack and to restore the security of the party attacked. As an illustration, assessing the proportionality of measures taken in self-defense may involve considerations of whether an actual or imminent attack is part of an ongoing pattern of attacks or what force is reasonably necessary to discourage future armed attacks or threats thereof.[56]

In the *ad bellum* context, the principle of proportionality therefore functions to frame the permissible strategic scope of military action in self-defense. While such scope is certainly not easily assessed at inception, it is unquestionably linked to *overall* necessity and not a consideration that should be treated as truly independent from the necessity for the military response. In short, overall necessity includes two critical considerations: first, whether the nature of the unlawful

54. USE OF FORCE REPORT, *supra* note 51, at 11.

55. *Id.* at 12.

56. DOD LAW OF WAR MANUAL, *supra* note 50, at 41.

threat triggers the right of self-help, and second, what is the permissible scope of that self-help action.

IV. *AD BELLUM* NECESSITY AND *AD BELLUM* PROPORTIONALITY AND THE STRATEGIC SCOPE OF SELF-DEFENSE OPERATIONS

The notion that *ad bellum* proportionality is the principle that dictates the permissible and *necessary* strategic scope of a self-defense response is not necessarily controversial. For example, Professor Michael Schmitt notes that "proportionality deals with the degree of force permissible in self-defense; it allows the application of no more force than required, in the attendant circumstances, to deter an anticipated attack or defeat one that is underway."[57] To violate proportionality, the victim state "must do no more than reasonably required in the circumstances to deter a threatened attack or defeat an ongoing one."[58]

But even in situations involving a response to what is assessed as an ongoing threat, it is the nature of the threat that dictates what type of response is necessary and therefore proportional within the *jus ad bellum*.[59] This raises an important question: Does proportionality demand a "tit-for-tat" response? Or may a state be justified in responding with much more force than was initially used against it, most notably when that initial use of force is assessed as the opening salvo in a broader campaign? David Kretzmer believes the latter approach is only logical in today's geopolitical climate, noting that "it does not seem reasonable to demand that the victim state restrict its response to halting and repelling the attack, even when it has well-founded fears that the aggressor may well mount another attack in the future."[60] Indeed, when a threat is reasonably assessed as *ongoing*, the determination of what is necessary to achieve the strategic self-protection objective is the decisive question related to what type of response is proportional and therefore necessary.[61] This reinforces the conclusion that proportionality is a component for assessing the *overall* necessity of the self-defense response. At the

57. Schmitt, *"Change Direction" 2006*, *supra* note 15, at 153.

58. *Id.* at 154.

59. David Kretzmer, *The Inherent Right to Self-Defence and Proportionality in* Jus Ad Bellum, 24 EUR. J. INT'L L. 235, 239 (2013) [hereinafter Kretzmer, *Self-Defence and Proportionality in* Jus Ad Bellum].

60. *Id.* at 267

61. *Id.* ("Several variables may affect the ends of the force used in self-defence, and hence the test for assessing its proportionality; whether the attack is ongoing, completed, or imminent; whether it was carried out by non-state actors and, if so, whether it can be imputed to a state; and, finally, the scale and effects of the attack, when judged in the context of the relations between those responsible for the attack and the victim state."); Schmitt, *"Change Direction" 2006*, *supra* note 15, at 153–55.

strategic/*ad bellum* level, this means the scale and duration of the response must be linked to the nature of the overall threat.

Proportionality can therefore be understood as the principle intended to ensure that only the force necessary to effectively defend the state from an unlawful armed attack or imminent armed attack may be used in self-defense.[62] When the nature of the force used in such an event is not reasonably proportional to the self-protection objective, it ceases to be necessary and is therefore unlawful. Thus, necessity and proportionality are not truly distinct requirements of self-defense, but instead integrated into an overall assessment of forcible action taken in self-defense. And, while it is certainly possible to analytically distinguish between a necessity element, which dictates when the right to act in self-defense arises, and a proportionality element, which is implicated only after that point, such a proportionality element nevertheless remains related to an overall necessity assessment. In short, overdoing the analytical divide between necessity and proportionality distorts the integrated role of these principles in the context of self-defense under international law.

Defining the self-defense objective is crucial, and it will often be a demanding task. This is the case especially when military action in self-defense is conducted in response to an assessed ongoing armed attack, such as what the United States characterized as its ongoing armed conflict with al-Qaida. Here it is important to distinguish the strategic self-defense objective from the military *campaign* initiated to achieve that objective. The military campaign must fall within the permissible proportional scope of the strategic response, meaning the *operational* objectives of the action (the "means") must be rationally linked to the *strategic* "self-help" protective goal (the "end").[63] Accordingly, in that self-defense context, it is unrealistic to expect that every attack against the organized armed group conducted as part of an overall self-defense campaign be subjected to an individual proportionality assessment. Instead, when gauging the appropriate scale of proportionality when the objective is to deter an imminent attack or subsequent

62. Paul H. Robinson & Adil Ahmad Haque, *Advantaging Aggressors: Justice & Deterrence in International Law*, 3 Harv. Nat'l Sec. J. 143, 155 (2011) ("The use of defensive force is indeed illegitimate—but only because the use of unnecessary force is *always* illegitimate, not because of any qualitative difference between limited unlawful aggression and armed attacks."); Amy J. Sepinwall, *Defense of Others and Defenseless "Others,"* 17 Yale J.L. & Feminism 327, 375 (2005).

63. *See* President Barack Obama, Report on the Legal and Policy Frameworks Guiding the United States' Use of Military Force and Related National Security Operations 9 (2016), https://fas.org/man/eprint/frameworks.pdf ("Under the *jus ad bellum*, a State may use force in the exercise of its inherent right of self- defense not only in response to armed attacks that have already occurred, but also in response to *imminent* attacks before they occur. When considering whether an armed attack is imminent under the *jus ad bellum* for purposes of the initial use of force against another State or on its territory, the United States analyzes a variety of factors."); Brian J. Egan, Legal Advisor, State Dep't, International Law, Legal Diplomacy, and the Counter-ISIL Campaign (Apr. 4, 2016), https://www.justsecurity.org/wp-content/uploads/2016/04/Egan-ASIL-speech.pdf.

attacks during an ongoing campaign, the state should be permitted to consider "the 'accumulation of events,' and not only the initial armed attack which triggered the forcible response."[64] Ultimately, what is a necessary military action in self-defense is inherently contextual, which extends not only to the question of imminence but also to the permissible scope of a responsive campaign.

This contextual assessment of the role proportionality plays in defining the permissible and therefore *necessary* scope of a responsive military campaign is central to the U.S. interpretation of the inherent right of self-defense. This understanding is reflected in the following extract from a speech by Brian Eagan, serving at that time as Legal Advisor to the Department of State:

> Under the jus ad bellum, a State may use force in the exercise of its inherent right of self-defense not only in response to armed attacks that have occurred, but also in response to imminent ones before they occur.
>
> When considering whether an armed attack is imminent under the jus ad bellum for purposes of the initial use of force against a particular non-State actor, the United States analyzes a variety of factors, including those identified by Sir Daniel Bethlehem in the enumeration he set forth in the American Journal of International Law—the ASIL's own in-house publication—in 2012. These factors include the nature and immediacy of the threat; the probability of an attack; whether the anticipated attack is part of a concerted pattern of continuing armed activity; the likely scale of the attack and the injury, loss, or damage likely to result therefrom in the absence of mitigating action; and the likelihood that there will be other opportunities to undertake effective action in self-defense that may be expected to cause less serious collateral injury, loss, or damage. The absence of specific evidence of where an attack will take place or of the precise nature of an attack does not preclude a conclusion that an armed attack is imminent for purposes of the exercise of the right of self-defense, provided that there is a reasonable and objective basis for concluding that an armed attack is imminent.
>
> In the view of the United States, once a State has lawfully resorted to force in self-defense against a particular armed group following an actual or imminent armed attack by that group, it is not necessary as a matter of international law to reassess whether an armed attack is imminent prior to every subsequent action taken against that group, provided that hostilities have not ended. Under the PPG, however, the concept of imminence plays an important role as a matter of policy in certain U.S. counterterrorism operations, even when it is not legally required.[65]

64. Kretzmer, *Self-Defence and Proportionality in* Jus ad Bellum, *supra* note 59, at 275; Kirklin M. Schweitzer, *Operation Cast Lead: A Perspective Through the Eyes of Sderot*, 9 Regent J. Int'l L. 145, 164 (2013) ("While a minor incident would not warrant a full armed conflict, proportionality is measured by the accumulation of attacks if they are recurring.").

65. Egan, *supra* note 63.

As Eagan's commentary illustrates, assessing what qualifies as a proportional response to an imminent threat when that response involves multiple military actions conducted within a broad self-defense campaign is perhaps the most challenging aspect of the proportionality analysis.[66]

Whether a military attack is viewed as a "one-off" action, or part of a broader military campaign to defend against an ongoing threat by achieving a broad self-defense strategic objective, the relationship between necessity and proportionality remains the same: the scope of the overall operation must be linked to the necessity of restoring the status quo ante.[67] Conceptualizing proportionality as an element of self-defense necessity might contribute to clarifying the important difference between the overall strategic scope of a self-defense military action and the operational campaign conducted to achieve this strategic objective.[68]

In this international law context, states must make this overall self-defense justification assessment based on intelligence and other reasonably available information.[69] Conceptualizing proportionality as an integral part of the overall necessity of the self-help action taken enhances the quality of the self-defense justification assessment because it will require a careful analysis of the scope and duration of any military action triggered by a threat assessed to render that action necessary.[70] There is no rational reason why scope and duration—the aspect of the action dictated by proportionality—should be relegated to a secondary consideration. Instead, any self-defense action must reflect the overall justification

66. Sloane, *The Cost of Conflation*, *supra* note 11, at 81 ("This disconnect has become increasingly apparent over time. It has led the ICJ, at times, to elide, confuse, or simply fail to engage with difficult but pressing questions raised by the jus ad bellum and the jus in bello in subsequent law-of-war opinions.").

67. *Id.* at 67 ("Any use of force must be necessary and proportional relative to both the jus ad bellum and the jus in bello.").

68. *Id.*

69. Amos Guiora, *Pre-Empting Terror Bombings: A Comparative Approach to Anticipatory Self-Defense*, 41 U. Tol. L. Rev. 801, 851 (2010) ("Anticipatory self-defense is dependent on intelligence gathering and analysis; international law must be re-articulated to enable the state to act proactively. While Article 51 of the United Nations Charter reflects a particular concern, the post 9/11 world (in particular in response to terror bombings) justifies a new paradigm based on intelligence information--the anticipatory self defense model."); Commander Roger D. Scott, *Territorially Intrusive Intelligence Collection and International Law*, 46 A.F. L. Rev. 217, 224 (1999) ("The right of self-defense may also justify the collection of intelligence. Intelligence is necessary to give substance and effect to the right of self-defense, including the customary international law right of anticipatory or peremptory self-defense. Appropriate defensive preparations cannot be made without information about potential threats.").

70. James A. Green & Francis Grimal, *The Threat of Force as an Action in Self-Defense Under International Law*, 44 Vand. J. Transnat'l L. 285, 325 (2011) ("Finally, in the context of 'traditional' self-defense involving the use of force, the criteria of necessity and proportionality together require that the response be of a limited duration: a response in self-defense must end when the defensive necessity ends.").

for the action. The touchstone for assessing the legitimacy of this asserted justification will inevitably be the operational and tactical execution of the self-defense mission. As a result, it is vital that proportionality dictates from inception the parameters of that military mission: the operational objectives defined to achieve the strategic self-defense goal.[71]

This "translation" of a strategic self-defense justification into military operational objectives requires that the state first make a credible determination that it is the victim of an unlawful armed attack or one that is imminent. This determination, if accompanied by a finding that an effective nonforcible response is of no avail, triggers the right to engage in a military response. However, proportionality must then dictate the scope and duration of that military response, as only then that response will be truly necessary. And if the international legal regulation of self-defense is to be meaningful, both these considerations must dictate the legality assessment *prior to* initiation of the military action even in the most time-sensitive situations.[72] Each element of self-defense must therefore guide the state's assessment of overall legal justification from the inception of the use of force decision-making process.[73] One may respond that there is no harm in treating each of these self-defense requirements as conceptually distinct. No matter how proportionality is conceptualized, it will still be a consideration central to both

71. Catherine Lotrionte, *State Sovereignty and Self-Defense in Cyberspace: A Normative Framework for Balancing Legal Rights*, 26 Emory Int'l L. Rev. 825, 892 (2012) ("Proportionality under jus ad bellum requires that any forcible response in self-defense be limited in size and magnitude to what is reasonably necessary to achieve the permissible objectives of the self-defense operation. Proportionality relates to the size, duration and target of the response.").

72. David Kaye, *Adjudicating Self-Defense: Discretion, Perception, and the Resort to Force in International Law*, 44 Colum. J. Transnat'l L. 134, 142 ("By contrast, the United States argued that '[t]he responsibility to determine the occurrence of an armed attack rests with the victim State, since by its very nature an "armed attack" requires the victim State to evaluate the threat to its security and the actions it must take to defend itself.' As a result, it said, 'any review should account for the victim State's assessment of the overall situation at the time it took action in self-defense.'"); Noam Chomsky, *The Rule of Force in International Affairs Nuremberg and Vietnam: An American Tragedy*, 80 Yale L.J. 1456, 1460 (1971) ("It was in Taylor's opinion permissible for the American Executive to determine unilaterally that North Vietnam was engaged in aggressive war prior to 1965, and to join South Vietnam in collective self-defense against the armed attack from the North, under Article 51 of the United Nations Charter. So uniquely competent is the United States to exercise this judgment, he seems to believe, that is was unnecessary even to adhere to the provision in Article 51 that measures taken in the exercise of the right of self-defense be immediately reported to the Security Council, or to the provision in Article 39 that 'the Security Council shall determine the existence of any threat to the peace, breach of the peace, or act of aggression' and shall determine what measures shall be taken.").

73. Kretzmer, *Self-Defence and Proportionality in* Jus ad Bellum, *supra* note 59, at 267 ("The point in time at which evaluation of proportionality is supposed to be made by the state using force is far more complicated in *jus ad bellum* than it is in *jus in bello*. . . . When deciding to use force in self-defence decision-makers in the state involved should ideally define the aims of such force and assess the scope of the force and the means necessary to achieve those aims. But once

legality and legitimacy—so the counterargument to the point made in this chapter might go.[74]

But any conception of proportionality that delays or "downstreams" proportionality considerations—considerations that must dictate the operational scope of military action—risks undermining the value of proportionality as a touchstone of alignment between strategic necessity and operational measures. This is because treating necessity and proportionality as distinct considerations may contribute to elevating necessity as the primary if not exclusive focus of the initial use of force decision-making process. This, in turn, may result in proportionality being viewed as a secondary or subsequent consideration.[75] In contrast, when the question is whether a use of force is genuinely necessary in the macro sense, proportionality should be conceptualized as an element of that self-help necessity assessment. This will ideally lead to considerations of military operational objectives (scope and duration of the military action) being "frontloaded" into the use of force decision-making process, increasing the likelihood that the military measures in response to the unlawful actual or imminent armed attack are rationally aligned with the necessity for that response.

The stakes involved in any state decision to use military force in self-defense, and the subsequent reaction by other members of the international community, are obviously profound.[76] In this regard, it is axiomatic that a state's assertion of self-defense justification does not ipso facto indicate the assertion is valid. If other states reject the asserted justification, they may respond by treating the state invoking the right of self-defense as the unlawful aggressor.[77] And when

force has been used in response to an armed attack the dynamics of the situation are likely to require ongoing decision-making.").

74. Lotrionte, *supra* note 71, at 890 ("Although these principles are not codified within the U.N. Charter, they are considered part of customary international law. State practice has shown that the principles of necessity and proportionality have played a central role in state justification of the use of force in self-defense and in international responses to attacks.").

75. Alan L. Schuller, *Inimical Inceptions of Imminence: A New Approach to Anticipatory Self-Defense Under the Law of Armed Conflict*, 18 UCLA J. Int'l L. & Foreign Aff. 161, 206 n.27 (2014) ("The proportionality aspect of self-defense comes into play if the necessity test has been met.").

76. Alan D. Surchin, *Terror and the Law: The Unilateral Use of Force and the June 1993 Bombing of Baghdad*, 5 Duke J. Comp. & Int'l L. 457, 486 (1995) ("In considering the generally favorable reaction to the Baghdad raid, it is clear that the international community has become more accepting of forceful responses to state-sponsored terrorism, at least if the terrorist act is targeted against a nation's former leader. This may mean that the international community accepts an expanded definition of self-defense. It almost makes more favorable the international reaction to reprisals, which the next section considers in detail.").

77. Saad Gul, *The Bells of Hell: An Assessment of the Sinking of Anr General Belgrano in the Context of the Falklands Conflict*, 18 N.Y. Int'l L. Rev. 81, 120 (2005) ("But the ultimate inference to be drawn from the episode may be that international law is simply not ready to pass

other states make this credibility assessment, they will naturally focus on two questions: first, was the state invoking self-defense actually a victim state left without any effective alternative to the use of force; and second, if so was the nature of the military response a proportional measure to achieve the self-defense interest.[78] Conceptualizing the proportionality requirement as intertwined with or part of the overall justification/necessity assessment may also enhance these external critiques, because it will focus them on what must be the ultimate legal question: whether both the decision to act in self-defense *and* the means utilized to accomplish the self-defense objective were legally justified because they were because both the response *and* the scope and duration of the response were truly necessary.

V. HOW TREATING PROPORTIONALITY AS AN ASPECT OF OVERALL JUSTIFICATION CONTRIBUTES TO STRATEGIC AND OPERATIONAL CLARITY

Emphasizing the link between *ad bellum* proportionality and the overall necessity of the use of force will produce additional potential advantages. First, and as noted previously, proportionality is the element of self-defense that is most central to the translation of a strategic objective into military operational objectives.[79] Conceptualizing

judgment on the rectitude of all military decisions taken in the heat of armed conflict. Critiques of the sinking seemingly are based not on the merits of the legal questions, but on larger questions of morality and the very existence of warfare as a tool of statecraft."); Patrick McLain, *Settling the Score with Saddam: Resolution 1441 and Parallel Justifications for the Use of Force Against Iraq*, 13 Duke J. Comp. & Int'l L. 233, 271 (2003) ("Nevertheless, the Security Council passed Resolution, condemning Israel's attack. The condemnation by the Security Council is especially significant considering that the United States voted for the resolution. It was unclear whether the Council's condemnation was directed at Israel's claim of anticipatory self-defense or a lack of necessity for action. Indeed, while some states implicitly acknowledged a right of anticipatory self-defense, they still condemned the action because, as the reactor was not yet finished, no Iraqi armed attack was imminent.").

78. Major Halil Murat Berberer, *The Right to Use Anticipatory Self Defense Against Terror: The Tomb of Suleyman Shah and Turkey's Challenges*, Army Law., Apr. 2015, at 34, 45 (2015) ("The author of this article is confident the international community's 'second opinion' on Turkey's election to respond with anticipatory self-defense will be that it was 'well-founded.'"); David A. Sadoff, *A Question of Determinacy: The Legal Status of Anticipatory Self-Defense*, 40 Geo. J. Int'l L. 523, 569 (2009) ("The international community's divided opinion on the legality of anticipatory self-defense was reflected in its debate on Israel's actions.").

79. Bohrer & Osiel, *supra* note 12, at 769 ("Israel's enemies seek to undermine the societal support for recourse to force in national self-defense. In other words, demoralizing Israeli society is the broader strategic goal of every discrete operational and tactical engagement."); Winston P. Nagan & Craig Hammer, *The New Bush National Security Doctrine and the Rule of Law*, 22 Berkeley J. Int'l L. 375, 426–27 (2004) ("Introducing the terrorism element into such strategic and operational concerns tests the foundations of the self-defense principle as it is traditionally understood.").

proportionality as part of the initial overall necessity assessment will better align the operational mission development process with the strategic end-state. This will ultimately enhance the legitimacy of the response, even if the only consequence of this approach is a more effective articulation of that relationship, it will be strategically beneficial.

The second benefit of conceptualizing proportionality as nested within the overall necessity of a self-defense response is that it may mitigate the tendency to assess strategic proportionality through an ex post lens. As an element of the overall necessity for the self-defense response, proportionality is an inherently ex ante consideration: the state should make an initial determination of the *necessary* nature and scope of military action justified by the strategic threat-neutralization justification.[80] However, it is increasingly common for proportionality to be judged by comparing the harm inflicted on the defending state to the harm that inflicted by the self-defense military action.[81] These effects are certainly *probative* when assessing the validity of a state's ex ante proportionality judgement as they provide objective evidence of the scope and intensity of the military action. However, treating military operational effects as the *dispositive* indication of compliance or noncompliance with the proportionality obligation distorts the function of the principle and any subsequent compliance critique.[82] Recognizing proportionality as an aspect of the initial self-defense justification will offset this effects-based

80. Yoo, *International Law and the War in Iraq*, *supra* note 17, at 567 ("It has become clearer since the war that Saddam Hussein had allowed Al Qaeda–linked terrorists to operate from Iraq. Nonetheless, these ex post developments do not directly bear on the justification for the use of force ex ante. What is important for *jus ad bellum* purposes is what the United States and its allies reasonably understood the facts to be at the start of hostilities, not what turned up afterwards.").

81. Laurie R. Blank, *A New Twist on an Old Story: Lawfare and the Mixing of Proportionalities*, 43 Case W. Res. J. Int'l L. 707, 729 (2011) ("Although, as explained above, past conflations have generally involved using jus ad bellum violations to excuse jus in bello violations, the report's use of purported jus in bello violations to find an overall jus ad bellum violation is equally problematic. The same arguments appeared in media coverage of the conflict as well, with one editorial stating: '[w]hatever pretext Israel has cited for launching massive air strikes on the Palestinian-controlled Gaza strip over the weekend, the high casualty figure among civilians makes this military action totally unacceptable.' This statement offers a clear example of how civilian casualties are simply substituted for the proportionality analysis required in the jus ad bellum, by directly disregarding the reason for the military operation, whether lawful or not under jus ad bellum, and treating civilian casualties as the definitive, indeed only, factor in any legal analysis.").

82. Yoo, *International Law and the War in Iraq*, *supra* note 17, at 567 ("It has become clearer since the war that Saddam Hussein had allowed Al Qaeda–linked terrorists to operate from Iraq. Nonetheless, these ex post developments do not directly bear on the justification for the use of force ex ante. What is important for *jus ad bellum* purposes is what the United States and its allies reasonably understood the facts to be at the start of hostilities, not what turned up afterwards.").

critique tendency and contribute to a more credible focus on whether the state made a reasonable assessment of the necessary operational scope of military action based on the information available when the use of force decision was made.[83]

This consideration also implicates the broader issue of how proportionality is properly assessed at inception of military self-help action. Some scholars assert that compliance with the proportionality obligations requires assessing a balance of harm between the victim state and the consequences of the self-defense action. Under this conception, any measure that produces substantially more harm in response to the actual or imminent armed attack would violate the obligation.[84]

But such an approach is problematic on a number of levels, not least of which is the assumption that the strategic objective of a self-defense military action should be defined by the level of anticipated harm inflicted as opposed to defeating, disrupting, or deterring the triggering threat. In some ways the appeal of this approach seems reflected in U.S. domestic self-defense law: an individual responding to unlawful aggression must use an analogous level of force in response, which is the foundation for the axiom that deadly force is justified only in response to a threat of death or grievous bodily harm.[85] But the international self-defense context is fundamentally different, because here the scope of the unlawful violence cannot be so easily assessed and isolated. Instead, the responding state will often be acting not only to repel an initial attack but also to prevent subsequent attacks from an ongoing threat.[86] Requiring the state to limit the response to only measures that inflict harm analogous to that which it suffered as the victim of an unlawful armed attack would frequently prevent the range of measures that would ensure the self-protection objective of the action.

This balance of harms approach may contribute to emphasis on operational effects as the principal if not exclusive indication of compliance with the *ad bellum* obligation. Such an approach is legally flawed, as it essentially imposes an "outcome-based" standard for compliance with a "predictive-based" principle. Indeed, it is almost instinctive that observers of any given self-defense action will gravitate toward a quantitative assessment of how much harm the defending state suffered and compare that with the amount of harm inflicted by the responsive military action when engaging in a balance of harms analysis. This, in turn will produce a secondary negative analytical distortion: conflating the obligations

83. *Id.*

84. For a more detailed exposition, *see* Tom Ruys, "Armed Attack" and Article 51 of the UN Charter: Evolutions in Customary Law and Practice 116–23 (2010).

85. *Id.* at 95; *see also* Wayne R. LaFave, Criminal Law § 10.4(b) (6th ed. 2017) ("[T]he law recognizes that the amount of force which he may justifiably use must be reasonably related to the threatened harm which he seeks to avoid. . . . He may justifiably use deadly force against the other in self-defense, . . . only if he reasonably believes that the other is about to inflict death or serious bodily harm upon him (and also that it is necessary to use deadly force to prevent it).").

86. Egan, *supra* note 63; *see also* Obama, *supra* note 63.

imposed by the *ad bellum* and *in bello* variants of the proportionality obligation and an accordant comparison between the extent of civilian casualties suffered by each party to the conflict (discussed in more detail later).

To be fair, this approach to applying a balance of harms theory is not necessarily consistent with those who advance the theory. Instead, the more rational application would be an expectation that the defending state assess, at inception of the self-defense action, the *overall* harm anticipated to result from the action and balance that harm against the extent of the risk presented by the triggering armed attack. But even this more rational approach risks reducing the assessment of strategic self-defense proportionality (defining the permissible operational scope of a military action conducted to produce a strategic self-defense outcome) to a somewhat arbitrary criteria of strategic success. First, this approach presupposes a certain degree of predictive clarity when comparing the harm produced or anticipated from an armed attack with the harm the responsive military action will inflict. Such predictions are fraught with complexity, and it may therefore be unrealistic to make such a comparison the focal point for assessing proportionality compliance.

More problematically, this approach presupposes that a balance of harms is always an effective touchstone of how and when a self-defense objective will be achieved. In this sense the approach is inherently overbroad and underinclusive. It is overbroad because in some situations, a state may be able to achieve its protective objective by inflicting much less harm than it suffered as the result of an armed attack. It is underinclusive because in other situations, a state may reasonably conclude that the protective objective necessitates more extensive harm than it suffered (especially in relation to a response to an ongoing threat). As a result, determining the scope of a self-defense action based on a balancing of anticipated effects distorts the fundamental strategic objective of such action. That objective is not to inflict analogous harm to the opponent but to produce a certain outcome. In some cases, a state might reasonably assess that this outcome may be produced by use of means that will produce less damage or destruction than the triggering act of aggression, in which case no more force should be used. And in other cases the opposite conclusion would be reasonable, when the state reasonably determines that infliction of more destruction is necessary to produce the protective strategic outcome.

Ultimately, this emphasis on balancing operational attack effects as the touchstone of strategic self-defense legitimacy compromises the basic tenet that there is no legal equivalence between the two sides. As noted in the introductory section of this chapter, the very notion of self-defense is a reflection of legal justification derived from the right of self-help triggered by *unlawful* aggression. Accordingly, the victim state is vindicating its right against an unlawful attack by another legal subject. The victim cannot therefore be required to abstain from taking action which is necessary to defend its right against unlawful attack just because this action on balance is to be anticipated (even assuming such a prediction is feasible) to inflict greater damage on the attacker than the latter is expected to cause on the victim. Instead, it is the anticipated *outcome* and not *effect* that must dictate the operational scope of the military action: infliction of that degree of harm reasonably necessary to reduce the threat and ensure the defending state is protected from the unlawful aggression.

A useful illustration of the fundamental difference between effects driven scope versus balance of harm is the 1989 U.S. military intervention in Panama, Operation Just Cause. Defense of nationals and the U.S. military facilities in Panama provided the primary asserted legal basis for the intervention, which was executed with a combined arms attack involving more than 25,000 military personnel. The strategic objective was to rapidly and decisively neutralize the capacity of the Panamanian Defense Force (PDF) to endanger U.S. personnel and civilians in Panama. While tensions had been building for more than a year between Panama and the United States, the event that triggered the attack decision was the killing of a U.S. naval officer while off duty when PDF forces confronted him at a checkpoint, along with the beating and sexual harassment of several other U.S. nationals at another checkpoint. The United States assessed these events as evidence of a major shift in PDF intentions, indicating that the restraint that had defined confrontations up to that point was no longer operative and a more substantial forcible action against U.S. targets by the PDF was reasonably to be expected in the near future. Evacuating the tens of thousands of U.S. personnel in Panama was never a feasible option, nor would that option have preserved U.S. presence rights pursuant to the Canal treaties. Certainly, a balance of harms approach would not have justified a massive invasion to disable the capacity of the PDF in its entirety. But it is equally clear that a "tit-for-tat" response—perhaps a raid to strike at a small group of PDF personnel—would have done little to ensure the protection of U.S. interests in Panama, or at least would have created substantial risk of further escalation. Proportionality in this situation required a reasonable assessment that the scope of the anticipated operation was necessary to fully secure the protection of U.S. interests endangered by the PDF armed attack.

This is not intended to suggest that consideration of the consequences of an action in self-defense is irrelevant to the proportionality assessment. But there is a substantial difference between treating the balance of harms as the dispositive touchstone of compliance as opposed to one of a number of considerations when assessing the necessary scope of a self-defense action. And as noted previously, it is simply impossible to predict consequences of complex collective action over time with anything close to complete accuracy.

Accordingly, a strict balance of harm approach is flawed for two reasons. First, it puts the victim state of an (imminent) armed attack in an unjustifiably weak normative position which could result in denying its right to defend itself. And second, if properly applied ex ante, it is fraught with too much uncertainty to be at all practicable.

There is yet a third reason why a balance of harm test at the level of *ad bellum* proportionality is inapposite. Setting out this reason also helps explain further why emphasis on the ex ante and strategic nature of the *ad bellum* proportionality obligation will contribute to more credible assessments of self-defense justification: it will better isolate this *ad bellum* proportionality consideration from the related—but distinct—*in bello* proportionality obligation.[87] The function of this *ad bellum* variant of proportionality is fundamentally different than the function of *jus in bello* proportionality, both in terms of the protective objective and the context in which the principle is applied.[88] In the *in bello* context, proportionality is an ongoing obligation that arises during the *operational execution* of military actions conducted to achieve the *strategic* self-defense objective.[89] And, while the strategic objective of such an ongoing military operation may be reassessed during

87. Geoffrey S. Corn, *Self-Defense Targeting: Blurring the Line Between the* Jus Ad Bellum *and the* Jus in Bello, 88 INT'L L. STUD. 57, 72 (2012) ("This aspect *of jus in bello* proportionality once again reflects the most fundamental difference between the two variants of the principle: the beneficiary of the protection is not the object of attack."); Blank, *supra* note 81, at 721 ("IHL's effectiveness depends in many ways on this separation of jus in bello and jus ad bellum. If the cause at arms influenced a state's obligation to abide by the laws regulating the means and methods of warfare and requiring protection of civilians and persons hors de combat, states would justify all departures from jus in bello with reference to the purported justness of their cause. The result: an invitation to unrestricted warfare. This article demonstrates one highly problematic example of how mixing jus in bello proportionality and jus ad bellum proportionality violates this long-standing proscription and, in doing so, undermines the core of IHL—the protection of civilians from the ravages of war.").

88. Corn, *supra* note 87, at 70 ("The *jus ad bellum* reflects an analogous conception of proportionality. First, the amount of force a State is permitted to employ in self-defense is strictly limited to that amount necessary to reduce the imminent threat. Second, the source of aggression is the beneficiary of the proportionality constraint. In other words, as in the criminal law context, a State (like an individual) responding to unlawful aggression may be authorized to employ force in self-defense, but is prohibited from responding to the source of aggression with any amount of force in excess of that necessary to reduce that immediate threat. In contrast, proportionality in *the jus in bello* context *does not* really mean proportionality. Again, this may seem like an odd proposition. Nonetheless, even a cursory review of the *jus in bello* proportionality principle validates this conclusion. First, unlike traditional proportionality, the *jus in bello* variant in no way protects the object of deliberate violence (the lawful target). Instead, the beneficiaries of the protection are the knowing but non-deliberate victims of a deliberate attack—civilians and civilian property in proximity to the lawful target. Protecting these potential victims from what is referred to in colloquial terms as collateral damage and incidental injury reflects a fundamentally different purpose for this proportionality constraint. Unlike in the self-defense context, *jus in bello* proportionality is not directly linked to the necessity of subduing an imminent threat.").

89. GEOFFREY CORN ET AL., THE LAW OF ARMED CONFLICT: AN OPERATIONAL APPROACH 272 (2d ed. 2019) ("Despite the principle of distinction and the prohibition on attacking civilians and civilian objects, it is inevitable in armed conflict that in the process of attacking combatants and military objectives, some death to civilians and/ or damage to civilian property will occur. Although this incidental damage is not prohibited per se, the principle of proportionality sets limits on how much incidental damage is acceptable."); Kretzmer, *Self-Defence and Proportionality in* Jus ad Bellum, *supra* note 59, at 267 ("The point in time at which evaluation of proportionality is supposed to be made by the state using force is far more complicated in *jus ad bellum* than it is in *jus in bello*. . . . When deciding to use force in self-defence decision-makers in the state involved should ideally define the aims of such force and assess the scope of the force and the means necessary to achieve those aims. But once force has been used in response to an armed attack the dynamics of the situation are likely to require ongoing decision-making.").

its course, this is not the same type of ongoing assessment obligation imposed by the *in bello* variant.[90] Instead, it is the nature of the triggering threat and the measures *necessary* to reduce that threat, that dictates what qualifies as a proportional response.[91]

Treating proportionality as a consideration that is subordinate or "secondary" to the necessity for a self-defense response creates a risk of contributing to the conflation of these two proportionality variants.[92] As Professor Yoram Dinstein explains, "[P]roportionality in these two branches of the law has disparate features and attributes. Consequently, any attempt to transplant rules or caveats

90. McMahan, *supra* note 17, at 23 ("If the Israeli attack on Gaza had been a reprisal, this way of assessing proportionality would have been appropriate. In law, a reprisal is a use of force intended to compel an adversary to halt or repair some breach of international law and it is generally held that the harm done by way of reprisal must be proportioned to the harm caused by the initial offense. In the International Criminal Tribunal for the Former Yugoslavia, for example, the Trial Chamber ruled that 'reprisals must not be excessive compared to the precedent unlawful act of warfare.' But it would be a mistake to conflate proportionality in reprisal with proportionality in defense. The aim of defensive violence is the physical prevention of harm by a threatener. Proportionality in defense is therefore essentially prospective. It weighs the harms that an act of defense will cause against those that it will prevent. For this reason, the harms that Palestinians in Gaza had inflicted on Israeli civilians in the past were relevant to the proportionality of the Israeli invasion only insofar as they provided evidence of the Palestinians' intentions and capabilities in causing further harm in the future. That proportionality in punishment is retrospective while proportionality in defense is prospective is only one difference between them."); Tony Rock, *Yesterday's Laws, Tomorrow's Technology: The Laws of War and Unmanned Warfare*, 24 N.Y. Int'l L. Rev. 39, 43–44 (2011) ("These laws may be broken down further into *jus ad bellum*, which governs the initial use of force, and *jus in bello*, which covers ongoing combat operations."); Yoo, *International Law and the War in Iraq*, *supra* note 17, at 567 ("Nonetheless, these ex post developments do not directly bear on the justification for the use of force ex ante. What is important for *jus ad bellum* purposes is what the United States and its allies reasonably understood the facts to be at the start of hostilities, not what turned up afterwards."); W. Michael Reisman, International Legal Responses to Terrorism, Order of the Coif Lecture, University of Houston Law Center (Mar. 12, 1999), *in* 22 Hous. J. Int'l L. 3, 17 (1999); Duncan B. Hollis, *Accountability in Chechnya-Addressing Internal Matters with Legal and Political International Norms*, 36 B.C. L. Rev. 793, 795 (1995).

91. Schmitt, *"Below the Threshold" Cyber Operations*, *supra* note 15, at 723–26; Lieutenant Colonel James C. Duncan, *A Primer on the Employment of Non-Lethal Weapons*, 45 Naval L. Rev. 1, 47 (1998) ("The two elements required for self-defense are necessity and proportionality. An understanding of these two elements is critical to the concept of self-defense and to the ROE. For it is necessity and proportionality, as amplified by the policy established in the Standing Rules of Engagement, 'that will be the basis for the judgment of the commander as to what constitutes an appropriate response' when acting in self-defense.").

92. Schuller, *supra* note 75, at 206 n.27 ("The proportionality aspect of self-defense comes into play if the necessity test has been met. It has been formulated in either of two ways. It could mean that the intensity of defensive force must be approximately the same as that defended against, or it could mean that the defensive force—even if more intensive—is permissible so long as it is not designed to do anything more than defend against the reasonably perceived

from one domain to the other is likely to cause confusion."[93] This conflation risks undermining the permissible scope of the *in bello* execution of *ad bellum* self-defense operations.[94] Unfortunately, this type of domain conflation seems to be an increasingly common response to the conduct of operations. This tendency is reflected in assertions that collateral damage and incidental injuries resulting from the execution of an ongoing armed conflict are unjustified because they indicate an imbalance of strategic harm.[95]

Conflating or "blending" the two variants of proportionality risks confusing credible assessments of self-defense military actions.[96] It is true, as noted previously, that the scale of a military operation justified based on *ad bellum* self-defense

threat. There is no authoritative international decision favoring one of these formulations over the other."); Sloane, *The Cost of Conflation*, *supra* note 11, at 53 ("Two forms of analytic conflation, in particular, afflict the modern law of war: (1) at the macro level, conflation of the jus ad bellum and the jus in bello generally, i.e., a failure to apply the dualistic axiom properly or at all; and (2) at the micro level, conflation of the distinct proportionality constraints imposed by each body of law. Both forms of conflation compromise the law's efficacy relative to the evolving nature of twenty-first-century hostilities. The dualistic axiom remains indispensable to the law of war. But it cannot be applied acontextually—for example, without considering, descriptively, the comparative power of the parties, the technology available to each, and the nature of the conflict.").

93. Dinstein, *supra* note 35, at 251–52.

94. Sloane, *The Cost of Conflation*, *supra* note 11, at 53 ("Two forms of analytic conflation, in particular, afflict the modern law of war: (1) at the macro level, conflation of the jus ad bellum and the jus in bello generally, i.e., a failure to apply the dualistic axiom properly or at all; and (2) at the micro level, conflation of the distinct proportionality constraints imposed by each body of law. Both forms of conflation compromise the law's efficacy relative to the evolving nature of twenty-first-century hostilities. The dualistic axiom remains indispensable to the law of war. But it cannot be applied acontextually—for example, without considering, descriptively, the comparative power of the parties, the technology available to each, and the nature of the conflict.").

95. *Id.* at 735 ("Beyond the misapplication of the law in conflating jus ad bellum with jus in bello, these practices have highly problematic results for the very people the law is designed to protect during armed conflict—civilians. 'The separation between jus ad bellum and jus in bello results in the uniform, neutral application of the latter, without reference to its distinctions between the rights and obligations of the parties.' Such neutral application simply cannot exist in these circumstances, however. The use of civilian casualties as an automatic trigger for claims of war crimes and of unjust war—regardless of the actual legal elements of either legal violation—holds the advanced military to an entirely different standard than the insurgent group. While the insurgent group faces what appear to be lower standards than those present in IHL, the military essentially faces a standard of strict liability rather than the standards actually set forth in both IHL and in the law governing the use of force. In the former, the law requires a measure of intent to find an IHL violation, whether in the intentional killing of civilians or in the launching of an indiscriminate attack on civilians, one that violates the principle of proportionality under jus in bello. In the latter, civilian casualties are not a relevant factor at all.").

96. *Id.*

is relevant to the assessment of whether that response is a proportional and therefore a necessary and justified response.[97] However, maintaining clarity between the two variants is important for two reasons. First, compliance with one type of proportionality does not ipso facto indicate compliance with the other type, and therefore compliance must be assessed independently.[98] For example, a military action responding to an unlawful armed attack may, in terms of scale and scope, be carefully tailored to the strategic objective of restoring the status quo ante.[99] However, the military forces executing that operation might employ force in an indiscriminate manner, thereby violating the *in bello* proportionality obligation.[100] In that instance, condemnation would be justified based on the operational use of force in an indiscriminate manner, even if the strategic scope of the military action was justified.[101] And it is equally conceivable that a military operation may far exceed the self-defense justification triggered by an actual or imminent armed

97. Kretzmer, *Self-Defence and Proportionality in* Jus ad Bellum, *supra* note 59, at 279 ("However, in the reaction of states and commentators to specific cases of force used in self-defence, the damage caused plays a major role in descriptions of the force as disproportionate. Thus, in their criticism of Israel's use of force in Lebanon in the summer of 2006 as being disproportionate, many states referred to the extensive damage caused to civilians and to infrastructure. In his analysis of this same case, Enzo Cannizzaro also mentions the threat to and harm sustained by civilians as one of the three factors which explained why Israel's use of force was regarded as disproportionate. The problem in such statements is not the consideration of the damage caused as a factor in assessing proportionality, but the absence of a serious analysis of the other side of the coin: the necessity of the force which caused the damage in advancing the legitimate ends of self-defence."); Sloane, *The Cost of Conflation*, *supra* note 11, at 99.

98. Kretzmer, *Self-Defence and Proportionality in* Jus ad Bellum, *supra* note 59, at 240 ("Use of force may be disproportionate under *jus ad bellum* even if all forcible measures are compatible with *jus in bello* in general, and the proportionality principle in *jus in bello* in particular.").

99. Richard Falk, *International Law and the United States Role in Viet Nam: A Response to Professor Moore*, 76 Yale L.J. 1095, 1158 n.22 (1967) ("In that case, Korea would appear to be an instance of Type I authorizing whatever military action is needed to restore the *status quo ante* the armed attack. On this basis I believe that the defensive armies should not have proceeded beyond the 38th Parallel, although it would have been permissible to commit war acts against North Korean territory so as to restore the *status quo ante*.").

100. Sloane, *The Cost of Conflation*, *supra* note 11, at 75 ("Second, Protocol I prohibits 'indiscriminate attacks.' That prohibition takes an absolute form insofar as civilians may never, whatever the utility, 'be the object of attack.' But it otherwise takes a qualified form. It prescribes a flexible calculus by describing as indiscriminate those attacks that 'may be expected to cause incidental loss of civilian life, injury to civilians, damage to civilian objects, or a combination thereof, which would be excessive in relation to the concrete and direct military advantage anticipated.'").

101. *Id.*; Int'l Comm. of the Red Cross, *Rule 12. Definition of Indiscriminate Attacks*, Customary IHL Database, https://ihl-databases.icrc.org/customary-ihl/eng/docs/v1_rul_rule12 (last visited Aug. 17, 2019) ("Rule 12. Indiscriminate attacks are those: (a) which are not directed at a specific military objective; (b) which employ a method or means of combat which cannot be directed at a specific military objective; or (c) which employ a method or means of

attack because the scale of the operation bore no rational relationship to that threat, even where the military action is executed in full compliance with the *in bello* proportionality obligation.[102]

The second reason distinct assessment of these proportionality obligations is important is because each variant has a distinct protective objective. *Ad bellum* proportionality protects the *intended* object of the self-help violence.[103] Proportionality in this context is intended to ensure that a *justified* response directed against the aggressor state or non-state organized armed group is not excessive in nature and is of a scale that is rationally related to the self-protection necessity produced by the unlawful threat.[104] Proportionality in this context focuses on whether such a response becomes disconnected from this objective, at which point it becomes excessive and therefore *unjustified*.[105] Thus, the protective object of the *ad bellum* proportionality obligation is the state or non-state group whose initial aggression triggered the self-defense necessity.[106] In contrast, the *in bello* variant of proportionality does not protect the *intended* object of a use of force.[107] Instead, this variant protects *incidental* victims of an attack

combat the effects of which cannot be limited as required by international humanitarian law; and consequently, in each such case, are of a nature to strike military objectives and civilians or civilian objects without distinction.").

102. Thomas S. Harris, *Can the ICC Consider Questions on Jus Ad Bellum in a War Crimes Trial?*, 48 Case W. Res. J. Int'l L. 273, 282–83 (2016); Kretzmer, *Self-Defence and Proportionality in* Jus ad Bellum, *supra* note 59, at 240 ("Use of force may be disproportionate under *jus ad bellum* even if all forcible measures are compatible with *jus in bello* in general, and the proportionality principle in *jus in bello* in particular.").

103. Schmitt, *"Below the Threshold" Cyber Operations*, *supra* note 15, at 723–26 ("Proportionality in the law of self-defense equally limits a State's defensive measures to those that are required to defeat the armed attack, even if they fall short of the intensity of the armed attack that precipitated them.").

104. *Id.*

105. Schmitt, *"Change Direction" 2006*, *supra* note 15, at 154 ("But recall that to breach the proportionality norm, the defender must do more than reasonably required in the circumstances to deter a threatened attack or defeat an ongoing one.").

106. *Id.* ("Most critics of Operation Change Direction in the jus ad bellum context focus on the proportionality criterion. The U.N. Secretary-General, for example, condemned Israeli operations on the ground that they had, borrowing the words of the Prime Minister Siniora, 'torn the country to shreds,' thereby producing results that ran counter to the Israeli need for the Lebanese military to exert its authority over southern Lebanon. Similarly, the European Union criticized Israel for acting in violation of the principle of proportionality.").

107. Corn, *supra* note 87, at 70 ("First, unlike traditional proportionality, the *jus in bello* variant in no way protects the object of deliberate violence (the lawful target)."); Lea Brilmayer & Geoffrey Chepiga, *Ownership or Use? Civilian Property Interests in International Humanitarian Law*, 49 Harv. Int'l L.J. 413, 418 (2008); Christopher L. Blakesley, *Ruminations on Terrorism & Anti-Terrorism Law & Literature*, 57 U. Miami L. Rev. 1041, 1096 (2003).

directed against a lawful military objective, meaning innocent persons and property that are proximate to the *intended* lawful target.[108]

And there are other problematic consequences. First, it creates the risk that the legal justification for a self-defense action may be improperly assessed by considering the incidental injury and collateral damage produced during the execution of the self-defense military action.[109] Second, it contributes to a false expectation that proportionality somehow limits the magnitude and intensity of force used against lawful military objectives during operational execution of that military action.[110] Treating *ad bellum* proportionality as an element of prima facie self-help necessity and justification will contribute to averting this type of conflation because it will lead to a strategic-response-oriented focus as opposed to an operational-execution-oriented focus.

This conflation also contributes to the expectation that every operational and tactical action conducted during the armed conflict must be analyzed as part of what should be a strategic assessment.[111] This is not the function of *ad bellum* proportionality, and it is operationally impracticable and illogical to assess compliance with this strategic-level principle of justification in such a manner. This is reflected in Brian Eagan's ASIL speech,[112] in which he emphasized that *ad bellum* self-defense justification is an initial strategic decision, not an ongoing obligation to engage in a new self-defense justification for every operational action conducted to achieve that strategic objective.[113] Emphasizing that *ad bellum*

108. Corn, *supra* note 35 ("The term 'proportionality' can be somewhat misleading. An attack does not become indiscriminate when the incidental injury to civilians or collateral damage to civilian property is slightly greater than the military advantage anticipated (as is suggested by the term 'disproportionate'), but only when those effects are *excessive*."); Corn, *supra* note 87, at 70 ("Instead, the beneficiaries of the protection are the knowing but non-deliberate victims of a deliberate attack—civilians and civilian property in proximity to the lawful target.").

109. Mark "Max" Maxwell & Richard V. Meyer, *The Innocent Combatant: Preserving Their* Jus in Bello *Protections*, 5 PENN ST. J.L. & INT'L AFF. 111, 163 (2017); Blank, *supra* note 81, at 726 ("As detailed above in Section I, jus ad bellum proportionality focuses on whether the force used in self-defense is commensurate with the need to repel or deter an armed attack. Civilian casualties do not enter the equation. In contrast, civilian casualties, often referred to as collateral damage, are a primary factor in assessing jus in bello proportionality.").

110. Schmitt, *"Change Direction" 2006*, *supra* note 15, at 153 ("Proportionality is frequently misapplied in one of two ways. First, the degree of force employed by the defender is sometimes assessed through comparison to that used by the aggressor on the basis of a false premise that the former may not exceed the latter. Yet, proportionality requires no such symmetry between the attacker's actions and defender's response.").

111. Bohrer & Osiel, *supra* note 12, at 822 n.222 ("Many argue that jus ad bellum proportionality assessments continue throughout the armed conflict. . . . In such a case, the benefits of the dual (ad bellum and in bello) proportionality assessment continue throughout the conflict.").

112. Egan, *supra* note 63.

113. Yoo, *International Law and the War in Iraq*, *supra* note 17, at 567 ("Nonetheless, these ex post developments do not directly bear on the justification for the use of force ex ante. What is

proportionality is linked to the assessment of overall strategic self-help necessity will contribute to mitigating the risk that every operational action is subjected to individualized *ad bellum* critique.

A good illustration of the negative effect of this type of conflation is provided by scrutiny of Israeli military operations in Gaza.[114] As a predicate question, Israel is obligated to assess the justification for military action directed against organized armed groups operating out of Gaza.[115] This requirement includes the question of what qualifies as a proportional strategic response to the threat, a question that will dictate the strategic scope of the self-defense military operation.[116] Beyond that point, *in bello* proportionality will play the dominant role in the selection of and attack against specified targets.[117] However, the legitimacy of Israel's self-defense

important for *jus ad bellum* purposes is what the United States and its allies reasonably understood the facts to be at the start of hostilities, not what turned up afterwards."); Chomsky, *supra* note 72, at 1460.

114. Noura Erakat, *It's Not Wrong, It's Illegal: Situating the Gaza Blockade Between International Law and the UN Response*, 11 UCLA J. Islamic & Near E. L. 37, 61–62 (2012) ("While the ICJ made clear that Article 51 self-defense is not available to occupying powers in the territories it occupies, Israel continues to insist that it is exercising its legal right to self-defense in its execution of military operations in the West Bank and the Gaza Strip. Its insistence is critical because as a legal matter the scope of self-defense is not settled as is reflected by varied legal scholarship on the topic."); Eyal Benvenisti, *Rethinking the Divide Between* Jus Ad Bellum *and* Jus in Bello *in Warfare Against Nonstate Actors*, 34 Yale J. Int'l L. 541, 544–45 (2009).

115. Yoo, *International Law and the War in Iraq*, *supra* note 17, at 567 ("Nonetheless, these ex post developments do not directly bear on the justification for the use of force ex ante. What is important for *jus ad bellum* purposes is what the United States and its allies reasonably understood the facts to be at the start of hostilities, not what turned up afterwards."); Chomsky, *supra* note 72, at 1460.

116. Schmitt, *"Below the Threshold" Cyber Operations*, *supra* note 15, at 723 ("Proportionality in the context of countermeasures must be distinguished from *jus ad bellum* proportionality, which refers to the amount of force required for a State to effectively defend itself against an armed attack.").

117. Corn, *supra* note 87, at 70 ("In contrast, proportionality in *the jus in bello* context *does not* really mean proportionality. Again, this may seem like an odd proposition. Nonetheless, even a cursory review of the *jus in bello* proportionality principle validates this conclusion. First, unlike traditional proportionality, the *jus in bello* variant in no way protects the object of deliberate violence (the lawful target). Instead, the beneficiaries of the protection are the knowing but non-deliberate victims of a deliberate attack—civilians and civilian property in proximity to the lawful target. Protecting these potential victims from what is referred to in colloquial terms as collateral damage and incidental injury reflects a fundamentally different purpose for this proportionality constraint. Unlike in the self-defense context, *jus in bello* proportionality is not directly linked to the necessity of subduing an imminent threat. Instead, the objective of the principle is to protect innocent people and property in the vicinity of a lawful object of attack from the consequences of employing combat power against lawful targets. As for the lawful target itself, the suggestion that an attack might be disproportionate is a legal oxymoron; the status alone justifies that amount of force determined necessary to bring about enemy submission, which justifies use of deadly force as a measure of first resort. The only limitation on that use of force is the prohibition against the use of methods (tactics) or means (weapons)

response is frequently gauged based on the extent of collateral damage inflicted during operational execution of that response.[118] Critics condemn the overall action as illegal and illegitimate not based on a careful assessment of whether the overall strategic scope of the response was proportional to the strategic threat, but instead based on the effects of specific attacks.[119] Such an assessment of *ad bellum* proportionality compliance reflects an expectation that the proportionality element of self-defense justification extends to the conduct of hostilities executed pursuant to that justification.[120] This distortion, in turn, creates an unrealistic expectation on tactical and operational commanders who are in no position to assess each attack in the context of the strategic justification for the operation.

Blurring the actual scope of tactical attack authority inherent in the *in bello* proportionality rule is another risk associated with the failure to clearly distinguish these two types of proportionality. As noted previously, *in bello* proportionality in no way protects the *intended* objects of attack. This means that there is no requirement to limit the intensity of attacks on lawful targets when executing a self-defense-based military operation. Indeed, at that level, the law permits the use of overwhelming force to promptly achieve tactical and operational objectives. When *ad bellum* proportionality is conceptualized as defining the overall strategic scope and duration of such military operations, it mitigates the risk that tactical execution will be impacted by an expectation that proportionality protects even the lawful targets within the scope of the operation.[121] But most problematically, it fails to account for the strategic context essential to the *ad bellum* proportionality assessment.[122] It is difficult to fully anticipate, at inception, the overall incidental

calculated or of a nature to cause superfluous injury or unnecessary suffering. However, this rule is not synonymous with the protections provided by the principle of proportionality, and rarely is considered a limitation on the employment of authorized weapon systems against enemy personnel, facilities or equipment."); Brilmayer & Chepiga, *supra* note 107, at 418; Blakesley, *supra* note 107, at 1096.

118. Blank, *supra* note 81, at 726 ("As detailed above in Section I, jus ad bellum proportionality focuses on whether the force used in self-defense is commensurate with the need to repel or deter an armed attack. Civilian casualties do not enter the equation. In contrast, civilian casualties, often referred to as collateral damage, are a primary factor in assessing jus in bello proportionality.").

119. *Id.*

120. *Id.*

121. Rock, *supra* note 90, at 43–44; Blank, *supra* note 81, at 735 ("In contrast, civilian casualties, often referred to as collateral damage, are a primary factor in assessing jus in bello proportionality.").

122. Corn, *supra* note 87, at 72 ("Furthermore, under the *ad bellum* construct, proportionality is traditionally assessed at the strategic (macro) level."); Blank, *supra* note 81, at 721; Sangero, *supra* note 5, at 457; Michael C. Bonafede, *Here, There, and Everywhere: Assessing the Proportionality Doctrine and U.S. Uses of Force in Response to Terrorism After the September 11 Attacks*, 88 Cornell L. Rev. 155, 167 (2002).

injury and collateral damage that may result from a military operation conducted pursuant to self-defense justification.[123] Those tactical attack effects are by their nature circumstance dependent, which includes the impact of enemy tactics and how those tactics increase or decrease the need to conduct attacks that endanger civilians and civilian property.[124] Asserting that such collateral damage is a touchstone for compliance with the predicate strategic proportionality assessment is, accordingly, unrealistic.[125]

When the scope of military action in self-defense is assessed as a component of the necessity for the response, that assessment will align with the strategic nature of the self-defense decision-making process. Beyond that point, operational and tactical execution of the *overall* mission will be subject to the distinct proportionality considerations derived from the *in bello* variant of the rule. This strategic focus will also better account for the risk that an operation may evolve in a way that increasingly distances it from the original self-defense justification. Self-defense proportionality should focus on the scope and duration of the overall strategic response, facilitating an initial and periodic reassessment of whether the overall operational scope of a mission is genuinely necessary to defeat or otherwise neutralize the triggering threat.[126] Thus, when proportionality is considered an element of overall response necessity, it will guide the adjustment of the strategic

123. Blank, *supra* note 81, at 717–18 ("Observers will often find it difficult to assess fairly whether collateral damage is excessive in practice because the military advantage from an attack may not be immediately apparent. The retrospective approach can therefore lead to departures from the accepted application of the principle of proportionality. The 'reasonable commander' forms the heart of this prospective analysis. Analogous to the 'reasonable person' in domestic criminal law, the reasonable commander is 'the reasonable man in the law of war [and] is based upon the experience of military men in dealing with basic military problems.' As numerous military manuals recognize: It will not always be easy for a commander to evaluate [whether an attack will be disproportionate] with precision. On the one hand, he must take into account the elements which are available to him, related to the military necessity necessary to justify an attack, and on the other hand, he must take into account the elements which are available to him, related to the possible loss of human life and damage to civilian objects.").

124. *Id.*

125. Maxwell & Meyer, *supra* note 109, at 163; Blank, *supra* note 81, at 726 ("As detailed above in Section I, jus ad bellum proportionality focuses on whether the force used in self-defense is commensurate with the need to repel or deter an armed attack. Civilian casualties do not enter the equation. In contrast, civilian casualties, often referred to as collateral damage, are a primary factor in assessing jus in bello proportionality.").

126. Kretzmer, *Self-Defence and Proportionality in Jus ad Bellum*, *supra* note 59, at 267 ("When deciding to use force in self-defence decision-makers in the state involved should ideally define the aims of such force and assess the scope of the force and the means necessary to achieve those aims. But once force has been used in response to an armed attack the dynamics of the situation are likely to require ongoing decision-making.").

scope of a self-defense response far more effectively than a focus on collateral damage and incidental injury caused by individual attacks.[127]

VI. CONCLUSION

Compliance with the proportionality requirement is central to ensuring the legality and legitimacy of any military action in self-defense.[128] This requirement applies equally to the individual right of self-defense in the domestic criminal context, and the state right of self-defense pursuant to international law, traditionally referred to as the *jus ad bellum*.[129] In the domestic criminal context, proportionality is often explained as a component of the ultimate necessity that provides legal justification for self-help protective measures. In that context, self-defense is a specialized application of the general necessity, or greater good, defense. As such, proportionality is not conceptualized as distinct from the necessity requirement but as an integral component of assessing whether it was in fact necessary for an individual to act in self-defense.

127. With that being said, a justified action in self-defense may morph into an unjustified use of force, and in that regard *ad bellum* proportionality is, to a certain extent, an ongoing element of strategic legal justification which could help mitigate the conflation risk: two distinct contexts; two distinct assessment points; two distinct objects of protection. *See* Corn, *supra* note 87, at 70 ("Like necessity, proportionality is a core principle of both the *jus ad bellum* and the *jus in bello*. And like necessity, the principle has a significantly different meaning in each branch of the *jus belli*."). But this variant of proportionality is unquestionably central to assessing the legality of the *initial* self-help response, and unlike the *in bello* variant, should be assessed as a strategic and not an operational or tactical consideration. *See* Bohrer & Osiel, *supra* note 12, at 752, 769 ("The first is jus ad bellum proportionality, governing the decision to resort to force in the first instance and determining what overall measure of force will be consistent with the goal of national self-defense. Second is jus in bello proportionality, regulating operational and tactical conduct during an armed conflict. . . . His legal analysis therefore speaks only to the former. Decisions about ad bellum proportionality concern strategic issues, however, and are made by high-ranking officials, for they are the only people authorized to establish those comprehensive goals. The conflation of in bello with ad bellum considerations, further discussed later, also plagues the other assayed authors' understandings of proportionality. To establish that the political or strategic rationale for force protection is irrelevant to in bello proportionality is not to show that it is immaterial to ad bellum proportionality, when it sometimes becomes highly pertinent and weighty."); Noura Erakat, *Operation Cast Lead: The Elusive Quest for Self Defense Under International Law*, 36 Rutgers U. L. Rev. 164, 169 (2009).

128. *Id.*

129. Sangero, *supra* note 5, at 466 ("As we have seen above, the rationale of self-defense dictates several conditions, central among them the requirements of necessity and proportionality."); Schmitt, *Preserving the Delicate Balance*, *supra* note 8, at 796. "Necessity and proportionality are the two central elements which must be present for the permissible use of coercion in self-defense under international law." Gehring, *supra* note 8, at 338.

In contrast, proportionality is often treated as distinct from necessity as an element of legal justification in international law.[130] Necessity focuses on whether the state has suffered an unlawful armed attack or whether such an attack is imminent and on whether there was an effective alternative to the use of force; proportionality on the scope of responsive forcible operations.[131] But as in the domestic context, the entire question of scope is really nothing more than an assessment of whether that scope and duration is genuinely *necessary* to protect against the unlawful threat.[132] Thus, there is logic in conceptualizing proportionality not as distinct from the necessity requirement but as an integral component of that requirement.

This proposed conceptualization is certainly no panacea. Indeed, it might not produce any dramatic modification in the way self-defense is analyzed and critiqued. After all, no matter how conceptualized, proportionality will remain an essential requirement for a valid assertion of self-defense. But this conceptualization may contribute to clarification and emphasis of the strategic nature of the *jus ad bellum* proportionality judgment, which must focus on the overall protection of the state, and not on isolated aspects of a broader self-defense campaign. When the *necessity* of the scope and duration of operations is assessed in terms of the strategic consideration of the unlawful threat, it will ideally contribute to careful tailoring of self-defense military operations to the overall nature of that threat. Of equal importance, this strategic-oriented focus will ideally offset the temptation to judge *jus ad bellum* proportionality by applying *jus in bello* principles. If nothing else, greater emphasis on the important differences between these two variants of the international legal proportionality requirement will enhance the significance of each.

130. These scholars have analyzed proportionality and necessity as two distinct elements. *See* Kretzmer, *Self-Defence and Proportionality in* Jus ad Bellum, *supra* note 59, at 239; Michael N. Schmitt, *Responding to Transnational Terrorism Under the Jus Ad Bellum: A Normative Framework*, 56 NAVAL L. REV. 1, 16 (2008); Schmitt, *"Change Direction" 2006*, *supra* note 15, at 153–55.

131. Ferzan, *supra* note 46, at 222 ("Both domestic and international law require that the self-defensive force be necessary. This necessity component has two parts: the actor may only act when necessary and to the extent necessary. The latter requirement is one of proportionality."); Schmitt, *Clipped Wings*, *supra* note 41, at 764 ("Many laymen interpret the requirement as 'proportional' to the force used against them. By this interpretation, one could not respond to small arms ground fire with bombs or use a missile to down a helicopter that has employed machine guns against an aircraft. This is clearly not the proper reading. The right to use self-defense is designed to protect without unnecessarily escalating the hostilities; it is not a rule designed to ensure a 'fair fight' on a level playing field.").

132. Schmitt, *Clipped Wings*, *supra* note 41, at 764 ("Many laymen interpret the requirement as 'proportional' to the force used against them. By this interpretation, one could not respond to small arms ground fire with bombs or use a missile to down a helicopter that has employed machine guns against an aircraft. This is clearly not the proper reading. The right to use self-defense is designed to protect without unnecessarily escalating the hostilities; it is not a rule designed to ensure a 'fair fight' on a level playing field.").

4

The Unwilling and Unable Test for Extraterritorial Defensive Force

Why Force Is Permitted against the Territorial State

JENS DAVID OHLIN*

I. THE PROBLEM OF EXTRATERRITORIAL FORCE

Perhaps no other issue regarding *jus ad bellum* is as controversial as a state's use of military force against a non-state actor (NSA) located on the territory of another state.[1]

The use of defensive force against NSAs generally is already controversial. In its 2004 *Wall* opinion, the International Court of Justice (ICJ) asserted, without much evidence or legal analysis, that the use of defensive force under international law was constrained to situations where a state was attacked by another state and that an attack by a NSA (not attributable to a host state by virtue of control or some other principle of state responsibility) was insufficient to trigger a right to self-defense against the NSA.[2] The ICJ presumably viewed this requirement as part

* Vice Dean and Professor of Law, Cornell Law School.

1. *See* Daniel Bethlehem, *Principles Relevant to the Scope of a State's Right of Self-Defense Against an Imminent or Actual Armed Attack by Nonstate Actors*, 106 AM. J. INT'L L. 700 (2012).

2. Legal Consequences of the Construction of a Wall in the Occupied Palestinian Territory, Advisory Opinion, 2004 I.C.J. Rep. 136, ¶ 139 (July 9) ("Article 51 of the Charter thus recognizes the existence of an inherent right of self-defence in the case of armed attack by one State against another State. However, Israel does not claim that the attacks against it are imputable to a foreign State. The Court also notes that Israel exercises control in the Occupied Palestinian Territory and that, as Israel itself states, the threat which it regards as justifying the construction of the wall originates within, and not outside, that territory. . . . Consequently, the Court concludes that Article 51 of the Charter has no relevance in this case.").

Jens David Ohlin, *The Unwilling and Unable Test for Extraterritorial Defensive Force* In: *Necessity and Proportionality in International Peace and Security Law.* Edited by: Professor Claus Kreß and Captain Robert Lawless, Oxford University Press (2021). © Oxford University Press. DOI: 10.1093/oso/9780197537374.003.0005.

of the architecture of Article 51, even though the bare terms of Article 51 simply refer to the criterion "if an armed attack occurs" without specifying *who* must launch that attack. The ICJ apparently was of the view that the provision should be interpreted with reference to an unwritten secret clause, such as "if an armed attack occurs by another state" or something similar.

If one accepts the ICJ interpretation of Article 51 as being dispositive of the issue of defensive force against NSAs, then the issue of extraterritorial defensive force largely disappears from view: it is not permitted under any circumstance. However, the ICJ view is largely rejected by many observers, including most notably the U.N. Security Council, which passed resolutions in the wake of 9/11 reaffirming the United States' right of defensive force at a time when it was largely understood that al-Qaida was responsible for the attack and that the conditions for state responsibility for al-Qaida's actions (by, for example, attributing the actions to Afghanistan) would not be satisfied.[3] So, assuming that the Security Council is right and that the ICJ is wrong, there is at least some latitude for exercising defensive force in response to an attack against a NSA that cannot be attributed to the actions of a state under principles of state responsibility.

However, the concept of defensive force, by itself, only explains why force can be used against the NSA. Assuming that the NSA is located on the territory of another state, as opposed to located on *terra nullius* or international waters, then the application of the defensive force against that NSA will entail, out of geographic necessity, some infringement on the territorial sovereignty of the host state. And *that* problem is one of the stickiest and messiest unresolved questions of *jus ad bellum*.

The standard answer is that extraterritorial defensive force is permitted when the territorial state is both unwilling or unable to resolve the threat on their own.[4] In other words, if the territorial state is willing but unable to respond to the situation, the external state is authorized to do what the territorial state is unable to do. Similarly, if the territorial state is able but unwilling—perhaps because its government is sympathetic to the aims of the NSA—then the external state is authorized to do what the territorial state is unwilling to do. Under this unwilling or unable test, the territorial state has the primary right of action, but the external state retains a residual right to remedial action that kicks in if the state holding the primary right fails to exercise it for any reason.[5]

3. *See* S.C. Res. 1368 (Sept. 12, 2001); S.C. Res. 1373 (Sept. 28, 2001).

4. *See, e.g.*, Yoram Dinstein, War, Aggression and Self-Defense 217 (3d ed. 2001).

5. Ashley S. Deeks, *"Unwilling or Unable": Toward a Normative Framework for Extraterritorial Self-Defense*, 52 Va. J. Int'l L. 483, 487–88 (2012) ("If the territorial state is willing and able, the victim state may not use force in the territorial state, and the territorial state is expected to take the appropriate steps against the nonstate group. If the territorial state is unwilling or unable to take those steps, however, it is lawful for the victim state to use that level of force that is necessary (and proportional) to suppress the threat that the nonstate group poses.").

Scholars who have written about the unwilling or unable test often cite the *Caroline* affair as the origin—or at the very least the best factual exemplar of the test—supporting the conclusion that the use of force is permitted against a NSA located on foreign territory.[6] In that case, Canadian rebels fighting against the British government were being supported, covertly, by sympathizers located in the United States.[7] The Canadian rebels were in command of the *Caroline*, which fled to the United States, specifically an American island in the Nicaragua River. The rebels were allegedly assisted by the American sympathizers. The Canadians (that is, the British) responded by crossing into American territory to engage and ultimately destroy the ship. This move was not endorsed by the American government, which was deeply angered by the infringement of sovereignty caused by the British military engagement.

The case is certainly on all fours with modern examples of extraterritorial defensive force. The rebels were responsible for attacks against British Canada, and the Americans were unwilling or unable to stop the attacks themselves. Indeed, the rebels apparently were being supported by Americans who were sympathetic, although that support was not governmental action, which would have made the rebel attacks attributable to the American government (which in turn would have radically simplified the legal analysis).[8] The famous Webster formulation—instant and overwhelming, leaving no room for deliberation—focused on the temporal element of the necessity and imminence requirements for defensive force.[9] If defensive force was necessary *at that moment in time* to alleviate the threat, then British Canada was permitted to cross into American territory to exercise defensive force. The *unstated assumption* behind the Webster formulation was that the hard question was whether British Canada jumped the gun and used force before it was strictly necessary; but reportedly no one in the controversy said that defensive force was impermissible once the rebels had crossed into American territory.[10] Had the relevant diplomats or international lawyers believed this, they would have said so. Their silence speaks volumes, some claim, suggesting that extraterritorial defensive force against a NSA is lawful when it is strictly necessary.

Several states have invoked the unwilling or unable rationale for using extraterritorial defensive force against the Islamic State (ISIS), al-Qaida, and other terrorist

6. *See* Craig Forcese, Destroying the Caroline: The Frontier Raid that Reshaped the Right to War (2018).

7. *Id.*

8. *Id.*

9. Letters between U.S. Secretary of State Daniel Webster and U.K. Foreign Secretary Lord Ashburton (July 27, 1842, July 28, 1842, Aug. 6, 1842), *reprinted in British American Diplomacy: The Caroline Case*, The Avalon Project (last visited Oct. 3, 2019), https://avalon.law.yale.edu/19th_century/br-1842d.asp.

10. *See* Forcese, *supra* note 6.

organizations. For example, the United States, the United Kingdom, France, and Italy have (explicitly or implicitly) invoked the criterion to justify their use of defensive force.[11] The cleanest, simplest example of the doctrine's application is in the context of defensive operations against ISIS. In 2016, ISIS controlled large swaths of territory in both Iraq and Syria. Defensive military operations against ISIS in Iraq are legally uncontroversial because Iraq consented to such operations by the United States, the United Kingdom, and coalition forces. In contrast, Syria has not consented to military operations on its territory except by Russian forces. Nor has the Security Council authorized member states to take collective military action on Syrian territory, again because Russia opposes these resolutions and is willing to exercise its veto power to defeat them.[12]

Consequently, the only way to legally justify the use of force against ISIS on Syrian territory is to appeal to the unwilling or unable test. The problem, of course, is that the unwilling or unable test is a *standard*, but it is a standard that does not effectively and transparently announce its own legal rationale. It simply articulates the *standard* by which extraterritorial force will be allowed without explaining why. In some situations, a legal doctrine has a name which adequately communicates its underlying principle—say, for example, self-defense. The name itself tells you that the force will be justified by virtue of the concept of self-defense, and then the doctrine leaves unsaid the standards that will be used to justify cases of self-defense. Unwilling or unable, by contrast, does the exact opposite: it articulates the standard itself but leaves the conceptual foundation covertly hidden. Perhaps that is because a large group of states all tacitly accept the standard but do not agree on a common conceptual foundation for it, thus producing an overlapping consensus on practical outcomes (modus vivendi) without any deeper agreement regarding fundamental notions of force, sovereignty, and intervention.[13]

Without that deeper conceptual foundation, it is totally unclear why the unable or unwilling standard confers a conceptual justification for the violation of the sovereignty of the territorial state. For the NSA, it is clear why force is permitted against it—it has launched an unlawful attack and defensive force is permitted against it (*pace* the ICJ) to alleviate that threat. But when exercising this defensive force requires crossing the sovereign territory of the host state, nothing in the unwilling or unable test explains why *that* sovereign intrusion is legally satisfied. The test explains *when* such force will be justified but does not articulate the *why* of it.

11. *See* Olivier Corten, *The "Unwilling or Unable" Test: Has It Been, and Could It Be, Accepted?*, 29 Leiden J. Int'l L. 777–99 (2016). Many of the official statements simply articulate that the state is using self-defense without explaining explicitly the legal rationale. *See also* Elena Chachko & Ashley Deeks, *Which States Support the "Unwilling and Unable" Test?*, Lawfare (Oct. 10, 2016, 1:55 PM), https://www.lawfareblog.com/which-states-support-unwilling-and-unable-test (noting that "[s]ome States have not been consistent in their positions, invoking the 'unwilling or unable' test in their own defense in one incident only to criticize other States for relying on it in others").

12. *See* Dan Bilefsky, *New Move to Condemn Syria in U.N.*, N.Y. Times, June 9, 2011, at A10.

13. *See* John Rawls, *The Idea of an Overlapping Consensus*, 7 Oxford J. Legal Stud. 1 (1987).

This chapter aims to explore this deeper conceptual question in the hopes that an answer can be found.

Before going any further, one must broach a difficult question of methodology. One must, in other words, settle on the ground rules for deciding this debate. Scholars who have disagreed with one another regarding the legitimacy of the unwilling or unable test have generally done so with a shared agreement regarding the terms of the debate. The debate usually involves a form of state counting: looking for the number of states that have exercised force in unwilling or unable situations and have invoked the unwilling or unable test, either explicitly or implicitly, as a justification for it.[14] Then the debate moves to the number of states that have explicitly criticized these invocations as well as the number of states that have remained silent and how one should interpret this silence.[15] Is it a form of tacit consent or is it a rejection of the doctrine? Or neither? In any evident, the evidence of state practice is taken as central to the formation of customary law, that is, trying to determine whether the unwilling or unable test is consistent with a new (or old, if one takes the *Caroline* affair as relevant) rule of customary international law regarding the use of extraterritorial force against NSAs.

I think there is reason to question this methodological assumption. The rules regarding the use of force are quite clear and laid out explicitly in the U.N. Charter. Article 2(4) prohibits the use of force, but then Article 42 carves out an exception for military action authorized by the Security Council, while Article 51 carves out an exception for self-defense, or the *droit naturel de légitime defense*, as the French language version of the Charter says. It seems odd to me to think that customary international law could change this structure, regardless of the content of the customary norm. The creation of the Charter was an explicit rejection of the idea that customary rules (primarily) govern the use of force; allowing customary law to widen the application of self-defense seems suspiciously like amending the U.N. Charter without going through the amendment process, which should be null and void.

Of course, the ICJ in *Nicaragua* recognized the application of customary rules of *jus ad bellum*—rules that allegedly run parallel to the Charter provisions.[16] This announcement has radically clouded matters, especially because it did not explain how the Charter rules would retain their centrality if they were simply widened or narrowed by the customary rules. While it is true that the existence of a treaty does not eliminate the application of custom that might apply to non-parties of the treaty—thus explaining why a customary law analysis should always be conducted—this is not the case with regard to the U.N. Charter. Almost all states

14. *See* Kevin Jon Heller, *The Absence of Practice Supporting the "Unwilling or Unable" Test*, Opinio Juris (Feb. 17, 2015), http://opiniojuris.org/2015/02/17/unable-unwilling-test-unstoppable-scholarly-imagination.

15. *Id.*

16. *See* Military and Paramilitary Activities in and Against Nicaragua (Nicar. v. U.S.), Judgment, 1986 I.C.J. 14 (June 27).

are members and are governed by the triumvirate legal norms of Article 2(4), Article 42, and Article 51, so there is no need to look to custom. Furthermore, even when one does look to custom, one does so to look for additional legal *constraints* that might apply even when a state is not constrained by the treaty (because they are not a party to it). But it is never acceptable for a state to say that it is constrained by treaty but nonetheless wants to look to custom to forum shop for a more permissive rule. The application of one constraint, wherever one finds it, is enough to determine that the behavior is illegal. So, I fail to see how the existence of a customary rule permitting the use of force in unwilling or unable situations could justify a state's use of force when that force is specifically condemned by the legal regime embodied by Articles 2(4), 42, and 51.

No, if there is an answer, it will not be found in the hallowed halls of custom. It will be found in treaty interpretation, and in the deep structure of self-defense and the use of force as embodied by Article 51. What difference does this make? The difference is that the rules of treaty interpretation are not the same as the rules for customary international law—the latter out of necessity involving a counting of states to see whether state practice is substantial enough to ground the existence of a customary norm.

True, there is some room for state practice even in the realm of treaty interpretation. International law will look at the practice of states in the application of the treaty provision as a gloss on what that treaty provision means. Just as in domestic contract law, where one might look to the commercial trade practice between two parties to understand the nature of the provision in a commercial contract, so too one might look at the way that states have applied Article 51 in the past as a gloss on what that provision means.[17] But that is not the same thing as a customary international law analysis and furthermore the recourse to subsequent practice must be balanced with the requirement that terms in treaties are to be give their ordinary meaning.[18] In other words, it cannot (or should not) displace an unambiguous treaty-based rule that either permits or denies the extraterritorial application of military force against NSAs.

With that in mind, the following section will look at the range of answers that have been posited to solve this problem—why military force is permitted despite the sovereignty of the host state—and whether the intervening state has violated a *jus ad bellum* prohibition with regard to the territorial state. Judged against

17. *See* Vienna Convention on the Law of Treaties arts. 31(3)(a), 31(3)(b), May 23, 1969, 1155 U.N.T.S. 331, *reprinted in* 8 I.L.M. 679 (1969); Rahim Moloo, *When Actions Speak Louder Than Words: The Relevance of Subsequent Party Conduct to Treaty Interpretation*, 31 Berkeley J. Int'l L. 39, 40–41 (2013); Jay Butler, *Responsibility for Regime Change*, 114 Colum. L. Rev. 503, 523 (2014) ("the ICJ has made clear that 'the subsequent practice of the parties, within the meaning of Article 31 (3) (b) of the Vienna Convention, can result in a departure from the original intent on the basis of a tacit agreement between the parties' ").

18. For more information, *see* Int'l L. Comm'n, Second Report on Subsequent Agreements and Subsequent Practice in Relation to the Interpretation of Treaties, U.N. Doc. A/CN.4/671 (Mar. 26, 2014); Treaties and Subsequent Practice (Georg Nolte ed., 2013).

the rule announced in Article 51, these doctrinal solutions each offer glimmers of truth, though each one fails to resolve the problem to complete satisfaction. Consequently, the following sections of this chapter will articulate a better solution that carefully explains why territorial states are in no position to object to the use of force, deployed against a NSA on their territory, that impinges on their territorial sovereignty.

II. THE EXISTING SOLUTIONS TO THE PROBLEM

There are numerous proposed solutions to help explain why violating the sovereignty of the territorial state is permitted. As I will explain in the following section, each of these solutions is somewhat unsatisfying.

First, one can simply assert that in order for defensive force to be used against the NSA, its actions must be attributed to the territorial state in order to justify the violation of sovereignty against the latter.[19] This solves the problem by dissolving it; the entire category of cases that the unwilling or unable test is designed to explain becomes a null set. In cases of attribution, the armed attack requirement is fulfilled against the state, making the intervention a straightforward application of defensive force under Article 51. The need to appeal to something like the unwilling or unable test disappears since legally speaking the attack came not just from the NSA but from the territorial state as well.

The problem with this position is that it simply denies the very possibility that any state can legally engage in defensive force against a NSA in situations where its acts cannot be attributed to the host state. If one has a liberal standard for principles of state responsibility the doctrine might work, but generally speaking, international law has eschewed broad principles of state responsibility and crafted extremely narrow ones.[20] This means that defensive force in these situations will be illegal and that the state threatened by the NSA will simply have to trust that the territorial state—or the international community—will deal with the situation. If the territorial state or the world community fails to do so, the threatened state will simply have to take its lumps and sacrifice its own security, perhaps even its own existence. No state will comply with an international legal regime which requires this amount of self-sacrifice.[21] International law, to be successful, must avoid utopian edicts that will be consistently ignored. Simply put, if a NSA has a

19. M.E. O'Connell, *Dangerous Departures*, 107 AM. J. INT'L L. 380, 383 (2013). For a discussion of the attribution requirement, *see* TOM RUYS, "ARMED ATTACK" AND ARTICLE 51 OF THE UN CHARTER 489–90 (2010).

20. For example, the debate between effective control versus overall control as principles of state responsibility embody this tension. *See* Antonio Cassese, *The Nicaragua and Tadić Tests Revisited in Light of the ICJ Judgment on Genocide in Bosnia*, 18 EUR. J. INT'L L. 649, 654 (2007).

21. Just as Justice Jackson once argued that the Bill of Rights was not "a suicide pact," Terminiello v. City of Chicago, 337 U.S. 1, 37 (1949), one might also argue that neither public international law nor *jus ad bellum* are suicide pacts.

nuclear weapon and plans to deploy it against an enemy state, and the territorial state is unwilling or unable to resolve the problem, the threatened state will defend itself and stop the NSA. Requiring the threatened state to forgo force in these circumstances is not just unreasonable, but absurd—a study in legal formalism. Instead of using that test case as a red flag to inform one's interpretation of the legal regime of *jus ad bellum*, some critics of the unwilling or unable test use the test case as inspiration to double down on a legal regime that is so restrictive that it requires self-sacrifice, knowing full well that no state will comply with it.

The second answer is to suggest that the defensive force is not applied against the territorial state just as long as the intervening state confines its attacks to the military and administrative resources of the NSA.[22] Under this view, as long as the intervening state refuses to engage the resources of the military forces of the territorial state, and refuses to bomb areas firmly under the control of the territorial state rather than the NSA, then the intervening state has not "attacked" the territorial state at all. If there is no attack against the territorial state, the territorial state has no right of defensive force against the intervening state. A closely resembling position holds that the use of defensive force might be illegal as to the territorial state but not rise to the level of an armed attack triggering a right of military response. This latter position is an uncomfortable liminal position, suggesting that the intervention is illegal but not illegal enough to trigger a right of response, though it is unclear how this could be so because defensive force should be triggered whenever there is a violation of the *jus ad bellum*.

As to the larger version of this argument, that the attack is not one against the territorial state at all, it is not consistent with the fact that the intervening state must cross the territorial boundary of the host state and engage assets on the territory of the host state. There is a grain of truth to this suggestion—that the territorial state has sovereignty over its land, yet that sovereignty does not extend so far that it can control the NSA on its territory. However, this position takes the grain of truth too far by ignoring entirely, without any explanation, the significance of the territorial violation. Crossing boundaries is significant for *jus ad bellum*, and the hypothetical intervention is no mere flyover designed to reach a third state far in the distance—it is a territorial incursion designed to engage targets located on the territory of the host state. It strains credulity to suggest that in the process of these interventions the host state is not attacked.

22. *See* Yoram Dinstein, War, Aggression and Self Defense 298–99 (6th ed. 2017); Noam Lubell, Extraterritorial Use of Force Against Non-State Actors 27–29 (2010) (discussing but not supporting the argument that a use of force against a NSA would not constitute an attack against the territorial state for purposes of Article 2 of the U.N. Charter). *But see* O'Connell, *supra* note 19, at 383 ("Attacking NSAs on the territory of another state is attacking that state as much as the NSAs."); Thomas Franck, Recourse to Force: State Action Against Threats and Armed Attacks 12 (2002).

Of course, one solution is to recognize the NSA as a new state, provided that there is a colorable argument that the NSA fulfills the traditional requirements for statehood. The United States and allied states could have used this strategy to justify its use of force against ISIS on Syrian territory.[23] If ISIS qualifies as a state, it is no longer—by definition—on Syrian territory; it exists on its own territory and is subject to defensive force on that basis. The United States was unwilling to pursue this option because it wanted to deny ISIS this ultimate prize—the legitimacy of statehood on the international stage. Rather than putting its intervention on stronger and less controversial legal ground, the United States and other states refused recognition based on a strategic calculation regarding the value of recognition. Of course, this option, like the attribution option discussed earlier in this chapter, ends up dissolving the problem of extraterritorial defensive force. Instead of unifying the NSA with the territorial state into one entity, the NSA is fully separated and emancipated from the territorial state. The conceptual method is totally different, but the result is the same: drop the non-state status from the equation and make the original attack, and the defensive force, between two states.

The third solution is to argue that the infringement of the territorial state's sovereignty is justified by its "complicity" for refusing to deal with the threat posed by the NSA's threat.[24] "Complicity" is in quotes because it is not typical to think of complicity in situations where the state fails to act. Usually, states are officially complicit under principles of state responsibility when they offer full-blown assistance to a group of individuals or another state.[25] In this case, complicity is being used in a vague sense rather than in the strict terms understood by the law of state responsibility. The obligation to act is difficult to identify, though perhaps one might conclude that all states have an obligation to prevent their territory from being used in a way that will harm the sovereignty or territorial integrity of other states—an *ergo omnes* obligation to the world community.[26] This could

23. Chelsea Elizabeth Bellew, *Secession in International Law: Could ISIS Become a Legally Recognized State?*, 42 Ohio N.U. L. Rev. 239, 265 (2015) ("With the United Nations and many other countries identifying ISIS as a terrorist organization, it is difficult to see how the international community could bless ISIS's rule in the Middle East through recognition of its government. People around the world would be outraged if the group was permitted to rule the population in the Middle East when it has plainly violated human rights norms in an egregious manner.").

24. *See, e.g.*, Steven R. Ratner, *Complicity and Compromise in the Law of Nations*, 10 Crim. L. & Phil. 559, 565 (2016) ("Though scholars disagree about just how far new norms have solidified, a number of states, including the United States, now assert that, when one state is 'unwilling or unable' to stop non-state actors on its territory from carrying out attacks against other states, the latter are legally permitted to use force against the 'host state.' And whether the victim state must limit its response to terrorist infrastructures in the host state or can actually attack the host state's facilities will also depend on the extent of the complicity.").

25. *See generally* Miles Jackson, Complicity in International Law (2015).

26. *See* Tom Ruys & Sten Verhoeven, *Attacks by Private Actors and the Right of Self-Defence*, 10 J. Conflict & Security L. 289, 306 (2005).

be described as a broader manifestation of the "no harm" principle that is often discussed in international environmental law, and also sometimes referred to as an emerging obligation to exercise "due diligence." But whether this obligation exists as a matter of *lex lata* is a bit controversial. That being said, it does articulate a common-sense and widely shared intuition: that states have a moral or diplomatic obligation to resolve threats on their territory and such states are accountable to the targets of those threats if they refuse to deal with them satisfactorily. And it certainly is a widely recognized *emerging* principle of public international law.

Naturally, the third argument fails to apply in cases where the state is willing to resolve the threat but is simply unable to do so. In that case, a new conceptual argument is required, leading to a fourth argument. In this new situation, one might argue that the state is a failed state, thus possessing no sovereignty at all.[27] In addition to being highly controversial as an argument, there are few places on earth that could legitimately qualify for this status where no government exists at all. The U.S. Department of Justice's Office of Legal Counsel famously made this argument about Afghanistan, which was widely ridiculed, though it might have been applicable to the facts of Somalia at one point in time.[28] But the point is that in most states where a NSA is located, there will be enough state power to conclude that a territorial state continues to exist, even if its ultimate control is partially compromised.

The argument could be reformulated so that the assertion is not that the territorial state has suffered a total elimination of sovereignty, but rather that the state has simply suffered a *diminution* of sovereignty sufficient to explain why the intervention fails to violate the state's sovereignty. If the state is genuinely unable to stop the NSA from using its territory to plan or launch attacks, this suggests that the state does not have complete control over its territory, that its government is not capable of exercising the police functions that one normally associates with sovereign authority, and that the notion of "control" associated with sovereign prerogative ("ought" implies "can") is decidedly lacking. In that case, the intervention would not be a violation of sovereignty as long as it aligns with the territorial state's lack of sovereignty over the NSA. If, on the other hand, the intervention goes to the core of the territorial state's existence and its central government, such an intervention would implicate the sovereignty that the state still retains despite its diminished character. When the state is unable, the state's sovereignty is

27. *See* Hannah Woolaver, *State Failure, Sovereign Equality and Non-Intervention: Assessing Claimed Rights to Intervene in Failed States*, 32 Wis. Int'l L.J. 595, 600 (2014) ("After the terrorist attacks of September 11, 2001, ('9/11'), this focus shifted from humanitarian to security-related concerns. Governments now commonly claim that failed states constitute a threat to national and international security, as the absence of effective government makes them vulnerable to use as havens for terrorist or other criminal organizations.").

28. John Yoo, *Fixing Failed States*, 99 Cal. L. Rev. 95, 104 (2011) ("Failed states present a challenge for both international law and policy.").

diminished in proportion to its level of control. This assumes that sovereignty has graduations, which is very controversial.

This argument is problematic insofar as it assumes a vision of sovereignty which is not very common—a variable concept that varies by degree depending on the degree of internal control exercised by the state. Typically, international lawyers view sovereignty as a creature of the formal legal personality of states, which does not depend on a factual inquiry of the *amount* of control that the state enjoys. In other words, most international lawyers think of sovereignty from outside military force (embodied in Article 2(4)) as being absolute, as an on-off switch that either applies or not. Either a state enjoys sovereignty or, if it does not, then it ceases to be a state, since sovereignty is constitutive of statehood. Internally strong states do not enjoy greater sovereignty than internally weaker states; each has equal rights to sovereignty once the *threshold* criteria for statehood are reached. Nonetheless, the argument does contain a grain of truth because it picks up a logical tension: the territorial state argues that it enjoys the freedom from external intervention that sovereignty bestows on it, yet at the same time the territorial state does not enjoy enough internal sovereignty that it can adequately squelch the NSA located on its territory. The result is an awkward tension: "yes" to one kind of sovereignty but "no" to another. Or, more properly, "yes" to sovereignty in one context but "no" to sovereignty in another. The territorial state uses sovereignty as a shield against foreign intervention but is unable to use sovereignty as a sword against the internal NSA. Something is fishy about this combination.

Each of these arguments contains insights that could be mined to produce a more satisfying answer. In the following section, this chapter lays out an approach that combines the best elements of each argument.

III. A SIMPLE ANSWER: SOVEREIGNTY ESTOPPEL

There is a way out of this mess—something more than simply bearing down and denying the possibility of extraterritorial military force against NSAs. The goal is to develop a legal doctrine that makes sense of the extensive state practice in favor of these unilateral defensive operations and yet explains how the doctrine might be consistent with Article 51 and the underlying structure of *jus ad bellum*.

The simple answer relies on the intuition that a right might be violated but not every party is in a position to object to it. This notion is common in domestic legal systems. One example of the idea is embodied in the equitable doctrine of clean hands.[29] Under this maxim, originally used in courts of equity, a party must come to the court with clean hands if she wants the court to vindicate her rights. Under

29. *See* T. Leigh Anenson, *Announcing the "Clean Hands" Doctrine*, 51 U.C. Davis L. Rev. 1827, 1837 (2018) ("The familiar maxim of equity that 'he [or she] who comes into equity must come with clean hands' is 'one of the elementary and fundamental conceptions of equity jurisprudence.'").

this doctrine, a party who is partly culpable in the situation cannot come to court and ask for a remedy for the other party's culpable conduct.[30]

Of course, the equitable maxim of clean hands does not apply in all situations. Parties frequently come into court having engaged in some wrongdoing and are still able to achieve a remedy. It is important to remember that clean hands is a *maxim* as opposed to an absolute rule. Courts of equity had jurisdiction to "balance the equities," in the sense that they would take into account the totality of the circumstances in order to achieve a just resolution of the controversy.[31] They would factor in the "clean hands" principle along with any other maxim that might be relevant to the situation.

The other example in domestic courts where parties are not in a position to complain about a rights violation is the broader concept of estoppel. In estoppel situations, a litigant might be prevented from making a particular claim in court—even if it might be true, even if it might have merit—because doing so would be inconsistent with prior statements made by the litigant. Usually those statements are ones that are made within the legal system, but in other situations they might be statements made or *conduct* by the party outside of the legal system to other parties. The doctrine of estoppel is closely related to the clean hands doctrine, and it is easy to see why. One common definition of estoppel states that it is a "bar that prevents one from asserting a claim or right that contradicts what one has said or done before or what has been legally established as true."[32] Of course, there are many different types of estoppel, but all of them involve this common structure: a prohibition on complaining (or making a legal claim) based on past statements or behavior of the party.

The language of estoppel is not common in public international law, much to the latter's detriment. The most likely explanation of its disuse is that it is a common law doctrine and public international law is loath to adopt general principles of law that do not share widespread adoption across the common law–civil law divide. In situations where estoppel *has* been adopted in the international context, it is in the limited circumstance of litigation before the ICJ and other international tribunals as a general prohibition against taking positions that are contrary to prior official statements.[33] With the exception of that limited context, the notion of estoppel has played little role in international legal discourse.

How might the principle of estoppel help explain why extraterritorial force is permitted against a territorial state hosting a NSA? It is the conceptual apparatus, the basic structure, of estoppel that is most useful here. The idea would be that the state exercising defensive force might have violated the territorial sovereignty

30. *See* Zechariah Chafee Jr., *Coming into Equity with Clean Hands*, 47 Mich. L. Rev. 877, 881 (1949).

31. Weinberger v. Romero-Barcelo, 456 U.S. 305, 311, 320 (1982).

32. *Estoppel*, Black's Law Dictionary (10th ed. 2014).

33. Ian Brownlie, Principles of Public International Law (8th ed. 2012).

of the territorial state, but the territorial state is estopped from asserting that its sovereignty was violated. In other words, it cannot, on the one hand, refuse to exercise its sovereign authority to stop the NSA and at the same time assert its sovereignty to complain about the putative infringement of its territorial boundaries. Call this notion *sovereignty estoppel.*

Essentially, sovereignty estoppel provides a legal gloss on the have-your-cake-and-it-too-ism of the host state that refuses to exercise its sovereignty to resolve the threat posed by the NSA but at the same time asserts its sovereignty as a barrier to the foreign state's intervention. Or, in the alternative, a state that does not have enough sovereign control (unable) to resolve the threat but then asserts its sovereignty enough to object to the intervention. Sovereignty estoppel suggests that you cannot object to the sovereign intrusion once you have made those original statements. Sovereignty is a package deal.

There are two objections to this conceptual structure that should be resolved immediately.

The first is the public nature of sovereignty violations. When a state violates the *jus ad bellum* regime, and the Article 2(4) prohibition on the use of force, there is some uncertainty about whether this should be viewed as a private or public wrong. If it is a private wrong, the victim of the aggression is the state that is the object of the sovereignty violation. On the other hand, there is another way of conceptualizing violations of *jus ad bellum*. Perhaps they are public wrongs, wherein the "victim" of the aggression is not just the target state but also the world community itself.[34] Just as a violent attack against an individual in the criminal law sense is more than just a private wrong, but also a public wrong triggering the machinery of the criminal justice system, so, too, perhaps, a violation of the prohibition against the use of force is not just a private dispute between two states but a public dispute involving the world community. It is for this reason that *jus ad bellum* disputes are resolved in part by the Security Council, which represents the interests of the world community, rather than simply worked out privately between the parties. If the latter conception is the correct one, then it is hard to see how an estoppel against the target of the use of force can in any way limit or bind the world community, which has a separate and distinct interest in maintaining stability and lowering instances of military force. The transformation of the dispute from a private one to a public one potentially sidelines the estoppel argument.

This argument raises an important point but ultimately is not fatal to the notion of sovereignty estoppel. Indeed, sovereignty estoppel is built for this very acoustic separation. Even assuming that violating the prohibition against the use of force is a public, rather than private, wrong, it is still the case that the victim state must either object, or not object, to the use of force against it. Consent always transforms an illegal use of force into a lawful one. Conversely, the lack of consent is what makes a military intervention illegal under public international law. Even

34. For more discussion, *see* George P. Fletcher & Jens David Ohlin, Defending Humanity (2008).

if we conceive of the *violation* as a violation of public law, the fact remains that the host state is not in a position to complain about the violation. If a shadow of the violation remains, it is not one for which the putative "victim" can ever seek redress. Just as a private litigant might be estopped from raising an argument before a court, so too the territorial state ought to be estopped from raising the territorial violation as a basis for a legal claim for redress, not just before a formal tribunal but also more generally before the world community as it sits in judgment over matters pertaining to *jus ad bellum*.

The second objection is that sovereignty usually means that the state is entitled to decide for itself whenever it wants to assert itself. In other words, if the state wants to forgo force against the NSA, it may, and that choice should not restrict its ability to object to violations of its sovereignty down the road. But in reality, it is already clear that public international law imposes an *obligation* on states not to allow their territory to be used in such a way as to threaten the security of other states. So, states are under an obligation to stop NSAs from launching attacks from their territory, and their failure to do so represents a violation of international law. This is already clear. Sovereignty estoppel clarifies that the law should connect this obligation, which is implicit in the notion of sovereign control, with the ability to use sovereignty as a shield against external interventions designed to resolve the very threat that the host state refuses to resolve on its own.

In practical terms, sovereignty estoppel would require that states articulate a consistent and coherent approach to their own sovereignty. If they assert that they will not redress the threat posed by a NSA, they cannot then assert their sovereignty as an objection to foreign interference to eliminate the threat, provided that the foreign intervention is strictly limited to resolving the threat and does not fall victim to "mission-creep," that is, launching attacks against the assets of the territorial state. Assuming that the intervening state confines its attacks to the NSA, the intervening state would be in a position where it has intervened against a territorial state that is in no position to object to that intervention.

Conceptually, this leaves open some room for classifying the foreign intervention as a wrong, in some sense. The external state may have violated a *general presumption* against military intervention underlying the entire international legal ecosystem. Perhaps one might even say that the intervention violates the underlying goals and purposes of the United Nations. At the same time, however, the territorial state is in no position to complain about that sovereignty violation. It would open up a space to say, in other words, that the intervention creates a violation against the general *jus ad bellum* presumption but that the territorial state is not in a position to complain about it. It threads the eye of the needle very carefully, suggesting that the intervening state *has* done something wrong, but also at the same time asserting that the territorial state is in no position to complain about it, and in no position to seek a remedy for the violation either. It basically says that if the territorial state wanted to avoid the violation of its sovereignty, it should have taken care of business by either willingly resolving the threat brewing on its territory or maintaining better control over its territory.

IV. AN ANALOGOUS FRAMEWORK

In this section, I hope to respond to a key objection to the notion of sovereignty estoppel. The language of "estoppel" gestures in the direction of Anglo-American common law and other legal traditions, including but not limited to civil law jurisdictions, will find the invocation of estoppel to be unfamiliar and foreign. This might lead to the objection that estoppel is an inappropriate addition to the *jus ad bellum* conceptual framework; core international legal doctrines should include concepts like self-defense or necessity that have broad appeal across national jurisdictions and across legal cultures.

This objection is important, and its spirit is laudable. International doctrine that is weighted too heavily toward common law or civil law concepts is less than ideal. On the other hand, it is important not to get bogged down with labels. Although the word "estoppel" has a distinctively common law ring to it, I hope to demonstrate that the basic conceptual structure of the solution that I have described might be found in other legal concepts, including some from civil law jurisdictions. In that vein, I am not wedded to the language of estoppel; it is the idea, not the language, that is most important. The key insight I have introduced is to recognize that the territorial state is in no position to complain about defensive force used to quell threats that emanate from its territory. This could be called "estoppel," or it could be called something else.

For example, German lawyers might be inclined to understand the situation under the rubric of *defensivnotstand*, or "defensive necessity." The theoretical concept, widely recognized in the German scholarly literature, stands somewhere in the netherworld between the defenses of necessity and self-defense but corresponding with neither.[35] The defense originally flows from German tort law and is codified in Section 228 of the German Civil Code.[36] The provision confers a defense on someone who uses force to destroy or damage a threatening object in order to avert a threat or risk to himself or someone else. The harm caused by the defensive force must not be disproportionate to the harm averted by the dangerous object.[37] The situation cannot be covered by a self-defense provision because the threatening harm does not necessarily come from a person who

35. For examples in the German literature, *see* Michael Pawlik, *Der Rechtfertigende Defensivnotstand im System Der Notrechte*, 2008, Goltdammer's Archiv für Strafrecht 12 (2008); Michael Pawlik, *Der Rechtfertigende Defensivnotstand*, 2002, Juristische Ausbildung 26 (2002).

36. Bürgerliches Gesetzbuch [BGB] [Civil Code] § 228 ("Wer eine fremde Sache beschädigt oder zerstört, um eine durch sie drohende Gefahr von sich oder einem anderen abzuwenden, handelt nicht widerrechtlich, wenn die Beschädigung oder die Zerstörung zur Abwendung der Gefahr erforderlich ist und der Schaden nicht außer Verhältnis zu der Gefahr steht. Hat der Handelnde die Gefahr verschuldet, so ist er zum Schadensersatz verpflichtet.").

37. *See* Russell Christopher, *Tripartite Structures of Criminal Law in Germany and Other Civil Law Jurisdictions*, 28 Cardozo L. Rev. 2675, 2686 (2007).

launches an unlawful attack.[38] On the other hand, the situation is not covered by a necessity provision either because the criminal defense of necessity, under the German penal code, requires a strict balancing requirement so that the harm avoided must be greater than the criminal conduct of the actor pleading necessity. In contrast, the civil law notion of "defensive necessity" has a much weaker proportionality requirement, simply requiring that the evil imposed on the originator of the threatening conduct not be disproportionate.[39] To see the difference between the strong and weak proportionality requirements, consider a situation where a life is taken to save a life. The taking of a life to save a life would not satisfy the requirements of necessity, which requires imposing a lesser harm, while it *would* satisfy the weaker requirement that one should not impose a disproportionate harm, since taking one life to save another is not disproportionate.

As noted, the concept of "defensive necessity" is codified in German civil law but not codified in the German Criminal Code, but the concept enjoys widespread support among some criminal law theorists.[40] However, the point of invoking the concept is not to argue whether the concept is, or is not, a recognized part of German criminal law. Rather, the point is far more abstract: it is to suggest that there are other conceptual "languages" that cover the same territory as sovereignty "estoppel" without using the same common-law language.

Defensive necessity covers the same conceptual ground because it articulates why someone should be subject to defensive measures if a threatening harm emerges from their territory and the only way to defeat that threat is for someone to take those defensive measures to neutralize the threat.[41] It is similar to sovereignty estoppel because it articulates a reason why the recipient of the defensive measures cannot complain; they cannot complain because the threatening conduct emerges from their own territory. In cases of defensive necessity, it would be somewhat odd for the source of the threatening harm to claim that they should be legally protected from the defensive action, even though the threatening harm flows from their territory.

38. *See* B. Sharon Byrd, *Till Death Do Us Part: A Comparative Law Approach to Justifying Lethal Self-Defense by Battered Women*, 1991 DUKE J. COMP. & INT'L L. 169, 206–207 (1991) ("The necessity or lesser evils defense generally requires not a present attack but a situation of imminent danger. It is exactly this distinction that separates the battered woman case from the typical self-defense case. Even though it is very difficult to maintain that the defendant in these cases was being attacked, the fact that her spouse has placed her in a general situation of danger is more plausible. A dangerous situation can be ongoing and need not represent a sudden threat posed by another's voluntary, aggressive conduct.").

39. *Id.* at 201.

40. *Id.* at 199.

41. Other scholars have suggested that the private law doctrine of "defensive necessity" could be applicable for *jus ad bellum*. *See, e.g.*, CLAUS KREß, GEWALTVERBOT UND SELBSTVERTEIDIGUNGSRECHT NACH DER SATZUNG DER VEREINTEN NATIONEN BEI STAATLICHER VERWICKLUNG IN GEWALTAKTE PRIVATER 290 (1995).

In fact, some of the classic objections to the concept of defensive necessity track exactly the objections to the sovereignty estoppel principle. For example, Fletcher argued that the category of defensive necessity should be disfavored because it unmoors responsibility from defensive force (in contrast with self-defense, which requires that the aggressor be responsible for committing an unlawful attack in order to be subject to defensive force).[42] Similarly, the underlying problem with sovereignty estoppel is that the territorial state is subject to defensive measures (the violation of its sovereignty) even though the original attack perpetrated by the NSA is not directly attributed to the territorial state under classic rules of state responsibility.

I have already argued earlier why defensive force in these situations is called for; although it involved a violation of the territorial state's sovereignty, the territorial state cannot complain about it because their territory was the source of the threatening harm against the defending state. Both defensive necessity and sovereignty estoppel coalesce around a common solution to this problem, albeit with different conceptual vocabularies. Again, this result is conceptually similar to my earlier description of sovereignty estoppel, which admits that the defending state has violated the interests of the territorial state, while at the same time insisting that the territorial state cannot complain that the intervening state has acted unreasonably in the encounter.

Finally, there is the question of whether a soft proportionality requirement should be imposed in the sovereignty estoppel situations that I have described in this chapter: situations where the intervening state uses military force to stop a terrorist organization using the territorial state as a base of operations. Recall that in German law, the doctrine of defensive necessity requires that the defender's imposition of harm should not be disproportionate to the harm faced by the defendant that they sought to avoid.[43] Given the similarities between sovereignty estoppel and defensive necessity, one might argue that a similar proportionality constraint should be imposed in the *jus ad bellum* cases described in this chapter. Applied to those situations, the proportionality element would require the following balancing assessment: whether the intervention against the territorial state would cause harm that is not disproportionate to the harm the intervening state is trying to avoid by using the defensive force. Although proportionality requirements are often imposed in self-defense cases—both in domestic criminal law and national self-defense under international law—the proportionality requirement in this case would be unique. It would require an estimate of the harm that would be caused by the terrorist group if it is allowed to continue its operations unfettered. Would it launch an attack against the defending state? How severe would that attack be? Then, on the other side of the analysis, one would estimate the harm to the

42. *See* George P. Fletcher, Rethinking Criminal Law 778 (Oxford reprint ed., 2000) ("One cannot but feel that adjusting the scales in this way puts too much emphasis on whether the injuring object happens to be in motion, rather than on the criteria of responsibility.").

43. For a discussion of the proportionality requirement, *see* Kress, *supra* note 41, at 290.

territorial state represented by the sovereignty violation of the defensive military operation. Would it be possible to defeat the terrorist organization without killing innocent civilians or destroying the civilian infrastructure that they depend on? Would the defending state attack the terrorist organization in sparsely population rural areas, or would it require aerial bombardment of heavily populated urban centers? Arguably, this balancing exercise would introduce a set of common-sense criteria into the legal decision-making. There is much to recommend prohibiting interventions in situations where the territorial violation represents a disproportionate imposition on the territorial state.

V. CONCLUSION

This result will aggravate both sides of the debate, while placating neither of them. For advocates of unilateral intervention, the notion that the intervention constitutes a violation of the host state's sovereignty will be cold comfort; these lawyers will want a full-throated defense of the state intervention, and the proposal here falls short of this idea. On the other hand, the critics of unilateral intervention will be equally bitter, because the conclusion falls far short of an unequivocal condemnation. At most, the conclusion is that the intervening state has violated a presumption against intervention, but the host state has no basis to complain about it. Nobody wins, but nobody loses either. It is a split decision designed to aggravate everyone.

Drones Programs, the Individualization of War, and the *Ad Bellum* Principle of Proportionality

REBECCA MIGNOT-MAHDAVI*

I. INTRODUCTION

Interest in drone wars should not fade for many reasons. First, the use of drones during armed conflict, which peaked for the United State in the early 2010s,[1] is now spreading. Following the United Kingdom, which started using combat drones in 2014,[2] France started using its first armed Reapers from its Niamey base in Niger against jihadist groups in Sahel in December 2019.[3] In addition,

* Researcher in International Law and Counter-terrorism at the T.M.C. Asser Institute, PhD candidate in Law at the European University Institute. This chapter greatly benefited from discussions with fellow members of the European Research Council–funded project "Individualisation of War," and with Professors Nehal Bhuta and Claus Kreß. All errors and omissions remain my own.

1. *See Drone Warfare*, The Bureau of Investigative Journalism, https://www.thebureauinvestigates.com/projects/drone-war (last visited Nov. 6, 2019).

2. *See U.K. Drone War Stats*, Drone Wars, https://dronewars.net/uk-drone-strike-list-2 (last visited Nov. 6, 2019).

3. Madame Florence Parly, Ministre des Armées, Université d'été de la Défense, Discours de Clôture (Sept. 5, 2017), https://www.defense.gouv.fr/salle-de-presse/discours/discours-de-florence-parly/discours-de-cloture-de-florence-parly-universite-d-ete-de-la-defense-2017; Loi de Programmation Militaire 2019–2025, statute n° 2018-607 (July 13, 2018), https://www.legifrance.gouv.fr/affichTexte.do?cidTexte=JORFTEXT000037192797&categorieLien=id (Fr.); *see also* Loi de Programmation Militaire 2019–2025, *supra*, report annexed to statute & contained in art. 65, https://www.legifrance.gouv.fr/affichTexteArticle.do;jsessionid=1AC201987855306124F24A5DEE727924.tplgfr23s_2?idArticle=LEGIARTI000037194585&cidTexte=LEGITEXT000037194533&dateTexte=20191122 (Fr.) [hereinafter Annexed Report]; Nathalie Guibert, *La France Entre dans l'ère des Drones Armés*, Le Monde (Mar. 21, 2019), https://www.lemonde.fr/international/article/2019/03/21/la-france-entre-dans-l-ere-des-drones-armes_5439209_3210.html.

Rebecca Mignot-Mahdavi, *Drones Programs, the Individualization of War, and the* Ad Bellum *Principle of Proportionality* In: *Necessity and Proportionality in International Peace and Security Law.* Edited by: Professor Claus Kreß and Captain Robert Lawless, Oxford University Press (2021). © Oxford University Press. DOI: 10.1093/oso/9780197537374.003.0006.

in February 2019, Australia announced the development of a locally designed combat drone, an innovation considered essential "in the early conceptual stages where [the Ministry of] Defence can explore concepts and define the role such capabilities can play in [Australia's] national security framework."[4]

The second reason interest in drone wars should not wane is that the technological capabilities of drones facilitate the emergence of an individualized warfare which, as I will show in this chapter, converges with the pressures put on the laws regulating the use of force against non-state armed groups. This individualized kind of warfare, facilitated by drones, also explains the recourse to the *jus ad bellum* in regulating the fight against transnational terrorist networks and the extension of the right of self-defense. This chapter explores how war, technology, and the law interact, and more specifically how drone programs facilitate an individualized kind of warfare, framed and legitimized by a revised version of the right of self-defense.

The essence of technology lies in how it encourages actors to re-perceive the world and their own practice in it. This contribution holds that the strategy of drone programs would not exist as such if it were not for drones' technological capacities. Furthermore, it suggests that the individualized use of force against terrorist networks,[5] understood here as the use of force against targets by reason of their personal features rather than to repel an armed attack, is facilitated and intensified by military drones.[6]

4. Press Release, Christopher Pyne, Minister for Defence, Australian-Designed Unmanned "Loyal Wingman" Aircraft to be developed with Industry (Feb. 27 2019), https://www.minister.defence.gov.au/minister/steven-ciobo/media-releases/australian-designed-unmanned-loyal-wingman-aircraft-be.

5. For a similar use of the terminology, *see* NILS MELZER, TARGETED KILLING IN INTERNATIONAL LAW 410 (2008) ("[O]ne of the central problems with the use of targeted killings as a method of the conduct of hostilities is that such 'individualized' warfare, particularly against non-State actors intermingling with the civilian population, requires extraordinarily reliable intelligence, and is prone to error and abuse."); *see also* IAN SHAW, PREDATOR EMPIRE: DRONE WARFARE AND FULL SPECTRUM DOMINANCE 18, 27, 111–12 (2016); Gabriella Blum, *The Individualization of War: From War to Policing in the Regulation of Armed Conflict*, *in* LAW AND WAR 48 (Austin Sarat, Lawrence Douglas, & Martha Merrill eds., 2014). Note, however, that Blum integrates different facets of individualization into her study. *See id.* at 59 ("[T]he combination of a greater normative commitment to individuals and the technological ability to distinguish among individuals has contributed not only to focusing harm on individuals who are threatening (and who are largely also viewed as 'guilty'), but also to voluntarily undertake to promote the welfare of those individuals who are innocent.").

6. There is something special about drones. The idea that drones are unique from a legal perspective, which is central to this chapter, contrasts sharply with the literature that considers drones to be just like other (discriminate) weapons and weapons systems. *See, e.g.*, Rosa Brooks, *Drones and the International Rule of Law*, 28 ETHICS & INT'L AFF. 83 (2014); Michael N. Schmitt, *Drone Attacks Under the* Jus ad Bellum *and* Jus in Bello: *Clearing the "Fog of Law,"* 12 Y.B. INT'L HUMANITARIAN L. 311, 313 (2010) ("The article concludes that there is little reason to treat drones as distinct from other weapons systems with regard to the legal consequences of their employment."); Jean-Baptiste Jeangène Vilmer, *Légalité et Légitimé des Drones Armés*, 78

As will be seen throughout this chapter, what is referred to using the term "drone program" consists of a network of interacting and interdependent factors including, among others, contemporary technological capacities of drones, the justifying rationale for the use of drones, the type of enemy that they are targeting, and the military strategy that is implemented. Viewed through a wider lens, drone programs are part of the extraterritorial counterterrorism policies that are said to "have had the very problematic effect of blurring and expanding the boundaries of the applicable legal frameworks."[7] While the present chapter focuses on the *jus ad bellum* framework, it must be acknowledged that it is part of a wider endeavor to assess the current pressures put on the three legal frameworks that are applicable to the extraterritorial use of force against non-state actors. That is, in addition to the *jus ad bellum*, drone programs place pressure on the *jus in bello* and international human rights law.

The next section of this chapter describes how drone programs facilitate the individualization of war and, as a corollary, the dematerialization of the decision to use force. For this, I show how, instead of force used in self-defense against an (imminent) act, force is used in self-defense against individuals based on their personal characteristics. In other words, drone programs are characterized by the objective of continuously addressing future threats before they materialize, and this objective leads to authorizing action against individuals who are not presently perpetrating, nor even clearly preparing to engage in, threatening acts. The absence of material circumstances amounting to the level of an armed attack, in the *jus ad bellum* sense, means that the use of force is focused not on material circumstances but on personal features. This is what I refer to respectively as the dematerialization and individualization of war. I argue that these changes are not merely the result of how states decide to use force in the current counterterrorism context but also are impacted by what technology allows them to do. As such,

Politique Étrangère 119 (2013); Stuart Casey-Malsen, *Pandora's Box? Drone Strikes Under* Jus ad Bellum, Jus in Bello *and International Human Rights Law*, 94 Int'l Rev. Red Cross 597 (2012). On the contrary studies or at least references to the potential consequences of drones' technological capacities, are included in: Mary Ellen O'Connell, Comment, *Seductive Drones: Learning from a Decade of Lethal Operations*, 21 J.L. Info. & Sci. 116 (2011); Laurie R. Blank, *After Top Gun: How Drone Strikes Impact the Law of War*, 33 U. Pa. J. Int'l L. 675 (2012); Grégoire Chamayou, Drone Theory (2015); Eyal Benvenisti, *The Legal Battle to Define the Law on Transnational Asymmetric Warfare*, 20 Duke J. Comp. & Int'l L. 339 (2010). Contributions on post-9/11 drone strikes against terrorists often revolve around two points. First, drones are not inherently legally problematic and should therefore be treated like any other weapon. And second, for underexplored reasons, the way drones are used has posed unprecedented challenges to the legal frameworks applicable to the use of force. While it is true that the legal and political discourses concerned with justifying drone use challenge the law, they are part of a larger dialogue. State agents' choices are generated by an evolving environment within which they, in turn, generate new habits and practices.

7. Human Rights Council, Report of the Special Rapporteur on Extrajudicial, Summary, or Arbitrary Executions, Philip Alston add., U.N. Doc. A/HRC/14/24/Add.6 (May 28, 2010).

drones facilitate and arguably intensify these phenomena of individualization and dematerialization of the use of force.

Section III focuses on one of the justifications for this practice, namely, the right of self-defense. I argue that the framework articulated by some states active in the transnational war on terror (the United States, the United Kingdom, Australia, Israel, and France), while still highly contested on some points, offers a framework for the continuous anticipation of armed attacks by individuals who show signs of continuing armed activity. I show that under pressure by state practice and rhetoric, some limitations on using force that were initially interpreted restrictively are currently interpreted extensively. More importantly, I argue that even if some limitations remain, the concessions to the extensive interpretation appear to have a direct cascade effect on the remaining limitations precisely because these limitations are interconnected. It is ultimately shown that this cascade effect is epitomized by the principle of proportionality, which is not only extended but also transformed to adapt to the individualization of war.

II. THE INDIVIDUALIZATION OF WAR INTENSIFIED BY DRONE PROGRAMS

Before delving into the characteristics of the individualization of war and the reasons why this phenomenon has been intensified by drone programs, it is necessary to contextualize the emergence of the individualization of war. The first subsection explains that the rise of a new type of non-state armed group has led to a new form of force used in self-defense, focused on the dispersed individuals composing transnational terrorist networks. This is important because the features of such "new" armed groups are emphasized when states assert legal justification to use force in self-defense by recourse to armed drones, which will be explored in section III. The second subsection shows how drones' technological capacities make ends meet by holding the promise of acute precision and enhanced anticipatory capacities.

A. Transnational Terrorist Networks: Calling for the Individualization of War

The emergence of a new type of non-state actor has led to a new form of hostilities. It is apparent that contemporary terrorist networks can be distinguished from traditional non-state armed groups. For the sake of clarity, I will refer to these two categories as "old" and "new" types of non-state armed groups, though it is worth noting that they may coexist. National or separatist non-state armed groups of the "old" type with formalized hierarchical structures still exist today.[8] At the same

8. The most recent reports of the U.S. National Counterterrorism Center clearly show that national/separatist terrorism still exists (for example, in India, Philippines, and Sri Lanka). Two-thirds of the terrorist attacks carried out in India in 2015 (67%) were attributed to the Communist Party of India-Maoist or Maoist perpetrators not specifically identified as belonging to a particular

time, contemporary warfare is broadly conducted by states and non-state armed groups of the new type—that is, of transnational character.[9] Old and new non-state armed groups differ from each other in fundamental ways. The former are territorialized and state-centered, while the latter are detached from state and territorial concerns. The distinction I make between these two types of non-state armed groups is based on three main criteria: the center of gravity, the agenda, and the structure of such groups.

"Old" non-state armed groups have a physical center of gravity. The physical center of gravity is a geographical focal point: either a country (or part of one) or a delineated territory that spills over multiple countries, from which the non-state armed group carries out its operations and recruits the majority of its members, and in which official authorities are the main targets.[10] The well-established center of gravity of old types of non-state armed groups does not exclude international cooperation. Yet, although "old" non-state armed groups are capable of forming international alliances around a common project or ideology, the actions of such groups mainly consist of a series of national campaigns.[11] Indeed, no matter how extensive the international activities of such groups are, they always aim to support the focal point of operations and to reinforce the group's core, nationalist agenda.[12]

By contrast, "new" non-state armed groups typically operate on a multiplicity of fronts, recruitment areas, and enemies. Such groups' lack of a center of gravity is not merely based on the cross-border operations of such groups. As Olivier Roy explains, "new" non-state armed groups vary in where they act, where they recruit, and where their members come from, reside, and radicalize.[13] As such, the theater of operations is geographically unconstrained: Spain, Indonesia, Britain,

organization. In the Philippines, the Moro Islamic Liberation Front, based in Mindanao, fights for the acquisition of an autonomous region of the Moro people from the central government. The Communist Party of the Philippines/New People's Army (CPP/NPA) perpetrates attacks to overthrow the Philippine government. *See* Bureau of Counterterrorism & Countering Violent Extremism, Country Reports on Terrorism 2016, 2017 & 2018, https://www.state.gov/country-reports-on-terrorism-2; Nat'l Consortium for the Study of Terrorism & Responses to Terrorism, Annex of Statistical Information: Country Reports on Terrorism 2015 (June 2016), https://2009-2017.state.gov/j/ct/rls/crt/2015//index.htm.

9. Uppsala Conflict Data Program, http://ucdp.uu.se/#/encyclopedia (last visited Nov. 11, 2019).

10. Peter Neumann, Old and New Terrorism 18 (2009).

11. David C. Rapoport, Inside Terrorist Organizations 34–38 (2d ed. 2013). For instance, the globalized nature of new non-state armed groups should be distinguished from the nineteenth-century anarchist movement that—if operating in and receiving support across Europe and North America—mainly consisted of a series of national campaigns with very few cross-border activity or exchange (common ideology but separate national-based campaigns).

12. Neumann, *supra* note 10, at 18.

13. Olivier Roy, Globalized Islam: The Search for a New Ummah (2006).

Tanzania, the United States, France, Germany, Yemen, India, and so forth.[14] In fact, these groups can be expected to increasingly target a multiplicity of fronts as they turn to cyberattacks and start using armed drones as a means of striking at their opponents.[15] The multiplicity of such groups takes on new meaning in light of the virtual spaces they begin to inhabit. Such virtual space is beyond the control or identity of any single state and crystallizes a new kind of social space, which lacks a single, permanent geographical point of reference. Indeed, cyber recruitment and operations have become a central feature of such groups.[16] Of course, the virtual community does not replace physical world relations. Nonetheless, it plays a role in the loosening of spatial constraints and in the changing nature of the relationship between non-state armed groups and states. Ultimately, such non-state armed groups do not follow state-based logic. Al-Qaida has moved its headquarters at least three times, and none of these moves has destroyed the organization altogether.[17] Drawing from a large sample of al-Qaida members, Olivier Roy observes that "relations between militants and their country of origin are weak or non-existent."[18]

If the organization of "new" non-state armed groups is transnational, so is their agenda. "Old" non-state armed groups, in addition to being territorially based, have a state-centered narrative and agenda. A comparison of al-Qaida or ISIS and the Revolutionary Armed Forces of Colombia (the FARC) reveals that, while both are non-state armed groups, the second—the FARC—has a state-centered and territorially delineated agenda. Indeed, the FARC's enemy has always been the Colombian security forces and their claim has mainly concerned control over land. Also, "old" non-state armed groups associated with struggles in the Middle East used to be linked to statist strategies in the 1980s, such as pro-Palestinian, pro-Syrian, and pro-Iranian operations. For instance, Ayatollah Khomeini's ideology and the Islamic Revolution in Iran in 1979 were aimed at conquering state power. Even if the Islamic Revolution of Iran was in part driven by the aim to

14. Tim Lester et al., *ISIS Goes Global: 143 Attacks in 29 Countries Have Killed 2043*, CNN (updated Feb. 12, 2018), https://edition.cnn.com/2015/12/17/world/mapping-isis-attacks-around-the-world/index.html; *Timeline: Al-Qaeda*, BBC News, http://news.bbc.co.uk/2/hi/7546355.stm (last updated Aug. 7, 2008).

15. Roy, Globalized Islam: The Search for a New Ummah, *supra* note 13, at 305; Thomas Gibbons-Neff, *ISIS Drones Are Attacking U.S. Troops and Disrupting Airstrikes in Raqqa, Officials Say*, Wash. Post (June 14, 2017), https://www.washingtonpost.com/news/checkpoint/wp/2017/06/14/isis-drones-are-attacking-u-s-troops-and-disrupting-airstrikes-in-raqqa-officials-say; Cody Poplin, *Look Who Else Has Drones: ISIS and Al Nusra*, Lawfare (Oct. 24, 2014, 10:11 AM), https://www.lawfareblog.com/look-who-else-has-drones-isis-and-al-nusra.

16. Neumann, *supra* note 10, at 20; Roy, Globalized Islam: The Search for a New Ummah, *supra* note 13.

17. Peter L. Bergen, Holy War, Inc.: Inside the Secret World of Osama Bin Laden ch. 4 (2002).

18. Roy, Globalized Islam: The Search for a New Ummah, *supra* note 13, at 305.

export an ideology of political Islam and to influence the political landscape of the Muslim world, the primary goals were state-centered.[19]

The agenda of "old" non-state armed groups, situated locally in the real world, is different from the global agenda of "new" non-state armed groups. First, it is hardly possible to identify a social or political cause driving the actions of the members of the non-state armed group of the latter type. Indeed, as Olivier Roy describes, there is no direct link between a specific conflict and how a jihadist justifies his actions. The concrete struggles of our contemporary world are ignored. The clearest illustration is the case of Palestine: even if the names Palestine and Gaza regularly arise in their campaigns, al-Qaida or Daesh members do not concretely support the Palestinian cause. Quite to the contrary, it is a fact that these groups fight against Muslim groups (for example, against Hamas in the Yarmuk camp and Hezbollah in the north of Damascus).[20] Therefore, the Muslim community that the jihad seeks to save is neither historically nor spatially specified.[21] In addition, the theaters of operation are mentioned loosely as part of a global conflict. The pictures used for propaganda are rarely dated and thus are interchangeable and sometimes have nothing to do with the cause in which they are used.[22] Thus, the narrative of these groups, such as al-Qaida and ISIS, builds a panoramic vision of a globally suffering Muslim population. The universal scope of this perspective also concerns the enemy: all infidels are enemies. As such, Olivier Roy concludes that there is almost no point in searching for a strategic justification for the attacks perpetrated against a specific country.[23]

Besides, "new" non-state armed groups follow a definition of jihad that departs from the traditional one. They define jihad as an individual, permanent, and global obligation rather than a collective and temporary one that concerns a specific territory.[24] If at first the priority of ISIS was to reterritorialize the jihad and create local political entities (contrary to al-Qaeda), ISIS—if it has not already—is moving toward joining global jihadism in two ways: firstly, through the creation of an international jihadist legion, and secondly, through the rejection of

19. Gilles Kepel, Jihad: The Trail of Political Islam 120 (Anthony F. Roberts trans., 2003) ("The Iranian revolution's propaganda . . . incited people to rise up against the impiety of their leaders, despite their claim to be following the dictates of the Koran and the sharia. The Saudi policy, on the other hand, was to finance the expansion of Islamism around the world, the better to control it . . . and to prevent groups bent on changing the status quo from appropriating Islam to themselves.").

20. Olivier Roy, Le Djihad et la Mort 81 (2016).

21. *Id.* at 80.

22. *Id.* Olivier Roy mentions the use of a picture of a massacre of Harkis, perpetrated by the FLN regime in Algeria but attributed to the French.

23. *Id.* at 85. For example, it is unclear why Spain would be targeted in 2004 and not Italy, given that both countries participated in the American-led occupation of Iraq.

24. *Id.* at 25, 137.

the nation-state concept, borders, and diplomatic "games."[25] Thus, the caliphate project of ISIS, as well as the project of global jihad of al-Qaeda, cultivates the fantasy of perpetual territorial expansion. Such projects do not allow any negotiation toward a political solution and stabilization of a society inside recognized borders.[26] Ultimately, even the prospect of creating a global Islamic society cannot be identified as the concrete agenda of these "new" non-state armed groups. Indeed, death and war are not the means toward the achievement of a political goal. Rather, war and death are ends in themselves: ISIS members are convinced of the imminence of the end of the world and the state that precedes apocalypse is a state of war.[27] All in all, the ideology of ISIS is essentially nihilistic in that it revolves around death, which is the only key to heaven.[28]

Finally, whereas "old" non-state armed groups used to be formalized structures built on hierarchical relationships, "new" non-state armed groups are characterized by loose networks based on multiple personal relationships.[29] At first, "old" non-state armed groups mimicked the structure of traditional armies and established "hierarchical systems with clear lines of command and control."[30] However, because such structure was too transparent, it was found unsuitable and replaced by a structure in cells. Neumann explains that "cells typically consisted of up to a dozen members, with only the cell leader having any contact or relations with the wider organization, so that—when individual members were caught—they could only betray the other members of their cell rather than implicating the entire organization."[31] Still, such cell structure implied the existence of both hierarchical control and central organization. In a different manner, "new" non-state armed groups' structure is mostly identified "decentralized," "networked" forms of organization. While the structure of such groups presents some hierarchical features, it is more diffuse. For instance, personal relationships (that is, who members know and what connections they can facilitate) can be more important than the formal rank held by the individual.

25. *Id.* at 140–41 ("Contrairement à l'émirat islamique d'Afghanistan fondé par les talibans, il n'est pas question pour Daech d'accepter le concept d'État-nation, avec les frontières et le jeu diplomatique induits. En ce sens, le terme « État islamique » est trompeur: ce projet n'a rien à voir avec celui des Frères musulmans de toute nature. Le califat n'existe que dans l'expansion, et donc dans la guerre, car il ne peut accepter aucune négociation.").

26. *Id.* at 11.

27. *Id.* at 97; William McCants, The ISIS Apocalypse: The History, Strategy, and Doomsday Vision of the Islamic State (reprint ed. 2016); Fawaz A. Gerges, ISIS: A History (reprint ed. 2017).

28. Roy, Le Djihad et la Mort, *supra* note 20, at 98.

29. Neumann, *supra* note 10, at 46.

30. *Id.* at 17.

31. *Id.*

These features of "new" non-state armed groups are emphasized by states in justifying the recourse to armed drones. For instance, the French Senate encouraged the recourse to armed drones on the basis that technological progress answers the needs of the armed forces in the war against a non-state enemy that is unpredictable, uncontrollable, hard to track, and cannot be fought without mastery over intelligence gathering.[32] American officials as well, and former President Barack Obama himself in 2015, evoked the evolution of the terrorist threat into a new phase characterized by the multiplication of "less complicated acts of violence" and the exploitation of the internet in that it "erases the distance between countries" and can be used to poison the minds of the people in diverse places.[33]

To a certain extent, states even inflate some characteristics of "new" non-state armed groups when referring to different non-state armed groups either as interchangeable entities, or at least as the same enemy in a unique conflict.[34] As has been shown, each "new" non-state armed group on its own, such as al-Qaida, is characterized by a multiplicity of fronts. When for instance al-Qaida is considered as part of the same enemy entity as ISIS, the Taliban, and other terrorist groups, the enemy appears as having an even greater number of fronts around the globe and a more significant mobility.

Although this chapter does not directly focus on the deterritorialized nature of the use of force against transnational terrorist networks, it should at least be noted that this spatial dimension is interrelated with the individualization of the use of force. The strategy against these groups consists in focusing on individuals in order

32. French Senate Report, N° 559, Drones d'Observation et Drones Armés: Un Enjeu de Souveraineté 14, 18, 77 (May 23, 2017), https://www.senat.fr/rap/r16-559/r16-559.html.

33. *Transcript: President Obama's Address to the Nation on the San Bernardino Terror Attack and the War on ISIS*, CNN (Dec. 6, 2015), http://edition.cnn.com/2015/12/06/politics/transcript-obama-san-bernardino-isis-address/index.html.

34. *READ: President Trump's speech to the UN General Assembly*, CNN (Sept. 19, 2017), http://edition.cnn.com/2017/09/19/politics/president-trump-united-nations-speech/index.html ("The United States and our allies are working together throughout the Middle East to crush the loser terrorists and stop the reemergence of safe havens they use to launch attacks on all of our people. Last month, I announced a new strategy for victory in the fight against this evil in Afghanistan. From now on, our security interests will dictate the length and scope of military operations, not arbitrary benchmarks and timetables set up by politicians. I have also totally changed the rules of engagement in our fight against the Taliban and other terrorist groups. In Syria and Iraq, we have made big gains toward lasting defeat of ISIS. In fact, our country has achieved more against ISIS in the last eight months than it has in many, many years combined."); French Parliament Hearing Transcript, Commission d'Enquête Parlementaire Relative aux Moyens Mis en œuvre par l'Etat pour Lutter Contre le Terrorisme [Committee of Inquiry on the Means Used by the State to Counter Terrorism], http://www2.assemblee-nationale.fr/14/autres-commissions/commissions-d-enquete/moyens-pour-lutter-contre-le-terrorisme/(block)/ComptesRendusCommission/(instance_leg)/14/(init)/0-14 (military and state officials identifying the enemy broadly as "jihadist" groups and individuals). Unlike in the United States and France, it should be noted that in the United Kingdom the identification of the enemy group is precise.

to face a dispersed enemy. Without individualized military operations, the geographical spread of the use of force would not significantly emerge and vice versa.

B. Drones: Tailor-Made Machines for Individualized Warfare

The strategy against this new type of enemy is explained as follows. Such an enemy cannot be successfully fought without accepting and responding to its dispersed nature and thus without focusing on the members of the group individually. Simultaneously, because of the new modes of organization and action of the enemy, it is implied that states involved in the fight against jihadist terrorism should not have to wait for the identification of a specific armed attack in order to use force, but rather should be able to identify and eliminate individuals who carry in concert a hostile intent.[35] The technological capabilities of drones allow this strategy to fully develop.

Drones' technological capacities facilitate a war conducted against a plethora of individuals and aimed at anticipating threats. This objective of anticipation requires being in control of time and being in control of time in that context means to possess knowledge. In this sense, it is important to emphasize that the characteristics of drone programs go beyond the possibility to target, as it also facilitates the aggregation of knowledge on individuals and the identification of the threat they may pose.

This is not to claim that military drones are a brand-new tool or that their current capabilities were not sought after and progressively reached. On the contrary, the idea of arming drones was contemplated since the beginning of their development.[36] The Digital Revolution, from the late 1950s to the late 1970s,

35. Daniel Bethlehem, *Self-Defense Against an Imminent or Actual Armed Attack by Nonstate Actors*, 106 Am. J. Int'l L. 770, 773 (2012). According to Bethlehem, "imminence" does not require "specific evidence of where an attack will take place or of the precise nature of an attack." His focus on the importance of tracing a "concerted pattern of activity" clearly supports my observation that material circumstances revealing an actual or forthcoming armed attack are considered by some as too demanding. It implies that a hostile intent is sufficient to act in self-defense. Jeremy Wright, the U.K. Attorney General, gave a speech at the International Institute for Strategic Studies on January 11, 2017, in which he asserted, "In a world where a small number of committed plotters may be seeking to inspire, enable and direct attacks around the world, and indeed have a proven track record of doing so, we will not always know where and when an attack will take place, or the precise nature of the attack. But where the evidence supports an assessment that an attack is imminent it cannot be right that a state is prevented from meeting its first duty of protecting its citizens without nailing down the specific target and timing of an attack. Apart from anything else, our enemies will not always have fixed plans. They are often opportunists." Jeremy Wright, Attorney General, Attorney General's Speech at International Institute for Strategic Studies: The Modern Law of Self-Defense, Jan. 11, 2017 (U.K.); *see also* George Brandis, *The Right of Self-Defense Against Armed Attack in International Law*, EJIL: Talk! (May 25, 2017), https://www.ejiltalk.org/the-right-of-self-defence-against-imminent-armed-attack-in-international-law.

36. Barry D. Watts, The Evolution of Precision Strike 17–18 (2013).

fostered the development of drones for surveillance purposes. Moving from technological development to practice, the United States started to use military drones to collect intelligence during the Vietnam War.[37] They were followed by Russia, who deployed surveillance drones for military intelligence purposes in Ukraine, Belarus, and Latvia.[38] In 1973, during the Yom Kippur War, Israel used surveillance drones and again in 1982 when invading Lebanon.[39] During the first Gulf War and during the Kosovo War, military drones were also used for intelligence, surveillance, and reconnaissance purposes.[40] It was between the Kosovo War and military intervention in Afghanistan that they metamorphosed from surveillance to surveillance *and* combat drones.[41] In February 2001, the U.S. Air Force carried out the first successful experimental strike at Nellis Air Force Base, where a Predator drone successfully deployed a Hellfire missile against its target.[42] Combat drones were first used in actual military operations against real targets later in the same year. U.S. drone operators stationed in the Nevada desert started conducting drone strikes extraterritorially in different zones around the globe. The United States was followed by the United Kingdom and Israel,[43] and more recently by France.[44] From 2001 onward, drone strikes were officially conducted in Afghanistan, Yemen, Pakistan, Somalia, Libya, Syria, Iraq, and the Occupied Palestinian Territories.

While drones are not new, contemporary drones possess unprecedented capabilities. These technological advances multiply operational efficiency by refining and accelerating each step of the decision-making process: orientation, observation, selection, surveillance, engagement, and targeting.[45] In other words,

37. David Cenciotti, *The Dawn of the Robot Age: U.S. Air Force Testing Air-Launched UCAVs Capable to Fire Maverick and Shrike Missiles in 1972*, The Aviationist (Mar. 14 2012), http://theaviationist.com/2012/03/14/the-dawn-of-the-robot-age; Shaw, *supra* note 5, at 71.

38. Yefim Gordon, Soviet/Russian Unmanned Aerial Vehicles 128 (2005); Océane Zubeldia, Histoire des Drones ch. 1 (2012).

39. Ben Hartman, *Ya'alon: IDF Cuts Revolutionary, Will Recreate Army*, Jerusalem Post (July 11, 2013), https://www.jpost.com/Defense/Yaalon-IDF-cuts-revolutionary-will-produce-new-army-319510.

40. David Jordon & Ben Wilkins, *Unmanned Aerial Vehicle Operations Since the 1980s*, *in* Air Power: UAVs: The Wider Context (Owen Barnes ed., 2009).

41. William Arkin, Unmanned Drones, Data, and the Illusion of Perfect Warfare ch. 9 (2015).

42. Steve Coll, Ghost Wars: The Secret History of the CIA, Afghanistan, and Bin Laden, from the Soviet Invasion to September 10, 2001 (2004).

43. U.K. Drone War Stats, *supra* note 2.

44. Parly, *supra* note 3; Loi de Programmation Militaire 2019–2025, *supra* note 3; *see also* Annexed Report, *supra* note 3; Guibert, *supra* note 3.

45. Arkin, *supra* note 41; Charlie Savage, Power Wars: The Relentless Rise of Presidential Authority and Secrecy 240, 273 (2015).

armed drones are equipped to "find, fix and finish" targets.[46] In other words, the enhancement of the military operational process is achieved because drones' current technological capabilities have two core objectives: precision and ubiquity. The objective of precision concerns not only surveillance and intelligence collection but also selection of targets and lethal strikes. The objective of ubiquity requires the capacity to be permanently everywhere in order to control, select, and terminate a target.

Drone programs are specific in that they apparently combine all the technologies necessary to determine the threat posed by individuals and targeting them on that basis rather than in responding to threatening acts or hostilities that have materialized or are materializing. First, drone programs involve a surveillance apparatus that allows a persistent collection of intelligence.[47] Unmanned aerial vehicles today have the capacity to gather several types of intelligence from the air such as signal intelligence (SIGINT) and image intelligence. Utilizing satellite communication links, unmanned aerial vehicles (UAVs) acquire real-time imagery beyond line-of-sight, which means that their radio communications capabilities allow them to connect with systems that are normally too distant or too obscured by terrain specificities (for example, weather situations and geological landform). For this reason, UAVs have replaced satellites and manned aircraft as the favored platform for intelligence collection. In countries where drones have not yet been armed, UAVs are already the first source of intelligence in external operations.

Following the surveillance step, drones' technological capacities facilitate the "fixing" and "finishing" parts of the process. Thanks to the black boxes (known in the United States as Gilgamesh) that are attached to them, drones are equipped with metadata analysis and cell-phone tracking technologies.[48] Each drone is equipped with a geolocation device that, as the drone circles, locates the SIM cards of potential targets. These black boxes give drones minute geolocation capacities that greatly enhance their power to find and fix targets. In addition to the black box device attached to UAVs, U.S. drones are combined with devices on the ground that relay GPS data to the drone,[49] to other data-collection tools such as the human intelligence collection (or HUMINT),[50] and to mini and micro

46. *The Drone Papers: Find, Fix, Finish*, The Intercept (Oct. 15, 2015), https://theintercept.com/drone-papers/find-fix-finish.

47. Jeremy Scahill et al., The Assassination Complex: Inside the Government's Secret Drone Warfare Program 44 (2016).

48. Jeremy Scahill & Glenn Greenwald, *Death by Metadata*, *in* The Assassination Complex, *supra* note 47, at 94.

49. In the United States, one of them is called ARTeMIS for Aerial Reconnaissance Tetraotor Mobile Intelligence System. *See* Arkin, *supra* note 41, at 23; *Ground Unit*, ESD ARTeMIS (Apr. 30, 2014), https://esdartemis.wordpress.com/2014/04/30/base-unit.

50. Arkin, *supra* note 41, at 10. HUMINT has been devalued in the face of technical collection's capacity to infiltrate denied physical spaces.

drones operating at lower altitudes.[51] To the end of "finishing" the target, reaper drones carry the Multi-Spectral Targeting System, which comprises a set of powerful visual sensors for targeting: an infrared sensor, a color/monochrome daylight TV camera, an image-intensified TV camera, a laser range finder/designator, and a laser illuminator. In addition, U.S. MQ-9 Reaper drones are equipped with Air-to-Ground Missile-114 Hellfire missiles, which is the primary air-to-ground precision weapon.

Unlike traditional airplanes, which were not designed with such an objective in mind, drones promise permanence in several ways. First, drones allow an economy of means—especially of ground refueling. The Reaper drone can stay airborne for up to 14 hours fully loaded and about 24 hours in total. General Atomic's updated drone, the Certifiable Predator B, is a turboprop-powered drone that can spend 40 hours in the air. Second, through a warden system, drones can ensure a 24/7 presence for each relevant area. This is a capacity that the French Senate emphasized as offering the perspective of permanent (and discrete) presence of drones, as facilitating an unprecedented control of time and space, and an essential to understanding the situation on the ground where the enemy is fleeting (*fugace*) and hides among civilians.[52] Third, the fact that drone pilots operate their vehicles remotely makes permanence possible, as it overcomes physiological constraints. The now-retired U.S. Air Force General T. Michael Moseley insisted that the capacity to "launch a UAV from a remote field on the other side of the globe, then pilot that aircraft from a base in the United States . . . offer[s] unprecedented flexibility to combatant commanders worldwide."[53] Finally, UAVs have a low maximum cruising speed of around 230 mph (200 knots), and thereby ensure that each specific area is continuously covered.[54]

All in all, drones are data machines that emerged from a long-lasting race for technological precision. By all accounts, there is a wide gap between official assessments of such casualties and nongovernmental reports on civilian casualties resulting from drone strikes. For instance, in 2011, then senior counterterrorism advisor John Brennan argued that "for the [previous] year, there ha[d]n't been a single collateral death because of the exceptional proficiency, precision of the capabilities that [they had] been able to develop."[55] On the other hand, for the year

51. *Id.* at 14.

52. French Senate Report, *supra* note 32.

53. Press Release, U.S. Air Force, "Reaper" Moniker Given to MQ-9 Unmanned Aerial Vehicle (Sept. 14, 2006), https://www.af.mil/News/Article-Display/Article/129780/reaper-moniker-given-to-mq-9-unmanned-aerial-vehicle.

54. *MQ-9 Reaper*, U.S. Air Force (Sept. 23, 2015), https://www.af.mil/About-Us/Fact-Sheets/Display/Article/104470/mq-9-reaper.

55. John O. Brennan, Assistant to the President for Homeland Security and Counterterrorism, Ensuring al-Qa'ida's Demise, June 29, 2010, https://obamawhitehouse.archives.gov/the-press-office/2011/06/29/remarks-john-o-brennan-assistant-president-homeland-security-and-counter.

2010 just in Pakistan, 89 to 197 civilian deaths were reported as having resulted from U.S. CIA-led drone strikes.[56] This data difference, rather than revealing the limits of the technological tool, flows from a conceptual disagreement: the largest number of civilian casualties reflects a restrictive interpretation of who can be lawfully targeted, and the smallest one on an extensive interpretation. In other words, drones do allow state agents to target who they intend to kill, it is the framework they use to identify legitimate targets that is overinclusive.

On the technical level, however, drones do allow to conduct warfare against individuals with high level of precision. In his detailed assessment of how these technological advances bring war ever closer to the realm of fighting against individuals, Arkin explains that from Desert Storm through Kosovo to Iraq and into the current day, "whether the task is synchronizing or searching deeper, the black box has grown smaller and smaller as the individual and minute target has also shrunk, all while operating on a larger and larger battlefield."[57] These capacities—the ability of geolocation devices that allow the machine to find individual cell phones even when they are not in use or that the caller does not answer;[58] the set of black boxes placed on aircrafts and on the ground, collecting intelligence and working together with the drones as a network—have altogether transformed the execution of war into a precision exercise focused on gathering knowledge on the individual targets before eliminating it. This does not mean that drones' technological capacities *caused* the military strategy focused on individuals—after all, this strategic objective was at the heart of the scientific research on how to improve the technology for the past decades—but rather that drones made possible the implementation of such strategy. Indeed, the military strategy of finding, fixing, and finishing could not be easily carried out without them.[59]

The technology not only facilitated the desired strategic change, it also intensified it by prioritizing drone use as the way of conducting contemporary warfare. The military, to use Arkin's words, "has been transformed and become hyperprecise, but it also has become able to do only one thing: drill down to the individual—a terrorist, a car, an armoured vehicle, a window in an office, the most hidden or fragile heart or brain of a machine or a network."[60] The essence of a war fought with a data machine and capable of precision strikes can only consist of

56. *Pakistan: Reported US Strikes 2010*, Bureau of Investigative Journalism, https://www.thebureauinvestigates.com/drone-war/data/obama-2010-pakistan-strikes (last visited Nov. 12, 2019).

57. Arkin, *supra* note 41, at 183–84.

58. Dana Priest & William M. Arkin, Top Secret America: The Rise of the New American Security State 242 (2012).

59. Arkin, *supra* note 41, at 119 ("The shift to the long war of individual targeting occurred silently"); *id.* at 120 ("None of this strategy could be implemented without black boxes and drones"); *id.* at 134 ("The changing of the doing itself thus also changed the very nature of war").

60. *Id.* at 18.

identifying, validating, locating, tracking, and eliminating individuals. Besides, as a matter of fact, the only two scenarios under which drone strikes are conducted are inherently centered on individuals. Drone strikes are either conducted as personality strikes against individuals appearing on a kill list because of their specific attributes,[61] or as signature strikes against individuals demonstrating an insurgent pattern of life, a suspicious behavior thought to suggest engagement in militant activity.[62] As reported by the *Intercept*, the target is always an individual person: "every mission that's triggered begins as an objective to find one person for whatever reason."[63]

In both drone strike scenarios, the intention to kill is aimed at specific persons. Even in the United Kingdom, where the government says that it does not have a "targeted killing policy" focused on individuals, the U.K. Parliamentary Joint Committee on Human Rights concluded in its 2016 report on the government's policy on the use of drones for targeted killings that although they "understand why the Government does not want to call its policy a 'targeted killing policy' . . . the Government's policy on the use of lethal force outside of areas of armed conflict does contemplate the possibility of pre-identified individuals being killed by the State."[64]

In the United States, the targeting process is facilitated by the existence of a "disposition matrix," a database that associates the names of suspected terrorists with the resources being used to track them down.[65] This database collects real-time data on the specific individuals the United States is interested in. A nominating agency prepares a profile for each individual chosen for lethal action on the basis of all relevant disseminated information, "as well as any other information needed to present as comprehensive and thorough a profile of the individual as possible."[66]

France is an interesting example of how military strategy and technological tools interact. France acquired armed drones at the beginning of 2019 and planned to start using them in Sahel by the end of that year. Notably, it has already

61. Human Rights Council, *supra* note 7.

62. *Id.*; Jeremy Scahill et. al., *supra* note 47, at 56; Grégoire Chamayou, Théorie du Drone (2013).

63. Ryan Devereaux, *Manhunting in the Hindu Kush*, *in* The Assassination Complex, *supra* note 47, at 158.

64. Joint Comm. on Hum. Rts., House of Lords & House of Commons, HC 574, HL Paper 141, Report on the Government's Policy on the Use of Drones for Targeted Killings (May 10, 2016).

65. Greg Miller, *Plan for Hunting Terrorists Signals U.S. Intends to Keep Adding Names to Kill Lists*, Wash. Post (Oct. 23, 2012), https://www.washingtonpost.com/world/national-security/plan-for-hunting-terrorists-signals-us-intends-to-keep-adding-names-to-kill-lists/2012/10/23/4789b2ae-18b3-11e2-a55c-39408fbe6a4b_story.html?hpid=z1&utm_term=.1143e2137871.

66. Presidential Policy Guidance, Procedures for Approving Direct Action Against Terrorist Targets Located Outside the United States and Areas of Active Hostilities (May 22, 2013), *reprinted in* 56 Int'l Legal Materials 1209 (2007).

shown signs of individualization of warfare. Former French President François Hollande admitted having personally authorized targeted killings in Syria and revealed the existence, beyond the Syrian situation, of a French kill list.[67] In this context, it was reported that the French military and the General Directorate for External Security have killed at least 40 "High Value Targets" in Mali between 2012 and 2016.[68] This number corresponds to an average of one targeted killing per month. In 2015 and 2016, state officials confirmed France's targeted killing practice in front of the Parliamentary Commission.[69]

The list of intelligence and communication systems that appears in the new French law on military programming for 2019–2025 officially ensures France's involvement in the era of data warfare.[70] The new law insists that technological innovations have to be acquired and adapted to evolving threats, in particular combat aerial vehicles. For strategic reasons, these drones will be connected to the data collection and communication systems both of other drone machines and of robots on the ground,[71] and will be capable of lethal action.[72] From DESCARTES,

67. Gérard Davet & Fabrice Lhomme, Un Président ne Devrait pas Dire Ça . . . les Secrets d'un Quinquennat (2016).

68. Vincent Nouzille, Erreurs Fatales: Comment nos Présidents ont Failli Face au Terrorisme 426–27 (2017) ("Devant les journalistes Gérard Davet et Fabrice Lhomme, il a confié avoir décidé des assassinats ciblés—« quatre, au moins »—et détenir une liste de personnes « à neutraliser »—un aveu inédit qui confirme ce que nous écrivions au début de 2015 et qui brise un tabou, créant la polémique. En réalité, selon des sources militaires et du renseignement, entre le déclenchement de l'opération au Mali et la fin de 2016, on peut estimer que les armées et la DGSE ont contribué à éliminer au moins une quarantaine de High Value Targets, les cibles de haute valeur, au Sahel, dans la corne de l'Afrique ou en Syrie, soit un rythme inédit d'environ une exécution par mois.").

69. *See, e.g.*, French Committee of Inquiry on the Means Used by the State to Counter Terrorism, Hearing of M. Didier Le Bret, National Intelligence Coordinator (May 18, 2016), http://www.assemblee-nationale.fr/14/cr-cemoyter/15-16/c1516024.asp. One should note that like its American allies, France underlined that the capture option was preferred to the kill option.

70. Annexed Report, *supra* note 3, ¶ 3.2.1.5.

71. *Id.* ¶ 3.2.1. ("Les programmes d'armement qui seront lancés d'ici à 2025 permettront de faire face à l'évolution des menaces notamment celles que font à nouveau peser les États puissances. A cette fin, les programmes intégreront des technologies innovantes adaptées. En particulier, l'autonomisation des systèmes constitue un axe important de modernisation et d'innovation des capacités. Ainsi, les programmes de drones aériens (comme le drone MALE européen ou le système de drones aéromaritimes embarqués SDAM), le système de guerre des mines futur (SLAMF) ou encore les robots du domaine terrestre intégrés aux systèmes d'information et de communication infovalorisés du programme SCORPION apporteront des concepts entièrement nouveaux fondés sur la collaboration entre des plateformes et des systèmes de drones. Ces nouveaux systèmes seront intégrés aux capacités actuelles afin d'en améliorer la performance globale.").

72. *Id.* ¶ 3.2.1.4 ("Les systèmes aéroportés de « drones aériens » poursuivront leur montée en puissance avec la mise en service des drones REAPER qui seront dotés de la capacité à délivrer des armements.").

to SYRACUSE IV, or Successeur MELCHIOR, to CONTACT, SCORPION, OMEGA, ASTRIDE, RIFAN, SIOC, SIA, GEODE, and ISSAN, the proposed law announces the modernization of the means of communication of the military by the implementation of these new (and multiple) data collection networks to ensure "informational superiority."[73] All in all, the French example is interesting because it will allow testing the above-mentioned hypothesis that, although drones do not initiate the individualization of warfare or cause a strategic change in that direction, their technological capacities intensify the individualization of war.

Not only do drones appear to facilitate and intensify the conduct of an individualized kind of warfare, they also provide a strong incentive for embracing some of the legal changes initially proposed by the Obama administration. The following section will examine how the proposed interpretation of the right of self-defense corresponds to the individualization of war that drone programs facilitate. In a context where behaviors could not be scrutinized from distance or where no tool would allow the surveillance of people's intimacy, habits, communication, and movements, such an extension of the right of self-defense would not appear as acceptable as it has in fact become. If such advanced technological capacities were not available, the idea that it could be lawful to target individuals who do not currently participate in the preparation of a forthcoming armed attack and who are far from areas of active hostilities and not objectively identified as members of an enemy group, likewise would not be as admissible as it has become. Conversely, the extended version of the right of self-defense appears as a plausible and acceptable means of anticipating a threat, even in the absence of an identified armed attack, in a world where drones' technological capacities combine the necessary elements to ensure persistent scrutiny of individuals and data collection, in other words elements that promise the minutiae of knowledge.

III. THE INDIVIDUALIZATION OF SELF-DEFENSE AND THE METAMORPHOSIS OF THE PRINCIPLE OF PROPORTIONALITY

The developments in states' drone programs discussed in the previous section form only part of the explanation for the individualization of self-defense posited in this chapter. The other part, which is the focus of the current section, involves a chain of propositions on how to interpret the right of self-defense against terrorists articulated by several states through the past two decades. This chain of propositions about the conditions and limits of self-defense is reasonably viewed as having expanded that right relative to an earlier series of propositions.[74] What has not been directly shown is the interconnectedness of these limitations. Yet, the co-dependence of these limitations is clear, to the extent that accepting some of

73. Loi de Programmation Militaire 2019–2025, *supra* note 3.

74. Christian Tams & James Devaney, *Applying Necessity and Proportionality to Anti-Terrorist Self-Defence*, 45 Isr. L. Rev. 91 (2012).

the proposed modifications to the different conditions of self-defense necessarily entails accepting others. So, even if many accept the proposed extensions of self-defense only partially, I suggest that the implications of such a choice necessarily entail greater consequences. The result of this cascade effect is the emergence of a right of self-defense that does not respond to threatening material circumstances but rather to threatening individuals in anticipation of their acts. The principle of proportionality, as ultimately suggested, is somewhat unique compared to the other elements because its very nature ends up being fully reshaped through the process rather than "merely" extended like the other conditions of self-defense.

A. The Extension of Self-Defense Conditions in a Cascade

Article 51 of the U.N. Charter provides that the right of self-defense is triggered by an armed attack. To date, although the initial restrictive interpretation of the armed attack criterion is challenged in some respects, several conditions for an armed attack to trigger a right to self-defense remain hardly contestable. The content of these conditions, however, may be evolving. The purpose here is not to describe what has been accepted as *lex lata*. Rather, it is to show that even if some elements of the chain of propositions formulated by a handful of states have not been accepted as such, accepting the extension of one of the conditions of self-defense tends to affect the other conditions in cascade. Going through each limitation of self-defense will bring their interconnected nature to light. I will start with the armed *ratione personae* limitation, followed by the *ratione materiae* limitation and *ratione temporis* limitation. The *ratione conditionis* limitation, the peak of the phenomenon, will be the object of section III.B. See Figure 5.1.

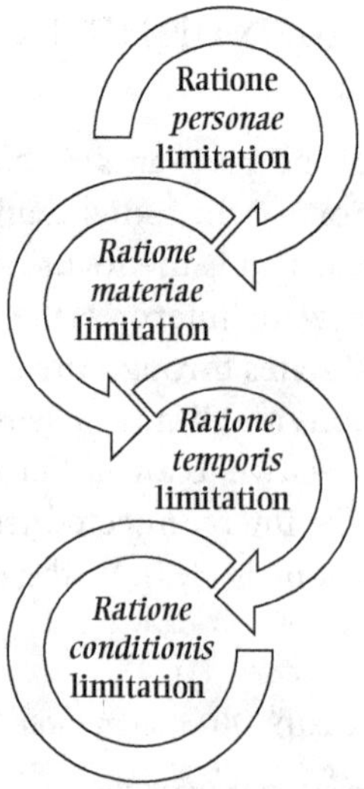

Figure 5.1. The interconnectedness of self-defense conditions

1. *Ratione Personae* Limitation: The Status of the Armed Attack Perpetrator, Link of Attribution, and "Unwilling/Unable"

The long-standing discussion concerning the *ratione personae* limitation of the right of self-defense, which predates 9/11[75] and goes beyond the link of attribution, concerns the necessary level of involvement of the host state when the litigious armed attack is perpetrated by non-state actors. My aim here is not to dive into this debate, which includes the evolution of the International Court of Justice's (ICJ) case law of this *ratione personae* requirement. This has been done with great care and scrupulousness elsewhere.[76] Rather, my goal is to focus on the reasoning used to argue that armed attacks perpetrated by jihadist non-state actors post 9/11 fall within the permissible bounds of the *ratione personae* limitation.

At the outset, it should be briefly noted that it is now widely accepted that non-state armed attacks can meet the *ratione personae* requirement, under certain conditions. However, these conditions are debated. In the *Nicaragua* case, the ICJ established that for the conduct of irregular forces to be attributable to a state, that state has to exercise "effective control [over] the military or paramilitary operations" that are carried out by the non-state group against another state.[77] Accordingly, only non-state actors' attacks that are effectively controlled by a foreign state can make the right of self-defense available to the victim state.[78] In a series of ulterior cases, the ICJ referred to its *Nicaragua* decision,[79] and maintained a requirement for a link of attribution between the host state and the non-state armed attack. In its 2004 *Wall* Advisory Opinion, the Court reaffirmed that Article 51 applied only to "an armed attack by one State against another State."[80]

75. Claus Kress, Gewaltverbot und Selbstverteidigungsrecht nach der Satzung der Vereinten Nationen bei staatlicher Verwicklung in Gewaltakte Privater (1995); Yoram Dinstein, War, Aggression and Self-Defense (1988).

76. Claus Kreß, *The International Court of Justice and the "Principle of Non-Use of Force," in* The Oxford Handbook of the Use of Force in International Law 561 (Marc Weller ed., 2015).

77. Military and Paramilitary Activities in and Against Nicaragua (Nicar. v. U.S.), Judgment, 1986 I.C.J. Rep. 14, ¶¶ 109, 115 (June 27); *id.* at 181, ¶ 17 (separate opinion of Ago, J.).

78. The effective control test has been subject to much discussion and is therefore covered in much of the literature. *See, e.g.*, Christian Henderson, *Non-State Actors and the Use of Force, in* Non-State Actors in International Law 88–89 (Math Noortmann, August Reinisch, & Cedric Ryngaert eds., 2015); Application of the Convention on the Prevention and Punishment of the Crime of Genocide (Bosn. & Herz. v. Serb. & Montenegro), Judgment, 2007 I.C.J. 241, ¶¶ 36–39 (Feb. 26) (dissenting opinion of Al-Khasawneh, J.); *id.* at 381, ¶¶ 113–17 (dissenting opinion of Mahiou, J.); *see also* 2 Indep. Int'l Fact-Finding Mission on the Conflict in Georgia, Report 260 (Sept. 2009).

79. *See, e.g.*, Application of the Convention on the Prevention and Punishment of the Crime of Genocide (Bosn. & Herz. v. Serb. & Montenegro), Judgment, 2007 I.C.J. 43, ¶ 391 (Feb. 26).

80. Legal Consequences of the Construction of a Wall in the Occupied Palestinian Territory, Advisory Opinion, 2004 I.C.J. Rep. 136, ¶ 139, at 195 (July 9).

Because there was no state to whom the discussed non-state actions could be attributed (Israel being the occupying power) Article 51 was deemed inapplicable. In the *DRC v. Uganda* case, the ICJ reaffirmed the necessity to attribute the acts perpetrated by non-state actors, which on another note could not be considered as constituting armed attacks in that case, to a state.[81] In the same vein, in the *Genocide* case, the Court defined the link of attribution as "acting on behalf of the state" by stating the following:

> Persons, groups of persons or entities may, for purposes of international responsibility, be equated with State organs even if that status does not follow from internal law, provided that in fact the persons, groups or entities act in "complete dependence" on the State, of which they are ultimately merely the instrument.[82]

According to this case law, for a non-state armed attack to qualify as an armed attack in the sense of Article 51, the non-state armed attack has to be attributed to another state under rather demanding rules of attribution. However, the alternative link of attribution of "effective control" used in *Nicaragua* is uncertain enough to engender discussion of a looser connection between the host state and the threatening non-state actors.[83]

There are some convincing arguments in support of the departure from a more restrictive interpretation of Article 51, starting with the fact that this article does not require that the armed attack be perpetrated by a state actor.[84] Indeed, the terminology used by Article 2(4), which speaks of a use of force by one "Member"

81. Armed Activities on the Territory of the Congo (Dem. Rep. Congo v. Uganda), Judgment, 2005 I.C.J. Rep. 168, ¶ 146, at 223 (Dec. 19) ("The attacks did not emanate from armed bands or irregulars sent by the DRC or on behalf of the DRC, within the sense of Article 3 (g) of General Assembly resolution 3314 (XXIX) on the definition of aggression, adopted on 14 December 1974. The Court is of the view that, on the evidence before it, even if this series of deplorable attacks could be regarded as cumulative in character, they still remained non-attributable to the DRC.").

82. *Bosn. & Herz. v. Serb. & Montenegro, supra* note 80, ¶ 392.

83. Kreß, *supra* note 76, at 584 ("Those requirements are, in the alternative, the complete dependence of a group of violent non-state actors on the support of the state concerned or the latter's effective control over the specific forcible actions carried out from within such a group. The 'harbouring' by a state of transnationally violent non-state actors on its territory, to take one specific and recently much discussed example, would seem to fall into that grey area.").

84. On this posture, *see* Claus Kreß, *The Fine Line Between Collective Self-Defense and Intervention by Invitation: Reflections on the Use of Force against IS in Syria*, JUST SECURITY (Feb. 17, 2015), https://www.justsecurity.org/20118/claus-kreb-force-isil-syria; Sean Murphy, *Terrorism and the Concept of "Armed Attack" in Article 51 of the UN Charter*, 43 HARV. INT'L L.J. 41, 50 (2002). For a seemingly more hesitant acceptance of non-state armed attacks entering the scope of Article 51, *see* Human Rights Council, *supra* note 7, ¶ 40. Alston is not drawing any conclusion on whether Article 51's armed attacks criterion includes attacks perpetrated by

against "any state" is not reiterated in Article 51. I agree with the argument that "there is nothing in Article 51 of the U.N. Charter that requires the exercise of self-defence to turn on whether an armed attack was committed directly by another state."[85] In addition to the letter of the norm, its purpose also excludes such a requirement. Given that Article 51 aims at exceptionally allowing states to use force when they face an attack that gravely endangers their security, and given that armed attacks perpetrated by non-state actors can actually reach this level of threat, the most relevant interpretation is that it can actually comprise the armed attacks of non-state actors.[86]

However, I also believe that establishing some sort of link of attribution, even a loose and indirect one, is in line with the U.N. Charter's logic.[87] Unless the principles of sovereign equality, non-use of force, and territorial integrity are depreciated, I do not see how the attribution logic can be replaced for instance by a balancing test between basic rights of physical persons and rights of innocent legal entities as suggested by Eliav Lieblich, even if this option is appealing from a normative standpoint.[88] At the same time, I argue that "unwilling or unable" can be considered as a link of attribution, as also comes out, it seems to me, from the compelling reasoning articulated by Lieblich on state fault.

Before I explain why I think "unwilling or unable" is a link of attribution and is, in my view because of this, receiving increasing support,[89] some elements must be recalled. First, the criterion of unwillingness or inability of the host state to counter the terrorist attacks that are perpetrated from its territory to recognize a

non-state actors. However, he underlines that "it will only be in very rare circumstances that a non-state actor whose activities do not engage the responsibility of any State will be able to conduct the kind of armed attack that would give rise to the right to use extraterritorial force."

85. Murphy, *supra* note 84, at 50.

86. Ashley Deeks, *Unwilling or Unable, Toward a Normative Framework for Extraterritorial Self-Defence*, 52 Va. J. Int'l L. 483, 493 (2012).

87. On the contrary, some scholars consider that attacks committed by non-state actors without any link of attribution to the state may constitute armed attacks under Article 51. *See, e.g.*, Thomas M. Franck, *Terrorism and the Right of Self-Defense*, 95 Am. J. Int'l L. 839, 840 (2001); Christopher Greenwood, *International Law and the Preemptive Use of Force: Afghanistan, al-Qaida, and Iraq*, 4 San Diego Int'l L.J. 7, 17 (2003); Raphaël Van Steenberghe, *Self-Defence in Response to Attacks by Non-State Actors in the Light of Recent State Practice: A Step Forward?*, 23 Leiden J. Int'l L. 183, 184 (2010); Dinstein, *supra* note 75, at 214.

88. Eliav Lieblich, *Self-Defense Against Non-State Actors and the Myth of the Innocent State*, *in* Global Governance and Human Rights (Nehal Bhuta & Rodrigo Vallejo eds., forthcoming OUP 2020).

89. Some scholars still very strictly interpret the armed attack criterion of Article 51. Olivier Corten, The Law Against War: The Prohibition on the Use of Force in Contemporary International Law ch. 7, § 1 (2012); Antonio Cassese, *The International Community's "Legal" Response to Terrorism*, 38 Int'l & Comp. L.Q. 589, 597 (1989). Eric Myjer & Nigel White, *The Twin Towers Attack: An Unlimited Right to Self-Defense*, 7 J. Conflict & Security L. 5, 7 (2002).

right of self-defense against non-state armed attacks was set forth by states and by scholars but was never endorsed (although neither was it rejected) by the ICJ.[90] Second, it is important to note that the doctrine predates 9/11 (and as such is not specific to use of force in the counterterrorism context) and was used as justification for action by numerous states as a trigger of the right to self-defense against non-state armed attacks.[91]

According to the "unwilling or unable" logic, a right to self-defense against non-state actors would exist if the foreign state is either supportive of the activities of terrorists or unable to stop them.[92] The reason why I think this logic can be characterized as an attribution link, although lenient and indirect, is that in the first scenario, the unwilling state still bears the fault of willingly letting non-state actors threaten the victim state, and the second scenario is a fantasy. In particular, the unable state that would allegedly be willing to counter the threat if able to, but simultaneously criticize a third state intervention, is a myth. A truly willing but unable state would either seek third-state support or at least consent to a third-state intervention, if not explicitly and prior to the intervention in self-defense, then implicitly or without contestation afterward. We could thereby easily exit the self-defense paradigm as there would be no violation of sovereignty. If on the contrary intervention within an unable state poses a diplomatic problem, such a host state could fairly be considered unwilling to address the threat posed by non-state actors from its territory.[93] Thus, for other reasons than those developed by Lieblich, I hereby suggest that the willing but unable state triggering a right of

90. Strong normative arguments against the "unwilling or unable" test are rare. For an exception, *see* Olivier Corten, *The "Unwilling or Unable" Test: Has It Been, and Could It Be, Accepted?*, 29 LEIDEN J. INT'L L. 777 (2016). Otherwise, *see, e.g.*, CHATHAM HOUSE, PRINCIPLES OF INTERNATIONAL LAW ON THE USE OF FORCE BY STATES IN SELF-DEFENCE ¶ 6 (2006), *reprinted in* 55 INT'L & COMP. L.Q. 963 (2006). For a more recent example, *see* N. Schrijver & L. van den Herik, *Leiden Policy Recommendations on Counter-terrorism and International Law*, 57 NETH. Y.B. INT'L L. 531 (2010).

91. For a detailed account and analysis of state practice and scholarly work in support and against this doctrine, *see* KRESS, *supra* note 75; *see also* Deeks, *supra* note 86, at 486–87. On Israel's practice, *see* TOM RUYS, "ARMED ATTACK" AND ARTICLE 51 OF THE UN CHARTER 421–28 (2010). For U.S. practice, *see* Permanent Rep. of the U.S. to the U.N., Letter Dated Sept. 23, 2014 from the Permanent Rep. of the U.S. to the U.N. Addressed to the Secretary-General, U.N. Doc. S/2014/695 (Sept. 23, 2014) ("ISIL and other terrorist groups in Syria are a threat not only to Iraq, but also to many other countries, including the United States and our partners in the region and beyond. States must be able to defend themselves, in accordance with the inherent right of individual and collective self-defence, as reflected in Article 51 of the Charter of the United Nations, when, as is the case here, the government of the State where the threat is located is unwilling or unable to prevent the use of its territory for such attacks.").

92. Deeks, *supra* note 86, at 486 ("More than a century of state practice suggests that it is lawful for State X, which has suffered an armed attack by an insurgent or terrorist group, to use force in State Y against that group if State Y is unwilling or unable to suppress the threat.").

93. In his forthcoming paper quoted previously, Eliav Lieblich expresses the idea that "[i]n effect, this view constructs the problem of self-defense against non-state actors as a crude form of

self-defense is a myth. Understood as such, the unwilling test, as well as what we could call, instead of "unable," the "unable *and* unwilling" test, correspond in my view to an attribution link between the host state and non-state armed attack as it recognizes state fault.

Following this analysis, the "unwilling and unable" test not only appears overall in line with the U.N. Charter's logic but also compatible with the ICJ case law requiring a link of attribution. Even if it would entail accepting a much more flexible connection between the host state and the threat posed by non-state actors from its territory, it would not be surprising to see the ICJ embrace the "unwilling and unable" test if it was clearly defined as analyzed here. This also could potentially reconcile differences among judges within the ICJ. While on the one hand the ICJ as a whole maintains that Article 51 requires an attribution link,[94] Judges Koojimans and Simma, who argued in favor of an express acceptance of non-state armed attacks in separate individual opinions, could very well be satisfied with the indirect and loose attribution link that an "unwilling and unable" test would require.[95]

To summarize, this possibility of defining "unwilling and unable" as an attribution link is in theory compatible both with maintaining the cornerstone principles of the international legal order (even if the principle of sovereign equality can be considerably harmed by such test if left undefined and open-textured), and with the (legally sound and reasonable) inclination to include non-state armed attacks within the scope of Article 51. I think it is because of this that a broad range of actors have shown interest, if not expressed approval, of the "unwilling and unable" doctrine. From scholars to U.N. special rapporteurs, such as Philip Alston,

an 'innocent threat' dilemma: the state's territory is being used by the non-state actor—against its will—to stage attacks against other states; but a response against the non-state actor will inevitably violate the innocent state's territory." Lieblich, *supra* note 88, at 4. To use Lieblich's vocabulary, but contrarily to what he and others consider, I believe that a response against the non-state actor does not violate the innocent state's territory if this state is indeed innocent (only unable).

94. Legal Consequences of the Construction of a Wall in the Occupied Palestinian Territory, Advisory Opinion, 2004 I.C.J. Rep. 136, ¶ 139, at 194 (July 9) (Article 51 recognizes the existence of an inherent right of self-defence in the case of an armed attack by one state against another. Since Israel did not claim that the attacks against it were imputable to a foreign state, however, Article 51 of the Charter had no relevance in the case of the wall.).

95. Armed Activities on the Territory of the Congo (Dem. Rep. Congo v. Uganda), Judgment, 2005 I.C.J. Rep. 306, ¶ 30 (Dec. 19) (separate opinion of Kooijmans, J.) (According to Judge Koojimans "[I]f armed attacks are carried out by irregular bands from such territory against a neighbouring State, they are still armed attacks even if they cannot be attributed to the territorial State. It would be unreasonable to deny the attacked State the right to self-defence merely because there is no attacker State, and the Charter does not so require."); *see also id.* at 334, ¶ 11, at 337 (separate opinion of Simma, J.) (declaring, in line with Judge Koojimans' argument, that "in the light of more recent developments not only in State practice but also with regard to accompanying *opinio juris*, [reading of Article 51] ought urgently to be reconsidered, also by the Court").

it has been noted that the use of force by one state in the territory of another state does not violate the second state's sovereignty either if the second state consents, or if the first state acts under its right to self-defense because "the second State is unwilling or unable to stop armed attacks against the first State launched from its territory."[96] The compromise that "unwilling and unable" can in principle achieve also explains, in my view, that it successfully legitimized post-9/11 extraterritorial use of force against non-state actors.

The U.S. interpretation of the *ratione personae* criterion as only requiring "an assessment that the relevant governmental authorities in the country where action is contemplated cannot or will not effectively address the threat to U.S. persons"[97] arose in a context where it became common for states to identify non-state threats in other states' territories. The looser attribution link constituted by "unwilling and unable" was therefore welcomed. As a result of the intense scholarly discussion that took place under the Obama administration, when the United Kingdom and France adopted a similar criterion to that of the United States, it has largely remained uncontroverted. The legal claim that strikes in Syria were justified by President Assad's unwillingness to deal with the attacks carried out by ISIL has been formulated by the United States,[98] followed by the United Kingdom,[99] France,[100] and Australia.[101] In their report of May 10, 2016, the U.K. House of Commons and House of Lords approved the U.K. government's position that there is a right of self-defense against armed attacks by non-state actors "such as ISIL/Daesh" if there is evidence that "the Assad regime is unwilling and/or unable

96. Human Rights Council, *supra* note 7.

97. Office of the Press Secretary, White House, Fact Sheet: U.S. Policy Standards and Procedures for the Use of Force in Counterterrorism Operations Outside the United States and Areas of Active Hostilities (May 23, 2013), https://www.whitehouse.gov/the-press-office/2013/05/23/fact-sheet-us-policy-standards-and-procedures-use-force-counterterrorism.

98. Letter from the President Concerning the War Powers Resolution Regarding Iraq to the Speaker of the House of Representatives and the President Pro Tempore of the Senate (Sept. 23, 2014), https://www.whitehouse.gov/the-press-office/2014/09/23/letter-president-war-powers-resolution-regarding-iraq.

99. Prime Minister David Cameron's Questions, House of Commons Debate (Nov. 25, 2015), https://www.parliament.uk/business/news/2015/november/prime-ministers-questions-25-november-2015 (begin at 12-minute mark) (U.K.).

100. Discours du Président de la République Devant le Parlement Réuni en Congrès (Nov. 16, 2015), http://www.elysee.fr/declarations/article/discours-du-president-de-la-republique-devant-le-parlement-reuni-en-congres-3. Interestingly, France meets the elements used for categorization by Elena Chachko and Ashley Deeks. Elena Chachko & Ashley Deeks, *Which States Support the "Unwilling and Unable" Test?*, LAWFARE (Oct. 10, 2016), https://www.lawfareblog.com/which-states-support-unwilling-and-unable-test. In my view, they wrongly categorize France as an ambiguous case.

101. Permanent Rep. of Aust. To the U.N., Letter Dated Sept. 9, 2015 from the Permanent Rep. of Austl. to the U.N. Addressed to the President of the Security Council, U.N. Doc. S/2015/693 (Sept. 9, 2015).

to take action necessary to prevent ISIL's continuing attack on Iraq, or indeed attacks on [the United Kingdom]."[102] A few commentators have raised questions concerning the use of the "unwilling and unable" test in the Syrian case[103] and have discussed the actual fulfilment of the unwillingness or inability of the Syrian government to deal with the armed attacks perpetrated by Daesh,[104] without putting the use of the doctrine itself into question.

Even if "unwilling and unable" is not *lex lata* yet, it is reasonable to assert that it is growingly accepted among states and scholars that the *ratione personae* criterion of self-defense is met for non-state armed attacks if the "unwilling and unable" test is positive.[105] In my view, as explained earlier, it can also be considered in line with the ICJ case law even if it would require an explicit loosening of the attribution link. It might be made even more acceptable in the context of individualized conduct of warfare (facilitated by the use of drones as we saw previously). Because the strikes conducted by combat drones are conducted remotely, are preceded by a process of intimate surveillance of specific individuals, and conclude by precisely finishing the target, there might be an impression that the intrusion into state sovereignty is limited in comparison to more traditional uses of force. This conclusion might very well be inaccurate. But, as is worth underlining, individualized warfare and acute technological capacities might intensify the idea that contemporary warfare does not require the establishment of a close link of attribution, or even attributability at all, between the members of transnational terrorist networks and their host state(s). In light of these different factors—drones'

102. Joint Comm. on Hum. Rts., *supra* note 64, at 41.

103. Jennifer Daskal, Ashley Deeks, & Ryan Goodman, *Strikes in Syria: The International Law Framework*, Just Security (Sept. 24, 2014), https://www.justsecurity.org/15479/strikes-syria-international-law-framework-daskal-deeks-goodman; Nehal Bhuta, *On Preventive Killing*, EJIL: Talk! (Sept. 17, 2015), http://www.ejiltalk.org/on-preventive-killing/#more-13651.

104. Kreß, *supra* note 84. According to Professor Kreß, it is impossible to say that Syria is unwilling to deal with ISIL's attacks considering President Assad's offer to fight the Islamic State in Syria in coordination with the United States and its partners. However, he considers Syria to be unable to deal with it on its own. Yet, he joins with Ryan Goodman's opinion that the inability is not sufficient to authorize self-defense measures. He says that "[i]f the goal to end a non-State armed attack can be effectively achieved through coordinated military action with the territorial State, then, in principle, this avenue must be pursued because it reconciles the needs to protect the sovereignty both of the victim and the territorial State. It follows, that, again in principle, the right of collective self-defense in case of a non-State attack is subsidiary to 'intervention by invitation.'" *Id.*; *see also* Ryan Goodman, *International Law on Airstrikes against ISIS in Syria*, Just Security (Aug. 28, 2014), https://www.justsecurity.org/14414/international-law-airstrikes-isis-syria.

105. This reasoning has been suggested in general by Malcolm Shaw. Malcolm N. Shaw, International Law 89 (6th ed. 2008) ("Generally, where states are seen to acquiesce in the behaviour of other states without protesting against them, the assumption must be that such behaviour is accepted as legitimate."); *see also* Monica Hakimi, *Defensive Force against Non-State Actors: The State of Play*, 91 Int'l L. Stud. 31 (2015); Bethlehem, *supra* note 35, at 773; Michael J. Glennon, *How International Rules Die*, 93 Geo. L.J. 939, 960 (2005).

technological capacities, the emergence of a new type of non-state actors, and the military strategy to fight transnational enemy groups—the initial strict necessity of linking the targets to the host state not only appears strategically undesirable but also practically and legally irrelevant to an increasing number of actors.

Finally, regarding the *ratione personae* requirement, it is necessary to underline that the *ad bellum* framework, other than international humanitarian law (IHL), does not establish any group-related requirement. While certain IHL criteria exist to avoid overinclusive characterization of non-international armed conflicts, in particular the requirement that the non-state group be sufficiently organized, the right of self-defense can be triggered even by one individual who is identified as posing a threat (the characteristics of which will be explored later). In addition, the right of self-defense applies without territorial limitation as it does not require any other contextual element than the forthcoming armed attack, and as long as—if we apply the above-mentioned reasoning—the host state is identified as unwilling and unable to address the threat. In this, if the "unwilling and unable" doctrine is accepted, I am not convinced that we can speak of a territorial limitation of the right of self-defense that would prevent defensive force against threats posed by transnational terrorist networks. Inasmuch as members of the violent non-state group or network are present on the territory of a state that is not willing to address the threat, a right of self-defense would legitimize violating the host state's sovereignty.

2. *Ratione Materiae* Limitation: The Armed Attack Requirement and the Accumulation Doctrine

If states are to address threats posed by transnational terrorist networks by resorting to the right of self-defense, we cannot ignore the features that characterize these threats. In other words, once one includes armed attacks perpetrated by non-state actors in the scope of self-defense through a link of attribution which is as loose and uncertain as "unwilling or unable," in situations that concern terrorist transnational networks, one has to consider adapting self-defense to the modes of action of these actors. The accumulation doctrine has developed over the past decades precisely because it is adapted to the use of force against threats posed by transnational terrorist networks.

The traditional interpretation of the *ratione materiae* limitation first entails that in order to give rise to a right of self-defense, the attack must be an armed attack. Therefore, it does not comprise economic or ideological aggressions. Secondly, the armed attack must present a certain degree of gravity and one has "to distinguish the most grave forms of the use of force (those constituting an armed attack) from other less grave forms."[106] A minor use of force that violates Article 2(4), even if it entails its author's responsibility, does not necessarily allow its victim

106. Military and Paramilitary Activities in and Against Nicaragua (Nicar. v. U.S.), Judgment, 1986 I.C.J. Rep. 14, ¶ 191 (June 27); Oil Platforms (Iran v. U.S.), Judgment, 2003 I.C.J. Rep. 161, ¶¶ 51, 64 (Nov. 6).

to respond with defensive force. It is important to note that there is an emerging view in the literature that the intensity requirement for non-state armed attacks should be more demanding.[107] However, this qualitative threshold, even when it is defined in more stringent terms, seems to be replaced by a quantitative one in light of the increasingly accepted accumulation of events doctrine. Therefore, although the introduction of a stricter intensity threshold could seem at first glance as a potential barrier against the cascade effect described here, the growing prominence of the accumulation of events doctrine seems to pull the evolution in the opposite direction.

Instead of having to identify one grave armed attack, the accumulation of events doctrine as discussed by the litigants in the *DRC–Uganda*[108] and *Oil Platforms*[109] cases entails that the armed attack criterion is fulfilled by the existence of "a series of minor incidents, taken together, [which] can be said to reach the threshold of an armed attack."[110] In other words, the doctrine admits a large-scale response both to a continuous series of attacks of a certain gravity and to less grave uses of force which amount to an armed attack when forming part of a chain of events.[111] Notably, in addition to the many occasions where states invoked the accumulation of events theory,[112] the ICJ has not explicitly rejected it, and, in the *Oil Platforms* case, the Court can even be considered to have implicitly followed the argument of the United States that the attacks should be considered together.[113]

107. Chatham House, *supra* note 90, ¶ 6; Schrijver & van den Herik, *supra* note 90, ¶¶ 38, 86; Claus Kreß, *Some Reflections on the International Legal Framework Governing Transnational Armed Conflicts*, 15 J. Conflict & Security L. 251 (2010); UN Gen. Assembly, Secretary-General's Transmission to the Gen. Assembly of the Report of the Special Rapporteur on Extrajudicial, Summary or Arbitrary Executions, ¶ 89, U.N. Doc. A/68/382 (Sept. 13, 2013).

108. Armed Activities on the Territory of the Congo (Dem. Rep. Congo v. Uganda), Judgment, 2005 I.C.J. Rep. 168, ¶ 146, at 223 (Dec. 19).

109. *Iran v. U.S.*, *supra* note 106.

110. Christian J. Tams, *The Use of Force against Terrorists*, 20 Eur. J. Int'l L. 388 (2009); *Iran v. U.S.*, *supra* note 106, ¶ 64 ("On the hypothesis that all the incidents complained of are to be attributed to Iran, and thus setting aside the question, examined above, of attribution to Iran of the specific attack on the Sea Isle City, the question is whether that attack, either in itself or in combination with the rest of the 'series of . . . attacks' cited by the United States can be categorized as an 'armed attack' on the United States justifying self-defence.").

111. Ruys, *supra* note 91, at 168.

112. *See, e.g.*, U.N. SCOR, 749th mtg., ¶¶ 33–39, U.N. Doc. S/PV.749 (Oct. 30, 1956) (Israel); *id.* ¶¶ 154–73 (France); *id.* ¶ 37 (Australia). For further examples and deeper analysis, *see* Ruys, *supra* note 91.

113. In the *Oil Platforms* case, even if the ICJ did not conclude that the incidents it analyzed constituted an armed attack, the judges were ready to "take them cumulatively" to conduct the qualification. Oil Platforms (Iran v. U.S.), Judgment, 2003 I.C.J. Rep. 161, ¶¶ 46–64 (Nov. 6). For concurring view and more detailed analysis, *see* Kreß, *supra* note 76, at 582 ("The question would lose some practical significance were the ICJ to finally endorse, as it seemed inclined to do in the *Oil Platforms* case as well as in the *Armed Activities* case, some form of accumulation

Recently, the U.N. Security Council, in its Resolution 2249 (2015), included what appears as an extensive version of the accumulation of events doctrine. It condemned

> the horrifying terrorist attacks perpetrated by ISIL also known as Da'esh which took place on 26 June 2015 in Sousse, on 10 October 2015 in Ankara, on 31 October 2015 over Sinaï, on 12 November 2015 in Beirut and on 13 November 2015 in Paris, and all other attacks perpetrated by ISIL also known as Da'esh, including hostage-taking and killing, and *notes* it has the capability and intention to carry out further attacks and regards all such acts of terrorism as a threat to peace and security.[114]

The threat is assessed based on past events revealing a continuing threat and the propensity of group members to maintain this posture of hostility. If this definition of "threat" is endorsed as a way of framing the armed attack requirement and the accumulation doctrine in self-defense, an additional step would be taken in the extension of this right. Indeed, it goes even further than the initial idea that "a series of minor incidents, taken together, can be said to reach the threshold of an armed attack." It means that action in self-defense could be taken on the basis of *past* hostile activity and the propensity of a group's members to maintain this posture of hostility. Some states have actually referred to this reasoning. Former U.K. Prime Minister David Cameron stated that it is clear "that ISIL's campaign against the U.K. and our allies has reached the level of an 'armed attack,' such that force may lawfully be used in self-defence to prevent further atrocities being committed by ISIL."[115] The validity of this more lenient interpretation of the armed attack criterion was affirmed on May 10, 2016, by the U.K. House of Lords and House of Commons' Joint Committee on Human Rights in their report on the government's policy on the use of drones for targeted killing.[116]

Former French President François Hollande, then Prime Minister Manuel Valls, and Minister of Defence Jean-Yves le Drian also built upon the right to self-defense for the strikes in Syria.[117] They argued that France may legitimately act

of events doctrine for the purpose of measuring gravity in cases of a series of attacks."); *see also* Tams, *supra* note 110, at 388.

114. S.C. Res. 2249 (Nov. 20, 2015).

115. UK House of Commons Debate, Questions Asked to Attorney General (Nov. 26, 2015), https://publications.parliament.uk/pa/cm201516/cmhansrd/cm151126/debtext/151126-0001.htm.

116. Joint Comm. on Hum. Rts., *supra* note 64, at 44.

117. Manuel Valls, Discours de Manuel Valls Devant l'Assemblée Nationale [Speech on the Operation in Syria in Front of Parliament] (Sept. 15, 2015), http://www.gouvernement.fr/syrie-la-france-est-en-guerre-contre-le-terrorisme-le-djihadisme-l-islamisme-radical-ce-sera-long-2873 ("Il s'agit ainsi d'identifier et de localiser le dispositif de Daech pour être en mesure de le frapper sur le sol syrien et d'exercer ainsi notre droit à la légitime défense, comme

under the right to self-defense to conduct strikes in Syria because of the attacks that are organized and perpetrated by ISIL members from Syria "against France and other countries."[118] On September 9, 2015, France addressed a letter to the Security Council, stating that

> [i]n accordance with Article 51 of the Charter of the United Nations, France has taken actions involving the participation of military aircraft in response to attacks carried out by ISIL from the territory of the Syrian Arab Republic.[119]

In the Bethlehem Principles,[120] and also in the DOJ White Paper, the U.K. Attorney General's January 2017 speech,[121] and the Australian Attorney General's Speech of June 2017,[122] it is apparent that the assessment of the threat draws on a behavioral diagnosis of the propensities of hostile individuals to act.

Turning the armed attack requirement into an identification of hostile intent on the basis of past attacks practically marks the departure from uses of force to face material circumstances: instead of using self-defense to repel a material threat, self-defense is used under this rationale to eliminate threatening individuals. As such, the proposed interpretation of the material condition of self-defense very well corresponds to the two scenarios of drone strikes that can be deduced from the practice, namely, drone strikes in targeted killings and in signature strikes, both of which focus on individual characteristics and not on current or forthcoming actions such as preparing or carrying out an attack meeting the threshold of an armed attack requirement. First, signature strikes are based on a suspicion of affiliation to a group identified as carrying a hostile intent, and this suspicion is deduced from an unusual feature in the pattern of life of the target. Second, drones are used in targeted killings against individuals who have been identified not necessarily as being involved in preparing imminent attacks, but at least as having committed in the past or showing signs they might commit attacks in the future.[123]

le prévoit l'article 51 de la Charte des Nations unies"); French National Assembly, Declaration of the Government on the Aerial Operations in Syria (Sept. 15, 2015), http://www.assemblee-nationale.fr/14/cri/2014-2015-extra2/20152001.asp.

118. 6th Press Conference of French President François Hollande (Sept. 7, 2015), https://www.youtube.com/watch?v=m6Gn59Zzk1g (begin at 9-minute mark).

119. Permanent Rep. of Fr. to the U.N., Identical Letters Dated Sept. 8, 2015 from the Permanent Rep. of Fr. to the U.N. Addressed to the Secretary-General and the President of the Security Council, U.N. Doc. S/2015/745 (Sept. 9, 2015).

120. Bethlehem, *supra* note 35, at 773.

121. Wright, *supra* note 35.

122. Brandis, *supra* note 35.

123. Human Rights Council, *supra* note 7, ¶ 40.

There remains, however, a possible barrier against a full-fledged dematerialized use of force in self-defense that is detached from the material circumstances and focused merely on individual hostile intents. This barrier lies in the idea that "in the case of a series of non-State attacks over time, none of which is large-scale of its own, a State may have recourse to self-defence if it can demonstrate that the attacks emanate from the same non-state group."[124] While force in self-defense generally can be used against individuals without any formally required consideration related to the group to which they belong, the accumulation of events doctrine could logically impose an obligation to identify a link between these accumulated events. Such link could very well be a group affiliation. Practically speaking, it would not halt the evolution toward accepting the accumulation of events doctrine, but it would make it less extensive. This requirement has to be further discussed and supported, as well as formally endorsed by the ICJ to concretely perform a restrictive function.

3. *Ratione Temporis* Limitation: Addressing Continuing Imminent Threats

The previous proposition about the *ratione materiae* condition of self-defense inevitably entails a temporal modification in comparison to a "responsive" version of self-defense. Responsive self-defense describes the use of force in response to an armed attack that may be completed or may still be ongoing, but which in any case, as Ruys points out, is "an observable fact of reality."[125] "Anticipatory" self-defense could include two very different kinds of self-defense: preemptive and preventive self-defense.[126] Preemptive self-defense refers to the use of force against an attack that has not occurred yet, but which is "imminent": the threat is "instant, overwhelming, leaving no choice of means and no moment for deliberation."[127] Preventive self-defense covers the use of force that seeks to counter several potential future attacks, even without any concrete indication that those attacks will actually occur. It seeks to prevent a prospective threat from becoming imminent.[128]

The legality of preemptive self-defense is already controversial in light of the wording of Article 51 of U.N. Charter.[129] Indeed, it entails to depart from the

124. Kreß, *supra* note 107, at 249; Tams, *supra* note 110, at 388.

125. Ruys, *supra* note 91, at 253.

126. *Id.*

127. For an explanation of the *Caroline* incident, *see* Matthew Allen Fitzgerald, Note, *Seizing Weapons of Mass Destruction from Foreign-Flagged Ships on the High Seas under Article 51 of the UN Charter*, 49 Va. J. Int'l L. 473, 477–79 (2009); Deeks, *supra* note 86, at 502 (quoting Fitzgerald's note).

128. Ruys, *supra* note 91, at 254.

129. Claus Kreß, *Extraterritorial Targeted Killings of non-State Actors by States in Response to Transnational non-State Violence, in* Targeted Killing, Unmanned Aerial Vehicles and EU Policy 3, ¶ 8 (Robert Schuman Centre for Advanced Studies Policy Papers 2013/17, 2013). For a detailed view of Article 51 as only including one form of self-defense, namely, in response to an

"inherently defensive character of the right"[130] as the armed attack is not an observable fact of reality yet; rather, it is anticipated. Yet this is not the main concern of this chapter. What I want to underline is that the accumulation of events doctrine not only affects the *ratione materiae* limitation of the armed attack criterion, but that it actually—and even more importantly—widens the temporal scope of the right of self-defense. This once more demonstrates the interconnectedness of the different conditions of that right.[131] Accepting the accumulation of events doctrine without carefully defining it, or expressly endorsing the backward-looking version of the accumulation of events doctrine, risks leading to a perpetuation of the time frame during which the right of self-defense may be exercised against a threat from a non-state armed group.[132]

For this reason, the Security Council took an important step in its Resolution 2249 (2015).[133] Joining and validating state practice and rhetoric, it considered that the accumulation of past attacks committed by ISIL in Sousse, in Ankara, over the Sinai, in Beirut, and in Paris revealed that ISIL has "the capability and intention to carry out further attacks."[134] Under this framework, it is not necessary to demonstrate that the threat is "instant, overwhelming, leaving no choice of means and no moment for deliberation." In affirming that an accumulation of past events can reveal a continuing threat of the non-state actors, the Council opened the door more widely to embrace the idea of a "permanent imminence" of the threat of armed attack.[135]

The idea that the right of self-defense is triggered because of the continuous imminence of the threat posed by certain individuals is not an American specificity. The U.K. drone strike against British national Reyaad Khan on August 24, 2014, initiated a discussion on the United Kingdom's interpretation of self-defense and showed that state practice beyond the United States could expand further the condition of imminence of self-defense. Early in the discussion, for instance when David Cameron made his first statement to the House of Commons, he did not specifically identify an imminent attack that the strike aimed to repel:[136]

armed attack, *see* Yoram Dinstein, War, Aggression and Self-Defence 67 (5th ed. 2011); Christine Gray, International Law and the Use of Force 480 (3d ed. 2008).

130. Tams, *supra* note 110, at 389.

131. *Id.* at 390.

132. Marc Weller, *Permanent Imminence of Armed Attacks: Resolution 2249 (2015) and the Right to Self Defence Against Designated Terrorist Groups*, EJIL: Talk! (Nov. 25, 2015), http://www.ejiltalk.org/permanent-imminence-of-armed-attacks-resolution-2249-2015-and-the-right-to-self-defence-against-designated-terrorist-groups.

133. *Id.*

134. S.C. Res. 2249, *supra* note 114, ¶ 1.

135. Weller, *supra* note 132.

136. David Cameron, Prime Minster, Oral Statement to Parliament Concerning Refugees and Counter-terrorism in Syria (Sept. 7, 2015), https://www.gov.uk/government/speeches/syria-refugees-and-counter-terrorism-prime-ministers-statement.

> Both Junaid Hussain and Reyaad Khan were British nationals based in Syria who were involved in actively recruiting ISIL sympathisers and seeking to orchestrate specific and barbaric attacks against the West, including directing a number of planned terrorist attacks right here in Britain, such as plots to attack high profile public commemorations, including those taking place this summer.

The language that David Cameron used in order to identify the attacks planned by Reyaad Khan remained indeterminate and the justification otherwise focused on the role played by Junaid Hussain and Reyaad Khan within ISIS. When analyzing this episode, we have to bear in mind that the requirements of national security could partly explain the lack of clarity and precision of official pronouncements on such matters. This cautions against deducing from this statement, without further consideration, that the United Kingdom was using force in self-defense against individuals for the threat they could pose in the future. However, the U.K. government later made it clear that "it favours a more flexible approach to the meaning of 'imminence,' to include an ongoing threat of a terrorist attack from an identified individual who has both the intent and the capability to carry out such an attack without notice."[137]

In his 2017 speech at the International Institute for Strategic Studies, the U.K. Attorney General Jeremy Wright directly referred to Bethlehem's principle and insisted on Principle 8 as endorsed by the British government:

> Another observation by Sir Daniel, as part of Principle 8 addressing imminence, also warrants comment, namely:
>
> "[t]he absence of specific evidence of where an attack will take place or of the precise nature of an attack does not preclude a conclusion that an armed attack is imminent for purposes of the exercise of a right of self-defence, provided that there is a reasonable and objective basis for concluding that an armed attack is imminent."
>
> This statement reflects and draws upon what has been a settled position of successive British Governments. Sir Daniel's formulation must be right. In a world where a small number of committed plotters may be seeking to inspire, enable and direct attacks around the world, and indeed have a proven track record of doing so, we will not always know where and when an attack will take place, or the precise nature of the attack.[138]

Hence, the United Kingdom has also endorsed a position which allows it to respond proactively to a "continuous imminent threat" by looking backward at an accumulation of events revealing the hostile intent of a terrorist network. By accepting that the use of force against terrorists cannot depend on the identification

137. JOINT COMM. ON HUM. RTS., *supra* note 64, ¶ 3.33.

138. Wright, *supra* note 35.

of a precise armed attack, self-defense is not only dematerialized and focused on individuals as previously shown but also takes de facto an anticipatory turn. Even if preventive self-defense is still officially widely rejected, accepting one of the previous propositions almost inevitably results in a cascade effect. The extension of the *ratione personae* condition affects the *ratione materiae* condition, which in turn impacts the *ratione temporis* requirement in a way that has not yet been fully recognized. Ultimately, it is the *ratione conditionis* requirement, namely, the necessity and proportionality criteria,[139] that epitomizes the metamorphosis of the objective of self-defense, from repelling threatening material acts to eliminating threatening individuals.

B. The Metamorphosis of the *Ratione Conditionis* Limitation: Proportionality to the Threat Posed by a Terrorist Network

Even though the conditions of proportionality and necessity are not expressly mentioned in Article 51 of the U.N. Charter, their existence under customary law has regularly been confirmed by the ICJ.[140] "Traditional self-defense" is used here to refer to the context where force in self-defense is used only to halt and repel an identified armed attack. Traditionally, then, the principle of necessity requires that the state attacked—or threatened with imminent attack—must not have had any means of halting the attack other than recourse to the armed force. The principle of proportionality entails that the attacked or threatened state must not have had any means of halting the attack other than recourse to this scale of armed force. If the attack could have been halted by using force on a lesser scale, the response is disproportionate. In other words, the whole necessity and proportionality test revolves around the armed attack. To use our lexicon, it is based on the analysis of "material circumstances."

Three judgments have been handed down by the ICJ in which the Court's condemnation notably was based on the grounds that the criteria of necessity and proportionality were not met. It should be emphasized that in none of the three cases did the defendant states succeed in proving that they had been victims of an armed attack. In the first case, *Military and Paramilitary Activities*, the United States defended the forcible measures they had taken against Nicaragua. The main offensive that U.S. measures were supposed to halt had occurred seven months before the U.S. measures produced their first effects. For this reason, the Court decided that the measures were not necessary. In *Oil Platforms*, the Court concluded

139. Corten, *supra* note 89, at 421 ("acceptance of preventive self-defence would consecrate the return to the 'law of necessity' that the Charter was devised to stamp out; the risk of abuse is greater when preventive self-defence makes the proportionality criterion inoperative").

140. Military and Paramilitary Activities in and Against Nicaragua (Nicar. v. U.S.), Judgment, 1986 I.C.J. Rep. 14, ¶ 194 (June 27); Oil Platforms (Iran v. U.S.), Judgment, 2003 I.C.J. Rep. 161, ¶¶ 73–77 (Nov. 6).

that the use of force did not lead to any military benefit for the United States. The judges underlined the fact that the use of force was not even thought to be necessary by the United States. Finally, in the *Armed Activities* case, the Democratic Republic of Congo argued that Uganda had not exhausted all peaceful means before using force. Therefore, according to the DRC, the necessity criterion had not been met. Uganda, for its part, argued that the criterion of exhaustion of peaceful means is not a proper definition of necessity, which only implies that "the conduct remains within the appropriate purpose."[141] The ICJ first decided that according to the facts of the case no prior armed attack had been proven and, accordingly, the judges did not need to discuss the question of necessity.[142] Then, the Court addressed the series of transborder attacks, which according to Uganda amounted to an armed attack and gave rise to the right of self-defense. The Court analyzed the necessity of the use of force, even though it pointed out that the series of transborder attacks mentioned by Uganda did not reach the threshold expected for an armed attack to be characterized in accordance with Article 51 of the U.N. Charter. The ICJ concluded that the riposte, the use of force "many hundreds of kilometres from Uganda's border," was not necessary.[143]

Hence, under traditional self-defense, the use of force cannot be considered a self-defense measure when it is used by the state to pursue an aim that goes beyond the objective of halting and repelling an armed attack.[144] For instance, a state cannot use force in self-defense to protect perceived security interests.[145] If the state acts beyond a simple occasional defense of its security, the measure cannot be considered necessary or proportionate under the terms of Article 51 U.N. Charter and the relevant case law.

The analytical problem with allegiance to traditional self-defense is that it often neglects the logical connection between the different limitations of self-defense. More concretely, it often disregards the fact that once all the above steps in the chain of propositions on the right of self-defense against terrorist networks have been accepted (or one directly accepted and the others as a result of the cascade effect), it is in fact impossible to stick to these assertions concerning necessity and proportionality. If the requirements of necessity and proportionality are

141. Armed Activities on the Territory of the Congo (Dem. Rep. Congo v. Uganda), Oral Proceeding, Remarks of Professor Ian Brownlie, Verbatim Record 2005/7, ¶ 82, at 31, https://www.icj-cij.org/files/case-related/116/116-20050418-ORA-01-00-BI.pdf.

142. It should be emphasized that in this case, the ICJ was not confronted to a threat of an armed attack or, in other words, anticipatory use of force. If it had been the case, it is most likely that even in the absence of an armed attack that had actually occurred, the Court would have analyzed whether the conditions of necessity and proportionality of the use of force to repel the threatening armed attack were met.

143. Armed Activities on the Territory of the Congo (Dem. Rep. Congo v. Uganda), Judgment, 2005 I.C.J. Rep. 168, ¶ 147 (Dec. 19).

144. *Id.* ¶ 304.

145. *Id.* ¶ 148.

necessarily affected by a ripple effect, it is because of one essential shift: the individualization/dematerialization of the use of force explored previously. If there is no identified armed attack in relation to which force should be necessary and proportionate, these requirements cannot be based on such an attack. The tests are de facto impossible to be conducted in relation to tangible or at least identified or expected material circumstances. Thus, the temporal and material changes of self-defense transform what is meant by proportionality and necessity. The essential change from a material use of self-defense (that is, to halt and repel an identified attack) to an individualized self-defense (that is, to eliminate an individual posing a continuing imminent threat) results in a fundamental change to the limitation flowing from the requirements of necessity and proportionality.

The dematerialization of self-defense directly calls for a proportionality test that differs from the test that demands that the scope and intensity of the response correspond to the (prospective assessment of the) harm to be caused by the armed attack. As Tams and Devaney rightly noted, acceptance of the idea of imminent threat already entailed an evolution in the proportionality test toward a more prospective comparison of the scope and intensity of the response to the threat posed by the armed attack.[146] The more prospective the test, the more attenuated the relation becomes between the intensity of the response and that of the armed attack. But what is missing in the analysis of how proportionality adapts to a new reality is the detachment of the proportionality test from any precisely identified armed attack. When self-defense is used in the "absence of specific evidence of where an attack will take place or of the precise nature of an attack"[147] to eliminate "plotters [who] may be seeking to inspire, enable[,] and direct attacks around the world, and indeed have a proven track record of doing so,"[148] the test cannot consist of measuring (even in a prospective way) the harm caused by an abstract threat.

Instead, several states are already prepared to accept that self-defense is used to weaken non-state armed groups.[149] And this is a direct consequence of the dematerialization and individualization of the use of force against terrorists. The restraining function of *ad bellum* proportionality is further diminished when the scope and intensity of the use of force are compared with the general threat posed by a transnational terrorist group or network. However, this conclusion should not be considered alarmist as the proportionality test so defined will still

146. Tams & Devaney, *supra* note 74, at 102.

147. Bethlehem, *supra* note 35.

148. Wright, *supra* note 35.

149. On Turkey's Operation Sun, *see* Tom Ruys, Quo Vadit Jus ad Bellum? *A Legal Analysis of Turkey's Military Operations against the PKK in Northern Iraq*, 12 Melbourne J. Int'l L. 334 (2008). On Israel's intervention in Lebanon, *see* Permanent Rep. of Isr. to the U.N., Identical Letters Dated July 12, 2006 from the Permanent Rep. of Isr. to the U.N. Addressed to the Secretary-General and the President of the Security Council, U.N. Docs. A/60/937, S/2006/515 (July 12, 2006); Yaël Ronen, *The 2006 Conflict in Lebanon*, 9 Y.B. Int'l Humanitarian L. 362 (2008).

involve the evaluation of circumstances. Such circumstances could include for instance (1) the intensity of the threat generally posed by the group to which the target is affiliated, and (2) the role played by the specific individual in the group (eliminating an individual might be excessive if this individual is a very low-value member of the group).

The metamorphosis of proportionality caused by the extension of the other conditions of self-defense also reveals the overlap between *jus ad bellum* and *jus in bello* proportionality. Force is used outside situations of active hostilities and hence justified under an *ad bellum* rationale in a way that is systemic. Drones have been used by the United States as part of a broader policy and as part of a system that functions permanently and without interruption, as revealed by the *Intercept* in the *Drone Papers*.[150] These official documents show that U.S. practice is institutionalized through the elaboration of a specific lexicon for drone strikes, the existence of a complex chain of command, of a formal kill list, of systematic processes, and so forth. It reveals that drone strikes are used for more than only responding to punctual armed attacks or threats. U.S., U.K., and French officials invoke the necessity of destroying ISIS in order to legitimize their strikes in Syria.[151] Therefore, these strikes cannot be considered as simply aiming at halting or repelling an armed attack (or to its threat). U.S., U.K., and French strikes converge toward a bigger and more abstract objective, not so big as protecting their general security interests but of killing individuals belonging to transnational terrorist groups or networks, who carry a hostile intent.

IV. CONCLUSION

This chapter argues that the principle of proportionality embodies the essential change from a material use of force in self-defense (that is, to repel an identified attack) toward an individualized self-defense against transnational terrorist networks through eliminating an individual posing a continuing imminent threat. It also brings to light the interaction between technology, war, and the law and showed how the evolution of the right of self-defense against transnational terrorist networks legitimizes and facilitates new military strategies, a use of force

150. *The Drone Papers*, *supra* note 46.

151. Barack Obama, Remarks by the President on the Military Campaign to Destroy ISIL (Dec. 14, 2015), https://obamawhitehouse.archives.gov/the-press-office/2015/12/14/remarks-president-military-campaign-destroy-isil; Discours du Président de la République Devant le Parlement Réuni en Congrès [Speech of President François Hollande to Parliament] (Nov. 16, 2015), http://www.elysee.fr/declarations/article/discours-du-president-de-la-republique-devant-le-parlement-reuni-en-congres-3; Memorandum from Prime Minster David Cameron to the Foreign Affairs Select Committee, Prime Minister's Response to the Foreign Affairs Select Committee's Second Report of Session 2015–16: The Extension of Offensive British Military Operations to Syria (Nov. 2015), https://www.parliament.uk/documents/commons-committees/foreign-affairs/PM-Response-to-FAC-Report-Extension-of-Offensive-British-Military-Operations-to-Syria.pdf.

detached from material threats and focused on individual hostile intentions. The chapter also shows how this military strategy, and the chain of legal propositions attached to it, are made more acceptable by drones' technological capacities and discursive practices on "new" non-state armed groups.

The rationale, strategy, and technology of drone programs allow the observation of the intimacy of people's daily life, the collection of data on them including by tracking cell phones, and striking them precisely.[152] The rationale is that the Hydra-headed enemy requires a change in military strategy and practice focused on individuals. It follows that this strategy can develop well through drone programs, which combine the advantages of intelligence gathering and the possibility to kill targets precisely, on the basis of that collected data. For all these elements, drone programs materialize the possibility of a full-fledged individualized warfare but also pave the way for the dematerialization of the right of self-defense. Ultimately, such a shift in the object of the use of force in self-defense results in a metamorphosis of the principle of proportionality.

Drone programs offer the possibility to collect individualized data, behavioral scrutiny on an almost permanent basis, and access into areas that were previously inaccessible. Accordingly, such programs could lead to a legal environment that permits targeting individuals for the hostile intent they carry, even if they are not preparing a threatening imminent attack. As a result, the de facto possibility to individualize the conduct of warfare and the associated legal authorization to do so extensively through a revised *jus ad bellum* framework, at least partly explain the phenomenon of extension of enmity in today's war on terror. As warfare appears to be individualizable and individualized, it may appear logical that the conflict is progressively extended to groups that have no link with the original enemy group. In such an environment, the only question that may remain is, "Is this individual an enemy?"

152. *The Drone Papers*, *supra* note 46; Arkin, *supra* note 41; Rosa Brooks, How Everything Became War and the Military Became Everything (2016); Shaw, *supra* note 5; *Drone Warfare*, *supra* note 1.

6

The Quest for an Internal *Jus Ad Bellum*: International Law's Missing Link, Mere Distraction, or Pandora's Box?

TOM RUYS*

I. INTRODUCTION: THE QUEST FOR AN INTERNAL *JUS AD BELLUM*

It is common knowledge that non-international armed conflicts (NIACs), rather than inter-state conflicts, today constitute "the most widespread, the most destructive, and the most characteristic form of organized human violence."[1] In spite hereof, as a matter of positive international law, there is (as yet) no "internal" *jus ad bellum*, restraining the recourse to force between the state, on the one hand, and rebels or insurgents, on the other hand. In other words, there is no *intra*-state equivalent to the "external" *jus ad bellum* governing *inter*-state recourse to force. The rudimentary contours of the existing legal framework governing "internal" use of force are relatively easy to

* Professor of International Law, Ghent Rolin-Jaequemyns International Law Institute (GRILI), Ghent University. The author wishes to thank the editors of this volume as well as the various participants in the workshop at the U.S. Military Academy at West Point on October 29–31, 2018, for their useful feedback. All errors remain, of course, my own.

1. David Armitage, Civil Wars: a History in Ideas 5–7 (2017). As Armitage observes: "[s]ince 1989, an average of twenty intrastate wars have been in progress at any moment—about ten times the annual average globally between 1816 and 1989. There have been roughly twenty-five million 'total battle deaths' in these wars since 1945. . . . The annual price tag for civil war has been about $123 billion—roughly what the Global North budgets for economic aid to the Global South each year. Not without reason, then, has civil war been chillingly described as 'development in reverse.'"

Tom Ruys, *The Quest for an Internal* Jus Ad Bellum*: International Law's Missing Link, Mere Distraction, or Pandora's Box?* In: *Necessity and Proportionality in International Peace and Security Law.* Edited by: Professor Claus Kreß and Captain Robert Lawless, Oxford University Press (2021). © Oxford University Press. DOI: 10.1093/oso/9780197537374.003.0007.

sketch. In essence, the assumption is that international law is "neutral" toward rebellion.[2] It neither permits nor prohibits rebels from taking up arms against the government. Conversely, as a matter of principle it accepts that states, enjoying full and exclusive enforcement jurisdiction within their own territory, deploy the state security apparatus to quell an uprising. By the same token, it accepts that the state employs the full range of its domestic legal system to criminally prosecute those that have taken up arms against it: rebels are not in principle endowed with the privilege of belligerency, irrespective of whether they comply with international humanitarian law (IHL).[3] Instead, all international law does is to regulate the *modalities* pertaining to specific instances involving the use of lethal force. To this end, international law relies on two different normative frameworks, found respectively in international human rights law (IHRL) and in IHL.

In recent years, this status quo has been challenged by several scholars arguing the need for an *ad bellum* regime for internal uses of force.[4] Two thoughtful and eloquent analyses in particular, by Eliav Lieblich and Jan Arno Hessbruegge, stand out and merit further consideration. The models put forward by both authors are considerably different. Lieblich, for one, asserts that the absence of a normative framework governing internal resort to force "undercuts the coherence of the international legal system and thus also its legitimacy."[5] More specifically, the author expresses concern at the existence of an accountability gap, in that "nobody can be held accountable on the international level for instigating the conflict, either on the level of state responsibility or on that of criminal liability."[6] This results in a lack of protection of the right to life "of both soldiers and armed opposition members, as well as civilians that can be incidentally harmed: their lives are simply not a matter for international law to consider."[7] Against this background, Lieblich construes the envisaged internal *jus ad bellum* in prohibitive terms, namely, as a ban on the first resort to internal hostilities.[8] This prohibition is deemed applicable both to the state and to non-state armed groups (NSAGs), albeit that the author acknowledges the additional difficulties of applying it to non-state actors[9]

2. *See* Olivier Corten, La Rébellion et le Droit International: Le Principe de Neutralité en Tension 53 (2016).

3. *See*, however, *infra* section III.A on the position of national liberation movements and section IV.A on the recognition of belligerency doctrine.

4. For an earlier suggestion along similar lines, *see, e.g.*, Jochen Frowein, *Globale und Regionale Friedenssicherung Nach 50 Jahren Vereinte Nationen*, 114 Zeitschrift für Schweizerisches Recht 269 (1995).

5. Eliav Lieblich, *Internal Jus ad Bellum*, 67 Hastings L.J. 687, 691 (2016).

6. *Id.* at 739.

7. *Id.*

8. *Id.* at 696.

9. *Id.* at 743–46. This difficulty stems from the claim that the prohibition is derived from the human right to life in combination with the fact that international human rights obligations are

and seems primarily concerned with government use of force.[10] Hessbruegge in turn seeks to identify a normative benchmark to distinguish those rare cases of legitimate armed resistance from the numerous rebels without a (just) cause.[11] Accordingly, the suggested *ad bellum* model takes the shape of a permissive norm, that is, an exceptional and conditional right of organized armed resistance, which is addressed to non-state actors only.[12]

At the same time, there are important common features in the models put forward by Lieblich and Hessbruegge. Thus, both are construed by extrapolating the right to life to the *ad bellum* level, albeit the theoretical underpinnings are not identical.[13] Lieblich starts from the observation that individuals can use (proportionate) lethal force only for "self-or-other-defense," lest there be an arbitrary deprivation of life. Building on the revisionist just war theory developed by McMahan and others,[14] Lieblich argues that the same "morality of killing" applies to collectives of individuals, such as governments or rebel groups, and that war must be seen as nothing more than "a web of forcible actions in self-or-other-defense."[15]

traditionally seen as binding only upon states to the exclusion of non-state actors. While the latter approach is increasingly challenged, *see, e.g.*, Daragh Murray, Human Rights Obligations of Non-State Armed Groups (2016); Katherine Fortin, The Accountability of Armed Groups under Human Rights Law (2017), especially in situations where non-state armed groups hold effective control over territory, Lieblich rightly concedes that consensus on the application of human rights obligations to non-state actors "remains elusive." Lieblich, *supra* note 5, at 745.

10. Recall also the different baseline under positive international law with regard to the internal use of force by states or by rebels. In the former case, international law is permissive in that it at least recognizes as a matter of principle that states can exercise enforcement jurisdiction within their territory. No such permissive baseline exists of course with regard to action undertaken by non-state actors against the state. The implication is that a prohibitive norm is more relevant from a state perspective.

11. Jan Arno Hessbruegge, Human Rights and Personal Self-Defense in international law 293–344 (2017).

12. Also construing the notion of "[a] new *jus contra bellum internum*" as something which is "addressed to non-state actors only," *see* Claus Kreβ, *Towards Further Developing the Law of Non-International Armed Conflict: A Proposal for a* Jus in Bello Interno *and a New* Jus Contra Bellum Internum, 96 Int'l Rev. Red Cross 30, 40 n.45 (2014) ("In light of the State monopoly on the internal use of force, this asymmetry is without alternative; the international legal limits upon the internal use of force by the State would continue to flow from international human rights law and the threat of international punishment would continue to result, in cases of the most egregious abuses, in the resort to internal violence by State officials from the international criminalization of genocide and crimes against humanity.").

13. Jan Arno Hessbruegge, *The Right to Life as the* Jus ad Bellum *of Non-International Armed Conflict (a Reply to Lieblich)*, Just Security (Oct. 27, 2016), https://www.justsecurity.org/33906/life-jus-ad-bellum-non-international-armed-conflict-a-reply-lieblich.

14. *See* Jeff McMahan, Killing in War (2009).

15. Lieblich, *supra* note 5, at 709–10.

Hessbruegge for his part grounds the suggested right of armed resistance in the right to life, read together with the human right to an effective remedy for human rights violations, and the right to personal self-defense as a general principle of law.[16]

The idea of extrapolating the right to life to the *ad bellum* level is not without precedent. Interestingly, the Human Rights Committee's (HRC) *General Comment Number 36* on the right to life asserts that "acts of aggression as defined in international law, resulting in deprivation of life, violate *ipso facto* article 6 of the Covenant."[17] At the same time, the extrapolation is limited here to breaches of the "external" jus *ad bellum*. No reference is made in the draft to any "internal" *ad bellum* dimension of the right to life.

Both Lieblich and Hessbruegge readily acknowledge that their proposals do not qualify as *lex lata*. Hessbruegge, for instance, insists that "at least *de lege ferenda*, . . . international law ought to recognize a right of organized armed assistance against mass atrocities amounting to genocide, crimes against humanity and war crimes."[18] Lieblich for his part aspires to "[spark] further discussion of this long averted issue."[19] The present chapter seeks to pick up the latter invitation by revisiting the proposed "internal *jus ad bellum*" models. The aim is to focus on the practical relevance and workability of these models, rather than their theoretical underpinning. While special consideration is given to the relevance of the criteria of necessity and proportionality in this context, it bears emphasizing that those standards cannot be assessed in isolation, but presuppose that a benchmark is first identified against which they are to be tested. Furthermore, while NIACs frequently tend to spill across borders, the current analysis will, for the sake of argument, be limited to purely internal uses of force, thus excluding any cross-border dimension. Internal violence between multiple non-state actors is similarly excluded.

Section II of this chapter takes a closer look at government use of force against rebels within the state's territory. Having regard to the extant regulation of the lethal use of force by the state under IHRL and IHL, it examines whether an additional *ad bellum* layer is needed in order to restrain government recourse to force against rebels, and shares some thoughts as to whether adding an *ad bellum* prohibition on government recourse to force against rebels is moreover feasible. Section III deals with internal use of force against the state. In particular, it revisits the common assertion that international law is "neutral" toward rebellion,

16. Hessbruegge, *supra* note 13.

17. Human Rights Committee, General Comment No. 36 on Article 6 of the International Covenant on Civil and Political Rights, on the Right to Life, Advance Unedited Version, ¶ 70, U.N. Doc. CCPR/C/GC/36 (Oct. 30, 2018). Violations of the right to life "may" also result when states "fail to take all reasonable measures to settle their international disputes by peaceful means." *Id.*

18. Hessbruegge, *supra* note 13, at 325.

19. Lieblich, *supra* note 5, at 692.

having regard to the growing web of multilateral counterterrorism instruments. Following a discussion of each individual's entitlement to personal self-defense and the related case law, the chapter proceeds to scrutinize the proposal to create a broader right of organized armed resistance at the *ad bellum* level. By way of epilogue, the concluding section of the chapter explores the links between the proposed internal *jus ad bellum*, on the one hand, and the concept of recognition of belligerency and third-state intervention in NIACs, on the other hand.

II. INTERNAL USE OF FORCE: GOVERNMENT USE OF FORCE AGAINST INSURGENTS AND REBELS

A. The Traditional Account in International Law and the Circularity Conundrum

As mentioned earlier, international law accepts that states resort to force when confronted with an insurgency or armed rebellion on their soil. It does not directly regulate the decision to employ force against rebels as such. Rather, all international law does in this context is to govern the modalities of specific instances of recourse to force, that is, the way in which force is being used in individual operations and confrontations. To this end, international law relies on two radically different frameworks, one found in IHRL, the other found in IHL.

As to the former, it is clear that states need not remain idle in the face of internal unrest and riots, but may respond in such settings, including by the use of force. This is recognized explicitly in Article 2(2) of the European Convention on Human Rights (ECHR). While most human rights instruments frame the right to life in general terms as a prohibition of "arbitrary deprivation of life,"[20] Article 2(2) enumerates three situations in which deprivation of life may be justified outside the context of armed conflict. One such exception pertains specifically to "action lawfully taken for the purpose of quelling a riot."[21] It would be erroneous to assume, however, on the basis of the foregoing provision, that the *deliberate* use of *lethal* force is normally justified in order to quell a riot, whether under the ECHR or under other human rights instruments.[22] Ample evidence supports the view

20. *See, e.g.*, International Covenant on Civil and Political Rights art. 6(1), Dec. 16, 1966, T.I.A.S. No. 92–108, 999 U.N.T.S. 171.

21. Convention for the Protection of Human Rights and Fundamental Freedoms art. 2(2)(c), Nov. 4, 1950, 213 U.N.T.S. 221 [hereinafter ECHR]. The other exceptions relate to "defence of any person from unlawful violence," *id.* art. 2(2)(a), and force "to effect a lawful arrest or to prevent the escape of a person lawfully detained," *id.* art. 2(2)(b).

22. The European Court of Human Rights has effectively stressed on numerous occasions that Article 2(2) "does not primarily define instances where it is permitted intentionally to kill an individual, but describes the situations where it is permitted to 'use force' which may result, as an unintended outcome, in the deprivation of life." Giuliani & Gaggio v. Italy, 2011-II Eur. Ct. H.R. 275, ¶ 175, http://hudoc.echr.coe.int/eng?i=001-104098. Article 2 of the ECHR "does not

that the deliberate use of lethal force is justified only in case of a threat to the life of an individual. What is more, the threat concerned must be *imminent*, implying that lethal force cannot in principle be used in anticipation of a future attack, nor in response to an attack that has already been concluded.[23] A strict necessity test applies. Principle 9 of the *U.N. Basic Principles on the Use of Force and Firearms*, asserts that "intentional lethal use of firearms may only be made when strictly unavoidable to protect life."[24] Principle 8 states that "exceptional circumstances such as internal political instability or any other public emergency may not be invoked to justify any departure from these basic principles,"[25] thus corroborating the position that offensive force by state agents would not be permissible for purposes of quelling a riot or insurrection.[26] Furthermore, according to the proportionality requirement, states should use "no more [force] than absolutely necessary"[27] to this end. It follows that states must, for instance, take into account the possible risk to innocent bystanders and balance the risk of harm to the latter against the expected harm if no force is used.[28]

Case law confirms that the aforementioned framework applies when states conduct law enforcement operations against suspected terrorists,[29] when they confront hostage crises[30] or violent demonstrations,[31] or seek to suppress prison

grant a *carte blanche*," but requires "that a balance . . . be struck between the aim pursued and the means employed to achieve it." Gülec v. Turkey, 1998-IV Eur. Ct. H.R. 58, ¶ 71.

23. On the "immediacy" of defensive action, *see* Hessbruegge, *supra* note 13, at 139–43.

24. The Eighth U.N. Congress on the Prevention of Crime and the Treatment of Offenders, Basic Principles on the Use of Force and Firearms by Law Enforcement Officials, U.N. Doc. A/CONF.144/28/Rev.1 (Sept. 7, 1990).

25. *Id.*

26. Ian Park, The Right to Life in Armed Conflict 29 (2018).

27. ECHR, *supra* note 21, art. 2(2); *see also* Human Rights Committee, *supra* note 17, ¶ 12 ("[T]he application of potentially lethal force by a person acting in self-defense, or by another person coming to his or her defence, must be strictly necessary in view of the threat posed by the attacker; it must represent a method of last resort after other alternatives have been exhausted or deemed inadequate; the amount of force applied cannot exceed the amount strictly needed for responding to the threat; the force applied must be carefully directed-only against the attacker, and the threat responded to must involve imminent death or serious injury.").

28. Hessbruegge, *supra* note 13.

29. McCann v. United Kingdom, 1995 Eur. Ct. H.R. 31.

30. Finogenov v. Russian Federation, I.H.R.L. 3798 (Eur. Ct. Hum. Rts. 2011).

31. For instance, in *Gülec v. Turkey*, the European Court of Human Rights found a breach of Article 2 of the ECHR where police officers had confronted a violent demonstration involving some 3,000 people by firing a tank-mounted machine gun to disperse the crowd. *See* Gülec v. Turkey, 1998-IV Eur. Ct. H.R. 58, ¶ 71. The use of live ammunition to disperse demonstrators throwing stones and fire bombs, and resulting in the death of 17 individuals, was similarly regarded as a breach of the right to life in *Simsek v. Turkey*. Simsek v. Turkey, 2005 Eur. Ct. H.R.

riots.[32] Thus, for purposes of quelling riots and other internal disturbances, law enforcement personnel must be properly equipped with necessary nonlethal and/or less lethal equipment. Even if they are not obliged to retreat in the face of a demonstration and may stand their ground, there is an obligation to show restraint inasmuch as possible and to attempt de-escalation measures in the handling of demonstrations.[33] This is not to say that human rights bodies are blind to the difficult circumstances in which security personnel may operate, or that the use of lethal force is *absolutely* prohibited in situations of riots.[34] Still, a "shoot-to-kill" approach is in principle incompatible with IHRL as it applies in times of peace.

The situation is, of course, fundamentally different when it comes to the use of force in the context of a NIAC. While IHRL continues to apply during armed conflict (and human rights bodies such as the European Court of Human Rights will not shy away from applying the relevant IHRL treaty provisions in times of war), what amounts to an "arbitrary" deprivation of life in such setting must be interpreted by reference to the targeting rules found in IHL, as was famously asserted by the International Court of Justice (ICJ) in the *Nuclear Weapons* Advisory Opinion.[35] The implication is that the normal necessity test under IHRL is replaced by the targeting rules of IHL pertaining to the identification of a lawful target for attack. The "necessity" dimension nonetheless remains implicit in the definition of a "military objective." Indeed, IHL operates a two-pronged definition of military objectives, which requires not only that the objects "by their nature, location, purpose or use make an effective contribution to military action" but also demands that the objectives' "partial or total destruction, capture or neutralization, in the circumstances ruling at the time, offers a definite military advantage."[36] At the same time, the second requirement may be partly superfluous, in that the destruction of an objective making "an effective contribution to military

546 (2005); *see also* Park, *supra* note 26, at 41–42 (claiming that the ECtHR's case law indicates that "any recourse to the use of lethal force to quell a riot would only be lawful with respect to Article 2 if there is an imminent threat to life").

32. *See, e.g.*, Montero-Aranguren (Detention Center of Catia) v. Venezuela, Preliminary Objection, Merits, Reparations & Costs, Inter-Am. Ct. H.R. (ser. C) No. 150 (July 5, 2006) (condemning the deliberate use of lethal force against rioting prisoners trying to stir up a mass prison break).

33. Hessbruegge, *supra* note 13, at 152–54.

34. Thus, the *Giuliani and Gaggio* case, relating to the riots during the G-8 Summit in Genoa in 2001, confirms that police officers can as a last resort use lethal force where their lives, or those of their colleagues, are being threatened. *See* Giuliani & Gaggio v. Italy, 2011-II Eur. Ct. H.R. 275, ¶¶ 188–97, http://hudoc.echr.coe.int/eng?i=001-104098.

35. Legality of the Threat or Use of Nuclear Weapons, Advisory Opinion, 1996 I.C.J. 226, ¶ 25 (July 8).

36. The cited definition, enshrined in Article 52(2) of the First Additional Protocol to the 1949 Geneva Conventions, is equally applicable in situations of non-international armed conflict.

action" will almost automatically offer "a definite military advantage" to the other side.[37] As far as the targeting of individuals, as opposed to objects, is concerned, IHL is commonly understood to permit the deliberate use of lethal force in NIACs against members of the state armed forces as well as of the military wing of the NSAG.[38] Other persons can only be targeted if, and for such time, as they take a direct part in hostilities.[39] *De lege lata*, the majority view is that the identification of a legitimate target pursuant to the principle of distinction as per the aforementioned suffices to justify the deliberate use of lethal force, without there being a need to additionally demonstrate any imminent threat to life.[40] In other words, the (military) necessity to use force against legitimate targets is *presumed*.[41] The proportionality principle and the concomitant duty to take precautions only operate so as to limit damage or injury to civilian objects and to civilians not taking direct part in hostilities, and require desisting from attacks that are expected to result in excessive collateral damage in comparison to the anticipated military advantage. The loss of life among those constituting lawful targets of attack, by contrast, does not enter the proportionality assessment.[42]

It follows from the aforementioned rudimentary synopsis that the regime governing the use of lethal force in situations of armed conflict is in principle far more permissive than that applicable in times of peace. Yet, the switch from one legal framework to another depends entirely on the facts on the ground: situations that previously qualified as mere "internal disturbances and tensions, such as riots, isolated and sporadic acts of violence and other acts of a similar nature"[43] may indeed gradually transform into NIACs. This will be the case where the situation meets the twin requirements of intensity and degree of organization, that

See, e.g., 1 INT'L COMM. OF THE RED CROSS, CUSTOMARY INTERNATIONAL HUMANITARIAN LAW: RULES 29 (Jean-Marie Henchaerts & Louise Doswald-Beck eds., 2005).

37. *E.g.*, YORAM DINSTEIN, THE CONDUCT OF HOSTILITIES UNDER THE LAW OF INTERNATIONAL ARMED CONFLICT 104 (3d ed. 2016).

38. Notably, whether membership of the military wing must be determined by reference to a person's "continuous combat function" or in a different manner remains controversial, yet this debate is beyond the scope of this chapter's analysis.

39. *E.g.*, Protocol Additional to the Geneva Conventions of 12 August 1949, and Relating to the Protection of Victims of Non-International Armed Conflict (Protocol II) art. 13(3), June 8, 1977, 1125 U.N.T.S. 609 [hereinafter AP II].

40. *But see infra* section II.B on the "capture or kill" controversy.

41. INT'L COMM. OF THE RED CROSS, THE USE OF FORCE IN ARMED CONFLICTS: INTERPLAY BETWEEN THE CONDUCT OF HOSTILITIES AND LAW ENFORCEMENT PARADIGMS 8 (Gloria Gaggioli ed., 2013).

42. *Id.* ("The legitimate target of an attack . . . is not covered by the principle of proportionality under IHL.").

43. AP II, *supra* note 39, art. 1(2).

is, where there is protracted armed violence ongoing and the non-state armed group is sufficiently organized to conduct sustained military operations. While the International Criminal Tribunal for the former Yugoslavia (ICTY) and the International Criminal Court (ICC) have helpfully identified a range of indicia that may be examined for purposes of assessing the requirements of intensity and organization,[44] it has been suggested that the existing regime creates a perverse incentive for states to deploy the military (in lieu of law enforcement personnel) and escalate the situation, so as to create a situation of armed conflict and trigger the more permissive regime governing the use of lethal force. Lieblich, for instance, speaks of an "awkward, circular result [whereby] a state is justified to resort to hostilities when hostilities exist," allowing states to "manipulate their way into an armed conflict through acts on the ground, thus gaining the *de facto* right to conduct hostilities while bearing no material legal costs."[45] Hessbruegge also flags the "conundrum whether a government can simply escalate an armed confrontation with violent non-state actors from law enforcement action to a non-international armed conflict with the result that its security forces can then rely on the more permissive hostilities paradigm to use force," acknowledging that "this would create a perverse incentive": "the more violence a government *de facto* uses, the more violence it is *de jure* entitled to use."[46] By the same token, a similar conundrum arises in respect of the continuation and termination of a NIAC: inasmuch as a NIAC continues to exist until a peaceful situation has been re-established, a government could arguably choose to continue fighting opponents by reference to the conduct of hostilities paradigm even if these opponents would no longer be in a position seriously to challenge the government.[47] Interestingly, the suggested circularity is presented by Lieblich as an important factor illustrating the need for an *ad bellum* prohibition on the first resort to internal hostilities.[48]

44. *See, e.g.*, Prosecutor v. Boškoski, Case No. IT-04-82-T, Judgment, ¶ 175, nn.702–708 (Int'l Crim. Trib. for the Former Yugoslavia July 10, 2008); Prosecutor v. Haradinaj, Case No. IT-04-84-T, Judgment, ¶¶ 32–60 (Int'l Crim. Trib. for the Former Yugoslavia Apr. 3, 2008); *see also* Sandesh Sivakumaran, The Law of Non-International Armed Conflict 167–82 (2012).

45. Lieblich, *supra* note 5, at 735–36; *see also id.* at 696 (referring to "a circular situation in which the factual existence of an armed conflict becomes a normative justification for the resort to hostilities").

46. Hessbruegge, *supra* note 13 (referring to "the conundrum whether a government can simply escalate an armed confrontation with violent non-state actors from law enforcement to a non-international armed conflict with the result that its security forces can then rely on the more permissive hostilities paradigm to use force. To say the least, this would entail a perverse incentive: the more violence a government *de facto* uses, the more violence it is *de jure* entitled to use.").

47. Gratitude to Claus Kreβ for signaling this scenario. *See* Claus Kreβ, *The Law of Naval Warfare and International Criminal Law: Germany's Federal Prosecutor on the* Gaza Flotilla Incident, Isr. Y.B. Hum. Rts. 1, 8.

48. Lieblich, *supra* note 5, at 696.

B. Challenging the Traditional Account: A False Dichotomy?

Before considering the desirability and feasibility of an *ad bellum* norm prohibiting the first resort to hostilities by the government, it is worth pausing an instant at the circularity paradox identified earlier and the underlying idea of two juxtaposed regimes governing the recourse to lethal force.

In particular, while the idea that states may have an incentive to inflate the intensity of the violence so as to trigger the more permissive targeting rules of IHL is intuitively appealing at first sight, reality is more complex. At the outset, it appears doubtful that concerns over the applicable legal framework are an autonomous driver steering the state's policy in confronting "internal disturbances and tensions." Other factors are likely to play a bigger part: a state may choose to respond by brutal force to deter its inhabitants from joining the insurgency; or it may opt for a softer posture in an attempt to "win the hearts and minds" and leave room for political dialogue.[49] Even if the activation of the more permissive IHL regime strikes as a perverse reward for a state's military escalation of the situation, it is recalled moreover that the "intensity" criterion does not operate in splendid isolation. In particular, the mere fact that hundreds, possibly thousands, of individuals are engaged in violent protests against the government is of its own insufficient to trigger the IHL regime on the use of force. For a NIAC to arise, it is further required that a sufficiently large group of rebels or insurgents organize themselves to such degree as to feature a responsible command, capable, on the one hand, of planning and carrying out sustained and concerted military operations, and, on the other, of imposing discipline on the members.[50] This, of course, is an element which is beyond the state's control.[51] It is accordingly doubtful whether states can—even if so desired—unilaterally manufacture a factual situation resulting in the activation of the IHL regime. To some extent then, the twin requirements of intensity and organization—and specifically the latter one—operate as an implicit proportionality barrier preventing the government from unduly moving from the law enforcement to the IHL paradigm.

The presumed incentive for states to escalate the conflict must also be put into perspective. Indeed, this presumption is based on a conception of two juxtaposed regimes, one conditioning the use of lethal force on the existence of an imminent threat to life and the other requiring little more than the identification of a lawful

49. Practice moreover suggests that states are generally reluctant to acknowledge the existence of a NIAC on their territory and will often flatly deny this.

50. *See* Sivakumaran, *supra* note 44, at 179.

51. Mutatis mutandis, a similar argument can be made in respect of the termination of a NIAC in the scenario where a non-state armed group is diminished to such extent that it no longer possesses the required degree of organization for purposes of IHL. On the various theories pertaining to the end of a NIAC, *see in particular* Dustin A. Lewis, Gabriella Blum, & Naz K. Modirzadeh, Indefinite War: Unsettled International Law on the End of Armed Conflict 97–103 (2017), http://blogs.harvard.edu/pilac/files/2017/03/Indefinite-War-February-2017-HLS-PILAC.pdf.

target. This dichotomy, however, is an oversimplification and is moreover increasingly challenged. A number of observations can be made in this respect.

First, even where a NIAC can be said to exist, the law enforcement paradigm will still continue to govern the use of force in various settings that do not form part of the actual conduct of hostilities. Typical illustrations include law enforcement operations against ordinary criminals or the conduct of guards in internment camps. Clearly, it is the factual context, rather than the identity of the security personnel involved (military or police), that determines the applicable regime. Importantly, demonstrations during a NIAC will normally be governed by the law enforcement paradigm. The International Committee of the Red Cross's (ICRC) *Interpretive Guidance on the Notion of Direct Participation in Hostilities* (*DPH Guidance*) explains in this regard that "violent forms of civil unrest, the primary purpose of which is to express dissatisfaction with the territorial or detaining authorities" must be distinguished from direct participation in hostilities, which is "specifically designed to support a party to an armed conflict against another."[52] Admittedly, the situation may become blurred where ordinary civilians are joined by persons taking direct part in hostilities and/or members of the military wing of the NSAG. Such a scenario presented itself during the Gaza border demonstrations in spring 2018, during which more than 100 Palestinians were killed by Israeli sniper fire.[53] The idea that in mixed scenarios the conduct

52. Int'l Comm. of the Red Cross, Interpretive Guidance on the Notion of Direct Participation in Hostilities Under International Humanitarian Law 63 (Nils Melzer ed., 2009).

53. Pursuant to a petition by a group of Israeli human rights organizations challenging the Israeli Defense Force's rules of engagement (and their implementation), the Israeli Supreme Court found that the situation was governed by a dual regime, applying interchangeably depending on the particular circumstances on the ground. On the one hand, the targeting of Hamas operatives (taking direct part in hostilities) was governed by the conduct of hostilities paradigm under IHL, implying that lethal force could be used against those operatives. On the other hand, for other demonstrators, including "central instigators," the Court (as per the lead opinion of Justice Melcer) held the law enforcement paradigm to be applicable. Rather than grounding this law enforcement paradigm in human rights law, however, the Court regarded it as a separate regime part and parcel of IHL itself. HCJ 3003/18, 3250/18 *Yesh Din et al. v. IDF Chief of Staff*, 24 May 2018, available at https://supremedecisions.court.gov.il/Home/Download?path=EnglishVerdicts%5C18%5C030%5C030%5Ck08&fileName=18030030.K08&type=4. The latter approach has rightly been criticized for inventing a novel law enforcement paradigm extraneous to international human rights law without adducing any meaningful evidence in support. For insightful critiques of this approach, *see* Amichai Cohen, *Analysis of Israel's Supreme Court Decision Allowing Lethal Force in Gaza*, Just Security (May 27, 2018), https://www.justsecurity.org/57033/analysis-israels-supreme-court-decision-allowing-lethal-force-gaza; Yuval Shany & Elena Chachko, *Supreme Court Dismisses a Petition Against Gaza Rules of Engagement*, Israel Democracy Institute (May 26, 2018), https://en.idi.org.il/articles/23583; Hannes Jöbstl, *Lost Between Law Enforcement and Active Hostilities: A First Glance at the Israeli Supreme Court Judgment on the Use of Lethal Force During the Gaza Border Demonstrations*, EJIL:Talk! (June 4, 2018), https://www.ejiltalk.org/

of hostilities and law enforcement paradigms apply in parallel finds substantial support among scholars, albeit that the operational challenges can be daunting.[54] During an ICRC expert meeting, the vast majority agreed that situations where fighters and civilians are closely intermingled ought to be addressed mainly through an "escalation of force" procedure, implying that the use of force should be a last resort and that other nonlethal means should be exhausted first.[55]

Second, reference must briefly be made to the "kill or capture" controversy in IHL. There is indeed growing support for the idea that, in situations of armed conflict, states should abstain from using lethal force against an individual who qualifies as a lawful target of attack when such individual can reasonably be captured without exposing the capturer to significant risk and should instead exhaust less harmful means. This position was famously endorsed in the context of the Israeli Supreme Court's *Targeted Killing* case, where the Court confirmed that "a civilian taking a direct part in hostilities cannot be attacked at such time as he is doing so, if a less harmful means can be employed."[56] It was also enshrined in the ICRC's *DPH Guidance*.[57] Different legal bases have been invoked in support of the alleged duty to "capture rather than kill," or to exercise restraint in the conduct of hostilities. The Israeli Supreme Court has suggested that the duty follows from the domestic law principle of proportionality, while drawing a parallel, in the same breath, to Article 2 of the ECHR and its application in the famous *McCann* case.[58] The *DPH Guidance* builds on the principle of humanity and a general principle of military necessity.[59] Others have instead relied on a broader understanding of the notion of hors de combat.[60] On the other hand,

lost-between-law-enforcement-and-active-hostilities-a-first-glance-at-the-israeli-supreme-court-judgment-on-the-use-of-lethal-force-during-the-gaza-border-demonstrations; *see also* Eliav Lieblich, *Collectivizing Threat: An Analysis of Israel's Legal Claims for Resort to Force on the Gaza Border*, JUST SECURITY (May 16, 2018), https://www.justsecurity.org/56346/collectivizing-threat-analysis-israels-legal-claims-resort-force-gaza-border (criticizing the position of the state ahead of the actual judgment). The Court moreover failed to shed clarity on the content of this new paradigm. The precise difference with the traditional human rights approach indeed remains unclear, albeit that it would appear to adopt a more flexible interpretation of the requirement of an imminent threat to life than under IHRL.

54. INT'L COMM. OF THE RED CROSS, *supra* note 41, at 25. In a similar vein, *see* Hessbruegge, *supra* note 13, at 222 (regarding this as the "prevailing" view).

55. INT'L COMM. OF THE RED CROSS, *supra* note 41, at 27–28.

56. HCJ 769/02 Pub. Comm. Against Torture v. Israel, 2006 (2) Isr. L. Rep. 459, 500–502 (2006).

57. INT'L COMM. OF THE RED CROSS, *supra* note 52, at 77–82 (Principle IX).

58. Pub. Comm. Against Torture, *supra* note 56, at 500–502.

59. INT'L COMM. OF THE RED CROSS, *supra* note 52, at 78–80.

60. *See* Ryan Goodman, *The Power to Kill or Capture Enemy Combatants*, 24 EUR. J. INT'L L. 819 (2013); *see also* Michael N. Schmitt, *Wound, Capture, or Kill: A Reply to Ryan Goodman's "The Power to Kill or Capture Enemy Combatants,"* 24 EUR. J. INT'L L. 855 (2013).

the alleged duty to kill or capture has been strongly objected to on the basis that it would lack any basis in international law, would be blind to the reality of the conduct of hostilities, and would create an imbalance between state armed forces and individuals taking direct part in hostilities.[61] Without revisiting the debate, what is important for present purposes is that supporters generally put forth two scenarios where the purported duty to capture rather than kill may be most relevant, that is, in occupied territories and in non-international armed conflicts.[62] This position is inspired in part by practical, operational considerations in that, in the two situations concerned, parties may exercise effective control over territory, thus creating an increased ability "to control the circumstances . . . in which its military operations are conducted"[63] (of course this assumption only holds true in respect of government-held territory, as opposed to military operations against rebels in rebel-held territory). In addition, it has been argued that the legal case for a duty to capture rather than kill is all the stronger in respect of NIACs, since—it is submitted—the notion of "combatants" is supposedly unknown to such type of conflicts.[64] If one accepts the foregoing, it is clear that the presumed incentive of states to escalate internal violence to the level of a NIAC is further reduced. At the same time, the existence of a duty to "capture, rather than kill" (and its possible scope) remains controversial.[65] It is telling in this respect that the HRC's *General Comment Number 6* states that in situations of armed conflict, "States parties should, in general, disclose . . . whether less harmful alternatives were considered," without, however, going as far as to embrace the idea that the use of lethal force against a fighter who could have been captured ipso facto breaches the right to life.[66]

Finally, the role of human rights law and of the various regional and international human rights bodies must not be underestimated. Some human rights bodies have indeed applied the law enforcement paradigm even when dealing with the use of force against persons who would be considered legitimate targets under IHL.[67] The European Court of Human Rights, for instance, has steered clear

61. *See* W. Hays Parks, *Part IX of the ICRC "Direct Participation in Hostilities" Study: No Mandate, No Expertise, and Legally Incorrect*, 42 N.Y.U. J. Int'l L. & Pol. 769, 799–812 (2010); Michael N. Schmitt, *The Interpretative Guidance on the Notion of Direct Participation in Hostilities: A Critical Analysis*, 1 Harv. Nat'l Sec. J. 5, 41–42 (2010).

62. Int'l Comm. of the Red Cross, *supra* note 52, at 81.

63. *Id.* at 80.

64. *See* David Kretzmer, Aviad Ben-Yehuda, & Meirav Furth, *"Thou Shall Not Kill": The Use of Lethal Force in Non-International Armed Conflicts*, 47 Isr. L. Rev. 191 (2014) (arguing inter alia that the permissive targeting rules applicable in IACs have never been imported in NIAC settings).

65. Sivakumaran, *supra* note 44, at 372.

66. Human Rights Committee, *supra* note 17, ¶ 64.

67. *See* Int'l Comm. of the Red Cross, *supra* note 41, at 14–15.

from applying IHL in cases involving the use of (potentially) lethal force, even where IHL was arguably or indisputably relevant, albeit that this attitude may be explained in part by the fact that states have generally denied, or refrained from invoking, the applicability of IHL.[68] Similar observations can be made in respect of the U.N. Human Rights Committee.[69]

At a more general level, it is hard to escape the conclusion that a state cannot unilaterally escalate a situation of internal unrest into a NIAC without committing multiple breaches of the right to life along the way. This follows by definition from the IHRL approach to the use of lethal force as sketched earlier, in particular by the requirements that lethal force can only be used when absolutely unavoidable to protect life and in a manner proportionate to that end and that states deploy nonlethal means to quell riots. Thus, the human right to life, as applied to specific instances involving government use of force, indirectly de facto prohibits the government to "militarize the confrontation by 'going to war.'"[70] Such militarization can only lawfully take place if non-state actors themselves provoke it by raising the level of violence. Such is indeed the result of human rights case law requiring states to graduate the level of force and to take measures of de-escalation in the face of riots and demonstrations, as well as of case law scrutinizing the planning, command, and control of operations (counterterrorist or other). Cases such as *McCann*[71] and *Zambrano Vélez*[72] indeed illustrate that human rights bodies such as the European Court of Human Rights or the Inter-American Court of Human Rights will critically examine the deployment of military personnel in times of peace and will scrutinize that the instructions, equipment, and training given to such personnel are suitable to the law enforcement context.

C. Toward an Internal *Ad Bellum* Prohibition on the Part of the State?

1. Feasibility

Although the human right to life indirectly prohibits the state from militarizing an insurrection, it is correct that its direct application by human rights bodies is limited to specific instances involving recourse to force. Such instances may concern the conduct of individual police officers, yet the right to life can also be

68. The result may well be that a more stringent test is sometimes applied than would be the case if IHL were applied directly. For a useful overview of the ECtHR's approach, *see* Françoise Hampson, *The Case-Law of the European Court of Human Rights and the Use of Force*, *in* Int'l Comm. of the Red Cross, *supra* note 41, app. 3, at 69.

69. *See, e.g.*, Camargo (on Behalf of Suarez de Guerrero) v. Colombia, Merits, Communication No. 45/1979, U.N. Doc. CCPR/C/15/D/45/1979 (U.N. Hum. Rts. Comm. Mar. 31, 1982).

70. *Cf.* Hessbruegge, *supra* note 13, at 115.

71. McCann v. United Kingdom, 1995 Eur. Ct. H.R. 31.

72. Zambrano Vélez v. Ecuador, Judgment, Inter-Am. Ct. H.R. (ser. C) No. 166 (July 4, 2007).

applied in a more general fashion to hold the state accountable for the preparation and conduct of various police or military operations, whether in times of peace or in times of armed conflict. By way of illustration, the European Court of Human Rights has applied the right to life to the shelling or aerial bombardment of villages in Turkey and in Chechnya.[73] However, what is missing, according to some, is an overarching norm to assess the internal use of force at the "macro" level, with a view to ascertaining which party—government or rebels—qualifies as the "aggressor" and which qualifies as the "victim."[74]

As mentioned earlier, Lieblich identifies such an overarching *ad bellum* norm through an extrapolation of the right to life to the collective level, and frames it as a prohibition on the first resort to internal hostilities—or more accurately perhaps a prohibition against "disproportionate" use of force—"qualified only by a right to self-and-other-defense, and subject to a necessity and proportionality requirements."[75] "Massive armed violence in the form of hostilities" is justified only as a necessary and proportionate reaction to "actions amounting to hostilities themselves."[76]

The focus on the *first* resort to hostilities mirrors the emphasis on the *first* use of force in the international legal framework governing the recourse to force between states. Thus, Article 2 of the U.N. General Assembly's *Definition of Aggression* stipulates that "[t]he first use of armed force by a State in contravention of the Charter shall constitute *prima facie* evidence of an act of aggression . . . ."[77] Lieblich draws another parallel to the law on the use of (inter-state) force with regard to the proposed threshold to identify a breach of the prohibition against the first resort to hostilities, and the concomitant right to respond to such hostilities by proportionate use of force. In particular, it is suggested that as "a viable rule of thumb, . . . the scale and effects of such actions must at least mirror that of an 'armed attack.' "[78]

It is questionable, however, whether the proposed focus on the *first* recourse to internal hostilities is workable in practice. When it comes to inter-state recourse to force, identifying the *first* use of force will often be a fairly straightforward

73. *E.g.*, Benzer v. Turkey, 2013 Eur. Ct. H.R. 1116, http://hudoc.echr.coe.int/eng?i=001-128036; Abdulkhanoy v. Russia, 2013 Eur. Ct. H.R. 918 (2013).

74. For example, in *Tagayeva*, the ECtHR suggests that its role is limited to the supervision of human rights obligations in connection with the "more operational aspects of the authorities' actions that have a direct bearing on the protected rights," as opposed to "the political choices made in the course of fighting terrorism." Tagayeva v. Russia, App. No. 26562/07, ¶ 481 (Eur. Ct. H.R. 2017).

75. Lieblich, *supra* note 5, at 696.

76. *Id.* at 742.

77. G.A. Res. 3314 (XXIX), U.N. Doc. A/RES/29/3314 (Dec. 14, 1974).

78. Lieblich, *supra* note 5, at 742.

exercise. This is so for the simple fact that the relevant protagonists are physically separated by their respective borders and neither is in principle permitted to exercise any form of enforcement jurisdiction in the territory of the other.[79] Thus, when the United States, France, and the United Kingdom decide to carry out air strikes against military facilities of the Syrian regime in reaction to a chemical weapons attack imputed to Damascus,[80] there can be little discussion that they are the *first* to act. The implication is that the onus is on them to justify their actions by explaining what triggered the strikes and why the proportionality and necessity criteria are fulfilled. True, at times the situation may be more complex in that states may be engaged in minor border incidents before large-scale hostilities erupt. The Ethiopia-Eritrea Claims Commission's *Partial Award* reveals how in such scenario it may be possible to make abstraction of incidents involving "geographically limited clashes . . . along a remote, unmarked, and disputed border" and to identify the party that escalated the situation by first conducting a large-scale armed attack on the territory of the other, and which accordingly incurs liability under the *jus ad bellum*.[81]

The situation is markedly different when it comes to internal use of force, where there is of course no physical separation between the government and its subjects to begin with, and the former is constantly exercising jurisdiction—including enforcement jurisdiction—vis-à-vis the latter. The implication is that it may be far more difficult, and oftentimes impossible, to identify the tip-off point where the proposed internal *jus ad bellum* norm is breached. NIACs indeed do not come out of the blue, but mostly follow a cycle of gradually escalating violence.[82] Consider the Libyan civil war in 2011, inspired by Libyans' fatigue with Gaddafi's decade-long authoritarian regime and pitted against the broader background of the Arab Spring. The events of February 2011 suggest a rapid escalation, with mass demonstrations by crowds armed with petrol bombs and stones, and the police initially responding with tear gas and rubber bullets.[83] In subsequent days, protests grew further, calling for an end of the Gaddafi regime. Libyan security

79. S.S. "Lotus" (Fr. v. Turk.), 1927 P.C.I.J. (ser. A) No. 10, at 14 (Sept. 7).

80. For further discussion, *see United States Bombs Government Facilities in Response to Chemical Weapons Use*, 112 Am. J. Int'l L. 522 (2018).

81. *Jus ad Bellum* (Eth. v. Eri.), Ethiopia's Claims 1–8, Partial Award, ¶ 12 (Eritrea-Ethiopia Claims Comm'n Dec. 19, 2005).

82. In a similar vein, *see* Kreβ, *supra* note 12, at 43 (referring to the possibility of an "escalation dynamic that [cannot] be disentangled with sufficient clarity to reliably attribute responsibility," and pointing to the situation in Syria since 2012 as an example of such dynamics).

83. *See, e.g.*, Jo Adetunji, Peter Beaumont, & Martin Chulov, *Libya Protests: More than 100 Killed as Army Fires on Unarmed Demonstrators*, The Guardian (Feb. 20, 2011), https://www.theguardian.com/world/2011/feb/20/libya-protests-benghazi-muammar-gaddafi; Ian Black & Matthew Taylor, *Libya Protesters Set Fire to Government Buildings in Tripoli*, The Guardian (Feb. 21, 2011), https://www.theguardian.com/world/2011/feb/21/libya-protesters-fire-government-tripoli.

forces fired live ammunition into the crowds, killing dozens, whereas protesters set fire to police stations and other government buildings. Another important development concerned the fact that some army personnel and police officers joined the antigovernment protesters. Such evolution is not uncommon in the early phase of a civil war, and has been similarly witnessed in the Syrian conflict.

How then to identify the party to *first* engage in "massive armed violence" in such settings? Can the deliberate use of lethal force to quell a violent demonstration—in gross violation of the right to life—qualify as the "first recourse to internal hostilities" as conceived by Lieblich, and, if so, as of when? Given the frequency of violent demonstrations turning deadly, from Libya to Venezuela,[84] and from the 2014 Maidan protests in Kiev[85] to the aforementioned 2018 Gaza border protests, the question is not without importance.

Furthermore, assuming, in spite of the foregoing, that the initial "aggressor" can effectively be identified, how must one assess a further escalation of the violence by the other side? Assuming, for instance, that the state has killed 50 unarmed demonstrators in city *X*, would that permit the inhabitants of city *Y*, far removed from *X*, to take up arms against the state? Would this raise proportionality concerns? Is it conceivable that both sides bear responsibility for escalating the situation and must somehow both be regarded as "aggressors"? Lieblich's concession that "[i]dentifying just exactly at what point . . . a forcible response [would be justified] is a complex factual question" strikes as an understatement.[86]

2. Added Value

Apart from the difficulty of applying a "first use" threshold, a related question is what added value is brought by an *ad bellum* norm prohibiting the first recourse to (disproportionate) internal force by the state. Leaving aside for now the possible implications with regard to third-state intervention in the conflict (see section IV.B), one aspect which Lieblich raises is its relevance for purposes of closing the existing accountability gap, namely, the lack of accountability at the international level "for instigating the conflict, either on the level of State responsibility or on that of criminal liability."[87] The underlying idea is that war crimes often take place at the lower echelons, so that IHL is not an effective tool to hold the leaders of states (and armed groups) criminally accountable.[88] While that may

84. *See, e.g.*, *Death Toll from Months of Anti-Maduro Protests in Venezuela Tops 100*, France 24 (July 21, 2017), https://www.france24.com/en/20170721-venezuela-death-toll-protests-100-nicolas-maduro-opposition.

85. *See, e.g.*, *Ukraine's Bloodiest Day: Dozens Dead as Kiev Protesters Regain Territory from Police*, The Guardian (Feb. 21, 2014), https://www.theguardian.com/world/2014/feb/20/ukraine-dead-protesters-police.

86. Lieblich, *supra* note 5, at 747.

87. *Id.* at 739.

88. *Id.*

be so, it is conceivable that the state's first resort to massive armed violence entails the commission of crimes against humanity—and perhaps even genocide.[89] *Pro memorie*, Article 7(1) of the Rome Statute defines "crimes against humanity" as, for example, acts of murder, extermination, enslavement, and torture, "when committed as part of a widespread or systematic attack directed against any civilian population with knowledge of the attack." Article 7(2) defines "attack directed against any civilian population" as "a course of conduct involving multiple commission of acts referred to in paragraph 1 against any civilian population, pursuant to or in furtherance of a State or organizational policy to commit such attack." The foregoing definitions are also copied in the International Law Commission's (ILC) *Draft Articles on Crimes Against Humanity*,[90] which will hopefully form the basis for a successful multilateral convention. The possibility to criminally prosecute (former)[91] state leaders who order the use of deadly force against unarmed demonstrators for crimes against humanity would seem to eclipse (at least partly) the need for a separate criminalization of "internal aggression."

Leaving aside the criminal aspect, the idea that the state could somehow be held internationally responsible at the international level and ordered to pay compensation for breaching an "internal" *jus ad bellum* presents daunting challenges. Precedents where aggressors breaching the prohibition against inter-state recourse to force were held internationally responsible and were moreover ordered to pay compensation for the damage caused—and extending beyond damage caused by specific breaches of human rights law or IHL—are few and far between. One rare precedent stems from the Ethiopia-Eritrea Claims Commission, which in its award on *Ethiopia's Damages Claims* also pronounced on Eritrea's liability for breaching the *jus ad bellum*. It is clear, however, from the *Award* that the Commission—partly due to a lack of precedents and other guidance—struggled greatly with this aspect, in particular with the definition and application of a causality link. In particular, the Commission held that the aggressor state was liable to pay compensation for the "foreseeable" consequences of its unlawful recourse to force.[92] Such consequences included deaths and injuries to civilians caused by shelling and gunfire, even if not contrary to the *jus in bello*.[93] At the same time,

89. In a similar vein, Kreβ refers to the "threat of international punishment . . . in cases of the most egregious abuses, in the resort to internal violence by State officials from the international criminalization of genocide and crimes against humanity." Kreβ, *supra* note 12, at 40.

90. Int'l L. Comm'n, Draft articles on Prevention and Punishment of Crimes against Humanity, with Commentaries, 2019, (2019) Vol. II, Part Two, *Yb. I.L.C.*

91. Acting heads of state, heads of government, and foreign ministers, of course, enjoy immunity from prosecution under current international law. *See, e.g.*, Arrest Warrant (Dem. Rep. Congo v. Belg.), Judgment, 2002 I.C.J. Rep. 3, ¶ 52 (Feb. 14).

92. Ethiopia's Damages Claims (Eth. v. Eri.), 26 Rep. Int'l Arbitral Awards 631, ¶ 289–90 (Eritrea-Ethiopia Claims Comm'n 2009).

93. *Id.* ¶ 334. By contrast, the Commission could not pronounce on liability of deaths and injuries of militiamen in combat, as Article 5(1) of the Algiers Agreement was deemed to exclude jurisdiction over such claims. *Id.* ¶ 338.

"given the uncertainties of armed conflict," it stressed that "if a party is deemed to foresee too wide a range of possible results of its action, reaching too far into the future, or too far from the battlefield, foreseeability loses meaning as a tool to assess proximate cause. If all results are foreseeable, the test is meaningless."[94] In the context of a NIAC, it is arguably all the more difficult to apply the causality requirement and ascertain what damage constitutes a "foreseeable" consequence of the state's initial recourse to hostilities. Add to this further hurdles, for example, in terms of *locus standi*: it is virtually unthinkable that a rebel group (for example, the Free Syrian Army) would bring a(n admissible) claim against a state (for example, the Damascus regime) before an international court or tribunal. It is also difficult to grasp who should pay compensation to whom, for example, when a NIAC ends with either the de jure government or the rebels being victorious, or with the two agreeing to a power-sharing agreement.[95]

Lieblich is absolutely right in denouncing the "glaring gap in the protection of the right to life of both soldiers and armed opposition members, as well as civilians that can be incidentally harmed." In the present situation, individuals who have suffered harm, without also having been the victims of a specific breach of IHRL or IHL, remain in the cold.[96] This gap, however, is not unique to NIACs but equally exists in international armed conflicts (IACs). True, when a member of the regular armed forces is killed in an exchange of fire with enemy troops, or when a civilian is killed as a result of an IHL-compliant attack against a military objective, such death may ultimately be a (foreseeable or unforeseeable) consequence of an initial unlawful decision by one state (either the individual's state of nationality or a third state) to use force against another state, in contravention of the U.N. Charter. Numerous hurdles exist, however, that would prevent the relatives of such individual from seeking compensation from the aggressor state before a domestic court of law or regional or international human rights body. Such hurdles may stem from domestic doctrines of crown or combat immunity, or separation of powers, as well as from the non-self-executing character of the *ad bellum* rules,[97] considerations of causality, and the doctrine of state immunity. The

94. *Id.* ¶ 290.

95. Even in the case in which a NIAC ends with a peace agreement between the "aggressor" government and the rebel group, it seems absurd to suggest that the government should pay compensation to the rebel group when both form part of the same state. The payment of compensation might possibly make more sense where the civil war results in the breakup of the state in two or more separate states (whether as a result of secession or *dismembratio*).

96. This is not to say that victims of human rights violations or breaches of IHL necessarily have a readily available remedy at their disposal. A directly enforceable right for victims of breaches of LOAC to obtain reparation, for instance, has yet to emerge. *See, e.g.*, Jurisdictional Immunities of the State (Germ. v. It.), 2012 I.C.J. 99, ¶ 108 (Feb. 3) (dodging the issue); Bundersverfassungsgericht [BVerfG] [Federal Constitutional Court] Aug. 13, 2013, 2 BvR 2660/06, ¶¶ 45–47 (Ger.).

97. *See, e.g.*, U.S. v. Khatallah, 160 F. Supp. 3d 144 (D.D.C. 2016).

expanding (extraterritorial) reach of human rights law may possibly open some (limited) room for soldiers to bring proceedings against their home state when it is possible to identify state negligence that has harmed their right to life.[98] Yet, it is hard to imagine—at least for the foreseeable future—tort proceedings being brought against a state solely or primarily on account of the state's unlawful recourse to force against another state. In a similar vein, notwithstanding the bold assertion in *General Comment Number 36* that acts of aggression violate the right to life,[99] it is clear that regional human rights bodies examining possible breaches of the right to life in situations of armed conflict have hitherto refrained from considering the *ad bellum* dimension of the conflict. The highly deferential attitude of human rights bodies with regard to state decisions to trigger the derogation clauses of human rights instruments[100] corroborates the view that this is unlikely to change. If the existence of the *ad bellum* norms on inter-state use of force has left unaffected the accountability gap which Lieblich identifies in respect of IACs, it is hard to see how the introduction of an *ad bellum* norm prohibiting the first recourse to hostilities at the internal level could of its own close this accountability gap with respect to NIACs.

In conclusion, the present section has raised doubts as to the suggested incentive on the part of states to escalate situations of internal violence in order to trigger the more permissive regime on the use of lethal force under IHL. In spite of the moral appeal, the section has also raised doubts with respect to the proposed *ad bellum* prohibition against the first (large-scale) use of force by the state at the internal level, primarily identifying difficulties in its application, but also questioning its added value in addressing the current accountability gap. In the end, the desire to restrain government use of force at the internal level may be better served through different avenues, for example, by a pragmatic narrowing of the divide between the IHL and IHRL approach to the use of lethal force—a trend

98. *See, e.g.*, Smith & Ors v. Ministry of Defence [2013] U.K.S.C. 41 (2013) (U.K.). Note, however, that the judges adopted a deferential attitude on the merits, separating those issues for which judicial scrutiny is appropriate from those for which it is not. Consider, for example, the following statement by Lord Hope (drawing from the jurisprudence of the ECtHR): "It will be easy to find that allegations are beyond the reach of article 2 [of the ECHR] if the decisions that were or ought to have been taken about training, procurement or the conduct of operations were at a high level of command and closely linked to the exercise of political judgment and issues of policy." *Id.* ¶ 76.

99. *See* Human Rights Committee, *supra* note 17.

100. *See, e.g.*, A & Others v. United Kingdom, 2009 EUR. Ct. H.R. 301, ¶ 173 (2009) ("The Court reiterates that it falls to each Contracting State . . . to determine whether that life is threatened by a 'public emergency' and, if so, how far it is necessary to go in attempting to overcome the emergency. By reason of their direct and continuous contact with the pressing needs of the moment, the national authorities are in principle better placed than the international judge to decide both on the presence of such an emergency and on the nature and scope of the derogations necessary to avert it. Accordingly, in this matter a wide margin of appreciation should be left to the national authorities."); *see also* Tagayeva v. Russia, App. No. 26562/07, ¶ 481 (Eur. Ct. H.R. 2017).

that is already materializing to some extent[101]—or by strengthening the international criminal law framework (including through the adoption of a multilateral treaty on crimes against humanity).

III. INTERNAL USE OF FORCE: REBEL USE OF FORCE AGAINST THE STATE

A. International Law's Neutrality toward Rebellion: Truth or Hoax?

Having examined the introduction of an internal *jus ad bellum* norm prohibiting government recourse to internal hostilities, the present section in turn looks at the possibility for the state's subjects to take up arms against the government, both from a *lex lata* and a *lex ferenda* perspective. The idea of a "right to rebel" against oppressive or tyrannical regimes has been a constant topic in scholarly literature throughout the centuries. The founding fathers of modern international law hotly debated the question,[102] and the topic continues to surface occasionally in contemporary legal doctrine.[103] The commonly accepted starting point is that—save for one partial exception discussed further later—international law does not currently recognize any right of armed resistance against the state, and accepts that individuals that take part in a NIAC against the state may be prosecuted pursuant to the state's domestic criminal law. It is true that a number of national constitutions recognize a certain right of resistance, but such examples remain the exception rather than the rule.[104] In a similar vein, it is true that the Universal Declaration of Human Rights states that "if man is not to be compelled to have recourse, as a last resort, to rebellion against tyranny and oppression, . . . human rights should be protected by the rule of law." This rebellion clause, however, seems little more than a cautious warning to states, and only made it to the preamble after suggestions to include an actual right to resist oppression in the Declaration were rejected.[105] The multilateral conventions that followed in subsequent years

101. *See supra* section II.B.

102. *See* 1 Hugo Grotius, De Jure Belli Ac Pacis Libri Tres ch. 4 (1625); 1 Emer De Vattel, Le Droit Des Gens ch. 4, ¶¶ 51, 54 (1758).

103. *E.g.*, Gwilym David Blunt, *Is There a Human Right to Resistance?*, 39 Hum. Rts. Q. 860 (2017); Jens David Ohlin, *The Right to Exist and the Right to Resist*, *in* The Theory of Self-Determination 70 (Fernando R. Tesón ed., 2016); Frédéric Mégret, *Le Droit International Peut-il être un Droit de Résistance? Dix Conditions pour un Renouveau de l'Ambition Normative Internationale*, 39 Études Internationales 39 (2008).

104. Hessbruegge, *supra* note 13, at 328–29. Hessbruegge finds that there are some 27 states that recognize resistance rights out of the world's 193 states. In addition, he states that there is no evidence to suggest that these constitutional resistance clauses reflect any *opinio juris* that customary international law recognizes such right.

105. *Id.* at 327.

do not hint at any right of armed resistance.[106] Conversely, as mentioned earlier, Article 2 of the ECHR effectively recognizes states' right to quell insurrections by force,[107] subject of course to the above-mentioned necessity and proportionality constraints. In all, the absence of a general right of armed resistance *de lege lata* is not in dispute.

A single exception to international law's principled neutrality toward rebellion is commonly put forward, specifically the struggle for self-determination of so-called "national liberation movements."[108] Throughout the 1960s and the 1970s the struggle for self-determination indeed dominated debates at the U.N. level, with a majority group of developing and socialist countries defending the right of national liberation movements to engage in armed struggle and to seek outside support, including military support, to achieve their legitimate aspirations.[109] Whether the campaign of developing and socialist states ultimately succeeded in the creation of a legal right to armed struggle on the part of "national liberation movements" is open to debate. Due primarily to the opposition of several Western states, key instruments, such as the 1970 Friendly Relations Declaration of the 1974 Definition of Aggression, were indeed framed in vague and ambiguous terms. The resolutions did recognize the "right" of peoples under colonial and racist regimes or other forms of alien domination to "struggle" in order to achieve self-determination, as well as to "seek and receive support" to this end. Whether that right to struggle included a right to "armed" struggle, and whether the right to receive third-state support included "armed" support was left unsettled.[110] While some scholars take the view that no positive right to rebellion for national liberation movements emerged from the debates,[111] the late Cassese suggests that

106. One exception is Article 20(2) of the African Charter on Human and Peoples' Rights, which states that "[c]olonized or oppressed peoples shall have the right to free themselves from the bonds of domination by resorting to any means recognized by the international community." This clause is, however, tied to the specific situation of wars of national liberation. *See infra* notes 109–19 and accompanying text.

107. *See supra* note 21 and accompanying text.

108. *See, e.g.*, Heather Wilson, International Law and the Use of Force by National Liberation Movements (1988); Natalino Ronzitti, Le Guerre di Liberazione Nazionale e il Diritto Internazionale (1974); Antonio Cassese, *Le Droit International et la Question de l'Assistance aux Mouvements de Libération Nationale*, 19 Revue Belge de Droit International 307 (1986).

109. The underlying legal arguments were diverse. While some regarded colonialism and racist domination as a "permanent" armed attack on subjected peoples triggering the right of self-defense, others framed the armed struggle for national liberation as a separate exception to the prohibition on the use of force, or as a use of force consistent with the purposes of the United Nations.

110. G.A. Res. 3314(XXIX), *supra* note 77, art. 7; G.A. Res. 2625(XXV), ¶ 5, U.N. Doc. A/RES/25/2625 (Oct. 24, 1970).

111. *E.g.*, Wilson, *supra* note 108, at 136 ("Practice in the UN, particularly the Declaration on Principles of International Law and the Declaration on Aggression, both adopted without vote,

it resulted in a "legal entitlement, . . . less than a right proper but more than an absence of any authorization whatsoever."[112]

What is certain, however, is that most states agreed that once an armed conflict erupted between a national liberation movement and a colonial, oppressive, or racist regime, such conflict should not be regarded as internal in nature, but rather as an IAC, with the result being that members of the national liberation movement and meeting the (watered down)[113] criteria for lawful combatancy benefited from the privilege of belligerency (and the concomitant POW protection upon capture) and could not be prosecuted for their mere participation in hostilities. This result was achieved through the introduction of Article 1(4) of the First Additional Protocol to the Geneva Conventions (AP I) in 1977.

While AP I, Article 1(4) would at first sight seem to put an important dent in the neutrality baseline, its impact should not be overestimated. This is primarily due to its limited scope. Indeed, the provision applies only to peoples "fighting against colonial domination and alien occupation and against racist regimes in the exercise of their right of self-determination." The first trigger is generally deemed to cover only cases of "saltwater colonialism," where the colonized territory is geographically separate from the colonial power. The third scenario extends only to the situation of apartheid regimes that are founded on racist criteria. "Alien occupation" normally presupposes that the territory did not yet form part of a state at the time of occupation but was populated by a distinct group.[114] By contrast, the provision does not in any way "internationalize" other wars of secession or rebellions against authoritarian regimes. What is more, the inclusion of Article 1(4) proved controversial at the time and explains at least in part why some countries that might be affected by its scope chose not to ratify the Protocol (Israel) or to postpone ratification until they would no longer be affected by it (Portugal and South Africa).[115] Attempts by the African National Congress (1980), the Palestinian Liberation Organization (1989), and the National Democratic Front of the Philippines (1996) to trigger Article 1(4) by submitting a declaration with

does not resolve the fundamental differences of opinion over the status of national liberation movement. . . .").

112. Antonio Cassese, Self-Determination of Peoples: A Legal Reappraisal 153 (1995).

113. *See* Protocol Additional to the Geneva Conventions of 12 August 1949, and Relating to the Protection of Victims of International Armed Conflict (Protocol I) arts. 43(3), 43(4), June 8, 1977, 1125 U.N.T.S. 3; *see also* the critique by Dinstein. Dinstein, *supra* note 37, at 61–64.

114. Hessbruegge, *supra* note 13, at 317; Kubo Mačák, Internationalized Armed Conflicts in International Law 67–69 (2018).

115. *See, e.g.*, Kubo Mačák, *Wars of National Liberation: The Story of One Unusual Rule*, OUPblog (July 23, 2018), https://blog.oup.com/2018/07/wars-national-liberation-unusual-rule-part-1 (noting that Portugal only ratified the Protocol after having relinquished control over its ex-colonies and South Africa did so after the end of apartheid).

the Protocol's depositary (the Swiss government) pursuant to AP I, Article 96(3) were all unsuccessful.[116] It is telling that the first, and so far only, activation of Article 1(4) took place in 2015, long after the end of the colonial era, and moreover relates to an essentially dormant conflict, namely, the conflict between the Polisario Front and the Kingdom of Morocco over the Western Sahara (note that the parties agreed to a ceasefire in 1991). Mačak rightly concludes that the practical impact of Article 1(4) has been "inversely proportional" to the amount of discussion and controversy it generated at the time of its drafting in Geneva.[117] Wilson for her part observes that even if Article 1(4) "opens a Pandora's box at all, it is an unexpectedly small one."[118]

Apart from its limited practical relevance, especially in the contemporary, post-colonial era, it stands to wondering if AP I, Article 1(4) would be maintained if the Protocol were to be renegotiated today. It does not take much effort indeed to observe that the widespread sympathy for national liberation movements that filled the U.N. corridors in past decades has long subsided and given way to a universal condemnation of terrorism. What is more, the wide net cast by international and regional counterterrorism instruments may well have put a much deeper—albeit less noticed—dent in international law's principled neutrality toward rebellion. Ever since the 1990s, and especially following the 9/11 attacks, numerous multilateral and regional treaties have indeed come into existence that provide for the criminalization of a wide variety of terrorist crimes. Reference can be made to a variety of U.N. conventions criminalizing specific terrorist offenses, such as the U.N. Convention for the Suppression of Terrorist Bombing (1997), which covers the bombing of any "State or government facility" with the intent to cause death or serious bodily injury or to cause extensive destruction of such place.[119] Admittedly, negotiations on a U.N. draft comprehensive convention against international terrorism have long been stuck in a deadlock,[120] illustrating that a generally agreed definition of "international terrorism" has yet to emerge.[121] At the same

116. Mačák, *supra* note 114, at 71.

117. *Id.* at 73.

118. Wilson, *supra* note 108, at 168.

119. International Convention for the Suppression of Terrorist Bombings, *opened for signature* Jan. 12, 1998, 2149 U.N.T.S. 256.

120. *See, e.g.*, Mahmoud Hmoud, *Negotiating the Draft Comprehensive Convention on International Terrorism: Major Bones of Contention*, 4 J. Int'l Crim. Just. 1031 (2006).

121. In 2011, the Appeals Chamber of the Special Tribunal for Lebanon did set forth a definition of transnational terrorism. Prosecutor v. Ayyash, Case No. STL-11-01/I, Interlocutory Decision on the Applicable Law, ¶¶ 83–113 (Special Tribunal for Lebanon, Appeals Chamber, Feb. 16, 2011). Whether the purported definition reflects customary international law is, however, highly questionable. For a critique, *see, e.g.*, Ben Saul, *Legislating from a Radical Hague: The UN Special Tribunal for Lebanon Invents an International Crime of Transnational Terrorism*, 24 Leiden J. Int'l L. 677 (2011); *see also* Kreβ, *supra* note 12, at 40 n.44.

time, regional instruments such as E.U. Directive 2017/541 on combating terrorism[122] or the Council of Europe Convention on the Prevention of Terrorism[123] have a very wide material scope of application, employing a broad definition of "terrorist acts" and criminalizing in broad terms assistance to, recruitment for, and financing of "terrorist groups." The E.U. Directive, for instance, qualifies as a "terrorist offense" numerous acts, including "attacks upon the physical integrity of a person" or acts "causing extensive destruction to a government or public facility," when committed with the aim of "seriously destabilising or destroying the fundamental political, constitutional, economic or social structures of a country or an international organisation."[124] It is prima facie hard to grasp what acts of rebellion would *not* be covered by the aforementioned definition. Importantly, the definitions of terrorist offenses generally do not distinguish between attacks against military objectives by IHL standards and attacks against civilians and civilian objects and are accordingly blind as to whether attacks by non-state actors are IHL compliant. They also tend to include an *aut dedere, aut judicare* obligation, while stipulating that the terrorist offenses concerned cannot be regarded as "political offenses" (for extradition purposes).[125]

One might object that many conventions do contain an exemption clause excluding from their purview the "activities of armed forces during an armed conflict, as those terms are understood under international humanitarian law, which are governed by that law." Such clauses—which leave open the possibility of prosecuting suspected war criminals—can be found, for instance, in the abovementioned Terrorist Bombings Convention[126] and in the preamble of the E.U. Directive.[127] While clauses of this type seemingly leave intact international law's neutrality toward rebellion, a number of observations are in order. First, the exemption does not extend to the pre-NIAC phase, that is, to the acts of violence committed before the internal unrest reaches the intensity threshold to trigger IHL. Second, the clause is not included in every counterterrorist treaty. In *R. v. Gul*, the U.K. Supreme Court found that out of 14 U.N. counterterrorism treaties, "(i) seven [included such clause], (ii) of the seven which have no such statement, six

122. Directive 2017/541 of the European Parliament and of the Council of 15 March 2017 on Combating Terrorism and Replacing Council Framework Decision 2002/475/JHA and Amending Council Decision 2005/671/JHA, 2017 O.J. (L-88) 6.

123. Council of Europe Convention on the Prevention of Terrorism, May 16, 2005, C.E.T.S. No. 196.

124. Directive 2017/541, *supra* note 122, arts. 1(a), 2(c).

125. *E.g.*, International Convention for the Suppression of Terrorist Bombings, *supra* note 119, arts. 9, 11.

126. *Id.* art. 19. The clause also exempts from its scope "the activities undertaken by military forces of a State in the exercise of their official duties, inasmuch as they are governed by other rules of international law."

127. Directive 2017/541, *supra* note 122, pmbl. ¶ 37.

provide that the treaty 'does not exclude any criminal jurisdiction exercised in accordance with national law.' "[128] At the E.U. level, while the exemption features in the preamble of Directive 2017/541, many E.U. member states (including the United Kingdom and France) have chosen to implement the Directive's provisions into national legislation, without, however, copying the clause concerned. In such countries, national courts have confirmed that, since no privilege of belligerency exists in NIACs, there is nothing that excludes the prosecution of participants in such conflicts for "terrorist offenses."[129] Furthermore, even in a state such as Belgium that has integrated the exemption into its criminal code,[130] it appears that judges have focussed on subjective considerations pertaining to a group's extremist agenda or its disregard for IHL, rather than on IHL's twin requirements of intensity and organization, to find that members (or supporters) of certain non-state armed groups can be prosecuted on account of terrorist offenses under the Belgian Criminal Code. The result is a series of judgments that appear internally inconsistent and difficult to reconcile with IHL, whereby a group such as the PKK is regarded as a party to a NIAC, but a group such as al-Nusra is not[131] (notwithstanding the group's large number of fighters and its control over large parts of Syria). In the end, whether members of a NSAG that is involved in a NIAC abroad will be prosecuted before the domestic courts of a third state is partly a question of prosecutorial discretion (in addition to practical and jurisdictional constraints).[132] That such approach may lead to contradictory and even absurd outcomes is well illustrated by a recent Dutch case involving the criminal prosecution on account of a person's membership of the "terrorist" group Jabhat al-Shamiya, while the very same group had previously received nonlethal assistance from the Dutch

128. R v. Gul, [2013] U.K.S.C. 64, ¶¶ 47–48 (2013) (U.K.).

129. *See id.*; *see also* High Council of the Netherlands, J.M.J., S 15/02147, April 4, 2017, ECLI:NL:HR:2017:574; High Council of the Netherlands, 02853/02 U, May 7, 2004, ECLI:NL:HR:2004:AF6988.

130. *See* Belgium Criminal Code art. 141bis.

131. *See* Sharia4Belgium, Antwerp Court of Appeals (Jan. 26, 2016), Cases 2015/FP/1-7 to FD35.98.47–12; Sharia4Belgium, Antwerp Court of First Instance, Correctional Chamber (Feb. 11, 2015), 2015 Nieuw Juridisch Weekblad 282, http://www.rechtbankeersteaanlegantwerpen.be/images/AN35F11809-12.pdf; PKK, Brussels Chambre des Mises en Accusation (Sept. 14, 2017), *excerpted in* 2017–18 Rechtskundig Weekblad 1611; PKK, Brussels Chambre des Mises en Accusation (Mar. 8, 2019); *see also* Rogier Bartels, *When Do Terrorist Organisations Qualify as "Parties to an Armed Conflict" Under International Humanitarian Law*, 56 Mil. L. & L. War Rev. 451 (2017–2018).

132. Criticizing such broad prosecutorial discretion, *see, e.g.*, R v. Gul, *supra* note 128, ¶¶ 36–37 (noting that such discretion "leaves citizens unclear as to whether or not their actions or projected actions are liable to be treated by the prosecution authorities as effectively innocent or criminal—in this case seriously criminal").

authorities.[133] The German Federal Criminal Court has similarly held that the concept of "terrorist offenses" under German criminal law would apply to armed groups involved in the Syrian civil war, irrespective of the Syrian regime's own human rights record and even with regard to armed groups receiving support from the German government.[134]

The spillover effect of counterterrorism law and discourse potentially also extends to questions of third-state intervention in NIACs. Indeed, among those that agree that de jure governments that are involved in a fully fledged civil war are no longer permitted to invite outside military assistance from third states, there is growing support for the view that an exception exists with regard to assistance to combat terrorism. We will return to this discussion in the final part of the chapter.

B. From Personal Self-Defense to an *Ad Bellum* Right of Armed Resistance?

1. A Limited Right to Personal Self-Defense under Positive International Law

It follows from the foregoing that international law's suggested neutrality toward rebellion may not be fully accurate, as acts that might fit the label of insurgency or rebellion are increasingly caught by the net of international and regional criminal law (as it relates to counterterrorism). On the other hand, it must be acknowledged that international law also leaves some—albeit limited—leeway for individuals to use force to defend themselves or others against unlawful violence, including by the state. Such limited right of resistance can be derived from the right to personal self-defense as a general principle of law recognized by nations.[135] Whether the same principle could serve as a basis to construe a broader right of organized armed resistance against the state in certain situations is a different matter altogether, one we will turn to in the next subsection.

National case law tends to confirm the existence of a right to personal self-defense in the face of manifestly unlawful police actions, in particular where

133. Nederland Steunde "Terreurbeweging" in Syrië, NOS (Sept. 10, 2018), https://nos.nl/nieuwsuur/artikel/2249806-nederland-steunde-terreurbeweging-in-syrie.html. For a comparable case in the UK, see R Norton-Taylor, *Terror Trial Collapses after Fears of Deep Embarrassment to Security Services*, The Guardian (June 1, 2015), https://www.theguardian.com/uk-news/2015/jun/01/trial-swedish-man-accused-terrorism-offences-collapse-bherlin-gildo.

134. Bundesgerichtshof [BGH] [Federal Court of Justice] Apr. 6, 2017, Beschl. V. 06.04.2017–3 StR 326/16 (2017) (Ger.) (with case comment by Nikolaos Gazeas and Thomas Grosse-Wilde). In particular, *see id.* ¶¶ 15, 18–20 ("*Der Angekl. Wäre deshalb dem Grunde nach dann strafrechtlich zu verfolgen gewesen, wenn er sich nach seiner Ausreise nach und Ausbildung in Syrien einger gegen das Assad-Regime kämpfenden Oppositionsgruppe hätte anschließen wollen, die von der Bundesregiering unterstützt wurde oder wird.*").

135. Hessbruegge, *supra* note 13, at 303.

police officers engage in abusive physical violence.[136] Such limited right of forcible resistance normally presumes the existence of a present or imminent unlawful attack. By contrast, the "prospective danger of the police getting out of hand and acting unlawfully" in a given situation is insufficient.[137] Furthermore, forcible resistance is permitted only if strictly necessary to avoid harm that is otherwise unavoidable. The implication is that protestors participating in a peaceful demonstration that is violently and unlawfully dispersed by the police should pursue safe escape options and do not normally have a right to fight the police.[138] In addition, case law confirms that the amount of force used in defense must be proportionate to the unlawful violence concerned.[139] A remarkable case suggesting that the right of personal self-defense may also operate at the collective level, when a group of persons is confronted with unlawful police action, concerns the Inter-American Court of Human Rights' judgment in *Miguel Castro-Castro Prison v. Peru*.[140] The case involved the large-scale use of deadly force by Peruvian security forces against prisoners linked to the *Sendero Luminiso*. The Court established that when the operation started, "the inmates were not in mutiny and it has not been proven that there was any cause that called from [*sic*] the legitimate use of force by the state agents in that first act of the attack."[141] Accordingly, the inmates' resistance following the attack constituted "a normal reaction to the offensive of the police officials, as the result of a natural instinct of defense of their life and physical integrity."[142] The Court observed how "the inmates spent four days looking for ways to survive the multiple and constant actions of the state that could lead to their death."[143] Without expressly stating this, the Court appeared to imply that the inmates had a right to defend themselves against deliberate attacks on their life.[144]

The existence of a limited right of personal self-defense is equally recognized in IHL. In particular, it is recognized in IHL that the use of necessary and proportionate force in individual self-defense or defense of others against violence prohibited under IHL does not mean that the individuals concerned are engaging

136. *See id.* at 302.

137. Devlin v. Armstrong, Northern Ireland, Court of Appeal, [1971] NILR 13, 33 (per Lord MacDermott, C.J.).

138. Hessbruegge, *supra* note 13, at 309–10.

139. *See, e.g.*, Bundesgerichtshof [BGH] [Federal Court of Justice] July 16, 1980, Judgment, Case No. 2 StR 127/80, 1981 JuristenZeitung 35 (1980) (Ger.); BGH, July 5, 2000, Judgment, Case No. 5 StR 629/99, 2000 Neure Juristische Wochenschrift 3079 (2000) (Ger.).

140. Miguel Castro-Castro Prison v. Peru, Judgment, 2006 Inter-Am. Ct. H.R. (ser. C) No. 160 (Nov. 25, 2006).

141. *Id.* ¶ 241.

142. *Id.*

143. *Id.* ¶ 242.

144. Hessbruegge, *supra* note 13, at 304.

in direct participation in hostilities. As the ICRC's *DPH Guidance* explains, such use of force, for example, against "unlawful attack or looting, rape, and murder by marauding soldiers," may well meet the threshold of harm, but lacks the required "belligerent nexus" to qualify as direct participation in hostilities.[145] The implication is that the persons concerned will not lose their immunity from attack as civilians. The preparatory works of the *DPH Guidance* indicate that experts were broadly in agreement on this point. During a meeting in 2003, "[a]ll the experts . . . stressed that individual civilians using a proportionate amount of force in response to an unlawful and imminent attack against themselves or their property should not be considered as directly participating in hostilities."[146] Similarly, during an expert meeting in 2004, the issue "did not generate any major controversy."[147] Some implicit support for this position can also be found in the case law of the international criminal tribunals. Thus, in *Blaskic*, the ICTY suggested that the presence of about 120 armed men conducting voluntary night watches, and forming "a sort of civil defence rather than an army strictly speaking," was insufficient to turn the area into a military objective.[148] In *Bagosora*, the ICTR similarly stated that it was "not satisfied" that the use of traditional weapons by refugees to defend themselves against repeated attacks by militiamen changed these persons' status.[149] Somewhat ambiguously, the Tribunal added that "[e]ven if those with weapons for self-defence could be characterised as combatants," their presence within groups of refugees did not deprive those that were noncombatants of their protected status.[150]

Whatever the precise contours of the right of personal self-defense, it is clear that it is narrow in scope. Thus, while there is some scholarly support for the view that under IHRL individuals are entitled to take proportionate action to defend themselves against extrajudicial killings and torture, a broader right for individuals to defend themselves against serious human rights violations has hitherto not been recognized and finds no support in the practice of international

145. Int'l Comm. of the Red Cross, *supra* note 52, at 61.

146. Jean-François Quéguiner, Summary Report: Direct Participation in Hostilities Under International Humanitarian Law 6 (2003), https://www.icrc.org/eng/assets/files/other/2003-03-report-dph-2003-icrc.pdf.

147. Nils Melzer, Direct Participation in Hostilities Under International Humanitarian Law: Background Paper 31 (2004), https://www.icrc.org/eng/assets/files/other/2004-03-background-doc-dph-icrc.pdf.

148. Prosecutor v. Blaskič, Case No. IT-95-14-T, Judgment, ¶ 407 (Int'l Crim. Trib. for the Former Yugoslavia Mar. 3, 2000), *see also* Bundesgerichtshof [BGH] [Federal Court of Justice] Apr. 6, 2017, Beschl. V. 06.04.2017-3 StR 326/16, ¶ 20(2) (Ger.) (hinting at a distinction between offensive and defensive conduct).

149. Prosecutor v. Bagosora & Ors., Case No. ICTR-98-41-T, Judgment, ¶ 2238 (Int'l Crim. Trib. for Rwanda Dec. 18, 2008).

150. *Id.*

human rights bodies. For instance, there exists no general right to resist arbitrary arrest, nor is there a right to use force to escape inhuman conditions of detention,[151] as the Inter-American Court's judgment in *Montero Aranguren* implicitly illustrates.[152] Similarly, IHL debates indicate that there is only a very narrow scope for individual and personal self-defense in armed conflict. During the preparatory works of the *DPH Guidance*, for instance, it was suggested that the scope was limited to defense of self or others against an unlawful imminent threat to life or bodily integrity,[153] whereas others stressed that it was necessarily "time-confined to the period of threat or actual violence."[154] Importantly, self-defense is limited to cases involving an unlawful attack. Efforts to defend a military objective or to otherwise support a party to the conflict undeniably give rise to direct participation in hostilities due to the existence of a belligerent nexus. The narrow construction of self-defense in this context is inspired by a desire to avoid creating a slippery slope where the distinction between the civilian population and those taking part in hostilities becomes blurred (to the detriment of the former group). It follows that personal self-defense as it is construed *de lege lata* does not justify individuals mounting offensive operations or transforming themselves into an organized armed group capable of conducting such operations.

2. Toward an *Ad Bellum* Right of Armed Resistance?

a. Feasibility

Dissatisfied with the current state of positive international law, several scholars have put forward *de lege ferenda* proposals—reminiscent of the doctrines set forth in earlier times by Vattel and others—and pleading for an *ad bellum* right of armed resistance against the state in certain, exceptional situations. Rather than pleading for a right of armed resistance against tyrannical or oppressive regimes on the basis of some vague and uncertain right to democracy, or on the basis of the right to self-determination—breaches of which come in various shapes and degrees of severity—several authors tie it to the right of life and the notion of personal self-defense.[155] The underlying idea appears to be that when a government engages in large-scale and systematic unlawful violence against its population, or part thereof, such conduct qualifies as a continuing attack triggering the right of self-defense of the population

151. Hessbruegge, *supra* note 13, at 304–307.

152. Montero-Aranguren (Detention Center of Catia) v. Venezuela, Preliminary Objection, Merits, Reparations & Costs, Inter-Am. Ct. H.R. (ser. C) No. 150, ¶¶ 60(8)–(15), 67–74 (July 5, 2006). In spite of the inhumane conditions at the Detention Center at Catia, the Court refrained from acknowledging that the inmates' violent breakout attempt could be regarded as an act of self-defense, and instead recognized that Venezuela had a right to use force to control the uprising (although the amount of force used was deemed disproportionate).

153. Int'l Comm. of the Red Cross, *supra* note 147, at 32.

154. *Id.*

155. *E.g.*, Kreβ, *supra* note 12, at 41.

(or the targeted part thereof). The exercise of this right remains subject to the necessity and proportionality criteria, yet both criteria must be applied at the "macro" level, that is, in their *ad bellum* version.

As explained earlier, an approach that would make the suggested right of armed resistance contingent on a first recourse to massive armed violence by the state may be unworkable in practice, since it may be impossible to isolate and pinpoint such first internal use of force in the chaos that marks the outbreak of civil war. Other scholars instead construe the "just cause" justifying organized armed resistance in terms of mass atrocities by the state against its own population[156]—an approach that bears parallels to the humanitarian intervention doctrine.

Hessbruegge's proposal is case in point. In particular, he argues that there is a right of organized armed resistance against mass atrocities, which would be triggered by "an ongoing or imminent state campaign of genocide, crimes against humanity, or widespread war crimes," as opposed to a "mere fear of future atrocities or historical grievances."[157] Similar to what is often suggested in the context of (*de lege ferenda*) proposals of a right of unilateral humanitarian intervention,[158] Hessbruegge stresses that there ought to be solid and objective evidence of such atrocities, consisting notably in the findings of credible and independent international human rights mechanisms (without, however, requiring a prior determination to this end by the (inevitably politicized) U.N. Security Council).[159] In addition, parallel to the treatment of national liberation movements under AP I, Articles 1(4) and 96(3), he argues that international law should only recognize as lawful those armed resistance movements that represent the affected population[160] and can credibly point to a popular mandate.[161] Otherwise, considerable emphasis is placed on the constraints resulting from the necessity and proportionality

156. *See, e.g.*, *id.* at 39 n.44 (referring to "massive internal violence"); *id.* at 41; *see also* Mégret, *supra* note 103.

157. Hessbruegge, *supra* note 13, at 334.

158. Consider, for example, the requirement that there be "convincing evidence, generally accepted by the international community as a whole, of extreme humanitarian distress on a large scale" in the (controversial) British position on unilateral humanitarian intervention. *See, e.g.*, Prime Minister's Office, Policy Paper: Syria Action—U.K. Government Legal Position ¶ 3 (Apr. 14, 2018) (U.K.), https://www.gov.uk/government/publications/syria-action-uk-government-legal-position/syria-action-uk-government-legal-position.

159. Hessbruegge, *supra* note 13, at 334.

160. Note that the qualifier that the resistance movement must be representative of the "affected population" seems of considerable importance. If, by contrast, the resistance movement ought to be representative of the state's population as a whole, this would, for instance, preclude a (ethnic, religious, or other) minority within a state from taking up arms in response to ethnic cleansing and other acts of unlawful violence by the state apparatus.

161. Hessbruegge, *supra* note 13, at 337.

requirements. For instance, Hessbruegge notes how armed resistance can only be a last resort, when nonviolent means have been exhausted, and must be directed only at those persons or institutions engaging in the mass atrocities that triggered it (but not, for instance, against regular police units that are not involved therein).[162] In addition, he notes how any violence outlawed under IHL would be ipso facto disproportionate,[163] a suggestion that nonetheless appears to conflate *ad bellum* and *in bello* considerations.

Although Hessbruegge, as well as others developing similar frameworks for lawful armed resistance, makes many sensible points, the suggested right of organized armed resistance also calls for some critical observations. At the outset, it is noted that, while there appears to be a compelling moral argument that people subjected to mass atrocities should be entitled to resist, the application of the suggested threshold may be problematic. It is open to debate, for instance, whether the (evidently unlawful) use of live fire to disperse peaceful demonstrators would suffice to activate the right to resist. Also, the reality on the ground may be chaotic, and atrocities may well be committed by both sides. Leaving aside the foregoing difficulties, it must be emphasized that the inevitable impact of accepting a right to resist in certain exceptional circumstances, is to exclude and delegitimize other situations of armed resistance: *inclusio unius est exclusio alterius*. For instance, if it is recognized that ethnic cleansing or genocide by the state justifies taking up arms against it, this would *a contrario* imply that no such right exists for people living under an authoritarian regime that stifles every form of dissent in various ways, for example, by jailing political opponents, but which does not go as far as to engage in large-scale extrajudicial killings. In a similar vein, a right to resistance would seemingly be excluded for peoples seeking to secede from a state where they enjoy no meaningful political participation and which denies their social and cultural rights. Those engaging in armed resistance would accordingly remain prone, for instance, to being caught in the net of international counterterrorism law. Identifying one or more just causes implies that other causes will be "unjust"; if the neutrality baseline is abandoned, this works both ways. Lest there be any misunderstanding: under the above-mentioned standard, both the American War of Independence and the French Revolution of 1789 would arguably have been contrary to the internal *ad bellum* norm, and those actively involved in either revolution would risk criminal prosecution, for example, for terrorist offenses.

The operation of the necessity and proportionality tests also poses challenges. Interestingly, similar to what is the case for the humanitarian intervention debate,[164] proponents of an *ad bellum* right of armed resistance tend to construe

162. *Id.* at 335.

163. *Id.* at 337–38.

164. *See, e.g.*, Int'l Comm. on Intervention & State Sovereignty, The Responsibility to Protect ¶¶ 4.39–4.41 (2001) (on the need for "reasonable prospects"); High-Level Panel on

the proportionality criterion as entailing a "balance-of-consequences" or a "likelihood of success" component.[165] Suggestions to this end were already present in the writings of the founding fathers of international law. Grotius, for instance, found that there was no right to resistance, even in extreme situations, if this would cause "great disturbance in the state, or prove the destruction of many innocents."[166] Contemporary scholars have similarly suggested that the positive human rights consequences of armed resistance must outweigh the negative impact on them, and that the chances of the armed struggle successfully stopping, or at least mitigating, the mass atrocities must be taken into account. In the words of Hessbruegge, "Plunging the country into a fully-fledged armed conflict without a discernible chance of success would be disproportional."[167] Yet, this requirement presupposes a degree of predictability which is generally lacking in the context of civil war. Indeed, while it is possible in the context of a specific targeting decision during an armed conflict to verify whether the person ordering the attack reasonably knew that the collateral damage would be "clearly excessive" in relation to the concrete and direct anticipated military advantage,[168] this exercise cannot easily be transplanted to the *ad bellum* sphere. Just as with a unilateral humanitarian intervention by a third state, the outcome of a civil war cannot be tested against a counterfactual scenario as it would have occurred absent military action.

The difficulty of anticipating the consequences and likelihood of success of a unilateral humanitarian intervention, and, more generally, of assessing its proportionality, is illustrated by NATO's 1999 air campaign against the Federal Republic of Yugoslavia with a view to halting the ethnic cleansing of the Kosovar minority.[169] Thus, the Independent International Commission on Kosovo notes how "NATO believed that a relatively short bombing campaign would persuade Milošević to sign the Rambouillet agreement. That was a major mistake."[170]

Threats, Challenges and Change, A More Secure World: Our Shared Responsibility ¶ 207 (2004), *annexed in* U.N. Doc. A/59/565 (Dec. 2, 2004).

165. *See* Nick Fotion & Bruno Coppieters, *Likelihood of Success*, *in* Moral Constraints on War 79, 79–90 (Bruno Coppieters & Nick Fotion eds., 2002).

166. Grotius, *supra* note 102, ch. 4, § 7.

167. Hessbruegge, *supra* note 13, at 336–37. Note that Lieblich also suggests that any right of armed resistance must "abide by a means-end requirement and be justified according to a cost-benefit analysis." At the same time, he concedes that the latter requirement "has generally been disregarded in the positive international law." Lieblich, *supra* note 5, at 742.

168. *Cf.* Rome Statute of the International Criminal Court art. 8(2)(b)(iv), July 17, 1998, 37 I.L.M. 999 (1998).

169. This paragraph is based on earlier work. *See* Tom Ruys, *Criminalizing Aggression: How the Future of the Law on the Use of Force Rests in the Hands of the ICC*, 29 Eur. J. Int'l L. 887, 904 (2018).

170. Indep. Int'l Comm. on Kosovo, The Kosovo Report 4 (2000).

Eventually, however, it took a 78-day bombing campaign, causing between 2,500 and 5,000 casualties, for Milošević to give in. In addition, there is room for debate as to whether the campaign achieved its stated aim and what its impact was beyond that aim.[171] How to limit the impact of an intervention to the halting of a humanitarian catastrophe proper, without further ripple effects, is not evident; the line between the protection of civilians and fostering regime change or secession may indeed be thin. The challenges related to the proportionality assessment are similarly illustrated by the NATO operation in Libya in 2011, where several states accused NATO of overstepping the U.N. Security Council's authorization to use force "to protect civilians and civilian populated areas under threat of attack" and instead pursuing an objective of regime change.[172]

The resulting dilemma is all the more problematic in cases of civil war, which a fortiori do not lend themselves to easy predictions. Consider, for instance, the Syrian civil war, with its manifold protagonists and changing coalitions, which since its eruption in 2011 has resulted in over 400,000 casualties and millions of refugees and internally displaced persons.[173] In September 2018, the Dutch government informed the national parliament that it had decided to halt its policy of providing nonlethal assistance to moderate rebel groups operating in Syria because of the "military advance of the [Assad] regime in large parts of Syria" and military victory of Assad seemed "imminent."[174] Assuming, for the sake of argument, that this position is or was correct, what would be the implications for the purported right of armed resistance? Does it imply that armed resistance, which may once have been lawful, suddenly becomes unlawful? Or that it becomes retroactively unlawful from the start? One might object that, as with the application of the proportionality test under IHL, the "balance of consequences" should not

171. Again, in the words of the Kosovo Report, "[T]he NATO war was neither a success nor a failure; it was in fact both. . . . [T]he intervention failed to achieve its avowed aim of preventing mass ethnic cleansing. . . . The Serbian people were the main losers. Kosovo was lost. Many Serbs fled or were expelled from the province. Serbia suffered considerable economic losses and destruction of civilian infrastructure." *Id.* at 5.

172. S.C. Res. 1973, ¶ 4 (Mar. 17, 2011); *see, e.g.*, Ashley Deeks, *The NATO Intervention in Libya—2011*, *in* THE USE OF FORCE IN INTERNATIONAL LAW: A CASE-BASED APPROACH 749, 754–55 (Tom Ruys, Olivier Corten, & Alexandra Hofer eds., 2018). Consider also the critique of Milanovic, who argues that the air strikes against Syria in April 2018 failed to meet the requirements for humanitarian intervention set forth by the U.K. government itself. Marko Milanovic, *The Syria Strikes: Still Clearly Illegal*, EJIL:TALK! (Apr. 15, 2018), https://www.ejiltalk.org/the-syria-strikes-still-clearly-illegal.

173. *See, e.g.*, *Syrian Civil War Fast Facts*, CNN (Apr. 9, 2019), https://edition.cnn.com/2013/08/27/world/meast/syria-civil-war-fast-facts/index.html.

174. DUTCH MINISTRY OF FOREIGN AFF., KAMERBRIEF OVER HET IOB-ONDERZOEK NAAR STABILISATIEPROGRAMMA'S IN SYRIË 2 (Sept. 7, 2018), https://www.rijksoverheid.nl/documenten/kamerstukken/2018/09/07/kamerbrief-over-het-iob-onderzoek-naar-stabilisatieprogramma%E2%80%99s-in-syrie (our translation).

be assessed ex post facto on the basis of hindsight, but should be assessed from the perspective of the rebel group as the situation presented itself at the start of the conflict. But is such exercise ultimately feasible? Historical precedents suggest a negative answer is in order. Even if one discounts the immediate risk that a rebellion may inspire the incumbent regime to commit yet more atrocities to quell the resistance,[175] the prospect of success—which depends on a range of variables, including the domestic and international support the rebels manage to secure—and the overall consequences—in terms of casualties, refugees, internally displaced persons, and state failure, to name but a few—appear impossible to predict. It is recalled in this context that civil war tends to breed further conflict. One of the main parameters to predict whether a state is likely to suffer violent conflict in future years is indeed exactly the prior occurrence of such conflict in its recent past.[176]

Assuming moreover that it is reasonably possible to conduct a "balance of consequences" test, the potentially perverse implications must not be overlooked. The implication would indeed be that in those cases where organized armed resistance is unlikely to succeed, or is likely to aggravate the situation, the individuals concerned would not have a right to rebel and would to the contrary be banned under international law from having recourse to force against the government.[177] A possible scenario that comes to mind is that of a minority threatened with or suffering ethnic cleansing or genocide at the hands of a regime with far superior military capacities. To hold that the minority concerned would not have a right of armed resistance not only appears difficult to accept from a moral perspective but also appears difficult to reconcile with the idea that the right of organized armed resistance finds its basis in the notion of personal self-defense, the application of which is not subject to any "likelihood of success" test.[178]

175. In this sense, *see* Hessbruegge, *supra* note 13, at 337.

176. On the "conflict trap," *see, e.g.*, Paul Collier, Breaking the Conflict Trap: Civil War and Development Policy (2003).

177. *See also* Ohlin, *supra* note 103. Apart from the perverse effect that the "success condition" renders defensive force—whether in the criminal or in the international context—"impermissible if it will be ineffectual," Ohlin points to a second concern. In particular, having regard to the U.S. intervention in Iraq in 1990–1991, he notes that there may be situations where the criterion would provide a reason "for a greater amount of defensive force, because the lesser amount of force would be ineffectual." Thus, the condition "pushes defensive force to either sides of the spectrum. Either the defendant should use enough overwhelming force to secure the legitimate aims of the defensive force, or the defendant should forego force entirely." *Id.* at 88.

178. *See, e.g.*, *id.* at 88–90. Ohlin criticizes the consequentialist reasoning upon which the "success condition" rests. Instead, he posits that "the rationale for the defensive force has nothing to do with the success condition. Rather, the victim has the right to resist force, regardless of whether doing so secures his or her existence, because doing so is an expression of the defender's autonomy as both a moral agent and a legitimate object of moral concern. The right to meet force with force is a natural right that all agents are endowed with, and to succumb to force just

Leaving aside the problems related to a "balance of consequences" and a "likelihood of success" criterion, operationalizing the proportionality and necessity requirements in the context of organized armed resistance within a state poses further challenges. The suggestion that nonviolent means, in the form of political negotiations, peaceful demonstrations, and so forth, must first be exhausted appears sensible, but must arguably be taken with a grain of salt. A parallel can be made in this context to the right of self-defense under Article 51 of the UN Charter. In particular, practice suggests that the need to exhaust peaceful means plays only a subsidiary role for the assessment of self-defense claims in response to a *prior* attack—as opposed to cases of anticipatory self-defense—and that unlawfulness will only result when a manifest unwillingness to address diplomatic channels can be demonstrated.[179] As Schachter puts it, "[A] State is not obliged to turn the other cheek when attacked."[180] By the same token, it is difficult to imagine a legal requirement to pursue nonviolent alternatives when a situation of ethnic cleansing or even genocide is already ongoing.

More generally, from a conceptual point of view, the necessity and proportionality criteria would presumably demand that organized armed resistance take place only when necessary to put an end to the mass atrocities triggering it and that it be limited to what is necessary to that end. This corresponds to the way in which the two criteria are used in the inter-state self-defense context. Indeed, as far as state recourse to self-defense is concerned, the necessity and proportionality criteria entail that defensive action should be constrained to the halting and repelling of an attack, and exceptionally, in the case of successive and interlinked armed attacks, to the preventing of their reoccurrence.[181] Thus, when a state *A* is confronted with a military intervention by state *B* and manages to successfully repulse the invading forces, state *A* cannot proceed to occupying part of state *B* without violating the proportionality principle and engaging in unlawful occupation. Similarly, proponents of unilateral humanitarian intervention—such as, most prominently, the United Kingdom—tend to argue that the force used "must be necessary and proportionate to the aim of relief of humanitarian suffering and

because the defense will be ineffectual is to passively accept the unjustified aggression." *Id.* at 90. Note that the perverse impact of the "likelihood of success" criterion in principle remains even if the criterion is interpreted narrowly so as to exclude *only* defensive action that is manifestly unlikely to be successful at a given point in time.

179. *See also* TOM RUYS, "ARMED ATTACK" AND ARTICLE 51 OF THE UN CHARTER 95–98 (2010).

180. Oscar Schachter, *The Lawful Resort to Unilateral Use of Force*, 10 YALE J. INT'L L. 291, 292 (1985).

181. RUYS, *supra* note 179, at 123. On the application of the proportionality principle to the (state) right of self-defense, *see also* David Kretzmer, *The Inherent Right to Self-Defence and Proportionality in* Jus ad Bellum, 24 EUR. J. INT'L L. 235 (2013); Georg Nolte, *Multipurpose Self-Defence, Proportionality Disoriented: A Response to David Kretzmer*, 24 EUR. J. INT'L L. 283 (2013).

must be strictly limited in time and in scope to this aim (i.e. the minimum necessary to achieve that end and for no other purpose)."[182]

If one attempts to put this approach into practice in the context of a civil war, hard questions abound. One such question was already hinted at earlier: If a state is engaging in large-scale unlawful violence in city *X* (such as the Libyan city of Benghazi), does that legally permit rebels to open a new "front" against the incumbent regime in other parts of the country, or would such escalation breach the proportionality principle? Or consider a different hypothesis, where the incumbent regime guilty of engaging in ethnic cleansing desires to put an end to an ongoing internal conflict (for example, for fear of ending on the losing end) and puts forward a ceasefire and power-sharing agreement. Could one argue that such offer prohibits the rebel group from continuing hostilities—in order not to breach the necessity and proportionality requirement—and that it would be required to accept the offer? Suggestions of a strict or "narrow" proportionality and necessity test in situations of civil war appear difficult—if not impossible—to reconcile with the actual practice of civil wars. Even if legal reform is not merely about reflecting practice but also about influencing and regulating behavior, the belief that civil wars can be so constrained may strike as a distant utopia. Alternatively, it could be argued that the gravity of the initial events triggering the right to organized armed assistance (namely, various forms of mass atrocities) warrants a more flexible interpretation. Again, a parallel can be drawn to the right of (inter-state) self-defense, where a more strict/narrow (and more quantitative) necessity and proportionality test would appear to apply in respect of small-scale armed attacks (allowing only for limited on-the-spot-reaction), as opposed to a more flexible (and qualitative/ends-based) approach that applies with regard to large-scale attacks.[183] The extreme position—akin to Dinstein's notion of (inter-state) wars of self-defense[184]—would be that the necessity and proportionality criteria are rendered moot when a state engages in large-scale and systematic unlawful violence against (part of) its population, particularly in the form of crimes against humanity, ethnic cleansing, and genocide. The upshot of the latter approach—which may better reflect the reality of internal hostilities, but is more apologetic in nature—is that, in cases where there exists a "just cause" justifying organized armed resistance, the necessity and proportionality requirements are essentially stripped of any constraining role, and rebellion can ultimately be pursued until regime change or (at least de facto) secession is secured. In all, introducing a very lenient proportionality standard, which is generally rejected in legal doctrine in cases of inter-state self-defense, in the proposed *jus ad bellum internum* makes little sense.

182. *See, e.g.*, Prime Minister's Office, *supra* note 158.

183. Ruys, *supra* note 179, at 117.

184. *See* Yoram Dinstein, War, Aggression and Self-Defence 279–88 (6th ed. 2017).

b. Added Value

In conclusion, the present section has examined the possibility for rebels to take up arms against their government under international law. It was observed that, while IHRL and IHL do provide for a limited right to personal self-defense in the face of unlawful violence (without such actions giving rise to direct participation in hostilities under IHL), this right must *de lege lata* be construed narrowly and does not justify any offensive military action against the state. Conversely, it was suggested that international law's stated neutrality toward rebellion has been eroded by the advance of international and regional counterterrorism law. With regard to calls for the recognition of an *ad bellum* right of organized armed resistance in the face of mass atrocities, it was noted that such a step will conversely result in international law's delegitimization of many cases of rebellion—all the more so if the legality of rebellion is subject to a "balance of consequences" test—as some would have it. Hessbruegge acknowledges this outcome, by admitting that "[f]ew, if any contemporary rebel would live up to [the conditions]."[185] Whether the "exposure" of the vast majority of cases of armed resistance "as not deserving of international legal recognition" is to be welcomed—as Hessbruegge suggests[186]—or rather turns the suggested right of armed resistance into a Trojan horse is open for debate. Furthermore, questions were raised as to whether the necessity and proportionality criteria can meaningfully restrict the exercise of the suggested right of armed resistance.

On a final note, Hessbruegge identifies a range of "legal implications" that would flow from the proposed right to resist mass atrocities.[187] Nonetheless, some of the suggested implications seem more political than legal in nature, and moreover appear rather speculative. It is indeed uncertain whether the recognition of such right would make governments "think twice" before engaging in atrocities and whether it would have a substantive impact on international sanctions practices.[188] By the same token, given the existing exposure to criminal prosecution, it may be naïve to expect the introduction of a *jus ad bellum internum* to effectively deter opposition groups from launching an armed struggle that would not meet the criteria for lawful resistance.

Other suggested benefits, such as the introduction of a bar against the provision of weapons and other support to governments committing mass atrocities, are already provided for by other norms, such as the duty to ensure compliance with IHL,[189] the

185. Hessbruegge, *supra* note 13, at 338.

186. *Id.*

187. *Id.* at 338–40.

188. This is suggested by Hessbruegge. *Id.* at 339–40.

189. For further discussion, *see, e.g.*, Knut Dörmann & Jose Serralvo, *Common Article 1 to the Geneva Conventions and the Obligation to Prevent International Humanitarian Violations*, 96 INT'L REV. RED CROSS 707 (2014).

complicity regime under the law of international responsibility,[190] or the Arms Trade Treaty.[191]

More important perhaps than the suggested legal implications identified by Hessbruegge is what the envisaged right of armed resistance does *not* purport to do. In particular, the proposed right of armed resistance would ostensibly leave unaffected the absence of a privilege of belligerency on the part of the rebel group, and the concomitant right of the de jure government to prosecute rebels under its domestic criminal law, possibly even the right of third states to prosecute such individuals for "terrorist offenses" under national and regional instruments.[192] Yet, if the ultimate aim is to reduce violence and human suffering in the context of a NIAC, there would seem to be more promising avenues than to create a distinction between the good and the bad. In particular, such a goal would perhaps be better served by attempts to revive the olden "recognition of belligerency" doctrine, and by strengthening the normative regime regulating third-state intervention in such conflicts.[193] It is these two issues, and their link to the proposed internal *jus ad bellum*, that we briefly turn to next.

190. *See* Draft Articles on Responsibility of States for Internationally Wrongful Acts art. 16, Rep. of the Int'l L. Comm'n on Its Fifty-Third Sess., U.N. Doc. A/56/10, at 26 (2001); Application of the Convention on the Prevention and Punishment of the Crime of Genocide (Bosn. & Herz. v. Serb. & Montenegro), Judgment, 2007 I.C.J. 43, ¶ 420 (Feb. 26); *see also* Helmut Aust, Complicity and the Law of State Responsibility (2011); Miles Jackson, Complicity in International Law (2015).

191. *See* Arms Trade Treaty art. 6(3), *opened for signature* June 3, 2013, 52 I.L.M. 988; *see also* Nina H.B. Jørgensen, *State Responsibility for Aiding or Assisting International Crimes in the Context of the Arms Trade Treaty*, 108 Am. J. Int'l L. 722 (2014).

192. The position of Hessbruegge is somewhat ambiguous in this regard. On the one hand, he takes the view that participants in a lawful rebellion have a right to rehabilitation and reparation after the conflict. In a similar vein, he argues that such rebels ought to not be refused refugee status due to the commission of serious nonpolitical crimes, since "[p]eople who merely participated in an armed struggle lawful under international law cannot be considered as having engaged in any crime." At the same time, he stops short of asserting that the government is prevented from prosecuting such rebels under domestic criminal law (instead referring descriptively to "resistance fighters who are punished for their participation in the rebellion"). Hessbruegge, *supra* note 13, at 339.

193. Another avenue would be a proper separation of the spheres of operation of counterterrorism instruments and the law of armed conflict, as envisaged in the exemption clauses found in several counterterrorism conventions—the operation of such clauses could possibly made contingent on a minimum degree of respect for IHL at the level of the non-state organized armed group.

IV. EPILOGUE

A. Internal *Jus Ad Bellum* and the Recognition Belligerency

Neither Lieblich nor Hessbruegge explicitly envisage the creation of an internal *jus ad bellum* as an opening to introduce the belligerent equality that is characteristic of IACs into the realm of NIACs. Put differently, neither suggests that members of an organized armed group that is engaged in a "lawful" rebellion—or that is the victim of an unlawful internal recourse to force by the government—enjoy the privilege of belligerency (POB). This is so in spite of the fact that the absence of a POB in NIACs is generally seen as one of the explanations for the lesser degree of compliance with IHL in NIACs, as compared to IACs, and for the higher rate of war crimes in NIACs, and might even be regarded as the Achilles heel of the law of NIACs.[194] Indeed, it is hard to ignore that a rebel that risks criminal prosecution at home (for murder, treason, and other crimes under domestic criminal law) or abroad (for example, for "terrorist offenses") irrespective of his (and his group's) compliance with the requirements of IHL, has a reduced incentive to refrain from committing war crimes (for example, by properly distinguishing between members of the state armed forces and civilians).[195] Even so, states have consistently resisted attempts to expand the POB to NIACs, including high-intensity NIACs with organized armed groups with effective control over part of the state's territory.[196] As is well known, the reason for this refusal is twofold. On the one hand, states are concerned—rightly or wrongly—that recognition of belligerency on the part of NSAGs will provide those groups with a

194. *See also* Tom Ruys, *The Syrian Civil War and the Achilles' Heel of the Law of Non-International Armed Conflict*, 50 STAN. J. INT'L L. 247 (2014).

195. In this sense, *see, e.g.*, Olivier Bangerter, *Reasons Why Armed Groups Choose to Respect International Humanitarian Law or Not*, 93 INT'L REV. RED CROSS 353, 377–78 (2011); INT'L COMM. OF THE RED CROSS, IMPROVING COMPLIANCE WITH INTERNATIONAL HUMANITARIAN LAW: BACKGROUND PAPER PREPARED FOR INFORMAL HIGH-LEVEL EXPERT MEETING ON CURRENT CHALLENGES TO INTERNATIONAL HUMANITARIAN LAW 4 (2004), https://www.icrc.org/en/doc/assets/files/other/improving_compliance_with_international_humanitarian_law.pdf; Marco Sassòli, *Taking Armed Groups Seriously: Ways to Improve Their Compliance with International Humanitarian Law*, 1 J. INT'L HUMANITARIAN LEGAL STUD. 5, 26 (2010). However, questioning this "general wisdom," *see* Frédéric Mégret, *Response to Claus Kreß: Leveraging the Privilege of Belligerency in Non-International Armed Conflict Towards Respect for the* Jus in Bello, 96 INT'L REV. RED CROSS 29, 59–61 (2014).

196. It is noted that, at times, de jure authorities involved in a NIAC have nonetheless adopted unilateral declarations or entered into agreements with non-state armed groups, providing for the application of certain rules of the law of international armed conflict to the NIAC concerned. For a useful overview and discussion, *see* SIVAKUMARAN, *supra* note 44, at 113–33. The key caveat, of course, is that such declarations or agreements are dependent on the political will of the de jure authorities (and are merely *recommended* by Common Article 3 of the Geneva Conventions).

legitimacy boost. On the other hand, states do not want to let go of the stick of criminal prosecution, so as to preserve a tool to deter individuals from starting, or joining, an insurgency.

Cognizant of the need for a further humanization of NIACs, Kreβ proposes a reformed international law of NIAC, "resting on two pillars, similar to those of its inter-state counterpart."[197] Specifically,

> It could embrace a privilege of combatancy in the *jus in bello interno* and at the same time prohibit any non-State organization from launching an armed attack against its government through a *new jus contra bellum*.[198]

According to Kreβ, "[A] move towards complete symmetry in the law of NIAC is dependent on the introduction of a new *jus contra bellum internum*, but this statement does not necessarily hold true the other way round."[199] The internal *jus ad bellum* is framed as a ban on the use of force which also applies to non-state armed organizations with a capacity to initiate massive violence[200] and is subject to a narrow exception allowing for "self-defense" by a civilian population under lethal attack.[201] Interestingly, on closer scrutiny, Kreβ sees the above-mentioned ban as operating primarily in the international criminal law sphere. Specifically, it is construed essentially as a leadership crime, the *ratione personae* scope of which is confined to the leadership of the rebels, analogous to what is the case for the extant crime of aggression under Article 8(bis) of the Rome Statute. Importantly, such an approach partly preserves the deterrent effect of criminal law against rebellion that states have been unwilling to surrender.

Kreβ's proposal illustrates that it is not impossible to reconcile an extension of the POB to NIACs (so as to improve compliance with IHL) with the legitimate interests of states in deterring rebellion. Two caveats are nonetheless in order. First, as Mégret points out, it is paradoxical to create a POB for NIACs in pursuit of the "Holy Grail" of improving compliance with IHL in such conflicts, yet without simultaneously making such grant conditional on a certain degree of compliance with IHL at the level of the non-state armed group(s) concerned. Indeed, as Mégret warns, a POB provides a "formidable license to kill."[202] Mégret may exaggerate the risk that NSAGs "would have an objective interest in bringing

197. Kreβ, *supra* note 12, at 39.

198. *Id.*

199. *Id.* at 43.

200. *Id.* at 41.

201. *Id.* at 40.

202. Mégret, *supra* note 195, at 54. Note that Mégret appears to assume that in IACs the POB is given "for free" to state armed forces, that is, without being in any way conditional upon compliance with IHL. *Id.* at 58. For a contrary position, *see, e.g.*, Dinstein, *supra* note 37, at 54, 59–60.

their campaign to the level of an armed conflict so as to benefit from the POB and, as a consequence, launder their individual behaviour."[203] After all, the leaders of an unlawful rebellion would still be exposed to criminal prosecution. Still, it is hard to argue with the suggestion that the granting of a POB must be conditional on some form of compliance with IHL at the group level, including in the form of a commitment of the group to (a) distinguish themselves from the civilian population by wearing a fixed distinctive sign recognizable at a distance, and (b) carry their arms openly during military engagements.[204]

Second, it is doubtful whether, as Kreβ proclaims, the extension of the POB to NIACs is necessarily "dependent on the introduction of a new *jus contra bellum internum*."[205] There is indeed an alternative to the "grand bargain" put forward by Kreβ, which simply does not require the creation of an internal *jus ad bellum*, with its inherently problematic distinction between just and unjust rebellions. In particular, instead of introducing a leadership crime for "internal aggression," why not simply exclude leaders in a position to effectively control the NSAG from the personal scope of the POB in the first place? In such a scenario, members of a non-state armed group, other than those in a leadership position, would benefit from the POB (and be immune from criminal prosecution, save in respect of war crimes and other core crimes) as soon as certain objective criteria are met. Such criteria can be linked to the intensity and duration of the conflict (and might

203. Mégret, *supra* note 195, at 55.

204. For the present author's position, in greater detail, *see* Ruys, *supra* note 194, at 274, a portion of which is provided here:

> The NSAG ought to make a formal declaration to the ICRC confirming that it will comply with the LOAC; that it will include it in the internal codes of conduct or instructions; and that it will disseminate and enforce said rules vis-à-vis its members.
>
> The NSAG ought to confirm specifically that captured combatants will be treated humanely and will not be executed (nor used as human shields). In addition, the ICRC should be allowed to visit captured combatants and, if it is unable to intern them, the NSAG ought to accept the transfer of captured combatants to a neutral, third-party State.
>
> The NSAG ought to confirm specifically that its members (a) will distinguish themselves from the civilian population by wearing a "distinctive sign recognizable at a distance," at least, "in all circumstances where concealment would directly jeopardize the lives or liberty of civilians," and (b) will carry their arms openly during each military engagement and during such time as they are visible to the adversary while engaged in a military deployment preceding the launching of an attack in which they are to participate.

Id. at 274. Note that the present author disagrees with Mégret's position that it would be better to retrospectively "grant amnesties to those groups that have broadly satisfied humanitarian exigencies over the course of a conflict," than to grant a POB ex ante, Mégret, *supra* note 195, at 63, as the remote prospect of being offered an amnesty creates less of an incentive to comply with IHL and the immediate recognition that rebels cannot be prosecuted for mere participation in hostilities. *See also* Ruys, *supra* note 194, at 276.

205. Kreβ, *supra* note 12, at 43.

include the requirement that the group control a substantial part of the state's territory) and would include a commitment to comply with IHL at the level of the non-state armed group (as per the aforementioned).[206] By contrast, states would retain the stick of criminal prosecution (and its concomitant deterrent effect) vis-à-vis the NSAG leadership, as well as vis-à-vis other individuals taking part in a rebellion that does not (or not yet) meet the aforementioned objective criteria. Of course, the reverse side of the medal is that rebel leaders could be prosecuted, even in case of a rebellion that many would regard as legitimate, unless the government voluntarily agrees to grant amnesty for past transgressions.[207] Yet, this may be a small and acceptable price to pay to reform the law of NIACs. In the end, by avoiding fruitless efforts to separate just from unjust rebellions, the approach sketched here may be more feasible than that put forward by Kreß. For the same reason, it could be more acceptable for states, and perhaps provide for a more "realizable utopia."[208]

In conclusion, it appears paradoxical to introduce an internal *jus ad bellum*, without simultaneously restricting the exposure to criminal prosecution (at home or abroad) for those exercising a purported right of armed assistance. Conversely, contrary to what some have argued, it is possible to create a conditional POB for non-state armed groups without introducing an internal *jus ad bellum*.

B. Implications for the Legal Quagmire of Third-State Intervention in Civil Wars

As a final point, it is worth pausing an instant at the issue of third-state intervention in civil wars. Indeed, apart from the prevalence of *non-international* armed conflict, another feature that is characteristic of contemporary warfare is the high degree of third-state intervention—in various forms—in such conflicts. Indeed, if proxy warfare was ever truly gone after the end of the Cold War, the conflicts in Syria, Iraq, Ukraine, Yemen, Mali, and Libya, among others, suggest it is more omnipresent than ever. Against this background, it is not difficult to see how the creation of an internal *jus ad bellum* might influence debates over the permissibility of third-state support to a state or non-state party involved in a NIAC.

As far as armed support to NSAGs fighting a de jure government is concerned, the traditional understanding is that third states are normally prohibited from providing such support. As the ICJ explained, it would be "difficult to see what would remain of the principle of non-intervention" if such support were to be

206. *See also* Ruys, *supra* note 194, at 272–75.

207. *Cf.* AP II, *supra* note 39, art. 6(5) (providing that "[a]t the end of hostilities, the authorities in power shall endeavour to grant the broadest possible amnesty to persons who have participated in the armed conflict . . .").

208. To paraphrase Kreß, Kreß, *supra* note 12, at 42, in turn alluding to the work of the late Antonio Cassese.

accepted.[209] The contrary view was found not to correspond to the present state of international law.[210] The position that—save perhaps in the case of wars of national liberation—states must refrain from financing, arming, training, or otherwise supporting rebel groups that are active in other countries has been confirmed in a range of U.N. General Assembly resolutions.[211] The prohibition also appears to be upheld—albeit imperfectly—in recent state practice. In particular, state support to rebel groups is frequently denounced as a form of unlawful intervention, and those accused of providing such support tend to adopt a policy of denial (even if often unconvincingly). Such is the situation, for instance, with regard to Russia's support to pro-Russian separatist fighters in eastern Ukraine. The situation in Syria points in the same direction, albeit perhaps more ambiguously. Thus, when in 2013 E.U. member states discussed a possible lifting of the arms embargo on Syria so as to permit the arming of (moderate) rebel forces, Austria, for one, argued that such arms supplies "would amount to a breach of the customary principle of non-intervention and the principle of non-use of force."[212] In a similar vein, the Dutch foreign minister asserted in a letter to the Dutch Parliament that the provision of military support and training to the armed opposition would amount to a breach of the non-intervention principle, notwithstanding the fact that the so-called Syrian Opposition Council had been recognized as the "legitimate representative of the Syrian people" by more than 100 countries.[213] U.S. Secretary of State John Kerry for his part similarly acknowledged that there is no legal right of forcible intervention on the side of the opposition in 2016.[214] The provision of arms to Syrian rebels has tended to take place on a covert basis.[215] Meanwhile, direct military involvement by the United States and other countries was framed (not uncontroversially) in the context of the right of collective

209. Military and Paramilitary Activities in and Against Nicaragua (Nicar. v. U.S.), Judgment, 1986 I.C.J. Rep. 14, ¶ 246 (June 27).

210. *Id.*; *see also* Armed Activities on the Territory of the Congo (Dem. Rep. Congo v. Uganda), Judgment, 2005 I.C.J. Rep. 168, ¶¶ 160–65 (Dec. 19).

211. *E.g.*, G.A. Res. 2625 (XXV), ¶ 9 (Oct. 24, 1970) (principle on the non-use of force); G.A. Res. 42/22, pt. I (Nov. 14, 1987).

212. Julian Borger, *The Austrian Position on Arms Embargo in Syria*, The Guardian (May 15, 2013), https://www.theguardian.com/world/julian-borger-global-security-blog/interactive/2013/may/15/austria-eu-syria-arms-embargo-pdf (reproducing a copy of the document).

213. Letter of the Dutch Minister of Foreign Affairs to the Staten-Generaal on the International Law Aspects of the Sanctions Regime Against Syria, Doc. 21 501–502, No. 1263 (June 4, 2013), https://www.parlementairemonitor.nl/9353000/1/j9vvij5epmj1ey0/vjaln94ywrwc.

214. *See* Christine Gray, International Law and the Use of Force 107 (4th ed. 2018).

215. *See, e.g.*, David E. Sanger, Eric Schmitt, & Ben Hubbard, *Trump Ends Covert Aid to Syrian Rebels Trying to Topple Assad*, N.Y. Times (July 19, 2017), https://www.nytimes.com/2017/07/19/world/middleeast/cia-arming-syrian-rebels.html; *but see CIA Starts Arming Syrian Rebels Overtly*, Russia Today (Sept. 12, 2013), https://www.rt.com/usa/us-weapons-syrian-rebels-745.

self-defense in support of Iraq following the cross-border advance by the Islamic State.[216]

It is conceivable that the introduction of an internal *jus ad bellum* would make it easier for third states to justify armed assistance for an NSAG supposedly exercising a right of armed resistance against a brutal and authoritarian regime, in particular one engaging in large-scale crimes against humanity and/or genocide. While this arguably remains a lone exception, it is worth observing, for instance, that in its 2013 Doha Declaration, the Arab League explained the legality of supplying weapons to the Free Syrian Army by reference to the right of self-defense of the Syrian people.[217] The notion that large-scale human rights violations or war crimes by the de jure regime remove the prohibition of providing military support to rebel groups has also received some support from scholars. Thus, Pustorino refers to a "growing although not yet consolidated trend that permits support, even military support, to . . . those that fight against dictatorial regimes that do not hesitate during civil war to employ brutal methods

216. *E.g.*, Permanent Rep. of the U.S. to the U.N., Letter Dated 23 September 2014 from the Permanent Rep. of the U.S. to the U.N. Addressed to the Secretary-General, U.N. Doc. S/2014/695 (Sept. 23, 2014); Permanent Rep. of the U.K. to the U.N., Identical Letters Dated 25 November 2014 from the Permanent Rep. of the U.K. to the U.N. Addressed to the Secretary-General and the President of the Security Council, U.N. Doc. S/2014/851 (Nov. 26, 2014); Chargé d'Affaires a.i. of the Permanent Mission of Can. to the U.N., Letter Dated 31 March 2015 from the Chargé d'Affaires a.i. of the Permanent Mission of Can. to the U.N. Addressed to the President of the Security Council, U.N. Doc. S/2015/221 (Mar. 31, 2015). On the other hand, there appears to be a discernible trend toward more open provision of so-called "nonlethal" assistance to non-state armed groups, even though such assistance—which may include items such as night vision goggles or armed personnel carriers—may well influence the conduct of hostilities and clearly does not fit the label of mere "humanitarian" aid (in the sense of the ICJ's *Nicaragua* case). *See* Military and Paramilitary Activities in and Against Nicaragua (Nicar. v. U.S.), Judgment, 1986 I.C.J. Rep. 14, ¶¶ 242–43 (June 27). For further discussion on nonlethal assistance, *see* Christian Henderson, *The Provision of Arms and "Non-Lethal" Assistance to Government and Opposition Forces*, 36 Univ. N.S.W. L.J. 642 (2013); Tom Ruys, *Of Arms, Funding and "Non-Lethal Assistance": Issues Surrounding Third-State Intervention in the Syrian Civil War*, 13 Chinese J. Int'l L. 13 (2014).

217. Press Release, Arab League, 24th Arab Summit Issues Doha Declaration (Mar. 21–27, 2013), http://arableaguesummit2013.qatarconferences.org/news/news-details-17.html. For another rare—and hesitant—exception, *see, e.g.*, the above-mentioned letter by Dutch Foreign Minister Timmermans to the Dutch parliament. Letter of the Dutch Minster, *supra* note 213. Having regard to the large-scale human rights violations by the Syrian authorities, the lack of legitimacy of the Assad regime, and the broad recognition of the Syrian Opposition Council (SOC) as the legitimate representative of the Syrian people, the letter suggests that "in exceptional cases and under strict conditions," the provision of military materiel to the SOC "would not have to be contrary to international law." *Id.* (our translation). Note that the statement appears at odds to the earlier finding in the same letter that the recognition of armed opposition as the legitimate representative of a people is a political decision only, without any international legal implications. Note also that the Dutch authorities eventually limited themselves to providing so-called "nonlethal" assistance.

against the civilian population."[218] In turn, Ohlin frames third-state humanitarian interventions as a collective application of a natural right of self-defense of nations or peoples.[219] Against this, while defending a right of armed resistance in the face of mass atrocities, Hessbruegge nonetheless expressly refuses to accept an analogy between state and personal self-defense that would permit third-state (humanitarian) intervention in support of such resistance.[220] In the end, the possible spillover effect of an (exceptional) right of armed resistance into the realm of inter-state relations and its potential for infecting the humanitarian intervention debate may constitute one more reason why such right is unlikely to be acceptable to states (the large majority of which continue to reject non-U.N.-authorized interventions in response to humanitarian crises).[221] What is more, it may be a valid reason to question the wisdom of such right, as third-state interventions often increase the intensity and duration of such NIACs and create the risk of spillover effects.[222] *Pro memorie*, already in 2013, the Independent International Commission of Inquiry on the Syrian Arab Republic observed that weapons supplies to the various protagonists "create[d] but an illusion of victory."[223] Seven years later, third-state intervention in the conflict continues unabated, with the death toll and the number of refugees and internally displaced persons ever rising.

What then about the possible implications of the proposed internal *jus ad bellum* with regard to third-state support to de jure authorities (as opposed to NSAGs) involved in a NIAC? Whether there would be more, or rather less, leeway for third states to intervene depends, of course, on the position one takes in respect of the permissibility of such support under existing law. Indeed, while the impermissibility of intervening in support of an NSAG is widely acknowledged, legal doctrine is admittedly more divided when it comes to pro-government support.[224]

218. Pietro Pustorino, *The Principle of Non-Intervention in Recent Non-International Armed Conflicts*, 53 QUESTIONS INT'L L. 17, 18, 26–28 (2018).

219. Jens David Ohlin, *The Doctrine of Legitimate Defence*, 91 INT'L L. STUD. 119, 140–47 (2015).

220. Hessbruegge, *supra* note 13, at 342.

221. For further discussion, *see* Ruys, *supra* note 169, at 895–96. Corten goes as far as to conclude that the illegality of humanitarian intervention is "one of the least complex" issues of contemporary international law. OLIVIER CORTEN, DROIT CONTRE LA GUERRE 799 (2014) (our translation).

222. *See also* Hessbruegge, *supra* note 13, at 342 (pointing at the "risks for global peace and international security that is created by the military involvement of third States").

223. Indep. Int'l Comm'n of Inquiry on the Syrian Arab Republic, Report of the Independent International Commission of Inquiry on the Syrian Arab Republic, summary, at 1, U.N. Doc. A/HRC/24/46 (Aug. 16, 2013).

224. For further discussion, *see, e.g.*, CHRISTIAN HENDERSON, THE USE OF FORCE AND INTERNATIONAL LAW 361–68 (2018); 2 Indep. Int'l Fact-Finding Mission on the Conflict in Georgia, Report 276–79 (2009), http://www.mpil.de/files/pdf4/IIFFMCG_Volume_II1.pdf.

On the one hand, proponents of the "government-preference" approach take the view that, even in situations of civil war, the incumbent government is still permitted to invite outside intervention. These scholars point out that this right was generally recognized in legal doctrine prior to the Charter era and has never truly been set aside by state practice during the Charter era.[225] At first sight, one might be inclined to think that for scholars adopting this approach, the introduction of an internal *jus ad bellum* could substantially reduce the scope for permissible third-state pro-government support. On closer scrutiny, however, as mentioned earlier, much the same outcome[226] is already brought about by other existing norms, including the duty to ensure compliance with IHL as per Common Article 1 of the Geneva Conventions, or the notion of complicity under the law of international responsibility.

By contrast, under the so-called "negative equality" approach, in situations of civil war, third states may support neither the rebels, nor the de jure regime.[227] In terms of the legal basis of such prohibition, reference is mostly made to the non-intervention principle, oftentimes in combination with the right of self-determination of peoples.[228] Seen from the "negative equality" perspective, the creation of an internal *jus ad bellum* might create more, rather than less, room for third-state support. In particular, it is not excluded that the supposed prohibition

225. *E.g.*, Yoram Dinstein, War, Aggression and Self-Defence 119 (5th ed. 2011); Erika De Wet, Military Assistance on Request and the Use of Force (2020); Pustorino, *supra* note 218, at 18, 20–21 (relying primarily on the "evident contradictions" in state practice).

226. That is, a ban on third-state support to a government engaged in a first recourse to hostilities against (part of) its population, or to a government committing mass atrocities.

227. This position is supported, for instance, in the 1975 Wiesbaden resolution of the Institut de Droit International, Institut de Droit International, The Principle of Non-Intervention in Civil Wars art. 2 (1975), http://www.idi-iil.org/app/uploads/2017/06/1975_wies_03_en.pdf, as well as in a document by the Planning Staff of the U.K. Foreign Office in 1984 and subsequently released as Foreign Policy Document No. 148. U.K. Foreign Office, Foreign Policy Document No. 148, *in* 57 Brit. Y.B. Int'l L. 614 (1986). The latter document states that "any form of interference or assistance is prohibited . . . when a civil war is taking place and control over the State's territory is divided between warring parties." Gray describes this as the "generally accepted position during the Cold War." Gray, *supra*, note 214, at 85.

228. Doswald-Beck in her seminal piece in the *British Yearbook of International Law* identifies the rule of non-intervention as the most realistic legal basis. Louise Doswald-Beck, *The Legal Validity of Military Intervention by Invitation of the Government*, 56 Brit. Y.B. Int'l L. 189, 207 (1986). At the same time, inasmuch as the non-intervention principle is sometimes suggested to exist only "for the benefit of sovereign States, and not for the benefit of groups or movements," Joined Cases T-208/11 & T-508/11, Liberation Tigers of Tamil Eelam v. Council of European Union, ¶ 69, 2014 ECLI:EU:T:2014:885 (General Court, 2014), the better view is that the prohibition rests on the combined application of the non-intervention principle and the "inalienable" right of self-determination of peoples. Another line of reasoning that is sometimes put forward is that a government engaged in a civil war, and which requires military support from a third state to remain in power, no longer possesses the sovereign authority to invite outside support. Unsurprisingly, the divide between the "government-preference" and "negative equality"

to render support to de jure authorities engaged in a NIAC would instead be reduced to a prohibition to prop up governments fighting a "lawful" rebellion (under the supposed internal *jus ad bellum*). Given the narrow scope for "lawful" rebellion as sketched earlier—recall Hessbruegge's assurance that "[f]ew, if any contemporary rebel groups would live up to [the conditions]"[229]—the implication would be that third states could, for instance, deploy ground troops or conduct air raids to aid governments combating secessionist groups. In short, the narrower one construes the supposed right of armed resistance, the less remains of the original "negative equality" approach.

It is noted that state practice and legal doctrine may already be moving in a direction where the legality of third-state pro-government intervention is made dependent on the *legitimacy* of the non-state armed group(s) confronting the government. Acknowledging that recent state practice is increasingly difficult to fit into the negative equality doctrine, several scholars have indeed suggested that a "purpose-oriented" approach be adopted, permitting third-state interventions

approaches is also characterized by a different methodological underpinning. Those who side with the former approach focus essentially on (physical) state practice (taken at face value by the beholder), and stress the frequency of third-state intervention in civil war. Adherents of the negative equality view, by contrast, pay greater importance to the surrounding *opinio juris*, as found primarily in various oral statements made at the U.N. level or elsewhere. True to the *Nicaragua* axiom, Military and Paramilitary Activities in and Against Nicaragua (Nicar. v. U.S.), Judgment, 1986 I.C.J. Rep. 14, ¶ 186 (June 27), these scholars argue that, since states generally refrain from expressly claiming a right to intervene in a civil war—instead relying on alternative justifications, including, most prominently, the notion of counterintervention, or denying involvement altogether—and since such interventions generally attract widespread condemnation from other states, the negative equality approach remains alive and well. The discrepancy between the two approaches must arguably not be exaggerated. Indeed, even supporters of the negative equality approach generally acknowledge that there is an exception to the prohibition of pro-government support in situations of civil war allowing for "counterintervention" when there has been prior third-state support to the benefit of the NSAG(s). *See, e.g.*, Doswald-Beck, *supra* note 228, at 213; U.K. Foreign Office, *supra* note 227, § II.7 ("It is widely accepted that outside interference in favour of one party to [a civil war] permits counter-intervention on behalf of the other."). The question arises in this context, however, what (minimum) level of third-state support to a rebel group must exist in order to trigger the possibility to engage in a counterintervention. A related question is whether and to what extent counterinterventions are subject to the proportionality principle. Answering in the affirmative, *see, e.g.*, John A. Perkins, *The Right of Counterintervention*, 17 GA. J. INT'L & COMP. L. 171, 179 (1986); *but see, e.g.*, ELIAV LIEBLICH, INTERNATIONAL LAW AND CIVIL WARS: INTERVENTION AND CONSENT 170 (2013). Clearly, if even the slightest form of pro-rebel support by a third state (for example, in terms of financial assistance or provision of weapons) would justify a large-scale and direct military intervention in support of the government, the presumed gap between the "negative equality" and the "government-preference" approaches may ultimately be little more than an exercise in semantics. The dilemma is well illustrated by the Saudi-led intervention in support of the Hadi regime in the context of the civil war in Yemen. For further discussion, *see* Tom Ruys & Luca Ferro, *Weathering the Storm: Legality and Legal Implications of the Saudi-led Military Intervention in Yemen*, 65 INT'L & COMP. L.Q. 61, 94–96 (2016).

229. HESSBRUEGGE, *supra* note 13, at 338.

upon invitation by the de jure authorities that take place *against the background of* a civil war, inasmuch as they do not (seek to) influence the actual civil war.[230] Crucially, it has been argued that third-state intervention remains permissible when third-state action targets "terrorist groups," as opposed to (other) rebel groups that are involved in a NIAC with the de jure government.[231] Some evidence in state practice in support of this approach can be derived from France's intervention in Mali in 2013.[232] France indeed took great pains at the time to stress that its military intervention in support of the government in Bamako would only target "terrorist elements,"[233] but would not take sides in the conflict between the Malian government and the Tuareg forces. The French operation was generally welcomed, and even drew support from the Tuareg rebels of the MNLA.[234] One might also point at Russia's intervention in Syria as of September 2015 as an illustration.[235] Thus, while Russia justified its intervention by reference to the invitation of the Assad regime, it stressed on multiple occasions that its actions were targeted against the Islamic State terrorist group and formed part of the fight against terrorism. For instance, in a letter to the Security Council dated October 15, 2015, Russia drew a distinction between the Islamic State and "other terrorist groups operating in Syria" and "the patriotic opposition."[236] Conversely,

230. In particular, *see* Theodore Christakis & Karine Bannelier, *Volenti non Fit Injuria? Les Effets du Consentement à l'Intervention Militaire*, 50 Annuaire Français de Droit International 102 (2014); Karine Bannelier-Christakis, *Military Interventions Against ISIL in Iraq, Syria and Libya, and the Legal Basis of Consent*, 29 Leiden J. Int'l L. 747 (2016). One possible illustration would concern a consensual noncombatant evacuation operation by a third state.

231. *E.g.*, Theodore Christakis & Karine Bannelier, *The Intervention of France and African Countries in Mali—2013*, *in* The Use of Force in International Law, *supra* note 172, at 812, 820.

232. *Id.* at 827.

233. Permanent Rep. of Fr. to the U.N., Identical Letters Dated 11 January 2013 from the Permanent Rep. of Fr. to the U.N. Addressed to the Secretary-General and the President of the Security Council, U.N. Doc. S/2013/17 (Jan. 14, 2013). France was referring in particular to three groups, namely, al-Qaida in the Islamic Maghreb (AQIM), the Movement for Oneness and Jihad in West Africa (MUJAO), and the Islamist group Ansar Dine.

234. *See* Christakis & Bannelier, *supra* note 231, at 817 n.29 (MNLA press releases cited therein).

235. *See, e.g.*, Olivier Corten, *L'Intervention de la Russie en Syrie: Que Reste-t-il du Principe de Non-Intervention dans les Guerres Civiles?*, 53 Questions Int'l L. 3, 8 (2018).

236. Permanent Rep. of Russian Federation to the U.N., Letter Dated 15 October 2015 from the Permanent Rep. of the Russian Federation to the U.N. Addressed to the President of the Security Council, U.N. Doc. S/2015/792 (Oct. 15, 2015). And in a television interview not long thereafter, Prime Minister Medvedev insisted that Russia's goal was to defeat the Islamic State, not to prop up Assad, recognizing that "[i]t is up to the Syrian people to decide who will be the head of Syria." *Russia's Aim in Syria Is Defeat of Islamic State, Not Prop Up Assad: Russian PM*, N.Y. Times (Oct. 17, 2015), https://www.reuters.com/article/us-mideast-crisis-syria-russia-idUSKCN0SB0GQ20151017.

third states did not suggest that Russia's intervention was unlawful under the *jus ad bellum*. Instead several countries cautiously welcome Russia's participation in the fight against the Islamic State, while nonetheless expressing concern that it was also targeting other ("non-terrorist") groups.[237] Shortly after Russia launched its operation, the Security Council adopted its famous Resolution 2249(2015), "call[ing] upon Member States . . . to take all necessary measures, in compliance with international law . . . on the territory under the control of ISIL . . . in Syria and Iraq, . . . to prevent and suppress terrorist acts committed . . . by [ISIL, al-Nusra, al-Qaida], and other terrorist groups, as designated by the United Nations Security Council,"[238] thus further legitimizing both coalition operations and Russian operations against the above-mentioned groups. Meanwhile, as the Russian operation went on, criticism of third states focused on indications that Russia was equally targeting moderate Syrian rebels,[239] as well as on apparent violations of IHL.[240]

While Russia's intervention in Syria could thus be construed as a precedent supporting a "terrorist" exception to the prohibition of third-state military intervention in support of a government involved in a civil war, it is obvious that it also illustrates the risks this entails. Indeed, it is undeniable that Western countries, including the United States, on the one hand, and Syria and Russia, on the other hand, held (and continue to hold) widely different views on which groups constitute "legitimate" rebel groups or (illegitimate) "terrorist groups," again illustrating the olden cliché that "one man's terrorist is another man's freedom fighter."[241] It follows that, in the absence of an internationally accepted definition of what constitutes a "terrorist group," the above-mentioned "terrorism" exception could easily become a recipe for abuse and arbitrariness.[242] So far, the best scholars have been able to come up with in order to mitigate such risk is to adopt a restrictive interpretation and acknowledge that the exception can apply only to non-state actors that have been denounced as "terrorist" groups by the large majority of the international community, principally in the form of a resolution of the U.N. Security Council (such as Resolution 2249(2015)) qualifying the actor as such or

237. *E.g.*, U.N. Security Council, Verbatim Record, 7527th mtg., at 24, U.N. Doc. S/PV.7527 (Sept. 30, 2015) (speech of U.K. representative).

238. S.C. Res. 2249, ¶ 5 (Nov. 20, 2015).

239. *See, e.g.*, G.A. Res. 71/203, ¶ 25 (Feb. 1, 2017) (in which the G.A. "strongly condemn[ed] all attacks against the Syrian moderate opposition, and calls for their immediate cessation," without, however, mentioning Russia by name).

240. Corten, *supra* note 235, at 12.

241. As mentioned earlier, in the Netherlands, the Department of Justice qualified as "terrorist" a group that had previously received nonlethal assistance from the Dutch authorities. *See supra* note 133.

242. In a similar vein, *see, e.g.*, GRAY, *supra*, note 214, at 118.

adding the group to the U.N. list of designated terrorist groups.[243] Whether it is feasible, or even desirable, to replace such legitimacy call on the part of the political organ with the primary responsibility for maintaining international peace and security by an international legal framework distinguishing between lawful and unlawful armed resistance is highly questionable.

In the end, just as the extension of the POB to NIACs is not necessarily contingent on the parallel creation of an internal *jus ad bellum*, neither is the latter invention to be welcomed as a tool to reshape the legal framework governing third-state intervention in non-international armed conflict. Rather, having regard to the degree of suffering and destruction caused, for instance, by the Saudi-led intervention in Yemen, in the present author's view, the more preferable route is to affirm and strengthen the negative equality approach and to limit the possibility for states to use the "counterintervention" argument as a fig leaf.

243. Such approach fits the language used in Paragraph 5 of S.C. Res. 2249. S.C. Res. 2249, *supra* note 238. Note also that, of the three "terrorist" groups targeted by France's operation Serval in Mali, two (AQIM and MUJAO) had already been put on the U.N. counterterrorism sanctions list, while the third group (Ansar Dine) was added shortly thereafter. *See* Christakis & Bannelier, *supra* note 231, at 823–24. Note also in this context that the Security Council increasingly appears to take sides in civil wars, by asserting the legitimacy of one party and thus disqualifying the other side. In this sense, *see* Corten, *supra* note 235, at 16 (referring to the Council's position with regard to the crises in Libya, the Central African Republic, or Gambia).

7

Article 51's Reporting Requirement as a Space for Legal Argument and Factfulness

LARISSA VAN DEN HERIK*

I. INTRODUCTION

It is generally accepted that the principles of necessity and proportionality apply to the exercise of self-defense. Nonetheless, disagreement remains regarding their function, contents, and application in concrete cases.[1] These disagreements and continuous uncertainties are discussed in detail in other chapters of this book. In light of this opacity, it may be useful to complement the substantive debate with some thoughts of a more institutional and procedural nature. This chapter explores possibilities of enhancing necessity and proportionality discourse through the widening and deepening of U.N. Security Council reporting requirements. The aim is to rethink and to design structures that pull states more clearly into the conversation. Building on ideas to "proceduralize Article 51,"[2] the

* Professor of Public International Law at the Grotius Centre for International Legal Studies at Leiden University. I am grateful to the editors and all participants of the Lieber Institute for Law and Land Warfareworkshop for their immensely valuable comments and suggestions on an earlier draft of this chapter. I am also grateful for research assistance offered by Charlotte Vercraeye, Teaching and Research Assistant, LLM advanced student at Leiden University 2017–2018.

1. *See generally* JUDITH GARDAM, NECESSITY, PROPORTIONALITY AND THE USE OF FORCE BY STATES (2004); David Kretzmer, *The Inherent Right to Self-Defence and Proportionality in* Jus ad Bellum, 24 EUR. J. INT'L L. 235 (2013); Christian J. Tams & James G. Devaney, *Applying Necessity and Proportionality to Anti-Terrorist Self-Defence*, 45 ISR. L. REV. 91 (2012); Enzo Cannizzaro, *Contextualizing Proportionality:* Jus ad Bellum *and* Jus in Bello *in the Lebanese War*, 88 INT'L REV. RED CROSS 779 (2006).

2. Larissa van den Herik, *Proceduralizing Article 51*, 77 ZEITSCHRIFT FÜR AUSLÄNDISCHES ÖFFENTLICHES RECHT UND VÖLKERRECHT 65 (2017).

Larissa van den Herik, *Article 51's Reporting Requirement as a Space for Legal Argument and Factfulness* In: *Necessity and Proportionality in International Peace and Security Law*. Edited by: Professor Claus Kreß and Captain Robert Lawless, Oxford University Press (2021). DOI: 10.1093/oso/9780197537374.003.0008.

chapter suggests the development of reporting requirements for any use of force. It also invites a more comprehensive architectural rethinking of the institutional environment in which adherence to and application of the proportionality and necessity principles are tested and contested. The central idea behind this is that the necessity and proportionality principles require strong institutions to gain meaning.

The chapter is inspired by Thomas Franck's scholarship on proportionality discourse.[3] Franck makes the argument that the proportionality principle can become more determinate through the "second opinion of legitimate institutions,"[4] whereby he points mainly to jurisprudential streams generated by different international courts. This chapter explores possibilities beyond courts. It looks at options for further proceduralization and institutionalization within political fora, in particular the Security Council setting. Building also on notions of legal diplomacy, a duty to explain, and a "culture of justification," the chapter interrogates through which structures necessity and proportionality discourse can be rendered more articulate and factful in concrete situations in which force is used.[5] The two leading questions that this chapter addresses are: First, which procedural or institutional structures at the Security Council level would strengthen necessity and proportionality discourse in concrete cases of use of force thereby also rendering the discourse more fact- and evidence-based? And second, what can be learned from the U.N. sanctions machinery in this regard?

The chapter starts the analysis in section II with a focus on self-defense and the unclarity surrounding the proportionality and necessity principles. Section III introduces Article 51's reporting requirement. Section IV then discusses the potential for deepening the discourse, and section V presents ideas to widen the discourse to other nonauthorized uses of force, specifically intervention by invitation.[6]

Finally, section VI makes a comparative analysis of the U.N. sanctions architecture to offer a first reflection regarding a platform for the discourse, followed by some brief concluding thoughts.

3. Thomas M. Franck, *On Proportionality and Countermeasures in International Law*, 102 AM. J. INT'L L. 715 (2008).

4. *Id.* at 717.

5. The word "factful" and the chapter title word "factfulness" refers to the book by Hans Rosling, which highlights contrasts between worldly understandings informed by instincts, preconceptions, and biases versus those based on data acquired through statistics,graphs, and questionnaires. HANS ROSLING ET AL., FACTFULNESS: TEN REASONS WE'RE WRONG ABOUT THE WORLD—AND WHY THINGS ARE BETTER THAN YOU THINK (2018).

6. This section was also published in slightly different form as Larissa van den Herik, *Replicating Article 51; A Reporting Requirement for Consent-Based Use of Force*, 79 HEIDELBERG J. INT'L L. 707 (2019).

II. SELF-DEFENSE AND NECESSITY AND PROPORTIONALITY DISCOURSE

Article 51 is the only Charter provision that offers a legal basis for nonauthorized use of force. As such, it has been invoked to justify different scenarios of self-defense and thus uses of force of different dynamic, intensity, and nature. The existing uncertainty as to how the necessity and proportionality principles condition the use of force in self-defense is exacerbated by this further differentiation of uses of force covered under the same general label of self-defense. In addition to inter-state self-defense, uses of force to protect own nationals, against (terrorist) threats by non-state actors, against anticipated attacks, and against cyberattacks have all been justified by reference to Article 51. What exactly application of the necessity and proportionality principles entails in these different scenarios may vary. This thus adds a layer of complexity to the existing discussions on temporal, geographical, and other dimensions of necessity and proportionality[7] and specifically on what constitutes the appropriate test for the *jus ad bellum* proportionality determination, a discussion that navigates between a tit-for-tat test, a means-end test, and a narrow proportionality test.[8] Different scenarios of self-defense may call for different types of proportionality tests. Moreover, specific scenarios of self-defense may give rise to new factors that should inform a proportionality calculus within a concrete test. For instance, in cases of self-defense against non-state actors, the contribution or attitude of the host state affects proportionality assessments including discussions on what constitutes a legitimate aim.[9] It may also be that there are multiple legal bases underlying a certain use of force all involving their own proportionality calculi and necessity tests, as was the case in the Islamic State strikes, which were justified by a combination of individual and collective self-defense and additionally consent.[10]

7. *See also* in this regard the discussion in Eliav Lieblich's chapter on the continuous versus the static approach to the proportionality principle. Eliav Lieblich, *On the Continuous and Concurrent Application of* Ad Bellum *and* In Bello *Proportionality*, *in* NECESSITY AND PROPORTIONALITY IN INTERNATIONAL PEACE AND SECURITY LAW (Claus Kreß & Robert Lawless eds., 2020). Similar to Lieblich, Gardam also makes the argument that *jus ad bellum* proportionality remains relevant through the course of the hostilities and must be constantly assessed, whereas Dinstein disputes this. *See* Judith Gail Gardam, *Proportionality and Force in International Law*, 87 AM. J. INT'L L. 391 (1993); YORAM DINSTEIN, WAR, AGGRESSION AND SELF-DEFENCE 262 (5th ed. 2011).

8. Kretzmer, *supra* note 1. Kretzmer's revisiting of the proportionality principle was critiqued by Georg Nolte. *See* Georg Nolte, *Multipurpose Self-Defence, Proportionality Disoriented: A Response to David Kretzmer*, 24 EUR. J. INT'L L. 283 (2013).

9. Dapo Akande & Thomas Liefländer, *Clarifying Necessity, Imminence, and Proportionality in the Law of Self-Defense*, 107 AM. J. INT'L L. 563 (2013).

10. Brian Egan, Legal Advisor, State Dep't, International Law, Legal Diplomacy, and the Counter-ISIL Campaign: Some Observations (Apr. 1, 2016), *in* 92 INT'L L. STUD. 235 (2016).

In addition to the variety of tests that may generally inform necessity and proportionality assessments in the different scenarios of self-defense as well as the variety of factors that may inform these tests in those distinct scenarios, the factual situations to which the principles are applied also offer endless variability. It has often been observed that ultimately concrete application of the necessity and proportionality principles hinges on the specific circumstances and contingencies of a situation.[11] Application of these principles thus also vastly depends on how the relevant facts of a situation are determined and measured.[12] This raises questions of evidentiary standards[13] and, even if standards are agreed upon, different perspectives may still give rise to different appreciation of the facts. As observed by Kretzmer, there is a self-evident bias of a state under attack, which extends to states that sympathize with the victim state, whereas the attitude of uninvolved states and outsiders may give rise to other perspectives, also informed by considerations of an entirely different nature.[14] Hence, in the words of Schmitt, "all such assessments [including necessity and proportionality assessments] are inherently subjective and contextual."[15]

These statements tie in with a louder chorus that depicts proportionality as extremely flexible and context-specific, dependent on circumstances at hand, and lacking certainty,[16] or even as a mere rhetorical tool.[17] In a 2008 article titled *On Proportionality of Countermeasures in International Law*, the late Thomas

11. Tams & Devaney, *supra* note 1, at 102.

12. Zimmerman submits that application of the *jus in bello* proportionality principle requires an "intense verification of the relevant facts on the ground." As for *jus ad bellum* proportionality, he states that "[i]t would accordingly be sufficient, in order for the reply to the armed attack to be considered legal under international law, that a bona fide claim could be made, that it could have ex ante been expected that the measures of self-defense, given the available information, would be proportionate in light of the anticipated armed attack." Andreas Zimmermann, *The Second Lebanon War:* Jus ad Bellum, Jus in Bello *and the Issue of Proportionality*, 11 Max Planck Y.B. U.N. L. 99, 125, 137 (2007).

13. Mary Ellen O'Connell, *Evidence of Terror*, 7 J. Conflict & Security L. 19 (2002). For the International Court of Justice's treatment of evidence in the self-defense context, *see* Armed Activities on the Territory of Congo (Dem. Rep. Congo v. Uganda), Judgement, 2005 I.C.J. Rep. 168, ¶¶ 120–34 (Dec. 19). For particular evidentiary problems and their limits in the context of risk-assessment to determine whether an attack is imminent and there is thus a basis for anticipatory self-defense, *see* Noam Lubell, *The Problem of Imminence in an Uncertain World*, *in* The Oxford Handbook of the Use of Force in International Law 697, 713–19 (Marc Weller ed., 2015).

14. Kretzmer, *supra* note 1, at 238.

15. Michael N. Schmitt, Counter-Terrorism and the Use of Force in International Law 70 (The Marshall Center Papers No. 5, 2002).

16. *See* Sina Etezazian, *The Nature of the Self-Defence Proportionality Requirement*, 3 J. Use Force Int'l L. 260 (2016) (including further references given therein).

17. Gardam, *supra* note 1, at 187.

Franck countered the idea that proportionality was like beauty, existing only in the eye of the beholder. Accepting the indeterminacy of proportionality, Franck argued that the dynamic quality of vague principles like proportionality lies in their operational effect of creating a space for second opinions.[18] Rather than seeing proportionality as a principle offering direct substantive guidance, Franck emphasized the institutional dimension of the proportionality principle and particularly the role of international courts in generating jurisprudence that clarifies the principle's contours through a precedential approach. In his article, Franck demonstrated how international courts had cast light on the concept of proportionality in different judicial settings also regarding trade disputes and human rights litigation. In the *jus ad bellum* context, the International Court of Justice's (ICJ) case law was spotlighted as offering guidance on proportionality.[19]

The ICJ is not always considered a beacon of clarity though, and various authors have in fact critiqued the ICJ for not offering sufficient guidance on what *jus ad bellum* proportionality means,[20] or for insisting on a retrospective approach that is out of tune with the generally accepted qualitative-prospective approach.[21] More generally the problem may be that *jus ad bellum* litigation at the ICJ remains sparse.[22] Therefore, the central premise of this chapter is to take Franck's idea one step further and to look beyond international courts to find other platforms that could offer a space for proportionality discourse. Parliamentary inquiries and debates can serve a useful role in this regard. Yet, given its primacy in matters of international peace and security, the Security Council is, of course, the inevitable and prime location to explore in this context. Article 51's reporting requirement may offer an entry for such explorations.

18. Franck, *supra* note 3, at 717.

19. *Id.* at 719–22.

20. *See, e.g.*, Akande & Liefländer, *supra* note 9, at 567. For an overall appraisal of the ICJ's *jus ad bellum* jurisprudence, *see* Christine Gray, *The International Court of Justice and the Use of Force*, *in* The Development of International Law by the International Court of Justice 237 (Christian J. Tams & James Sloan eds., 2013).

21. Christian J. Tams, *The Necessity and Proportionality of Anti-Terrorist Self-Defense*, *in* Counter-Terrorism Strategies in a Fragmented International Legal Order: Meeting the Challenges 373, 387–88 (Larissa van den Herik & Nico Schrijver eds., 2013).

22. For a general inquiry on rationale for states to present *jus ad bellum* cases to the ICJ, *see* Christine Gray, *Why State Resort to Litigation in Cases Concerning the Use of Force*, *in* Litigating International Law Disputes: Weighing the Options 305 (Natalie Klein ed., 2014). For an analysis of the ICJ's case law on the use of force, *see* Claus Kreß, *The International Court of Justice and the "Principle of Non-Use of Force," in* The Oxford Handbook of the Use of Force in International Law 561 (Marc Weller ed., 2015).

III. THE REPORTING REQUIREMENT OF ARTICLE 51

As per Article 51, states retain the inherent but temporary right to defend themselves, "until the Security Council has taken measures necessary to maintain international peace and security." The second sentence of Article 51 reads:

> Measures taken by Members in the exercise of this right of self-defence shall be immediately reported to the Security Council and shall not in any way affect the authority and responsibility of the Security Council under the present Charter to take at any time such action as it deems necessary in order to maintain or restore international peace and security.

Article 51 thus prescribes that states acting in self-defense shall report their actions immediately to the Security Council and that the Security Council may then take over, thereby subscribing to the Charter's τέλος (goal) of centralization of military action, which—as is well known—has not materialized in practice.[23]

The word "shall" has been understood as being directive but not mandatory in the sense that failure to report does not invalidate the claim of self-defense as such,[24] nor does mere fulfillment of the reporting requirement render the underlying self-defense action legal per se. In this sense, the reporting requirement rather has a procedural or technical function, and is not substantive in nature. It thus follows, also flowing from the ICJ's dicta in the *Nicaragua* case, that the reporting requirement pertains to Article 51 only and does not exist in parallel under customary international law,[25] but the relevance of this finding is rather limited given the U.N. Charter's universal ratification.

The word "reported" is not further elaborated on. Early incarnations of Article 51 required that the Security Council "be kept fully informed."[26] The subsequent

23. Monica Hakimi, *The* Jus ad Bellum*'s Regulatory Form*, 112 AM. J. INT'L L. 151, 158 (2018) ("[T]he more Article 51 permits defensive force . . . , the more its shifts decisionmaking from the Council to state acting unilaterally.").

24. D.W. Greig, *Self-Defence and the Security Council: What Does Article 51 Require?*, 40 INT'L & COMP. L.Q. 366, 384 (1991). For an analysis on the status of the reporting obligation, *see* DINSTEIN, *supra* note 7, at 239–41, as well as the ICJ's statement in the *Nicaragua* judgment that "the absence of a report may be one of the factors indicating whether the State in question was itself convinced that it was acting in self-defence." Military and Paramilitary Activities in and Against Nicaragua (Nicar. v. U.S.), Judgment, 1986 I.C.J. Rep. 226, ¶ 200 (July 8). On this topic *also see* James A. Green, *The Article 51 Reporting Requirement for Self-Defense Actions*, 55 VA. J. INT'L L. 563 (2015); TOM RUYS, "ARMED ATTACK" AND ARTICLE 51 OF THE UN CHARTER: EVOLUTION IN CUSTOMARY LAW AND PRACTICE 68–74 (2010).

25. "Whatever influence the Charter may have had on customary international law in these matters, it is clear that in customary international law it is not a condition of the lawfulness of the use of force in self-defence that a procedure so closely dependent on the content of a treaty commitment and of the institutions established by it, should have been followed." *Nicar. v. U.S.*, *supra* note 24, ¶ 200.

26. Green, *supra* note 24, at 603.

use of the word "report" seems to pose a lower bar as to the level of legal and factual detail that should be provided. The wording of the other authentic languages varies: Arabic (تبلغ = reported); Chinese (应立向安全理事会报告 = shall be immediately reported); French (portées à la connaissance = brought to the attention); Russian (сообщены = communicated; сообщить means to inform or to send a message); and Spanish (communicadas = communicated). The French, Russian, and Spanish texts may imply a mere notification requirement without any need for further substantiation. Indeed, one of the main purposes of the reporting requirement is to publicize a claim of self-defense and thus to put it on the agenda of the Security Council and the international community more broadly. Nonetheless, serious engagement at a central level does require a certain substantiation to allow for a meaningful discussion. Scholarly arguments have been advanced that reports must include evidence regarding the alleged circumstances that triggered the attack and some information on defensive measures taken.[27] This raises questions of the extent to which such disclosure obligations can apply, also taking into account the highly sensitive nature of underlying intelligence information.[28] These questions tie in with other rationales of the reporting requirement regarding transparency and justification.[29] These broader rationales may also inform timing and frequency of reporting and in this respect the argument has been made that states "must report afresh when the material facts have changed, for example, where self-defense is used as a basis for the use of force on the territory of a new State, or new parties are added to the conflict."[30]

In a comprehensive piece on Article 51's reporting requirement, Green analyzed the practice of reporting. His findings were that, in the period 1998–2013, a majority of self-defense actions was reported to the Security Council.[31] On substantive quality of the reports, Green noted that reports were "extremely cursory, for the most part including little factual or legal detail."[32] By way of example, Green pointed out that only three of the 200 reports submitted between 1998 and 2013 referred to the proportionality principle, and only one of those made an actual attempt to substantiate the claim that the proportionality principle had been

27. Yutaka Arai-Takahashi, *Shifting Boundaries of the Right of Self-Defence—Appraising the Impact of the September 11 Attacks on* Jus Ad Bellum, 36 Int'l Law. 1081 (2002).

28. *See id.* at 1095; Michael Wood, *International Law and the Use of Force: What Happens in Practice?*, 53 Indian J. Int'l L. 345, 350 (2013); Schmitt, *supra* note 15, at 69–72.

29. Report of the Special Rapporteur on Extrajudicial, Summary or Arbitrary Executions, ¶ 93, U.N. Doc. A/68/382 (Sept. 13, 2013).

30. *Id.*, ¶ 94.

31. Green, *supra* note 24, at 585. The reporting is still not 100 percent complied with. *See, e.g.*, Ashley Deeks, *A Call for Article 51 Letters*, Lawfare (June 25, 2014), https://www.lawfareblog.com/call-article-51-letters (noting the absence of Article 51 letters following the Kenyan strikes in Somalia against al-Shabaab, the Israeli air strikes in Syria in response to a cross-border attack killing of an Israeli teenager, and the Syrian air strikes in western Iraq against ISIS).

32. Green, *supra* note 24, at 604.

adhered to.[33] These figures may not have taken account of letters which did not refer to the proportionality principle expressly, but which did make indirect reference to the spirit of the principle, for instance, by highlighting the aim of operations. Specifically in the context of the operations against al-Qaida, the majority of Article 51 letters did pay tribute to the proportionality principle, emphasizing that the self-defense measures were targeting al-Qaida as a terrorist organization and the Taliban regime as their host, but not the Afghan population.[34] In contrast, France was more evasive, stating only,

> On instructions from my Government, following the terrorist attacks perpetrated in the United States of America on 11 September 2001, I have the honour to inform you that, in accordance with the exercise of the inherent right of individual or collective self-defence (Article 51 of the Charter), referred to in Security Council resolution 1368 (2001), and in response to the encouragement addressed to Member States by the Council in paragraph 5 of its resolution 1378 (2001), France has undertaken action involving the participation of military air, land and naval forces.[35]

Such a letter does not offer much beyond mere notification.

Practice since 2013 has been rather different. In the context of operations against the Islamic State specifically, a variety of states have more expressly reported on

33. *Id.* at 605.

34. Permanent Rep. of the U.S. to the U.N., Letter Dated Oct. 7, 2001 from the Permanent Rep. of the U.S. to the U.N. Addressed to the President of the Security Council, para. 4, U.N. Doc. S/2001/946 (Oct. 7, 2001); Chargé d'Affaires a.i. of the Permanent Mission of the U.K. to the U.N., Letter Dated Oct. 7, 2001 from the Chargé d'Affaires a.i. of the Permanent Mission of the U.K. to the U.N. Addressed to the President of the Security Council, paras. 3–4, U.N. Doc. S/2001/947 (Oct. 7, 2001); Chargé d'Affaires a.i. of the Permanent Mission of Can. to the U.N., Letter Dated Oct. 24, 2001 from the Chargé d'Affaires a.i. of the Permanent Mission of Can. to the U.N. Addressed to the President of the Security Council, para. 2, U.N. Doc. S/2001/1005 (Oct. 24, 2001); Permanent Rep. of Austl. to the U.N., Letter Dated Nov. 23, 2001 from the Permanent Rep. of Austl. to the U.N. Addressed to the President of the Security Council, para. 6, U.N. Doc. S/2001/1104 (Nov. 23, 2001); Permanent Rep. of Germ. to the U.N., Letter Dated Nov. 29, 2001 from the Permanent Rep. of Germ. to the U.N. Addressed to the President of the Security Council, para. 2, U.N. Doc. S/2001/1127 (Nov. 29, 2001); Permanent Rep. of the Neth. to the U.N., Letter Dated Dec. 6, 2001 from the Permanent Rep. of the Neth. to the U.N. Addressed to the President of the Security Council, para. 3, U.N. Doc. S/2001/1171 (Dec. 6, 2001); Permanent Rep. of N.Z. to the U.N., Letter Dated Dec. 17, 2001 from the Permanent Rep. of N.Z. to the U.N. Addressed to the President of the Security Council, para. 3, U.N. Doc. S/2001/1193 (Dec. 18, 2001); Permanent Rep. of Pol. to the U.N., Letter Dated Mar. 15, 2002 from the Permanent Rep. of Pol. to the U.N. Addressed to the President of the Security Council, para. 1, U.N. Doc. S/2002/275 (Mar. 15, 2002).

35. Permanent Rep. of Fr. to the U.N., Letter Dated Nov. 23, 2001 from the Permanent Rep. of Fr. to the U.N. Addressed to the President of the Security Council, U.N. Doc. S/2001/1103 (Nov. 23, 2001).

necessity and proportionality. In their Article 51 letters, states almost invariably posited that they took "necessary and proportionate measures" in individual and/or collective self-defense.[36] Going beyond *Operation Enduring Freedom*, which targeted the terrorist organization as well as the supportive Taliban regime, the Article 51 letters regarding Islamic State operations consistently underscored that they targeted the Islamic State specifically, thereby subscribing to an interpretation

36. The United States indicated that it had "initiated necessary and proportionate military actions in Syria." Permanent Rep. of the U.S. to the U.N., Letter Dated Sept. 23, 2014 from the Permanent Rep. of the U.S. to the U.N. Addressed to the Secretary-General, U.N. Doc. S/2014/695 (Sept. 23, 2014) [hereinafter U.S. Letter, U.N. Doc. S/2014/695]. The United Kingdom reported that it "fully supports these international efforts, whose purpose is to end the continuing attack on Iraq, to protect Iraqi citizens and to enable Iraqi forces to regain control of the borders of Iraq by striking ISIL sites and military strongholds in Syria, as necessary and proportionate measures." Permanent Rep. of the U.K. to the U.N., Identical Letters Dated Nov. 25, 2014 from the Permanent Rep. of the U.K. to the U.N. Addressed to the Secretary-General and the President of the Security Council, U.N. Doc. S/2014/851 (Nov. 26, 2014) [hereinafter U.K. Letter, U.N. Doc. S/2014/851]. On a later occasion, the United Kingdom reported that it "carried out a precision air strike against an ISIL vehicle in which a target known to be actively engaged in planning and directing imminent armed attacks against the United Kingdom was travelling. This air strike was a necessary and proportionate exercise of the individual right of self-defence of the United Kingdom." Permanent Rep. of the U.K. to the U.N., Letter Dated Sept. 7, 2015 from the Permanent Rep. of the U.K. to the U.N. Addressed to the President of the Security Council, para. 2, U.N. Doc. S/2015/688 (Sept. 8, 2015). Yet again later, the United Kingdom reported that it "is taking necessary and proportionate measures against ISIL/Daesh in Syria, as called for by the Council in resolution 2249 (2015), in exercise of the inherent right of individual and collective self-defence." Permanent Rep. of the U.K. to the U.N., Letter Dated Dec. 3, 2015 from the Permanent Rep. of the U.K. to the U.N. Addressed to the President of the Security Council, para. 2, U.N. Doc. S/2015/928 (Dec. 3, 2015). *See also* Chargé d'Affaires a.i. of the Permanent Mission of Can. to the U.N., Letter Dated Mar. 31, 2015 from the Chargé d'Affaires a.i. of the Permanent Mission of Can. to the U.N. Addressed to the President of the Security Council, para. 1, U.N. Doc. S/2015/221 (Mar. 31, 2015) [hereinafter Canada Letter, U.N. Doc. S/2015/221]; Permanent Rep. of Austl. to the U.N., Letter Dated Sept. 9, 2015 from the Permanent Rep. of Austl. to the U.N. Addressed to the President of the Security Council, paras. 5–6, U.N. Doc. S/2015/693 (Sept. 9, 2015) [hereinafter Australia Letter, U.N. Doc. S/2015/693]; Chargé d'Affaires a.i. of the Permanent Mission of Germ. to the U.N., Letter Dated Dec. 10, 2015 from the Chargé d'Affaires a.i. of the Permanent Mission of Germ. to the U.N. Addressed to the President of the Security Council, paras. 1, 3, U.N. Doc. S/2015/946 (Dec. 10, 2015) [hereinafter Germany Letter, U.N. Doc. S/2015/946]; Permanent Rep. of Den. to the U.N., Letter Dated Jan. 11, 2016 from the Permanent Rep. of Den. to the U.N. Addressed to the President of the Security Council, para. 1, U.N. Doc. S/2016/34 (Jan. 13, 2016); Chargé d'Affaires a.i. of the Permanent Mission of the Neth. to the U.N., Letter Dated Feb. 10, 2016 from the Chargé d'Affaires a.i. of the Permanent Mission of the Neth. to the U.N. Addressed to the President of the Security Council, paras. 1–2, U.N. Doc. S/2016/132 (Feb. 10, 2016) [hereinafter Netherlands Letter, U.N. Doc. S/2016/132]; Permanent Rep. of Nor. to the U.N., Letter Dated June 3, 2016 from the Permanent Rep. of Nor. to the U.N. Addressed to the President of the Security Council, paras. 1, 3, U.N. Doc. S/2016/513 (June 3, 2016) [hereinafter Norway Letter, U.N. Doc. S/2016/513]; Permanent Rep. of Belg. to the U.N., Letter Dated June 7, 2016 from the Permanent Rep. of Belg. to the U.N. Addressed to the President of the Security Council, paras. 1, 3, U.N. Doc. S/2016/523 (June 9, 2016) [hereinafter Belgium Letter, U.N. Doc. S/2016/523].

of proportionality that excludes attacks against the host state.[37] In addition, the letters generally adhered to a prospective understanding of the proportionality principle, presenting their actions as a response to a threat while also referring to constant and continuing armed attacks on Iraq from safe havens in Syria. In their letters, states articulated concrete purposes of their actions, such as "to end the continuing attacks on Iraq, to protect Iraqi citizens, and ultimately to enable and arm Iraqi forces to perform their task of regaining control of the Iraqi borders";[38] to aim at "further degrading ISIL's ability to carry out attacks";[39] and "to prevent and suppress terrorist acts committed by ISIL and to eradicate the safe haven that ISIL has established over significant parts of Iraq and Syria."[40] This may offer insight into which aims are considered and presented as legitimate. Yet, as is well known, significant debate remains as to whether the Article 51 letters can be interpreted as offering support for the unwilling and unable test, and some states' deliberate ambiguity is not particularly helpful in this regard.[41] The claim has also been made that certain states attempt to rewrite the U.N. Charter through their Article 51 letters.[42]

It is also the case that letters and their contents often remain uncontested—apart from the victim state's response.[43] In this regard, Turkey's reporting on *Operation Olive Branch* can be mentioned. It reads as follows:

37. For example, the letters of Canada, Canada Letter, U.N. Doc. S/2015/221, *supra* note 36, para. 4, and Australia, Australia Letter, U.N. Doc. S/2015/693, *supra* note 36, para. 5, specify, "These military actions are not aimed at Syria or the Syrian people, nor do they entail support for the Syrian regime." Similarly, Germany, Germany Letter, U.N. Doc. S/2015/946, *supra* note 36, para. 1, Norway, Norway Letter, U.N. Doc. S/2016/513, *supra* note 36, para. 3, and Belgium, Belgium Letter, U.N. Doc. S/2016/523, *supra* note 36, para. 3, each stated, "These measures are directed against ISIL, not against the Syrian Arab Republic."

38. U.S. Letter, U.N. Doc. S/2014/695, *supra* note 36; U.K. Letter, U.N. Doc. S/2014/851, *supra* note 36.

39. Canada Letter, U.N. Doc. S/2015/221, *supra* note 36, para. 4.

40. Netherlands Letter, U.N. Doc. S/2016/132, *supra* note 36, paras. 1–2.

41. For the argument that there is no broad support for the unwilling and unable standard, *see, e.g.*, Jutta Brunnée & Stephen J. Toope, *Self-Defense Against Non-State Actors: Are Powerful States Willing but Unable to Change International Law?*, 67 INT'L & COMP. L.Q. 263 (2018). For a different assessment, *see* Elena Chachko & Ashley Deeks, *Which States Support the "Unwilling and Unable" Test?*, LAWFARE (Oct. 10, 2016), https://www.lawfareblog.com/which-states-support-unwilling-and-unable-test. On strategic ambiguity, *see* Marko Milanovic, *Belgium's Article 51 Letter to the Security Council [UPDATED]*, EJIL: TALK! (June 17, 2016), https://www.ejiltalk.org/belgiums-article-51-letter-to-the-security-council.

42. Heads of State or Gov't of the Movement of Non-Aligned Countries, Final Document of the 17th Summit of Heads of State and Government of the Non-Aligned Movement, ¶ 25.2, NAM 2016/CoB/DOC.1.Corr.1 (Sept. 17–18, 2016).

43. In response to the letters and operations, Syria has pointed out that the self-defense actions did not meet various criteria, including the requirement that the response be temporary.

> In countering the threat of terrorism, our response has always been proportionate, measured and in line with the right of self-defence, as defined in Article 51 of the Charter of the United Nations. Accordingly, Turkey successfully concluded Operation Euphrates Shield last year, through which 2,015 km2 of land was cleared of Deash and a safe haven free of terror could be established, which enabled some of the displaced Syrians to return safely and voluntarily to their homes. However, the threat of terrorism from Syria targeting our borders has not ended. The recent increase in rocket attacks and harassment fire directed at Hatay and Kilis provinces of Turkey from the Afrin region of Syria, which is under the control of the PKK/KCK/PYD/YPG terrorist organization, has resulted in the deaths of many civilians and soldiers and has left many more wounded. The risk of Deash elements infiltrating Turkey via this area and targeting the security of Turkey as well as the European countries is also heightened owing to the recent movements of Deash terrorists coming into the Afrin region from other parts of Syria. In order to counter this terrorist threat, Turkey initiated a military operation on 20 January 2018 against these terrorist elements. The operation is aimed at ensuring our border security, neutralizing terrorists in Afrin and saving the brotherly Syrians. Accordingly, the operation will target only terrorists and their hideouts, shelters, emplacements, weapons, vehicles and equipment. All precautions have been taken to avoid collateral damage.[44]

This letter, and particularly the underlying operation, has been critiqued for not meeting Article 51's requirements, in particular the requirement that there be an (imminent) armed attack, for not adhering to the principles of necessity and proportionality, and for failing to sufficiently substantiate its claims.[45] Such critique has not been echoed at the Security Council level though.

The Article 51 letters, when taken together, offer insight into views and practices regarding the application of the necessity and proportionality principles,

Permanent Rep. of Syria to the U.N., Identical Letters Dated Dec. 29, 2015 from the Permanent Rep. of Syria to the U.N. Addressed to the Secretary-General and the President of the Security Council, U.N. Docs. A/70/673 & S/2015/1048 (Jan. 4, 2016). It also argued that the operations caused destruction of Syrian infrastructure, economic facilities, and social institutions. Permanent Rep. of Syria to the U.N., Identical Letters Dated Sept. 29, 2016 from the Permanent Rep. of Syria Addressed to the Secretary-General and the President of the Security Council, U.N. Doc. S/2016/820 (Sept. 30, 2016).

44. Chargé d'Affaires a.i. of the Permanent Mission of Turk. to the U.N., Identical Letters Dated Jan. 20, 2018 from the Chargé d'Affaires a.i. of the Permanent Mission of Turk. to the U.N. Addressed to the Secretary-General and the President of the Security Council, paras. 4–8, U.N. Doc. S/2018/53 (Jan. 22, 2018).

45. Anne Peters, *The Turkish Operation in Afrin (Syria) and the Silence of the Lambs*, EJIL: Talk! (Jan. 30, 2018), https://www.ejiltalk.org/the-turkish-operation-in-afrin-syria-and-the-silence-of-the-lambs.

specifically in a non-state actor context. This underscores that reporting may generate further clarity on the contents of the necessity and proportionality principles in different scenarios. However, as can be expected, scholars disagree on the meaning of the reports, and third states generally withhold from disclosing a view on other states' letters unless they are the victim state or otherwise involved. Scholarly disagreement results, in part, from the fact that the reports are still fairly general without concrete assessments and factual detail.[46] Moreover, reporting which does not match the facts on the ground is not necessarily exposed as such at the Security Council level.

IV. DEEPENING ARTICLE 51'S REPORTING REQUIREMENT: TOWARD A DUTY TO EXPLAIN AND SUBSTANTIATE CLAIMS OF PROPORTIONAL SELF-DEFENSE?

Hence, despite a possible peak in necessity and proportionality reporting, the current practice still leaves room for arguments favoring a more meaningful approach to Article 51's reporting requirement. Such arguments find a basis in relevant policy and scholarly documents on self-defense, such as the *Leiden Policy Recommendations*[47] and the Chatham House *Principles of International Law on the Use of Force by States in Self-Defence.*[48]

The *Leiden Policy Recommendations* underscore the obligation of states to justify and explain their actions. The *Recommendations* specifically concern self-defense against non-state actors, but the core idea has broader application. As the following excerpts demonstrate, the *Recommendations* insist on several occasions on the burden of states using force in self-defense to make their case. They state:

> Self-defence may also be necessary if the armed attack cannot be repelled or averted by the territorial state. States relying on self-defence **must therefore show** that the territorial state's action is not effective in countering the terrorist threat.
>
> . . . .

46. For a similar observation made in a different context, *see* Tams, *supra* note 21, at 418–21.

47. The *Leiden Policy Recommendations* were the outcome of a consultative expert process, organized with the full support of the Netherlands Ministry of Foreign Affairs. They offer expert perspectives aimed at clarifying the law, and they highlight areas in which greater consensus needs to be pursued in particular also regarding self-defense against non-state actors. *See* Leiden Policy Recommendations on Counter-Terrorism and International Law (Nico Schrijver & Larissa van den Herik eds., 2010) [hereinafter Leiden Policy Recommendations], *reprinted in* 57 Neth. Int'l L. Rev. 531 (2010).

48. Chatham House, The Chatham House Principles of International Law on the Use of Force in Self-Defence (2005) [hereinafter Chatham House Principles], *reprinted in* 55 Int'l & Comp. L.Q. 963 (2006).

> Any use of force in anticipatory self-defence should be justified publicly by reference to the evidence available to the state concerned; the facts do not speak for themselves, and the state should explain, as fully as it is able to do, the nature of the threat and the necessity for anticipatory military action.[49]

Specifically on proportionality, the *Leiden Policy Recommendations* add,

> In order to be proportionate, measures of self-defence must be limited to what is required to repel or avert the armed attack. Proportionality in this sense requires states regularly to monitor on-going measures of self-defence and ensure that they remain defensive in character. This may entail limitations on the intensity and duration of force employed and on the theatre and target of operations. In particular, it will normally mean that measures of self-defence against suspected terrorists must be directed primarily against the terrorist groups responsible for the armed attack in question or their facilities. Only in exceptional circumstances will self-defence justify the use of force against the armed forces or facilities of the territorial state, for example, in circumstances where the territorial state is supporting suspected terrorists, as in Afghanistan in 2001.
>
> Unnecessary or disproportionate use of force cannot be justified as a measure of self-defence under international law. As the application of both factors is heavily fact-dependent, states using force in self-defence should be prepared to make publicly available information and data that will support the necessity and proportionality of their conduct. International law does not prevent third states from scrutinising the necessity and proportionality of self-defence operations or from requesting further evidence.[50]

These excerpts underscore the requirement to factually substantiate a claim of self-defense.

The Chatham House *Principles of International Law on the Use of Force by States in Self-Defence* also accentuate the eminence of facts and public justification. Principle 4 on anticipatory self-defense states that "force may be used only on a proper factual basis and after a good faith assessment of the facts." This is further elaborated as follows:

> Each case will necessarily turn on its own facts.
>
> . . . .
>
> The determination of "imminence" is in the first place for the relevant state to make, but it must be made in good faith and on grounds which are capable of objective assessment. Insofar as this can reasonably be achieved, the evidence should be publicly demonstrable. Some kinds of evidence cannot be

49. Leiden Policy Recommendations, *supra* note 47, ¶¶ 42, 48 (emphasis added).

50. *Id.* ¶¶ 43, 44.

> reasonably produced, whether because of the nature or source, or because it is the product of interpretation of many small pieces of information. But evidence is fundamental to accountability, and accountability to the rule of law. The more far-reaching, and the more irreversible its external actions, the more a state should accept (internally as well as externally) the burden of showing that its actions were justifiable on the facts. And there should be proper internal procedures for the assessment of intelligence and appropriate procedural safeguards.[51]

The principles on self-defense against an imminent or actual armed attack by non-state actors as proposed by Bethlehem and published in the *American Journal of International Law* require a strong, reasonable, and objective basis for relevant conclusions, but they do not articulate a concomitant obligation to explain how exactly such conclusions are drawn and corroborated.[52]

Nonetheless, given the centrality of the prohibition of the use of force and its cornerstone nature in the present-day international legal order, it is not entirely illogical to require substantiated justification of unilateral nonconformity. Indeed, it flows from the exceptional nature of self-defense, as well as the spirit of the U.N. Charter and the framing of relevant provisions, that states invoking Article 51 of the U.N. Charter should not only notify the Security Council, but that the word "report" is more demanding and that states should additionally and in light of all relevant circumstances provide appropriate justification.[53] Following this reasoning, states relying on self-defense should construct their justifications in a legally plausible sense that adheres to the strictures and phraseology of Article 51. In addition, the duty to justify and explain can be said to encapsulate the requirement to factually substantiate a claim of proportional self-defense. In case of more exceptional uses of self-defense, such as self-defense against non-state actors, anticipatory self-defense, and anticipatory self-defense against non-state actors, an even greater imperative to explain exists, as in these cases the exceptionality of self-defense is pushed even further. The exact contents of the duty to report may vary in the different scenarios though. Anticipatory self-defense hinges on the notion of "imminence" and thus involves a threat assessment which leaves even greater scope for subjectivity in the analysis.[54] Inevitably, this affects the factual

51. CHATHAM HOUSE PRINCIPLES, *supra* note 48, princ. 4 & cmt.

52. Daniel Bethlehem, *Self-Defense Against an Imminent or Actual Armed Attack by Nonstate Actors*, 106 AM. J. INT'L L. 770, princs. 7, 12, at 775, 776 (2012). The Principles were critiqued for this lacuna by Elizabeth Wilmshurst and Michael Wood. Elizabeth Wilmshurst & Michael Wood, *Self-Defence Against Nonstate Actors: Reflections on the Bethlehem Principles*, 107 AM. J. INT'L L. 386, 394 (2013) ("The principles would have done well to insert cautionary words, as in the Chatham House principles, about the need for a good faith assessment of the facts.").

53. LEIDEN POLICY RECOMMENDATIONS, *supra* note 47, ¶ 36.

54. Lubell, *supra* note 13, at 718.

contents of reporting, but it does not remove the rationale of explaining and justifying per se.

The idea of necessity and proportionality discourse and use of force reporting ties in with notions of legal diplomacy, a duty to explain, and "a culture of justification," presented by Brian Egan, Chimène Keitner, and Harold Koh. With specific reference to the counter-ISIL campaign, Brian Egan underscored that public explanations of legal positions are an important element of legal diplomacy.[55] Egan indicated that a public conversation on legal positions may be informed by concurrent private consultations, and he sees such intertwined public and private engagements as an indispensable ingredient of international partnerships and coalitions.[56] Publicizing legal positions may also be the start of a broader conversation with other states. Adversary or other disagreeing states may react on legal and factual positions taken and this conversation can subsequently create a feedback loop that ultimately contributes to clarifying and crystallizing the contents of the law and legal principles at stake. Portrayed this way, nonreporting effectively amounts to an omission or at least a diminished ability to shape public discourse.[57] Hence, bypassing the question regarding the legal nature of the obligation, the more compelling argument may be that reporting is generally in states' self-interest. Reporting allows states to shape the normative environment in which they operate in addition to cultivating partnerships.[58] More concretely, reporting on the necessity and proportionality requirements with legal substantiation and factual articulation specifies and consolidates what necessity and proportionality require, thereby also operationalizing these principles in nontraditional invocations of self-defense. Additionally, reporting as an accountability process also has the effect of improving the ex ante integrity of decision-making and thereby contributes to norm-internalization.[59]

Despite such advantages, states have been diagnosed as being generally hesitant to state their legal and factual position in detail. They prefer to keep maximum flexibility and to preserve the possibility to change position at a later stage. States tend to present skeletal arguments, possibly also to ensure that they do not prejudice potential ICJ proceedings or other accountability processes. The criminalization of the use of force may inadvertently have enhanced this reflex, and it may further disincentivize states to present their case.[60] Such transparency

55. Egan, *supra* note 10, at 244.

56. *Id.*

57. For a similar argument in relation to covert action, *see* Alexandra H. Perina, *Black Holes and Open Secrets: The Impact of Covert Action on International Law*, 53 Colum. J. Transnat'l L. 507, 511 (2015) ("But the void created by a silent state compels courts to turn to other sources.").

58. Chimène Keitner, *Explaining International Acts*, 63 McGill L.J. 649 (2018).

59. *See id.*; *see also* Harold Koh, *The Legal Adviser's Duty to Explain*, 41 Yale J. Int'l L. 189 (2016).

60. The criminalization of the use of force was enacted through amendment to the Statute of the International Criminal Court adopted at the ICC Review Conference in Kampala on June 11,

cost of operationalizing the crime of aggression within the ICC statute is not a given though. States retain an overarching interest not to lose sway over use of force discourse and thus to participate in it. As underlined by Schmitt and Watts in relation to international humanitarian law, state silence may cede the initiative and power over law development to others.[61] Moreover, denial and secrecy over the facts of concrete cases can also be costly in a different respect, as widespread and inaccurate claims may fill the void left by a silent state.[62] Secrecy will in any event be increasingly difficult to sustain, given open source investigations through new cybertechnologies by private agencies such as Bellingcat, the Bureau of Investigative Journalism and Forensic Architecture.[63] While third states may often be reticent to express claims of illegality,[64] exemplified by the deafening silence over Yemen, private actors are not governed by similar diplomatic instincts. Hence, different actors are driven by different interests, and while states may make strategic use of Article 51 letters to expand the law on the one hand, they may be ambiguous as to precise legal basis and reserved in providing factual evidence on the other. A more structured approach to Article 51's reporting requirement could thus well serve as a countervailing force to such dynamics.

V. WIDENING THE REPORTING REQUIREMENT TO INTERVENTION BY INVITATION

The initial rationale of Article 51's reporting requirement was to alert the Security Council that force in self-defense had been used and to place the matter on the international agenda with a view to enabling the Council to exercise its primary responsibility to maintain peace and security.[65] As the system of collective security is becoming more decentralized and as the Security Council has been adopting

2010. Review Conference of the Rome Statute, The Crime of Aggression, Resol. RC/Res.6 (June 11, 2010), https://treaties.un.org/Pages/ViewDetails.aspx?src=TREATY&mtdsg_no=XVIII-10-b&chapter=18&clang=_en. The ICC's jurisdiction was subsequently activated on December 14, 2017. Assembly of States Parties, Activation of the Jurisdiction of the Court over the Crime of Aggression, Resol. ICC-ASP/16/Res.5 (Dec. 14, 2017), https://asp.icc-cpi.int/en_menus/asp/resolutions/sessions/Pages/2017-16th-session.aspx (click on the link next to "ICC-ASP/16/Res.5).

61. Michael N. Schmitt & Sean Watts, *State* Opinio Juris *and International Humanitarian Law Pluralism*, 91 Int'l L. Stud. 171 (2015).

62. Koh illustrated this argument with reference to the killing of Anwar Al Aulaqi, which the U.S. government only acknowledged two years later and only then offered legal justification. Koh, *supra* note 59, at 207. *See generally* Perina, *supra* note 57.

63. Forensic Architecture, https://forensic-architecture.org (last visited Aug. 20, 2019).

64. On the normative effects of silence, *see* Paulina Starski, *Silence Within the Process of Normative Change and Evolution of the Prohibition on the Use of Force: Normative Volatility and Legislative Responsibility*, 4 J. Use Force & Int'l L. 14 (2017).

65. Green, *supra* note 24, at 568.

a new role recently whereby it condones or blesses nonauthorized uses of force rather than authorizing use of force itself,[66] the reporting requirement has taken on new meaning. In such constellation, the purpose of the reporting requirement is not mainly to notify or alert so that the Council can take over, but rather to report in the ordinary sense, namely, to offer information and to account so as to enable the Security Council and the international community at large to discuss whether the use of force was in accordance with the applicable rules and requirements.

In addition to self-defense as an exception, consent is also relied on to justify the use of force, and it has increasingly been invoked as an additional basis for counter-terrorism operations. Also in the context of consent situations, a practice has emerged whereby the Security Council refrains from authorizing the use of force itself, and instead it may appraise the circumstances surrounding the formulation of the invitation thereby endorsing the consent. Whether the Security Council makes such appraisal in concrete situations depends, inter alia, on whether the use of force is reported and whether the matter is placed on the Security Council's agenda. This raises the question regarding the existence of a reporting requirement for consent-based use of force.

Since the U.N. Charter is silent on intervention by invitation, any legally binding reporting requirement would have to be construed under customary international law. Scholarly arguments have been made in this respect, proposing that Article 51's reporting requirement should be applied mutatis mutandis to consent-based use of force.[67] In its resolution on military assistance on request, the *Institut de Droit International* also stated that "any request that is followed by military assistance shall be notified to the Secretary-General of the United Nations."[68] Suggesting the Secretary-General as recipient of notifications rather than the Security Council might be explained by political sensitivities and reluctance of states to accept any hard core reporting obligation. In this vein, the following U.S. statement may be noted when reporting on missile strikes in Houthi-controlled territory in Yemen in 2016:

> These actions were taken with the consent of the Government of Yemen. Although the United States therefore does not believe notification pursuant

66. As also discussed by Monica Hakimi. Hakimi, *supra* note 23.

67. Karine Bannelier & Théodore Christakis, *Under the UN Security Council's Watchful Eyes: Military Intervention by Invitation in the Malian Conflict*, 26 Leiden J. Int'l L. 855, 870 (2013). For a more tentative approach, *see* Olivier Corten, *Intervention by Invitation: The Expanding Role of the UN Security Council*, *in* 4 Max Planck Trialogues on the Law of Peace and War: Intervention by Invitation (Anne Peters & Christian Marxsen eds., forthcoming).

68. M. Gerhard Hafner, Rapporteur, Tenth Commission, Sub-group C, Institut de Droit International, Present Problems of the Use of Force in International Law: Military Assistance on Request (Sept. 8, 2011), http://www.idi-iil.org/app/uploads/2017/06/2011_rhodes_10_C_en.pdf.

to Article 51 of the Charter of the United Nations is necessary in these circumstances, the United States nevertheless wishes to inform the Council that these actions were taken consistent with international law.[69]

This can be read as implying that no reporting requirement exists at all, or that Article 51 cannot serve as a legal basis for a reporting requirement on consent-based use of force. It is, in any event, not self-evident to construe a legally binding reporting requirement for consent-based use of force under customary international law. Even if there is a certain practice of informing the Security Council of forceful action taken pursuant to an invitation,[70] there are also clear examples of nonreporting.[71] Reporting on consent-based use of force may be sensitive in particular when the consent is not public. Moreover, to construe a customary reporting rule for consent-based use of force, there also needs to be *opinio juris*, which at this point in time does not yet seem to clearly exist. States outside the Security Council as well as nonpermanent members could perhaps play a role in contributing to the expression and formation of such *opinio juris*. In this regard, Brazil's statements in 2018 are noteworthy, as it insisted on a more meaningful reporting requirement for Article 51,[72] as well on the need for periodic reporting on military operations pursuant to Article 42 of the U.N. Charter,[73] thus suggesting a more holistic reporting requirement.

69. Permanent Rep. of the U.S. to the U.N., Letter Dated Oct. 15, 2016 from the Permanent Rep. of the U.S. to the U.N. Addressed to the President of the Security Council, U.N. Doc. S/2016/869 (Oct. 17, 2016).

70. For example, Saudi Arabia in Yemen, the United States in Iraq, Russia in Syria, France in Mali, and Senegal in the Gambia.

71. *See* Deeks, *supra* note 31. On U.S. nonreporting of its drone strikes and other operations in Yemen, Somalia, and Pakistan, *see* Colum. L. Sch. Hum. Rts. Clinic & Sana'a Ctr. for Strategic Stud., Out of the Shadows: Recommendations to Advance Transparency in the Use of Lethal Force 54 (2017); *see also* David Bosco, *Letters from the Front Lines: State Communications to the U.N. Security Council During Conflict*, 54 Colum. J. Transnat'l L. 341 (2016).

72. Mission of Braz. to the U.N., Letter Dated Oct. 15, 2018 from the Mission of Braz. to the U.N. Addressed to the Chairman of the Special Committee on the Charter of the U.N. and on the Strengthening of the Role of the Organization (Oct. 15, 2018), http://statements.unmeetings.org/media2/20303642/brazil-85.pdf.

73. Duque Estrada Meyer, Rep. to Braz., Statement During 8262d Meeting of the U.N. Security Council Concerning Upholding International Law within the Context of the Maintenance of International Peace and Security, U.N. Doc. S/PV.8262, at 44–45 (May 17, 2018). On effective monitoring and accountability, *see* Ambassador Maria Luiza Ribeiro Viotti, Permanent Rep. of Braz. to U.N., Letter Dated Nov. 9, 2011 from the Permanent Rep. of Braz. to the U.N. Addressed to the Secretary-General, annex, Responsibility While Protecting: Elements for the Development and Promotion of a Concept ¶¶ 11(h), 11(i), U.N. Docs. A/66/551 & S/2011/701 (Nov. 11, 2011).

In considering a reporting requirement for consent-based use of force specifically, complex questions arise on timing and modalities, as well as on when and how consent-based use of force that is very temporary or that involves a one-off action must be reported, and on what exactly must be reported under this heading, that is, whether a reporting requirement would also cover pure aiding.

Absent a clear requirement thus far, states nonetheless tend to rely on multiple justifications including consent, and they have reported on this to the Security Council. Given this existing practice, the issue whether a perceived duty to explain translates into a hard legal obligation to report and whether this obligation extends to consent-based use of force in addition to self-defense is perhaps not the most pressing one. Even absent overall agreement that reporting on all uses of force is legally required, states have in fact reported beyond Article 51's requirement or at least they are often inclined to make statements that are meant to be explanatory. The bigger problem is that the reporting and related discourse is not always centralized and sometimes done at other venues such as the Human Rights Council, the European Union, domestic parliaments, or the media. A second bigger problem concerns ambiguous or superficial language and absence of reasoning and legal argument, as well as failure to adduce any supporting factual material and evidence.[74] This raises the question how states may be persuaded to engage in more structured and meaningful reporting and use of force discourse.

VI. ENHANCING USE OF FORCE DISCOURSE: LESSONS FROM THE U.N. SANCTIONS ARCHITECTURE

Enhancing use of force discourse presupposes the creation or existence of an enabling environment which entices states invoking self-defense or justificatory grounds to take part in the conversation in a meaningful way and which similarly animates third states to challenge or scrutinize claims of self-defense and other justifications. What should such an "enabling environment" look like?[75]

The most sophisticated institutional architecture that exists at the Security Council level has been designed in the past decades in the context of U.N. sanctions and counterterrorism. It may be explored to what extent ideas to build a more elaborate enabling environment to discuss claims of self-defense and other justifications of unilateral use of force can be patterned upon the bodies or platforms created as part of the U.N. sanctions architecture.

74. On strategic ambiguity, *see* Milanovic, *supra* note 41. On intentional ambiguity within the Security Council, outside the context of self-defense, *see* Michael Byers, *Agreeing to Disagree: Security Council Resolutions 1441 and Intentional Ambiguity*, 10 Global Governance 165 (2004).

75. On the Security Council as a forum for justificatory discourse, *see* Ian Johnstone, *Security Council Deliberations: The Power of the Better Argument*, 14 Eur. J. Int'l L. 437, 452–64 (2003). On reason-giving in the Security Council, *see* Daniel Moeckli & Raffael Fasel, *A Duty to Give Reasons in the Security Council: Making Voting Transparent*, 14 Int'l Orgs. L. Rev. 13 (2017). Both articles rely on Jürgen Habermas's theory of communicative action.

The elaborate U.N. sanctions machinery is, in a sense, quite spectacular given the Security Council's reticence to settling on any generic procedures or working methods.[76] Despite the Council's preference for ad hoc–ism, which better allows it to keep control, a certain U.N. sanctions apparatus including notable elements of independence has come into place. An important component of the U.N. sanctions architecture is the sanctions committees, which are created under Article 29 of the U.N. Charter as subsidiary organs. Each U.N. sanctions regime has its own sanctions committee, which is composed of the 15 members of the Security Council. The core mandate of a sanctions committee is to monitor implementation, which includes the listing of individuals that are to be subjected to sanctions. The exact working methods and procedures differ per sanctions regime, although recent streamlining attempts have been made pursuant to external criticisms on the political and arbitrary nature of the functioning of these committees. These criticisms were particularly strong in the context of the Taliban/al-Qaida/Daesh sanctions, which ultimately led to the creation of the Ombudsperson for this sanctions regime.[77] The Ombudsperson was established for the al-Qaida sanctions regime only. When the Taliban/al-Qaida sanctions regime split up into two separate regimes, the Taliban sanctions regime was brought outside of the scope of the Ombudsperson's "jurisdiction."[78] Yet, when the al-Qaida sanctions regime was expanded to also cover the Islamic State in 2015, the Ombudsperson's powers grew accordingly.[79]

The Ombudsperson can receive petitions by individuals to be delisted, and its mandate and procedures are detailed in Resolutions 1904 (2009), 1989 (2011), 2083 (2012), 2161 (2014), 2253 (2015), and 2368 (2017). The Ombudsperson can recommend delisting, which will take effect unless the sanctions committee disagrees by consensus or refers the matter to the Security Council.[80] This procedure has been criticized by human rights lawyers as not offering fair process to individuals since a recommendation is not binding, yet such criticism fails to recognize the revolutionary step that the Security Council took to accept a nearly binding independent second opinion in its decision-making processes.[81] The Ombudsperson process is also interesting in its treatment of confidential

76. For a similar finding and a general appraisal of the U.N. sanctions apparatus, *see* Joanna Weschler, *The Evolution of Security Council Innovations in Sanctions*, INT'L J. 31 [Winter 2009–2010] (2010).

77. For an analysis, *see* Kimberly Prost, *Security Council Sanctions and Fair Process*, *in* RESEARCH HANDBOOK ON UN SANCTIONS AND INTERNATIONAL LAW 213 (Larissa van den Herik ed., 2017).

78. S.C. Res. 1988 (June 17, 2011); S.C. Res. 1989 (June 17, 2011).

79. S.C. Res. 2253 (Dec. 17, 2015).

80. S.C. Res. 2161, ¶ 43, annex II. ¶ 14 (June 17, 2014).

81. *See* DEVIKA HOVELL, THE POWER OF PROCESS: THE VALUE OF DUE PROCESS IN SECURITY COUNCIL SANCTIONS DECISION-MAKING (2016).

information. For instance, Resolution 2368 (2017) encourages states to offer as much information as possible that can serve as a statement of case explaining the reasons why a person has been listed, and it also indicates that this statement of case shall be releasable.[82] Obviously, there may be intel involved and underlying the listing proposals, but this does not necessarily need to be disclosed if sufficient reasons can be given otherwise, for instance, based on open-source materials. In this respect, it is interesting to note that certain actors, such as the United Kingdom and the European Union, have indicated that they are turning to open source information to substantiate domestic listings pursuant to U.N. and E.U. designations with a view to circumventing disclosure problems.[83]

Attempts to broaden the Ombudsperson process to other regimes have failed so far, and this reluctance is mainly inspired by a desire to keep the fullest control possible over nonproliferation regimes.[84] Yet, all U.N. sanctions regimes do have—on paper—independent elements in the form of panels of experts. These experts are appointed by the Secretary-General after consultation with the Sanctions Committee. Typically, the experts assist the Committee in carrying out its mandate, including through providing information relevant to the potential designation of individuals and entities, and they also assist the Committee in refining and updating information on the list of individuals subject to the assets freeze, travel ban, and targeted arms embargo, including through the provision of identifying information and additional information for the publicly available narrative summary of reasons for listing. The experts thus have a strong fact-finding mandate, and they are tasked to gather, examine, and analyze information from states, relevant U.N. bodies, regional organizations, and other interested parties regarding the implementation of the sanctions. It is already the case that information gathered by panels of experts may have *jus ad bellum* relevance. For instance, the panel of experts for Yemen has reported on the relationship between Iran and the Houthis, a factor of relevance to proportionality assessments in the context of the consent-based use of force by the Gulf Coalition Forces.[85]

The panels of experts do not receive much guidance on how to find and establish facts, and they are largely dependent on state cooperation. Nonetheless, procedural advancements are being made with a view to ensure proper fact-finding, and the investigative methodology developed by the panel of experts for Yemen

82. S.C. Res. 2368, ¶ 51 (July 20, 2017).

83. *See, e.g.*, U.K. House of Lords, The Legality of EU Sanctions ¶¶ 105–106 (2017), https://publications.parliament.uk/pa/ld201617/ldselect/ldeucom/102/10203.htm.

84. Larissa van den Herik, *Peripheral Hegemony in the Quest to Ensure Security Council Accountability for Its Individualized UN Sanctions Regimes*, 19 J. Conflict & Security L. 427 (2014).

85. Benjamin Nußberger, *Military Strikes in Yemen in 2015: Intervention by Invitation and Self-Defence in the Course of Yemen's "Model Transitional Process,"* 4 J. Use Force & Int'l L. 110, 139 (2017).

is particularly instructive in this regard.[86] This panel has also begun to use social media, commercial satellite imagery, and navigation-tracking databases for its fact-finding exercises.[87] Also in the more comprehensive sanctions regimes, such as the nonproliferation regimes, panels of experts are part of the apparatus. Their level of independence may be slightly more circumspect, as was illustrated by a recent incident in which Russia allegedly suppressed parts of an expert panel report that detailed Russian sanctions evasion.[88] But this example can also be taken as indicative of the independent potential of panels of experts.

Obviously, the legal framework governing U.N. sanctions is very different from the rules on *jus ad bellum* and self-defense specifically. U.N. sanctions have come to be more focused on individuals, which has been one of the incentives for the push toward proceduralization. Nonetheless, some of the elements of the U.N. sanctions architecture may still be useful as a very general blueprint for thinking about ways to design an enabling environment for use of force discourse. Currently, not all use of force communication is always done in the form of formal reporting letters. Other types of written state communications may include use of force discourse too. Information can also be shared orally in Security Council meetings, to which an state that is involved in the use of force but is not a Security Council member may be invited pursuant to Article 32, but only if the concrete use of force in which it is involved is placed on the agenda. Even information that is presented at the Security Council level thus remains scattered. Academic initiatives may fill the void, such as the Harvard Law School databases,[89] but these should not replace formal structures or the need to develop more refine institutional structures at the Security Council level.

To be more concrete, proceduralizing Article 51 and concomitant reporting obligations could include some of the following:

- Placing unilateral use of force on the Security Council agenda;
- Holding a routine debate once Article 51 or another *jus ad bellum* justificatory ground is invoked;
- The setup of a database collecting Article 51 and other reporting letters;

86. Panel of Experts on Yemen, Final Report of the Panel of Experts on Yemen, annexes I, 2, at 62–66, U.N. Doc. S/2017/81 (Jan. 31, 2017).

87. *Id.* at 7–8.

88. Nikki Haley, U.S. Ambassador to the U.N., Remarks at a UN Security Council Briefing on Nonproliferation and the Implementation and Enforcement of UN Sanctions on North Korea (Sept. 17, 2018); *see also* Julian Borger, *US Accuses Russia of Covering Up North Korea Sanctions Violations*, The Guardian (Sept. 17, 2018), https://www.theguardian.com/world/2018/sep/17/us-russia-north-korea-sanctions-violations-nikki-haley.

89. Harv. L. Sch. Program on Int'l L. & Armed Conflict, https://pilac.law.harvard.edu/about-menu (last visited Aug. 21, 2019).

- Developing best practices on when exactly and how often letters should be submitted;
- Developing best practices on what letters should contain;
- The creation of a subsidiary body that collects and monitors submission of Article 51 and other letters; and
- The creation of panels of experts to gather, examine, and analyze relevant information from states, including from third states, and possibly to make prima facie evaluations.[90]

A modest role for independent panels of experts would reflect the interests that the entire international community has in upholding the prohibition of the use of force as a central norm. Notably, Mexico has taken this matter up and has drafted an elaborate working paper entitled "Analysis of the application of Articles 2(4) and 51 of the Charter of the United Nations" that it submitted to the Special Committee on the Charter of the United Nations and on the Strengthening of the Role of the Organization.[91] Mexico specified that its aim was not to conduct analysis of specific communications, but rather to create space for discussion on the scope and limits of self-defense. It proposed a number of substantive, procedural, and transparency/publicity issues that were relevant to guide the discussion.

VII. CONCLUSION

This chapter has presented the argument that Article 51's reporting requirement goes beyond mere notification, and that it also demands that states make formal articulations on the scope of self-defense in concrete situations and that they make an effort to substantiate claims of self-defense, both legally and factually. This call seems to conflict with recent concerns expressed by the Community of Latin American and Caribbean States over "the increase in the number of letters to the Security Council under Article 51 of the Charter submitted by some States in order to have recourse to the use of force in the context of counter-terrorism, most of the times 'ex post facto.'"[92] Also, the Non-Aligned Movement has underlined that "Article 51 of the UN Charter is restrictive and should not be re-written or re-interpreted."[93] One-sided Article 51 letters can indeed have this effect of rewriting the exception of self-defense. The argument regarding a deepening and widening of the reporting requirement thus must be connected with broader reflections

90. For similar suggestions put forward by Brazil, *see supra* note 73.

91. Report of the Special Committee on the Charter of the United Nations and on the Strengthening of the Role of the Organization, U.N. Doc. A/75/33 (Mar. 2, 2020).

92. Permanent Mission of El Sal. to the U.N., Measures to Eliminate International Terrorism, Statement by the Permanent Mission of El Sal. to the U.N. on Behalf of the Community of Latin American and Caribbean States (CELAC) (Oct. 2, 2017), https://enaun.cancilleria.gob.ar/en/measures-eliminate-international-terrorism.

93. Heads of State or Gov't of the Movement of Non-Aligned Countries, *supra* note 42, ¶ 25.2.

on how to create a space for formal self-defense discourse. Such a space should encourage and facilitate all states, including third states, to be explicit in their position on the scope of self-defense and other uses of force. Broad participation in use of force discourse is essential given the central place of Article 2(4) of the U.N. Charter and its status as a cornerstone of our international legal order. As noted by Oona Hathaway, "States that do not use force need to be more active in voicing their legal positions. . . . If the only states that take legal positions on the use of force are those *using* force, the exceptions will continue to expand until they swallow the rule."[94] Acknowledging the warning inherent in this observation, it is submitted that some consideration of countervailing structures at the Security Council level, and Mexico's working paper in particular, certainly might not be superfluous.

94. Oona Hathaway (@oonahathaway), Twitter (Oct. 22, 2018, 4:15 PM), https://twitter.com/oonahathaway/status/1054466271360753665.

PART FOUR

The International Law of Armed Conflicts

8

Sequences of Military Necessity for the *Jus in Bello*

DINO KRITSIOTIS*

I. INTRODUCTION

Military necessity was once described in grandiose terms as "the 'lord paramount' of war,"[1] though its significance has never been too distant or too attenuated within laws of war (or *jus in bello*).[2] As an idea or value system or set of practices, it has had its time dictating the terms of hostilities as well as the conditions of any ensuing peace,[3] and, for better or for worse, an appreciation of those laws is not possible without a full and frank appraisal of what it was that military necessity entailed or was said to entail. In theoretical terms, then, it could be contended that the very idea of a (or any) benchmark of "necessity" embodied what the *jus in bello* itself fundamentally stands for: the injection of an essential economy of

* Professor of Public International Law, University of Nottingham.

1. J.M. Spaight, War Rights on Land 428 (1911) (occurring in a passage where it is said that military necessity "puts its veto upon any endeavour to collect the wounded and dead after a fight—whether because tactical considerations require that the ground on which they lie must be swept with shot and shell, to prevent the enemy from seizing it . . . or because the holders of a jealously-guarded position cannot allow the enemy's search-parties to approach their line and spy out the secrets of the defence works").

2. For a particularly important discussion, *see* Charles de Visscher, *Les Lois de la Guerre et la Théorie de la Nécessité*, 24 Revue Générale de Droit International Public 74 (1917).

3. Christopher Greenwood, *Historical Development and Legal Basis*, *in* The Handbook of the International Law of Military Operations 1, 35–36 (Terry Gill & Dieter Fleck eds., 2d ed. 2008); *see also* Michael N. Schmitt, *Military Necessity and Humanity in International Humanitarian Law: Preserving the Delicate Balance*, 50 Va. J. Int'l L. 795 (2010).

Dino Kritsiotis, *Sequences of Military Necessity for the* Jus in Bello In: *Necessity and Proportionality in International Peace and Security Law.* Edited by: Professor Claus Kreß and Captain Robert Lawless, Oxford University Press (2021).
 DOI: 10.1093/oso/9780197537374.003.0009.

violence into the context of war or armed conflict—a constitution, if you will, against violence for violence's sake and the beckoning of the thought of the *unnecessary* in warfare.[4] An inherent duality has therefore come to define the concept—its relentless capacities of quantification of the permissible as well as the impermissible—though its function, status, and standing historically is really deserving of more serious study.

In this contribution, we have therefore designated a series of discrete snapshots or "sequences" of military necessity as told through or over time, commencing with its relationship with the cognate proposition of self-preservation within the laws of war and peace. From there, we shall consider an associated logic existing within the *jus ad bellum* (specifically with respect to the right of self-defense), before examining the first sustained iterations of military necessity made during the American Civil War (1861–1865) and how these came to be received as part of the "Hague tradition" of the *jus in bello*. The chapter moves toward its conclusion by assessing the impact of military necessity within the more recent contexts of the current law on targeting, the advisory jurisprudence of the International Court of Justice (ICJ) and, finally, customary international humanitarian law (IHL) as computed by the International Committee of the Red Cross.

II. SELF-PRESERVATION IN WAR AND PEACE

First, of course, must be the matter of terminological formulation or framing. We refer in this chapter specifically to the proposition of "military necessity" rather than to necessity *simpliciter*—that is, to necessity pure and simple—because the adjectival qualification has become standard fare for the purpose of indicating the specific *context* in which the principle at hand is designed to operate, namely, the laws of war or armed conflict (*jus in bello*). It is for this reason, for example, that we also find reference made to *belligerent* reprisals within the laws of the *jus in bello*, to be distinguished from *armed* reprisals once known and accepted under the laws of the *jus ad bellum*. The legal arrangements for armed and belligerent reprisals have followed separate trajectories since the end of the Second World War to be sure,[5] and it is out of respect for these differing contexts that such

4. Yoram Dinstein has written of military necessity as "lubricating the wheels" of the law of armed conflict. YORAM DINSTEIN, THE CONDUCT OF HOSTILITIES UNDER THE LAW OF INTERNATIONAL ARMED CONFLICT 9 (3d ed. 2016). Though consider the formulation of the solitary reference to military necessity in Article 8(2)(a)(iv) of the 1998 Rome Statute of the International Criminal Court, regarding "[e]xtensive destruction and appropriation of property, not justified by military necessity and carried out unlawfully and wantonly." Rome Statute of the International Criminal Court art. 8(2)(a)(iv), July 17, 1998, 2187 U.N.T.S. 90. *See*, too, the fifth preambular recital of U.N. General Assembly Resolution 47/37, which stresses "that destruction of the environment, not justified by military necessity and carried out wantonly, is clearly contrary to existing international law." G.A. Res. 47/37, at 2 (Feb. 9, 1993).

5. *Cf., e.g.*, G.A. Res. 2625 (XXV), annex, Declaration on Principles of International Law Concerning Friendly Relations and Co-operation Among States in Accordance with the

distinctions are made and maintained. Yet a further manifestation of this practice may be proffered by way of "belligerent occupation" (a discrete emendation of the *jus in bello*) as distinct from "occupation" (once recognized as a mode of title to territory within public international law),[6] where, emphatically, belligerent occupation involved no transfer of sovereignty whatsoever.[7] In each of these cases, the appellation of "military" or "belligerent" is not accidental. It carries with and within it a signaling element that we are operating within the confines of the *lex specialis* of the *jus in bello*.

Let us now try to set down more of the general historical and conceptual background in anticipation of our concentration on some of the iterations of military necessity within the *jus in bello*. In the first edition of Lassa Oppenheim's treatise on public international law, we find the following passage:

> [T]here are exceptions to the protection of the qualities which constitute the International Personality of the States, and these exceptions are likewise characteristic of the position of the States within the Family of Nations. Thus, in time of war belligerents have a right to violate one another's Personality in many ways; even annihilation of the vanquished State, through subjugation after conquest, is allowed. Thus, further, in time of peace as well as in time of war, such violations of the Personality of other States are excused as are committed in self-preservation or through justified intervention.[8]

This passage directs itself toward the legal position of states "in time of peace as well as in time of war," even though Oppenheim is sharing this general observation in the first volume of his treatise (which was concerned with the laws of peace). Even so, in this formulation, self-preservation is counterposed against "another's Personality" in *both* of the situations of war and peace, though there is an embellishment of more of the detail in the second volume of the treatise (which focused on the laws of war and neutrality). There, at one point, Oppenheim concedes "the fact that a general devastation [of a locality, be it a town or a larger part of enemy

Charter of the United Nations (Oct. 24, 1970) ("States have a duty to refrain from acts of reprisal involving the use of force."); 1 Int'l Comm. of the Red Cross, Customary International Humanitarian Law: Rules r. 145, at 513 (Jean-Marie Henckaerts & Louise Doswald-Beck eds., 2005) [hereinafter ICRC Customary IHL Study] ("Where not prohibited by international law, belligerent reprisals are subject to stringent conditions."); *see also* Frits Kalshoven, Belligerent Reprisals (2d ed. 2005); Christopher Greenwood, *The Twilight of the Law of Belligerent Reprisals*, 20 Neth. Y.B. Int'l L. 35 (1989).

6. *See, e.g.*, Donald W. Greig, *Sovereignty, Territory and the International Lawyer's Dilemma*, 26 Osgoode Hall L.J. 127, 140 (2000).

7. L.F. Oppenheim, *The Legal Relations Between an Occupying Power and the Inhabitants*, 33 L.Q. Rev. 363 (1917).

8. 1 Lassa Oppenheim, International Law: Peace § 114, at 161 (1905).

territory] can be lawful must be admitted."[9] "And it is, for instance," he goes on to write, "lawful in case of a levy *en masse* on already occupied territory, when self-preservation obliges a belligerent to take refuge in the most severe measures."[10] He continues with the citation of an additional example of when general devastation may well be called for:

> It is . . . further lawful when, after the defeat of his main forces and occupation of his territory, an enemy disperses his remaining forces into small bands which carry on guerrilla tactics and receive food and information, so that there is no hope of ending the war except by a general devastation which cuts off supplies of every kind from the guerrilla bands. But is must be emphasized that only imperative necessity and the fact that there is no better and less severe way open to a belligerent [than to] justify general devastation.[11]

An equation—one might even contend a synonymy—between self-preservation and military necessity ("imperative necessity") is being intimated with these words,[12] and it is a relation that is repeated at various points in the second volume of the treatise. We find it in the suggestion of the occupation of neutrality territory by belligerents,[13] as well as in the delicate "compromise" of "the principle of freedom of commercebetweensubjectsofneutralsandeitherbelligerent," which "includedfrom

9. 2 Lassa Oppenheim, International Law: War and Neutrality § 154, at 153 (1905).

10. *Id.*

11. *Id.* § 154, at 153–54.

12. Coming as they do after the statement made by Oppenheim on general devastation that "[t]here cannot be the slightest doubt that such devastation is as a rule absolutely prohibited and exceptionally only permitted when, to use the words of article 23 (*g*) of the Hague Regulations, it is 'imperatively demanded by the necessities of war.'" *Id.* § 154, at 154. However, the distinction as been maintained elsewhere. N.C.H. Dunbar, *Military Necessity in War Crimes Trials*, 29 Brit. Y.B. Int'l L. 442, 443 (1952) ("[T]he phrase 'necessity in self-preservation' is more properly employed to describe a danger or emergency of such proportions as to threaten immediately the vital interests, and, perhaps, the very existence of the state itself. Military necessity should be confined to the plight in which armed forces may find themselves under stress of active warfare.").

13. 2 International Law: War and Neutrality, *supra* note 9, § 326, at 349 ("[T]he neutral must even use force to prevent belligerents from occupying any part of his neutral territory. The question whether such occupation on the part of a belligerent could be justified in the case of extreme necessity on account of the neutral's inability to prevent the other belligerent from making use of the neutral territory as a base for his military operations must, I think, be answered in the affirmative, since an extreme case of necessity in the interest of self-preservation must be considered an excuse."); *see also id.* § 336, at 361 ("according to the present rules of International Law, the duty of either belligerent to treat neutrals according to their impartiality must—the case of extreme necessity for self-preservation excepted—prevent them from violation the territorial supremacy of neutrals").

the beginning the right of either belligerent to punish carriage of contraband on the sea"[14] and, also, of the case "where a vessel has such enemy persons and despatches on board as she is allowed to carry, but whom a belligerent believes it to be necessary in the interest of self-preservation to seize."[15]

As "an excuse for an illegal act,"[16] it is in the first volume of his treatise that Oppenheim schematizes the appropriate significance of self-preservation within the broader taxonomy of public international law. He does so under the rubric of intervention where we learn that

> [w]herever there is no right to intervention, although it may be admissible and excused, an intervention violates either the external independence or the territorial or the personal supremacy [of a state] [b]ut if an intervention takes place by right, it never contains such a violation, because the right of intervention is always based on a legal restriction upon the independence or territorial or personal supremacy of the State concerned, and because the latter is in duty bound to submit to the intervention.[17]

No such duty to submit to self-preservation on behalf of other states applies—for, according to this schemata, self-preservation exists as an *excuse* and not a *right* as a matter of public international law,[18] and, as such, it is to be accorded a different

14. *Id.* § 398, at 432 ("[a]nd the reason obviously is the necessity for belligerents in the interest of self-preservation to prevent the import of such articles as may strengthen the enemy, and to confiscate the contraband cargo, and eventually the vessel also, as a deterrent to other vessels").

15. *Id.* at 413 ("[s]ince necessity in the interest of self-preservation is, according to International Law, an excuse for an illegal act, a belligerent can seize such persons and despatches, provided that such seizure is not only desirable, but absolutely necessary in the interest of self-preservation").

16. *Id.* Akin, thus, to "intervention in the interest of the balance of power"—where "it is likewise obvious that it must be excused." 1 International Law: Peace, *supra* note 8, § 136, at 185. Oppenheim does mention a third example of admissible or excusable interventions "when exercised in the interest of humanity for the purpose of stopping religious persecution and endless cruelties in time of peace and war." *Id.* § 137, at 186 ("whether there is really a rule of the Law of Nations which admits such interventions may well be doubted").

17. 1 International Law: Peace, *supra* note 8, at § 135, at 183.

18. *Id.* § 129, at 178 ("[A]lthough self-preservation is in certain cases an excuse recognized by International Law, no State is obliged patiently to submit to violations done to it by such other State as acts in self-preservation, but can repulse them. It is a fact that in certain cases violations committed in self-preservation are not prohibited by the Law of Nations. But they remain nevertheless violations and can therefore be repulsed."). Consider, however, self-preservation as one of "the *absolute* international rights of states," as depicted by Henry Wheaton. Henry Wheaton, Elements of International Law: With a Sketch of the History of Science 81 (1836); *see also* Alejandro Alvarez, *The State's Right of Self-Preservation*, 3 St. Louis L. Rev. 113, 118 (1919) (self-preservation as one of the instances of "fundamental right"). For his part, Hans Kelsen considered that "[i]t is . . . hardly possible to prove the existence of such a right

status from those interventions occurring by right (for example, the right of protection over nationals abroad and the right of states to intervene to make a delinquent state submit to principles of the Law of Nations, which are universally recognized).[19]

That said, it is interesting that self-preservation could not—or, better, that it could no longer—be pleaded by mere motivation ("as long as it was caused by the motive of self-preservation"),[20] for Oppenheim had formed the view that "it becomes more and more recognised that violations of other States in the interest of self-preservation are excused in cases of *necessity* only."[21] This is important because, although no precise chronological path is charted for the change, it is clear that, the old order (which was dictated by considerations of state subjectivity or whim) was caught in this very moment by Oppenheim as giving way—gradually, incrementally, but nevertheless surely—to a newer order (that somehow promised

of self-preservation as being established by general international law." HANS KELSEN, THE PRINCIPLES OF INTERNATIONAL LAW 59 (1952); *see also id.* at 60 ("If the exercise of the so-called right of self-preservation is a delict, there can be no 'right' of self-preservation. What is meant by the 'right' of a state to violate in case of necessity the rights of another state is probably only that such a violation of the rights of another state is morally excusable").

19. Appearing among the "several grounds" of a right of intervention itemized by Oppenheim. The other instances were: the right of the suzerain state to intervene in many affairs of the vassal; the state which holds a protectorate having the right to intervene in all the external affairs of the protected State; any right provided by treaty for intervention where a state does not comply with the restrictions imposed upon its internal independence or its territorial or personal supremacy by that treaty; where an external affair of a state is simultaneously an affair of another state. 1 INTERNATIONAL LAW: PEACE, *supra* note 8, § 135, at 183–84.

20. *Id.* § 130, at 178. Note how Oppenheim invokes self-preservation in this passage dealing with alternatives to the death penalty for war crimes: "If a belligerent has a right to pronounce capital punishment, it is obvious that he can select a more lenient penalty and carry the latter out even beyond the duration of the war. And it would in no wise be in the interest of humanity to deny this right, for otherwise belligerents would have always to pronounce and carry out capital punishment in the interest of self-preservation." 2 INTERNATIONAL LAW: WAR AND NEUTRALITY, *supra* note 9, § 257, at 270.

21. 1 INTERNATIONAL LAW: PEACE, *supra* note 8, § 130, at 178; *see also* IAN BROWNLIE, INTERNATIONAL LAW AND THE USE OF FORCE BY STATES 42 (1963) ("The right of self-preservation is in some cases asserted parallel to, or as a form of, a doctrine of necessity. There would seem analytically to be no distinction between the two and the discussions in works of international law certainly treat them as identical except in so far as necessity is a wider legal category and may, for example, appear in the context of the laws of war."). Brownlie further observes "that the protection of vital interests as a reserved sphere of competence on the part of a state can be regarded as yet another form of the plea of necessity or self-preservation." *Id.* at 43–44. The "more or less interchangeab[ility] [of] terms" does seem to have been a rather common practice of this period. *Id.* at 43. *See also* ELLERY C. STOWELL, INTERVENTION IN INTERNATIONAL LAW 392 (1921) (regarding self-preservation ("the preservation of [a state's] existence") as an instance of "this doctrine of necessity").

greater objectivity and certainty for the law).[22] And it is a shift that occurs by reference to the idea of necessity:

> Such acts of violence in the interest of self-preservation are exclusively excused as are necessary in self-defence, because otherwise the acting State would have to suffer or have to continue to suffer a violation against itself. If an imminent violation or the continuation of an already commenced violation can be prevented and redressed otherwise than by violation of another State on the part of the endangered State, this latter violation is not necessary, and therefore not excused and justified. When, to give an example, a State is informed that on neighbouring territory a body of armed men is being organised for the purpose of a raid into its own territory, and when the danger can be removed through an appeal to the authorities of the neighbouring country, no case of necessity has arisen. But if such an appeal is fruitless or not possible, or if there is danger in delay, a case of necessity arises and the threatened State is justified in invading the neighbouring country and disarming the intending raiders.[23]

From these transcriptions, it will be appreciated that "necessity" came to be the ready and viable conduit for a state to harness the relevant proofs for making any claim to self-preservation. Evidently, this meant that the state would have to channel its argumentative as well as evidential energies toward demonstrating to other states that "a case of necessity arises" in the name of self-preservation, since this could no longer occur on a state's mere say-so. Hence, in the previous passage, Oppenheim's bevy of hypotheticals really seems designed toward illustrating the kind of considerations that would either sustain or undermine any appeal made to "necessity" (for example, prevention or redress other than that violation of another state; removal through appeal to the authorities of the neighboring

22. For Wheaton, "the exercise of these absolute sovereign rights can be controlled only by the equal correspondent rights of other states, or by special compacts freely entered into with others to modify the exercise of these rights." WHEATON, *supra* note 18, at 82. In discussing the right of intervention as part and parcel of the right of self-preservation (or, as it is colorfully described, "the . . . primeval right of self-preservation"), it is interesting that Wheaton does not make any reference to "necessity" as such—but we do find the following passage which surely touches upon that thematic:

> Where the exercise of this right by any of these means directly affects the security of others, as where it immediately interferes with the actual exercise of sovereign rights of other states, there is no difficulty in assigning precise limits. But where it merely involves a supposed contingent danger to the safety of others, arising out of the undue aggrandizement of a particular state, or the disturbance of what has been called the balance of power, questions of the greater difficulty arise, which belong to the science of politics rather than of public law.

Id. at 82–83.

23. 1 INTERNATIONAL LAW: PEACE, *supra* note 8, § 130, at 178–79.

country; or the danger(s) of delay). In the broader scheme of things, it should be said that while "every State must decide for itself whether vital interests of its own are at stake and whether a case of necessity in the interest of self-preservation has arisen" at all,[24] this was to be the position in the first instance. It would then be for other states to reflect on the merits of that proclaimed necessity, since it is by virtue of that "necessity" that an intervention stood any chance of being "admitted by the Law of Nations and . . . excused in spite of the violation of the Personality of the respective States they involve."[25]

III. NECESSITY AND SELF-DEFENSE

It will be recalled that, in his exegesis on self-preservation, Oppenheim made the passing observation that "[s]uch acts of violence in the interest of self-preservation are exclusively excused as are necessary in self-defence."[26] He then proceeded to reflect on the *Caroline* incident of December 1837 in these terms—an incident where Great Britain "was in a position to prove that her act" of entering the territory of the United States and of the destruction of the *Caroline* "was necessary in self-preservation, since there was not sufficient time to prevent the imminent invasion of her territory through application to the United States Government."[27] This stylization of the "right" of self-defense alongside—indeed, in the same breath as—"self-preservation" should give prolonged pause for thought in particular

24. *Id.* § 138, at 187. Consider that in the most recent edition of Oppenheim's treatise—its ninth, published in 1992—the observation is made that "this alleged right, if it ever existed, was often a barely colourable excuse for violations of another's sovereignty." 1 Oppenheim's International Law: Peace § 126, at 416 (Robert Jennings & Arthur Watts eds., 9th ed. 1992).

25. 1 International Law: Peace, *supra* note 8, § 134, at 182. Though, not apparently so for Brownlie. *See* Brownlie, *supra* note 21, at 42 ("[a]s the state taking such action was regarded as the judge of the situation, necessity, like self-preservation, usually appears as the window of *raison d'état*").

26. *See* quote in main text accompanying note 23 *supra*.

27. 1 International Law: Peace, *supra* note 8, § 133, at 180–81. For further details of the incident and correspondence, *see* Craig Forcese, Destroying the Caroline: The Frontier Raid that Reshaped the Right to War (2018). Admittedly, in one of its earliest formal iterations following the *Caroline* incident, Henry S. Fox, British Minister at Washington, D.C., advised U.S. Secretary of State David Forsyth on Feb. 6, 1838, that "[t]he piratical character of the steam boat *Caroline* and the necessity of self-defense and self-preservation, under which Her Majesty's subjects acted in destroying that vessel, would seem to be sufficient established." 3 Diplomatic Correspondence of the United States: Canadian Relations 1784–1860, Doc. No. 1426, at 422 (William R. Manning ed., 1943). By the time that Lord Ashburton became one of the principal interlocutors of the correspondence as successor to Minister Fox, this language appeared to have changed, as is evident from the formulation of a letter to Secretary of State Webster dated July 28, 1842: "Self defence is the first law of our nature and it must be recognized by every code which professes to regulate the condition and relations of man." *Id.* Doc. No. 1593, at 766–67.

view of the proclaimed feature of self-preservation as "an excuse recognised by International Law,"[28] whereas much is made today of the "right" of self-defense under public international law and of the "inherent" nature of this right at that.[29]

Be this as it may, it would appear that in this rendition of the "necessity" of self-preservation and self-defense, not much if anything was made of any difference in its function or significance depending on one context or the other. Necessity appeared to mean one and the same thing for self-preservation as it did for self-defense, but doubtless the better explanation derives from the fact that, on this account, self-defense was seen to be but one manifestation of self-preservation,[30] which, it will be recalled, applied "in cases of *necessity* only."[31] Yet, when one probes deeper into the *Caroline* correspondence between Great Britain and the United States from January 1838 to August 1842, one finds that "necessity" was deliberately announced by U.S. Secretary of State Daniel Webster in terms of the right of self-defense—the "necessity of self-defence" as he so robustly put it[32]—and that, more tellingly, it was also conceived as part of a more detailed framework for regulating that right as a matter of law.[33] It was not a simple affair of pleading necessity alone—that is, on its own terms and without more—but, rather, it was envisaged as forming part of a more intricate matrix of normativity.

28. 1 International Law: Peace, *supra* note 8, § 129, at 178.

29. *See also* Federica Paddeu, Justification and Excuse in International Law: Concept and Theory of General Defences 347 (2018). Hence the adroit reflection of Derek Bowett: "[i]n so far as self-preservation and necessity find a use as concepts justifying conduct which, *though not lawful (and therefore distinct from self-defence) is yet excusable*, their scope is necessarily limited." D.W. Bowett, Self-Defence in International Law 10 (1958) (emphasis added). Bowett is of the view that it is the "precondition of delictual conduct" which "distinguishes self-defence from the 'right' of self-preservation and the 'right' of necessity." *Id.* at 9. Consider, however, the claim that "[i]t was in the *Caroline case* that self-defence was changed from a political excuse to a legal doctrine." R.Y. Jennings, *The* Caroline *and* McLeod *Cases*, 32 Am. J. Int'l L. 82, 82 (1938).

30. *See* Brownlie, *supra* note 21, at 43; *see also* James Crawford, Brownlie's Principles of Public International Law 724 (9th ed. 2019).

31. 1 International Law: Peace, *supra* note 8, § 130, at 178; *see also* Brownlie, *supra* note 21, at 43.

32. 3 Diplomatic Correspondence of the United States: Canadian Relations 1784–1860, *supra* note 27, Doc. No. 1269, at 145; *see also* Judith Gardam, Necessity, Proportionality and the Use of Force 40 (2004); Tadashi Mori, Origins of the Right of Self-Defence in International Law: From the *Caroline* Incident to the United Nations Charter 27 (2018); Jennings, *supra* note 29, at 92 (Self-defense "whether inadvertently or by design, crept into the correspondence. In using that phrase the diplomatists were almost certainly not consciously attempting to introduce a new concept into the law. But once the phrase had been introduced, it would be possible for lawyers of a later day to give it a legal content.").

33. *See also* Jennings, *supra* note 29; Brownlie, *supra* note 21, at 261 (maintaining that "[t]he Webster correspondence in reality merely stated a right of self-defence which had a more

Both of these characteristics of "necessity"—relating to its essential function but also to the scheme of which it formed so crucial a part—are handsomely borne out in the following excerpt from the letter that Secretary Webster wrote to Henry S. Fox, the British Minister at Washington, D.C., on April 24, 1841, which contained the celebrated formulation for regulating the right of self-defense:

> Under these circumstances, and under those immediately connected with the transaction itself, it will be for Her Majesty's Government to show, upon what state of facts, and what rules of national law, the destruction of the *Caroline* is to be defended. It will be for that Government to show a necessity of self-defence, instant, overwhelming, leaving no choice of means, and no moment for deliberation. It will be for it to show, also, that the local authorities of Canada,—even supposing the necessity of the moment authorized them to enter the territories of the United States at all,—did nothing unreasonable or excessive; since the act justified by the necessity of self-defense, must be limited by that necessity, and kept clearly within it. It must be strewn that admonition or remonstrance to the persons on board the *Caroline* was impracticable, or would have been unavailing; it must be strewn that daylight could not be waited for; that there could be no attempt at discrimination, between the innocent and the guilty; that it would not have been enough to seize and detain the vessel; but that there was a necessity, present and inevitable, for attacking her, in the darkness of the night, while moored to the shore, and while unarmed men were asleep on board, killing some, and wound[ing] others, and then drawing her into the current, above the cataract, setting her on fire, and careless to know whether there might not be in her the innocent with the guilty, or the living with the dead, committing her to a fate, which fills the imagination with horror. A necessity for all of this, the Government of the United States cannot believe to have existed.[34]

Evidently, the principles or "canons"[35] emerging from the *Caroline* correspondence were conceived in order that the right of self-defense could "be defended" in law and in legal terms.[36] Their operational premise would appear to have been that while "[i]t is of the essence of the legal conception of self-defence that recourse

limited application than the vague right of self-preservation and the broad and political concept of self-defence found in nineteenth century thought and practice").

34. 3 Diplomatic Correspondence of the United States: Canadian Relations 1784–1860, *supra* note 27, Doc. No. 1269, at 145.

35. Military and Paramilitary Activities in and Against Nicaragua (Nicar. v. U.S.), Judgment, 1986 I.C.J. Rep. 14, ¶ 237, at 122 (June 27); *see also id.* (referring to "the criteria of necessity and proportionality").

36. 3 Diplomatic Correspondence of the United States: Canadian Relations 1784–1860, *supra* note 27, Doc. No. 1269, at 145.

to it must, in the first instance, be a matter for the judgement of the State concerned,"[37] it could not have remained thus. To have maintained otherwise would have meant that each and every invocation of the right of self-defense would have ultimately proved determinative, and, so, some basic system had to be devised to help shift the meritorious appeals to the right of self-defense from those that were less so. Secretary Webster made this very clear in placing the argumentative and evidential burden at the doorstep of the state exercising its right of self-defense. The idea is that they would be involved in a process of persuasion—an exercise most definitely involving other states—as to why their recourse to the right of self-defense should be deemed permissible, and Secretary Webster devoted the remainder of the passage above to explicating what "principles" were in issue. Two such principles can be identified: the principles of necessity and proportionality.[38]

According to this framework, the self-defending state would first have to attend to and address the principle of "necessity" ("a necessity of self-defence, instant, overwhelming, leaving no choice of means, and no moment for deliberation"), which, crucially, was not to be argued as a freestanding principle but would involve recourse to a (second) principle—that of proportionality ("nothing unreasonable or excessive").[39] Satisfaction of both of these principles was required if the right of self-defense was to be lawfully exercised, so that, crucially for present purposes, the successful pleading of the "necessity" of self-defense would not in and of itself prove conclusive. For the self-defending state, all that the "necessity of the moment" would have done on the available facts of December 1837 is to have "authorized them to enter the territories of the United States at all,"[40] and it would have then been for them to make the case that the resulting action involved "nothing unreasonable or excessive"—in other words, that it also accorded with the principle of proportionality as imparted in the *Caroline* correspondence.[41]

37. Hersch Lauterpacht, The Function of Law in the International Community § 15, at 187 (1933).

38. Not, as Yoram Dinstein has sought to argue, three principles—so as to include the principle of immediacy (which Secretary Webster addressed as an aspect of the principle of necessity). *See* Yoram Dinstein, War, Aggression and Self-Defence ¶ 652, at 249 (6th ed. 2017); *see also* Gardam, *supra* note 32, at 31.

39. *See* Gardam, *supra* note 32, at 41; *see also* Brownlie, *supra* note 21, at 261.

40. 3 Diplomatic Correspondence of the United States: Canadian Relations 1784–1860, *supra* note 27, Doc. No. 1269, at 145.

41. *See also* Christine Gray, International Law and the Use of Force 158 (4th ed. 2018). It is interesting that, in seeking to elaborate the meaning of this principle of proportionality, Secretary Webster noted that "since the act justified by the necessity of self-defense, must be limited by that necessity, and kept clearly within it." 3 Diplomatic Correspondence of the United States: Canadian Relations 1784–1860, *supra* note 27, Doc. No. 1269, at

IV. THE LIEBER CODE

Let us now try to make some headway with the principle of military necessity in view of this more general (and hopefully useful) background. For the remainder of this chapter, our focus shall be on the meaning and function of military necessity within the *jus in bello*, where we shall be especially sensitive to any shifts in its significance that the principle has endured over time. Perhaps as good a place to start as any is the General Orders No. 100, the Instructions for the Government of Armies of the United States in the Field—otherwise known as the Lieber Code, which was issued by President Abraham Lincoln on April 24, 1863.[42] The Lieber Code is calling out for particular attention because, somewhat unusually, it provides something of a general prospectus of military necessity that is not really repeated in any of the subsequent endeavors of codification.[43] In short and in sum, there are an array of important insights contained in the Code on military necessity that are waiting to be dissected and distilled—so much so that it has been said that "the Lieber Code's greatest theoretical contribution to the modern law of war was its identification of military necessity as a general legal principle to limit violence, in the absence of any other rule."[44]

These insights occur in two forms: first, there appear three provisions of a prefatory and expository character in the opening section of the Code (devoted to martial law, military jurisdiction, military necessity, and retaliation) before the Code goes on to mark out specific conditions for the use or application of military necessity. Article 14 is the first of these general provisions from the Code, setting the scene to the effect that military necessity "consists in the necessity of those measures which are indispensable for securing the ends of the war, and which are lawful according to the modern law and usages of war." This might be thought to

145. This formulation suggests that proportionality is to be understood or defined by ideas or imperatives of necessity—and that necessity is (necessarily) a precursor principle to the principle of proportionality.

42. Francis Lieber, U.S. War Dep't, General Order No. 100: Instructions for the Government of Armies of the United States in the Field art. 14 (Apr. 24, 1863) [hereinafter Lieber Code], *reprinted in* The Laws of Armed Conflicts: A Collection of Conventions, Resolutions and Other Documents 3 (Dietrich Schindler & Jiri Toman eds., 4th ed. 2004). The full text of General Orders No. 100 is also available at the Avalon Project of Yale Law School. General Orders No. 100: The Lieber Code, The Avalon Project: Documents in Law, History and Diplomacy, https://avalon.law.yale.edu/19th_century/lieber.asp (last visited Oct. 25, 2019). For more of the background behind its promulgation, *see* John Fabian Witt, Lincoln's Code: The Laws of War in American History (2012); Richard Shelly Hartigan, Lieber's Code and the Law of War (1983).

43. Richard Baxter, *The First Modern Codification of the Law of War: Francis Lieber and General Orders No. 100*, 3 Int'l Rev. Red Cross 171 (1963).

44. Burrus M. Carnahan, *Lincoln, Lieber and the Laws of War: The Origins and Limits of the Principle of Military Necessity*, 92 Am. J. Int'l L. 213, 213 (1998); *see also* James G. Garner, *General Order 100 Revisited*, 27 Mil. L. Rev. 1, 8–10 (1965).

be a singularly unhelpful interposition for its lack of indication or precision on the practical measures that may be deemed "indispensable for securing the ends of war," but what is significant is how this provision appears to deny any overarching relevance for the principle of military necessity in respect of the modern law and usages of war in their entirety. We are led to believe that the principle is there to be validated from one occasion to the next by that law and by those usages, as indeed the Code goes on to do itself.[45]

That said, on only two occasions does the Code mention military necessity *eo nomine*: Article 3 and Article 38. Article 3 asserts that "[m]artial law in a hostile country consists in the suspension, by the occupying military authority, of the criminal and civil law, and of the domestic administration and government in the occupied place or territory, and in the substitution of military rule and force for the same, as well as in the dictation of general laws, as far as military necessity requires this suspension, substitution, or dictation."[46] Article 38 states that "[p]rivate property, unless forfeited by crimes or by offences of the owner, can be seized only by way of military necessity, for the support or other benefit of the army or of the United States."[47] To be sure, these references may be said to be enjoined by other iterations of the principle of military necessity even if it is not mentioned in those terms. Consider, for instance, the refrain of Article 5 that "[t]o save the country is paramount to all other circumstances."[48] Consider, too, that "[s]urprise may be a necessity";[49] that "[t]he principle has been more and more acknowledged that the unarmed citizen is to be spared in person, property, and honour as much as the exigencies of war will admit";[50] that "deception in war is admitted as a just and necessary means of hostility";[51] that "[a]n honourable

45. *See* HARTIGAN, *supra* note 42, at 15.

46. Lieber Code, *supra* note 42, art. 3(1).

47. *Id.* art. 38(1).

48. *Id.* art. 5(2). Article 5 had earlier professed that "[m]uch greater severity may be exercised [in respect of Martial Law] in places or regions where actual hostilities exist, or are expected and must be prepared for. Its most complete sway is allowed—even in the commander's own country—when face to face with the enemy, *because of the absolute necessities of the case*, and of the paramount duty to defend the country against invasion." *Id.* art. 5(2) (emphasis added); *see also* Rotem Giladi, *A Different Sense of Humanity: Occupation in Francis Lieber's Code*, 94 INT'L REV. RED CROSS 81 (2012).

49. Lieber Code, *supra* note 42, art. 19. This follows through from the earlier stipulation of Article 19 that "[c]ommanders, *whenever admissible*, inform the enemy of their intention to bombard a place, so that the noncombatants, and especially the women and children, may be removed before the bombardment commences. But it is no infraction of the common law of war to omit thus to inform the enemy." *Id.* (emphasis added).

50. *Id.* art. 22.

51. *Id.* art. 101.

belligerent allows himself to be guided by flags or signals of protection as much as the contingencies and the necessities of the right will permit";[52] and that "[t]he commander of an occupying army may require of the civil officers of the enemy, and of its citizens, any pledge he may consider necessary for the safety or security of his army."[53]

The second and third general provisions of the Code on military necessity are forthcoming with more detail on what the principle involves or what it does not involve, with Article 15 outlining what could come within its compass and Article 16 setting forth what comes without. According to Article 15,

> [m]ilitary necessity admits of all destruction of life or limb of armed enemies, and of other persons whose destruction is incidentally unavoidable in the armed contests of the war; it allows of the capturing of every armed enemy, and every enemy of importance to the hostile government, or of peculiar danger to the captor; it allows of all destruction of property, and obstruction of the ways and channels of traffic, travel, or communication, and of all withholding of sustenance of means of life from the enemy; of the appropriation of whatever an enemy's country affords necessary for the subsistence and safety of the army, and of such deception as does not involve the breaking of good faith either positively pledged, regarding agreements entered into during the war, or supposed by the modern law of war to exist. Men who take up arms against one another in public war do not cease on this account to be moral beings, responsible to one another and to God.

One cannot miss or mistake the totalizing rubric that is being summoned here—and being summoned at repeated intervals, it must be said—in order to convey the full and forbidding realities of warfare ("all destruction of life or limb of armed enemies"; "the capturing of every armed enemy, and every enemy of importance to the hostile government"; "all destruction of property"; "all withholding of sustenance of means of life from the enemy"; "whatever an enemy's country affords necessary for the subsistence and safety of the army"); though, in this, there is a curious, possibly even despairing, allusion to the moderating influence of men as

52. *Id.* art. 116 (coming on the heels of Article 116's claim that "[h]onourable belligerents often request that the hospitals within the territory of the enemy may be designated, so that they may be spared"). Note that according to the 1864 Geneva Convention for the Amelioration of the Condition of the Wounded in Armies in the Field, ambulances and military hospitals "shall be acknowledged to be neuter." Convention for the Amelioration of the Condition of the Wounded in Armies in the Field art. 1(1), Aug. 22, 1864, 129 Consol. T.S. 361, https://ihl-databases.icrc.org/ihl/INTRO/120 ("and, as such, shall be protected and respected by belligerents so long as any sick or wounded may be therein"). However, "[s]uch neutrality shall cease if the ambulances or hospitals should be held by a military force." *Id.* art. 1(2). In contrast, evacuations of wounded or sick soldiers "together with the persons under whose direction they take place" were protected by "an absolute neutrality." *Id.* art. 6(5).

53. Lieber Code, *supra* note 42, art. 134.

"moral beings," apparently responsible "to one another and to God."[54] Still, this candid calibration of military necessity was somehow thought to fall on the right side of the line as against "the internecine wars of savages" that is also mentioned in the Code.[55] But there is a crucial inference to be drawn from these references, and that relates to the impact that any principle of military necessity may have had in the very framing of the laws all told. Note how "all withholding of sustenance of means of life from the enemy" and "of the appropriation of whatever an enemy's country affords necessary for the subsistence and safety of the army" contrasts with the position of a separate provision in the Code—that "[i]t is lawful to starve the hostile belligerent, armed or unarmed, so that it leads to the speedier subjection of the enemy."[56]

To turn to Article 16 and the negative definition of the principle,

> [m]ilitary necessity does not admit of cruelty—that is, the infliction of suffering for the sake of suffering or for revenge, nor of maiming or wounding except in fight, nor of torture to extort confessions. It does not admit of the use of poison in any way, nor of the wanton devastation of a district. It admits of deception, but disclaims acts of perfidy; and, in general, military necessity does not include any act of hostility which makes the return to peace unnecessarily difficult.

Cruelty therefore becomes an organizing idiom for the definition of military necessity in this formulation, which is then explained by reference to four examples of what military necessity does not entail—two of which appear impermissible ab initio (suffering ("for the sake of suffering") and revenge) and two of which seem impermissible under certain specified conditions ("maiming or wounding except in fight" and "torture to extort confessions").

It is not immediately apparent how these clarifications are intended to assist our overall understanding of how military necessity is pressed into service in the Code. After all, Article 3 deals with the "suspension, substitution, or dictation" of general laws in the event of the emplacement of martial law in a hostile country, and Article 38 is concerned with the seizure of private property. By virtue of this negative definition, there might therefore be something of a hint that a more general significance is intended for military necessity than might at first be gleaned from the Code. However, what is striking about the illustrations given in Article

54. Presumably in pursuit of "honourable warfare," *id.* art. 101, a recurring thematic of the Code. *See id.* arts. 4, 22, 30, 72, 78, 107, 116, 120.

55. In the context of unjust or inconsiderate retaliation, *see id.* art. 28(2); *see also id.* art. 27 ("the repetition of barbarous outrage").

56. Famously set forth in Article 17 of the Code. For further assessment of the role of military necessity in this context, *see* Esbjörn Rosenblad, *Starvation as a Method of Warfare—Conditions for Regulation by Convention*, 7 INT'L LAW. 252 (1973); George Alfred Mudge, *Starvation as a Means of Warfare*, 4 INT'L LAW. 228 (1970).

16 is that they find expression elsewhere in the Code, but do so without any further reference being made to military necessity. So, on suffering, we find that Article 56 of the Code addresses itself to the treatment of prisoners of war ("subject to no punishment for being a public enemy, nor is any revenge wreaked upon him by the intentional infliction of any suffering, or disgrace, by cruel imprisonment, want of food, by mutilation, death, or any other barbarity"), as does Article 75 ("subject to confinement or imprisonment such as may be deemed necessary on account of safety, but they are to be subjected to no other intentional suffering or indignity"). On revenge, Article 28 provides that "[r]etaliation will . . . never be resorted to as a measure of mere revenge, but only as a means of protective retribution, and, moreover, cautiously and unavoidably"; Article 60 specifies that "[i]t is against the usage of modern war to resolve, in hatred and revenge, to give no quarter"; and Article 68 makes clear that "[u]nnecessary or revengeful destruction of life is not lawful."[57] On maiming, Article 44 could not be clearer in providing that "all rape, wounding, maiming, or killing of such inhabitants [of an invaded country] are prohibited under penalty of death."[58] And, on wounding, Article 71 provides that

> [w]hoever intentionally inflicts additional wounds on an enemy already wholly disabled, or kills such an enemy, or who orders or encourages soldiers to do so, shall suffer death, if duly convicted, whether he belongs to the Army of the United States, or is an enemy captured after having committed his misdeed.[59]

No further reference is made to torture elsewhere in the Code.

There is a further, and final, point to be raised at this moment of the analysis, and it concerns how military necessity—as an idea, as a set of practices, and, yes, as a principle—is defined by its relation to other principles known to or recognized by the laws of war.[60] The difficulty here is that these principles—or, better, these normative imperatives—were not necessarily operating by the appellations that

57. Lieber Code, *supra* note 42, art. 68(2). There is, of course, also "revenge" as mentioned in Article 56 (on prisoners of war).

58. *See also id.* art. 47 ("Crimes punishable by all penal codes, such as arson, murder, maiming, assaults, highway robbery, theft, burglary, fraud, forgery, and rape, if committed by an American soldier in a hostile country against its inhabitants, are not only punishable as at home, but in all cases in which death is not inflicted, the severer punishment shall be preferred.").

59. *See also id.* art. 57 ("So soon as a man is armed by a sovereign government and takes the soldier's oath of fidelity, he is a belligerent; his killing, wounding, or other warlike acts are not individual crimes or offences.").

60. In this respect, consider the (more recent) claim that "[l]aw of war principles work as interdependent and reinforcing parts of a coherent system." Off. of the Gen. Couns., U.S. Dep't of Def., Department of Defense Law of War Manual 52 (June 2015, updated Dec. 2016) (where military necessity is defined as "the principle that justifies the use of all measures

we know or use them today,[61] but they are imperatives nevertheless that came to steer the meaning of military necessity as presented in the Code. Consider, for instance, the emphasis that Article 15 puts on "armed enemies," in order to delimit the scope of "all destruction of life or limb" and of capture. Military necessity endorses these practices but, evidently, only when they are directed against such armed enemies—who are set against "other persons," "whose destruction, the Code advises, is incidentally unavoidable in the armed contests of the war."[62] There is, thus, something akin to the principle of distinction at work here,[63] but the same may be said of the principle of proportionality. Military necessity evidently can transcend the principle of distinction, but, notably, the destruction of "other persons" is made contingent on that being "incidentally unavoidable in the armed contests of the war"; that contingency comes to replace the totalizing impact of military necessity envisaged for armed enemies ("all destruction of life or limb"). At the same time, too, there are indications of reasoning innate to the principle of unnecessary suffering as articulated in the 1868 St. Petersburg Declaration Renouncing the Use, in Time of War, of Explosive Projectiles under 400 Grammes in Weight, which asserted "[t]hat [the] object [to disable the greatest possible number of men] would be exceeded by the employment of arms which uselessly aggravate the sufferings of disabled men, or render their death inevitable."[64] This emerges in the negative definition of military necessity in Article 16,[65] although it should be said that the remit of the principle of

needed to defeat the enemy as quickly and efficiently as possible that are not prohibited by the law of war"). In the Manual, the principle of military necessity appears alongside the principles of distinction, humanity, proportionality, and honor. *Id.* at 50–69.

61. *See*, however, the interaction between "general principles" and "specific rules of humanitarian law" developed by Greenwood. Greenwood, *supra* note 3, ¶ 131, at 35.

62. Lieber Code, *supra* note 42, art. 15.

63. Note, too, how "armed enemies" (or "the army") is developed in contradistinction to more the more rhetorical formulations of "every enemy of importance to the hostile government, or of peculiar danger to the captor" and, indeed, to the enemy per se ("all withholding of sustenance of means of life from the enemy; of the appropriation of whatever an enemy's country affords necessary for the subsistence and safety of the army")—cohering with another general thematic of the Code. In particular, *see id.* arts. 81–85.

64. Declaration Renouncing the Use, in Time of War, of Explosive Projectiles Under 400 Grammes Weight pmbl., Dec. 11, 1868 [hereinafter St. Petersburg Declaration], *reprinted in* The Laws of Armed Conflicts: A Collection of Conventions, Resolutions and Other Documents 91 (Dietrich Schindler & Jiri Toman eds., 4th ed. 2004).

65. *See* Carnahan, *supra* note 44, at 215 (that the Declaration "applied the code's principle of military necessity to ban the use of small-caliber explosive bullets because they would cause 'unnecessary suffering' "); *id.* at 213 (prior to the previous quotation, proclaiming that "[t]his principle soon achieved international recognition in the St. Petersburg Declaration of 1868").

unnecessary suffering as developed in the St. Petersburg Declaration is one that is confined to combatants—or, in the parlance of the Code, to "armed enemies."[66]

V. THE 1907 HAGUE REGULATIONS

Our previous section has raised several possibilities for interpreting how the Lieber Code interacts with the principle of military necessity: first, we identified the limited occasions—there were two—where the principle was given explicit expression; then, we considered situations where the Code makes approximate appeals to the idea of military necessity where that term as such is not employed; and, finally, we explored how the principle might be said to have a more discerning influence on the fashioning of various other provisions in the Code. Let us now take this framework and turn to the Hague Regulations annexed to the Hague Convention (IV) Respecting the Laws and Customs of War on Land of October 1907.[67] These do not benefit from explanatory capsules of the sort contained in Articles 14, 15, and 16 of the Lieber Code, although the preamble of that Convention does announce that its provisions, "the wording of which ha[ve] been inspired by the desire to diminish the evils of war, as far as military requirements permit, are intended to serve as a general rule of conduct for belligerents in their mutual relations and in their relations with inhabitants."[68]

This preambular formulation does tend to suggest that the provisions of the Hague Regulations are to be treated as a product of the calibrations already made on behalf of or in the name of military necessity ("as far as military requirements permit")—that, in consequence, we can expect the sublimation of military

66. Hence Judge Rosalyn Higgins's observation in her dissenting opinion in *Legality of the Threat or Use of Nuclear Weapons* that "the 'unnecessary suffering' provision does not operate as a generalized prohibition, but is rather directed at the protection of combatants." Legality of the Threat or Use of Nuclear Weapons, Advisory Opinion, 1996 I.C.J. 226, ¶ 13, at 585 (July 8); *see also* Henri Meyrowitz, *The Principle of Superfluous Injury or Unnecessary Suffering: From the Declaration of St. Petersburg of 1868 to Additional Protocol 1 of 1977*, 34 INT'L REV. RED CROSS 98 (1994). For what it is worth, the Declaration contained its own iteration of the principle of distinction. *See* St. Petersburg Declaration, *supra* note 64, pmbl. ("the only legitimate object which States should endeavour to accomplish during war is to weaken the military forces of the enemy"); *see also* Janina Dill & Henry Shue, *Limiting the Killing in War: Military Necessity and the St. Petersburg Assumption*, 26 ETHICS & INT'L AFF. 311 (2012); Michael G. Cowling, *The Relationship between Military Necessity and the Principle of Superfluous Injury and Unnecessary Suffering in the Law of Armed Conflict*, 25 S. AFR. Y.B. INT'L L. 131 (2000).

67. Convention (IV) Respecting the Laws and Customs of War on Land and Its Annex: Regulations Concerning the Laws and Customs of War on Land annex, Oct. 18, 1907, 26 Stat. 2277, 207 Consol. T.S. 277 [hereinafter Hague IV].

68. *Id.* This is a verbatim repetition of the sixth preambular recital of the 1899 Hague Convention. *See* Convention (II) with Respect to the Laws and Customs of War on Land and Its Annex: Regulations Concerning the Laws and Customs of War on Land pmbl., July 29, 1899, 187 Consol. T.S. 429 [hereinafter 1899 Hague Convention].

necessity within the various provisions of the Convention itself. However, we do find that there is one—only one—specific reference made to military necessity in the Regulations, and this comes in the form of Article 15, which provides that "[r]elief societies for prisoners of war, which are properly constituted in accordance with the law of their country and with the object of serving as the channel for charitable effort, shall receive from the belligerents, for themselves and their duly accredited agents, every facility for the efficient performance of their humane task within the bounds imposed by military necessities and administrative regulations." This suggests that further assessments will almost invariably need to occur on the ground and that these will need to be argued in terms of what the "military necessities" governing at that time may warrant (it is not immediately clear how the pluralization of the term (or principle) was thought to add anything substantive to proceedings).

Next we come to analogous references in the Hague Regulations. Perhaps most famously, Article 23 forbids (or, rather, it states that "it is especially forbidden" to bring about) the destruction or seizure of the enemy's property "unless such destruction or seizure be imperatively demanded by the necessities of war."[69] Then, Article 24 provides that "[r]uses of war and the employment of measures necessary for obtaining information about the enemy and the country are considered permissible,"[70] and, as far as Article 54 is concerned, "[s]ubmarine cables connecting an occupied territory with a neutral territory shall not be seized or destroyed except in the case of absolute necessity." Furthermore, there are two provisions dealing with the treatment of prisoners of war: Article 5, providing that "[p]risoners of war may be interned in a town, fortress, or other place, and bound not to go beyond certain fixed limits, but they cannot be confined except as in indispensable measures of safety and only while the circumstances which necessitate the measure continue to exist"; and Article 8, stating that "[p]risoners of war shall be subject to the laws, regulations, and orders in force in the army of the State in whose power they are. Any act of subordination justifies the adoption towards them of such measures of severity as may be considered necessary." And this is not to mention any attenuated influences the principle of military necessity may be said to have (had) on other aspects of the Regulations.[71]

69. Hague IV, *supra* note 67, annex art. 23(g).

70. Here we see evidence of the long shadow of Article 101 of the Lieber Code. *See* Lieber Code, *supra* note 42, art. 101.

71. Consider, for instance, Article 32 on the parlementaire's "right to inviolability," also belonging to the trumpeter, bugler, or drummer, the flag-bearer, and interpreter who may accompany him. Hague IV, *supra* note 67, annex art. 32. Article 33 of the Regulations specifies that the commander to whom a parlementaire is sent "is not in all cases obliged to receive him," *id.* art. 33, and Article 34 makes clear that the parlementaire "loses his rights of inviolability if it is proved in a clear and incontestable manner that he has taken advantage of his privileged position to provoke or commit an action of treason," *id.* art. 34. In none of these provisions is any reference made to military necessity, yet Spaight has argued that "[m]ilitary necessity may make

We are left with the sense, then, that, as understood and deployed in the Hague Regulations of October 1907, the principle of military necessity was never intended to have an overarching relevance for the Regulations from first provision to last—so we are not to draw any grand inferences from the relative silence of the Regulations on military necessity.[72] If the laws of war merit the general epithet of prohibitive law,[73] then it needs to be understood that the principle of military necessity does not exist in latent or residual form as a potential release from any or, indeed, all of these prohibitions. We might therefore seek to distinguish *this* version of military necessity as found in the Hague Regulations from that derived from *Kriegsraison*, where it is "conceived as a kind of resolutory condition implied in all the particular prescriptions of the law of war."[74] This matter arose with particular acuity in the *United States v. List* in February 1948—where the U.S. Military Tribunal was confronted with "the German theory of expediency and military necessity (*Kriegsraeson geht vor Kriegsmanier*) [which] superseded established rules of International Law," and found that it was not in favor with it, concluding that "the rules of International Law must be followed even if it results

it necessary to refuse to admit [a flag of truce] while a secret movement is being executed, or in the midst of an engagement when 'to suspend the fighting at the very moment the *parlementaire* presents himself, would be to risk sacrificing the victory at the decisive moment or paralysing the pursuit.'" *See* Spaight, *supra* note 1, at 220 (citing Henry Bonfils, Manuel de Droit International Public (Droit des Gens) (5th ed. 1908)). Furthermore:

> To fire on an envoy deliberately and without warning would be a breach of war law, but if, having presented himself and having been signalled or warned to retire, he persists in advancing, then military necessity would justify his being shot at. If a commander has the right to refuse admission to an envoy, he must have the right to take adequate steps to prevent the man's forcing admission—perhaps just at the critical stage of some important secret operation.

Id. at 221; *see also* Dinstein, *supra* note 4, at 195.

72. To this extent, we are in accord with the analysis of Spaight in respect of the Regulations annexed to the 1899 Hague Convention (II), that "it is incorrect to state generally that the Hague Regulations are subject to military necessities. . . . Some of the rules are so subject—for instance, those which lay down that private property, or religious institutions, are to be respected. But the most imperative military necessity could not justify the use of poison or the torture ('inhuman treatment') or a prisoner of war, or assassination." Spaight, *supra* note 1, at 8.

73. As they have from Baxter. Richard R. Baxter, *So-Called "Unprivileged Belligerency": Spies, Guerrillas, and Saboteurs*, 28 Brit. Y.B. Int'l L. 323, 324 (1951) ("The law of war is . . . 'prohibitive law' in the sense that it forbids rather than authorizes certain manifestations of force.").

74. Myres S. McDougal & Florentino F. Feliciano, The International Law of War: Transnational Coercion and World Public Order 672 (1994) ("In capsular form, this doctrine is to the effect that military necessity or, as it is sometimes called, the necessities of war (*Kriegsraison*) overrides and renders inoperative the ordinary laws and customs of war (*Kriegsmanier*)."); *see also* Dunbar, *supra* note 12, at 445.

in the loss of a battle or even a war. Expediency or necessity cannot warrant their violation."[75]

Given that the Hague Regulations informed much of the deliberations of the Military Tribunal, it is worth considering at some length what it said about military necessity. One of the general observations it made of the principle, that "[m]ilitary necessity permits a belligerent, subject to the laws of war, to apply any amount and kind of force to compel the complete submission of the enemy with the least possible expenditure of time, life and money,"[76] bore shades of similarity to the conception found in the Lieber Code—of military necessity as being "subject to the laws of war."[77] The Military Tribunal had no difficulty in seizing on this formulation to frame its quantification of the significance of military necessity for the laws of war more generally:

> It is apparent from the evidence of these defendants that they considered military necessity, a matter to be determined by them, a complete justification of their acts. We do not concur in the view that the rules of warfare are anything less than they purport to be. Military necessity or expediency do not justify a violation of positive rules. International Law is prohibitive law. Articles 46, 47 and 50 of the Hague Regulations of 1907 make no such exceptions to its enforcement. The rights of the innocent population therein set forth must be respected even if military necessity or expediency decree otherwise.[78]

75. United States v. List (The Hostage Case) (U.S. Mil. Tribunal Feb. 19, 1948), *reprinted in* 8 U.N. War Crimes Comm'n, Law Reports of Trials of War Criminals 34, 67 (1949). Apparently, while military necessity was pleaded on more than one occasion in war crimes trials held after the Second World War, "it did not, as a defence to a criminal charge, enjoy the prominence accorded to the highly controversial please of superior orders." Dunbar, *supra* note 12, at 452.

76. *List*, *supra* note 75, at 66.

77. In particular, *see* Lieber Code, *supra* note 42, art. 14; *see also id.* arts. 15, 16 (on what military necessity "sanctions," "admits," and "does not admit"); *List*, *supra* note 75, at 66 ("The destruction of property to be lawful must be imperatively demanded by the necessities of war. Destruction as an end in itself is a violation of International Law."). Consider, however, Article 6(b) of Charter of the International Military Tribunal at Nuremberg which identifies (in part) the crimes coming within the jurisdiction of the Tribunal: "*War Crimes*: namely, violations of the laws or customs of war. Such violations shall include, but not be limited to, murder, ill-treatment or deportation to slave labour or for any other purpose of civilian population of or in occupied territory, murder or ill-treatment of prisoners of war or persons on the seas, killing of hostages, plunder of public or private property, wanton destruction of cities, towns or villages, or devastation *not justified by military necessity*." Agreement for the Prosecution and Punishment of the Major War Criminals of the European Axis art. 6(b), Aug. 8, 1945, 82 U.N.T.S. 279 (emphasis added).

78. *List*, *supra* note 75, at 66. To similar effect, consider the judgment of the U.S. Military Tribunal in Nuremberg in *Trial of Alfred Felix Alwyn Krupp von Bohlen und Halbach and Eleven Others* in response to a plea of "national emergency." The Tribunal asserted that "the contention that the

One of those defendants in the case, Lothar Rendulic, had become Commander-in-Chief of the *Wehrmacht*'s Twentieth Mountain Army in July 1944, and had been charged with the wanton destruction of private and public property in the province of Finnmark, in northern Norway, during the retreat of the army that had been organized by him in advance of—and in order to forestall—any liberation strategy pursued by Soviet armed forces.[79] According to Rendulic, military necessity required "that he do as he did in view of the military situation as it then appeared to him,"[80] and this included the evacuation of the population

rules and customs of warfare can be violated if either party is hard pressed in any way must be rejected on other grounds. War is by definition a risky and hazardous business. . . . It is an essence of war that one or the other side must lose and the experienced generals and statesmen knew this when they drafted the rules and customs of land warfare. In short these rules and customs of warfare are designed specifically for all phases of war. They comprise the law for such emergency. To claim that they can be wantonly—and at the sole discretion of any one belligerent—disregarded when he considers his own situation to be critical, means nothing more or less than to abrogate the laws and customs of war entirely." *See* United States v. Krupp (The Krupp Case), Case No. 10 (July 31, 1948), *reprinted in* 9 Trials of War Criminals Before the Nuremberg Military Tribunals Under Control Council Law No. 10, at 138–39 (1950).

Some of the similar reasoning is evident more recently in *Legal Consequences of the Construction of A Wall in the Occupied Palestinian Territory*:

> The Court would observe . . . that the applicable international humanitarian law contains provisions enabling account to be taken of military exigencies in certain circumstances.
>
> Neither Article 46 of the Hague Regulations of 1907 nor Article 47 of the Fourth Geneva Convention contain any qualifying provision of this type. With regard to forcible transfers of population and deportations, which are prohibited under Article 49, paragraph 1, of the Convention, paragraph 2 of that Article provides for an exception in those cases in which "the security of the population or imperative military reasons so demand". This exception however does not apply to paragraph 6 of that Article, which prohibits the occupying Power from deporting or transferring parts of its own civilian population into the territories it occupies. As to Article 53 concerning the destruction of personal property, it provides for an exception "where such destruction is rendered absolutely necessary by military operations".
>
> The Court considers that the military exigencies contemplated by these texts may be invoked in occupied territories even after the general close of the military operations that led to their occupation. However, on the material before it, the Court is not convinced that the destructions carried out contrary to the prohibition in Article 53 of the Fourth Geneva Convention were rendered absolutely necessary by military operations.

Legal Consequences of the Construction of a Wall in the Occupied Palestinian Territory, Advisory Opinion, 2004 I.C.J. Rep. 136, ¶ 135, at 192 (July 9).

79. For a description, *see* James F. Gebhardt, The Petsamo-Kirkenes Operation: Soviet Breakthrough and Pursuit in the Arctic, October 1944 (Leavenworth Papers No. 17, 1989); *see also* Vincent Hunt, Fire and Ice: The Nazis' Scorched Earth Campaign in Norway (2014).

80. Again, as summarized by the Tribunal. *See* United States v. List (The Hostage Case) (U.S. Mil. Tribunal Feb. 19, 1948), *reprinted in* 8 U.N. War Crimes Comm'n, Law Reports of Trials

of Finnmark. Apparently, from the public record, no loss of life resulted directly from what then occurred, but the broader toll of Rendulic's decision was set forth in the judgment in the following terms:

> Villages were destroyed. Isolated habitations met a similar fate. Bridges and highways were blasted. Communication lines were destroyed. Port installations were wrecked. A complete destruction of all housing, communication and transport facilitates was had. This was not only true along the coast and highways, but in the interior sections as well. The destruction was as complete as an efficient army could do it. Three years after the completion of the operation, the extent of the devastation was discernible to the eye.[81]

In reflecting on these facts from the prism of the Hague Regulations, the Military Tribunal then concluded that "[t]he prohibitions therein contained control and are superior to military necessities of the most urgent nature except where the Regulations themselves specifically provide to the contrary," such that military necessity required some acknowledgment in conventional form. A rare instance of this occurs in Article 23(*g*) of the Regulations on the destruction or seizure of the enemy's property,[82] a provision which served as the platform for the following set of observations:

> The destructions of public and private property by retreating military forces which would give aid and comfort to the enemy, may constitute a situation coming within the exceptions contained in Article 23 (*g*). We are not called upon to determine whether urgent military necessity for the devastation and destruction in the province of Finnmark actually existed. We are concerned with the question whether the defendant at the time of its occurrence acted within the limits of honest judgment on the basis of the conditions prevailing at the time. The course of a military operation by the enemy is loaded with uncertainties, such as the numerical strength of the enemy, the quality of his equipment, his fighting spirit, the efficiency and daring of his commanders,

of War Criminals 34, 67 (1949); *see also* Brian J. Bill, *The Rendulic "Rule": Military Necessity, Commander's Knowledge, and Methods of Warfare*, 12 Y.B. Int'l Humanitarian L. 119 (2009).

81. *List, supra* note 80, at 68.

82. *See also* Geneva Convention Relative to the Protection of Civilians Persons in Time of War art. 53, Aug. 12, 1949, 6 U.S.T. 3516, 75 U.N.T.S. 287 [hereinafter GC IV] ("Any destruction by the Occupying Power of real or personal property belonging individually or collectively to private persons, or to the State, or to other public authorities, or to social or cooperative organizations, is prohibited, except where such destruction is rendered absolutely necessary by military operations"); Protocol Additional to the Geneva Conventions of 12 August 1949, and Relating to the Protection of Victims of International Armed Conflict (Protocol I) art. 54(5), June 8, 1977, 1125 U.N.T.S. 3 [hereinafter AP I]; Int'l Comm. of the Red Cross, Commentary on the Additional Protocols of 8 June 1977 to the Geneva Conventions of 12 August 1949, at 659 (Yves Sandoz, Christophe Swinarski, & Bruno Zimmerman eds., 1987).

> and the uncertainty of his intentions. These things when considered with his own military situation provided the facts or want thereof which furnished the basis for the defendant's decision to carry out the "scorched earth" policy in Finnmark as a precautionary measure against an attack by superior forces. It is our considered opinion that the conditions as they appeared to the defendant at the time were sufficient, upon which he could honestly conclude that urgent military necessity warranted the decision made. This being true, the defendant may have erred in the exercise of his judgment but he was guilty of no criminal act. We find the defendant not guilty on this portion of the charge.[83]

The importance of this passage is that it locates the meaning of military necessity subsequent to its anchoring within the Hague Regulations.[84] That meaning is grounded in what may be described as a deference to the "honest judgment" of the relevant commander operating at ground level, as understood by "the conditions prevailing at the time"—quite evidently an effort made by the Military Tribunal to avoid or minimize the privilege (or unfair advantage) of hindsight. The idea would very much seem to be to create a certain intimacy or empathy with the conditions faced by the military commander himself or herself as confronted in or by real time, and once the evidential burden had been redeemed by the defendant—"that the conditions as they appeared to [him] were sufficient"—the Military Tribunal found that there was no choice other than to find him not guilty for his actions.[85]

VI. THE LAW OF STATE RESPONSIBILITY

Let us now consider by way of important contrast the plea of necessity as it appears within the entirely separate context of the *lex generalis* of state responsibility, where it features as one of six circumstances precluding wrongfulness in the International Law Commission's Articles on Responsibility of States for Internationally Wrongful Acts released in August 2001. Here, each of the six circumstances has been described as "a shield against an otherwise well-founded claim for the breach of an international obligation,"[86] and is also stated

83. *List*, *supra* note 80, at 69.

84. We are at one with Dunbar. *See* Dunbar, *supra* note 12, at 452 ("It seems likely that courts will be disinclined to enlarge the doctrine of military necessity beyond that countenanced by express reservations appearing in the Hague and Geneva Conventions."). On the practice side of things, however, *see*, more recently, Scott Horton, Kriegsraison *or Military Necessity? The Bush Administration's Wilhelmine Attitude Towards the Conduct of War*, 30 FORDHAM INT'L L.J. 576 (2007).

85. *But see* GEOFFREY BEST, WAR AND LAW SINCE 1945, at 328–30 (1997) ("Far from acting with the understandable temporary wildness of a frightened man in the dark, Rendulic was methodically executing in daylight a preplanned policy of vindictive desertification.").

86. JAMES CRAWFORD, THE INTERNATIONAL LAW COMMISSION'S ARTICLES ON STATE RESPONSIBILITY: INTRODUCTION, TEXT AND COMMENTARIES 160 (2002). The other

to be "of general application,"[87] though their application does not entail the actual annulment or termination of the obligation in question. They provide instead "a justification or excuse for non-performance while the circumstance in question subsists."[88] Such is the position, then, with respect to the plea of necessity,[89] but, crucially, the Articles go on to stipulate the limitation that none of the aforementioned circumstances "precludes the wrongfulness of any act of a State which is not in conformity with an obligation arising under a peremptory norm of general international law."[90] Nonperformance of a given obligation these circumstances precluding wrongfulness may well underwrite, but, evidently, that does not pertain to all obligations in the international legal order.

Those Articles identify the narrow conditions for any plea of necessity to be successfully made. Specifically, according to Article 25, an act must be "the only means for the State to safeguard an essential interest against a grave and imminent peril,"[91] and it must not "seriously impair an essential interest of the State or States towards which the obligation exists, or of the international community as a whole."[92] The setting of the standard of this order—of "an essential interest against a grave and imminent peril"—is such that it can be predicted with some confidence that necessity "will only rarely be available to excuse non-performance

circumstances precluding wrongfulness appearing in the International Law Commission's Articles of August 2001 are: consent (Article 20), self-defense (Article 21), countermeasures (Article 22), *force majeure* (Article 23), and distress (Article 24). Draft Articles on Responsibility of States for Internationally Wrongful Acts arts. 20, 21, 22, 23, 24, Rep. of the Int'l L. Comm'n on Its Fifty-Third Sess., U.N. Doc. A/56/10, at 26 (2001) [hereinafter Draft Articles]. Defended by reference to the "essential coherence of the category" of circumstances precluding wrongfulness—that "[l]ike analogous defences in domestic law, they preclude the *wrongfulness* of an act." James Crawford, State Responsibility: The General Part 275 (2013).

87. Unless it is otherwise provided—for example, by a treaty to the contrary, which would be regarded as an instance of *lex specialis* under Article 55. *See* Draft Articles, *supra* note 86, art. 55. We can presume that such an instance of *lex specialis* occurs with self-defence as a circumstance precluding wrongfulness—because Article 21 specifically refers to "a lawful measure of self-defence taken in conformity with the Charter of the United Nations." *Id.* art. 21.

88. Crawford, *supra* note 86, at 160.

89. Draft Articles, *supra* note 86, art. 25. Very much "a reality in international practice," as it is put by Sandra Szurek. Sandra Szurek, *The Notion of Precluding Wrongfulness*, *in* The Law of International Responsibility 427, 429 (James Crawford, Alain Pellet, & Simon Olleson eds., 2010); *see also* Roman Boed, *State of Necessity as a Justification for Internationally Wrongful Conduct*, 3 Yale Hum. Rts. & Dev. L.J. 1 (2000).

90. Draft Articles, *supra* note 86, art. 26.

91. *Id.* art. 25(1)(a).

92. *Id.* art. 25(1)(b).

of an obligation,"[93] though it has been said that the precedents rallied in its name expand to cover "three factual rubrics," those of state security, fiscal crises, as well as ecological harms.[94] This broad berth of possibility for the plea of necessity is interesting because it suggests a general disciplinary reach for this circumstance precluding wrongfulness,[95] and it has been contended that—at least as far as the first of these rubrics is concerned—there is some association to be made with "a state's natural right to self-preservation."[96]

Still, the question does need to be posed in the present context as to whether Article 25 is sufficiently expansive so as to encompass or accommodate claims to "military necessity" itself. This has been answered in the negative, by James Crawford, the Special Rapporteur on State Responsibility (1997–2001), who cast emphasis instead on the relevance of necessity in the "formulation and interpretation" of "primary obligations" under the *jus in bello*:

> As embodied in article 25, the plea of necessity is not intended to cover conduct which is in principle regulated by the primary obligations. This has a particular importance in relation to the rules relating to the use of force in international relations and to the question of "military necessity". It is true that in a few cases, the plea of necessity has been invoked to excuse military action abroad, in particular in the context of claims to humanitarian intervention. The question whether measures of forcible humanitarian intervention, not sanctioned pursuant to Chapters VII or VIII of the Charter of the United Nations, may be lawful under modern international law is not covered by article 25. The same thing is true of the doctrine of "military necessity" which is, in the first place, the underlying criterion for a series of substantive rules of the law of war and neutrality, as well as being included in terms in a number of treaty provisions in the field of international humanitarian law. In both respects, while considerations akin to those underlying article 25 may have a role, they are taken into account in the context of the formulation and interpretation of the primary obligations.[97]

93. Crawford, *supra* note 86, at 178.

94. Robert D. Sloane, *On the Use and Abuse of Necessity in the Law of State Responsibility*, 106 Am. J. Int'l L. 447, 454 (2012).

95. Consider, though, in contrast, self-defense in Article 21 ("The wrongfulness of an act of State is precluded if the act constitutes a lawful measure of self-defence taken in conformity with the Charter of the United Nations."). *See* Crawford, *supra* note 86, at 166–67.

96. Sloane, *supra* note 94, at 454 (describing state security as an instance of classical (or existential) necessity).

97. Crawford, *supra* note 86, at 185–86; *see also* Roberto Ago, Special Rapporteur, Int'l L. Comm'n, Addendum to the Eighth Report on State Responsibility, U.N. Doc. A/CN.4/318/ADD.5-7, ¶ 49, at 34 (1980), *reprinted in* [1980] 2 (pt. 1) Y.B. Int'l L. Comm'n 13, ¶ 49, at 34 (1980) ("There is . . . nothing to prevent a belligerent State from pleading 'necessity', even if it arises from the very fact that a state of war exists and from the resulting constraints, as a ground for not complying with a peacetime international obligation still binding on it, notwithstanding the

VII. 1977 ADDITIONAL PROTOCOL I

Now, to a much more recent transcription of military necessity and its purpose within the *jus in bello*: it has been said that it is a "legal concept" that is used "as part of the legal justification for attacks on legitimate military targets that may have adverse, even terrible, consequences for civilians and civilians objects."[98] According to this view, "military forces in planning military actions are permitted to take into account the practical requirements of a military situation at any given moment and the imperatives of winning" so that military necessity "acknowledges that even under the laws of war, winning the war or battle is a legitimate consideration, though it must be put alongside other considerations" of the *jus in bello*.[99] In the words of the relevant rule from the Protocol Additional to the Geneva Conventions of 12 August 1949, and Relating to the Protection of Victims of International Armed Conflicts (Additional Protocol I), "[a]ttacks shall be limited strictly to military objectives," which are defined as "those objects which by their nature, location, purpose or use make an effective contribution to military action and whose total or partial destruction, capture or neutralization, in the circumstances ruling at the time, offers a definite military advantage."[100] Evidently, there is no mention at all in this formulation of "military necessity" per se, though its influence on the overall content of the rule—in the primary obligation—cannot be doubted. Its eminent practicality is demonstrated by fidelity to conditions on the ground ("nature, location, purpose or use") as set against the broader military landscape or position ("effective contribution to military action" and "definite military advantage").[101] When all is said and done, the law has been honed with

supervision of a state of belligerence with another State, vis-à-vis a third country with which it remains at peace. In time of war, however, the idea of 'necessity' materializes mainly in a form other than that of a circumstance precluding, by way of exception, the wrongfulness of an act of the State not in conformity with the requirements of an obligation imposed on it by a rule of international law. In making this statement, we have in mind the function assigned to the concept of necessity 'of war' or 'military necessity' as the basic underlying intention of the rules of the international law of war and neutrality. In this special sector or international law, the concept in question is not regarded, at least not primarily, as a kind of subcategory of 'state of necessity' in the sense in which we have tried to define it in the context of peacetime law."); *see also* Claus Kreß, *The International Court of Justice and the Law of Armed Conflicts*, *in* The Development of International Law by the International Court of Justice 263, 276 (Christian J. Tams & James Sloan eds., 2013).

98. Françoise Hampson, *Military Necessity*, *in* Crimes of War 2.0: What the Public Should Know 297 (Anthony Dworkin, Roy Gutman, & David Rieff eds., revised & expanded ed. 2007).

99. *Id.*

100. AP I, *supra* note 82, art. 52(2).

101. Or, as the Commentary to the Additional Protocol puts it, "it is not legitimate to launch an attack which only offers potential or indeterminate advantages." Int'l Comm. of the Red Cross, *supra* note 82, at 636. Note how Dinstein refers to military necessity as one of "two diametrically opposed stimulants" (alongside humanitarian considerations). Dinstein, *supra* note 4, at 9.

military considerations very much in mind, and, to this end, it has been expressed in terms of an abiding temporal intimacy ("in the circumstances ruling at the time") in relation to those considerations.

To be sure, although the *jus in bello* has not always benefited from the clarity of the rule as set forth in Additional Protocol I, echoes of this reasoning are evident from the earlier law concerning targeting. Consider, for instance, Article 25 of the Hague Regulations ("[t]he attack or bombardment, by whatever means, of towns, villages, dwellings, or buildings which are undefended is prohibited"), which carried with it the inescapable implication that *defended* towns, villages, dwellings, or buildings would be lawful objects of attack or bombardment. One can imagine how military necessity might have been invoked, even if rhetorically, to realize the same ambition as set out in this provision.[102] Consider, too, Article 27 of the Regulations: "[i]n sieges and bombardments all necessary steps must be taken to spare, as far as possible, buildings dedicated to religion, art, science, or charitable purposes, historic monuments, hospitals, and places where the sick and wounded are collected, provided they are not being used at the time for military purposes." The appearance of the (undefined) "military purposes"[103] makes all the difference: the fate of the affected buildings can switch in an instant from the threadbare protection afforded by the provision to no protection at all.[104]

This aspect of the Regulations was all succeeded by an obligation to respect cultural property enunciated in the 1954 Hague Convention for the Protection

102. The same goes for Article 43 of the Hague Regulations. Hague IV, *supra* note 67, annex art. 43 ("The authority of the legitimate power having in fact passed into the hands of the occupant, the latter shall take all the measures in his power to restore, and ensure, as far as possible, public order and safety, while respecting, unless absolutely prevented, the laws in force in the country."). It has been argued that the term "absolutely prevented"—"empêchement absolu"—"means nothing but 'absolute necessity.'" Edmund H. Schwenk, *Legislative Power of the Military Occupant under Article 43 Hague Regulations*, 54 Yale L.J. 393, 401 (1945).

103. A phrase that resurfaces in Article 24(2) of the Hague Draft Rules on Aerial Warfare. Comm'n of Jurists Nominated by the Washington Conference of 1922 on the Limitation of Armaments, Rules Concerning the Control of Wireless Telegraphy in Time of War and Air Warfare pt. 2, art. 24(2) (adopted Feb. 19, 1923), *reprinted in* Int'l Comm. of the Red Cross: Treaties, State Parties & Commentaries, https://ihl-databases.icrc.org/applic/ihl/ihl.nsf/Article.xsp?action=openDocument&documentId=8F0205182641A279C12563CD00518530 (last visited Oct. 26, 2019) ("Such bombardment is legitimate only when directed exclusively at the following objectives: military forces; military works; military establishments or depots; factories constituting important and well-known centres engaged in the manufacture of arms, ammunition, or distinctively military supplies; lines of communication or transportation used for military purposes."); *see also id.* pt. 2, art. 26.

104. An immunity that "is far from absolute." Dinstein, *supra* note 4, at 204. Nobuo Hayashi regards this as nothing other than a "rudimentary framework." Nobuo Hayashi, *Requirements of Military Necessity in International Humanitarian Law and International Criminal Law*, 28 B.U. Int'l L.J. 39, 48 (2010).

of Cultural Property in the Event of Armed Conflict,[105] although that obligation was hemmed by waiver "only in cases where military necessity imperatively requires such a waiver."[106] A regime of special protection is contained in Article 8 of that Convention (as opposed to the system of general protection introduced by Article 4), but, even here, "immunity shall be withdrawn from cultural property under special protection only in exceptional cases of unavoidable military necessity, and only for such time as that necessity continues."[107] The Hague Convention is thus responsible for enhanced rhetorical flourishes akin to that found in Article 23(g) of the 1907 Hague Regulations,[108] though it is surely legitimate to inquire as to whether these intimations were intended to deliver more than just that.[109] What exactly is meant by an *imperative*

105. Convention for the Protection of Cultural Property in the Event of Armed Conflict art. 4(1), May 14, 1954, S. Treaty Doc. No. 106-1 (1999), 249 U.N.T.S. 240.

106. *Id.* art. 4(2). In point of fact, Article 4(2) makes mention of the "obligations" of Article 4(1), and rightly so, since High Contracting Parties must respect cultural property situated in their own territory "as well as within the territory of other High Contracting Parties." As a matter of law, that respect involves "refraining from any use of the property and its immediate surroundings or of the appliances in use for its protection for purposes which are likely to expose it to destruction or damage in the event of armed conflict" *and* "by refraining from any act of hostilities" directed against such property.

107. *Id.* art. 11(2); *see also* Jan Hladik, *The 1954 Hague Convention for the Protection of Cultural Property in the Event of Armed Conflict and the Notion of Military Necessity*, 81 Int'l Rev. Red Cross 621 (1999).

108. *See supra* note 69 and accompanying text; *see also* 1899 Hague Convention, *supra* note 68, art. 23 ("[t]o destroy or seize the enemy's property, unless such destruction or seizure be imperatively demanded by the necessities of war").

109. Consider, too, the four occasions on which this occurs in Additional Protocol I. Article 54 of that Protocol, for example, recognizes "the vital requirements of any Party to the conflict in the defence of its national territory against invasion" and provides for the derogation from the prohibitions contained earlier in Article 54(2) "by a party to the conflict within such territory under its own control where required by imperative military necessity." AP I, *supra* note 82, art. 54(5). In addition to Article 54: Article 62(1) on general protection, *id.* art. 62(1) ("Civilian civil defence organizations and their personnel shall be respected and protected, subject to the provisions of this Protocol, particularly the provisions of this Section. They shall be entitled to perform their civil defence tasks except in case of imperative military necessity."); Article 67 on members of the armed forces and military units, *id.* art. 67 ("The *matériel* and buildings of military units permanently assigned to civil defence organizations and exclusively devoted to the performance of civil defence tasks shall, if they fall into the hands of an adverse Party, remain subject to the laws of war. They may not be diverted from their civil defence purpose so long as they are required for the performance of civil defence tasks, except in case of imperative military necessity, unless previous arrangements have been made for adequate provision for the needs of the civilian population."); and Article 71(3) on personnel participating in relief actions, *id.* art. 71(3) ("Each Party in receipt of relief consignments shall, to the fullest extent practicable,

military necessity? What of an *unavoidable* military necessity? Are these terms to be taken to mean one and the same thing?[110] And are they intended to suggest a difference from an ordinary or unqualified military necessity—a necessity perchance that is neither "imperative" nor "unavoidable"? What, too, of other kindred terms that have crept into the conventional lexicon—the "absolute necessity" of the Hague Regulations,[111] for instance?

First appearances could be taken to suggest that a taxonomy of military necessity—or, better, military necessities—is indeed being crafted here. Shifts in formulation, including shifts that seem slight, do not exist by accident, and the temptation is to believe that they are loaded within some greater meaning, some sublimated significance. However, upon closer inspection, it transpires that "[i]n order that there should be no abuse of so-called military necessities, it has been provided in [Article 4] of the Convention, that the obligation to respect cultural property situated within the territory of another Contracting Party shall lapse only in cases of 'imperative' military necessity."[112] And the shift to "exceptional cases of unavoidable military necessity" in Article 11 of the Hague Convention was generally understood "as reflecting the greater degree of protection" afforded by the Convention as a whole,[113] such that the preferred view is that each of these references has been "devised to accentuate that military necessity has to be mulled over attentively and not acted upon flippantly."[114] It has also been contended that the "difference" of formulations evident in the Hague Convention is not one "which would commend itself to a court, especially one adjudicating charges of war crimes,"[115] so one is left with the impression that, since the Hague Convention does not itself provide relevant explications for these stipulations, they await

assist the relief personnel referred to in paragraph 1 in carrying out their relief mission. Only in case of imperative military necessity may the activities of the relief personnel be limited or their movements temporarily restricted.").

110. Not for Hladik, who views the "not very strict conditions" of Article 4(2) of the Hague Convention against the "stricter conditions" of Article 11(2). *See* Hladik, *supra* note 107, at 622.

111. Hague IV, *supra* note 67, annex art. 54; *see also supra* note 108.

112. Government of the Netherlands, Records of the Conference Convened by the United Nations Educational, Scientific and Cultural Organization, Held at The Hague, from 21 April to 14 May 1954, 309 (1961).

113. In the words of the Committee of Experts: UNESCO Doc. Record of the General Conference, 7th Session, Paris, 1952, Proceedings, 7 C/PRG/7, Annex I, p. 10.

114. Dinstein, *supra* note 4, at 12; *see also id.* at 208 (in respect of the 1954 Hague Convention, stating that "the added value of the adverb 'imperatively' is far from self-evident, and the attacking force is prone to regard almost any military necessity as satisfying this requirement").

115. Roger O'Keefe, The Protection of Cultural Property in Armed Conflict 159 (2006).

clarification in the form of any subsequent agreement or practice by the High Contracting Parties to the Hague Convention.[116]

VIII. THE *LEGALITY OF THE THREAT OR USE OF NUCLEAR WEAPONS* ADVISORY OPINION (1996)

And, so, to our penultimate sequence, in the form of the advisory opinion of the International Court of Justice in *Legality of the Threat or Use of Nuclear Weapons* in July 1996, where the Court observed that

> in view of the current state of international law, and of the elements of fact at its disposal, the Court cannot conclude definitively whether the threat

116. Hladik, *supra* note 107, at 624. Consider, thus, Article 6 of the Second Protocol to the Hague Convention of 1954 for the Protection of Cultural Property in the Event of Armed Conflict ("Respect for Cultural Property"):

> With the goal of ensuring respect for cultural property in accordance with Article 4 of the Convention:
> a. a waiver on the basis of imperative military necessity pursuant to Article 4 paragraph 2 of the Convention may only be invoked to direct an act of hostility against cultural property when and for as long as:
>   i. that cultural property has, by its function, been made into a military objective; and
>   ii. there is no feasible alternative available to obtain a similar military advantage to that offered by directing an act of hostility against that objective;
> b. a waiver on the basis of imperative military necessity pursuant to Article 4 paragraph 2 of the Convention may only be invoked to use cultural property for purposes which are likely to expose it to destruction or damage when and for as long as no choice is possible between such use of the cultural property and another feasible method for obtaining a similar military advantage;
> c. the decision to invoke imperative military necessity shall only be taken by an officer commanding a force the equivalent of a battalion in size or larger, or a force smaller in size where circumstances do not permit otherwise;
> d. in case of an attack based on a decision taken in accordance with sub-paragraph (a), an effective advance warning shall be given whenever circumstances permit.
>
> Second Protocol to the Hague Convention of 1954 for the Protection of Cultural Property in the Event of Armed Conflict art. 6, Mar. 26, 1999, 2253 U.N.T.S. 172. With its concern of the loss of enhanced protection as contained in the Hague Convention, Hladik considers that Article 13 of the Second Protocol to the Hague Convention "*de facto* develops the definition of 'unavoidable military necessity'" from Article 11 of the Hague Convention by providing that:
> 1. Cultural property under enhanced protection shall only lose such protection:
>   a. if such protection is suspended or cancelled in accordance with Article 14; or
>   b. if, and for as long as, the property has, by its use, become a military objective.
> 2. In the circumstances of sub-paragraph 1(b), such property may only be the object of attack if:
>   a. the attack is the only feasible means of terminating the use of the property referred to in sub-paragraph 1(b);

> or use of nuclear weapons would be lawful or unlawful in an extreme circumstance of self-defence, in which the very survival of a State would be at stake.[117]

Perhaps one striking feature of this statement is the Court endearing (or endeavoring) itself toward a position of *non liquet*.[118] Perhaps another is the careful identification by the Court of the "extreme circumstance" of self-defense where "the very survival of a State would be at stake,"[119] presumably part of the elements of fact that were not then before the Court. That, in turn, might well stoke perceptions that there might exist conditions of "military necessity" for the use of nuclear weapons at some anonymous point hence. But, as far as the Court was concerned, the better view seems to be that the ambition of state survival had to be addressed—at least initially—by reference to the right of self-defense and, presumably, to its principle of proportionality.[120] However, much like self-preservation, which was discussed earlier in this chapter,[121] the survival of states is a thematic that apparently spans the laws of the *jus ad bellum* as well as those of the *jus in bello*. It is in the latter context that we find Judge Rosalyn Higgins making the observation in her dissent to that advisory opinion that

> b. all feasible precautions are taken in the choice of means and methods of attack, with a view to terminating such use and avoiding, or in any event minimising, damage to the cultural property;
> c. unless circumstances do not permit, due to requirements of immediate self-defence:
>   i. the attack is ordered at the highest operational level of command;
>   ii. effective advance warning is issued to the opposing forces requiring the termination of the use referred to in sub-paragraph 1(b); and
>   iii. reasonable time is given to the opposing forces to redress the situation.

See Hladik, *supra* note 107, at 629.

117. *Nuclear Weapons*, *supra* note 66, ¶ 105(2)(E), at 266 (July 8). Christopher Greenwood described this as "more than a little enigmatic." Christopher Greenwood, Jus ad Bellum *and* Jus in Bello *in the* Nuclear Weapons *Advisory Opinion*, *in* INTERNATIONAL LAW, THE INTERNATIONAL COURT OF JUSTICE AND NUCLEAR WEAPONS 247, 249 (Laurence Boisson de Chazournes & Philippe Sands eds., 1999).

118. What Judge Higgins regarded as a "formula of non-pronouncement." *Nuclear Weapons*, *supra* note 66, ¶ 29, at 590; *see also* Prosper Weil, *"The Court Cannot Conclude Definitively . . ."* Non Liquet *Revisited*, 36 COLUM. J. TRANSNAT'L L. 109 (1998).

119. Shades, here, of Article 5 of the Lieber Code ("[t]o save the country is paramount to all other circumstances"), *supra* note 48. For further assessment, *see* Marcelo G. Kohen, *The Notion of "State Survival" in International Law*, *in* INTERNATIONAL LAW, THE INTERNATIONAL COURT OF JUSTICE AND NUCLEAR WEAPONS, *supra* note 117, at 293.

120. *See* Greenwood, *supra* note 117, at 258–59.

121. *See supra* Section II.

> [i]t must be that, in order to meet the legal requirements that a military target may not be attacked if collateral civilian casualties would be excessive in relation to the military advantage, the "military advantage" must indeed be one related to the very survival of a State or the avoidance of infliction (whether by nuclear or other weapons of mass destruction) of vast and severe suffering on its own population; and that no other method of eliminating this military target must be available.[122]

There is thus an essential context marked out in this reasoning for the making and measuring of military calculations, which must resonate with the animating logic for violence in the first place as well as take into account any available alternatives or methods of elimination.

IX. THE ICRC STUDY ON CUSTOMARY INTERNATIONAL HUMANITARIAN LAW (2005)

For our final sequence, we shall turn to the Study on Customary International Humanitarian Law of the International Committee of the Red Cross (ICRC) published in March 2005, where "military necessity" is once again announced in terms of the requirements of "imperative military necessity," but, on this occasion, it also features as one of "[t]he general principles on the conduct of hostilities" applicable to the natural environment.[123] According to Rule 43 of that Study:

> A. No part of the natural environment may be attacked, unless it is a military objective.
> B. Destruction of any part of the natural environment is prohibited, unless required by imperative military necessity.

122. *Nuclear Weapons*, *supra* note 66, ¶ 21, at 588; *see also* Kohen, *supra* note 119, at 299. Consider in this respect the position of Burns Weston:

> Assuming even the so-called "worst case" scenario—e.g., a Soviet conventional assault against Western Europe or the oilfields of the Middle East—where is the military necessity in incinerating entire urban populations, defiling the territory of neighboring and distant neutral countries, and ravaging the natural environment for generations to come simply for the purpose of containing or repelling a conventional attack? Surely a failure to provide for an adequate conventional defense or to develop alternative energy sources does not excuse these probable results. If so, then we are witness to the demise of Nuremberg, the triumph of *Kriegsraison*, the virtual repudiation of the humanitarian rules of armed conflict in at least large-scale warfare.

Burns H. Weston, *Nuclear Weapons Versus International Law: A Conceptual Reassessment*, 28 McGill L.J. 542, 578 (1983). The relation of "military necessities" and "the legality of actions carried out by belligerent in neutrality territory" was also mentioned by Judge Gilbert Guillaume in his separate opinion in the *Nuclear Weapons* advisory opinion.

Nuclear Weapons, *supra* note 66, ¶ 6, at 289–90 (July 8).

123. ICRC Customary IHL Study, *supra* note 5, at 143.

C. Launching an attack against a military objective which may be expected to cause incidental damage to the environment which would be excessive in relation to the concrete and direct military advantage anticipated is prohibited.[124]

There is a second occasion for "general principles" to be articulated in the Study, and this occurs in chapter 20 in relation to the use of weapons—concerning weapons of a nature to cause superfluous injury or unnecessary suffering (Rule 70) or that are by nature indiscriminate (Rule 71).[125]

It is perhaps worth reflecting on the supposed generality of each of these principles. As a preliminary matter, we might be disposed to thinking of a "principle" as the statement of a general proposition or paradigm in contrast to the specificity of a given "rule" of law,[126] although, as we proceed, it should be noted that the Study does announce the contents of Rule 43 elsewhere as "general rules."[127] It may also be, of course, that the generality of the principle is intended to indicate its normative pedigree, as is done with the "general principles of law recognized by civilized nations" of Article 38(1)(c) of the 1945 Statute of the International Court of Justice.[128] Here, in articulating its rule that "[t]he dead must be disposed of in a respectful manner and their graves respected and properly maintained,"[129] the ICRC appears to have had this formal source of law in mind by claiming that "this rule" regarding the decent disposal of the dead "reflects a general principle of law requiring respect for the dead and their graves."[130] The same goes for its

124. *Id.*

125. By way of comparison, consider the so-called "cardinal principles contained in the texts constituting the fabric of international humanitarian law" as expressed by the International Court of Justice in its advisory opinion in July 1996—distinction, unnecessary suffering, and neutrality—where there was no reference made to military necessity. *Nuclear Weapons, supra* note 66, ¶ 78, at 257 (July 8). In the same breath as the principle of distinction, the Court also referred to the Martens Clause of the 1899 Hague Convention (II). *Id.* The Court stayed its hand on the "character" of the principles and rules of international humanitarian law—or their status as *jus cogens. Id.* ¶ 83, at 258.

126. I am thinking here of the "logical distinction" developed for "principles" and "rules" by Ronald Dworkin: "Both sets of standards point to particular decisions about legal obligation in particular circumstances, but they differ in the character they give. Rules are applicable in all-or-nothing fashion. If the facts a rule stipulates are given, then either the rule is valid, in which case the answer it supplies must be accepted, or it is not, in which case it contributes nothing to the decision." Ronald M. Dworkin, *The Model of Rules*, 35 U. Chi. L. Rev. 14, 25 (1967).

127. In its table of contents. ICRC Customary IHL Study, *supra* note 5, at vii.

128. Statute of the International Court of Justice art. 38(1)(c), June 26, 1945, https://www.icj-cij.org/en/statute.

129. ICRC Customary IHL Study, *supra* note 5, r. 115, at 414.

130. *Id.* at 416. Note, too, in respect of Rule 133 ("[t]he property rights of displaced persons must be respect"), the ICRC Study states that "it should . . . be noted that the legislation of most,

articulation of the prohibition of pillage, which it regards as "a specific application of the general principle of law prohibiting theft."[131]

Be this as it may, the first general principle to appear in Rule 43 is the principle of distinction,[132] which specifies that attacks may only be directed against military objectives,[133] defined as "those objects which by their nature, location, purpose or use make an effective contribution to military action and whose partial or total destruction, capture or neutralisation, in the circumstances ruling at the time, offer a definitive military advantage."[134] As we have already intimated, this rule (or principle), coming forward as it does from Article 52(2) of Additional Protocol I,[135] encodes some of the logic of military necessity on economies of violence without making any explicit reference to military necessity itself.[136] That said, in a separate targeting rule in the Study—Rule 37 on the prohibition of directing attacks against nondefended localities[137]—it is notable that in the iteration of this rule for *non-international* armed conflicts, the ICRC Study reasons that "the idea of prohibiting attacks on non-defended localities is based on the more general concept of military necessity: there is no need to attack a town, village, dwelling or building that is open for occupation."[138]

When military necessity *is* mentioned in Rule 43 of the Study, it is clearly intended to carry an authorizing function in respect of the possible destruction of any part of the natural environment ("unless required by imperative military necessity"). In its remarkably short explication of what is entailed by this aspect of

if not all, countries in the world guarantees a form of protection against arbitrary or illegal seizure of property which can be said to constitute a general principle of law." *Id.* at 474.

131. *Id.* r. 52, at 185.

132. *Id.* at 143–44.

133. Though, to be sure, this is framed as part of Rule 7. *Id.* at 25 ("The parties to the conflict must at all time distinguish between civilian objects and military objectives. Attacks may only be directed against military objectives. Attacks must not be directed against civilian objects.").

134. *Id.* r. 8, at 29.

135. AP I, *supra* note 82, art. 52(2).

136. Consider especially how military necessity has been defined by reference to "military objective" in the Second Protocol to the 1954 Hague Convention. Second Protocol to the Hague Convention of 1954 for the Protection of Cultural Property in the Event of Armed Conflict, Mar. 26, 1999, 2253 U.N.T.S. 172.

137. ICRC Customary IHL Study, *supra* note 5, at 122.

138. *Id.* at 124 ("This rule is an application of the principle that no more destruction may be wrought upon an adversary than absolutely necessary, a rule which is also applicable in non-international armed conflicts (Rule 50)."); *see also* Dinstein, *supra* note 4, at 11. To be contrasted with the iteration of this rule in *international* armed conflicts, which is based for the most part on an array of conventional stipulations. *See* ICRC Customary IHL Study, *supra* note 5, at 122–23; The Companion to International Humanitarian Law 201 (Drazan Djukic & Niccolò Pons eds., 2018).

the rule,[139] the Study simply advises that "imperative military necessity" demands the same as that provided for by Rule 50 in the Study ("[t]he destruction or seizure of the property of an adversary is prohibited, unless required by imperative military necessity").[140] Yet, when one turns to the explanation provided for Rule 50,[141] the detail there is found rather wanting. Nothing especial is made of the reference to "imperative" military necessity as contained in *that* rule,[142] and it is interesting that in its evidence for the rule in respect of international armed conflicts, the Study juxtaposes conventional stipulations whether they indulge—or do not indulge—that particular formulation.[143] We are therefore left with the impression that the "imperativeness" of military necessity is not intended to introduce or reinforce a hierarchy of necessities where one is to be regarded as any more important or exacting than any other. Rather, the imperativeness is inherent to, and one could say determining of, that necessity, and warring parties should thereby be in no doubt about the evidential demands that shall be made of them in that regard.[144]

139. ICRC Customary IHL Study, *supra* note 5, at 143–44.

140. *Id.* at 175.

141. *Id.* at 176–77.

142. *See* Dinstein, *supra* note 4, at 208.

143. *Compare* Hague IV, *supra* note 67, annex art. 23(g) *and* Rome Statute of the International Criminal Court, *supra* note 4, art. 8(2)(b)(xiii) ("[d]estroying or seizing the enemy's property unless such destruction or seizure by imperatively demanded by the necessities of war"), *with* Geneva Convention for the Amelioration of the Condition of the Wounded and Sick in Armed Forces in the Field art. 50, Aug. 12, 1949, 6 U.S.T. 3114, 75 U.N.T.S. 31 ("Grave breaches to which the preceding Article relates shall be those involving any of the following acts, if committed against persons or property protected by the Convention: wilful killing, torture or inhuman treatment, including biological experiments, wilfully causing great suffering or serious injury to body or health, and extensive destruction and appropriation of property, not justified by military necessity and carried out unlawfully and wantonly."); *see also* Geneva Convention for the Amelioration of the Condition of Wounded, Sick and Shipwrecked Members of Armed Forces at Sea art. 51, Aug. 12, 1949, 6 U.S.T. 3217, 75 U.N.T.S. 85; GC IV, *supra* note 82, art. 147. Importantly, the equivalent provision—Article 130—of the third Geneva Convention: "Grave breaches to which the preceding Article relates shall be those involving any of the following acts, if committed against persons or property protected by the Convention: wilful killing, torture or inhuman treatment, including biological experiments, wilfully causing great suffering or serious injury to body or health, compelling a prisoner of war to serve in the forces of the hostile Power, or wilfully depriving a prisoner of war of the rights of fair and regular trial prescribed in this Convention." Geneva Convention Relative to the Treatment of Prisoners of War art. 130, Aug. 12, 1949, 6 U.S.T. 3316, 75 U.N.T.S. 135. On the evidence for this rule for non-international armed conflicts, *see* Rome Statute of the International Criminal Court, *supra* note 4, art. 8(2)(e)(xii) ("[d]estroying or seizing the property of an adversary unless such destruction or seizure be imperatively demanded by the necessities of the conflict").

144. Dinstein, *supra* note 4, at 208. Curiously, in its adumbration of the second general principle of Rule 43, the Study omits to mention the term "imperative": "Destruction of property not justified by military necessity." *See* ICRC Customary IHL Study, *supra* note 5, at 144.

The final general principle to be mentioned in Rule 43—"[l]aunching an attack against a military objective which may be expected to cause incidental damage to the environment which would be excessive in relation to the concrete and direct military advantage anticipated is prohibited"—concerns, of course, the principle of proportionality.[145] The restraining effect of this principle contrasts with the authorizing function attributed to the existence of a military objective and to military necessity—both, also, contained in Rule 43. The idea is that the occurrence of excessive incidental damage to the environment would make the overall attack unlawful.[146] But it is also clear that a certain coherence prevails in this cohort of general principles: proportionality obtains in respect of that which is a military objective; if something is not a military objective, the principle of proportionality does not apply. But there remains a lurking question about the relevance of the principle of proportionality as far as the second general principle—that concerning (imperative) military necessity—is concerned because, here, the "[d]estruction of any part of the natural environment" is actively contemplated by the Study, and it is unclear what (if any) qualifying power proportionality can have in the face of destruction so deliberately envisaged.[147] This is not to mention how the second general principle of Rule 43 comports with the specification in Rule 45 that "[d]estruction of the natural environment may not be used as a weapon,"[148] including whether an action undertaken in the name of military necessity can and should be said to weaponize the natural environment in some meaningful way.

X. CONCLUSION

Through a series of discrete sequences arising from the 1863 Lieber Code through to the 2005 ICRC Study on Customary International Humanitarian Law, this chapter has sought to recall or reconstruct military necessity within a range of contexts existing within the *jus in bello* itself—that is to say, for the purpose or purposes which it has been variously invoked but also the differing language that has been used to bring it to legal life. Throughout the chapter, though, we have also tried to make some sense of kindred propositions appearing in public international law as a greater whole—such as self-preservation, necessity under the laws of the *jus ad bellum*, and necessity, too, as it features within the realm of the law of state responsibility. The principal intention behind this structure for the

145. *See* ICRC Customary IHL Study, *supra* note 5, at 145. Or to proportionality in attack, as it is put in Rule 14. *Id.* at 46.

146. Rule 43 specifically applies the principle of proportionality to the environment.

147. Recall Oppenheim's mention of the "annihilation of the vanquished State." 1 International Law: Peace, *supra* note 8, § 114, at 161.

148. A rule applicable in international armed conflicts and arguably in non-international armed conflicts. ICRC Customary IHL Study, *supra* note 5, at 151.

chapter has not been to identify a steady or even coherent philosophy or meaning for military necessity occurring through time but, rather, to invite the reader to make appropriate connections between the explicit uses that have been made of military necessity in the conventional and customary form and, perhaps more fundamentally, to be alert to the more subtle influence it may be said to have had on how certain laws of the *jus in bello* have been fashioned.[149]

149. Though, to be sure, much will depend on the juxtaposition of the laws of the *jus ad bellum* with those of the *jus in bello*. Greenwood, *supra* note 117, at 258–59. Note, too, Judge Higgins's observation in the *Nuclear Weapons* advisory opinion that the "non-pronouncement" of the Court in Paragraph 105(2)(E) of its *dispositive* "necessarily leaves open the possibility that a use of nuclear weapons contrary to humanitarian law might nonetheless be lawful." *Nuclear Weapons*, *supra* note 66, ¶ 29, at 590.

9

Practical and Conceptual Challenges to Doctrinal Military Necessity

MAJOR ROBERT LAWLESS*

I. INTRODUCTION

Military necessity plays a foundational role in the law of armed conflict (LOAC). It echoes throughout this body of law and is referenced extensively by states, international organizations, courts, non-state humanitarian organizations, and scholars. However, it is also controversial and confounding. It has been said that "[n]o principle is more central [to the LOAC], nor more misunderstood" than military necessity.[1] If you put three or four LOAC scholars and practitioners in a room and asked them to define military necessity, you may be likely to get three or four quite different responses.[2]

Sometimes practitioners avoid the challenges of military necessity by ignoring them, or by referencing military necessity without any explanation or analysis. For

* Major and Judge Advocate, U.S. Army. I am grateful for the support of Colonel David Wallace, Lieutenant Colonel Shane Reeves, Professor Michael Schmitt, the Lieber Institute for Law and Land Warfare, and the participants of the 2018 Lieber Institute workshop at West Point. I owe special thanks to Professor Claus Kreß and Professor Sean Watts, each of whom read drafts of this chapter and provided helpful and encouraging feedback. The views expressed here are mine and do not necessarily represent the views of the U.S. Military Academy, the U.S. Army, or the U.S. government.

1. Michael N. Schmitt, *Military Necessity and Humanity in International Humanitarian Law: Preserving the Delicate Balance*, 50 Va. J. Int'l L. 795, 796 (2010).

2. As will be explored in this chapter, this in part is due to the fact that military necessity is conceptualized in vastly different ways. For example, some conceptualize military necessity in positive or vesting terms; others understand it in prohibitive terms.

Major Robert Lawless, *Practical and Conceptual Challenges to Doctrinal Military Necessity* In: *Necessity and Proportionality in International Peace and Security Law.* Edited by: Professor Claus Kreß and Captain Robert Lawless, Oxford University Press (2021). © Oxford University Press. DOI: 10.1093/oso/9780197537374.003.0010.

example, in a 2016 speech entitled *Applying the Law of Targeting to the Modern Battlefield*, the General Counsel of the U.S. Department of Defense discussed the application of the LOAC in the context of U.S. military operations against the Islamic State in the Middle East.[3] One might expect military necessity to arise during a speech on this topic, and indeed it did. In a section of the speech concerning the targeting process, the General Counsel stated that when the U.S. military engages in lethal targeting operations, the legal analysis of such operations "would include [the LOAC] principles of distinction, proportionality, military necessity, and so forth."[4] However, nowhere in the speech did the General Counsel explain how such a legal analysis would *apply* the principle of military necessity.[5] While the speech included discussion of the practical applications of distinction and proportionality, it did not explain how military necessity functions in an operational context. In general, during practical discussions of the LOAC, it is not uncommon to find similar references to military necessity with little or no analysis.[6]

This trend may be related to the surprising difficulty of finding an authoritative definition of military necessity in primary sources of the LOAC, especially conventional LOAC. The most prominent LOAC conventions—the four Geneva Conventions of 1949 and their two Additional Protocols of 1977—refer at times to "military necessity" (usually in its narrower usage as an exception to particular LOAC rules[7]), but do

3. Jennifer M. O'Connor, Gen. Couns., Dep't of Def., Applying the Law of Targeting to the Modern Battlefield (Nov. 28, 2016), *reprinted in "Applying the Law of Targeting to the Modern Battlefield"—Full Speech Given by DOD General Counsel Jennifer O'Connor*, JUST SECURITY (Nov. 28, 2016), https://www.justsecurity.org/34977/applying-law-targeting-modern-battlefield%E2%80%8E-full-speech-dod-general-counsel-jennifer-oconnor.

4. *Id.*

5. The General Counsel references Francis Lieber's definition of military necessity earlier in the speech. *Id.*; *see infra* notes 11–13 and accompanying text. However, it is referred to only as a basis for the principle of proportionality, and is not directly analyzed or applied. *See* O'Connor, *supra* note 3.

6. Furthermore, it is not uncommon to see practitioners, as well as scholars, conflate military necessity with aspects of the principle of distinction. Perhaps most commonly, military necessity is often referenced in connection with the notion of military objective under Article 51 of the First Additional Protocol to the 1949 Geneva Conventions. However, the two are not completely overlapping concepts. *See, e.g.*, Wolff Heintschel von Heinegg, *Considerations of Necessity Under Article 57(2)(a)(ii), (c), and (3) and Proportionality Under Article 51(5)(b) and Article 57(2)(b) of Additional Protocol I: Is There Room for an Integrated Approach?*, *in* NECESSITY AND PROPORTIONALITY IN INTERNATIONAL PEACE AND SECURITY LAW 325, 331 (Claus Kreß & Robert Lawless eds., 2020).

7. This chapter is concerned with military necessity in its broad sense within the LOAC. Military necessity also has a distinct, narrow application in the LOAC in the form of an express exception to specific rules. This narrow application is not the subject of this chapter. *See infra* note 18 and accompanying text.

not define it.[8] Purported restatements of customary LOAC likewise have not offered a definition.[9] Some may find evidence of its shape in notable historical documents, but these references are veiled and indirect.[10]

The most famous and influential definitions of military necessity come not from conventional LOAC but from a U.S. Civil War–era doctrinal publication written by Francis Lieber (the Lieber Code), and from *United States v. List*, a post–Second World War case arising in one of the national military commissions in Nuremberg. The Lieber Code, for its part, asserts that military necessity, "as understood by modern civilized nations, consists in the necessity of those measures which are indispensable for securing the ends of war, and which are lawful according to the modern law and usages of war."[11] It "admits of all direct destruction

8. *See* Geneva Convention for the Amelioration of the Condition of the Wounded and Sick in Armed Forces in the Field, Aug. 12, 1949, 6 U.S.T. 3114, 75 U.N.T.S. 31; Geneva Convention for the Amelioration of the Condition of Wounded, Sick and Shipwrecked Members of Armed Forces at Sea, Aug. 12, 1949, 6 U.S.T. 3217, 75 U.N.T.S. 85; Geneva Convention Relative to the Treatment of Prisoners of War, Aug. 12, 1949, 6 U.S.T. 3316, 75 U.N.T.S. 135 [hereinafter GC III]; Geneva Convention Relative to the Protection of Civilians Persons in Time of War, Aug. 12, 1949, 6 U.S.T. 3516, 75 U.N.T.S. 287 [hereinafter GC IV]; Protocol Additional to the Geneva Conventions of 12 August 1949, and Relating to the Protection of Victims of International Armed Conflict (Protocol I), June 8, 1977, 1125 U.N.T.S. 3 [hereinafter AP I]; Protocol Additional to the Geneva Conventions of 12 August 1949, and Relating to the Protection of Victims of Non-International Armed Conflict (Protocol II), June 8, 1977, 1125 U.N.T.S. 609.

9. *See, e.g.*, 1 INT'L COMM. OF THE RED CROSS, CUSTOMARY INTERNATIONAL HUMANITARIAN LAW: RULES 124–31, 143–47, 175–81, 201–202 (Jean-Marie Henckaerts & Louise Doswald-Beck eds., 2005) [hereinafter 1 ICRC CUSTOMARY IHL STUDY]; *cf.* TALLINN MANUAL 2.0 ON THE INTERNATIONAL LAW APPLICABLE TO CYBER OPERATIONS (Michael N. Schmitt & Liis Vihul eds., 2017).

10. *See, e.g.*, Declaration Renouncing the Use, in Time of War, of Explosive Projectiles Under 400 Grammes Weight pmbl., Dec. 11, 1868 [hereinafter St. Petersburg Declaration], *reprinted in* THE LAWS OF ARMED CONFLICTS: A COLLECTION OF CONVENTIONS, RESOLUTIONS AND OTHER DOCUMENTS 91 (Dietrich Schindler & Jiri Toman eds., 4th ed. 2004) ("[T]he only legitimate object which States should endeavor to accomplish during war is to weaken the military forces of the enemy . . . [and] for this purpose it is sufficient to disable the greatest possible number of men . . . ."); Convention (IV) Respecting the Laws and Customs of War on Land annex art. 22, Oct. 18, 1907, 26 Stat. 2277, 207 Consol. T.S. 277 [hereinafter Hague IV] ("The right of belligerents to adopt means of injuring the enemy is not unlimited."); The Laws of War on Land arts. 3, Sept. 9, 1880 (citing St. Petersburg Declaration, *supra*), *reprinted in* THE LAWS OF ARMED CONFLICTS, *supra*, at 29 ("The only legitimate end that States may have in war being to weaken the military strength of the enemy."); *id.* art. 4 ("The laws of war do not recognize in belligerents an unlimited liberty as to the means of injuring the enemy."); Project of an International Declaration Concerning the Laws and Customs of War art. 12, Aug. 27, 1874, *reprinted in* THE LAWS OF ARMED CONFLICTS, *supra*, at 23 ("The laws of war do not recognize in belligerents an unlimited power in the adoption of means of injuring the enemy.").

11. Francis Lieber, U.S. War Dep't, General Orders No. 100: Instructions for the Government of Armies of the United States in the Field art. 14 (Apr. 24, 1863) [hereinafter Lieber Code], *reprinted in* THE LAWS OF ARMED CONFLICTS, *supra* note 10, at 3.

of life or limb" of enemy combatants, as well as "of other persons whose destruction is incidentally unavoidable" during hostilities.[12] According to Lieber, military necessity does not license unlimited warfare,[13] but it does marshal starkly broad and permissive language in describing admissible acts of hostilities. In *United States v. List*, a national military commission building on Lieber's definition influentially asserted that military necessity "permits a belligerent, subject to the laws of war, to apply any amount and kind of force to compel the complete submission of the enemy with the least possible expenditure of time, life, and money."[14] By way of reference, this chapter will refer to these definitions in combination as the "Lieber/Nuremberg model" for military necessity.

Notwithstanding the shortage of authoritative guidance in LOAC conventions concerning the definition of military necessity, states have consistently over time included definitions of military necessity within national doctrinal publications. In particular, military LOAC manuals, produced by states' defense departments or ministries and expressing comprehensive statements of the content of the LOAC, virtually always identify military necessity as a core principle or concept.[15] These doctrinal publications also define military necessity according to the Lieber/Nuremberg model, the language of which appears, at least at first glance, quite concrete and practicable: in essence, it authorizes belligerents to use those military measures that are needed to defeat the opposing belligerent's armed forces—that is, to *win the war*—quickly and efficiently.

The concrete and practicable terms used by states to define military necessity contrast with the views of many prominent scholars who have concluded that the

12. *Id.* art. 15.

13. Military necessity "does not admit of cruelty—that is, the infliction of suffering for the sake of suffering or for revenge, nor of maiming or wounding except in fight, nor of torture to extort confessions. It does not admit of the use of poison in any way, nor of the wanton devastation of a district. It admits of deception, but disclaims acts of perfidy; and, in general, military necessity does not include any act of hostility which makes the return to peace unnecessarily difficult." *Id.* art. 16.

14. United States v. List (The Hostage Case), Case No. 7 (Feb. 19, 1948), *reprinted in* 11 Trials of War Criminals Before the Nuremberg Military Tribunals Under Control Council Law No. 10, at 757, 1253 (1950).

15. An important question, which is beyond the scope of this chapter, is whether and to what extent military manuals contribute to the formation of international law generally and the LOAC in particular. *See, e.g.*, David Turns, *Military Manuals and the Customary Law of Armed Conflict*, *in* National Military Manuals on the Law of Armed Conflict (Nobuo Hayashi ed., 2d ed. 2010). Indeed, one challenge to seeking authoritative statements of the law—or states' assertions of their official interpretations of the law—in LOAC manuals is that such manuals are not exclusively reflective of law; they also include guidance or direction based on policy determinations. This chapter assumes for the sake of its analysis that the careful reader of military manuals will find that such publications offer substantial insight into states' views about the content of the LOAC.

principle is more theoretical and conceptual than practicable in nature.[16] Indeed, the weight of academic thought about military necessity holds that it is best understood not as a practicable principle of the LOAC but rather as a conceptual or foundational *interest* that underlies the LOAC.[17] According to these theorists, military necessity and the coordinate interest of humanity dialectically form and shape concrete principles, such as distinction and proportionality, and specific rules of the LOAC.[18] In other words, on this view military necessity is not a *part* of the LOAC in the sense that combatants and other fighters must routinely *apply* such a principle or rule to factual circumstances they encounter during hostilities, but rather constitutes one of two "driving forces" behind the concrete and practicable principles and rules of the LOAC.[19] Given the widespread acceptance of this theory in the academy, it is thus curious that states continue both to articulate military necessity according to the Lieber/Nuremberg model, with its concrete and practicable rather than conceptual language, as well as decline in large part to explain *how* it must be applied in operational practice.[20]

This chapter explores the implications of states' persistence in articulating the Lieber/Nuremberg version of military necessity in doctrinal publications. In doing so, it breaks down the general model of military necessity into its constituent parts. Specifically, states generally articulate military necessity as

(a) a principle
(b) that confers a right, permission, or justification
(c) to use any military measures or force
(d) required to defeat the enemy
(e) as quickly and efficiently as possible
(f) so long as they are not otherwise prohibited by the LOAC.

16. *See, e.g.*, Schmitt, *supra* note 1, at 798–801; Yoram Dinstein, The Conduct of Hostilities under the Law of International Armed Conflict 8–10 (3d ed. 2016).

17. *See, e.g.*, Schmitt, *supra* note 1, at 799.

18. Military necessity has a distinct, narrow application in the LOAC in the form of an express exception to specific rules. *See, e.g.*, Hague IV, *supra* note 10, annex art. 23(g) ("[I]t is especially forbidden . . . [t]o destroy or seize the enemy's property, unless such destruction or seizure be imperatively demanded by the necessities of war"); Convention for the Protection of Cultural Property in the Event of Armed Conflict art. 4, May 14, 1954, S. Treaty Doc. No. 106-1 (1999), 249 U.N.T.S. 240 (permitting narrowing of protections provided to cultural property "in cases where military necessity imperatively requires such a waiver"); AP I, *supra* note 8, arts. 54(5), 67(4), 62(1), 71(3) (when demanded by "imperative military necessity," permitting derogation by some measure of "scorched earth" tactics; use of enemy "*materiel* and buildings of military units permanently assigned to civil defense organizations"; and restriction on the conduct of civil defense and relief personnel). This narrow application of military necessity is not the subject of this chapter.

19. Dinstein, supra note 16, at 8.

20. One noteworthy, partial exception is the U.S. Department of Defense's Law of War Manual, which attempts to analyze military necessity in greater than normal detail. (Of course, at 1,236 total pages, the manual addresses most LOAC issues in greater than normal detail.) However,

Each of these components of the overall definition of military necessity poses significant practical and conceptual challenges. For example, what is the significance of characterizing military necessity as a "principle"? Does this characterization signal that military necessity serves more as a theoretical concept or instead fulfills a practical regulatory function during hostilities? If the latter, then how effective is it at providing combatants with guidance concerning what conduct is permitted and what is forbidden? Does military necessity "permit" certain conduct, and, if so, what is the nature of this legal "permission"? Furthermore, what conclusions about military necessity's value as a guide for combatants should be drawn from the broadly permissive terms used in the Lieber/Nuremberg model? Does it also serve a "forbidding" function? Does it prohibit combatants to engage in specific conduct that is *not* precluded by rules found elsewhere in the LOAC?

This is only a sample of the significant conceptual and practical questions raised by states' continued insistence on defining military necessity in this manner in military LOAC manuals and other doctrinal publications. Section II of this chapter engages in a systematic analysis of each of the previously identified components of military necessity. Through this analysis it is shown that, although states' definitions of military necessity vary in minor ways, many adopt the general model based on the Lieber Code and Nuremberg jurisprudence. For each component of the model, Section II provides examples of state doctrinal articulations. Each component is also examined in detail to reveal the practical and conceptual challenges it poses to military operators' clear understanding of military necessity's role in the LOAC. It is shown that states' continued insistence on this model of military necessity raises, and fails to adequately answer, crucial questions about the nature and application of the LOAC. Therefore, Section III recommends that states reformulate how they define military necessity in doctrinal publications such as military manuals. Reformulation will benefit practitioners by providing conceptual clarity and hopefully will result in fewer instances of uncritical recitation of military necessity. Section IV provides brief concluding remarks.

II. CHALLENGING DOCTRINAL MILITARY NECESSITY

This section evaluates in turn each of the six previously identified components of the Lieber/Nuremberg model of military necessity. These six components of the general model include (a) its identification as a "principle"; (b) its granting of a "right," "permission," or "justification"; (c) its authorization of "any measures" or "force" (d) "required to defeat the enemy" (e) "as quickly and efficiently as possible"; (f) and its proviso that any such use of military measures or force must comply with the LOAC. For each of these components, examples are provided of

as will be discussed at length in the following section, the Department of Defense Manual's attempt to explain the practical applicability of military necessity leaves important questions unanswered and at times seems even self-contradictory.

language used by states in articulating military necessity. Each component is also evaluated to reveal the practical and conceptual challenges it poses.

It must be conceded that, although this chapter attempts to survey as many states' military doctrinal publications as possible, it cannot be claimed to have done so exhaustively. Most states do not publish much of their LOAC doctrine, and for many others there were language challenges (although translations were made when possible). Furthermore, the reader will undoubtedly note the prominence of publications of the U.S. government. This is due in part to the relative quantitative wealth of material published by the United States, as well as its prominent role in many past and present armed conflict situations around the world. Nonetheless, I have sought to include examples from the doctrine of a broad sample of states.

A. Is Military Necessity a LOAC "Principle"?

States often refer to military necessity as a LOAC "principle,"[21] usually as one of a number of core, fundamental, or foundational principles.[22] Furthermore,

21. *E.g.*, Off. of the Gen. Couns., U.S. Dep't of Def., Department of Defense Law of War Manual 50, 52 (June 2015, updated Dec. 2016) [hereinafter U.S. LOAC Manual]; Dep't of the Army & U.S. Marine Corps, FM 6-27/MCTP 11-10C, The Commander's Handbook on the Law of Land Warfare 1-6 (2019) [hereinafter U.S. Army LOAC Manual]; Ministerio de Defensa, Manual de Derecho Internacional de los Conflictos Armados 24–25 (2010) (Arg.) [hereinafter Argentina LOAC Manual]; Austl. Def. Force, Exec. Series ADDP 06.4, Law of Armed Conflict 2-1, 2-2 (2006) (Austl.) [hereinafter Australia LOAC Manual]; Austl. Def. Force, Operations Series ADDP 3.14, Targeting 3-1 (2009) (Austl.) [hereinafter Australia Targeting Doctrine]; Ministry of Nat'l Def., CFJP 01, Canadian Military Doctrine 2-15 (2009) (Can.) [hereinafter Canada Military Doctrine]; Ministère de la Défense, Manuel de Droit des Conflits Armés 8 (2012) (Fr.) [hereinafter France LOAC Manual] (calling it "necessity" rather than "military necessity"); Bundesministerium der Verteidigung, Joint Serv. Reg. (ZDv) 15/2, Law of Armed Conflict Manual 25 (2013) (Ger.) [hereinafter Germany LOAC Manual]; Ministry of Def., JSP 381, Aide Memoire on the Law of Armed Conflict 1 (2010) (U.K.) [hereinafter U.K. Aide Memoire]; Ministry of Def., JDP 3-46, Legal Support to Joint Operations 22 (3d ed. 2018) (U.K.) [hereinafter U.K. Legal Support Doctrine]; Ministry of Def., JSP 383, The Joint Service Manual of the Law of Armed Conflict 21 (2004) (U.K.) [hereinafter U.K. LOAC Manual]; North Atlantic Treaty Org., NATO Legal Deskbook 248 (2d ed. 2010) [hereinafter NATO Legal Deskbook]. *But see, e.g.*, Off. of the Judge Advoc. Gen., Ministry of Def., Law of Armed Conflict at the Operational and Tactical Levels 2-1 (2001) (Can.) [hereinafter Canada LOAC Manual] (identifying military necessity, humanity, and chivalry as primary "concepts" of the LOAC); Royal Austl. Air Force, AAP 1003, Operations Law for RAAF Commanders 47 (2d ed. 2004) (Austl.) [hereinafter Australia Air Force Doctrine] (referring to the "three fundamental LOAC *concepts* of military necessity, humanity and proportionality," and to "related LOAC *principles*") (emphasis added); *id.* at 49 (defining the *concept* of military necessity).

22. *See* U.S. LOAC Manual, *supra* note 21, at 50 ("foundational principles"); U.S. Army LOAC Manual, *supra* note 21, at 1-6 (same); U.K. LOAC Manual, *supra* note 21, at 21 ("fundamental

states include military necessity as one of often several other LOAC "principles." Examples of other principles states include alongside military necessity include (with each of the following varying in commonality of usage) distinction,[23] proportionality,[24] humanity,[25] unnecessary suffering,[26] precautions in attack,[27] nonreciprocity,[28] and good faith.[29] While states vary in the number of LOAC principles they identify, military necessity remains constant as a fundamental principle for those states that endeavor to list such principles.[30]

principles"); NATO Legal Deskbook, *supra* note 21, at 248 ("core principles"). *But see* Canada LOAC Manual, *supra* note 21, at 2-1 ("primary concepts"); Australia Air Force Doctrine, *supra* note 21, at 47 (referring to the "three fundamental LOAC *concepts* of military necessity, humanity and proportionality," and to "related LOAC *principles*") (emphasis added); Germany LOAC Manual, *supra* note 21, at 25 (separating military necessity and humanity from other rules and principles).

23. U.S. LOAC Manual, *supra* note 21, at 50, 62–65; U.S. Army LOAC Manual, *supra* note 21, at 1-6, 1-9 to 1-10; Argentina LOAC Manual, *supra* note 21, at 25; Australia Air Force Doctrine, *supra* note 21, at 51–52; Australia LOAC Manual, *supra* note 21, at 2-7 ("Although not a basic principle, distinction is said to be a related principle [of the LOAC]."); Australia Targeting Doctrine, *supra* note 21, at 3-1; Comando General de las Fuerzas Militares, FF.MM 3-41 Público, Manual de Derecho Operacional 37 (2009) (Colom.) [hereinafter Colombia LOAC Manual]; France LOAC Manual, *supra* note 21, at 8; U.K. Aide Memoire, *supra* note 21, at 1; U.K. Legal Support Doctrine, *supra* note 21, at 23; U.K. LOAC Manual, *supra* note 21, at 21, 24; NATO Legal Deskbook, *supra* note 21, at 248.

24. U.S. LOAC Manual, *supra* note 21, at 50, 60–62; U.S. Army LOAC Manual, *supra* note 21, at 1-6, 1-11; Argentina LOAC Manual, *supra* note 21, at 25; Australia Air Force Doctrine, *supra* note 21, at 50–51; Australia LOAC Manual, *supra* note 21, at 2-1, 2-4 to 2-6; Australia Targeting Doctrine, *supra* note 21, at 3-1; Colombia LOAC Manual, *supra* note 23, at 38; France LOAC Manual, *supra* note 21, at 8; Germany LOAC Manual, *supra* note 21, at 53; U.K. Aide Memoire, *supra* note 21, at 1; U.K. Legal Support Doctrine, *supra* note 21, at 23; U.K. LOAC Manual, *supra* note 21, at 21, 25; NATO Legal Deskbook, *supra* note 21, at 248.

25. U.S. LOAC Manual, *supra* note 21, at 50, 58–60; U.S. Army LOAC Manual, *supra* note 21, at 1-6, 1-8; Argentina LOAC Manual, *supra* note 21, at 24; Australia Air Force Doctrine, *supra* note 21, at 50; Australia LOAC Manual, *supra* note 21, at 2-2; Canada Military Doctrine, *supra* note 21, at 2215; Colombia LOAC Manual, *supra* note 23, at 38; France LOAC Manual, *supra* note 21, at 8; U.K. Aide Memoire, *supra* note 21, at 1; U.K. Legal Support Doctrine, *supra* note 21, at 23; U.K. LOAC Manual, *supra* note 21, at 21, 23; NATO Legal Deskbook, *supra* note 21, at 248.

26. Australia LOAC Manual, *supra* note 21, at 2-1, 2-4; Australia Targeting Doctrine, *supra* note 21, at 3-1; U.S. Army LOAC Manual, *supra* note 21, at 1-6.

27. Colombia LOAC Manual, *supra* note 23, at 38–39.

28. *Id.* at 39.

29. Argentina LOAC Manual, *supra* note 21, at 26.

30. *See supra* note 21 and accompanying text. Some states refer instead to the principle of "necessity." *E.g.*, France LOAC Manual, *supra* note 21, at 8. Notably, other international law

"Principle" is a general legal term that is difficult to define precisely, perhaps due to its varied usage.[31] Sometimes it refers to a subtype of those functional legal units[32] that are preceptual in nature.[33] Conceived of in this way, a principle functions like a generalized rule: it informs addressees of actions that may, must, or may not occur, or conduct or behavior that they may, must, or may not engage in.[34] Like other legal precepts (such as rules and norms), a principle is applied by practitioners and other legal subjects to concrete factual scenarios to reach legal decisions about what conduct or behavior is permissible or prohibited.

Another usage of the term "principle" serves a nonpreceptual legal function.[35] Specifically, a legal principle may refer to a foundational interest or concept that underlies a legal system or regime.[36] Seen in this way, a principle serves as a

commentators and scholars also refer to military necessity as a "principle." 1 How Does Law Protect in War? pt. I, ch. 8, at 8, pt. I, ch. 9, at 9, pt. I, ch. 12, at 20 (Marco Sassòli, Antoine A. Bouvier & Anne Quinton eds., 3d ed. n.d.); Hum. Rts. Watch, Losing Humanity: The Case Against Killer Robots 26, 35 (2012), https://www.hrw.org/report/2012/11/19/losing-humanity/case-against-killer-robots (click on "Download the full report"); Schmitt, *supra* note 1, at 796; Brian J. Brill, The *Rendulic "Rule": Military Necessity, Commander's Knowledge, and Methods of Warfare*, 12 Y.B. Int'l Humanitarian L. 119, 120 (2009). It must be acknowledged that states and organizations are not always consistent in how they categorize and describe military necessity. *Cf. infra* notes 159–61 and accompanying text; *see also* 1 How Does Law Protect in War?, *supra*, pt. I, ch. 4, at 10 (referring to "necessity" instead of "military necessity").

31. It goes without saying that the term "principle" is also used outside the legal context. In fact, it is used so frequently and in so many different contexts that a precise definition, even regarding narrow contexts, may not be possible. *Cf. infra* note 48 and accompanying text.

32. Summers uses this term to refer to a legal system's various formal components, which include institutions such as legislatures and courts, legal precepts such as rules and principles, nonpreceptual legal forms such as contracts and property interests, legal methodologies, and sanctions and remedies. Robert S. Summers, Form and Function in a Legal System: A General Study 3–4 (2009).

33. *Id.* at 136 ("Legal systems recognize varied functional units that are preceptual in nature, including rules, principles, maxims, and general orders."); *see Precept*, Black's Law Dictionary (8th ed. 2004) (defining it in relevant part as a "standard or rule of conduct; a command or principle").

34. Summers, *supra* note 32, at 137; *see also* Scott J. Shapiro, Legality 409 n.8 (2011) (using the term "norm" to encompass principles, rules, and standards, each of which is a normative entity that informs the addressee "*what to do* or what is valuable, desirable, [or] acceptable") (emphasis added).

35. Analytical philosophy of law is concerned with the metaphysical foundations of law. Shapiro, *supra* note 34, at 2, 3. As previously noted, *see supra* note 32 and accompanying text, legal formalists have sought to distinguish the various formal elements of a legal system or regime, including "its purposes, its overall form, constituent features thereof, and complementary material or other components." Summers, *supra* note 32, at 5.

36. Every legal regime has a "scheme of interests or goals or *principles* the [regime] can be taken to serve or express or exemplify. Ronald Dworkin, Law's Empire 52 (1986) (emphasis added).

reference point or lodestar, representing a conceptual motivating force or purpose of a legal regime.[37] Thus, a legal principle is an abstract element of the law, perhaps informing but nonetheless existing outside of the preceptual legal provisions that are applied to concrete factual circumstances. Although this more abstract, conceptual usage serves no independent regulatory role, it nonetheless provides value to the law's practitioners and others as an interpretive tool to understanding the law.[38] In this regard, Ronald Dworkin insightfully referred to law's "purpose"—similar to a motivating force or interest—as the "formal structure of all interpretive claims"[39] as well as a "structural requirement" of any interpretation of law.[40]

It is difficult to draw a precise definition of the term "principle" as states use it in articulating and defining the content of the LOAC. Once again, in this regard Dworkin's theoretical work is useful in highlighting the elusive boundaries around what law refers to as "principles." Dworkin distinguished between "principles" and "rules."[41] A rule functions in an "all-or-nothing fashion":[42] if it applies in a given situation, "the answer it supplies must be accepted";[43] but if it does not, the rule is irrelevant and "contributes nothing to the decision."[44] In contrast, a principle does not "purport to set out conditions that makes its application necessary."[45] Rather, it provides reasons that argue in one direction, but do not necessitate a particular

37. A common form of legal analysis involves seeking to interpret and understand the law's "purpose . . . in order to make of it the best possible example of the form or genre to which it is taken to belong." *Id.* Purposive analysis endeavors to show a legal system in its "best light, to achieve equilibrium between legal practice . . . and the best justification of that practice." *Id.* at 90.

38. *See id.* at 52.

39. *Id.* at 58.

40. *Id.* at 59. Identifying or ascribing the purpose of a legal system, legal regime, or one or more rules within a regime is necessary because often the "raw behavioral data of the practice," that is, "what people do in what circumstances," will undermine the value of the practice. *See id.* at 52. Furthermore, interpretation of a legal system or one or more aspect of such a system "is by nature the report of a purpose." *Id.* at 58. Such an interpretive endeavor "proposes a way of seeing what is interpreted" as if the system or the principle or rule in question "were the product of a decision to pursue one set of themes or visions or purposes, one 'point' rather than another." *Id.* at 58–59. Indeed, the rules, principles, and other positive law we intentionally and purposefully apply to factual disputes "could not even have been drafted in the first place without first formulating the purposes, desired form, features," and other defining aspects of the law. Summers, *supra* note 32, at 5.

41. *See* Ronald Dworkin, *The Model of Rules*, 35 U. Chi. L. Rev. 14, 23–29 (1967).

42. *Id.* at 25.

43. *Id.*

44. *Id.*

45. *Id.* at 26.

decision.[46] If relevant, a principle must be taken into account "as a consideration inclining in one direction or another."[47] This suggests that legal principles may reside in a conceptual, nebulous zone between concrete legal precepts such as rules and abstract legal concepts such as motivating forces, interests, or purposes. Thus, the contrast drawn earlier between the two possible manifestations of "principles" may be somewhat artificial. However, instead of undermining this subsection's analysis, it furthers it by highlighting the conceptual challenges posed by states' insistence on referring to military necessity as a LOAC principle.[48]

Before directing these considerations toward the principle of military necessity, it is worth noting that legal "principles" play a significant role in general international law. In doing so, general international law suggests both the preceptual usage of the term as well as the abstract, conceptual usage. For example, the Statute of the International Court of Justice identifies "general principles of law," along with customary and conventional international law, as primary sources of international law.[49] This suggests a view of principles that serve a preceptual function and thus may be applied to concrete factual situations, such as the cases submitted to the court. In at least partial contrast, others refer to "general principles of international law" that may refer to "certain logical propositions underlying judicial reasoning on the basis of existing international law," which are "primarily abstractions."[50] In short, perhaps in the broader international legal context, as well as within the LOAC, usage of the term may be inconsistent, or perhaps even necessarily nebulous.[51] This may be seen as a virtue, as "law in the form of discretion

46. *Id.*

47. *Id.* In this way, principles have a "dimension of weight or importance" that rules do not. *Id.* at 27.

48. As suggested in this paragraph, the term "principle" is sufficiently amorphous that usage may be inconsistent, even within a legal regime or component of such a regime (for example, in a particular statute or doctrinal publication). The preceptual usage of "principle" is quite abstract relative to other precepts such as rules and direct or general orders. This may be seen as their virtue, as "law in the form of discretion exercisable in accord with general principles may allow decisionmakers to engage in somewhat more context-sensitive exploration of the merits of alternative decisions in varied sets of particular circumstances." Summers, *supra* note 32, at 185.

49. Statute of the International Court of Justice art. 38(1), July 17, 1998, 2187 U.N.T.S. 3.

50. James Crawford, Brownlie's Principles of Public International Law 37 (8th ed. 2012).

51. *See supra* notes 41–48 and accompanying text. Both usages of the term "principles" within general international law have been suggested by other influential writers. *See, e.g.*, J.L. Brierly, The Law of Nations 63 (5th ed. 1955) (describing "a sort of reserve store of principles upon which [the law] has been in the habit of drawing" and referring to "general principles of law" as secondary rules reflecting legal concepts directed at dispute resolution and other enforcement concerns such as "[p]rescription, estoppel, and *res judicata*"); *id.* at 63–64 (describing "general principles of law" as "a source to which international courts have instinctively and properly

exercisable in accord with general principles may allow decisionmakers to engage in somewhat more context-sensitive exploration of the merits of alternative decisions in varied sets of particular circumstances."[52]

Moving now to military necessity, states' doctrinal definitions suggest that states either alternate between these usages of the term "principle" or else have been less than careful about the distinction. Sometimes states suggest that the principle of military necessity serves a preceptual function in the LOAC. For example, states refer to the practical application of the principle of military necessity to factual situations.[53] The U.S. Department of Defense notes that LOAC principles, including military necessity, may be *applied* by combatants during hostilities,[54] serving as a "general guide for conduct during war when no specific rule applies."[55] Other states implicitly characterize military necessity in preceptual terms by

referred to in the past"); GEORG SCHWARZENBERGER, 1 A MANUAL OF INTERNATIONAL LAW 23–24, 29–30 (4th ed. 1960) (referring to "general principles of law recognized by civilized nations" as one of three "law-creating processes . . . whereby rules of positive international law are *created*") (emphasis added). Common examples of these general principles of law are "the principles of consent, reciprocity, equality of states, finality of awards and settlements, the legal validity of agreements, good faith, domestic jurisdiction, and the freedom of the seas." CRAWFORD, *supra* note 50, at 37.

52. SUMMERS, *supra* note 32, at 185.

53. *See, e.g.*, U.K. AIDE MEMOIRE, *supra* note 21, at 1 ("All personnel must be aware of the basic rules of the law of armed conflict, including the *practical application* of the principles of military necessity, proportionality, distinction and humanity.") (emphasis added). Prominent commentators and publicists sometimes refer to military necessity as a "rule." *See, e.g.*, HUM. RTS. WATCH, *supra* note 30, at 3, 24, 30; Brill, *supra* note 30, at 13. Some refer to military necessity using rule-like language. *See, e.g.*, HUM. RTS. WATCH, *supra* note 30, at 34 (quoting Benjamin Kastan, *Autonomous Weapons Systems: A Coming Legal "Singularity"?*, 2013 U. ILL. J.L. TECH. POL'Y 45 (2013)).

54. *See* U.S. LOAC MANUAL, *supra* note 21, at 51 ("When no specific rule applies, the principles of the law of war form the general guide for conduct during war."); *id.* at 56 (noting military necessity "is a difficult concept to define and *apply*") (emphasis added); *see also* U.S. ARMY LOAC MANUAL, *supra* note 21, at 1-5 ("When no specific rule applies, the principles of LOAC form the general guide for conduct during war.") (citation omitted); *id.* at 1-8 (referring to the "difficulties in applying military necessity").

55. U.S. LOAC MANUAL, *supra* note 21, at 51; *see also id.* at 51 ("When no specific rule applies, the principles of the law of war form the general guide for conduct during war."); *id.* at 56, 57, 58 (identifying other, secondary rules designed to ameliorate the "difficulties of *applying* military necessity") (emphasis added); U.S. ARMY LOAC MANUAL, *supra* note 21, at 1-5, 1-6. Additionally, the Martens Clause, which is included in several important international instruments, states that situations not covered by treaty law remain governed by principles of international law. *See, e.g.*, Hague IV, *supra* note 10, pmbl. para. 8 ("Until a more complete code of the laws of war has been issued, the High Contracting Parties deem it expedient to declare that, in cases not included in the Regulations adopted by them, the inhabitants and the belligerents remain under the protection and the rule of the principles of the law of nations, as they result from the usages established among civilized peoples, from the laws of humanity, and the dictates of public conscience.").

situating it among other principles understood to serve preceptual functions.[56] For example, many states place military necessity within a group of core or foundational principles, including distinction and proportionality, both of which are thought to serve a preceptual role in the LOAC.[57] Furthermore, inclusion of military necessity within doctrinal publications intended to serve combatants with practical guidance about how lawfully to engage in warfare suggests, at least in part, that it has a preceptual function.[58] Finally, when defining the principle of military necessity, states virtually always use a rule-like structure, that is, they describe it as a principle that "permits," "justifies," or grants a "right" to combatants to engage in certain conduct.[59]

At other times, states describe military necessity as serving a more conceptual, abstract role. In this way, states appear to understand military necessity as a motivating force, interest, or purpose underlying the LOAC rather than (or perhaps in addition to) a preceptual role.[60] For example, Canada signals this view of military

56. It is debatable whether and to what extent other LOAC "principles" such as distinction, proportionality, and humanity serve a preceptual role or, alternatively, serve a more abstract role as animating interests that drive the development of concrete LOAC rules. For example, the International Court of Justice refers to distinction and the prohibition against unnecessary suffering as the LOAC's two "cardinal principles," which arguably suggests the latter. *See* Legality of the Threat or Use of Nuclear Weapons, Advisory Opinion, 1996 I.C.J. 226, 257 (July 8). On the other hand, states' doctrinal definitions suggest perceptual roles for some of these principles, particularly distinction and proportionality. *See infra* notes 75–77 and accompanying text. This question is particularly relevant with regard to the principle of humanity, as many of the considerations addressed to military necessity in this and other subsections apply equally or similarly to humanity. *See infra* notes 63 and accompanying text.

57. *See, e.g.*, U.S. LOAC Manual, *supra* note 21, at 50 (identifying military necessity, a foundational principle of the LOAC, as "a recognized *part* of international law") (emphasis added); *see also* Statute of the International Court of Justice art. 38(1)(c) (stating that general principles of law are a "source" of applicable law for the court); U.S. LOAC Manual, *supra* note 21, at 50 (referring to military necessity as one of the "general principles of law" recognized in Article 38(1)(c) of the Statute of the International Court of Justice). This raises a deeper philosophical question, which will not be explored further in this chapter, of what is meant by "law" or what it means for some rule, principle, concept, or notion to be "part" of the law. *See generally The Nature of Law*, Stan. Encyc. of Phil. (last updated Aug. 7, 2013), https://plato.stanford.edu/entries/lawphil-nature.

58. *See, e.g.*, U.S. LOAC Manual, *supra* note 21, at 1 ("The purpose of this manual is to provide information on the law of war to DoD personnel responsible for implementing the law of war and executing military operations."); Australia LOAC Manual, *supra* note 21, at iii (asserting that the manual "promulgates guidance to commanders for the planning and conduct of [Australian Defence Force (ADF)] operations in armed conflict and details responsibilities and obligations for ADF members").

59. Section II.B *infra* examines the significance of states' articulation of military necessity as a right, justification, or permission.

60. As such, military necessity serves as one in a "scheme of interests or goals or principles the [LOAC] can be taken to serve or express or exemplify." *See* Dworkin, *supra* note 36, at 52.

necessity by identifying it not as a principle but rather as a LOAC "concept."[61] Other states suggest this view of military necessity by conceptually separating it from other, less abstract (and thus more practicable or functional) LOAC principles. The U.S. Department of Defense, for instance, identifies military necessity as a "foundational" principle, which (in conjunction with the other foundational principles of humanity and honor) gives rise to the other LOAC principles of distinction and proportionality.[62] Perhaps most significantly, states often note the inextricability and interdependence of military necessity with other foundational LOAC principles, such as the principles of unnecessary suffering and humanity.[63] The interdependence of these foundational principles suggests that states, despite some indications to the contrary, understand military necessity (along with humanity) as a motivating interest rather than as a preceptual rule that may be applied in isolation from other LOAC principles.[64]

It should be noted that a clear majority of prominent LOAC scholars understands military necessity in this latter sense rather than as serving a preceptual or

61. CANADA LOAC MANUAL, *supra* note 21, at 2-1. But other Canadian military doctrinal publications refer to military necessity as a LOAC "principle." *See supra* note 21 and accompanying text.

62. U.S. LOAC MANUAL, *supra* note 21, at 50; *see also* U.S. ARMY LOAC MANUAL, *supra* note 21, at 1-6.

63. *See, e.g.*, AUSTRALIA LOAC MANUAL, *supra* note 21, at 2-2 ("The three principles [of military necessity, avoidance of unnecessary suffering, and proportionality] must be considered together in that no single principle can be considered in isolation from the other two. In other words, whilst military necessity may justify a particular action, the action may cause unnecessary suffering including civilian death, or damage may be totally disproportionate to the military advantage to be gained. If so, the action should not proceed because the military necessity is outweighed by proportionality and humanitarian considerations."); CANADA LOAC MANUAL, *supra* note 21, at 2-1 (cautioning that military necessity "is not a concept that can be considered in isolation" and that humanity is "related to the concept of [military] necessity and implicitly contained within it"); U.S. LOAC MANUAL, *supra* note 21, at 51 (LOAC "principles work as interdependent and reinforcing parts of a coherent system."); U.S. ARMY LOAC MANUAL, *supra* note 21, at 1-6 (referring to military necessity, humanity, and honor as "[t]hree interdependent principles").

64. In his philosophical works on the nature of law, *see supra* notes 41–48 and accompanying text, Dworkin notes that the difference between rules and principles may not always be clear. *See* Dworkin, *supra* note 41, at 28. In this regard, and as already noted, states may not have these considerations and distinctions in the forefront of their minds when defining military necessity in doctrinal publications. Furthermore, as a practical matter, not much may depend alone on the characterization of a particular precept as either a rule or principle. *See id.* The practical effect of "applying" it may be the same. Similarly, not much may depend solely on the characterization of military necessity as serving a preceptual role or, alternatively, a role as a conceptual, motivating interest or driving force. This chapter argues that the lack of conceptual clarity in this regard in combination with other underanalyzed aspects of the Lieber/Nuremberg model of military necessity justify reformulation of its doctrinal definition.

functional role. On this view, military necessity primarily constitutes an overarching, conceptual force that, along with the interest of humanity, animates and drives the formation of the LOAC.[65] Accordingly, military necessity serves no preceptual function, either as a permission to combatants to engage in otherwise lawful hostilities,[66] or as a limitation that imposes additional restrictions on combatants above what is required by the other concrete rules contained in the LOAC.[67]

This similarity of thought among scholars notwithstanding, the question of how states understand military necessity's doctrinal role remains relevant. First, even if states understand military necessity as *generally* not serving a preceptual function, this is not to say that combatants will never have to "apply" it during hostilities. For example, the Martens Clause, which is contained in a number of widelyratified LOAC treaties, directs armed conflict participants to apply "principles of international law" when a treaty provides no specific rule to govern a particular circumstance.[68] In such a situation, combatants would presumably have to apply the principles of military necessity and humanity in good faith to come to a reasonable legal decision as to permissible means and methods of warfare.[69] In other words, while the best view of the principle of military necessity

65. *See* Schmitt, *supra* note 1, at 798 (The LOAC "represents a carefully thought out balance between the principles of military necessity and humanity. Every one of its rules constitutes a dialectical compromise between these two opposing forces."). On this view, military necessity "constitutes the IHL mechanism for safeguarding" states' interest in pursuing "vital national interests" by ensuring "legal norms [that do] not unduly restrict their freedom of action on the battlefield, such that national interests might be affected." *Id.* at 799. Put another way, military necessity constitutes one of "two driving forces energizing the motion of" the LOAC. Dinstein, *supra* note 16, at 8. It "lubricates the wheels" of the LOAC, and accounts within the LOAC's specific rules for "the exigencies of war impelling each Belligerent Party to take the requisite steps to engage the enemy and defeat it." *Id.*

66. *See* Michael N. Schmitt, *Wound, Capture, or Kill: A Reply to Ryan Goodman's "The Power to Kill or Capture Enemy Combatants,"* 24 Eur. J. Int'l L. 855, 857 (2013) (asserting that military necessity (as well as its counterpart humanity) "is not in itself a separate prescriptive norm with independent valence").

67. *See* Schmitt, *supra* note 1, at 799; *see also* W. Hays Parks, *Part IX of the ICRC Direct Participation in Hostilities Study: No Mandate, No Expertise, and Legally Incorrect*, 42 N.Y.U. J. Int'l L. & Pol. 769, 804 (2010) ("There is no 'military necessity' determination requirement for an individual soldier to engage an enemy combatant or a civilian determined to be taking a direct part in hostilities, any more than there is for a soldier to attack an enemy tank.").

68. *See, e.g.*, Hague IV, *supra* note 10, pmbl. para. 8; AP I, *supra* note 8, art. 1(2); *see also supra* note 55.

69. *Cf.* Schmitt, *supra* note 1, at 800 ("The Martens Clause demonstrates that IHL is excluded from any positivist assertion to the effect that all which is not forbidden is international law is permitted. . . . Consequently, the mere absence of an express IHL rule on point does not necessarily justify an action on the basis of military necessity; actions in warfare must equally reflect respect for humanity.").

may be that it does not serve as a precept to be routinely consulted and applied during hostilities, it may nonetheless maintain a minimal preceptual role insofar as situations arise in which combatants lack a relevant concrete rule and thus must endeavor to balance the forces of military necessity and humanity to guide their conduct.[70] Second, and in light of the previous point, notwithstanding nearly universal support from publicists and others for the notion that military necessity serves as an overarching interest for the LOAC, states persist in articulate and discussing military necessity in ways that suggest, at least in part, that it has a preceptual function. The implications of this doctrinal decision by states warrant further exploration.

B. Does Military Necessity Grant a "Right," "Permission," or "Justification"?

Another common feature of military necessity as articulated by states (and based on the Lieber/Nuremberg model) is its textual characterization as a right,[71] permission,[72] or justification.[73] This may be contrasted with how states characterize

70. This raises the question of how individual combatants engage in the practice of applying the LOAC during hostilities. *See infra* Section III.

71. *See* U.S. LOAC MANUAL, *supra* note 21, at 60 (implying that applying military necessity during hostilities constitutes the "[e]xercise of a [r]ight"); CANADA MILITARY DOCTRINE, *supra* note 21, at 2-15 ("Military necessity is defined as the principle whereby a belligerent has the *right* to apply any measures that are required to bring about the successful conclusion of a military operation and that are not forbidden by the LOAC.") (emphasis added); FRANCE LOAC MANUAL, *supra* note 21, at 8; MINISTRY OF DEF., JSP 383, THE JOINT SERVICE MANUAL OF THE LAW OF ARMED CONFLICT 5 (amend. 3 Sept. 2010) (U.K.) [hereinafter U.K. LOAC MANUAL AMENDMENT 3] (referring to military necessity as "the principle whereby a belligerent has the *right* to apply any measures which are required to bring about the successful conclusion of a military operation and which are not forbidden by the [LOAC]") (emphasis added); NORTH ATLANTIC TREATY ORG., AAP-06, NATO GLOSSARY OF TERMS AND DEFINITIONS 73 (2017) [hereinafter NATO GLOSSARY] ("the principle whereby a belligerent has the *right*") (emphasis added).

72. AUSTRALIA LOAC MANUAL, *supra* note 21, at 2-2 (Military necessity "*permits* the killing of enemy combatants and other persons whose death is unavoidable. It *permits* the destruction of property if that destruction is imperatively demanded by the necessities of war.") (emphasis added); GERMANY LOAC MANUAL, *supra* note 21, at 25 ("According to the principle of military necessity, all military measures are *permissible* in armed conflict which are required for the successful execution of military operations in order to engage an enemy, provided that these measures are not forbidden by [the] LOAC.") (emphasis added); U.K. LEGAL SUPPORT DOCTRINE, *supra* note 21, at 23 ("Military necessity *permits* a state engaged in an armed conflict to use only that degree and kind of force, not otherwise prohibited by the LOAC, that is required to achieve the legitimate purpose of the conflict, namely the complete or partial submission of the enemy at the earliest possible moment with the minimum expenditure of life and resources.") (emphasis added).

73. U.S. LOAC MANUAL, *supra* note 21, at 52 ("Military necessity may be defined as the principle that *justifies* the use of all measures needed to defeat the enemy as quickly and efficiently as

other LOAC principles, namely, as limitations, prohibitions, or obligations.[74] For example, the principle of avoiding unnecessary suffering is said to *forbid* "the use of means or methods of warfare which are calculated to cause suffering which is excessive in the circumstances."[75] Distinction *obligates* parties to an armed conflict and armed conflict participants "to distinguish between legitimate military targets and civilian objects and the civilian population."[76] The principle of proportionality is characterized as a *limitation* on attacks against lawful targets, prohibiting those attacks "which may be expected to cause incidental loss of civilian life, injury to civilians, damage to civilian objects, or a combination thereof, which would be excessive in relation to the concrete and direct military advantage anticipated."[77]

possible that are not prohibited by the [LOAC]") (emphasis added); U.S. Army LOAC Manual, *supra* note 21, at 1-6, 1-7; Australia LOAC Manual, *supra* note 21, at 2-2 ("The principle of military necessity states that a combatant is *justified* in using those measures, not forbidden by international law, which are indispensable for securing complete submission of an enemy at the soonest moment.") (emphasis added); Canada LOAC Manual, *supra* note 21, at 2-1 ("Military necessity is related to the primary aim of armed conflict—the complete submission of the enemy at the earliest possible moment with the least possible expenditure of personnel and resources. The concept of military necessity *justifies* the application of force not forbidden by International Law, to the extent necessary, for the realization of the purpose of armed conflict.") (emphasis added).

74. However, as will be discussed, semantics play a role here, as some LOAC principles may be articulated in both prohibitive and permissive ways. *See infra* notes 94–97 and accompanying text. For example, distinction may be said to prohibit the targeting of civilians but in another sense may be said to "permit" the targeting of combatants.

75. Australia LOAC Manual, *supra* note 21, at 2-4. Similarly, "[h]umanity may be defined as the principle that forbids the infliction of suffering, injury, or destruction unnecessary to accomplish a legitimate military purpose." U.S. LOAC Manual, *supra* note 21, at 58; U.S. Army LOAC Manual, *supra* note 21, at 1-6, 1-8. "Humanity forbids the infliction of suffering, injury, or destruction not actually necessary for the accomplishment of legitimate military purposes." U.K. LOAC Manual, *supra* note 21, at 23.

76. Canada LOAC Manual, *supra* note 21, at 2-2. "Distinction . . . [requires states] to maintain the distinction between combatants and non-combatants or civilian and military personnel" and to "distinguish[] between legitimate military targets and civilian objects." Australia LOAC Manual, *supra* note 21, at 2-7. Distinction "requires that belligerents maintain the clear distinction between armed forces and civilians taking no direct part in hostilities; that is, between combatants and non-combatants, and between objects that might legitimately be attacked and those protected from attack." *Id.* "[D]istinction will be made at all times between civilian population and combatants and between civilian assets and military objectives and, consequently, operations will be directed only against military objectives." Argentina LOAC Manual, *supra* note 21, at 25. Distinction is an "obligation" to "distinguish between civilian objects and military targets." U.K. LOAC Manual, *supra* note 21, at 24. Distinction "requires a force to identify and differentiate between civilians and combatants and between valid military targets, which may be lawfully attacked, and civilian objects, which are not valid targets." NATO Legal Deskbook, *supra* note 21, at 249.

77. U.K. LOAC Manual, *supra* note 21, at 25 n.15. "Proportionality may be defined as the principle that even where one is justified in acting, one must not act in a way that is unreasonable or

States articulate military necessity in terms that suggest it functions as a belligerent right, permission, or justification for certain battlefield conduct.[78] This potentially raises two separate but related questions. The first is whether the LOAC provides belligerent parties, and by extension the individuals who fight on their behalf, with legal authority to engage in hostilities.[79] If it does, then the second question is whether military necessity is wholly or partially the source of that legal authority. If the LOAC does not supply legal authority to fight, then one is left to wonder how states' use of the words "right," "permission," and "justification" should be interpreted.[80]

The question whether the LOAC contains authorities to use military force is currently receiving significant attention from scholars.[81] Adil Haque recently argued against such legal authority derived from the LOAC. On this view, the LOAC,

excessive." U.S. LOAC MANUAL, *supra* note 21, at 60; U.S. ARMY LOAC MANUAL, *supra* note 21, at 1-11. "The principle of proportionality requires that the losses resulting from a military action should not be excessive in relation to the expected military advantage." U.K. LOAC MANUAL, *supra* note 21, at 25. The principle of proportionality "means that attacks on military objectives which may be expected to cause incidental loss of civilian life, injury to civilians, damage to civilian objects, or a combination of these, which and would be excessive in relation to the concrete and direct military advantage anticipated are prohibited." GERMANY LOAC MANUAL, *supra* note 21, at 53. "Proportionality requires that the incidental loss of civilian life or damage to civilian objects, the humanitarian interest, must not be excessive compared to the concrete and direct military advantage anticipated, the military interest." NATO LEGAL DESKBOOK, *supra* note 21, at 250.

78. *See, e.g.*, U.S. LOAC MANUAL, *supra* note 21, at 15 (The LOAC "may be viewed as permissive or even as a source of authority. For example, the principle of military necessity in the customary law of war may be viewed as justifying or permitting certain acts.") (citations omitted).

79. The question whether the LOAC provides armed conflict participants such as combatants with legal authority to use military force must be distinguished from use of force questions under other legal regimes. Service members, as lawfully designated agents of their state's armed forces, act as state agents empowered to carry out the state's objectives, including the use of military force. States, as sovereigns and as parties to the U.N. Charter and subjects of customary international law on the use of force, in certain circumstances have or may be given authority to use armed force. These questions refer to domestic law and the *jus ad bellum*, or the international law pertaining to the use of force. In contrast, the present question is whether the LOAC provides legal authority to states and their armed forces members (and, even more controversially, non-stated armed groups engaged in armed conflict and their members) to use lethal and nonlethal force during armed conflict.

80. This chapter will sidestep the significant and interesting question whether and how "justification" is legally distinct in meaning from "permission" or a "right." This chapter treats these three terms as roughly equivalent, that is, as potentially serving an authorizing function.

81. *See, e.g.*, ADIL HAQUE, LAW AND MORALITY AT WAR ch. 2 (2017); Janina Dill, *Towards a Moral Division of Labour Between IHL and IHRL During the Conduct of Hostilities*, *in* LAW APPLICABLE TO ARMED CONFLICT (Ziv Bohrer, Janina Dill, & Helen Duffy eds., 2020); Eliav Lieblich, *The Facilitative Function of* Jus in Bello, 30 EUR. J. INT'L L. 321 (2019); Sean Aughey & Aurel Sari, *Targeting and Detention in Non-International Armed Conflict:* Serdar Mohammed *and the Limits of Human Rights Convergence*, 91 INT'L L. STUD. 60 (2015).

particularly "the law of targeting and attack[,] contains no [legal] permissions but instead contains only prohibitions."[82] As a textual matter, international law provides lawful combatants with "the *right* to participate directly in hostilities."[83] However, on Haque's view, this does not amount to a legal privilege or liberty in the Hohfeldian sense,[84] but instead only constitutes a limited immunity from criminal prosecution by foreign states under those states' domestic criminal law.[85] Accordingly, the so-called "combatant's privilege" is not a license to kill in war, nor does it suggest that killing in war is presumptively lawful.[86] Rather, "killing in war, as elsewhere, is presumptively *criminal*"[87] and combatants "[o]ften . . . have committed crimes, albeit crimes for which they may not be prosecuted."[88] Thus, the

82. Haque, *supra* note 81, at 20. Haque largely avoids the permissive implications of LOAC rules related to detention and occupation. He appears to acknowledge that the LOAC may provide legal authority to use military force in these contexts. *Id.* at 31 n.43 (citing GC III, *supra* note 8, art. 21—"The Detaining Power may subject prisoners of war to internment. It may impose on them the obligation of not leaving, beyond certain limits, the camp where they are interned, or if the said camp is fenced in, of not going outside its perimeter."—and GC IV, *supra* note 8, art. 42—"The internment or placing in assigned residence of protected persons may be ordered only if the security of the Detaining Power makes it absolutely necessary.").

83. AP I, *supra* note 8, art. 43(2) (emphasis added).

84. A "Hohfeldian privilege" derives from Wesley Hohfeld's analytic system concerning the form of rights. *See generally* Wesley Newcomb Hohfeld, *Some Fundamental Legal Conceptions as Applied in Judicial Reasoning*, 23 Yale L.J. 16 (1913), *reprinted in* Wesley Newcomb Hohfeld, Fundamental Legal Conceptions as Applied in Judicial Reasoning and Other Legal Essays 23 (Walter Wheeler Cook ed., 1923). A person has a "privilege" (or "liberty") to do *X* if and only if he has no duty not to do *X*. Haque argues that, since international law nowhere prohibits anyone (either combatants or civilians) from participating in hostilities, it cannot be the case that combatants have a Hohfeldian privilege to participate in hostilities. Furthermore, the combatant's "right" to participate in hostilities also cannot be understood as a Hohfeldian claim-right. *See generally* Hohfeld, *supra*. No other subject of the LOAC, for example, "a combatant's own state, the enemy belligerent[,] or other individuals[,] has a duty to not impede a combatant's participation in war." Dill, *supra* note 81, at 8.

85. *See* Haque, *supra* note 81, 26. Haque stresses that legal immunities have a legal function and moral foundation than differs markedly from legal permissions, exemptions from legal prohibitions, justifications, excuses, and denials of responsibility. *Id.* at 27. In contrast to these others, "a legal immunity is a bar to criminal prosecution that applies irrespective of the wrongdoing and blameworthiness of the actor." *Id.*

86. *Id.* at 27.

87. *Id.* (emphasis added).

88. *See id.* at 29. Here Haque is speaking of lawful combatants who kill "in pursuit of an unjust cause." But under Haque's logic, this argument appears to apply equally to lawful combatants who kill in pursuit of a just cause.

LOAC serves solely a restrictive legal function and does not provide combatants with legal authority or permission to fight.[89]

This view of the LOAC as only restrictive and as never providing legal authority to use military force encounters difficulty when faced with some textual and practical aspects of the LOAC. As already noted, the widely (although not universally) ratified Additional Protocol I to the Geneva Conventions of 1949 explicitly affords combatants with "the *right* to participate directly in hostilities."[90] This aligns with specific LOAC rules, particularly in the context of detention and internment, which appear to grant legal authority to belligerent parties.[91] For example, the 1949 Geneva Convention Relative to the Treatment of Prisoners of War provides that a "Detaining Power may subject prisoners of war to internment."[92] Furthermore, as Janina Dill recently noted, the fact that the LOAC provides for positive obligations to act—for example, to take precautions in attack—may reasonably lead states and combatants to believe that compliance with such obligations entails legal authority to engage in hostilities.[93] Related to this debate, as pointed out by Eliav Lieblich, is the special dialectic between prohibitions and permissions in law, which plays a role in how the LOAC is interpreted.[94] For example, Article 48(1) of Additional Protocol I provides that belligerent parties "shall direct their operations only against military objectives."[95] In deciding whether the LOAC is permissive or instead only prohibitive, it may matter which language in Article 48(1) one emphasizes: "shall direct" or "only against."[96] Thus, "prohibitive law might be understood formally as also implying what is allowed."[97] Staying within the legal realist lens, if the LOAC were understood to be only prohibitive (and not permissive), we would expect states—at least the ones with the most powerful militaries and that are relatively frequently involve in armed conflict situations—to argue for its limited applicability and we would expect human rights advocates to argue for its wide applicability; however, the opposite is usually true.[98] On this view,

89. Haque's argument also relies significantly on the conceptual distinction between the *jus ad bellum* and the *jus in bellum*. This issue is addressed in Section II.D *infra*.

90. AP I, *supra* note 8, art. 43(2) (emphasis added).

91. Haque largely brushes these provisions aside. *See supra* note 82.

92. GC III, *supra* note 8, art. 21; *see also* GC IV, *supra* note 8, art. 42; *supra* note 82.

93. Dill, *supra* note 81, at 17.

94. Lieblich, *supra* note 81, at 329. Indeed, one's view of the nature of the LOAC in this regard may be informed by how one refers to the regime: as the LOAC or as international humanitarian law. *Id.*

95. AP I, *supra* note 8, art. 48(1).

96. Lieblich, *supra* note 81, at 329–30.

97. *Id.* at 330.

98. *Id.* at 331.

"permissions are in fact implied in the law, even though they may not be stated expressly. [For example,] the duty of distinction channels lawful violence, exposing military objectives to attack while shielding civilians."[99]

States suggest a permissive view of the LOAC in their military doctrine and elsewhere.[100] The U.S. Department of Defense asserts that combatants have "certain *rights*," including "to engage in hostilities,"[101] and members of armed forces of a party to an armed conflict "receive [a] general license to commit belligerent acts."[102] In public speeches, U.S. government officials have referred to the authorities afforded to combatants by the LOAC. For example, in a 2012 speech, the General Counsel of the U.S. Central Intelligence Agency, after noting the well-established legal authority to use force that derives from the *jus ad bellum*, made the remarkable assertion that "[t]he existence of an armed conflict might also provide an additional justification for the use of force under international law."[103] Other states show support for a rights-based view of combatants' participation in armed conflict. For example, the Canadian Ministry of Defense defines "combatants" in part as being "*entitled* to take a direct part in armed conflict and, in particular, to engage in hostilities."[104] Furthermore, in a recent high-profile military detention case in the United Kingdom, *Al-Waheed v. Ministry of Defence*, the government argued that the LOAC provides authority to state armed forces, among other things, to detain enemy combatants and civilians under certain circumstances.[105] It must be emphasized that it would be a significant overstatement to say that there is anything close to uniformity on this matter, or even that states have fully thought through the implications and expressed a coherent, overarching theory of the LOAC as affording belligerent rights to use military

99. Aughey & Sari, *supra* note 81, at 93.

100. Additionally, the International Committee of the Red Cross identifies art. 43(2) of Additional Protocol I as a rule of customary international law, 1 ICRC Customary IHL Study, *supra* note 9, at 11–14, and points to numerous articulations of state practice. 2 Int'l Comm. of the Red Cross, Customary International Humanitarian Law: Practice 78–86 (Jean-Marie Henchaerts & Louise Doswald-Beck eds., 2005). In its famous report on the notion of direct participation in hostilities, the ICRC asserted that the LOAC "provides an express 'right'" to combatants in an armed conflict to directly participate in hostilities. Int'l Comm. of the Red Cross, Interpretive Guidance on the Notion of Direct Participation in Hostilities under International Humanitarian Law 83 (Nils Melzer ed., 2009).

101. U.S. LOAC Manual, *supra* note 21, at 105 (emphasis added); *see also* U.S. Army LOAC Manual, *supra* note 21, at 1-12.

102. U.S. LOAC Manual, *supra* note 21, at 108.

103. Stephen W. Preston, Gen. Couns., U.S. Cent. Intelligence Agency, *Remarks Concerning the CIA and the Rule of Law* (Apr. 10, 2012), https://www.cia.gov/news-information/speeches-testimony/2012-speeches-testimony/cia-general-counsel-harvard.html.

104. *See, e.g.*, Canada LOAC Manual, *supra* note 21, at 3-1 (emphasis added).

105. Al-Waheed v. Ministry of Def. [2017] UKSC 2, [2014] EWHC 2714 (QB).

force.[106] Nevertheless, it may fairly be said that there is some evidence that states are open to the idea of legal permissions deriving from the LOAC.

Even if the LOAC is not merely restrictive but also offers authority to use military force, it must be determined the role that military necessity plays in such authorization. As already noted, states articulate military necessity in a way that expressly provides for a right, permission, or justification to use military measures or force.[107] A reasonable interpretation of this language is that military necessity serves a permissive function, authorizing states and their combatants engaged in armed conflict to use "those measures of warfare that are reasonably required for the effective conduct of hostilities."[108] In other words, it could be argued that, if the LOAC is permissive, military necessity as articulated by states constitutes the source of such authority.

This view of military necessity is of course controversial and raises several challenges. First, military necessity may not be "sufficiently precise to provide detailed guidance on what are permissible aims, means and methods of warfare, and what are not"[109]—and given the dynamic and evolving nature of combat and of international security, it likely could never do so. Thus, the argument that military necessity confers a legal privilege on combatants requires a more sophisticated argument. This typically takes the form of arguing that military necessity is "woven into the fabric" of the LOAC by "feed[ing] into the creation of positive rules as a permissive principle."[110] As such, legal permissions are implied within the LOAC. For example, distinction, while usually framed as a prohibitive principle,[111] also "channels lawful violence, exposing military objectives to attack while shielding civilians."[112] According to this argument, "the permissive aspect of the principle of military necessity confers . . . Hohfeldian liberties on States party to an armed

106. For example, if the LOAC is indeed permissive (that is, force-authorizing), then the principle of equal application suggests that armed conflict fighters who are part of non-state groups also have the *right* to engage in hostilities. Furthermore, what implications does a permissive theory of the LOAC have for other legal regimes that may apply during military operations, such as the *jus ad bellum* or international human rights law?

107. *See supra* notes 71–73 and accompanying text.

108. Nils Melzer, Targeted Killing in International Law 279–80 (2008).

109. Aughey & Sari, *supra* note 81, at 93.

110. *Id.*

111. *See supra* note 76 and accompanying text.

112. Aughey & Sari, *supra* note 81, at 93; *see also id.* at 93–94 ("This permissive element of the duty of distinction is confirmed by the longstanding, consistent and general practice of States of exercising their liberty to conduct status-based operations against enemy military objectives within the limits laid down by the law of armed conflict."); *supra* notes 94–97 and accompanying text.

conflict *within* the framework of the law of armed conflict."[113] Thus, on this view, military necessity is an integral part of a larger system that in its sum affords belligerent parties and their combatants a Hohfeldian liberty to use military force to defeat the enemy.[114]

It must be acknowledged that scholars generally reject the force-authorizing view of military necessity.[115] Of course, this rejection alone does not preclude states from conceptualizing military necessity as a legal principle capable of being applied during hostilities and conferring a Hohfeldian privilege upon combatants. Nevertheless, as already noted, the evidence that states take this view is conflicting. On the one hand, states that articulate military necessity virtually always characterize it as a right or permission.[116] The U.S. Department of Defense asserts that the LOAC "may be viewed as permissive or even as a source of authority," for example "the principle of military necessity . . . may be viewed as justifying or permitting certain acts."[117] On the other hand, states assert that military necessity does not function in isolation but rather must be applied in conjunction with the principle of humanity.[118] The intertwined nature of these two LOAC principles suggests the complex, conceptual role attributed to military necessity by many scholars. Additionally, as will be discussed in more detail subsequently, the precise conduct that a rights-granting principle of military necessity authorizes is far from clear. It thus lacks the definition or clarity one might expect or desire in an authorization, especially one included within military doctrine designed to guide battlefield conduct. Perhaps relatedly, and again as will be discussed more fully, a fair argument may be made that military necessity does not authorize anything that is not already permitted (or, if one likes, not otherwise prohibited) under other rules of the LOAC.

For these reasons, and setting aside the question whether the LOAC generally contains legal permissions or authorities, the preferred interpretation of the

113. Aughey & Sari, *supra* note 81, at 110.

114. Some would say that the legal authority to do what is militarily necessary lies deeper than the LOAC and even precedes it. On this view, such authority constitutes an essential component of state sovereignty. Accordingly, the legal framework recognized in the *Lotus* case suggest the correct answer to the permissive-restrictive debate. *See* S.S. "Lotus" (Fr. v. Turk.), 1927 P.C.I.J. (ser. A) No. 10, at 14 (Sept. 7) ("The rules of law binding upon States . . . emanate from their own free will as expressed in conventions or by usages generally accepted as expressing principles of law and established in order to regulate the relations between these co-existing independent communities or with a view to the achievement of common aims.") My thanks to Professor Sean Watts for sharing this insightful point.

115. Some prominent scholars who take this view define military necessity without reference to a "right," "permission," or "justification." *See, e.g.*, Schmitt, *supra* note 1, at 799; Dinstein, *supra* note 16, at 8–10. *But see* Aughey & Sari, *supra* note 81.

116. *See supra* notes 71–73 and accompanying text.

117. U.S. LOAC Manual, *supra* note 21, at 15.

118. *See supra* notes 63–64 and accompanying text.

principle of military necessity, at least for the purposes of states in articulating military LOAC doctrine that is useful for service members, is that it is not the source of legal authority to use force or engage in hostilities. It is better thought of as a meta-principle or overarching interest of the LOAC.[119] Military necessity and humanity thus act as guiding forces, shaping the development and in some cases interpretation of the LOAC. Notwithstanding this interim conclusion, it is worth continuing this exploration of states' definitions of military necessity. Doing so highlights additional conceptual and practical challenges, and thus raises further questions as to whether including these definitions advances military doctrine's primary purpose: to provide service members with clear and concise guidance on what the LOAC requires, allows, and prohibits.

C. Broad and Undefined Terminology: "Any Measures" or "Force"

States often articulate military necessity using broad, sweeping language.[120] The principle is said to permit "all measures needed to defeat the enemy as quickly and efficiently as possible,"[121] as well as to justify "the application of force" required to ensure "the complete submission of the enemy at the earliest possible moment with the least possible expenditure of personnel and resources."[122] Put another (equally broad) way, military necessity constitutes a "right . . . to use the degree of

119. *See supra* note 65 and accompanying text.

120. It must be acknowledged that some states articulate military necessity in much narrower terms. *See, e.g.*, ARGENTINA LOAC MANUAL, *supra* note 21, at 24–25 ("All combat activity must be justified for military reasons; activities that are not militarily necessary are prohibited. It is forbidden to attack peaceful civilians or those who are out of combat, because this does not obtain a military advantage. . . . Any action taken to destroy enemy assets and required by military necessity has to comport with the principles of distinction and proportionality. One cannot resort to military necessity as an excuse for laziness, indifference or unprofessional behavior."); COLOMBIA LOAC MANUAL, *supra* note 23, at 37 (Necessity "implies that all combat activity must be justified for military reasons, for it prohibits activities that are not militarily necessity."); *id.* at 88 ("The concept of military necessity contains in itself an important element of restriction: only the force necessary to comply with the military purposes; any use of force that exceeds that objective goes against military necessity."). Other states are inconsistent in the way they define military necessity. *See supra* notes 71–73 (states defining military necessity differently in doctrinal publications); *see also infra* note 161.

121. U.S. LOAC MANUAL, *supra* note 21, at 52; U.S. ARMY LOAC MANUAL, *supra* note 21, at 1-7; *see also* AUSTRALIA LOAC MANUAL, *supra* note 21, at 2-2 ("those measures . . . indispensable for securing complete submission of an enemy at the soonest moment"); CANADA MILITARY DOCTRINE, *supra* note 21, at 2-15 ("the right to apply any measures that are required to bring about the successful conclusion of a military operation and that are not forbidden by the LOAC").

122. CANADA LOAC MANUAL, *supra* note 21, at 2-1.

force that is . . . necessary in order to achieve the purpose of the conflict—namely, partial or total submission of the enemy at the lowest human, economic and temporal cost."[123]

In the LOAC, the term "hostilities" embraces all forms of hostile acts parties to an armed conflict take against one another.[124] It includes attacks as well as activities that precede attacks, such as the planning of operations and operational decision-making process.[125] The parties conduct hostilities by engaging in means and methods of

123. FRANCE LOAC MANUAL, *supra* note 21, at 8. "According to the principle of military necessity, all military measures are permissible in armed conflict which are required for the successful execution of military operations in order to engage an enemy, provided that these measures are not forbidden by [the] LOAC." GERMANY LOAC MANUAL, *supra* note 21, at 25. "Military necessity is . . . the principle whereby a belligerent has the right to apply any measures which are required to bring about the successful conclusion of a military operation and which are not forbidden by the laws of war." U.K. LOAC MANUAL AMENDMENT 3, *supra* note 71, at 5; *see also* NATO GLOSSARY, *supra* note 71, at 73. "Put another way, a state engaged in an armed conflict may use that degree and kind of force, not otherwise prohibited by the law of armed conflict, that is required in order to achieve the legitimate purpose of the conflict, namely the complete or partial submission of the enemy at the earliest possible moment with the minimum expenditure of life and resources." U.K. LOAC MANUAL AMENDMENT 3, *supra* note 71, at 5. It "justifies" certain battlefield conduct, including "destroying and seizing persons and property." U.S. LOAC MANUAL, *supra* note 21, at 52; U.S. ARMY LOAC MANUAL, *supra* note 21, at 1-7; *see also* AUSTRALIA LOAC MANUAL, *supra* note 21, at 2-2 (Military necessity "permits the killing of enemy combatants and other persons whose death is unavoidable" and "permits the destruction of property if" there is a "reasonable connection between the destruction of property and the overcoming of enemy forces."). It also permits "certain incidental harms that inevitably result from" the lawful conduct of hostilities, including civilian death, injury, damage, and destruction that is nonexcessive. *See* U.S. LOAC MANUAL, *supra* note 21, at 53; U.S. ARMY LOAC MANUAL, *supra* note 21, at 1-7; AUSTRALIA LOAC MANUAL, *supra* note 21, at 2-2.

124. DINSTEIN, *supra* note 16, at 2; *see also* MELZER, *supra* note 108, at 269 ("Generally speaking, the concept of hostilities is equivalent to the sum of all conduct regulated by the law of hostilities, namely the choice of and use by the parties to an armed conflict of means and methods of injuring the enemy."); Hague IV, *supra* note 10, annex § 2 (concerning the regulation of "hostilities").

125. MELZER, *supra* note 108, at 270–71. Hostilities may be synonymous with military operations. *Id.*; *see also* INT'L COMM. OF THE RED CROSS, COMMENTARY ON THE ADDITIONAL PROTOCOLS OF 8 JUNE 1977 TO THE GENEVA CONVENTIONS OF 12 AUGUST 1949 § 1943, at 618–19 (Yves Sandoz, Christophe Swinarski, & Bruno Zimmerman eds., 1987) ("It seems that the word 'hostilities' covers not only the time that the civilian actually makes use of a weapon, but also, for example, the time that he is carrying it, as well as situations in which he undertakes hostile acts without using a weapon."); MELZER, *supra* note 108, at 275 ("The preceding examination of positive international law and the legal doctrine allows the conclusion that the concept of 'hostilities' is both narrower than the concept of 'armed conflict' and wider than that of 'attack' and that it approximately corresponds to the sum of all 'military operations' or 'hostile acts' conducted against an adversary by a party to an armed conflict.").

warfare.[126] Means of warfare are weapons and materiel.[127] Methods of warfare are operational modalities, such as attacks, intelligence gathering, and logistics.[128]

In defining military necessity, states do not adopt any of this terminology, but rather use broader, less precise terms: "measures" and "force."[129] The former is not defined within the LOAC, nor is it defined in any of the military manuals that adopt it. Presumably, states adopted this language for two reasons. The first is historical. As already discussed, the origins of the principle of military necessity, in the Lieber Code and subsequent doctrinal publications, as well as in the influential Nuremberg jurisprudence, use these terms to define the principle of military necessity. Specifically, the Lieber Code permits "those measures" indispensable for securing the ends of war,[130] and the Nuremberg jurisprudence refers to "any amount and kind of force."[131] Second, the use of broad terminology coincides with the theme of military necessity as a broadly "permissive" principle. Indeed, the term "measures" is used throughout military manuals to indicate many different kinds of battlefield conduct, including both acts of violence and nonviolence.[132] In establishing doctrine, states may seek maximum breadth and flexibility by choosing the term "measures" precisely for its lack of definition and its lack of status as a term of art.

However, the same cannot be said for those states that refer to "force" in defining military necessity. The term "force" is a term of art; not in the LOAC, but in the *jus ad bellum*. Most significantly, the U.N. Charter, in its foundational rule contained in Article 2(4), prohibits the threat or use of force against other states. This raises the possibility of conflation between the two legal regimes, which generally are thought to remain conceptually separate. This issue is addressed in the next subsection.

126. DINSTEIN, *supra* note 16, at 2.

127. *Id.*

128. *Id.*

129. *See supra* notes 71–73 and 121–23 and accompanying text.

130. *See* Lieber Code, *supra* note 11, arts. 14, 15; *see also* WAR DEP'T, RULES OF LAND WARFARE ¶ 11, at 14 (1914) [hereinafter 1914 RULES OF LAND WARFARE]; WAR DEP'T, FM 27-10, RULES OF LAND WARFARE ¶ 4(a), at 1 (1940) [hereinafter 1940 RULES OF LAND WARFARE]; DEP'T OF THE ARMY, FM 27-10, THE LAW OF LAND WARFARE ¶ 3(a), at 4 (1956); DEP'T OF THE ARMY, FM 27-10, THE LAW OF LAND WARFARE ¶ 3(a), at 4 (change 1 1976).

131. United States v. List (The Hostage Case), Case No. 7 (Feb. 19, 1948), *reprinted in* 11 TRIALS OF WAR CRIMINALS BEFORE THE NUREMBERG MILITARY TRIBUNALS UNDER CONTROL COUNCIL LAW NO. 10, at 757, 1253 (1950).

132. *See, e.g.*, AUSTRALIA LOAC MANUAL, *supra* note 21, at 4-7 ("remedial measures" and "preventive measure"); *id.* at 6-6 ("Belligerents passing through, under or over neutral straits or archipelagic sea lanes are permitted to take defensive measures consistent with their security, including launching and recovery of aircraft, screen formation steaming, and acoustic

D. The Risk of Conflating Legal Regimes: "To Defeat the Enemy"

The "measures" or "force" that military necessity envisions are tied conceptually to a particular end, namely, the submission or defeat of the enemy as quickly and efficiently as possible. The language used by states varies to some extent, but all generally come to the same idea: that military necessity permits the military force required to defeat the opposing armed forces as soon as possible and with the least possible cost.[133]

It is, of course, no surprise that states engaged in armed conflict are concerned with defeating the enemy belligerent's forces. This is the long recognized and studied object of warfare.[134] However, the relationship between the object of war and the LOAC itself may be more complex than it first appears.[135] It is certainly true that the LOAC accounts for both the nature[136] and object of war. However, it accounts for another interest as well, namely, the humanitarian interest in

and electronic surveillance."); *id.* at 6-12 to 6-20 (detailing "measures of naval warfare against trade"); *id.* at 7-1 ("Ruses of war and the employment of measures necessary for obtaining information about the enemy and the enemy country are permissible."); CANADA LOAC MANUAL, *supra* note 21, at 7-1 to 7-2 ("If the neutral state cannot or does not prevent violations of its airspace by one belligerent, opposing belligerents are entitled to take appropriate measures including entry into the neutral airspace to attack the adversary."); *id.* at 7-10 ("A hospital ship that persists, after warning, in violating a condition of its protection renders itself liable to capture or other necessary measures to enforce compliance."); GERMANY LOAC MANUAL, *supra* note 21, at 75 ("In times of international armed conflicts, reprisals are coercive measures that are as such in violation of international law and that are conducted by armed forces against an adversary; such measures are justified in exceptional cases if a Party to a conflict conducts such measures to end violations of international law committed by the adversary.").

133. *See supra* notes 71–73 and 121–23 and accompanying text.

134. U.S. LOAC MANUAL, *supra* note 21, at 16 ("The object of war has been understood to be the submission of the enemy as quickly and efficiently as possible. The military defeat of the enemy in war is intended to advance political objectives. Even where those political objectives are limited, the object of war is nonetheless to ensure the submission of the enemy as quickly and efficiently as possible.") (citations omitted); 1940 RULES OF LAND WARFARE, *supra* note 130 ¶ 22, at 7 ("The object of war is to bring about the complete submission of the enemy as soon as possible by means of regulated violence."); 1914 RULES OF LAND WARFARE, *supra* note 130 ¶ 10, at 14 (same); United States v. von Leeb (The High Command Case), *reprinted in* 11 TRIALS OF WAR CRIMINALS BEFORE THE NUREMBERG MILITARY TRIBUNALS UNDER CONTROL COUNCIL LAW NO. 10, at 485 ("War is the exerting of violence by one state or politically organized body against another. In other words, it is the implementation of a political policy by means of violence.").

135. *See* U.S. LOAC MANUAL, *supra* note 21, at 17 ("The object of war informs the principle of *military necessity* and what uses of force may be justified in war. Nevertheless, the law of war limits what uses of force the object of war may justify.") (citations omitted).

136. *See* U.S. LOAC MANUAL, *supra* note 21, at 17 ("War has been described as a violent clash of interests characterized by the use of force. The fact that violence is an essential element of war has been viewed as important in understanding the nature of war. The violent nature of war has

"alleviating as much as possible the calamities of war."[137] Thus, while the LOAC recognizes states' interest in pursuing the object of war, care must be taken to avoid the misunderstanding that the LOAC generally, and military necessity in particular, justifies the unencumbered pursuit of war aims.

Furthermore, incorporating the defeat or submission of the enemy into the definition of military necessity risks conflating the LOAC with another body of law, namely, the *jus ad bellum*, or the law governing the resort to military force by states. The *jus ad bellum* prohibits the threat or use of force against the territorial integrity or political independence of another state.[138] This general prohibition has exceptions, including the right to use force in self-defense against an armed attack[139] and the authorization of military force by the U.N. Security Council deemed necessary to maintain or restore international peace and security.[140] Uses of force in conformity with these exceptions are limited. Thus, it is a matter of debate whether and to what extent the *jus ad bellum* permits a state to "defeat or ensure the submission of" opposing armed forces.[141] However, notwithstanding the lawfulness of defeating the enemy under the *jus ad bellum*, it is a question to be analyzed under that legal regime rather than under the LOAC.

This re-raises the previously highlighted debate about the nature of the LOAC either as authorizing states and by extension their combatants to use force necessary

also meant to that suffering has been an unfortunate and tragic, but unavoidable consequence of war.") (citations omitted); DEP'T OF THE ARMY, FM 3-24, COUNTERINSURGENCY ¶ 1-1, at 1-1 (2006) (While characteristics of insurgency and counterinsurgency operations "have certainly influenced contemporary conflict[,] . . . warfare in the 21st century retains many of the characteristics it was exhibited since ancient times. Warfare remains a violent clash of interests between organized groups characterized by the use of force. Achieving victory still depends on a group's ability to mobilize support for its political interest . . . and to generate enough violence to achieve political consequences."); MARINE CORPS, MCDP 1, WARFIGHTING 3 (1997) (War is "a violent clash of interests between or among organized groups characterized by the use of military force."); *id.* at 14 ("War is among the greatest horrors known to humanity; it should never be romanticized. The means of war is force, applied in the form of organized violence. It is through the use of violence, or a credible threat of violence, that we compel our enemy to do our will. Violence is an essential element of war, and its immediate result is bloodshed, destruction, and suffering. While the magnitude of violence may vary with the object and means of war, the violent essence of war will never change. Any study of war that neglects this basic truth is misleading and incomplete.").

137. St. Petersburg Declaration, *supra* note 10, pmbl.

138. *See* U.N. Charter art. 2(4).

139. *Id.* art. 51.

140. *Id.* art. 42.

141. *See* YORAM DINSTEIN, WAR, AGGRESSION AND SELF-DEFENCE 262–67 (5th ed. 2012); Eliav Lieblich, *On the Continuous and Concurrent Application of* ad Bellum *and* in Bello *Proportionality, in* NECESSITY AND PROPORTIONALITY IN INTERNATIONAL PEACE AND SECURITY LAW, *supra* note 6, at 45.

to defeat the enemy or, alternatively, as merely tolerating or tacitly acknowledging such force to the extent that it complies with the positive dictates embodied in the LOAC.[142] As noted, Haque argues that the LOAC is only restrictive and contains no legal permissions. In doing so, he relies significantly on the conceptual distinction between the *jus ad bellum* and the *jus in bello*. While the *jus ad bellum* "sometimes authorizes the use of force by states, the *jus in bello* never authorizes acts of violence by armed forces. Under international law, authorization for acts of violence, if any, must come from the *jus ad bellum*."[143] On this view, legal authority derived from the LOAC would lead to illogical results: the *jus ad bellum* might prohibit a use of force while the *jus in bello* "authorized the acts of violence that make up that use of force."[144] Because the *jus in bello* applies equally to just and unjust combatants, the notion of legal authority deriving from the LOAC is logically incompatible with the *jus ad bellum* prohibitions.

This argument is based on the logical distinction between the *jus ad bellum* and the *jus in bello* and an appeal to the coherence of law.[145] But, as Lieblich has shown, it is susceptible to a rebuttal based in legal realism.[146] Viewed through this lens, the LOAC may serve a "facilitative function," for example, by legitimating war and empowering states' executives.[147] Furthermore, even if the argument for a restrictive approach to the LOAC based on logic and coherency is correct as a matter of principle, the generality of the *jus ad bellum* and its lack of "concrete and detailed guidance on how to act in war" leave space for the LOAC to play a facilitative role in the question of when military force is authorized.[148] In other words, the generality of the *jus ad bellum* and the relative specificity of the LOAC may lead states to consult the LOAC for guidance on when they are legally authorized to use military force.

Notwithstanding the ongoing debate in the academy, it may in fact be the case that, by referencing the defeat of the enemy in the definition of military necessity, states intend to assert the view that the LOAC provides legal authority to use military force. However, the evidence is far from clear. For example, as discussed earlier, the U.S. Department of Defense appears to distinguish between the object of war and the LOAC.[149] If states were interested in asserting such a conceptually radical view of the LOAC, one might expect a more definitive statement of

142. *See supra* notes 81–99 and accompanying text.

143. Haque, *supra* note 81, at 31.

144. *Id.*

145. Lieblich, *supra* note 81, at 325.

146. *Id.* at 326.

147. *Id.*

148. *Id.* at 328.

149. *See supra* note 135 and accompanying text.

their intent. State intent aside, the invocation of defeating the enemy within the definition of military necessity may further potential conceptual confusion, particularly among practitioners and legal advisors who rely on military manuals to provide guidance on the nature of the LOAC as well as its general principles and specific rules.

E. Conceptual Necessity: "As Quickly and Efficiently as Possible"

There are two aspects of military necessity that, at least theoretically, countervail the sweeping language of doctrinal military necessity detailed in the previous subsections. First, states at least nominally invoke the concept of necessity—that is, in its strict sense—within their definitions of military necessity.[150] Second, states universally condition the broad language they use to define military necessity on compliance with other rules contained within the LOAC.[151] This subsection examines the former. The latter is examined in the following subsection.

150. U.S. LOAC MANUAL, *supra* note 21, at 52 ("all measures *needed*") (emphasis added); U.S. ARMY LOAC MANUAL, *supra* note 21, at 1-7; *id.* at 53 ("certain incidental harms that *inevitably* result") (emphasis added); AUSTRALIA LOAC MANUAL, *supra* note 21, at 2-2 ("those measures . . . which are *indispensable*") (emphasis added); *id.* at 2-2 ("unavoidable"); CANADA LOAC MANUAL, *supra* note 21, at 2-1 ("to the extent necessary") (emphasis added); CANADA MILITARY DOCTRINE, *supra* note 21, at 2-15 ("required" and "to the extent necessary"); FRANCE LOAC MANUAL, *supra* note 21, at 8, 65–66 ("necessary"); GERMANY LOAC MANUAL, *supra* note 21, at 25 ("required"); U.K. LEGAL SUPPORT DOCTRINE, *supra* note 21, at 23 ("only that degree and kind of force . . . that is *required*") (emphasis added); U.K. LOAC MANUAL AMENDMENT 3, *supra* note 71, at 5 ("required"); NATO GLOSSARY, *supra* note 71, at 73 ("required"); NATO LEGAL DESKBOOK, *supra* note 21, at 248 ("necessary or required"); *see also supra* notes 71–73 and 121–23.

151. U.S. LOAC MANUAL, *supra* note 21, at 52; U.S. ARMY LOAC MANUAL, *supra* note 21, at 1-6, 1-7; AUSTRALIA LOAC MANUAL, *supra* note 21, at 2-2 ("The principle cannot be used to justify actions prohibited by law, as the means to achieve victory are not unlimited."); CANADA LOAC MANUAL, *supra* note 21, at 2-1 (military necessity "justifies the application of force not forbidden by International Law"); CANADA MILITARY DOCTRINE, *supra* note 21, at 2-15 ("that are not forbidden by the LOAC" and "within the bounds of international law"); FRANCE LOAC MANUAL, *supra* note 21, at 8, 65–66 ("not prohibited by the law of armed conflict"); GERMANY LOAC MANUAL, *supra* note 21, at 25 ("provided that these measures are not forbidden by LOAC" and "[c]onsiderations of military necessity can therefore not justify a departure from the rules of humanitarian law; to seek a military advantage using forbidden means is not permissible"); U.K. LEGAL SUPPORT DOCTRINE, *supra* note 21, at 23 ("not otherwise prohibited by the law of armed conflict"); U.K. LOAC MANUAL AMENDMENT 3, *supra* note 71, at 5 ("which are not forbidden by the laws of war" and "not otherwise prohibited by the law of armed conflict"); *see also* NATO LEGAL DESKBOOK, *supra* note 21, at 248; NATO GLOSSARY, *supra* note 71, at 73; *supra* notes 71–73 and 121–23.

It is a complex question how military necessity relates to the general (nonlegal) concept of necessity and as it is used in the peacetime legal context.[152] A deep exploration of the relationship between military necessity on the one hand and the general legal principle and concept of necessity on the other hand is beyond the scope of this chapter. It will suffice to observe briefly how states frame military necessity and how that framing contrasts with the general concept and legal principle of necessity.

It is true that in some sense states invoke the concept of necessity within the principle of military necessity. Specifically, necessity links the measures military necessity permits with the permitted end of defeating the enemy as quickly and efficiently as possible.[153] However, in doing so states significantly distort the concept of necessity.[154]

To see how, consider the logic of necessity as it is used in its strict sense in many legal regimes.[155] Some end, call it *Y*, is recognized as having significant importance. Accordingly, the law is endowed with normal rules designed to facilitate the consistent achievement of *Y*. Naturally, sometimes the achievement of *Y* will be at risk, even under these normal rules. In such cases, necessity may provide a legal basis for allowing normal rules to be overridden to ensure *Y*. Of course, such an allowance carries significant risk of potential abuse. Accordingly, necessity is cabined in careful ways. First, it is only available when the jeopardized interest, *Y*, is of exceptional importance. Second, means available under normal rules must be demonstrably incapable of achieving *Y*. Third, means taken pursuant to necessity must be narrowly tailored. In other words, necessity contains qualitative and quantitative limits on the means taken to achieve *Y*. Finally, the justification for means taken pursuant to necessity ceases once those means yield *Y*.

152. *See generally* Jens David Ohlin & Larry May, Necessity in International Law (2016).

153. *See supra* note 150 and accompanying text.

154. For an example in U.S. domestic law in which the concept of necessity is distorted, *see McCulloch v. Maryland*, a landmark case in which the U.S. Supreme Court interpreted the constitutional power of Congress under Article I, Section 8 of the Constitution to "make all Laws which shall be necessary and proper for carrying into Execution" Congress's express powers enumerated elsewhere in Article I. McCulloch v. Maryland, 17 U.S. 316 (1819). In that case, the Court interpreted the word "necessity" not in its strict, logical sense but in a broadly permissive sense. *See id.* at 413 (declining to interpret the word "necessary" as limiting Congress's authority "to pass laws for the execution of the granted powers to such as are indispensable, and without which the power would be nugatory"). In other words, the Court identified the term with convenience and utility rather than with compulsion. *See id.* The Court also contrasted the term as it appears in Article I, Section 8 with the term "absolutely necessary" as it appears in Article I, Section 10. *Id.* at 414.

155. For a domestic criminal law example, see Model Penal Code § 3.04 (Am. L. Inst., Proposed Official Draft 1962). For an example in the international human rights law context, see McCann v. United Kingdom, 21 Eur. Ct. H.R. 97 (1996). For an example in the context of general international law, see Draft Articles on Responsibility of States for Internationally Wrongful Acts art. 25, Rep. of the Int'l L. Comm'n on Its Fifty-Third Sess., U.N. Doc. A/56/10, at 26 (2001).

Military necessity defies these aspects of conceptual necessity in numerous ways.[156] First, the LOAC operates under the assumption that "normal" rules have failed in some fundamental way. After all, wartime generally looks nothing like peacetime. In wartime, law enforcement rules, which *do* incorporate strict conceptual necessity, have given way to the carrying out of general, intense, and protracted armed violence between two competing armed forces. As such, virtually all acts of hostilities would violate "normal" rules.

Second, and relatedly, the end to which military necessity justifies acts of violence is not special in the sense that it is exceptional and limited temporally or geographically, as is the case during peacetime. Rather, military necessity deems "necessary" any measure required to defeat the enemy forces. Textually, it does nothing to limit the type of conduct ("any measures"). Furthermore, any measure is justified—that is, "necessary"—so long as it can be said to achieve the desired end as quickly as possible and as efficiently as possible. So far as the concept of necessity applies in such cases, it is stretched perhaps beyond recognition by incorporation of the words "as quickly and efficiently as possible." The crucial questions are what alternatives to the proposed military measure must states consider, and how possible must they be. While military necessity does not answer these questions, answers are provided elsewhere in the LOAC. For example, combatants are not required to use the least restrictive amount of force during hostilities—there is no requirement to capture or wound instead of kill, even if capturing or wounding is feasible.[157]

In fact, one might argue that military necessity's "as quickly and efficiently as possible" language goes far toward transforming it from an application of the concept of necessity to an application of the concept of sufficiency. It is true that military necessity uses the language of conceptual necessity—states may use those measures *required* to achieve military necessity's permissible ends.[158] However, the permission it gives to achieve those ends *as soon as possible* and in the *least costly way possible* seemingly releases the parties from any real limits. Indeed, it is hard to imagine—except perhaps in the most egregious cases—a situation in which a combatant acting in good faith could not justify a proposed military measure under this standard.

In this regard, it is interesting to note an example of how changing the definition of military necessity can lead to significant conceptual shift. In the 2004 version of its military manual, the United Kingdom defined military necessity as

156. It is worth re-emphasizing that this chapter is not concerned with the narrow version of military necessity, which functions much more strictly and hews more closely to conceptual necessity compared with the broad, structural version of military necessity addressed in this chapter. The narrow version of military necessity is incorporated into particular LOAC rules; it does not function within the LOAC in an independent, stand-alone manner. *See supra* note 18.

157. *See* Schmitt, *supra* note 66. *But see* Ryan Goodman, *The Power to Kill or Capture Enemy Combatants*, 24 Eur. J. Int'l L. 819 (2013).

158. *See supra* note 150 and accompanying text.

permitting "*only* that degree and kind of force" required to defeat the enemy.[159] The use of the word "only" is a cardinal signal of conceptual necessity. However, in a 2010 update to the manual, the United Kingdom changed the definition to remove the word "only."[160] This suggests at least an implicit recognition of a definition of military necessity that is unconstrained in any practical way by strict necessity.[161]

This is not to say that military necessity ought to incorporate strict, conceptual necessity. As previously noted, the LOAC does not impose a "least restrictive means" analysis on belligerents and combatants. Because military necessity does not contain such a requirement, its doctrinal definition is not infelicitous, at least not in this regard, to the LOAC. By the same token, it would be a mistake to believe that the LOAC, beyond military necessity, is completely free of the stricter form of necessity. Certain LOAC rules incorporate conceptual necessity in its stricter sense.[162] However, it is clear that the disjointed relationship between military necessity, as articulated by states, and conceptual necessity may cause confusion, particularly among practitioners and operators who are often not experts on the LOAC.

159. U.K. LOAC Manual, *supra* note 21, at 21 (emphasis added).

160. U.K. LOAC Manual Amendment 3, *supra* note 71, at 5.

161. Other examples show that there may be a trend toward an increasingly permissive definition of military necessity. *Compare* Ministry of Def., Humanitarian Law in Armed Conflicts: Manual § 130 (1992) (Ger.) ("In war, a belligerent may apply only that amount and kind of force necessary to defeat the enemy."), *with* Germany LOAC Manual, *supra* note 21, at 25; *compare* U.K. LOAC Manual, *supra* note 21, at 21 ("Military necessity permits a state engaged in an armed conflict to use only that degree and kind of force . . ."), *with* U.K. LOAC Manual Amendment 3, *supra* note 71, at 5 ("Military necessity is . . . the principle whereby a belligerent has the right to apply any measures . . ."); *compare* NATO Legal Deskbook, *supra* note 21, at 248 (Under the principle of military necessity, states "can use force not otherwise prohibited by LOAC that is necessary or required for the submission of the enemy."), *with* NATO Glossary, *supra* note 71, at 73 (defining military necessity as the "principle whereby a belligerent has the right to apply any measures that are required to bring about the successful conclusion of a military operation and that are not forbidden by the Law of War."); *compare* Australia Air Force Doctrine, *supra* note 21 (defining military necessity relatively narrowly as requiring the "use [of] such force as is reasonably necessary to achieve a military objective" that "result[s] in the least expenditure of life and damage to property, as is possible under the prevailing circumstances"), *with* Australia LOAC Manual, *supra* note 21, at 2-2 (asserting relatively broadly that military necessity "justifies . . . those measures, not forbidden by international law, which are indispensable for securing complete submission of an enemy at the soonest moment" and "permits the destruction of enemy combatants and other persons whose death is unavoidable").

162. Use of "military necessity" in the strict sense, as well as use of the standard "absolutely or imperatively necessary," in the LOAC are examples in which conceptual necessity is invoked. These terms are contained in particular LOAC rules. *See supra* note 18.

F. A Pointless Proviso (?): "Not Forbidden by the LOAC"

In light of the broadly permissive principle of military necessity as defined by states, one might believe the proper question is not what the principle permits (in either the strong or weak sense), but rather what it does *not* permit. Indeed, as demonstrated by the previous analysis, it is quite clear that military necessity reflects states' interests in operational flexibility and mission accomplishment during armed conflict. However, it must be recognized that, notwithstanding the otherwise sweeping language, all definitions of military necessity incorporate the proviso that it does not justify conduct that violates other LOAC rules.[163]

While this was not always the case,[164] the idea today that military necessity may justify deviation from the LOAC cannot be taken as a serious argument, particularly by those states examined in this chapter that have gone through the effort to publish military manuals on the LOAC.[165] It is therefore worth thinking about why this proviso is included within the definition of military necessity. In other words, the proviso is perhaps objectionable not because it is wrong but because it is redundant.

163. *See supra* note 151 and accompanying text. "Military necessity does not justify actions that are prohibited by the law of war." U.S. LOAC MANUAL, *supra* note 21, at 53; U.S. ARMY LOAC MANUAL, *supra* note 21, at 1-7. This is because "states have crafted the law of war specifically with war's exigencies in mind. In devising law of war rules, States considered military requirements. Thus, prohibitions on conduct in the law of war may be understood to reflect States' determinations that such conduct is militarily unnecessary per se." U.S. LOAC MANUAL, *supra* note 21, at 54 (citations omitted); *see also* U.S. ARMY LOAC MANUAL, *supra* note 21, at 1-7.

164. The idea that war necessity could overcome the LOAC derives from the nineteenth-century German doctrine of *kriegsraeson geht vor kriegsmanier* ("necessity in war overrules the manner of warfare"). *See* 2 L. OPPENHEIM, INTERNATIONAL LAW: A TREATISE § 69, at 231–33 (H. Lauterpacht ed., 7th ed. 1952); *see also* United States v. Göring, Case No. 1 (Oct. 1, 1946), *reprinted in* 1 TRIALS OF THE MAJOR WAR CRIMINALS BEFORE THE INTERNATIONAL MILITARY TRIBUNAL 226–27 (1947) ("The truth remains that War Crimes were committed on a vast scale, never before seen in the history of war. . . . There can be no doubt that the majority of them arose from the Nazi conception of 'total war', with which the aggressive wars were waged. For in this conception of 'total war', the moral ideas underlying the conventions which seek to make war more humane are no longer regarded as having force or validity. Everything is made subordinate to the overmastering dictates of war. Rules, regulations, assurances, and treaties all alike are of no moment."); United States v. List (The Hostage Case), Case No. 7 (Feb. 19, 1948), *reprinted in* 11 TRIALS OF WAR CRIMINALS BEFORE THE NUREMBERG MILITARY TRIBUNALS UNDER CONTROL COUNCIL LAW NO. 10, at 757, 1255–56 (1950) ("It is apparent from the evidence of these defendants that they considered military necessity, a matter to be determined by them, a complete justification of their acts. We do not concur in the view that the rules of warfare are anything less than they purport to be. Military necessity or expediency do not justify a violation of positive rules.").

165. Indeed, many of the manuals surveyed in this chapter explicitly raise and reject the *kriegsraeson* argument. *See, e.g.*, CANADA LOAC MANUAL, *supra* note 21, at 2-1.

Most obviously, the "not otherwise prohibited" proviso may be included simply as a reminder and guard against the evils of *kriegsraeson*. Additionally, perhaps states continue to include it as a counterweight to the otherwise sweepingly broad language of military necessity. Indeed, as argued elsewhere in this section, it is unclear whether any other part of the definition limits military operations in any practical way. But if this is the case, then one is left wondering what is the practical significance of the principle of military necessity. In effect, as articulated in state doctrinal publications, it seems to be an assertion that states may seek to achieve the object of war—namely, the defeat of the enemy's armed forces—so long as they comply with the rules contained in the LOAC. If this is all military necessity stands for, then it is certainly among the most uncontroversial assertions within the LOAC and accordingly warrants much less attention than it typically receives from scholars and practitioners. Furthermore, in this light it is unclear why such a principle must be included within doctrinal publications such as military manuals, adjacent to the much more practical principles of distinction and proportionality as well as the many concrete rules of the LOAC.

III. REFORMULATING DOCTRINAL MILITARY NECESSITY

As demonstrated in the previous section, military necessity, as states generally define it in LOAC doctrinal publications such as military manuals, raises significant practical and conceptual problems. Accordingly, this definition, based on the Lieber/Nuremberg model, should be abandoned in favor of a definition that explains military necessity as an overarching, conceptual interest or motivating force, rather than a preceptual principle, of the LOAC.

How one receives this recommendation will naturally depend, at least in part, on one's views concerning the nature of the LOAC. For example, those who believe that the LOAC affords states and combatants legal authority to use military force (that is, authorities separate from and in addition to the authorities derived from the *jus ad bellum*)[166] may not object in principle to the version of military necessity currently favored in state LOAC doctrine. Indeed, those who take this view of the LOAC may find merit in that definition because it suggests that military necessity plays a role in the larger, structural force-authorizing aspects of the LOAC—even if military necessity does not itself provide much guidance to combatants concerning what particular conduct is permitted.[167]

166. This issue may best be analyzed by distinguishing between states and individual combatants. For example, regarding the latter, the so-called "combatant's privilege" plays a legal role in resolving the difficult questions surrounding those combatants who fight on behalf of a state with an unjust cause. Another example, regarding the former, involves questions about how such authority under the LOAC interacts, if at all, with the prohibition under Article 2(4) of the U.N. Charter and its exceptions. *See infra* note 181.

167. *See* Aughey & Sari, *supra* note 81, at 93 ("As a general principle, military necessity is not sufficiently precise to provide detailed guidance on what are permissible aims, means and methods of warfare, and what are not. Rather, it falls to the positive rules of the law of armed

However, even assuming for the moment that the LOAC is not only restrictive but also contains legal permissions,[168] it does not necessarily follow that states are best served by continuing to include the current definition of military necessity in doctrinal publications. First, if the LOAC imbues combatants with some form of legal authority, it is not necessarily the case that military necessity must be the source of such authority. Second, even if the current definition of military necessity provides some value as part of the larger force-authorizing or permissive aspects of the LOAC, the costs resulting from its lack of complete coherency and its likelihood to cause confusion for practitioners may well outweigh that value. Furthermore, the better conceptualization of military necessity—that it constitutes a conceptual interest or driving force of the LOAC, rather than a functional or practicable principle—is by no means inconsistent with the view that the LOAC permits (either strongly or weakly) combatants to engage in hostilities aggressively to achieve their states' war aims, so long as they do so within the bounds set by the positive rules contained in the LOAC.

These considerations as well as those outlined in the previous section reveal the potential for confusion and distortion. Combatants require and deserve clear and concise guidance on the principles and rules that apply during armed conflict. As currently defined in military doctrine, military necessity at the very least is prone to mislead practitioners and combatants. What is worse, it may constitute a bold and wildly undertheorized assertion of legal authority that casts a thick conceptual haze over the international law that applies to military operations.

Military necessity is best understood as one of two conceptual interests—the other being humanity—underlying the LOAC.[169] As the U.S. Department of Defense states, "Humanity is related to military necessity, and these principles complement one another. Humanity may be viewed as the logical inverse of the principle of military necessity."[170] These two principles represent the sometimes complementary, sometimes competing interests that underlie the LOAC: first, the

conflict, as laid down in the applicable treaties and embodied in customary international law, to provide that guidance and thereby give military necessity concrete meaning.").

168. This is a complex question that is only touched upon in this chapter. Since this chapter may achieve its aims without resolving the question, I do not take a definitive position on the matter.

169. *See* U.S. LOAC MANUAL, *supra* note 21, at 51 ("Law of war principles work as interdependent and reinforcing parts of a coherent system.").

170. *Id.* at 59; *see also* CANADA LOAC MANUAL, *supra* note 21, at 2-1 ("Military necessity is not a concept that can be considered in isolation."); FRANCE LOAC MANUAL, *supra* note 21, at 65 ("The law of armed conflict is a compromise between the search for military efficiency on the one hand and the demands of humanity on the other."); GERMANY LOAC MANUAL, *supra* note 21, at 25 ("LOAC is a compromise between military and humanitarian requirements. Its rules take account of both military necessity and the dictates of humanity."); U.K. LOAC MANUAL, *supra* note 21, at 21 ("The law of armed conflict is consistent with the economic and efficient use of force. It is intended to minimize the suffering caused by armed conflict rather than impede military efficiency.").

interest of states in achieving their war aims; second, their interest in minimizing suffering during war.[171] These two motivating forces are engaged in a constant and continuing "dialectical compromise," the result of which is the formation and development of principles and rules of the LOAC.[172]

Accordingly, states should abandon the definition of military necessity based on the Lieber/Nuremberg model within their doctrinal publications. Most radically, states could decline to include military necessity within doctrinal publications, whose intended audience is tactical military operators. After all, on the view adopted in this chapter, military necessity is a conceptual notion rather than a practicable principle, and thus including it within doctrinal guidance directed toward relatively low echelons of military command may be inappropriate.

Alternatively, states could include a version of military necessity defined in conceptual rather than practical terms. It should not be identified as a "principle," given the previously discussed confusion that term may engender.[173] One possibility is to model it on Professor Michael Schmitt's influential description:

> In the arena of [armed] conflict, states harbor two prevailing aims. The first is an ability to pursue and safeguard vital national interests. When crafting [the LOAC], states therefore insist that legal norms not unduly restrict their freedom of action on the battlefield, such that national interests might be affected. The principle of military necessity constitutes the [LOAC] mechanism for safeguarding this purpose. . . . [It] recognizes the appropriateness of considering military factors in setting the rules for warfare.[174]

Professor Yoram Dinstein's definition may also serve as a model:

> Military necessity lubricates the wheels of the [LOAC]. When [LOAC] norms are crafted, the law-makers cannot be oblivious to the exigencies of war impelling each Belligerent Part to take the requisite steps to engage the enemy and defeat it. Military necessity is associated with the attainment of some discernible military advantage over the enemy. Differently put, the measures taken in an [international armed conflict] must be leveraged to gaining a military advantage—in the circumstances ruling at the time—as a direct result of their use.[175]

Although improving conceptual clarity in states' LOAC doctrine is valuable in its own right, the reformulation of doctrinal military necessity in this way will

171. *See* Schmitt, *supra* note 1, at 798–99.

172. *Id.* at 798.

173. *See supra* Section II.A.

174. Schmitt, *supra* note 1, at 799.

175. DINSTEIN, *supra* note 16, at 8.

also serve a much greater purpose: it will benefit military service members who after all are the principal audience of military doctrine. To see why, one must consider how service members make decisions on the battlefield during the stress and quick pace of combat. Anyone with combat experience or who has worked closely with those who engage in combat can attest to the considerations that remain at the center of the combatant's focus: mission plans and objectives, tactical guidance, direct orders, and rules of engagement. Those men and women engaged in hostilities—not in operations centers assisted by staff officers and lawyers, but rather "in the fight" as part of small, tactical groups of soldiers—do not recollect and consult deep sets of rules, such as those found in a military LOAC manual or the first Additional Protocol. Time restraints simply will not permit this. Rather, they make decisions informed and guided by general principles, such as distinction—"do not target civilians and civilian objects"—and proportionality—"do not cause *excessive* collateral damage." In this regard, combatants' conceptualization and understanding of the LOAC may be deep in one sense: they must internalize a few broad principles and rules capable of being applied quickly in a wide variety of situations. However, such conceptualization and understanding is also necessarily generalized. In other words, the reality of combat involves the need to greatly distill LOAC rules into general principles that may be internalized and applied on the battlefield under great stress.[176] For example, the complex set of rules surrounding the principle of distinction—the baseline prohibitions against targeting civilians and civilian objects; the exceptions to those rules for direct participation in hostilities and the nature/location/purpose/use test for military objectives; as well as the controversial role of tactical self-defense—are distilled and generalized within rules of engagement into broad notions such as hostile acts and demonstrated hostile intent. Furthermore, it has been the practice of states to distill (yet again) rules of engagement into pocket-sized cards containing lists of short rules for combatants to remember.[177]

In light of service members' reliance on general principles, "rules of thumb," and other broad guidance, it is crucial that states refine doctrinal guidance to the "bare bones." While general principles such as distinction and proportionality usefully serve combatants, military necessity as currently defined does not. Reformulating the definition as described earlier will allow military necessity (and humanity, for that matter) to provide the conceptual basis for, and thus a deeper understanding of, the practical principles and rules they will apply during hostilities. In this regard, recall Dworkin's assertion that the forces or interests that underlie law constitute in large part the "formal structure of all interpretive claims,"[178] as well as a "structural

176. *Cf.* Sean Watts, *The DOD Law of War Manual's Return to Principles*, JUST SECURITY (June 30, 2015), https://www.justsecurity.org/24270/dod-law-war-manuals-return-principles.

177. GARY D. SOLIS, THE LAW OF ARMED CONFLICT: INTERNATIONAL HUMANITARIAN LAW IN WAR 485, 501–504 (2d ed. 2016).

178. DWORKIN, *supra* note 36, at 58.

requirement"[179] of any interpretation of law. In other words, providing combatants with the LOAC's structural underpinnings is valuable because improving their understanding of the foundational interests behind the law will improve the way they apply the law during combat. As the previous section of this chapter detailed, military necessity as currently defined in state LOAC doctrine does not productively serve this clarifying role.

It must be acknowledged that—quite obviously—reformulation of military necessity will not resolve all conceptual challenges involved in operationalizing international law during hostilities. Certainly, reformulation will remove the temptation to cite—lazily, improperly—military necessity in the manner of a force-authorizing rule or, perhaps worse, as a mindless justification for battlefield conduct that must be analyzed under and comport with more specific legal and operational guidance. However, the notion of wartime authority will remain conceptually challenging. For instance, reformulation of military necessity is not sufficient to address the larger questions related to whether and how the *jus ad bellum* continues to apply during hostilities[180] or, relatedly, whether and to what extent the LOAC affords distinct armed conflict authorities. Furthermore, there remain important questions about the interaction between the LOAC and international human rights law,[181] as well as complex questions about the interaction between international and domestic law as they relate to authorities and limitations in the use of military force.[182]

That said, reformulation of doctrinal military necessity would be a step toward conceptual clarification of the LOAC and, more importantly, would provide service members with better, clearer guidance. At bottom, the trouble with the current definition of military necessity, based on the Lieber/Nuremberg model, is it suggests that military necessity is a *part* of the applicable body of rules encompassed within the LOAC. Even if seeing military necessity in this way was

179. *Id.* at 59.

180. *See* Lieblich, *supra* note 141. It must be emphasized that whatever the nature of the LOAC as either "permissive" or "restrictive," no additional justification regarding the prohibition of the use of force is required for a state acting lawfully under the *jus ad bellum*. In other words, a state using force lawfully pursuant to the U.N. Charter need not consult the LOAC for further authority to use force. By the same token, under current law the LOAC, including military necessity, provides no separate justification for a state to use force within the meaning of Article 2(4) of the U.N. Charter. Where no such justification exists, the state concerned violates Article 2(4) by every use of force regardless of what military necessity may say.

181. For example, does international human rights law continue to apply, and if so how, during armed conflict? If the LOAC affords combatants with legal authority to engage in hostilities, then how does this authority coincide with states' human rights obligations? How does the applicability of international human rights law during armed conflict impact combatants who fight for a state whose cause is unjust and in violation of the *jus ad bellum*?

182. *Cf.* Eric Holder, Att'y Gen., *Remarks at Northwestern University School of Law*, Mar. 5, 2012, 2012 Digest of United States Practice in International Law 577.

potentially beneficial, the current definition fails to guide service members usefully or productively. Accordingly, doctrine should define military necessity as a force or interest that recognizes operational reality; that is, as representing what the conditions of the enemy and the political objectives demand military forces act on to be successful. The LOAC reflects the limitations states have agreed to notwithstanding those realities and demands. Any attempt to distill military necessity into a regulatory form will be fleeting at best and at worst is a fool's errand.

IV. CONCLUSION

This chapter examined the ways in which states articulate military necessity in doctrinal publications, including military LOAC manuals. Based on the model prescribed by the Lieber Code and the Nuremberg jurisprudence, the version of military necessity currently favored by states has several aspects that are liable to mislead practitioners of the LOAC. This version of military necessity is especially unhelpful in military doctrine, whose purpose is to provide concise and clear guidance to warfighters on how to carry out military operations in compliance with the LOAC.

It has been said that "[t]here is no conception in International Law more elusive, protean, wholly unsatisfactory, than that of war necessity."[183] For scholars, this is a job-creating, and therefore welcome, challenge. Indeed, it is unsurprising that fierce debate would evolve around the role of necessity during armed conflict, as necessity "is quite possibly the most powerful concept in the law."[184] But this debate does not belong in the pages of military doctrine. The current doctrinal definition of military necessity raises, and fails to resolve, many practical and conceptual challenges. Instead, states should reformulate doctrinal military necessity to reflect its role as an overarching conceptual interest in the LOAC, and minimize the risk that combatants will engage in the fruitless task of searching within it for that which it does not afford: clear and practicable guidance for warfighting.

183. J.M. Spaight, War Rights on Land 113 (1911).

184. Ohlin & May, *supra* note 152, at 1.

Considerations of Necessity under Article 57(2)(a)(ii), (c), and (3) and Proportionality under Article 51(5)(b) and Article 57(2)(b) of Additional Protocol I

Is There Room for an Integrated Approach?

WOLFF HEINTSCHEL VON HEINEGG*

I. INTRODUCTION

This brief analysis examines whether and to what extent military necessity has a bearing on the obligation to take certain precautions in attack and on the proportionality assessment required by the prohibition of excessive collateral damage and by other pertinent rules of the law of armed conflict. It will be shown that the relevant factors must be taken account of in their entirety in the course of any targeting decision and that the question whether there is room for an integrated approach must be answered in the affirmative. An integrated approach that combines the prohibition of excessive collateral damage, precautions in attack, and considerations of military necessity is not an option but rather is required by the law of armed conflict.

The analysis is based upon the 1977 Additional Protocol I (AP I),[1] which, according to the position taken here, is reflective of the customary law of armed

* Chair of Public Law, in particular Public International Law, European Law, and Foreign Constitutional Law, European University Viadrina, Frankfurt (Oder), Germany.

1. Protocol Additional to the Geneva Conventions of 12 August 1949, and Relating to the Protection of Victims of International Armed Conflicts (Protocol I), 8 June 1977, 1125 U.N.T.S. 3 [hereinafter AP I].

Wolff Heintschel von Heinegg, *Considerations of Necessity under Article 57(2)(a)(ii), (c), and (3) and Proportionality under Article 51(5)(b) and Article 57(2)(b) of Additional Protocol I* In: *Necessity and Proportionality in International Peace and Security Law.* Edited by: Professor Claus Kreß and Captain Robert Lawless, Oxford University Press (2021).
 DOI: 10.1093/oso/9780197537374.003.0011.

conflict at least insofar as the prohibition of excessive collateral damage[2] and the obligation to take precautions in attack are concerned.[3]

II. THE RELATIONSHIP BETWEEN MILITARY NECESSITY AND PRECAUTIONS IN ATTACK ACCORDING TO AP I, ARTICLE 57(2)(A)(II), (C), AND (3)

"Military necessity" has been defined as "the principle that justifies the use of all measures needed to defeat the enemy as quickly as possible that are not prohibited by the law of war."[4] A more precise definition is provided for in the 2004 U.K. Law of Armed Conflict Manual: "Military necessity permits a state engaged in an armed conflict to use only that degree and kind of force, not otherwise prohibited by the law of armed conflict, that is required in order to achieve the legitimate purpose of the conflict, namely the complete or partial submission of the enemy at the earliest possible moment with the minimum expenditure of life and resources."[5]

At first glance, military necessity as defined seems to have no role to play in the context of precautions in attack. The obligation to take precautions is closely linked to the principle of distinction, which is designed to protect civilians and civilian objects.[6] Hence, the protective humanitarian purpose underlying the obligation to take precautions in attack seems to clearly prevail over any considerations of military necessity.

While military necessity may be considered a principle of the law of armed conflict,[7] it certainly does not justify deviations from the law of armed conflict

2. Although the United States is not a party to AP I, the recent DoD Law of War Manual seems to recognize that AP I, Article 51(5)(b) is reflective of customary international law. *See* Office of the Gen. Counsel, U.S. Dep't of Def., Department of Defense Law of War Manual ¶¶ 2.4, 5.10, 5.12 (June 2015, updated Dec. 2016) [hereinafter DoD Manual]; *see also* Yoram Dinstein, The Conduct of Hostilities under the Law of International Armed Conflict ¶¶ 317–30 (2d ed. 2010); William H. Boothby, The Law of Targeting 94–97 (2012); Ian Henderson, The Contemporary Law of Targeting 180–82 (2009).

3. DoD Manual, *supra* note 2, ¶¶ 5.11, 5.14; Dinstein, *supra* note 2, ¶¶ 340–57; Boothby, *supra* note 2, at 118–40.

4. DoD Manual, *supra* note 2, ¶ 2.2.

5. Ministry of Def., JSP 383, The Joint Service Manual of the Law of Armed Conflict ¶ 2.2 (2004) (U.K.) [hereinafter U.K. Manual]; *see also* Int'l Comm. of the Red Cross, Commentary on the Additional Protocols of 8 June 1977 to the Geneva Conventions of 12 August 1949 ¶¶ 1389–97 (Yves Sandoz, Christophe Swinarski, & Bruno Zimmerman eds., 1987) [hereinafter ICRC Commentary].

6. Boothby, *supra* note 2, at 118–40; Dinstein, *supra* note 2, ¶ 340.

7. Boothby, *supra* note 2, at 59; Yoram Dinstein, *Military Necessity*, *in* The Law of Armed Conflict and the Use of Force 710, 711 (Frauke Lachenmann & Rüdiger Wolfrum eds., 2017).

such that a party to an armed conflict could absolve itself from its obligations.[8] The law of armed conflict "is a product of reconciliation between demands of military necessity and humanitarian considerations."[9] Accordingly, the law "cannot be overridden by [military] necessity, except in those special cases where the law itself makes provisions for that eventuality."[10] Considerations of military necessity may be recognized by the law either explicitly or implicitly.[11]

This section aims at identifying those elements of the obligation to take precautions in attack according to which considerations of military necessity may have an impact on the scope of the precautionary obligations. Such considerations do not necessarily result in widening military options. They may also limit military options.

A. Military Necessity as an Element of the Obligation under AP I, Article 57(2)(a)(ii)

AP I, Article 57(2)(a)(ii) obliges those who plan or decide upon an attack to "take all feasible precautions in the choice of methods and means of attack with a view to avoiding, and in any event to minimizing, incidental loss of civilian life, injury to civilians, and damage to civilian objects."

While this obligation certainly applies in situations in which an attack is expected to cause "collateral damage," it may not be misunderstood as coming into operation only if the "collateral damage" is expected to be excessive in relation to the military advantage anticipated. Rather to the contrary. If there is an expectation of excessive collateral damage, the attack will be unlawful according to AP I, Article 51(5)(b). Of course, by taking precautionary measures the extent of collateral damage could be reduced below the threshold of excessiveness. This, however, would not per se imply full compliance with the obligation to avoid or minimize collateral damage. In other words, the obligation under Article 57(2)(a)(ii) comes into operation if there is an expectation of collateral damage even if that collateral damage is not expected to be excessive in relation to the military advantage anticipated.[12] It needs to be emphasized, however, that the reduction of collateral damage by certain precautionary measures may exhaust what is feasible[13] with a view to avoiding or minimizing nonexcessive collateral damage.

8. ICRC Commentary, *supra* note 5, ¶ 1389; Dinstein, *Military Necessity*, *supra* note 7, at 711.

9. Dinstein, *Military Necessity*, *supra* note 7, at 711.

10. *Id.* at 712 (quoting In re von Lesinski (called von Manstein) (Brit. Mil. Ct. at Hamburg Dec. 19, 1949), *reprinted in* 16 Ann. Dig. & Rep. Pub. Int'l L. Cases 509, 512 (1949)).

11. *Id.* at 713–14.

12. Wolff Heintschel von Heinegg, *Precautions in Attack*, *in* The Law of Armed Conflict and the Use of Force, *supra* note 7, at 1008, 1010; Boothby, *supra* note 2, at 123–29.

13. For feasibility, *see infra* text accompanying note 15.

Accordingly, and because there is no link to an anticipated military advantage, considerations of military necessity do not seem to allow for a mitigation of the obligation to avoid or minimize collateral damage.

The ICRC Commentary on Article 57(2)(a)(ii) contains the following statement: "As regards weapons, their precision and range should be taken into account; such precautions coincide with the concerns of military commanders wishing to economise on ammunition and to avoid hitting point of no military interest. . . . However, it is clear that the circumstances of combat and the control of airspace may render it more difficult to observe this rule."[14] This statement is not all too helpful because it does not clarify the standard of feasibility and because it seems to confuse it with "economy of force," which is neither a principle of the law of armed conflict nor helpful in determining the meaning of feasibility or military necessity. An attack may very well be considered as serving the overall aim of defeating the enemy as quickly as possible, although the standards of "economy of force" have been disregarded. Nevertheless, the ICRC Commentary seems to acknowledge that the obligation under Article 57(2)(a)(ii) could be subject to military considerations.

This, however, is rather due to the inclusion of the standard of "feasibility," which has been defined by states "to mean that which is practicable or practically possible, taking into account all circumstances ruling at the time, including humanitarian and military considerations."[15] This definition has been formally endorsed in Article 3(10) of the Second Protocol to the Conventional Weapons Convention[16] and in the HPCR Manual on Air and Missile Warfare[17] and may therefore be considered as reflective of customary international law.[18]

14. ICRC Commentary, *supra* note 5, ¶ 2200.

15. *See* Corrected Letter of 28 January 1998 from Ambassador Christopher Hulse of the U.K. to the Swiss Government, ¶ (b), *reprinted in* Declarations and Reservations of the U.K. Regarding Additional Protocol I to the Geneva Conventions, Treaties, State Parties and Commentaries, https://ihl-databases.icrc.org/applic/ihl/ihl.nsf/Notification.xsp?action=openDocument&documentId=0A9E03F0F2EE757CC1256402003FB6D2 (last visited Oct. 6, 2019) [hereinafter U.K. Declaration]. Similar declarations were made by Belgium, Canada, Germany, Italy, and Spain. *See also* Federal Ministry of Defence, Joint Serv. Reg. 15/2, Law of Armed Conflict Manual ¶ 412 (2013) (Ger.) [hereinafter Germany Manual]. An English translation of the German manual is available at https://usnwc.libguides.com/ld.php?content_id=5616055.

16. Protocol on Prohibitions or Restrictions on the Use of Mines, Booby-Traps and Other Devices as Amended on 3 May 1996 (Protocol II as Amended on 3 May 1996) Annexed to the Convention on Prohibitions or Restrictions on the Use of Certain Conventional Weapons Which May Be Deemed to Be Excessively Injurious or to Have Indiscriminate Effects art. 3(10), May 3, 1996, 2048 U.N.T.S. 93, 35 I.L.M. 1206.

17. Program on Humanitarian Policy and Conflict Research, Manual on International Law Applicable to Air and Missile Warfare r. 1(q) (2013).

18. *See* Dinstein, *supra* note 2, ¶ 342. Interestingly, the DoD Law of War Manual does not distinguish between "feasible," "reasonable," and "practical" precautions. *See* DoD Manual, *supra* note 2, ¶ 5.2.3.1.

Hence, the extent of the obligation to take feasible precautions to reduce the risk of harm to the civilian population and other protected persons and objects is to be determined in light of feasibility and, thus, also of military necessity. While the standard of feasibility is circumstantial and, thus, does not provide for an absolute or specific standard,[19] its scope depends upon both humanitarian and military considerations. Accordingly, in the circumstances ruling at the time, those who plan or decide upon an attack may lack the means or information necessary to take measures aimed at avoiding or minimizing collateral damage. Or, more importantly, the respective means may be available, but they are crucial for the success of another attack or operation directed at a military objective offering a considerably higher military advantage or neutralization of which is likely to contribute to an earlier termination of the hostilities. The U.S. Department of Defense Law of War Manual provides some useful guidance as to the military (and humanitarian) considerations that may be taken account of and that may justify a deviation from the obligation under Article 57(2)(a)(ii). Such military considerations may include:

- the effect of taking the precaution on mission accomplishment;
- whether taking the precautions poses a risk to one's own forces or presents other security risks;
- the likelihood and degree of humanitarian benefit from taking the precaution;
- the cost of taking the precaution, in terms of time, money, or other resources; or
- whether taking the precaution forecloses alternative course of action.[20]

Since feasibility includes military considerations and, thus, allows a course of action that will result in a "minimum of expenditure"[21] of own personnel and assets, "force protection is a valid concern that can be factored in any attack."[22] "The [LOAC] obligation does not imply that minimizing incidental civilian injury/damage must be achieved at all costs to the attacking force, and there is no obligation incumbent on the attacker to sustain unnecessary military losses with the sole purpose of minimizing collateral damage to enemy civilians (or civilian objects)."[23]

19. DoD Manual, *supra* note 2, ¶ 5.2.3.2.

20. DoD Manual, *supra* note 2, ¶ 5.2.3.2.

21. *See* U.K. Manual, *supra* note 5, ¶ 2.2 (defining "military necessity").

22. Dinstein, *supra* note 2, ¶ 348.

23. *Id.*

B. Military Necessity and the Obligation of Advance Warnings

According to AP I, Article 57(2)(c), "[E]ffective advance warning shall be given of attacks which may affect the civilian population, unless circumstances do not permit." An advance warning that would allow the civilian population to get out of harm's way may be considered one way of avoiding or minimizing nonexcessive collateral damage. Accordingly, Article 57(2)(c) may be understood as providing a potential option for compliance with the obligation under AP I, Article 57(2)(a)(ii).

The phrase "unless circumstances do not permit" has been formulated in the negative, which means that a warning need not be given "whenever circumstances permit" or "at all times."[24] In other words, whether a warning must be given does not exclusively depend upon whether it is feasible. Rather, even if feasible, giving a warning is not required if otherwise, in the circumstances ruling at the time, the success of the attack could be compromised. The prime example provided is a surprise attack which would become futile if the enemy were to become aware of it because of an advance warning to the civilian population or to individual civilians. "The practice of States shows that the desire to achieve surprise may frequently preclude warnings in non-assault situations or instigate warnings which are too vague to alert the civilian population to the impending peril."[25] Accordingly, the exception of Article 57(2)(c) can be considered the "prime example of a military necessity to avoid giving a warning."[26]

C. Military Necessity and AP I, Article 57(3)

AP I, Article 57(3) provides: "When a choice is possible between several military objectives for obtaining a similar military advantage, the objective to be selected shall be that the attack on which may be expected to cause the least danger to civilian lives and to civilian objects."

Before addressing the question whether the obligation under Article 57(3) can be mitigated by considerations of military necessity, it is important to briefly clarify its relationship with AP I, Article 57(2)(a)(ii). Interestingly, this aspect has not yet been dealt with either in military manuals or in the literature. Arguably, Article 57(3) merely offers one option of avoiding or minimizing collateral damage and, thus, could be understood as a specification of the obligation according to Article 57(2)(a)(ii). Both obligations have in common that they apply in situations in which there is an expectation of nonexcessive collateral damage. Whereas the obligation to avoid or minimize always applies, if it is feasible for the

24. ICRC Commentary, *supra* note 5, ¶ 2223 ("other delegations would have preferred the expression 'whenever circumstances permit', or even no derogation").

25. Dinstein, *supra* note 2, ¶ 357.

26. Dinstein, *Military Necessity*, *supra* note 7, at 714.

attacker to choose "between means and methods to minimize collateral loss,"[27] the obligation to select another target only applies in a very specific situation, namely, if a target offering a similar military advantage exists. Moreover, it presupposes that the expected (nonexcessive) collateral damage of an attack against the alternative target will be less than the collateral damage resulting from an attack on the other target. The obligation to avoid or minimize is stricter insofar as it is not governed by the standard of feasibility but requires the attacker to choose the target of attack upon which will result in lesser collateral damage. Finally, the obligation does not apply to "those who plan or decide upon an attack." Rather, the obligation "usually devolves on relatively high echelons, inasmuch as they are the only ones who normally have the prerequisite 'overview of the military situation' (although senior commanders need to rely on military intelligence gathered and evaluated by lower ranks)."[28]

The obligation under Article 57(3) may come into operation if it sufficed to attack railway tracks outside inhabited areas instead of attacking a railway station located in the center of a town.[29] While this example is illustrative, it must not be misunderstood to mean that railway stations may never be attacked. The scope of the obligation depends upon whether the military advantage of attacking the railway tracks is similar to the attack on the train station. If the military advantage is similar, the concept of military advantage may have a limiting effect such that, according to Article 57(3), a similar military advantage may render an attack on another object unlawful. Accordingly, it is crucial to determine the respective military advantage.

Being closely linked to attacks on military objectives, the concept of military advantage is also related to military necessity. Yet, the latter concept is broader than the former because it may justify measures other than attacks, such as the capture of enemy (or neutral) property. Such measures may be militarily necessary although they do not offer a definite military advantage.[30] Nevertheless, military advantage and military necessity cannot be entirely separated from each other. Firstly, if an attack is militarily unnecessary, it cannot result in a definite military advantage.[31] Secondly, states have linked the concept of military advantage to military necessity. According to the United Kingdom, "[T]he military advantage anticipated from an attack is intended to refer to the advantage anticipated from the attack considered as a whole and not only from isolated or particular parts of the attack."[32] Similar statements have been made by

27. Boothby, *supra* note 2, at 129.

28. Dinstein, *supra* note 2, ¶ 347; *see also* Stefan Oeter, *Methods and Means of Combat*, *in* The Handbook of International Humanitarian Law 116, 203 (Dieter Fleck ed., 3d ed. 2013).

29. ICRC Commentary, *supra* note 5, ¶ 2227.

30. DoD Manual, *supra* note 2, ¶ 2.2.1.

31. Dinstein, *Military Necessity*, *supra* note 7, at 715.

32. U.K. Manual, *supra* note 5, ¶ 5.4.4(j); *see also* Agnieszka Jachec-Neale, The Concept of Military Objectives in International Law and Targeting Practice 120–24 (2015).

Germany,[33] Belgium,[34] Canada,[35] Italy,[36] Netherlands,[37] Spain,[38] New Zealand,[39] and Australia.[40] According to the declarations of New Zealand and Australia,

33. Notification by the Depositary Addressed to the ICRC on 15 February 1991, ¶ 5, *reprinted in* Declarations and Reservations of Germany Regarding Additional Protocol I to the Geneva Conventions, INT'L COMM. OF THE RED CROSS, TREATIES, STATE PARTIES AND COMMENTARY, https://ihl-databases.icrc.org/applic/ihl/ihl.nsf/Notification.xsp?action=openDocument&documentId=3F4D8706B6B7EA40C1256402003FB3C7 (last visited Oct. 7, 2019) [hereinafter Germany Declaration].

34. Interpretive Declarations Made at the Time of Ratification, May 20, 1986, ¶ 5, *reprinted in* Declarations and Reservations of Belgium Regarding Additional Protocol I to the Geneva Conventions, INT'L COMM. OF THE RED CROSS, TREATIES, STATE PARTIES AND COMMENTARY, https://ihl-databases.icrc.org/applic/ihl/ihl.nsf/Notification.xsp?action=openDocument&documentId=EA2560B9B790488EC1256402003FB2BC (last visited Oct. 7, 2019) [hereinafter Belgium Declaration].

35. Reservations Made at the Time of Ratification, Nov. 20, 1990, *reprinted in* Declarations and Reservations of Canada Regarding Additional Protocol I to the Geneva Conventions, INT'L COMM. OF THE RED CROSS, TREATIES, STATE PARTIES AND COMMENTARY, https://ihl-databases.icrc.org/applic/ihl/ihl.nsf/Notification.xsp?action=openDocument&documentId=172FFEC04ADC80F2C1256402003FB314 (last visited Oct. 7, 2019) [hereinafter Canada Declaration].

36. Declarations Made at the Time of Ratification, Feb. 27, 1986, *reprinted in* Declarations and Reservations of Italy Regarding Additional Protocol I to the Geneva Conventions, INT'L COMM. OF THE RED CROSS, TREATIES, STATE PARTIES AND COMMENTARY, https://ihl-databases.icrc.org/applic/ihl/ihl.nsf/Notification.xsp?action=openDocument&documentId=E2F248CE54CF09B5C1256402003FB443 (last visited Oct. 7, 2019) [hereinafter Italy Declaration].

37. Notification by the Depositary Addressed to the ICRC on 10 July 1987, ¶ 5, June 26, 1987, *reprinted in* Declarations and Reservations of Netherlands Regarding Additional Protocol I to the Geneva Conventions, INT'L COMM. OF THE RED CROSS, TREATIES, STATE PARTIES AND COMMENTARY, https://ihl-databases.icrc.org/applic/ihl/ihl.nsf/Notification.xsp?action=openDocument&documentId=E6EF925C67966E90C1256402003FB532 (last visited Oct. 7, 2019) [hereinafter Netherlands Declaration].

38. Notification by the Depositary Addressed to the ICRC on 24 November 1989, *reprinted in* Declarations and Reservations of Spain Regarding Additional Protocol I to the Geneva Conventions, INT'L COMM. OF THE RED CROSS, TREATIES, STATE PRACTICE AND COMMENTARY, https://ihl-databases.icrc.org/applic/ihl/ihl.nsf/Notification.xsp?action=openDocument&documentId=FC622F31C9E2236EC1256402003FB660 (last visited Oct. 7, 2019) [hereinafter Spain Declaration].

39. Notification by the Depository Addressed to the ICRC on 12 February 1988, ¶ 3, *reprinted in* Declarations and Reservations of New Zealand Regarding Additional Protocol I to the Geneva Conventions, INT'L COMM. OF THE RED CROSS, TREATIES, STATE PRACTICE AND COMMENTARY, https://ihl-databases.icrc.org/applic/ihl/ihl.nsf/Notification.xsp?action=openDocument&documentId=8FEC3861203ABE21C1256402003FB53B (last visited Oct. 7, 2019) [hereinafter New Zealand Declaration].

40. Notification by the Depository Addressed to the ICRC on 24 June 1991, *reprinted in* Declarations and Reservations of Australia Regarding Additional Protocol I to the Geneva Conventions, INT'L COMM. OF THE RED CROSS, TREATIES, STATE PRACTICE AND COMMENTARY, https://ihl-databases.icrc.org/applic/ihl/ihl.nsf/Notification.xsp?action=openDocument&

"[M]ilitary advantage involves a variety of considerations including the security of attacking forces."[41] These declarations provide sufficient evidence that considerations of military necessity may also have a (positive) impact on the determination of a military advantage.[42] According to the U.S. Department of Defense (DoD) Law of War Manual,

> [M]ilitary necessity may consider the broader imperatives of winning the war and not only the demands of the immediate situation. For example, in assessing the military advantage of attacking an object, one may consider the entire war strategy rather than only the potential tactical gains from attacking that object. An interpretation of military necessity that only permitted consideration of the immediate situation could prolong the fighting and increase the overall suffering caused by the war.[43]

Thirdly, the definition of military objectives "may be viewed as a way of evaluating whether military necessity exists to attack an object."[44]

It follows from the foregoing that, in the context of Article 57(3), considerations of military necessity do play a role insofar as the military advantage of attacks on the separate targets is concerned. In other words, for each of the targets, the military advantage has to be determined independently. This may include considerations of military necessity with a view to the overall aim of defeating the enemy as quickly as possible with the least expenditure of own assets or personnel. This may well result in different military advantages. By way of illustration, the military advantage of attacking railway tracks will result in depriving the enemy forces of a connection between two stations, whereas an attack on the railway station would result in a breakdown of an important hub and would thus deprive enemy forces from using train connections in an entire region, which will eventually limit the enemy's freedom of movement and result in an overall success. Thus, the military advantage accruing to an attack on the railway tracks will hardly be similar to an attack on the railway hub. Then, the train station may be chosen as a target although an attack on the railway track would "cause the least danger to civilian lives and to civilian objects." This finding is, of course, without prejudice to the prohibition of excessive collateral damage and to the obligation to take all feasible precautions to avoid or minimize nonexcessive collateral damage.

documentId=10312B4E9047086EC1256402003FB253 (last visited Oct. 7, 2019) [Australia Declaration].

41. *Supra* notes 39, 40.

42. *See also* Dinstein, *supra* note 2, ¶ 329.

43. DoD Manual, *supra* note 2, ¶ 2.2.3.1.

44. *Id.* ¶ 5.6.3.

D. Preliminary Conclusions

Military necessity as such does not absolve the parties to the conflict from the obligations to avoid or minimize collateral damage, to give an advance warning, or to choose a target offering a similar military advantage if this results in a reduction of dangers to the civilian population, civilians, and civilian objects. However, considerations of military necessity are relevant for the determination of the scope of these obligations. An advance warning is subject to the circumstances and, thus, to military necessity. The obligation to avoid or minimize collateral damage depends on "feasibility," which includes military considerations. The obligation to choose a target of attack upon which results in reduced dangers to civilians or civilian objects presupposes a similar military advantage, which is to be determined in light of not only tactical but also strategic considerations and, thus, of military necessity.

III. PROHIBITION OF EXCESSIVE COLLATERAL DAMAGE AND THE OBLIGATION TO CANCEL OR SUSPEND AN ATTACK

AP I, Article 51(5)(b) describes as indiscriminate, and thus prohibits, "an attack which may be expected to cause incidental loss of civilian life, injury to civilians, damage to civilian objects, or a combination thereof, which would be excessive in relation to the concrete and direct military advantage anticipated." AP I, Article 57(2)(b) provides that "an attack shall be cancelled or suspended if it becomes apparent that the objective is not a military one or is subject to special protection or that the attack may be expected to cause incidental loss of civilian life, injury to civilians, damage to civilian objects, or a combination thereof, which would be excessive in relation to the concrete and direct military advantage anticipated." For the purposes of the present chapter, the obligation to cancel or suspend an attack if the target is not a military objective or subject to special protection can be ignored.

In light of the findings of the preceding section, the excessiveness of the expected collateral damage of an attack against a lawful target is to be determined in light of the anticipated military advantage, which may include considerations of military necessity.[45] Of course, this "may not lead to the conclusion that the act of approximating proportionality is 'left to the unfettered discretion of the combatants.'"[46] Insofar, the same standards apply to Article 51(5)(b) and Article 57(2)(b). However, despite their close relation to excessive collateral damage, the provisions of Article 51(5)(b) and Article 57(2)(b) address two different situations. Moreover, the conditions triggering the respective prohibition or obligation differ considerably.

45. *Id.* ¶ 5.6.6.2; DINSTEIN, *supra* note 2, ¶ 326.

46. DINSTEIN, *supra* note 2, ¶ 327.

A. Proportionality

The present section deals with proportionality, that is with collateral damage expected to be excessive (as distinct from extensive[47]) in relation to the military advantage anticipated.[48] Arguably, "the principle of proportionality described in a more general sense . . . also underlies the affirmative duties to take feasible precautions for the protection of civilians and other protected persons and objects."[49] However, this may not lead to the conclusion that all precautions in attack required by the law of armed conflict are governed by proportionality. This merely holds true for Articles 57(2)(a)(ii) and (iii), Article 57(2)(b), Article 57(2)(a)(ii), and Article 57(3).

B. The Differences between AP I, Article 51(5)(b) and Article 57(2)(b)

As stated previously, the two provisions, while both applying if there is an expectation of excessive collateral damage thus obliging the parties to the conflict to either disapprove, cancel, or suspend an attack against a lawful target, differ considerably as to their temporal, personal, and material scope of applicability.

Both provisions have in common that they do not depend upon the "actual outcome of the attack but [on] the initial expectation and anticipation."[50] There is no "hindsight rule."[51] Accordingly, there is an expectation of excessive collateral damage only if "a reasonably well-informed person in the actual circumstances . . . , making reasonable use of the information available to him or her, could have expected excessive civilian casualties to result from the attack."[52] As stated in the U.K. Declaration, "[M]ilitary commanders and others responsible for planning, deciding upon, or executing attacks necessarily have to reach decisions on the basis of their assessment of the information from all sources which is reasonable available to them at the relevant time."[53] Still, the two provisions apply in different

47. The ICRC Commentary seems to confuse the two standards. *See* ICRC Commentary, *supra* note 5, ¶ 1979.

48. Dinstein, *supra* note 2, ¶ 326.

49. DoD Manual, *supra* note 2, ¶ 2.4.2.

50. Dinstein, *supra* note 2, ¶ 325.

51. *See* Germany Declaration, *supra* note 33; *see also* Australia Declaration, *supra* note 40; Belgium Declaration, *supra* note 34; Canada Declaration, *supra* note 35; Italy Declaration, *supra* note 36; Netherlands Declaration, *supra* note 37; New Zealand Declaration, *supra* note 39; Spain Declaration, *supra* note 38.

52. Dinstein, *supra* note 2, ¶ 327.

53. *See* U.K. Declaration, *supra* note 15. Similar declarations were made by Australia, *see* Australia Declaration, *supra* note 40, Germany, *see* Germany Declaration, *supra* note 33, Italy, *see* Italy Declaration, *supra* note 36, and Spain, *see* Spain Declaration, *supra* note 38. *See also* Notification by the Depositary Addressed to the ICRC on 16 August 1982, *reprinted in* Declarations and Reservations of Austria Regarding Additional Protocol I to the Geneva

phases. Whereas Article 51(5)(b) applies at the point in time in which the decision on an attack is made, Article 57(2)(b) applies after an attack has been approved and when the circumstances have changed in light of newly available information. By way of illustration, the Kunduz Incident may serve as an example.[54] On the basis of the information available to the German colonel, the decision to attack the tank trucks and the individuals present on the sandbank was in accordance with the law of armed conflict because the expected collateral damage on houses in the vicinity of the sandbank had been taken account of by choosing two 500-pound bombs instead of two 2,000-pound bombs. Hence, there was no longer an expectation of collateral damage, and the attack was not in violation of Article 51(5)(b). The obligation under Article 57(2)(b) was inapplicable because there was no new information reasonably available according to which not only Taliban fighters but also civilians were present on the sandbank.

The prohibition of Article 51(5)(b) applies to all involved in the planning and decision-making process who must reasonably expect the respective attack to cause excessive collateral damage. Accordingly, the personal scope of application is considerably wide, and all concerned are obliged to either disapprove or refrain from an attack. This is different insofar as an attack has been initially approved but circumstances have changed because in view of newly available information the attack is expected to cause excessive collateral damage (although the initial decision had been in accordance with the rules and principles of targeting law). The obligation under Article 57(2)(b) to cancel or suspend the attack does not apply to all involved in the planning or decision-making process but "only extends to those who have the authority and practical possibility to cancel or suspend the attack."[55]

Finally, the obligation to cancel or suspend an attack is limited to situations in which it becomes apparent that the attack may be expected to cause excessive collateral damage. The word "apparent" is used in the beginning of the if clause and accordingly sets the same standard for all three situations addressed in Article 57(2)(b). "Apparent" means "readily perceived or understood; obvious."[56] This is a considerably different standard than the one underlying Article 51(5)(b), although both provisions apply if there is an expectation of excessive collateral damage.[57] In the case of Article 57(2)(b), the newly available information on changed or new circumstances has to be such that the determination whether there is an

Conventions, INT'L COMM. OF THE RED CROSS, TREATIES, STATE PRACTICE AND COMMENTARY, https://ihl-databases.icrc.org/applic/ihl/ihl.nsf/Notification.xsp?action=openDocument&documentId=C5CD201B43C3E56AC1256402003FB262 (last visited Oct. 7, 2019).

54. For the 2009 Kunduz Incident, *see* Wolff Heintschel von Heinegg & Peter Dreist, *The 2009 Kunduz Air Attack: The Decision of the Federal Prosecutor-General on the Dismissal of Criminal Proceedings Against Members of the German Armed Forces*, 53 GER. Y.B. INT'L L. 833 (2010).

55. *See* U.K. Declaration, *supra* note 15.

56. *Apparent*, CONCISE OXFORD ENGLISH DICTIONARY 62 (12th ed. 2011).

57. For the elements to be taken into consideration, *see* DINSTEIN, *supra* note 2, ¶¶ 325–27.

expectation of excessive collateral damage is obvious. In other words, any reasonable commander receiving the new information, without a further "process of pondering dissimilar considerations,"[58] will have to arrive at the conclusion that there is an expectation of excessive collateral damage. This is due to the temporal phase in which the obligation applies. Whereas the decision according to Article 51(5)(b) will usually, albeit not exclusively, be taken in the planning phase of an attack, the decision according to Article 57(2)(b) has to be taken after an attack has already been approved. Moreover, it needs to be emphasized that the three situations addressed in that provision differ considerably. The fact that in light of newly available information a target is not a lawful military objective or subject to special protection can be ascertained without considerable difficulties. For instance, a pilot may recognize by visual means that the assigned target is an ambulance and he or she will have to cancel the attack because it has, thus, become apparent that the attack would be unlawful. Certainly, the determination whether an attack originally approved of as being in accordance with targeting law is expected to cause excessive collateral damage in light of newly available information is more difficult.

C. Preliminary Conclusions

The term "proportionality" is not a legal term of art under the law of armed conflict, nor is there a general "principle of proportionality" that would govern the law of armed conflict in a manner similar to the principle of distinction. Rather, the primary relevance of proportionality relates to the prohibition of attacks expected to cause excessive collateral damage—AP I, Articles 51(5)(b) and 57(2)(a)(iii)—and to the obligation to cancel or suspend an attack, if it becomes apparent that it is expected to cause excessive collateral damage—AP I, Article 57(2)(b). In order to ensure that excessive collateral damage will not be caused by an attack against a lawful target, the law of armed conflict does not satisfy itself with regulating merely the initial phase of the planning of, or decision on, an attack. It also regulates situations, in which circumstances change because of newly available information. Whereas the former situation is governed by rather strict standards, the latter triggers an obligation to cancel or suspend an attack only insofar as it becomes apparent that an originally approved and initiated attack is expected to cause excessive collateral damage.

In a wider sense, proportionality considerations also apply to situations in which there is no expectation of excessive collateral damage.[59] As seen, the obligations to avoid or minimize, to choose an alternative target, and to give an advance warning apply if there is an expectation of nonexcessive collateral damage. This, however, does not justify the conclusion that the law of armed conflict recognizes a general

58. *Id.* ¶ 326.

59. DoD Manual, *supra* note 2, ¶ 2.4.2.

principle of proportionality.[60] Proportionality considerations are at stake only if the respective rules so require.

IV. AN INTEGRATED APPROACH

A. The Interplay between Prohibited Attacks and Precautions in Attack

The prohibitions of attacks against nonmilitary objectives and of attacks expected to cause excessive collateral damage according to AP I, Article 51(5)(b) may not be considered in isolation. It is but one of a variety of factors that must be taken into account when planning, deciding upon, or executing an attack against a lawful target, including the obligation to take precautions. Already AP I, Article 57(2)(a)(iii), which re-emphasizes the prohibition of AP I, Article 51(5)(b), provides sufficient evidence to that effect. The same holds true for AP I, Article 57(2)(b), which obliges the parties to the conflict to cancel or suspend an attack if it becomes apparent that it is expected to cause excessive collateral damage. The parties to the conflict may, however, not satisfy themselves with complying only with these provisions. In other words, it does not suffice to merely ensure that there is no expectation of excessive collateral damage. Unless there is no expectation of collateral damage—a determination to be based upon the information reasonably available in the given circumstances—the law of armed conflict obliges the parties to the conflict to exert additional efforts aimed at either avoiding or minimizing collateral damage (Article 57(2)(a)(ii)), which may be accomplished by an advance warning according to Article 57(2)(c), or by choosing an alternative target offering a similar military advantage but an attack upon which will result in least danger to civilians and civilian objects (Article 57(3)). Accordingly, a targeting decision to be in compliance with the law of armed conflict must be the result of a complex process. It must include all the aforementioned considerations in order to eventually result in a lawful targeting decision. The aforementioned considerations are the elements that must by necessity be included in the decision-making process in order to form a whole, which means that the final decision must be the result of an integrated approach.

It is important to re-emphasize that the scope of the prohibition and of the respective precautionary obligations depends upon the circumstances ruling at the time and is subject to considerations of military necessity. This holds true for the determination of the military advantage when deciding upon the legality of the target and on whether the collateral damage is expected to be excessive, for the choice of an alternative target, for assessing the feasibility of precautions, and for the obligation to give an advance warning.

60. *See* Wolff Heintschel von Heinegg, *Proportionality and Collateral Damage*, *in* The Law of Armed Conflict and the Use of Force, *supra* note 7, at 1055, 1055.

B. The "Targeting Cycle"

The targeting process that must be based upon an integrated approach may be summarized as follows.

The first step is the verification of the lawfulness of the target under AP I, Article 57(2)(a)(i), which not only includes the determination of the military advantage anticipated from the attack, but which is also dependent on feasibility, which includes humanitarian and military considerations.

The second step is to determine whether there is an expectation of collateral damage. This step may be considered the crossroad in the decision-making process. If, based upon the information reasonable available, there is no collateral damage to be expected, the attack may be approved and, apart from the obligation to take constant care according to AP I, Article 57(1), no further precautions need to be taken.

If there is an expectation of collateral damage, those responsible for the attack decision will, in a third step, have to assess whether it is expected to be excessive. This assessment "entails a mental process of pondering dissimilar considerations—to wit, civilian losses/damage and military advantage—and is not an exact science. . . . There is no objective possibility of quantifying the factors of the equation, and the process necessarily contains a large subjective element."[61] Military necessity, including the reduction of own losses and the overall aim of neutralizing the enemy forces, is a decisive factor in that assessment, which may eventually result in either an affirmative or a negative determination. If collateral damage is expected to be excessive, the attack may not be approved or executed because it would be in violation of AP I, Articles 51(5)(b) and 57(2)(a)(iii).

If the assessment results in a decision that the collateral damage is expected to be nonexcessive, those responsible are obliged to comply with the further precautions in attack. In that fourth step, they are required to consider whether it is feasible to avoid or minimize nonexcessive collateral damage, as provided for in AP I, Article 57(2)(a)(ii). Feasibility is to be assessed in light of humanitarian and military considerations. Again, there is no objective quantifying factor that will equally apply to all attacks expected to result in nonexcessive collateral damage. It all depends upon the circumstances ruling at the time and on what is reasonably available to the responsible commanders. In that context, commanders should consider an advance warning according to AP I, Article 57(2)(c), a decision clearly governed by military necessity.

In a fifth step, commanders must take a decision according to AP I, Article 57(3). If there is an alternative target offering a similar military advantage, the attack must be directed against that target, if it is expected to cause the least danger to civilians and civilian objects. The similarity of the expected military advantage is to be assessed in light of military necessity and is, therefore, dependent upon the circumstances ruling at the time. The determination of the extent of the

61. Dinstein, *supra* note 2, ¶ 326 (citing further references).

collateral damage or dangers for civilians and civilian objects must by necessity be based upon a comparison of the effects of the initial and of the alternative target.

Unless circumstances change, the attack may eventually be approved, which regularly marks the end of the decision-making process, which is "a matter of pre-attack expectation and anticipation [and thus] embedded in probabilities."[62] This, however, does not relieve those responsible for the targeting decision from taking constant care according to AP I, Article 57(1). If the circumstances underlying the attack decision change, for instance in light of newly available information, they will have to take a sixth step, that is, the attack has to be canceled or suspended according to AP I, Article 57(2)(b), if it becomes apparent that the target is not a military objective, is subject to special protection, or if the (originally lawfully approved) attack is expected to cause excessive collateral damage. The expected excessiveness is, again, determined in light of the anticipated military advantage and, thus, also by considerations of military necessity. It is important to note that in view of the fact that the expected excessiveness must be "apparent," there is no legal requirement of re-entering the complex process of assessing excessiveness.[63]

The Annex to this chapter provides a schematic illustration of the targeting process as required by the law of armed conflict.

V. CONCLUDING REMARKS

It has been shown that targeting decisions to be in full compliance with the law of armed conflict must be based on a complex assessment of a variety of factors that in their entirety (as distinguished from a selective approach) will eventually result in either the legality or illegality of an attack decision. Unfortunately, military manuals do not necessarily capture this complexity.[64] Instead of taking an integrated approach, which is required by the law of armed conflict, the respective provisions are dealt with separately without providing an explanation of their combined effect on the legality or illegality of an attack decision. Military commanders, and to a certain degree also those executing attacks, must be aware of their obligation to not merely satisfy themselves with avoiding excessive collateral damage. The law of armed conflict imposes upon them much stricter obligations, in particular with regard to the required precautions in attack. While many of the factors, such as military necessity, military advantage, and feasibility, are not absolute but circumstantial, military commanders must be aware of their fundamental importance in the interplay between the various applicable provisions.

Finally, it must be born in mind that noncompliance with the aforementioned requirements under the law of armed conflict will not necessarily result in international criminal responsibility of those responsible for the attack decision. The war crime under Article 8(2)(b)(iv) of the ICC Statute is limited to an intentional

62. *Id.*

63. *See supra* text accompanying note 60.

64. *See, e.g.*, Germany Manual, *supra* note 15, ¶ 416.

attack "in the knowledge that such attack will cause incidental loss of life or injury to civilians or damage to civilian objects . . . which would be clearly excessive in relation to the concrete and direct overall military advantage anticipated." Arguably, the intentional launching of an attack in disregard of the fact that, due to changed circumstances, it has become apparent that the attack may be expected to cause excessive collateral damage, is a war crime under Article 8(2)(b)(iv). The unlawful failure to avoid or minimize nonexcessive collateral damage or to choose an alternative target as provided for by AP I, Article 57(3) is not sufficiently grave to be considered a war crime *stricto sensu*.

ANNEX: *THE "TARGETING CYCLE" IN LIGHT OF THE PROHIBITION OF EXCESSIVE COLLATERAL DAMAGE AND THE OBLIGATION TO TAKE PRECAUTIONS IN ATTACK*

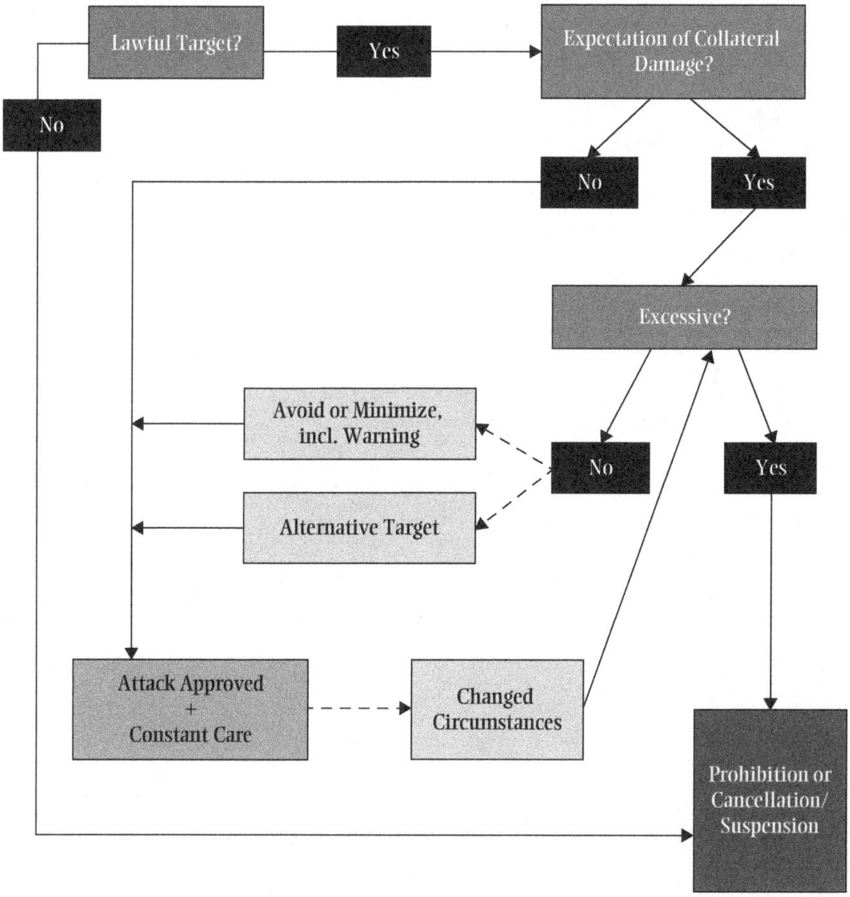

11

Specifying the Proportionality Test and the Standard of Due Precaution: Problems of Prognostic Assessment in Determining the Meaning of "May Be Expected" and "Anticipated"

STEFAN OETER*

I. INTRODUCTION

The operational issues raised by the prohibition of indiscriminate warfare, and the proportionality requirement in assessing the legality of collateral damage in particular, probably belong to the most complex and difficult questions in the law of armed conflict. This chapter will examine a number of particularly challenging issues in that respect, but will leave aside the question whether the rules of Articles 51 and 57 of the First Additional Protocol to the 1949 Geneva Conventions (AP I) actually mirror the inherited rules of customary law.[1] The chapter simply assumes that by and large the relevant rules of Articles 51(5) and 57(2) may be seen as identical with the parallel standards of customary law.[2]

* Professor for German and Comparative Public Law and Public International Law, Faculty of Law, University of Hamburg.

1. *See* Robert D. Sloane, *Puzzles of Proportion and the "Reasonable Military Commander": Reflections on the Law, Ethics, and Geopolitics of Proportionality*, 6 Harv. Nat'l Sec. J. 299, 310–12 (2015).

2. *See* 1 Int'l Comm. of the Red Cross, Customary International Humanitarian Law: Rules 48–49 (Jean-Marie Henckaerts & Louise Doswald-Beck eds., 2005) [hereinafter ICRC Customary IHL Study]; Shane Darcy, Judges, Law and War: The Judicial Development of International Humanitarian Law 204–15 (2014). *But see* Aaron

Stefan Oeter, *Specifying the Proportionality Test and the Standard of Due Precaution: Problems of Prognostic Assessment in Determining the Meaning of "May Be Expected" and "Anticipated"* In: *Necessity and Proportionality in International Peace and Security Law.* Edited by: Professor Claus Kreß and Captain Robert Lawless, Oxford University Press (2021). © Oxford University Press. DOI: 10.1093/oso/9780197537374.003.0012.

The starting point of the following reflections are the two rules contained in AP I that concern issues of proportionality of collateral damage: Article 51(5)(b) and Article 57(2)(b).[3] The first one defines—under the umbrella of the heading "protection of civilians"—the nature and form of (prohibited) indiscriminate attacks. The chapeau of Article 51(5) reads, "Among others, the following types of attacks are to be considered as indiscriminate," and then continues with several cases. Subparagraph (b) of Article 51(5) indicates as one version of indiscriminate attacks "an attack which may be expected to cause incidental loss of civilian life, injury to civilians, damage to civilian objects, or a combination thereof, which would be excessive in relation to the concrete and direct military advantage anticipated."

Article 57 is the norm that regulates precautions in attack.[4] The first paragraph of that article provides, "In the conduct of military operations, constant care shall be taken to spare the civilian population, civilians and civilian objects." In Paragraph 2, the required measures of "constant care" are further detailed. Subparagraph (b) of Article 57(2) explains that

> an attack shall be cancelled or suspended if it becomes apparent that the objective is not a military one or is subject to special protection or that the attack may be expected to cause incidental loss of civilian life, injury to civilians, damage to civilian objects, or a combination thereof, which would be excessive in relation to the concrete and direct military advantage anticipated.[5]

The following reflections will first concentrate on the fundamental issue dealt with in Article 51(5)(b): What makes an attack that unavoidably must include incidental loss of civilian lives or civilian property an "indiscriminate attack"? And in more concrete terms, how can we operationalize the formula of collateral damage—"which would be excessive in relation to the concrete and direct military advantage anticipated"—in combat situations? This formula foresees a basic structure of three analytical steps that must be taken in order to come to a sound judgment whether expected collateral damage is legitimate or, to the contrary,

Fellmeth, *The Proportionality Principle in Operation: Methodological Limitations of Empirical Research and the Need for Transparency*, 45 Isr. L. Rev. 125, 131–35 (2012).

3. Protocol Additional to the Geneva Conventions of 12 August 1949, and Relating to the Protection of Victims of International Armed Conflict (Protocol I), June 8, 1977, 1125 U.N.T.S. 3 [hereinafter AP I].

4. *See* ICRC Customary IHL Study, *supra* note 2, at 51–57; Stefan Oeter, *Methods and Means of Combat*, *in* The Handbook of International Humanitarian Law 119, 207–12 (Dieter Fleck ed., 2d ed. 2009); Isabel Robinson & Ellen Nohle, *Proportionality and Precautions in Attack: The Reverberating effects of Using Explosive Weapons in Populated Areas*, 98 Int'l Rev. Red Cross 107, 113–31 (2016).

5. AP I, *supra* note 3, art. 57(2)(b).

makes the attack a (prohibited) act of indiscriminate warfare.[6] Two of the three analytical steps involve strong prognostic elements. One must first project which forms of collateral damage an attack will cause, and what amount of incidental loss to civilian lives and civilian property will happen. Like any other prognosis of future events under conditions of (at least partial) epistemic insecurity, such an assessment contains significant risk of error. The other step with prognostic elements requires an identification of the "concrete and direct military advantage anticipated." The projection of such an anticipated military advantage strongly relies on the operational planning of the armed forces involved. The responsible military commander will know his (or his own forces') planning, but obviously not the planning of the adversary. Experience may allow some degree of learned speculation about the planning and the intentions of the other side, but of course these considerations remain largely unknown. Nevertheless, it is the interaction of the commander's own military planning and the countermoves of the other side that finally determines the "concrete and direct military advantage anticipated." As a result, such military advantage will always remain dynamic to a certain degree.[7] Operational situations evolve dynamically and might make previous operational planning obsolete. These two (highly insecure) elements must then be related to each other, in the sense of a proportionality assessment. In essence, this requires comparing apples with pears. It can be done—indeed, this calculation is required under the law—but the intellectual operation underlying such assessment inevitably will be highly subjective.[8]

These reflections will then move to the issue of necessary precautions under AP I, Article 57(2)(b). What will be of most interest is not the ordinary situation of a diligent planner providing for a sequence of operational moves, but rather the much more chaotic decisional constellation of a field commander who must make the decision whether a certain operation (for example, an attack) shall be undertaken. As said previously, operational situations evolve dynamically, and one may not always rely on the previous judgment of the planner. Situations naturally change, and accordingly, commanders have a duty to make their own judgment whether the planned operation is still justifiable. This requires strong reconnaissance and intelligence, as a source of constant updating of the informational fundaments of assessing the concrete proportionality of an operation at a specific point in time.

6. *See* Nils Melzer, *The Principle of Distinction Between Civilians and Combatants*, *in* The Oxford Handbook of International Law in Armed Conflict 296 (Andrew Clapham & Paola Gaeta eds., 2014); Oeter, *supra* note 4, at 197–207; Yoram Dinstein, The Conduct of Hostilities under the Law of International Armed Conflict 121–55 (3d ed. 2016).

7. *See* Oeter, *supra* note 4, at 183–86; Judith G. Gardam, Necessity, Proportionality and the Use of Force by States 102 (2004).

8. *See* Sloane, *supra* note 1, at 301–303.

II. THE PROPORTIONALITY TEST: RELATING THE EXPECTED INCIDENTAL LOSS TO THE MILITARY ADVANTAGE ANTICIPATED

The introduction indicated that the intellectual operation underlying the proportionality test is a tricky issue. The entire doctrine of proportionality (or, in functional terms, of the banning of "excessive collateral damage") might sound awkward for military practitioners, but it is unavoidable since it secures basic tenets of the principle of distinction and the prohibition of indiscriminate warfare. Before codifying these principles in the text of AP I, it had already been widely accepted that attacks on military objectives are subject to elementary restrictions.[9] There was agreement that if collateral damage is likely to affect the civilian population and civilian goods as a consequence of the attack, then the anticipated damage must not be excessive in relation to the intended military advantage.[10] It is not clear, however, whether AP I, Article 51(5)(b) goes beyond that minimum requirement and settles that all damaging effects of military operations must be measured against the yardstick of proportionality (in a broader sense).[11] The collateral damage which inevitably occurs on the occasion of nearly every attack is justifiable only in so far as losses to the "innocent" civilian population are commensurate with the military advantage which the operation sought to achieve.[12] As a general rule this sounds reasonable. However, the principle of proportionality

9. *See* 2 L. Oppenheim, International Law: A Treatise 346 (H. Lauterpacht ed., 7th ed. 1952); *see also* ICRC Customary IHL Study, *supra* note 2, at 46–50; Enzo Cannizzaro, *Proportionality in the Law of Armed Conflict*, *in* The Oxford Handbook of International Law in Armed Conflict, *supra* note 6, at 332.

10. On the customary rule of proportionality, *see* W. Hays Parks, *Air War and the Law of War*, 32 Air Force L. Rev. 1, 168–75 (1990); George Aldrich, *New Life for the Laws of War*, 75 Am. J. Int'l L. 764, 778 (1981); Marco Sassòli, Bedeutung einer Kodifikation für das allgemeine Völkerrecht mit besonderer Betrachtung der Regeln zum Schutze der Zivilbevölkerung vor den Auswirkungen von Feindseligkeiten 412–15 (1990); Joseph Holland, *Military Objective and Collateral Damage: Their Relationship and Dynamics*, 7 Y.B. Int'l Humanitarian L. 35, 51–52 (2004).

11. Concerning the rather controversial debate on including criteria of proportionality in AP I, *see* William J. Fenrick, *The Rule of Proportionality and Protocol I in Conventional Warfare*, 98 Mil. L. Rev. 91 (1982); Int'l Comm. of the Red Cross, Commentary on the Additional Protocols of 8 June 1977 to the Geneva Conventions of 12 August 1949 ¶¶ 2204–18 (Yves Sandoz, Christophe Swinarski & Bruno Zimmerman eds., 1987) [hereinafter ICRC Commentary]; Sassòli, *supra* note 10, at 415–18. As to the combination of indiscriminate and disproportionate attacks in AP I, Article 51(5), *see* Gardam, *supra* note 7, at 93–96.

12. *See* Michael Bothe, Karl Josef Partsch, & Waldemar A. Solf, New Rules for Victims of Armed Conflicts: Commentary on the Two 1977 Protocols Additional to the Geneva Conventions of 1949, at 310 (1982); *see also* Int'l Comm. of the Red Cross, The Principle of Proportionality in the Rules Governing the Conduct of Hostilities under International Humanitarian Law 8 (2016), https://www.icrc.org/en/download/file/79184/4358_002_expert_meeting_report_web_1.pdf (last visited Oct. 7, 2019) [hereinafter ICRC, The Principle of Proportionality].

creates serious difficulties in practice, since it necessarily remains loosely defined and is open to subjective assessment and balancing. In the framework of the required evaluation, the actors enjoy a considerable margin of appreciation.[13]

This is particularly true in view of the strongly prognostic character of any such assessment, which must always be an assessment of the future effects of the operation.[14] Objective standards for the appraisal and balancing of expected collateral damage and intended military advantage are virtually nonexistent. Proportionality requires that two very unlike values be weighed and balanced against each other, without any objective method to compare two such disparate categories.[15] In the final result, therefore, it is for the competent military commander and the staff planning the operation—who should know best the possible results and repercussions—to assess the consequences of the operation and to ensure its proportionality.[16] Final responsibility is thus laid in the hands of the military, which can act only on the basis of the information available at the time of the decision. For example, Germany, like most other NATO members that ratified AP I, filed a declaration that "the decision taken by the person responsible has to be judged on the basis of all information available to him at the relevant time, and not on the basis of hindsight."[17] In a second interpretative declaration Germany

13. As to these problems, *see* Fenrick, *supra* note 11, at 126; Bothe, Partsch, & Solf, *supra* note 12, at 310.

14. *See* Sloane, *supra* note 1, at 312–16.

15. *See* Holland, *supra* note 10, at 46–47; *see also* ICRC, The Principle of Proportionality, *supra* note 12, at 52.

16. *See* Frits Kalshoven & Lisbeth Zegveld, Constraints on the Waging of War: An Introduction to International Humanitarian Law 115 (3d ed. 2001). For the subsequent difficulties with respect to the criminal responsibility according to Article 8(2)(b)(iv) of the Rome Statute, *see* Torsten Stein, *Collateral Damage, Proportionality and Individual International Criminal Responsibility*, *in* International Humanitarian Law Facing New Challenges 158–61 (Wolff Heintschel von Heinegg & Volker Epping eds., 2007); *see also* ICRC, The Principle of Proportionality, *supra* note 12, at 58–59.

17. *See* Notification by the Depositary Addressed to the ICRC on 15 February 1991, ¶ 4, *reprinted in* Declarations and Reservations of Germany Regarding Additional Protocol I to the Geneva Conventions, Int'l Comm. of the Red Cross, Treaties, State Parties and Commentary, https://ihl-databases.icrc.org/applic/ihl/ihl.nsf/Notification.xsp?action=openDocument&documentId=3F4D8706B6B7EA40C1256402003FB3C7 (last visited Oct. 7, 2019) [hereinafter Germany Declaration]; Interpretive Declarations Made at the Time of Ratification, May 20, 1986, ¶ 5, *reprinted in* Declarations and Reservations of Belgium Regarding Additional Protocol I to the Geneva Conventions, Int'l Comm. of the Red Cross, Treaties, State Parties and Commentary, https://ihl-databases.icrc.org/applic/ihl/ihl.nsf/Notification.xsp?action=openDocument&documentId=EA2560B9B790488EC1256402003FB2BC (last visited Oct. 7, 2019); Declarations Made at the Time of Ratification, Feb. 27, 1986, *reprinted in* Declarations and Reservations of Italy Regarding Additional Protocol I to the Geneva Conventions, Int'l Comm. of the Red Cross, Treaties, State Parties and Commentary, https://ihl-databases.icrc.org/applic/ihl/ihl.nsf/Notification.xsp?action=openDocument&documentId=E2F248CE54CF09B5C1256402003FB443 (last visited Oct. 7, 2019); Notification by the Depositary Addressed to the ICRC on 10 July 1987, ¶ 5, June 26, 1987, *reprinted in* Declarations and Reservations

stated that by "definite military advantage" in AP I, Article 51(5)(b), it understood "the advantage anticipated from the attack considered as a whole and not only from isolated or particular parts of the attack."[18] This means that the point of reference of the required balancing is not the gain of territory or other advantage expected from the isolated action of a single unit; rather, what counts is the context of the overall military campaign of which that action forms part. Only in the framework of the overall campaign plan of a belligerent can one assess the relative military value of the specific purpose of an individual attack.[19] In essence this should be self-evident: actions of individual units are not ends in themselves in modern integrated warfare. To the contrary, they must be placed in their operational context.

There are further problems that make the handling of the proportionality requirement of AP I, Article 51(5)(b) extremely difficult. In practice, the circumstances usually involve combatants and civilians, military objects or installations and civilian settlements, industrial plants, and infrastructure installations of dual use. Such a complicated mixture of categories not only makes it difficult to meet the requirements of distinction but also makes (considerable) collateral damage inevitable. To prevent excessive losses and damage to the civilian population proves extremely difficult in such situations, unless the adversary takes it upon itself to ensure a certain minimum separation between military objectives and civilian population.[20] A particularly difficult problem is caused for the attacker if the

of Netherlands Regarding Additional Protocol I to the Geneva Conventions, INT'L COMM. OF THE RED CROSS, TREATIES, STATE PARTIES AND COMMENTARY, https://ihl-databases.icrc.org/applic/ihl/ihl.nsf/Notification.xsp?action=openDocument&documentId=E6EF925C67966E90C1256402003FB532 (last visited Oct. 7, 2019); Notification by the Depositary Addressed to the ICRC on 24 November 1989, *reprinted in* Declarations and Reservations of Spain Regarding Additional Protocol I to the Geneva Conventions, INT'L COMM. OF THE RED CROSS, TREATIES, STATE PRACTICE AND COMMENTARY, https://ihl-databases.icrc.org/applic/ihl/ihl.nsf/Notification.xsp?action=openDocument&documentId=FC622F31C9E2236EC1256402003FB660 (last visited Oct. 7, 2019); THE LAWS OF ARMED CONFLICTS: A COLLECTION OF CONVENTIONS, RESOLUTIONS, AND OTHER DOCUMENTS 707, 712, 714, 717 (Dietrich Schindler & Jiri Toman eds., 4th ed. 2004). As to the underlying problem, *see* Brian J. Bill, *The Rendulic "Rule": Military Necessity, Commander's Knowledge, and Methods of Warfare*, 12 Y.B. INT'L HUMANITARIAN L. 119, 133–42 (2009).

18. *See* Germany Declaration, *supra* note 17, ¶ 5. As to the background of the declaration, *see* Fenrick, *supra* note 11, at 107; Parks, *supra* note 10, at 172; BOTHE, PARTSCH, & SOLF, *supra* note 12, at 311, 325; SASSÒLI, *supra* note 10, at 417; YORAM DINSTEIN, THE CONDUCT OF HOSTILITIES UNDER THE LAW OF INTERNATIONAL ARMED CONFLICT 92–95 (2d ed. 2010) [hereinafter DINSTEIN, 2d ed.].

19. *See* SASSÒLI, *supra* note 10, at 414; *see also* Noam Neuman, *Applying the Rule of Proportionality: Force Protection and Cumulative Assessment in International Law and Morality*, 7 Y.B. INT'L HUMANITARIAN L. 79, 96–100 (2004); Kenneth Watkin, *Assessing Proportionality: Moral Complexity and Legal Rules*, 7 Y.B. INT'L HUMANITARIAN L. 3, 19–21 (2005); ICRC, THE PRINCIPLE OF PROPORTIONALITY, *supra* note 12, at 13–17.

20. For critical observations, *see* Parks, *supra* note 10, at 152–56.

opposing side illegally uses the civilian population to shield military activities, whether by transferring parts of the civilian population deliberately to military installations,[21] or by calculatedly establishing military objectives among the civilian population and civilian objects.[22] A common and prominent example of such geographical mixing is subcontracting in the armaments industry, which transforms seemingly civilian industrial installations into military objectives.[23] Nevertheless, AP I, Article 51(8) expressly confirms that the violation of international legal obligations by the adversary does not exempt the attacker from his legal obligations with regard to the civilian population.[24]

The problem is obviously not solved by that provision—quite to the contrary. The attacker will face extreme difficulties of justification, without having the alternative of accepting a higher level of collateral damage, if it wants effectively to counter the moves of the opponent.[25] Also, the role of civilians deliberately incorporated into the military organization of the belligerent, such as workers in arms factories or civilian drivers of munitions transports, has remained unclear in that regard.[26] Does the loss of thousands of workers in an attack on a munitions factory have the same relative value, in terms of the proportionality of collateral damage, as the predictable deaths of women and children caused by an attack on a military command center located in the midst of a densely populated civilian quarter? Does the rule of proportionality allow measures avoiding risks of casualties among one's own soldiers to the detriment of the civilian population?[27] Many would argue no, but it must be admitted that many questions are left open.[28]

The role of the commander responsible for the operation is not made easier by these uncertainties, although one should not exaggerate demands for exact detail in such a rule. What is required is no more than a sincere effort to cope with the problem of collateral damage, and a proper application of common sense.

21. Concerning the issue of "human shields," *see* IAN HENDERSON, THE CONTEMPORARY LAW OF TARGETING 203–206 (2009).

22. *See* Oeter, *supra* note 4, ¶ 446, at 188.

23. As to the resulting problems, *see* HENDERSON, *supra* note 21, at 106–10; Parks, *supra* note 10, at 159–68; Stefan Oeter, *Comment: Is the Principle of Distinction Outdated?*, *in* INTERNATIONAL HUMANITARIAN LAW FACING NEW CHALLENGES, *supra* note 16, at 53, 59–60.

24. *See* Parks, *supra* note 10, at 163–64; SASSÒLI, *supra* note 10, at 447–53; ICRC COMMENTARY, *supra* note 11, ¶¶ 1989–93.

25. For critical remarks on this point, *see* Parks, *supra* note 10, at 164–65.

26. *Id.* at 174–79.

27. *See* Neuman, *supra* note 19, at 90–96.

28. *See, e.g.*, DINSTEIN, 2d ed., *supra* note 18, at 131, 136; Christine Byron, *International Humanitarian Law and Bombing Campaigns: Legitimate Military Objectives and Excessive Collateral Damage*, Y.B. INT'L HUMANITARIAN L. 175, 195 (2010). For a military ethics perspective, *see* Cheryl Abbate, *Assuming Risk: A Critical Analysis of a Soldier's Duty to Prevent Collateral Casualties*, 13 J. MIL. ETHICS 70 (2014).

Humanitarian law in that regard is dependent on an inherent sense of humanity, whose impulse is to avoid attacks causing catastrophic collateral damage when the objective is of only marginal importance. In other words, the law shuns blatant disproportionality. Judging proportionality thus is, in essence, a decision that appeals to morality and professional ethics and relies on moral judgment of deciding commanders.[29]

Some further reflections on the tricky details of the proportionality test are needed if one shall understand fully the intricacies of the prohibition of excessive collateral damages. The introductory remarks already highlighted the prognostic character of two of the three analytical steps that must be undertaken in assessing the proportionality of military operations with respect to their incidental losses. Let us first look at the determination of the expected incidental losses to civilian lives and civilian goods. There are two factors creating quite some insecurity in that regard. The first is the dynamic character of the distinction between military objectives and civilian goods, making it challenging to decide at one point in time whether a certain installation is and will remain of a military character or falls and will remain to fall under the protection of civilian persons and goods.[30] The second factor creating epistemic uncertainty is the time lag between operational planning (and decision-making) and the effective execution of the operation. What may have been totally harmless at one point in time may later become extremely problematic. Consider the notorious "Kunduz incident" involving the German district commander Colonel Klein.[31] Initially, there were two military fuel trucks hijacked by Taliban forces that had got stuck in a river ford. Attacking these two trucks in clinical isolation somewhere out in the empty countryside would have been a safe issue. However, soon the Taliban called the villagers from nearby hamlets for help, first to move the trucks out of the ford, then to unload the fuel into canisters, with more and more civilians assembling in the area. This significantly complicated the situation, and thus provides an example of how the determination of "expected incidental loss" can become tricky.

The dynamic character of distinguishing military objectives from (protected) civilian goods finds its expression in AP I, Article 52(2). The second sentence of this provisions states that "military objectives are limited to those objects which by their nature, location, purpose or use make an effective contribution to military action and whose total or partial destruction, capture or neutralization, in the circumstances ruling at the time, offers a definite military advantage."[32] Such conceptualization of "military objective" contains two structuring elements:

29. *See* Holland, *supra* note 10, at 73–74; ICRC, The Principle of Proportionality, *supra* note 12, at 51–59.

30. *See* Oeter, *Comment*, *supra* note 23, ¶ 444.

31. *See* Wolff Heintschel von Heinegg, *The 2009 Kunduz Air Attack*, 53 Ger. Y.B. Int'l L. 833 (2010).

32. As to the notion of "definite military advantage," *see* ICRC Customary IHL Study, *supra* note 2, at 49–50; Oeter, *Methods and Means of Combat*, *supra* note 4, at 185–86.

- objects which by their nature, location, purpose, or use make an effective contribution to military action
- whose total or partial destruction, capture, or neutralization, in the circumstances ruling at the time, offers a definite military advantage.

This includes elements susceptible to change in time.[33] The nature and location of an object may be relatively static elements. Purpose and use, however, are definitely not static concepts. These elements contain the inherent assumption of a fluid situation in which an object that at its origin was purely civilian in purpose and use, may under changed circumstances easily become a military objective. There are plenty of examples for such a dynamic. Let us think of the civilian infrastructure for energy delivery, in particular electricity networks.[34] Depending on the characteristics of the network, they may suddenly become extremely important military objectives with the outbreak of armed conflict. The same often happens with the civilian transport infrastructure, for example roads, bridges, and railway lines. If such infrastructure attains central significance for military logistics, something quite probable during armed conflict, it is likely to transform into a military objective.[35] On a smaller scale, this often happens also with seemingly harmless objects, such as a church tower which is then used as a looking point for artillery observers, or a farmhouse on a strategic site transformed into a military position manned by armed forces.[36] These examples show that the difference between military objectives and civilian objects is context dependent and cannot be resolved irrespective of the particular circumstances.

The largely context-dependent character of the definition of military objective may lead to significant phenomena of mixing military resources with the civilian population and civilian objects—the farmhouse may suddenly become a military objective, but the farmer's family may still be present in the house; or roads and bridges may simultaneously serve military and civilian traffic. It is also due to topographic and urbanistic features of certain locations that military installations and civilian objects cannot always be separated neatly. State parties should do the utmost to avoid operating in such a vicinity, but—as indicated—this is often not possible for geographical, economic, or other reasons.[37] The mentioned dynamics of sudden transformation of civilian objects into military objectives certainly creates dilemmas for application of the principle of distinction. But for all the reasons mentioned, an attack on (definite) military objectives will also likely cause in a lot of cases incidental losses of civilian lives and civilian goods.

33. On the (dynamic) definition of military objectives, *see generally* HENDERSON, *supra* note 21, at 43–78, 79–124.

34. *See id.* at 139–41.

35. *See* DINSTEIN, 2d ed., *supra* note 18, at 98.

36. *See* Oeter, *Comment*, *supra* note 23, ¶ 444.5.

37. *Id.*

If reflected upon on a very fundamental level of moral philosophy and military ethics, it becomes clear that simply banning any type of incidental loss of civilian lives and goods is impossible if you do not rule out any use of military force.[38] As soon as one accepts that states may legitimately use military force, for example in self-defense against a foreign aggressor or in restoring law and order internally by oppressing an insurgency, it is more or less unavoidable to accept a certain degree of incidental loss. One may try to limit such incidental losses by imposing severe restrictions and obligations of "due care" on the armed forces.[39] However, banning collateral damage altogether would create perverse incentives: malicious parties to the conflict would then be tempted to "immunize" their troops and military installations, creating a situation of moral hazard where the moral actor can only lose, and the immoral actor structurally wins.

Behind the ethical dilemma of collateral damage thus lies an intricate problem of "normative asymmetry"—we must avoid making the law so rigid that an actor loyal to the law is prevented from achieving its aims in the conflict.[40] In a world full of heinous actors and cynical rulers ready to use force in ignorance of all legal rules, the normative setup for military action in armed conflict must be construed in a way that realistically allows the state trying to obey the law to conduct hostilities without being doomed to failure. This calls for a delimitation of sustainable levels of incidental loss that allow the conduct of military operations while drawing boundary lines that demarcate where the extent and nature of collateral damage becomes so problematic that it cannot be legally tolerated.[41]

Any attempt to draw such boundary lines inevitably ends up in an act of balancing.[42] It is not the fault of the drafters of AP I that the rules on collateral damage and proportionality are rather vague and open-ended, leaving room for subjective assessment.[43] It is a result of the structure of the problem. The proportionality rule of Article 51(5)(b) does justice to the underlying ethical dilemma by providing that armed forces in an armed conflict are prohibited to lead operations "expected to cause incidental loss of civilian life, injury to civilians, damage to civilian objects, or a combination thereof, which would be excessive in relation to the concrete and direct military advantage anticipated."

38. *See* Frances Kamm, *Justifications for Killing Noncombatants in War*, 24 MIDWEST STUD. PHIL. 219–28 (2000).

39. *See* MICHAEL WALZER, JUST AND UNJUST WARS: A MORAL ARGUMENT WITH HISTORICAL ILLUSTRATIONS 155–56 (3d ed. 2000); Anne Schwenkenbecher, *Collateral Damage and the Principle of Due Care*, 13 J. MIL. ETHICS 94 (2014).

40. *See also* Michael Walzer, *Noncombatant Immunity and Military Necessity*, *in* 2 ETHICS OF WAR AND CONFLICT: JUST WAR DOCTRINE 341, 352–54 (Asa Kasher ed., 2014).

41. *See also* Thomas Hurka, *Proportionality in the Morality of War*, 33 PHIL. & PUB. AFF. 34 (2005).

42. *See* C.A.J. COADY, MORALITY AND POLITICAL VIOLENCE 137 (2008).

43. *See* Sloane, *supra* note 1, at 312–15.

The norm requires belligerents to relate the expected incidental loss to the "concrete and direct military advantage anticipated." This is not the place to go in detail concerning what "concrete and direct" means[44]—a topic for a paper on its own. The focus here, rather, is on the fact that the pair of concepts that must be related to and compared with each other consists on both sides of strongly prognostic character: "expected incidental loss" to the civilian population on the one side, "anticipated military advantage" on the other side. The prognostic character of both essential elements of the analytical operation of balancing makes the proportionality test dependent on prognoses of future consequences of a planned action.[45]

This seems relatively easy in the case of the "anticipated military advantage." The expectations concerning certain concrete operational moves ("attacks" in the sense of AP I) are embedded in the operational plans of the armed forces in which planners and commanders operates. These individuals should know which tactical and strategic objectives and goals are intended to be achieved by certain operations. Bearing this planning horizon of the operational planning in mind should make it possible to determine the relevance of the "anticipated military advantage" of a specific operation (and its context in a given operational plan). However, things are not always as easy as the doctrines of operational planning tell us. Problems tend to arise as a result of speculative assumptions underlying certain planning. Indeed, it is not easy to forecast what one's own troops might achieve under given circumstances; it is even more difficult to forecast the objectives and the action of the opposing side. These assumptions often prove to be false, which forces adaptation of plans under time pressure. The problem is most acute in the dynamic situation of combat on the ground, where there is pressure to constantly adapt plans to an ever-changing combat situation. Such constant adaptation of tactical planning raises problems for the overall operational planning, including the tactical and strategic objectives. In these dynamic situations in ongoing combat, it is much less easy to determine the "definite military advantage" anticipated as a result of a cluster of combined operations.

The prognostic problem becomes even more dramatic in assessing (probable) forms of incidental loss of civilian lives and civilian goods. It is quite common that the planner (and the responsible commander) do not have firm intelligence regarding whether (and to what degree) civilians might be affected by certain planned military operations.[46] This is why precautions play such an important role in the avoidance of excessive collateral damages.[47] The military planners and commanding officers must make all feasible use of the capabilities of reconnaissance

44. *See* Henderson, *supra* note 21, at 200–202; Sloane, *supra* note 1, at 318–20; ICRC, The Principle of Proportionality, *supra* note 12, at 12–19.

45. *See also* Sloane, *supra* note 1, at 312–15.

46. *See* Jason D. Wright, *"Excessive" Ambiguity: Analysing and Refining the Proportionality Standard*, 94 Int'l Rev. Red Cross 819 (2012).

47. For a detailed look at the system of precautions, *see* Henderson, *supra* note 21, at 157–96.

and intelligence. This effort depends on the availability of such capabilities in general, its qualities, and the "feasibility" of further reconnaissance. Military action often is action under extreme time pressure. A commander may not be in a position to use more means of reconnaissance in order to get a clear picture: as time passes, situations change rapidly—thus, the stressing of "feasible" reconnaissance. As a result, planners and commanding officers often will have insufficient information and must rely on experience and "rules of thumb," content to work with rough estimations.[48] Such estimations may prove to be erroneous in dynamically changing situations, but "rules of thumb" based on experience may give reliable indications as far as the risk involved is concerned: the risk for the lives of the soldiers involved, but also for the civilians potentially affected.[49] One may sum up this issue by giving a simplistic formula: the military actors responsible for planning and decision-making in an operation must exhaust all "feasible" means of information, and the feasibility must be judged taking into consideration the limited time horizon under which operational decisions must be made.[50]

Prognoses are always prone to failure and open to errors. For that reason, a strong "error tolerance" in assessing the anticipated military advantage and the expected incidental losses is built into the rule system. There have been discussions whether the (judicial) control of the proportionality test should follow a "subjective" approach based on a reconstruction of the specific decisional horizon of the actors involved; or whether elements of a more "objective" control should be added, for example, by inquiring whether the actors making the decision acted diligently according to "objective" standards by implementing reasonable precautions and analytical steps required from a "reasonable military commander."[51]

The preference for a "subjective" approach protects the military commander and military planner against accusations of error leading to huge numbers of incidental losses of civilian lives and property which in the hindsight might be deemed excessive. On this view, if the decision maker began with a "subjective" assessment conducted in good faith and concluded that incidental losses would be proportionate to the anticipated military advantage, there can be no claim of a "faulty" assessment. The result may be unhappy, but the commander may be

48. *See* Wright, *supra* note 46.

49. As to the (relative) weight of protecting one's own soldiers versus the lives of foreign civilians, *see* Ziv Bohrer, *Protecting State Soldiers, Compatriot Civilians or Foreign Civilians: Proportionality's Meanings at the Tactical, Operational and Strategic Level of War*, 46 Isr. Y.B. Hum. Rts. 171 (2016); *see also* Asa Kasher, *Combatants' Life and Human Dignity*, 44 Isr. Y.B. Hum. Rts. 219 (2014); Ziv Bohrer & Mark Osiel, *Proportionality in Military Force at War's Multiple Levels: Averting Civilian Casualties vs. Safeguarding Soldiers*, 46 Vand. J. Transnat'l L. 747 (2013); Robin Geiss, *The Principle of Proportionality: "Force Protection" as a Military Advantage*, 45 Isr. L. Rev. 71 (2012); Eyal Benvenisti, *Human Dignity in Combat: The Duty to Spare Enemy Civilians*, Isr. L. Rev. 81 (2006).

50. *See* Oeter, *Methods and Means of Combat*, *supra* note 4, at 208–209.

51. *See* Sloane, *supra* note 1, at 302; *see also* ICRC, The Principle of Proportionality, *supra* note 12, at 53.

said to have made a justifiable decision based on what he knew at the time. Such a purely "subjective" approach leaves a strong unease with any outside observer. Accordingly, there are good arguments for incorporating a more "objective" element to the test. The burden shifts to a certain degree with the passage toward a more "objective" control, where the obligation to invest enough efforts in a careful prognosis of the expected incidental losses and the anticipated military advantage tends to become akin to a "due diligence" obligation. Even a "due diligence" standard, however, still contains a significant degree of "error-tolerance," since the fact as such that too large incidental losses occurred in the result is irrelevant as long as the military decision maker was diligent enough in preparing his decision. This seems to be a delicate point which is difficult to convey to the public at large in democratic states, which may tend to assume a violation of the proportionality requirement as soon as incidental losses ex post seem unbearable in relation to the anticipated military advantage. The focus on the epistemic horizon of decision-making at the time of making the decision is important, however, if efficient military action under conditions of limited knowledge and strong time pressure shall remain possible. It is often preferable that the commander makes a decision which might prove erroneous in the hindsight than taking no decision at all, an alternative often seriously endangering his own troops.

The question of "error tolerance" is of utmost importance since prognostic estimations, such as the assessment of future consequences of certain actions, are open to a number of typical errors. The sources of these typical errors are relatively well known from the research in the field of social psychology.[52] Research results of social psychologists warn us against investing too much confidence in the prognostic capabilities of human beings. The capacity of humans to achieve a reliable (and unbiased) assessment of consequences and risks of a given course of behavior is exceedingly limited. Professional training and the long-standing experience of commanding officers may moderate such shortages in weighing all the relevant factors, but the fundamental sources of error and deficient weighing of all the relevant factors remain. These epistemic deficiencies in risk estimation comprise:

- forms of cognitive bias;
- distortions in risk perception;
- decisional routines leading to the marginalization of important aspects in a concrete situation; and
- phenomena of cognitive dissonance.

It is beyond the scope of this chapter to dive deeply into the implications of these findings of cognitive sciences, and social psychology in particular. It should suffice to be aware of these sources of deficiencies in prognostic estimations (and the resulting decisions). Nonetheless, commanding officers are expected to make

52. *See* Gerd Gigerenzer, Simply Rational: Decision-Making in the Real World (2015).

these difficult decisions under adverse conditions, thus necessitating to some degree the above-mentioned "error tolerance."

The difficulties culminate in the final balancing that constitutes the essence of the proportionality test. Comparing and balancing rather different types of (expected) positive and negative consequences of a certain action raises systematic problems of a fundamental nature.[53] The significance of (estimated) consequences must be contextualized in varying internal logic of different societal subsystems and must be evaluated in the light of different value-systems. These different "valuations" then must be related to each other. This is far from easy and may leave the decision maker with a strong feeling of unease. Training and experience may help to overcome that unease and assist in developing a sufficiently differentiated moral judgment. It is moral judgment that is finally brought to the stage in the proportionality test, thus the strong element of subjectivity that accompanies the decisive balancing.[54] There have been proposals to develop some kind of a decisional matrix, that is, decisional schemes that give some (rough) indication how the balancing should look. Indeed, different forms of such a matrix have been used in military practice.[55] One of the most advanced proposals in that direction stems from Jason D. Wright, a military attorney who proposed in a 2012 article in the *International Review of the Red Cross* a rather advanced and elaborate matrix.[56] The article proposes a scaling of the values of anticipated military advantages as well as expected incidental losses in three categories, which would allow subsequently to draw up a kind of matrix where certain fields must be seen as evidently problematic, while others are clearly unproblematic and signal a permissible course of conduct. One may be skeptical toward these types of endeavors, as they may only create a semblance, if not outright illusion, of clarity in judgment. In the end, such endeavors hide the problems in the way of scaling and artificial categorization of cases that may not bear such distillation. This is unhelpful, as the moral judgment of commanding officers cannot be replaced as the decisive element in decision-making.

In operative practice, the balancing is usually done in an intuitive way,[57] a way forward that is not necessarily wrong, since current research of social psychologists demonstrates that a professional intuition trained over time and enriched with vast experience is astonishingly secure in making adequate decisions.[58] Admittedly,

53. *See* Sloane, *supra* note 1, at 321–23; Wright, *supra* note 46, at 846–48.

54. *See also* Emanuela-Chiara Gillard, *Protection of Civilians in the Conduct of Hostilities*, *in* Routledge Handbook of the Law of Armed Conflict 157, 169 (Rain Liivoja & Tim McCormack eds., 2016).

55. *See* ICRC, The Principle of Proportionality, *supra* note 12, at 65.

56. *See* Wright, *supra* note 46, at 849–53.

57. *See id.* at 839–40.

58. *See* Elijah Chudnoff, Intuition (2013); Gerd Gigerenzer, Bauchentscheidungen: Die Intelligenz des Unbewussten und die Macht der Intuition (2007); Tony Bastick, Intuition: Evaluating the Construct and Its Impact on Creative Thinking (2003); David G. Myers, Intuition: Its Powers and Perils (2002); Amos Tversky & Daniel

this makes the reliability of the balancing strongly dependent on the ethical sensibility of the deciding actors and couples the intricacies of balancing with the kind of professional ethics that actors develop over a long process of professional socialization.[59] But this may be the best option, as more clear-cut rules will not help against heinous actors and will not discipline brute military elites of armed forces in certain parts of the world, nor militias and armed groups raised ad hoc.[60]

III. NECESSARY PRECAUTIONS AND THE ANTICIPATION OF POTENTIAL EFFECTS

The inexorably subjective nature of the involved balancing—and of the proportionality test in general—refers us to the moral intuition of the deciding actors. This may sound disappointing. But there is a procedural safeguard that should not be underestimated: the precautions provided for in AP I, Article 57 (in military ethics, discussed as "due care" supplementing the "doctrine of double effects").[61]

Article 57(1) holds that, before engaging an objective, every responsible military leader shall

- verify the military nature of the objective to be attacked;[62]
- choose means and methods minimizing incidental injury and damage to civilian life and objects;[63]
- refrain from launching any attack which may be expected to cause incidental injury and damage to civilian life and objects which would be excessive in relation to the concrete and direct military advantage anticipated;[64]

Kahneman, *Extensional Versus Intuitive Reasoning*, *in* HEURISTIC AND BIASES: THE PSYCHOLOGY OF INTUITIVE JUDGMENT 19 (Thomas Gilovich, Dale Griffin, & Daniel Kahneman eds., 2002).

59. *See also* Sloane, *supra* note 1, at 316–18.

60. As an aside, the fact that even the actors in non-international armed conflict are required to balance the anticipated military advantage with the expected incidental losses assumes that the rule on the prohibition of excessive collateral damage applies also in situations of non-international armed conflict, an assumption largely shared in international legal doctrine. *See* ICRC CUSTOMARY IHL STUDY, *supra* note 2, at 48–49; MIRIAM BRADLEY, PROTECTING CIVILIANS IN WAR: THE ICRC, UNHCR, AND THEIR LIMITATIONS IN INTERNAL ARMED CONFLICTS 72 (2016); Sten Verhoeven, *The Protection of Civilians and Civilian Objects Against Hostilities*, *in* ARMED CONFLICTS AND THE LAW 259, 300 (Jan Wouters, Philip De Man, & Nele Verlinden eds., 2016); YORAM DINSTEIN, NON-INTERNATIONAL ARMED CONFLICTS IN INTERNATIONAL LAW 214–15 (2014).

61. Concerning the principle of "double effects," *see* Warren S. Quinn, *Actions, Intentions, and Consequences: The Doctrine of Double Effect*, 18 PHIL. & PUB. AFF. 334 (1989).

62. AP I, *supra* note 5, art. 57(2)(a)(i).

63. *Id.* art. 57(2)(a)(ii).

64. *Id.* art. 57(2)(a)(iii).

- give the civilian population advance warning of attacks which may affect it, unless circumstances do not permit this;[65] and
- when a choice is possible between several military objectives of equal importance, engage that objective the attack on which is likely to cause the least incidental injury or damage.[66]

The military authorities responsible for preparing and implementing an attack are required by Article 57 to implement certain elementary safeguards and are subject to stringent standards in their attempts to protect the civilian population from collateral damage.[67] Article 57(1) begins by stating the general principle underlying the whole provision, namely, that the attacker shall take "constant care" to spare the civilian population and civilian objects in the conduct of military operations, or—as formulated in a 1967 ICRC memorandum—to minimize the damage inflicted upon noncombatants.[68] This rule may be deduced from the general principle of military necessity provided by customary law.[69] With regard to non-international armed conflicts the same set of obligations applies as a result of customary law standards.[70]

Although the general rule requiring precautions is undisputed, one essential problem remains, namely, which individuals are addressed by Article 57. The obligations should be understood to address primarily commanders and staff officers who are directly responsible for specific operations, and only to a lesser degree the individual soldiers participating directly in the attack.[71] Due to the lack of sufficient information, even noncommissioned officers and unit commanders up to the level of company command will usually not have the overview of the military situation which is required for an adequate evaluation of the legality of operations under Articles 48 through 57 of AP I, in particular for the assessment of proportionality. Without an adequate idea of the operational framework and of the nature and importance of the target, the safeguard measures provided for in Article 57 cannot be implemented satisfactorily.

65. *Id.* art. 57(2)(c).

66. *Id.* art. 57(3).

67. As to the history and substance of AP I, Article 57, *see* Sassòli, *supra* note 10, at 459–89; Bothe, Partsch, & Solf, *supra* note 12, at 361–69; ICRC Commentary, *supra* note 11, ¶¶ 2184–88.

68. *See* Sassòli, *supra* note 10, at 458.

69. *See* Erik Castrén, The Present Law of War and Neutrality 202 (1954); Sassòli, *supra* note 10, at 456–64.

70. *See* Verhoeven, *supra* note 60, at 300.

71. As to the question of who is primarily affected by Article 57, *see* Sassòli, *supra* note 10, at 461, 463; ICRC Commentary, *supra* note 11, ¶ 2197; Kalshoven & Zegveld, *supra* note 16, at 115; Byron, *supra* note 28, at 200; Bohrer & Osiel, *supra* note 49, at 787–99.

Article 57(a)(ii) calls upon commanders and planning staff officers to "take all feasible precautions in the choice of means and methods of attack with a view to avoiding, and in any event to minimizing, incidental loss of civilian life, injury to civilians and damage to civilian objects."[72] The required measures relate in particular to the problems of "targeting," including target development and battle damage assessment, and to the choice of weapons and ammunition used in the attack.[73] How to select and locate the objective, and the linked question of selecting the weapons best suited for the attack, is probably the essential question in the practical implementation of the principles of distinction and proportionality.[74] Only if the target becomes, as far as possible, precisely demarcated and if, in selecting the means of attack and establishing the mission parameters, it is ensured that the effects of the use of force are as far as possible limited to the military objective, can the "rule of proportionality" be realized in military practice.[75] Yet the logistics of such mission parameters are so complex and depend on so many factors that it is impossible to express the consequences of distinction and proportionality in a precise formula. The flexibility of the clauses contained in AP I reflect the recognition by the international community that it is not possible to regulate all the infinite variables affecting military operations in a stringent provision. Many factors may be decisive in the analysis: a nonexhaustive list includes the location and physical character of the objective; the configuration of the surrounding terrain; the presence of civilians in the vicinity of the objective; the adjacency of military and civilian objects; the degree to which the target is defended and the resulting risks for the attacker's personnel and equipment; the quality of the weaponry used by attacker and defender (in particular the relative accuracy of artillery, bombs, and missiles); the standards of technical training of combatants and their physical and psychological condition; and meteorological conditions.[76] Furthermore, the "rules of engagement" governing the operating forces may play a key role in conforming with Article 57(2)(a)(ii). In general, the weapon with most accurate delivery parameters should be employed to attack a military objective with civilian objects in its vicinity.[77] In some cases there may also be a requirement to use infantry operations in circumstances where superior firepower (air support or artillery) would traditionally have been employed. However, it is not to be expected that one could ever structure the whole question in a short

72. ICRC Customary IHL Study, *supra* note 2, r. 17; *cf.* Dep't of the Army, ATTP 3-37.31, Civilian Casualty Mitigation (July 18, 2012) [hereinafter Civilian Casualty Mitigation].

73. ICRC Commentary, *supra* note 11, ¶ 2200. *But see* Watkin, *supra* note 19, at 23–25.

74. *See* Sassòli, *supra* note 10, at 470; Castrén, *supra* note 69, at 202; Kalshoven & Zegveld, *supra* note 16, at 113–14; Byron, *supra* note 28, at 197.

75. ICRC Commentary, *supra* note 11, ¶ 2200.

76. Bothe, Partsch, & Solf, *supra* note 12, at 364.

77. *See also* Byron, *supra* note 28, at 197.

and precise formula; the individual responsibility of the competent commander will therefore be sanctioned only in extreme cases, such as deliberate attacks on obviously civilian objects, because the previously mentioned uncertainties must be taken into account when assessing ex post facto the legality of an operation. What is required is a decision taken in good faith according to the standard of a "reasonable military commander," and nothing more.[78]

However, some general safeguards will also apply in nearly every case at the level of high command. In order to avoid precipitate decisions without sufficient information, also certain procedural safeguards must be taken in order to counter the inherent cognitive biases that inevitably might accompany the decision. It is advisable to follow the example of U.S. forces during "Operation Desert Storm" (Kuwait and Iraq in 1991) and a number of other recent operations, which provided for the control of targeting decisions and operations plans by legal advisors to the armed forces who were specially trained for that task.[79] Admittedly, such an additional precaution is not required by Article 57(2)(a)(ii), but the mechanism is effective in assisting the competent commander in the exercise of his responsibilities, as long as the legal advice is properly taken into account.

Article 57(2)(a)(iii) reiterates the rule of proportionality. Command authorities and planning staff must ensure that operations remain within the bounds of proportionality, that is, that they do not cause collateral damage which is excessive in relation to the expected military advantage.[80] Article 57(3) stresses the self-evident consequence of the principle of proportionality and the corresponding general principle of optimal minimization of collateral civilian damage:[81] the need to choose, when several military objectives provide equal military advantage, the objective "the attack on which is likely to cause the least danger to civilian lives and objects."[82] An example often cited is the option to attack, instead of a railway station inside a city, an equally important railway junction or line at a strategically important point outside a densely populated area, on the basis that the destruction of such a crucial point causes as much disruption to the enemy lines of communication as the destruction of an urban station.[83]

78. *See* Holland, *supra* note 10, at 48–49.

79. *See* Thomas P. Keenan, *Die Operation "Wüstensturm" aus der Sicht des aktiven Rechtsberaters*, 4 Humanitäres Völkerrecht 34, 36 (1991).

80. As to background and legal effects of AP I, Article 57(2)(a)(iii), *see* Sassòli, *supra* note 10, at 473–74; Bothe, Partsch, & Solf, *supra* note 12, at 364–65; ICRC Commentary, *supra* note 11, ¶¶ 2204–19; *see also* ICRC Customary IHL Study, *supra* note 2, r. 18; Civilian Casualty Mitigation, *supra* note 72, ¶ 1-10.

81. *See* Sassòli, *supra* note 10, at 485; Bothe, Partsch, & Solf, *supra* note 12, at 368.

82. As to the interpretation of AP I, Article 57(3), *see* Sassòli, *supra* note 10, at 485–89; Bothe, Partsch, & Solf, *supra* note 10, at 368–69; Gardam, *supra* note 7, at 96–98; ICRC Customary IHL Study, *supra* note 2, r. 21.

83. *See* ICRC Commentary, *supra* note 11, ¶ 2227; Sassòli, *supra* note 10, at 487.

The duties of military leaders to take precautions in favor of the civilian population relates not only to the planning and preparation prior to an attack but also to its implementation.[84] The officers responsible for carrying out each operation must minimize collateral damage to the civilian population even during the course of combat operations.[85] They must call off the attack immediately if it becomes clear that the attacked objective does not have the supposed military character, but constitutes a purely civilian object.[86] They must halt fire if it becomes apparent that the incidental danger to the civilian population is more serious than had been expected.[87] The commanders responsible for the attack must also call off the attack if the military advantage which can still be obtained from the operation becomes too small in relation to the probable collateral damage to the civilian population.[88] Military leaders therefore must ensure for the entire course of the operation that the attack remains inside the limits drawn by the rules of humanitarian law. All this relates primarily to military leaders, as was made clear by the wording of the preceding phrases. Whether a corresponding duty also affects the lower levels of hierarchy actually engaged in combat remains in doubt. On one hand, if there is a duty on ordinary soldiers to halt fire or break off an attack in the case of flagrant indiscriminate attack, this can relate only to the decisive phase of immediate combat.[89] Yet ordinary soldiers and junior officers have no authority to resist their superiors' orders and to break off an operation; they would risk sanction under domestic martial law if in following their personal judgment they refused to obey orders, except in blatant cases of misjudgment where the principle of manifest illegality under Article 33 of the Statute of the International Criminal Court (ICC Statute) applies. Beyond these blatant cases, the obligation in AP I, Article 57(2)(b) cannot extend below the level of commanders with authority to stop or modify an operation.[90] If time allows, they should report any new information on the changed situation to their superior command levels, but low-level commanders usually will not be in a position to modify the operational orders. The limit is reached only in the extraordinary cases in which the acting soldier can evidently see that the order would force him to commit a war crime (which in this respect means an order to attack an obviously purely civilian object or to attack despite blatantly excessive collateral damage). In these extraordinary cases,

84. ICRC Commentary, *supra* note 11, ¶ 2220.

85. AP I, *supra* note 5, art. 57(2)(b).

86. *See* Bothe, Partsch, & Solf, *supra* note 12, at 366; Sassòli, *supra* note 10, at 474–77; ICRC Commentary, *supra* note 11, ¶ 2221; Kalshoven & Zegveld, *supra* note 16, at 113–14.

87. *See* Sassòli, *supra* note 10, at 474–76; Byron, *supra* note 28, at 198.

88. Bothe, Partsch, & Solf, *supra* note 12, at 366–67; Gardam, *supra* note 7, at 98.

89. *See* Bothe, Partsch, & Solf, *supra* note 12, at 366.

90. *See* Dieter Fleck, *Military Manuals on the Law of Armed Conflicts*, *in* National Implementation of International Humanitarian Law 185, 192 (Michael Bothe, P. Macalister-Smith, & Thomas Kurzidem eds., 1990).

the order must not be obeyed; to the contrary, in such cases a superior order is no defense to a combatant in criminal proceedings, who bears individual criminal responsibility.[91]

All of these considerations hinge upon the flow of recurrent information about the changing operational circumstances on the ground. It is only possible to adapt operational plans if there is a relatively reliable flow of information from the ground to the planners and commanders, which may allow the latter to abstain from an operation that might threaten to cause excessive collateral damage under the circumstances prevailing. AP I, Article 57(2)(b) states that an attack shall be canceled or suspended if it becomes apparent "that the attack may be expected to cause incidental loss of civilian life, injury to civilians, damage to civilian objects, or a combination thereof, which would be excessive in relation to the concrete and direct military advantage anticipated." Featured prominently are the words "may be expected" and "anticipated." The prognostic problem does not end with finalizing the operational planning. It continues, and requires planners and commanders, as well as in certain cases lower-level officers, to monitor the situation (which, of course, they will do for operational purposes anyway) and to correct evidently wrong prognostic elements in the planning and adapt the operational details accordingly. In the phase of the operation in which the plans are executed, one is much nearer to the time when the effects are actually realized, thus giving better ground for estimation. At the same time, planners and commanders are acting under significant time pressure in these situations, which gives them less leeway to proceed and weigh the incoming information diligently in order to decide whether an attack shall be canceled or suspended. There is a conflict of goals, namely, between efficiency and diligence, in mitigating the effects. One cannot resolve in favor of one of these interests. Rather, the relevant question is what degree of diligence ought to be expected from a "reasonable military commander."

IV. EXCESSIVE COLLATERAL DAMAGE AS A WAR CRIME UNDER INTERNATIONAL CRIMINAL LAW

The analysis has shown that the substantive rule on the prohibition of excessive collateral damage as well as the procedural requirements of precautions in attack in essence must be understood as "due diligence" obligations, which in substance leave room for a large degree of "error tolerance." Such "error tolerance" here means that one cannot describe an attack as having been illegal simply because it resulted in hindsight in a large degree of incidental losses that are not justified by the military advantage achieved. The attack becomes illegal only if the responsible military commander did not exercise sufficient diligence with regard to the precautions in attack, ordered the attack (or did not halt it) despite warning signs that incidental losses might be excessive or simply acted careless in not seeking

91. For a general discussion on the topic of "obedience to orders," *see* Gary D. Solis, The Law of Armed Conflict 341–64 (1st ed. 2010).

enough information to come to a reliable prognosis of expected incidental losses. It is the decisional horizon of the decision maker that is essential, complemented by a background control whether a "diligent commander" would have decided so in light of applicable due diligence requirements.

International criminal law corroborates this analysis of a deeply encoded "error tolerance." According to Article 8(2)(b)(iv) of the ICC Statute, which makes a war crime "intentionally launching an attack in the knowledge that such attack will cause incidental loss of life or injury to civilians or damage to civilian objects or widespread, long-term and severe damage to the natural environment which would be clearly excessive in relation to the concrete and direct overall military advantage anticipated." As seen in this standard, the conditions required to qualify an attack with excessive collateral damages as a war crime are extremely high.[92] Article 8(2)(b)(iv) requires express "knowledge" that incidental losses will be excessively high, and subjects commanders to potential criminal responsibility only if they acted with the intention to inflict excessive collateral damage, or if they accept (knowingly) that the attack will result in clearly excessive collateral damage.[93] Although largely adopting the wording of AP I, Article 51(5)(b) and of the grave breach provision of AP I, Article 85(3)(b), the standard is much more strict in its requirements than the due diligence standard of AP I, Articles 51 and 57, since it does not suffice for an attack to be qualified as criminal that due diligence in precautions was evidently neglected; rather the commander must positively anticipate the expected (excessive) losses and thus be aware of the tilted balance that would have required him to abstain from attacking (or to halt or modify the ongoing attack).[94] A commander deciding on an attack on the erroneous factual assumption that incidental losses will not be clearly excessive compared with the anticipated military advantage will accordingly not subject himself to potential war crime liability. As long as his decisional horizon caused him to come reasonably to his conclusion, he will not be liable in terms of international criminal law, even if he obviously neglected his due diligence obligations, inter alia by not exhausting all the available sources of information. As far as the normal range of modes of decision-making in planning and commanding military operations is concerned, the provision accords a wide margin of appreciation, and there is thus practically little risk of individual criminal liability.[95] The definition of the

92. As to Article 8(2)(b)(iv) of the Rome Statute, *see* Gerhard Werle & Florian Jessberger, Principles of International Criminal Law 491–94 (3d ed. 2014); Roberta Arnold, *Article 8 (2)(b)(iv)*, *in* Commentary on the Rome Statute of the International Criminal Court 338 (Otto Triffterer ed., 2d ed. 2008); Didier Pfirter, *Elements of Crime—Article 8(2)(b)(iv)*, *in* The International Criminal Court: Elements of Crimes and Rules of Procedure and Evidence 147 (Roy S. Lee ed., 2001).

93. *See* Arnold, *supra* note 92, at 339.

94. *See also* Knut Dörmann, Elements of War Crimes Under the Rome Statute of the International Criminal Court: Sources and Commentary 164 (2003).

95. *See also* Pfirter, *supra* note 92, at 148.

crime thus requires a clear criminal intent in order to be individually liable under Article 8(2)(b)(iv), whereas the relevant courts and tribunals should respect military judgments made reasonably and in good faith, even if they lead to catastrophic results.[96]

Despite this clear orientation toward not sanctioning mistakes in the decisional process, the borderlines between accepted practices and criminal behavior raise significant difficulties in judicial operationalization.[97] When does a military commander have knowledge of the dramatic consequences of an attack? The issue of how to distinguish between attacks on legitimate military targets and attacks on civilians and civilian objects led to heated disputes in the famous *Gotovina* case before the International Criminal Tribunal for the Former Yugoslavia (ICTY),[98] although one must bear in mind that the Tribunal did not apply Article 8(2)(b)(iv) of the ICC Statute with its particularly high mental standard. The Trial Chamber devised an effects test apparently based on the claim that one might reasonably interpret AP I, Article 51 in the sense "that those artillery projectiles which impacted within a distance of 300 metres of an identified military target were deliberately fired at that target."[99] The Trial Chamber gave no specific reasoning for this (rather schematic) rule of thumb and concluded on its basis that the artillery fire directed at the town of Knin in an overall judgment "constituted an indiscriminate attack on the town and thus an unlawful attack on civilians and civilian objects," although certain targets inside the town were clearly military objectives legitimately fired upon.[100] In general it concluded that the firing of shells from approximately 25 kilometers away risked disproportionate harm to civilians and civilian property and would have been excessive in relation to the military advantage anticipated.[101]

These generalized statements are clearly too broad and sweeping, and accordingly the Appeals Chamber of the ICTY criticized the first instance judgment for providing neither an evidentiary basis nor a reasoned opinion as to why such "impact analysis" was relied upon.[102] The Appeals Chamber noted that the absence of "an established range of error" meant that it could not exclude the possibility that the shelling was lawful,[103] again a very far-reaching statement

96. *See id.* at 149–50.

97. *See* DARCY, *supra* note 2, at 204–15; Fellmeth, *supra* note 2, at 128–30.

98. *See* Prosecutor v. Gotovina, Case No. IT-06-90-T, Judgment (Int'l Crim. Trib. for the Former Yugoslavia Trial Chamber Apr. 15, 2011) [hereinafter *Gotovina* Trial Judgment]; Prosecutor v. Gotovina, Case No. IT-06-90-A, Judgment (Int'l Crim. Trib. for the Former Yugoslavia Appeals Chamber Nov. 16, 2012) [hereinafter *Gotovina* Appeals Judgment].

99. *Gotovina* Trial Judgment, *supra* note 98, ¶ 1898.

100. *Id.* ¶ 1911.

101. *Id.* ¶ 1910.

102. *Gotovina* Appeals Judgment, *supra* note 98, ¶¶ 58–65.

103. *Id.* ¶ 65.

since there were a number of factual grounds putting the artillery bombardment of Knin in a very dubious light. Admittedly it depends on the concrete circumstances, but a commander of a new army with artillery units having very limited professional training and experience may face significant challenges regarding the precision of his artillery. In such circumstances, a long-distance fire from more than 20 kilometers directed to a densely populated area may indeed raise intricate questions concerning the risk of excessive collateral damage, a point not seriously dealt with in the appeals judgment. The Appeals Chamber judgment in consequence received much criticism.[104] The case is interesting because it demonstrates the difficulties of operationalizing the elements of the crime of indiscriminate attack on civilians, either by lodging an attack solely directed against civilians and civilian objects or launching an attack with clearly excessive collateral damages. In practice, these two different cases are often difficult to distinguish.

If one turns attention back to the relevant crime under the ICC Statute, one point is beyond doubt: the war crime articulated in Article 8(2)(b)(iv) was constructed in a very narrow way that limits rigidly its scope of application to the most clear-cut cases. Only attacks that intentionally run the risk of clearly excessive collateral damages fall under the definition, and not the much broader range of negligent acts that ignore the relevant rules of precaution set out in AP I. This strict limitation safeguards effectively the military against overblown accusations, but the extremely narrow construction of the crime may leave the legal analyst with a strong unease. Article 8(2)(b)(iv) covers only a core segment of the grave breaches provision of AP I, Article 85(3)(b). The whole range of precautions that minimize collateral damage as much as possible are removed from the realm of criminal liability, despite the wording and spirit of AP I, Article 86, which obliges states parties to sanction all other violations of the treaty that result from inaction in violation of explicit obligations under AP I. If one would like to define the crime in a manner which provides a more comprehensive sanction for the nonobservance of the due diligence obligations, the mental standard of knowledge would have to be lowered. Instead, the point of reference would have to be the due diligence obligations under AP I, Articles 51(5)(b) and 57(2). Risking seriously the lives of civilians by ignorant behavior in neglect of the due diligence obligations falling upon military planners, commanders, and responsible officers warrants the possibility of individual criminal liability, just as attacks that intentionally accept excessive collateral damages. In a future revision of the ICC Statute, it would be advisable to modify the crime under Article 8(2)(b)(iv) accordingly.

104. *See, e.g.*, Laurie R. Blank, Operational Law Experts Roundtable on the Gotovina Judgment: Military Operations, Battlefield Reality and the Judgment's Impact on Effective Implementation and Enforcement of International Humanitarian Law, Emory Public Law Research Paper No. 12-186 (Jan. 28, 2012), http://dx.doi.org/10.2139/ssrn.1994414.

V. CONCLUSION

This chapter revisited the structural problems of proportionality under the *jus in bello* and reconstructed the approach that practice has taken in operationalizing it. The findings of the investigation into the logic of the proportionality test, the involved elements of prognosis, and the diligence required in collecting and processing information provide a lesson of caution. Admittedly, there is some degree of "due care" that we must expect from military planners and responsible commanders, but also from officers executing the plans on the ground. They should constantly proceed and weigh the incoming information and monitor whether the prognostic parts of the estimation of effects comply with the standard or whether the course of action shows severe mistakes in planning (and in the underlying assessment of potential effects and the resulting balancing). We should remain reasonable, however, in what we expect from military actors. Planning and directing military operations is a risky business, naturally prone to errors and mistakes. While not completely avoidable, mistakes should be learned from. Accordingly, the rules have properly incorporated a large degree of "error tolerance." Military planners and commanders should exercise "due care" in collecting, processing, and acting on information to develop a sound basis for operational decisions. The yardstick, however, cannot be perfection—a world in which every decision maker is expected to be omniscient. Rather, the standard should be the normative *leitbild* of a "reasonable military commander" possessing the intuition to determine when the underlying information is too patchy to justify a risky operation and when there is sufficient ground to decide to launch an attack. The reality of warfare is that decisions must be made, even when information is imperfect, as indecisiveness may endanger personnel entrusted to one's care. Thus, there is no alternative to relying on educated moral intuition. But that intuition must be trained and must be sensitized in a constant process of questioning and reflecting on decisions in terms of a professional military ethic.[105] Military organizations—and in particular institutions such as West Point that train future officers—should always be aware of the importance of the task of preparing officers to lead operations on the battlefield. This task includes training ethical and normative sensibility. The reasonable application of the law of armed conflict depends on such training, as this chapter's deep analysis of the proportionality requirements makes clear. Avoiding excessive collateral damages is a stringent requirement of humanity in warfare, but the respect of such demand hinges upon common sense and the professional ethics of soldiers.

105. *See* ICRC, The Principle of Proportionality, *supra* note 12, at 63–64; *see also* Paul Robinson, *Ethics Training and Development in the Military*, *in* 4 Ethics of War and Conflict: Issues 66 (Asa Kasher ed. 2014).

12

The Proportionality Rule and Mental Harm in War

SARAH KNUCKEY,* ALEX MOOREHEAD, AUDREY MCCALLEY,*** AND ADAM BROWN******

I. INTRODUCTION

The foundational international humanitarian law (IHL) rule of proportionality that parties to an armed conflict may not attack where any expected incidental loss of civilian life, civilian injury, or civilian object damage would be excessive in relation to the anticipated military advantage is normally interpreted to encompass only civilian *physical* injuries, such as loss of a limb, organ damage, burns, or blindness. Attacks risk causing significant mental harms also, yet current interpretations and applications of international law lag behind science in understanding and recognizing these kinds of harms.

* Clinical Professor of Law; Director, Human Rights Clinic; Faculty Co-Director, Human Rights Institute, Columbia Law School. The authors thank Marion Crepet, Emma DiNapoli, Aarthi Sridharan, and Sean Yau for their excellent research assistance. We also thank Claus Kreß, Michael Schmitt, Colonel David Wallace, Colonel Shane Reeves, and Robert Lawless for the invitation to prepare this chapter, and the participants in the October 2018 Lieber Institute for Law and Land Warfare workshop at the U.S. Military Academy at West Point, as well as Dr. Lindsay Stark and Emanuela Chiara-Gillard for their comments on an earlier draft.

** Human Rights Officer, U.N. Office of the High Commissioner for Human Rights. This chapter has been written in a personal capacity. The views expressed are those of the author and do not necessarily reflect the views of the United Nations.

*** MPH, Department of Sociomedical Sciences, Mailman School of Public Health, Columbia University.

**** Associate Professor of Psychology, The New School for Social Research; clinical psychologist; and Director, Trauma and Global Mental Health Lab. Adjunct Assistant Professor, Department of Psychiatry, New York University School of Medicine.

Sarah Knuckey, Alex Moorehead, Audrey McCalley, and Adam Brown, *The Proportionality Rule and Mental Harm in War* In: *Necessity and Proportionality in International Peace and Security Law.* Edited by: Professor Claus Kreß and Captain Robert Lawless, Oxford University Press (2021). © Oxford University Press. DOI: 10.1093/oso/9780197537374.003.0013.

Exposure to a potentially traumatic event, such as an air strike, shooting, or an attack with a rocket or an improvised explosive device, risks serious and long-term harm to mental health. Such exposure can cause a range of mental health harms, including post-traumatic stress disorder (PTSD), which can involve significant distress and functional impairment and lowered quality of life, including symptoms such as flashbacks and trauma-related reactivity (aggression, hypervigilance). PTSD, the subject of thousands of scientific studies,[1] is also associated with reduced educational and work performance, physical health harms, destructive behaviors, and a range of physiological concerns including hormone and neurochemical dysregulation and neuroimmune system dysfunction. Those diagnosed with PTSD may experience symptoms for months, years, or even a lifetime.

In this chapter, we first provide an overview of the extent of recognition of mental harms in international law generally, and outline existing scholarship on mental harms in IHL specifically. Building on earlier analyses of mental harms, we then focus on the proportionality rule, examining existing scientific research in light of policy considerations and legal requirements. We argue that the humanitarian and military interests in reducing civilian suffering and the extensive scientific research into the serious nature of conditions like PTSD, are compelling reasons of principle and policy to include mental harms in a proportionality analysis. The difficult issue is whether the inclusion of mental harms is operationalizable in practice. In the final section of this chapter, we explore the feasibility of a commander incorporating serious mental harms such as PTSD into a proportionality assessment, examining the legal elements of proportionality alongside public health, psychology, and neuroscience research. Where scientific research deepens understanding about how civilians may be harmed by attacks, this updated knowledge should be incorporated into a military's training, policies, and operations. We argue that while PTSD is complex, existing scientific research demonstrates that PTSD is subject to measurement and that it is a reasonably foreseeable consequence of exposure to a traumatic event such as a violent attack. Extensive scientific research into the causes and consequences of PTSD for populations exposed to violent attack or armed conflict suggests that, at minimum, militaries should take seriously these harms not only for their own forces but also for civilian populations, and that they should take steps to assess how to include the risk of serious mental harms in proportionality assessments.

However, scientific research into PTSD continues to develop and has gaps and limitations which challenge the feasibility of incorporating mental harms into the proportionality assessment in practice. There are difficult questions about which civilian populations potentially harmed by traumatic event exposure should be considered in a proportionality analysis, as well as of predicting the likelihood of harms resulting from different kinds of attacks and in varying circumstances,

1. Paola Rodriguez et al., *Assessment of Posttraumatic Stress Disorder-Related Functional Impairment: A Review*, 49 J. Rehabilitation Res. & Dev. 649, 649–66 (2012).

particularly for civilian populations living in insecure locations who may have significant trauma exposure from myriad sources. We recommend that states bring military, human rights, IHL, and mental health experts together to assess how to include mental health in proportionality assessments and to clarify the research and operational knowledge needs that would improve the feasibility of doing so. States should also facilitate new scientific research to improve, through the long term, the integration of mental health into methods for assessing the risks of civilian harm.

II. MENTAL HEALTH HARMS IN CURRENT LAW AND SCHOLARSHIP

> *Law, marching with medicine but in the rear and limping a little, has today come a long way. . . . An illness of the mind set off by shock is not the less an injury because it is functional, not organic, and its progress is psychogenic.*[2]

International law recognizes mental health harms of varying forms through a patchwork of protections in human rights, criminal, and humanitarian law. In humanitarian law, there is protection against certain intentional mental harms, but no existing explicit protection for such harms where incidental. The proportionality rule might be able to encompass excessive mental harms, but applying the elements of the rule in the case of mental harms raises a number of feasibility challenges. While scholarship exploring mental harms as "injury" for the purposes of a proportionality analysis is minimal, a number of recent analyses and expert group discussions have begun to move the debate forward, setting out both possibilities and challenges for the law's recognition of incidental war-related mental harms.

A. International Law and Mental Health

In international law, mental health and mental harm are recognized to varying extents in human rights law, international criminal law, IHL, and the law of remedies.

Under international human rights law, the right to mental health is specifically guaranteed as part of the right to health.[3] The elements of the right to mental health have been developed through international and domestic jurisprudence, U.N. General Assembly and Human Rights Council resolutions, U.N. treaty

2. David Schwartz, *The Ongoing Development of the Law on Pure Psychiatric Injury*, 138 PRECEDENT 32 (2017), http://classic.austlii.edu.au/au/journals/PrecedentAULA/2017/9.html (referring to Windeyer J., remarking in the 1970 case of *Mount Isa Mines Ltd v. Pusey*).

3. *See, e.g.*, International Covenant on Economic, Social and Cultural Rights art. 12, Dec. 16, 1966, 993 U.N.T.S. 3 (stating that everyone has the right "to the enjoyment of the highest attainable standard of physical and mental health"); Convention on the Rights of Persons with Disabilities art. 1, Dec. 13, 2006, 2515 U.N.T.S. 3 (referring to mental impairments).

bodies, scholarly writing, and the work of the World Health Organization, U.N. Special Rapporteurs, and the U.N. High Commissioner for Human Rights.[4] States must take steps to progressively realize the right, and may not engage in activities aimed at destroying the right. The right requires that mental health care goods,

4. *See, e.g.*, Tribunal Constitucional de Bolivia [Constitutional Tribunal of Bolivia], Nov. 25, 2003, Case 1716-2003-R (Bol.); Corte Constitucional [Constitutional Court], Sala Primera de Revisión, Feb. 2, 2010, Case T-045/10 (Colom.); Corte Constitucional [Constitutional Court], Fourth Revision Chamber, Apr. 13, 1999, Case T-209/99 (Colom.); Sudan Human Rights Organisation, et al. v. Sudan, Communication 279/03-296/05, African Commission on Human and Peoples' Rights [Afr. Comm'n H.P.R.], (May 27, 2009), http://www.achpr.org/files/sessions/45th/comunications/279.03-296.05/achpr45_279.03_296.05_eng.pdf; Association for the Defence of Human Rights in Romania-Helsinki Committee on Behalf of Ionel Garcea v. Romania, App. No. 2959/11, 2015, Eur. Ct. H.R., http://hudoc.echr.coe.int/eng?i=001-153027; Lazariu v. Romania, App. No. 31973/03, 2015, Eur. Ct. H.R., http://hudoc.echr.coe.int/eng?i=001-147865; M.H. v. United Kingdom, App. No. 11577/06, 2014, Eur. Ct. H.R., http://hudoc.echr.coe.int/eng?i=001-127107; Ximenes-Lopes v. Brazil, 12.237, Inter-Am. Comm'n H.R., Report No. 38/02 (2002); Victor Rosario Congo v. Ecuador, 11.427, Inter-Am. Comm'n H.R., Report No. 63/99 (1999); Ituango Massacres v. Colombia, Merits, Reparations, and Costs, Preliminary Objection, Inter-Am. Ct. H.R., (ser. C) No. 148 (July 1, 2006); Moiwana Community v. Suriname, Merits, Reparations, and Costs, Preliminary Objections, Inter-Am. Ct. H.R. (ser. C) No. 124 (June 15, 2005); G.A. Res. 58/173, The Right of Everyone to the Highest Attainable Standard of Physical and Mental Health (Dec. 22, 2003); G.A. Res. 46/118, The Protection of Persons with Mental Illness and the Improvement of Mental Health Care (Dec. 17, 1991); G.A. Res. 217 (III) A, Universal Declaration of Human Rights (Dec. 10, 1948); Human Rights Council Res. 36/13, Mental Health and Human Rights, U.N. Doc. A/HRC/RES/36/13 (Sept. 28, 2017); Human Rights Council Res. 32/18, Mental Health and Human Rights, U.N. Doc. A/HRC/RES/32/18 (July 1, 2016); African Charter on the Rights and Welfare of the Child art. 14, July 11, 1990, CAB/LEG/24.9/49; African Charter on Human and Peoples' Rights art. 16, June 27, 1981, 1520 U.N.T.S. 217; U.N. Comm. on Econ., Soc. and Cultural Rights, Substantive Issues Arising in the Implementation of the International Covenant on Economic, Social and Cultural Rights, General Comment No. 14: The Right to the Highest Attainable Standard of Health, U.N. Doc. E/C.12/2000/4 (Aug. 11, 2000); Comm. on the Elimination of Discrimination Against Women, L.C. v. Peru, Communication No. 22/2009, U.N. Doc. CEDAW/C/50/D/22/2009 (2011); U.N., Econ. & Soc. Council, Comm'n on Human Rights, Economic, Social and Cultural Rights: Report of the Special Rapporteur on the Right of Everyone to the Highest Attainable Standard of Physical and Mental Health, U.N. Doc. E/CN.4/2005/51 (Feb. 11, 2005); U.N. Gen. Assembly, Human Rights Council, Report of the Special Rapporteur on the Right of Everyone to the Enjoyment of the Highest Attainable Standard of Physical and Mental Health, U.N. Doc. A/HRC/35/21 (Mar. 28, 2017); U.N. Human Rights Council, Annual Report of the United Nations High Commissioner for Human Rights and Reports of the Office of the High Commissioner and the Secretary-General, Mental Health and Human Rights, U.N. Doc. A/HRC/34/32 (Jan. 31, 2017); U.N. Human Rights Comm., Williams v. Jamaica, Communication No. 609/1995, U.N. Doc. CCPR/C/61/D/609/1995 (Nov. 4, 1997); U.N. Human Rights Comm., Francis v. Jamaica, Communication No. 606/1994, U.N. Doc. CCPR/C/54/D/606/1994 (Aug. 12, 1994); Lawrence O. Gostin & Lance Gable, *The Human Rights of Persons with Mental Disabilities: A Global Perspective on the Application of Human Rights Principles to Mental Health*, 63 Md. L.R. 20 (2004); Jonathan M. Mann et al., *Health and Human Rights*, 1 Health & Hum. Rts. J. 7, 7 (1999); Carla A. Arena Ventura, *International Law, Mental Health and Human Rights*, Ctr. for Civil & Hum. Rts. (June 2014); Dr. Michelle Funk et al., *Mental Health and*

facilities, and services be available, accessible, acceptable, of good quality, and nondiscriminatory.[5]

Under international criminal law, a number of acts that involve the infliction of "mental pain or suffering," or that involve forms of "psychological oppression," are specifically criminalized. These include, for example, the war crimes of torture,[6] inhuman treatment,[7] biological experiments,[8] willfully causing great suffering,[9] mutilation,[10] and the crimes against humanity of

Development: Targeting People with Mental Health Conditions as a Vulnerable Group, World Health Org. [WHO] (2010), https://apps.who.int/iris/bitstream/handle/10665/44257/9789241563949_eng.pdf?sequence=1&isAllowed=y; Dr. Michelle Funk et al., *WHO Resource Book on Mental Health, Human Rights and Legislation*, World Health Org. [WHO] (2005), https://ec.europa.eu/health/sites/health/files/mental_health/docs/who_resource_book_en.pdf; World Health Org. [WHO], Div. of Mental Health and Prevention of Substance Abuse, *Guidelines for the Promotion of Human Rights of Persons with Mental Disabilities*, WHO/MNH/MND/95.4 (1996), https://apps.who.int/iris/bitstream/handle/10665/41880/WHO_MNH_MND_95.4.pdf?sequence=1&isAllowed=y; World Health Org. [WHO], Dept. of Mental Health & Substance Abuse in Collaboration with the Victorian Health Promotion Found. & the Univ. of Melbourne, *Promoting Mental Health: Concepts, Emerging Evidence, Practice* (Helen Herrman et al. eds., 2004), https://apps.who.int/iris/bitstream/handle/10665/43286/9241562943_eng.pdf?sequence=1&isAllowed=y;

5. U.N. Comm. on Econ., Soc. & Cultural Rights (CESCR), General Comment No. 14: The Right to the Highest Attainable Standard of Health (Art. 12 of the Covenant), U.N. Doc. E/C.12/2000/4 (Aug. 11, 2000).

6. Rome Statute of the International Criminal Court art. 8(2)(a)(ii), July 17, 1998, 2187 U.N.T.S. 90 [hereinafter Rome Statute]; Assembly of States Parties to the Rome Statute of the International Criminal Court, First Session, New York, 3–10 September 2002, Official Records, at 126, U.N. Doc. ICC-ASP/1/3, U.N. Sales No. E.03.V.2 (2002) [hereinafter Elements of Crimes] (describing the first element for the war crime of torture as "the perpetrator inflicted severe physical or mental pain or suffering upon one or more persons.").

7. Rome Statute, *supra* note 6, art. 8(2)(a)(ii)-2 (war crime of inhuman treatment); Elements of Crimes, *supra* note 6, at 126 (describing the first element of the crime as "the perpetrator inflicted severe physical or *mental pain or suffering* upon one or more persons") (emphasis added).

8. Rome Statute, *supra* note 6, at art. 8(2)(a)(ii); Elements of Crimes, *supra* note 6, at 127 (describing the second element of the war crime of biological experiments as requiring that "the experiment seriously endangered the physical or mental health or integrity of such person or persons").

9. Rome Statute, *supra* note 6, at art. 8(2)(a)(iii) (war crime of willfully causing great suffering); Elements of Crimes, *supra* note 6, at 127 (describing the first element of the crime as "the perpetrator caused *great physical or mental pain or suffering* to, or serious injury to body or health of, one or more persons") (emphasis added).

10. Rome Statute, *supra* note 6, at art. 8(2)(b)(x)-1 (war crime of mutilation); Elements of Crimes, *supra* note 6, at 136 (describing the second element of the crime as "the conduct caused death or seriously endangered the physical or *mental health* of such person or persons") (emphasis added).

torture,[11] inhumane acts,[12] rape,[13] enforced prostitution,[14] and sexual violence.[15] The crime of genocide explicitly includes the act of "causing serious bodily or mental harm" within its definition.[16]

International law has also increasingly addressed the issue of mental harm through the law of remedies, recognizing that victims include those who have suffered "mental injury" or "emotional suffering," and that compensation and other remedies should be provided for "mental harm."[17] The European Court of Human Rights, for example, has awarded reparations to the families of victims of enforced disappearance due to the "anguish and distress" they have suffered.[18] The Inter-American Court of Human Rights has held that the "non-pecuniary damage inflicted on the victims is evident" because it was clear "all those subjected to brutal acts in the context of this case experienced intense suffering, anguish,

11. Rome Statute, *supra* note 6, at art. 7(1)(f) (crime against humanity of torture); Elements of Crimes, *supra* note 6, at 119 (describing the first element of the crime as "the perpetrator inflicted severe physical or *mental pain* or suffering upon one or more persons") (emphasis added).

12. Rome Statute, *supra* note 6, at art. 7(1)(k) (crime against humanity of other inhumane acts); Elements of Crimes, *supra* note 6, at 124 (describing the first element of the crime as "the perpetrator inflicted great suffering, or serious injury to body or *to mental or physical health*, by means of an inhumane act") (emphasis added.).

13. Rome Statute, *supra* note 6, at art. 7(1)(g); Elements of Crimes, *supra* note 6, at 119 (describing the second element of the crime against humanity of rape as requiring that "the invasion was committed by force, or by threat of force or coercion, such as that caused by fear of violence, duress, detention, *psychological oppression* or abuse of power, against such person or another person, or by taking advantage of a coercive environment, or the invasion was committed against a person *incapable of giving genuine consent*") (emphasis added).

14. Rome Statute, *supra* note 6, at art. 7(1)(g)-3; Elements of Crimes, *supra* note 6, at 120 (describing the first element of the crime as "the perpetrator caused one or more persons to engage in one or more acts of a sexual nature by force, or by threat of force or coercion, such as that caused by fear of violence, duress, detention, *psychological oppression* or abuse of power, against such person or persons or another person, or by taking advantage of a coercive environment or such person's or *persons' incapacity to give genuine consent*") (emphasis added).

15. Rome Statute, *supra* note 6, at art. 7(1)(g)-6; Elements of Crimes, *supra* note 6, at 121 (describing the first element of the crime as "the perpetrator committed an act of a sexual nature against one or more persons or caused such person or persons to engage in an act of a sexual nature by force, or by threat of force or coercion, such as that caused by fear of violence, duress, detention, *psychological oppression* or abuse of power, against such person or persons or another person, or by taking advantage of a coercive environment or such person's or *persons' incapacity to give genuine consent*") (emphasis added).

16. Rome Statute, *supra* note 6, at art. 6(b) ("'[G]enocide' means any of the following acts committed with intent to destroy, in whole or in part, a national, ethnical, racial or religious group, as such . . . (b) Causing serious bodily *or mental harm* to members of the group . . .").

17. G.A. Res. 60/147, ¶¶ 8, 20, 21 (Dec. 16, 2005).

18. Cakici v. Turkey, App. No. 23657/94, 1999 Eur. Ct. H.R., http://hudoc.echr.coe.int/eng?i=001-58282.

terror and insecurity."[19] International law also recognizes that in the cases of mental harm, reparation should aim at psychological remedy. For example, compensation should include "costs required for . . . psychological and social services," and that rehabilitation includes "medical and psychological care."[20]

B. International Humanitarian Law and Mental Health

IHL provides numerous protections for civilians generally, including some protections related to mental health specifically.

Generally, IHL protects against intentional attacks on civilians and against certain kinds of attacks that result in incidental harm. Parties to a conflict must distinguish between civilians and combatants, and between civilian objects and military objectives, and may only direct attacks at combatants and military objectives.[21] Indiscriminate attacks are prohibited,[22] as are attacks that would result in excessive expected civilian harm compared to the anticipated military advantage ("the proportionality rule," discussed in detail later).[23] Parties to a conflict are obliged to take "constant care to spare the civilian population" during military operations.[24]

19. Case of the Pueblo Bello Massacre v. Colombia, Merits, Reparations and Costs, Judgement, at § 384, Inter-Am. Ct. H.R., (ser. C) No. 140 (Jan. 31, 2006).

20. G.A. Res. 60/147, ¶¶ 20, 21 (Dec. 16, 2005). *See also* U.N. Comm. Against Torture, General Comment No. 3: Implementation of Article 14 by States Parties, § 13, U.N. Doc. CAT/C/GC/3 (Dec. 13, 2012) (Reparations "may include a wide range of inter-disciplinary measures, such as medical, physical and psychological rehabilitative services; re-integrative and social services; community and family-oriented assistance and services; vocational training; education etc. A holistic approach to rehabilitation which also takes into consideration the strength and resilience of the victim is of utmost importance.").

21. Protocol Additional to the Geneva Conventions of 12 August 1949, and Relating to the Protection of Victims of International Armed Conflicts (Protocol I) arts. 48, 51(2), 52(2), June 8, 1977, 1125 U.N.T.S. 3 [hereinafter AP I]; Protocol Additional to the Geneva Conventions of 12 August 1949, and Relating to the Protection of Victims of Non-International Armed Conflicts (Protocol II) art. 13(2), June 8, 1977, 1125 U.N.T.S. 609 [hereinafter AP II]; Rome Statute, *supra* note 6, arts. 8(2)(b)(i)–(ii), 8(2)(e)(i); 1 Int'l Comm. of the Red Cross, Customary International Humanitarian Law: Rules 3, 25 (Jean-Marie Henckaerts & Louise Doswald-Beck eds., 2005), https://www.icrc.org/en/doc/assets/files/other/customary-international-humanitarian-law-i-icrc-eng.pdf [hereinafter ICRC Customary IHL Study] (Rules 1 and 7).

22. AP I, *supra* note 21, art. 51(4); Protocol on Prohibitions or Restrictions on the Use of Mines, Booby-Traps and Other Devices to the Convention on Prohibitions or Restrictions on the Use of Certain Conventional Weapons art. 3(8), May 3, 1996, 2048 U.N.T.S. 93 [hereinafter Amended Protocol II]; ICRC Customary IHL Study, *supra* note 21, at 37 (Rule 11).

23. AP I, *supra* note 21, arts. 51(5)(b), 57; Amended Protocol II, *supra* note 22, art. 3(8)(c); ICRC Customary IHL Study, *supra* note 21, at 46 (Rule 14).

24. AP I, *supra* note 21, art. 57(1); ICRC Customary IHL Study, *supra* note 21, at 51 (Rule 15); Amended Protocol II, *supra* note 22, art. 3(10); *see also* AP II, *supra* note 21, art. 13(1) (explaining that in a non-international armed conflict "[t]he civilian population and individual civilians shall enjoy general protection against the dangers arising from military operations").

They must take "all feasible precautions in the choice of means and methods of attack with a view to avoiding, and in any event minimizing, incidental loss of civilian life, injury to civilians and damage to civilian objects."[25]

IHL specifically prohibits certain kinds of intentional mental harm. Article 51(2) of Additional Protocol I to the Geneva Conventions prohibits "acts or threats of violence the primary purpose of which is to spread terror" among civilians.[26] As Lieblich has written, in the most detailed examination and analysis of the issue of mental harm and IHL to date, Additional Protocol I does not provide a definition of "terror," but the notion of "terror" can reasonably be assumed to include mental harm,[27] and is focused on the intentional—not incidental—infliction of such harm.[28]

A question that has received increased attention in recent years is whether and the extent to which *incidental* mental harms are protected by IHL. None of the rules in IHL that protect civilians from incidental harm explicitly refer to mental harms. For instance, the proportionality and feasible precautions in the choice of means and methods of attack rules protect against civilian "injury." Some commentators have also argued that the obligation to take constant care to spare the civilian population "is not limited to the types of harm expressly referred to in the rule of proportionality,"[29] and that mental harm is within its remit.

1. The Proportionality Rule in International Humanitarian Law

IHL prohibits disproportionate attacks: those attacks that "may be expected to cause incidental loss of civilian life, injury to civilians, damage to civilian objects, or a combination thereof which would be excessive in relation to the concrete and direct military advantage anticipated."[30] Commanders must refrain from

25. AP I, *supra* note 21, art. 57(2)(a)(ii); Amended Protocol II, *supra* note 22, art. 3(10); ICRC Customary IHL Study, *supra* note 21, at 51 (Rule 15).

26. AP I, *supra* note 21, art. 51(2).

27. Eliav Lieblich, *Beyond Life and Limb: Exploring Incidental Mental Harm Under International Humanitarian Law*, *in* Applying International Humanitarian Law in Judicial and Quasi-Judicial Bodies: International and Domestic Aspects 195 (Derek Jinks, Jackson Nyamuya Maogoto, & Solon Solomon eds., 2014); *see also* Tallinn Manual on the International Law Applicable to Cyber Warfare 108 (Michael N. Schmitt ed., 2013) [hereinafter Tallinn Manual].

28. Lieblich, *supra* note 27, at 195–96.

29. Emanuela-Chiara Gillard, *Proportionality in the Conduct of Hostilities: The Incidental Harm Side of the Assessment*, Chatham House 33 (Dec. 2018), https://www.chathamhouse.org/sites/default/files/publications/research/2018-12-10-proportionality-conduct-hostilities-incidental-harm-gillard-final.pdf; Michael N. Schmitt & Chad Highfill, *Invisible Injuries: Concussive Effects and International Humanitarian Law*, 9 Harv. Nat'l Sec. J. 72, 95–96 (2018) (noting that the "constant care" obligation requires military personnel to avoid any harm to civilians "not just that which qualifies as incidental injury or collateral damage pursuant to the rule of proportionality").

30. AP I, *supra* note 21, arts. 51(5)(b), 57; Amended Protocol II, *supra* note 22, art. 3(8) (applicable in NIACs); ICRC Customary IHL Study, *supra* note 21, at 46 (Rule 14).

undertaking such attacks and cancel or suspend them where "it becomes apparent" that the attack would be disproportionate.[31]

In broad terms, this involves a balancing exercise—between the civilian harm anticipated at the time and the expected military advantage to be gained from carrying out the attack. This is a notoriously difficult test, due to the challenges of weighing up two completely different, and, many have argued, incommensurable, factors.[32]

The focus in this chapter is on the incidental civilian harm side of the test—and specifically the question of whether mental harm is and can be included—so we do not address in detail the issue of military advantage. However, it is important to note that the military advantage must be "concrete and direct."[33] This means it must be "substantial and clearly identifiable," and either directly enhancing "friendly military operations" or hindering enemy ones.[34] It is also important to highlight that, even if mental harm is taken into account in a proportionality analysis, this would not make all attacks which cause such harm unlawful. The test of proportionality is a balancing exercise, and if the overall anticipated civilian harm is not excessive in relation to the military advantage, then the attack would not violate the proportionality rule.

When assessing incidental civilian harm, the lawfulness of the attack is judged on its reasonably foreseeable consequences at the time the attack is carried out, not the actual consequences that ensue.[35] The standard is that of the reasonable military commander,[36] and the commander's interpretation must be one of

31. AP I, *supra* note 21, arts. 57(2)(a)(iii), 57(2)(b).

32. *See, e.g.*, Henry Shue, *Proportionality in War*, *in* THE ENCYCLOPEDIA OF WAR 7 (Gordon Martel ed., 2012); Michael Schmitt, *The Principle of Discrimination in 21st Century Warfare*, 2 YALE HUM. RTS. & DEV. L.J. 143 (1999); Amichai Cohen, The Lebanon War and the Application of the Proportionality Principle, Research Paper No. 6-07 (Apr. 2007), https://ssrn.com/abstract=983436; GARY D. SOLIS, THE LAW OF ARMED CONFLICT: INTERNATIONAL HUMANITARIAN LAW IN WAR 273 (2010); Adil Haque, *A Theory of* Jus in Bello *Proportionality*, *in* WEIGHING LIVES IN WAR 192 (Jens David Ohlin, Larry May, & Claire Finkelstein eds., 2015) [hereinafter Haque, *Jus in Bello*].

33. AP I, *supra* note 21, arts. 51(5)(b), 57.

34. Adil Haque, *Necessity and Proportionality in International Law*, *in* THE CAMBRIDGE HANDBOOK OF THE JUST WAR 268–69 (Larry May ed., 2016); PROGRAM ON HUMANITARIAN POL'Y & CONFLICT RES., COMMENTARY TO THE HPCR MANUAL ON INTERNATIONAL LAW APPLICABLE TO AIR AND MISSILE WARFARE 45 (2010).

35. *See* Haque, *Jus in Bello*, *supra* note 32, at 189; OFFICE OF THE GEN. COUNSEL, U.S. DEP'T OF DEF., DEPARTMENT OF DEFENSE LAW OF WAR MANUAL 61 (June 2015, updated Dec. 2016) [hereinafter DOD LAW OF WAR MANUAL]; TERRY GILL ET AL., INT'L LAW ASS'N STUDY GRP., THE CONDUCT OF HOSTILITIES AND INTERNATIONAL HUMANITARIAN LAW: CHALLENGES OF 21ST CENTURY WARFARE, FINAL REPORT 2 (2017); William J. Fenrick, *Applying IHL Targeting Rules to Practical Situations: Proportionality and Military Objectives*, 27 WINDSOR Y.B. ACCESS JUST. 271, 277 (2009).

36. *See, e.g.*, DOD LAW OF WAR MANUAL, *supra* note 35, at 244 (§ 5.10.2.2); Schmitt & Highfill, *supra* note 29, at 84.

"common sense" and "good faith."[37] The assessment should be based on all sources of information available at the time of the assessment.[38] For example, what may be foreseeable to a reasonable commander may be different depending on whether the attack is preplanned, an opportunistic attack on a target, or a defensive response to an enemy attack.[39] What exactly may be reasonably foreseeable may partly depend on prior lessons learned and empirical data.[40]

The harm must be "caused" by the attack.[41] While the Additional Protocols and their commentaries do not offer specific guidance on how far down the chain of causation the effects of attacks may be, the generally accepted view—including that of the International Committee of the Red Cross (ICRC)—is that both "direct" and "indirect" effects are included, where they are reasonably foreseeable.[42]

2. Scholarly Literature and Expert Discussion on the Proportionality Rule and Mental Harm

The scholarly literature and expert discussion on mental health harms in IHL is still nascent. The more traditional view is that the current state of the law on proportionality does not encompass mental

37. Isabel Robinson & Ellen Nohle, *Proportionality and Precautions in Attack: The Reverberating Effects of Using Explosive Weapons in Populated Areas*, 98 Int'l Rev. Red Cross 107, 119–21 (2016); Prosecutor v. Galić, Case No. IT-89-29-T, Judgement, ¶ 58 (Int'l Crim. Trib. for the Former Yugoslavia Dec. 5, 2003); Off. of the Judge Advoc. Gen., Ministry of Def., Law of Armed Conflict at the Operational and Tactical Levels 4–5 (2001) (Can.), https://www.fichl.org/fileadmin/_migrated/content_uploads/Canadian_LOAC_Manual_2001_English.pdf [hereinafter Canada Joint Doctrine Manual]; Yoram Dinstein, The Conduct of Hostilities Under the Law of International Armed Conflict 159 (2016); Michael N. Schmitt & Jeffrey S. Thurnher, *"Out of the Loop": Autonomous Weapon Systems and the Law of Armed Conflict*, 4 Harv. Nat'l Sec. J. 231, 256 (2013); A.P.V. Rogers, Law on the Battlefield 151 (2012); *see also* Int'l L. Ass'n Study Grp., The Conduct of Hostilities and International Humanitarian Law: Challenges of 21st Century Warfare 24 (2017) [hereinafter ILA Study Group].

38. ILA Study Group, *supra* note 37, at 24.

39. Robinson & Nohle, *supra* note 37, at 121.

40. *Id.* at 122–24.

41. AP I, *supra* note 21, arts. 51(5)(b), 57; Amended Protocol II, *supra* note 22, art. 3(8) (applicable in NIACs); ICRC Customary IHL Study, *supra* note 21, at 46 (Rule 14).

42. Int'l Comm. of the Red Cross, International Humanitarian Law and the Challenges of Contemporary Armed Conflicts 41–43, 52 (2015), http://e-brief.icrc.org/wp-content/uploads/2016/08/4-international-humanitarian-law-and-the-challenges-of-contemporary-armed-conflicts.pdf; ILA Study Group, *supra* note 37, at 23–24; Tallinn Manual, *supra* note 27, at 472 (Rule 113); Schmitt & Highfill, *supra* note 29, at 87–88; Robinson & Nohle, *supra* note 37, at 112–13; Laurent Gisel, *Relevant Incidental Harm for the Proportionality Principle*, *in* Proceedings of the Bruges Colloquium 125 (Luis Bouza García et al. eds., 2015) [hereinafter Gisel, *Relevant Incidental Harm*].

harms.[43] From what is publicly verifiable, military practice appears generally to include within "injury" only physical harms when applying the proportionality rule.[44] However, a growing number of experts argue that there is "no reason to categorically exclude mental health from the principle of proportionality,"[45] and that serious mental harm either already is part of the law on proportionality, or should be.[46]

In one of the most detailed contributions on this topic, Lieblich argues that the law's silence on mental harms is not determinative, and that a teleological interpretation that reads incidental mental harm into the rules is both tenable and consistent with the humanitarian principles that underpin humanitarian law.[47] What remains, he argues, is to overcome the various legal and policy obstacles (e.g., causation, foreseeability, and measurability), which he suggests is possible, for example, by examining other bodies of law that have dealt with similar issues such as tort law and international criminal law.[48]

In a short piece examining Houthi rebel missile strikes on Saudi Arabia and other kinds of recurrent attacks, Solomon highlighted the seriousness of mental harms to civilians around the world from conflict-related violence.[49] He discussed some of the practical considerations which could make taking mental health into account difficult at the operational level, but argued that in recurrent attacks, it might be possible to make some "operational adjustments" to take mental harms

43. Int'l Comm. of the Red Cross, The Principle of Proportionality in the Rules Governing the Conduct of Hostilities under International Humanitarian Law 35 (Laurent Gisel ed., 2016), https://www.icrc.org/en/download/file/79184/4358_002_expert_meeting_report_web_1.pdf [hereinafter ICRC, Principle of Proportionality].

44. Gillard, *supra* note 29, at 33 (noting that "the majority of state practice considered for this paper does not take mental harm into account"); ICRC, Principle of Proportionality, *supra* note 43, at 35 (explaining that, in the view of several experts, "while collateral damage estimate (CDE) methodology has developed to enable a better assessment to be made of the magnitude of the expected losses of life, physical injuries and damage, this is not the case for mental injury").

45. ICRC, Principle of Proportionality, *supra* note 43, at 35.

46. ILA Study Group, *supra* note 37, at 23–24; Tallinn Manual, *supra* note 27, at 417; ICRC, Principle of Proportionality, *supra* note 43, at 35; Robinson & Nohle, *supra* note 37, at 129; Gisel, *Relevant Incidental Harm*, *supra* note 42, at 120; Steve Wilkinson, *Incidental Yet Monumental: Incorporating Mental Health Impacts into IHL Proportionality Assessments*, Harvard Humanitarian Initiative (Apr. 7, 2017), https://reliefweb.int/report/world/incidental-yet-monumental-incorporating-mental-health-impacts-ihl-proportionality.

47. Lieblich, *supra* note 27, at 200–201.

48. *Id.* at 201–15.

49. Solon Solomon, *Bringing Psychological Civilian Harm to the Forefront: Incidental Civilian Fear as Trauma in the Case of Recurrent Attacks*, EJIL: Talk! (Apr. 25, 2018), https://www.ejiltalk.org/bringing-psychological-civilian-harm-to-the-forefront-incidental-civilian-fear-as-trauma-in-the-case-of-recurrent-attacks.

into account.[50] In a short exploratory piece on mental harms, Wilkinson similarly noted the severe harms of war-related trauma.[51] He argued that the relevance of mental harms to IHL is "often overlooked," and had "clear gap[s] in research," and he called for more scrutiny of the issue.[52] He also highlighted challenges to incorporating it, including measurability, foreseeability, and severity.[53]

In an expert discussion hosted by the ICRC, opinion was divided on the current state of the law. Some of the participants maintained that states did not "sign up" or intend for mental harms "to be part of the assessment" when they adopted Additional Protocol I.[54] However, Gillard, the author of a detailed 2018 paper on proportionality, argues that mental health was "probably" not addressed at the time because it was "not considered" then that attacks could have such mental effects.[55] She cites two representatives who had been involved in the negotiations and who told her that "mental harm had simply not been considered" by states during the drafting.[56] Some experts at the ICRC meeting argued that the law is dynamic and needs to respond to the emerging scientific knowledge around conditions like PTSD and the fact that "in the 21st century, mental health has the same status as physical health."[57]

In the International Law Association's 2016 discussion of this issue by the study group on the Conduct of Hostilities and International Humanitarian Law (the ILA Study Group), different views were expressed among participants. The Final Report summarized that "[v]arious members . . . agreed on the importance of this issue, bearing in mind however that mental harm could only be included within the proportionality analysis when it is measurable and when a causal link to a specific attack can be established (war is intrinsically harmful)."[58] When discussing the definition of "cyber attack," the international expert group that collectively drafted the *Tallinn Manual on the International Law Applicable to Cyber Warfare* stated that "while the notion of attack encompasses injury and death caused to individuals, the International Group of Experts agreed that it is, in light of the law of armed conflict's underlying humanitarian purposes, reasonable to extend the definition to serious illness and severe mental suffering that are tantamount to injury."[59]

50. Solomon, *supra* note 49.

51. Wilkinson, *supra* note 46.

52. *Id.*

53. *Id.*

54. ICRC, Principle of Proportionality, *supra* note 43, at 35 (discussing the views of some experts).

55. Gillard, *supra* note 29, at 32.

56. *Id.* at 32 n.95 (referencing the recollections of two representatives at the negotiations).

57. ICRC, Principle of Proportionality, *supra* note 43, at 35.

58. ILA Study Group, *supra* note 37, at 28–29.

59. Tallinn Manual, *supra* note 27, at 417.

A key question that arises in the literature is how feasible it is for commanders to incorporate a mental harm assessment into their proportionality analysis. The notion that commanders should be expected to anticipate and account for mental harms has been subject to several key criticisms. The primary concerns relate to whether mental harm is sufficiently measurable, quantifiable, or definable to enable it to be weighed against the expected military advantage, and whether it is possible to sufficiently assess causation and for commanders to foresee such harms.[60]

In the context of proportionality, the concern about causation can in part be understood as the difficulty of making a risk assessment. The question is not whether the particular attack caused mental harm in a specific incident (although that may be important for accountability, redress, and to inform future mitigation measures, including precautions in attack), but rather whether the attack may be expected to cause such mental harm, as proportionality is always a forward-looking test. Lieblich has argued that it may be possible to carry out such an assessment, using domestic tort law in the United States to show that this kind of test is already applied in other legal contexts.[61]

Building on existing scholarship on mental harms, as well as Schmitt and Highfill's comprehensive analysis of the science and law related to traumatic brain injury,[62] the next section of this chapter delves into the scientific literature on PTSD to examine whether such serious mental harm can and should be included in assessments of proportionality under IHL. We evaluate the state of public health, psychology, and neuroscience research on PTSD to examine the extent to which scientific research on the etiology, symptoms, nature, and consequences of PTSD might enable commanders to make proportionality assessments.

III. SHOULD PTSD BE INCLUDED AMONG THE TYPES OF CIVILIAN INJURIES CONSIDERED IN A PROPORTIONALITY ANALYSIS?

The underlying purpose of the proportionality rule is to balance the goal of reducing incidental civilian harm during war with the goal of enabling military action necessary to achieve military purposes.[63] The rule recognizes the importance of constraining military action, and it developed against a backdrop of

60. ILA Study Group, *supra* note 37, at 29; Lieblich, *supra* note 27, at 201–11.

61. Lieblich, *supra* note 27, at 201–11; *see also* Wilkinson, *supra* note 46.

62. Schmitt & Highfill, *supra* note 29 (evaluating the state of scientific research on traumatic brain injury (TBI) and assessing whether the understanding of TBI is at a level that would make it possible to include in assessments of proportionality and precautions in attack).

63. *See, e.g.*, Cohen, *supra* note 32, at 17; Dep't of the Army, ATTP 3-37.31, Civilian Casualty Mitigation 1-10 (July 18, 2012), https://fas.org/irp/doddir/army/attp3-37-31.pdf [hereinafter Dep't of the Army, Civilian Casualty Migration]; Canada Joint Doctrine Manual, *supra* note 37, at § 204.4–204.6.

growing recognition of civilian suffering during war.[64] It seeks to reduce collateral damage and unnecessary civilian suffering.[65] In addition to minimizing civilian deaths, the rule seeks to minimize civilian injuries, such as loss of a leg, damage to intestines from a blast, blindness, or burns.[66] Civilian physical injuries are taken into account in planning military attacks out of recognition of the immediate pain caused to the individual and the serious consequences that the injury can have for the individual's well-being and functioning. Militaries and leaders often stress the humanitarian values inherent in their efforts to reduce civilian harm.[67] The

64. Judith Gail Gardham, *Proportionality and Force in International Law*, 87 Am. J. Int'l L. 391, 397–400 (1993).

65. *See, e.g.*, Cohen, *supra* note 32, at 14; Dep't of the Army, Civilian Casualty Migration, *supra* note 63, at 1–10; Ziv Bohrer & Mark Osiel, *Proportionality in Military Force at War's Multiple Levels: Averting Civilian Casualties vs. Safeguarding Soldiers*, 46 Vand. J. Transnat'l L. 747, 771 (2013); Int'l Comm. of the Red Cross, *Iraq: Practice Relating to Rule 14. Proportionality in Attack*, § A(VI), Customary IHL, https://ihl-databases.icrc.org/customary-ihl/eng/docs/v2_cou_iq_rule14 (last visited Oct. 4, 2019) (citing statements made by the Iraqi president); Int'l Comm. of the Red Cross, *Benin: Practice Relating to Rule 14. Proportionality in Attack*, § A(III), Customary IHL, https://ihl-databases.icrc.org/customary-ihl/eng/docs/v2_cou_bj_rule14 (last visited Oct. 4, 2019) (citing Benin's military manual).

66. *See, e.g.*, ILA Study Group, *supra* note 37, at 24.

67. *See, e.g.*, David J. Petraeus, General, U.S. Army, Address at 45th Munich Security Conference: The Future of the Alliance and the Mission in Afghanistan (Feb. 8, 2009); Parliament of the U.K., Reporting of All Civilian Casualties Admitted to a UK Military Field Hospital on Future Combat Operations: Written Statement—HLWS479 (Feb. 27, 2018), https://www.parliament.uk/business/publications/written-questions-answers-statements/written-statement/Lords/2018-02-27/HLWS479 (statement of Earl Howe, Minister of State, Ministry of Defence). Reducing harms among civilians also aligns with military operational and strategic interests. *See* U.S. Joint Forces Command, Joint Ctr. for Operational Analysis, Adaptive Learning for Afghanistan: Final Recommendations 4 (Feb. 10, 2011), https://info.publicintelligence.net/JCOA-ALA-Afghanistan.pdf; Joint Staff J7, Joint and Coalition Operational Analysis, Reducing and Mitigating Civilian Casualties: Enduring Lessons (Apr. 12, 2013); Gregory S. McNeal, *New Approaches to Reducing and Mitigating Harm to Civilians*, *in* Counterinsurgency: New Directions in Asymmetric Warfare 127, 127–40 (William C. Banks ed., 2013); Sarah B. Sewall, Chasing Success: Air Force Efforts to Reduce Civilian Harm (2016); Sahr Muhammedally, *Minimizing Civilian Harm in Populated Areas: Lessons from Examining ISAF and AMISOM Policies*, 98 Int'l Rev. Red Cross 225 (2016); *see also* Open Soc'y Founds., The Strategic Costs of Civilian Harm: Applying Lessons from Afghanistan to Current and Future Conflicts (June 2016), https://www.opensocietyfoundations.org/sites/default/files/strategic-costs-civilian-harm-20160622.pdf (finding that civilian harm can be fatal to counterinsurgency and counterterrorism strategies); E.L. Gaston & Rebecca Wright, Ctr. for Civilians in Conflict, Losing the People: The Costs and Consequences of Civilian Suffering in Afghanistan (Feb. 2009), https://civiliansinconflict.org/wp-content/uploads/2017/09/losing-the-people_2009.pdf; Dep't of the Army, Civilian Casualty Migration, *supra* note 63, at 1–5 ("In addition to legal and humanitarian reasons, Army units must mitigate CIVCASs because they create lasting repercussions that impair post-conflict reconstruction and reconciliation. CIVCASs lead to ill will among the host-nation population and political pressure that can limit freedom of action

rationale for reducing unnecessary civilian suffering by protecting against excessive physical injuries applies equally to mental harms to the extent that they are similarly serious in the suffering caused. In this section, we examine in detail existing scientific literature on the nature and harms of PTSD and find that it is a serious disorder entailing significant suffering. Indeed, militaries already recognize the seriousness of PTSD. They have increasingly recognized the harms of PTSD among their soldiers, and devote significant resources to prevent and respond to PTSD.

A. Mental Harms Can Cause Significant Civilian Suffering and Impairment of Functioning

Like already-recognized physical injuries, mental harms resulting from military attacks can cause significant suffering and impairment of functioning. We focus here on PTSD because it is clearly defined, has a clear etiology tied to trauma, is the subject of significant scientific research as to causes, symptomology, and effects,[68] and because "PTSD is the most prevalent psychopathological consequence of exposure to traumatic events."[69]

A PTSD diagnosis requires a traumatic stressor, such as "exposure to actual or threatened death, serious injury, or sexual violence."[70] A traumatic event is necessary for the onset of PTSD. In the armed conflict context, the traumatic stressor could be witnessing a shooting, experiencing a bombing, surviving an act of terrorism, seeing dead bodies or injuries, the sudden death of a loved one, or being physically injured in an attack.[71] These war-related traumas can be

of military forces. If Army units fail to protect civilians, for whatever reason, the legitimacy of U.S. operations is likely to be questioned by the host nation and other partners. . . . Focused attention on CIVCAS mitigation is an important investment to maintain legitimacy and ensure eventual success. Failure to prevent CIVCASs will undermine national policy objectives as well as the mission of Army units, while assisting adversaries. Adversaries will exploit CIVCAS incidents.").

68. Paola Rodriguez, Darren W. Holowka, & Brian P. Marx, *Assessment of Posttraumatic Stress Disorder-Related Functional Impairment: A Review*, 49 J. Rehabilitation Res. & Dev. 649–66 (2012) (noting that there are over 10,000 scientific articles about PTSD).

69. Arieh Shalev, Israel Liberzon, & Charles Marmar, *Post-Traumatic Stress Disorder*, 376 New England J. Med. 2459, 2459 (2017). We hope that future research in this area could examine other conditions, including depression.

70. Am. Psychiatric Ass'n, Diagnostic and Statistical Manual of Mental Disorders (2013).

71. *See, e.g.*, R. Srinivasa Murthy & Rashmi Lakshminarayana, *Mental Health Consequences of War: A Brief Review of Research Findings*, 5 World Psychiatry 25, 25–30 (2006); *Trauma Types*, Nat'l Child Traumatic Stress Network, https://www.nctsn.org/what-is-child-trauma/trauma-types (last visited Oct. 4, 2019).

singular, or chronic in nature with multiple traumas occurring over a span of years.[72]

PTSD is a serious condition which can lead to severe dysfunction and "devastating" impairment,[73] significantly lowering the quality of life.[74] The requirements for a PTSD diagnosis have been clarified and refined by many experts over the past 40 years. A PTSD diagnosis requires the presence of the following set of symptoms for at least one month and requires that the symptoms cause "distress or functional impairment":[75]

- Re-experiencing symptoms, such as nightmares, flashbacks, and emotional distress after exposure to a reminder;
- Avoidance of trauma-related stimuli;
- Persistent and recurring negative beliefs, thoughts, or feelings; and
- Trauma related reactivity, such as aggression, hypervigilance, difficulty sleeping, or a heightened startle reaction.

PTSD can lead to lengthy suffering. It is associated with functional impairment, including to educational and work performance; physical health harms; harm to relationships; additional harm to psychological well-being and suicide risk; harmful behaviors; physical brain abnormalities; hormone and neurochemical dysregulation; and neuroimmune system dysfunction. Children are particularly

72. Abraham Sagi-Schwartz, *The Wellbeing of Children Living in Chronic War Zones: The Palestinian–Israeli Case*, 32 INT'L J. BEHAVIORAL DEV. 322, 322–36 (2008).

73. Jonathan E. Sherin & Charles B. Nemeroff, *Post-Traumatic Stress Disorder: The Neurobiological Impact of Psychological Trauma*, 13 DIALOGUES CLINICAL NEUROSCIENCE 263, 263 (2011); Rodriguez, Holowka, & Marx, *supra* note 68; JUDITH LEWIS HERMAN, TRAUMA AND RECOVERY (1992); AM. PSYCHIATRIC ASS'N, *supra* note 70 (PTSD is "associated with high levels of social, occupational, and physical disability, as well as considerable economic costs and high levels of medical utilization. Impaired functioning is exhibited across social, interpersonal, developmental, educational, physical health, and occupational domains. In community and veteran samples, PTSD is associated with poor social and family relationships, absenteeism from work, lower income, and lower educational and occupational success.").

74. Domenico Giacco, Aleksandra Matanov, & Stefan Priebe, *Symptoms and Subjective Quality of Life in Post-Traumatic Stress Disorder: A Longitudinal Study*, 8 PLoS ONE 1 (2013); Aleksandra Matanov et al., *Subjective Quality of Life in War-Affected Populations*, 13 BMC PUB. HEALTH 1 (2013); Paula P. Schnurr et al., *Posttraumatic Stress Disorder and Quality of Life: Extension of Findings to Veterans of the Wars in Iraq and Afghanistan*, 29 CLINICAL PSYCH. REV. 727, 727–35 (2009); F.B. Danielsson, M. Schultz Larsen, B. Nørgaard, & J.M. Lauritsen, *Quality of Life and Level of Post-Traumatic Stress Disorder Among Trauma Patients: A Comparative Study Between a Regional and a University Hospital*, 26 SCANDINAVIAN J. TRAUMA RESUSCITATION & EMERGENCY MED. 1 (2018) (finding that severe trauma has a substantial impact on quality of life).

75. AM. PSYCHIATRIC ASS'N, *supra* note 70. Children have, in general, similar criteria, but the symptom presentation can look different in children and signs of illness can present through a child's play.

vulnerable to PTSD, and can suffer significant, long-term harm as a result of trauma exposure in childhood.

Children. It is clear that children are particularly susceptible to the impacts of trauma exposure. A large body of scientific evidence has shown that exposure to early childhood trauma has severe and negative consequences on the brain and body, in sometimes irreversible ways, and is harmful in a dose-dependent manner.[76] Childhood exposure may have adverse effects that can continue through a lifetime.[77] The landmark Adverse Childhood Experiences (ACEs) Study, completed with over 17,000 children, found that such experiences had:

> a strong influence on adolescent health; reproductive health; smoking; alcohol abuse; illicit drug abuse; sexual behaviour; mental health; the risk of violence and re-victimization; stability of relationships, homelessness; and performance in the workforce. Via these behaviours and other neurobiological pathways, ACEs increase the risk of: heart disease; chronic lung disease; liver disease; suicide; and other risks for the leading causes of death.[78]

A meta-analysis of ACEs including 253,719 people from all over the world found that exposure to multiple ACEs affected all of the health outcomes examined, with the strongest relationships to increased expressed violence, mental illness, and problematic substance abuse later in life.[79] In a study of 22,256 respondents in five African countries, exposure to physical violence was moderately to strongly associated with mental health problems, substance abuse behaviors, and risky sexual behaviors.[80] A study of refugees found that childhood war exposure was

76. Niclas Olofsson et al., *Long-Term Health Consequences of Violence Exposure in Adolescence: A 26-year Prospective Study*, 12 BMC Pub. Health 1 (2012); B.D. Perry, *The Neurodevelopmental Impact of Violence in Childhood*, *in* Textbook of Child and Adolescent Forensic Psychiatry 221–38 (D. Schetky & E.P. Benedek eds., 2001); *About the CDC-Kaiser ACE Study*, Ctrs. for Disease Control & Prevention, https://www.cdc.gov/violenceprevention/acestudy/about.html (last reviewed Apr. 2, 2019) [hereinafter *CDC-Kaiser ACE Study*].

77. D. Kuh et al., *Life Course Epidemiology*, 57 J. Epidemiology & Community Health 778, 778–83 (2003).

78. *CDC-Kaiser ACE Study*, *supra* note 76; *see also* World Health Org., Addressing Adverse Childhood Experiences to Improve Public Health: Expert Consultation, 4–5 May 2009, https://www.who.int/violence_injury_prevention/violence/activities/adverse_childhood_experiences/global_research_network_may_2009.pdf (last visited Apr. 7, 2019).

79. Karen Hughes et al., *The Effect of Multiple Adverse Childhood Experiences on Health: A Systematic Review and Meta-Analysis*, 2 Lancet Pub. Health 356, 356–66 (2017).

80. David W. Brown et al., *Exposure to Physical and Sexual Violence and Adverse Health Behaviours in African Children: Results from the Global School-Based Student Health Survey*, 87 Bull. World Health Org. 447, 447–55 (2009).

significantly associated with mental health problems and reduced the quality of life in adulthood.[81]

Lengthy suffering. Individuals can suffer from PTSD for many months, years, or even a lifetime. A study of the PTSD prevalence among survivors of the September 11 attacks in Manhattan found that 12 percent of respondents who lived near the twin towers still had PTSD two to three years later, and those who worked in the towers at the time had a PTSD prevalence of 15 percent.[82] (The global prevalence of PTSD commonly ranges from approximately 0.5 to 3.5 percent in the general population.[83]) Five years after the conflict in Yugoslavia, 22 percent of civilians met PTSD criteria.[84] Fourteen years after the Rwandan genocide, 26 percent were found to meet the criteria for PTSD.[85] In Lebanon, 43 percent of people with PTSD were found to still have the disorder 10 years after their initial diagnosis.[86]

81. Marianne Opaas & Sverre Varvin, *Relationships of Childhood Adverse Experiences with Mental Health and Quality of Life at Treatment Start for Adult Refugees Traumatized by Pre-Flight Experiences of War and Human Rights Violations*, 203 J. Nervous & Mental Disease 684, 684–95 (2015).

82. David S. Fink & Sandro Galea, *Life Course Epidemiology of Trauma and Related Psychopathology in Civilian Populations*, 17 Current Psychiatry Reps. 1 (2015).

83. Am. Psychiatric Ass'n, *supra* note 70.

84. Stefan Priebe et al., *Experience of Human Rights Violations and Subsequent Mental Disorders—A Study Following the War in the Balkans*, 71 Soc. Sci. & Med. 2170, 2170–77 (2010).

85. Ariel Eytan et al., *Long-Term Mental Health Outcome in Post-Conflict Settings: Similarities and Differences Between Kosovo and Rwanda*, 61 Int'l J. Soc. Psychiatry 363, 363–72 (2015); *see* Lamaro P. Onyut et al., *Trauma, Poverty and Mental Health Among Somali and Rwandese Refugees Living in an African Refugee Settlement—An Epidemiological Study*, 3 Conflict & Health 1 (2009) (noting that over 10 years post-conflict, 32 percent of Rwandans and 48.1 percent of Somalis still screened positive for PTSD). Symptoms can continue decades later. *See* Matthew Brooks et al., *Long-Term Effects of Military Service on Mental Health among Veterans of the Vietnam War Era*, 173 Mil. Med. 570, 570–75 (2008) (finding that 28 years following the Vietnam war, the point prevalence of PTSD in Vietnam veterans was 9.1 percent); I. Bramsen & H.M. Ploeg, *Fifty Years Later: The Long-Term Psychological Adjustment of Ageing World War II Survivors*, 100 Acta Psychiatrica Scandinavica 350, 350–58 (1999) (finding that 4 percent of civilian war victims or resistance participants were still suffering from PTSD 50 years post–WWII, compared to 1.5 percent of controls who were not survivors of WWII and were in the same age group).

86. Jawad Fares et al., *Post-Traumatic Stress Disorder in Adult Victims of Cluster Munitions in Lebanon: A 10-Year Longitudinal Study*, 7 BMJ Open 1 (2017); *see also* Christiane Steinert et al., *The Course of PTSD in Maturalistic Long-Term Studies: High Variability of Outcomes. A Systematic Review*, 69 Nordic J. Psychiatry 483, 483–96 (2015) (finding that existing studies showed a range of 18–50 percent of people who had a stable recovery within 3–7 years). The more trauma events types experienced, the lower the chances of spontaneous remission from PTSD. *See* Iris-Tatjana Kolassa et al., *Spontaneous Remission from PTSD Depends on the Number of Traumatic Event Types Experienced*, 2 Psych. Trauma: Theory Res. Prac. & Pol'y 169, 169–74 (2010).

Education and employment impairment. PTSD is associated with significant functional impairment,[87] including to educational participation and outcomes,[88] and work performance and employment status.[89] Impaired functioning may be a result of cognition difficulties or sleep disturbances associated with PTSD.[90] PTSD symptoms of avoidance, numbing, and hypervigilance have also been strongly associated with poor work and academic performance.[91]

Physical health. PTSD is associated with the increased risk of acute and chronic physical health problems,[92] including gastrointestinal

87. Rodriguez, Holowka, & Marx, *supra* note 68. This is large review completed by the U.S. Department of Veteran Affairs shows that there is a large body of evidence supporting a strong and reliable association between PTSD and functional impairment.

88. Sheryl Kataoka et al., *Responding to Students with Posttraumatic Stress Disorder in Schools*, 21 Child & Adolescent Psychiatric Clinics North Am. 119, 119–33 (2012); Virginia Delaney-Black et al., *Violence Exposure, Trauma, and IQ and/or Reading Deficits Among Urban Children*, 156 Archives Pediatrics & Adolescent Med. 280, 280–85 (2002); Hallam Hurt et al., *Exposure to Violence: Psychological and Academic Correlates in Child Witnesses*, 155 Archives Pediatrics & Adolescent Med. 1351, 1351–56 (2001); Holly Foster & Jeanne Brooks-Gunn, *Children's Exposure to Community and War Violence and Mental Health in Four African Countries*, 146 Soc. Sci. & Med. 292, 292–99 (2015) (longitudinal study finding that as exposure to community violence increased, grade-point average decreased and days of missed school increased).

89. Mark W. Smith, Paula P. Schnurr, & Robert A. Rosenheck, *Employment Outcomes and PTSD Symptom Severity*, 7 Mental Health Servs. Res. 89, 89–101 (2005) (finding that male Vietnam veterans with more severe PTSD symptoms were less likely to be employed full-time, if they were employed at all); Maarten J. Kunst, *Employment Status and Posttraumatic Stress Disorder Following Compensation Seeking in Victims of Violence*, 26 J. Interpersonal Violence 377, 377–93 (2011) (finding that PTSD severity was positively correlated with a higher unemployment rate, and those with PTSD were more likely to be unemployed than those without PTSD); Christopher R. Erbes et al., *Mental Health Diagnosis and Occupational Functioning in National Guard/Reserve Veterans Returning from Iraq*, 48 J. Rehabilitation Res. & Dev. 1159, 1159–70 (2011) (finding lower levels of work performance and a deterioration of functioning in the workplace over time for combat veterans with PTSD, depression, and/or alcohol abuse); Susan Evans et al., *Anger and Its Association to Distress and Social/Occupational Functioning in Symptomatic Disaster Relief Workers Responding to the September 11, 2001, World Trade Center Disaster*, 19 J. Traumatic Stress 147, 147–52 (2006); Kallio Hunnicutt-Ferguson et al., *Posttraumatic Stress Disorder, Functional Impairment, and Subjective Distress in World Trade Center Disaster Workers*, 31 J. Traumatic Stress 234, 234–43 (2018) (finding that PTSD was associated with "deficits in social and occupational functioning, over time").

90. Rodriguez, Holowka, & Marx, *supra* note 68.

91. *Id.*

92. Maria L. Pacella, Bryce Hruska, & Douglas L. Delahanty, *The Physical Health Consequences of PTSD and PTSD Symptoms: A Meta-Analytic Review*, 27 J. Anxiety Disorders 33, 33–46 (2013) (meta-analysis of 62 studies found a significantly increased risk of general health symptoms, general medical conditions, poorer health-related quality of life, and a greater frequency and severity of pain, cardio-respiratory symptoms, and gastrointestinal (GI) complaints for PTSD and high PTSD symptom individuals); Olofsson, *supra* note 76; Anna W. Wright et al., *Systematic*

dysfunction,[93] cardiovascular and respiratory problems,[94] arthritis,[95] autoimmune disorders,[96] dermatological, genitourinary, musculoskeletal, neurological, and pulmonary functioning,[97] sexual and erectile dysfunction,[98]

Review: Exposure to Community Violence and Physical Health Outcomes in Youth, 42 J. Pediatric Psych. 364, 364–78 (2017); Benjamin J. Morasco et al., *The Relationship Between PTSD and Chronic Pain: Mediating Role of Coping Strategies and Depression*, 154 Pain 609, 609–16 (2013) (finding that those with PTSD had a significantly increased severity of pain and interference of pain in daily life); Dinu-Stefan Teodorescu et al., *Chronic Pain in Multi-Traumatized Outpatients with a Refugee Background Resettled in Norway: A Cross-Sectional Study*, 3 BMC Psych. 1 (2015); Marie-Jo Brennstuhl, Cyril Tarquinio, & Sebastien Montel, *Chronic Pain and PTSD: Evolving Views on Their Comorbidity*, 51 Perspectives Psychiatric Care 295, 295–304 (2015).

93. Maria L. Pacella, Bryce Hruska, & Douglas L. Delahanty, *The Physical Health Consequences of PTSD and PTSD Symptoms: A Meta-Analytic Review*, 27 J. Anxiety Disorders 33, 33–46 (2013); Wendy D'Andrea et al., *Physical Health Problems After Single Trauma Exposure*, 17 J. Am. Psychiatric Nurses Ass'n 378, 378–92 (2011).

94. Pacella et al., *supra* note 93; D'Andrea et al., *supra* note 93; Melanie Arenson & Beth Cohen, *Posttraumatic Stress Disorder and Cardiovascular Disease*, 28 PTSD Res. Q. 1 (2017) (The U.S. Department of Veteran Affairs found that among a diverse population, "including Veterans and active-duty military personnel, nurses, and 9/11 survivors," those with PTSD were more likely to develop and die from cardiovascular disease. They found that in a sample of Vietnam veterans, "[p]atients with PTSD had double the risk of death from heart disease during a 15-year follow-up period, and each 5-point increase in PTSD symptom score corresponded with a 20% increase in risk of heart disease mortality."); Monika A. Waszczuk et al., *Pathway from PTSD to Respiratory Health: Longitudinal Evidence from a Psychosocial Intervention*, 36 Health Psych. 429, 429–37 (2017) (longitudinal study of PTSD and lower respiratory symptoms (LRS) found that PTSD and LRS were significantly linked and that when PTSD symptoms were decreased through intervention, so were LRS); C. Spitzer et al., *Association of Airflow Limitation with Trauma Exposure and Post-Traumatic Stress Disorder*, 37 Eur. Respiratory J. 1068, 1068–75 (2011) (study of 1,772 participants found that PTSD and asthma symptoms were significantly related); Viola Vaccarino et al., *Post-Traumatic Stress Disorder and Incidence of Coronary Heart Disease*, 62 J. Am. C. Cardiology 970, 970–78 (2013) (a study of 562 Vietnam veteran twins, one twin with PTSD and one twin without PTSD, the twin with PTSD had a significantly higher risk of developing coronary heart disease).

95. Joseph A. Boscarino, Christopher W. Forsberg, & Jack Goldberg, *A Twin Study of the Association Between PTSD Symptoms and Rheumatoid Arthritis*, 72 Psychosomatic Med. 481, 481–86 (2010); Kim Korinek, Peter Loebach, & Bussarawan Teerawichitchainan, *Physical and Mental Health Consequences of War-Related Stressors Among Older Adults: An Analysis of Posttraumatic Stress Disorder and Arthritis in Northern Vietnamese War Survivors*, 72 Js. Gerontology Series B 1090, 1090–1102 (2017).

96. Huan Song et al., *Association of Stress-Related Disorders with Subsequent Autoimmune Disease*, 319 J. Am. Med. Ass'n 2388, 2388–400 (2018).

97. Jennifer Schuster Wachen et al., *Posttraumatic Stress Symptomatology as a Mediator of the Relationship Between Warzone Exposure and Physical Health Symptoms in Men and Women*, 26 J. Traumatic Stress 319, 319–28 (2013).

98. Daniel J. Cosgrove et al., *Sexual Dysfunction in Combat Veterans with Post-Traumatic Stress Disorder*, 60 Urology 881, 881–84 (2002).

diabetes,[99] obesity,[100] and overall mortality.[101] Women with PTSD have also been found to have an increased risk for health symptoms when compared to men with PTSD.[102] The scientific literature has heavily documented the mind-body connection, including connections between the immune, endocrine, neurologic, and psychic systems. Trauma has been found to temporally occur prior to negative health outcomes and has been found to be highly associated with decreased immune functioning, increased inflammation, and alteration in neurologic and psychological functioning, thus leading to a sequela of possible illnesses.[103]

Relationships and family harm. PTSD is associated with relationship difficulties, interpersonal conflict, interpersonal violence, and divorce.[104] As per the diagnostic criteria, a person suffering from PTSD can have alterations in cognition and mood leading to persistent negative beliefs about self and others

99. Andrea L. Roberts et al., *Posttraumatic Stress Disorder and Incidence of Type 2 Diabetes Mellitus in a Sample of Women*, 72 J. Am. Med. Ass'n Psychiatry 203, 203–10 (2015) (22-year long longitudinal study of 49,739 women found that "women with the highest number of PTSD symptoms had a nearly 2-fold increased risk of [type 2 diabetes] over follow-up than women with no trauma exposure"); Sara A. Miller-Archie et al., *Posttraumatic Stress Disorder and New-Onset Diabetes Among Adult Survivors of the World Trade Center Disaster*, 66 Preventive Med. 34, 34–38 (2014) (longitudinal study of 9/11 survivors found that 11 years post-9/11, those with 9/11-related PTSD had a significantly increased risk of developing new-onset diabetes).

100. Kanaklakshmi Masodkar, Justine Johnson, & Michael J. Peterson, *A Review of Posttraumatic Stress Disorder and Obesity*, 18 Primary Care Companion For CNS Disorders 1 (2016) (those with PTSD have an increased risk of becoming obese and developing cardiovascular and metabolic illnesses; these findings were proposed to be potentially related to increased inflammation, renin-angiotensin-aldosterone system (RAAS) endocrine pathway alterations, decreased telomere length, mitochondrial dysfunction, and a host of other problems often found in those with PTSD).

101. J. Boscarino, *Posttraumatic Stress Disorder and Mortality Among U.S. Army Veterans 30 Years After Military Service*, 16 Annals Epidemiology 248, 248–56 (2006) (study of 15,288 male veterans 30 years post military service, found that all-cause mortality, cardiovascular death, and cancer were associated with PTSD); James B. Lohr et al., *Is Post-Traumatic Stress Disorder Associated with Premature Senescence? A Review of the Literature*, 23 Am. J. Geriatric Psychiatry 709, 709–25 (2015).

102. Amie R. Schry et al., *The Relationship Between Posttraumatic Stress Symptoms and Physical Health in a Survey of U.S. Veterans of the Iraq and Afghanistan Era*, 56 Psychosomatics 674, 674–84 (2015).

103. Sherin & Nemeroff, *supra* note 73, at 263–78.

104. *See, e.g.*, Jennifer L. Price & Susan P. Stevens, U.S. Dep't of Veterans Affairs, Partners of Veterans with PTSD: Research Findings, https://www.ptsd.va.gov/professional/treat/specific/vet_partners_research.asp (last visited Nov. 12, 2019) (Vietnam veterans with PTSD had a two to three times higher divorce rate than their non-PTSD veteran counterparts); Steven L. Sayers et al., *Family Problems Among Recently Returned Military Veterans Referred for a Mental Health Evaluation*, 70 J. Clinical Psychiatry 163, 163–70 (2009); Gabriela Misca & Mary Ann Forgey, *The Role of PTSD in Bi-Directional Intimate Partner Violence in Military and Veteran Populations: A Research Review*, 8 Frontiers Psych. 1 (2017).

which can impact all relationships.[105] There are also neurobiological associations which link PTSD to aggression, irritability, and mood dysregulation.[106] There is a consistency within the literature that PTSD and family dysfunction are associated.[107] There are also recent studies of aggression and interpersonal difficulties in U.S. war veterans with PTSD. On the higher end of the spectrum, one study found that of those veterans without PTSD, 13.5 percent engaged in physical intimate partner violence (IPV), but in veterans with PTSD, there was a 33 percent prevalence of physical IPV within the past year, and 91 percent engaged in verbal abuse and emotional manipulation toward their partner in the past year.[108] It has also been found that anger is one of the most common symptoms following air raids in veterans, civilians, and emergency responders.[109] Children of parents with PTSD can also be impacted and have been found to have "significant behavioral problems, higher level of neuroticism, internalizations, posttraumatic stress reactions, symptoms of intrusion and avoidance as well as significantly higher level of stress compared to children of parents without PTSD."[110]

Further psychological harm and suicidal behavior. Beyond the symptoms of PTSD that are described in the DSM-5, PTSD is also associated with increases in risk for other mental health disorders and psychological difficulties. Those with PTSD also often have comorbid, or co-occurring, psychological conditions "such as depressive disorders, substance dependence, panic disorder, agoraphobia, generalized anxiety disorder, social phobia, bipolar disorder, and somatization."[111]

105. Sherin & Nemeroff, *supra* note 73, at 263–78.

106. *Id.*

107. Tara Galovski & Judith A. Lyons, *Psychological Sequelae of Combat Violence: A Review of the Impact of PTSD on the Veterans Family and Possible Interventions*, 9 Aggression & Violent Behavior 477, 477–501 (2004).

108. Casey T. Taft et al., *Intimate Partner and General Aggression Perpetration Among Combat Veterans Presenting to a Posttraumatic Stress Disorder Clinic*, 79 Am. J. Orthopsychiatry 461, 461–68 (2009); A. Marshall, J. Panuzio, & C. Taft, *Intimate Partner Violence Among Military Veterans and Active Duty Servicemen*, 25 Clinical Psych. Rev. 862, 862–76 (2005).

109. Alberta Engelbrecht et al., *The Symptomatology of Psychological Trauma in the Aftermath of War (1945–1980): UK Army Veterans, Civilians and Emergency Responders*, 49 Psych. Med. 811 (2019).

110. Zihnet Selimbasic, Osman Sinanovic, & Esmina Avdibegovic, *Psychosocial Problems Among Children of Parents with Posttraumatic Stress Disorder*, 66 Med. Archives 304, 304–308 (2012); *see also* Jessica E. Lambert, Jessica Holzer, & Amber Hasbun, *Association Between Parents' PTSD Severity and Children's Psychological Distress: A Meta-Analysis*, 27 J. Traumatic Stress 9, 9–17 (2014); Galovski & Lyons, *supra* note 107; Miro Klarić et al., *Psychological Problems in Children of War Veterans with Posttraumatic Stress Disorder in Bosnia and Herzegovina: Cross-Sectional Study*, 49 Croatian Med. J. 491, 491–98 (2008).

111. Comm. on the Assessment of Ongoing Efforts in the Treatment of Posttraumatic Stress Disorder, Inst. of Med. of the Nat'l Acads., Treatment for Posttraumatic Stress Disorder in Military and Veteran Populations: Initial Assessment (2012), https://www.ncbi.nlm.nih.gov/books/NBK201098/pdf/Bookshelf_NBK201098.pdf [hereinafter

There is also a "highly significant" association between PTSD and suicidality and completed suicide, with one study of veterans showing that those with PTSD had a 5.3 times increased rate of completed suicide than those veterans without PTSD.[112] In a study of 3,238 veterans, for example, "combat exposure was significantly associated with PTSD-depression, which was in turn associated with suicidal behavior."[113] A Danish study of 22,716 individuals found that those with stress disorders were 12 to 29 times more likely to die from suicide when compared to the general population.[114]

Harmful behaviors. PTSD is associated with a number of unhealthy behaviors that can exacerbate physical and mental health problems. A recent systematic review and meta-analysis was completed using studies from 1980 to 2016 to assess the association between PTSD and behavioral health problems.[115] A review of the literature found that trauma exposure is associated with a significantly increased risk of smoking behaviors, and PTSD poses even more risk.[116] These behaviors

National Academies, Veterans and PTSD]; Jitender Sareen, *Posttraumatic Stress Disorder in Adults: Impact, Comorbidity, Risk Factors, and Treatment*, 59 Canadian J. Psychiatry 460, 460–67 (2014) (large nationally representative study finding that "90% of people with PTSD have at least 1 lifetime comorbid mental disorder"); Jenna L. Mccauley et al., *Posttraumatic Stress Disorder and Co-Occurring Substance Use Disorders: Advances in Assessment and Treatment*, 19 Clinical Psych. 283, 283–304 (2012) (those with PTSD have a 2–4 times increased risk of suffering from co-occurring substance use disorders).

112. Maria Panagioti, Patricia A. Gooding, & Nicholas Tarrier, *A Meta-Analysis of the Association Between Posttraumatic Stress Disorder and Suicidality: The Role of Comorbid Depression*, 53 Comprehensive Psychiatry 915, 915–30 (2012); *see also* Mccauley et al., *supra* note 111, at 283–304; Christine Lehmann, *PTSD Raises Suicide Risk in Major Depression*, Psychiatric News (Apr. 18, 2003), https://psychnews.psychiatryonline.org/doi/full/10.1176/pn.38.8.0037; N. Tarrier & L. Gregg, *Suicide Risk in Civilian PTSD Patients*, 39 Soc. Psychiatry & Psychiatric Epidemiology 655, 655–61 (2004); Maria Panagioti, Patricia Gooding, & Nicholas Tarrier, *Post-Traumatic Stress Disorder and Suicidal Behavior: A Narrative Review*, 29 Clinical Psych. Rev. 471, 471–82 (2009); J.L. Gradus et al., *Posttraumatic Stress Disorder and Completed Suicide*, 171 Am. J. Epidemiology 721, 721–27 (2010).

113. Kirsten H. Dillon et al., *Examination of the Indirect Effects of Combat Exposure on Suicidal Behavior in Veterans*, 235 J. Affective Disorders 407, 407–13 (2018).

114. Jaimie L. Gradus et al., *Trauma, Comorbidity, and Mortality Following Diagnoses of Severe Stress and Adjustment Disorders: A Nationwide Cohort Study*, 182 Am. J. Epidemiology 451, 451–58 (2015).

115. Carissa Van Den Berk-Clark et al., *Association Between Posttraumatic Stress Disorder and Lack of Exercise, Poor Diet, Obesity, and Co-Occurring Smoking: A Systematic Review and Meta-Analysis*, 37 Health Psych. 407, 407–16 (2018).

116. M. Feldner, K. Babson, & M. Zvolensky, *Smoking, Traumatic Event Exposure, and Post-Traumatic Stress: A Critical Review of the Empirical Literature*, 27 Clinical Psych. Rev. 14, 14–45 (2007); *see also* Samantha G. Farris et al., *Trauma Exposure and Cigarette Smoking: The Impact of Negative Affect and Affect-Regulatory Smoking Motives*, 33 J. Addictive Diseases 354, 354–65 (2014); Berna Güloğlu, *Psychiatric Symptoms of Turkish Combat-Injured Non-Professional Veterans*, 7 Eur. J. Psychotraumatology 1 (2016); Steven Fu et al., *Post-Traumatic Stress*

extend to alcohol and other substances as well.[117] In a study of U.S. veterans from the wars in Iraq and Afghanistan, those who screened positive for PTSD and depression were twice as likely to have alcohol misuse problems.[118] PTSD has also been associated with unhealthy eating behaviors and a decrease in physical activity following PTSD onset.[119] These behaviors are hypothesized to contribute to the physical health concerns discussed earlier, such as cardiovascular disease, metabolic disease, and other comorbidities that lead to increased mortality.[120]

Brain abnormalities. Some research has addressed the structural and functional brain abnormalities of those who have had traumatic experiences and those with PTSD. A number of studies have found that PTSD is associated with decreased brain volume,[121] yet many of the studies collected data post-trauma and thus it is difficult at this stage of the scientific research to determine causality. However, some data suggests that brain volume may atrophy more rapidly among those with chronic PTSD compared to those who do not develop PTSD or whose symptoms remit.[122]

Neurochemical dysregulation. Studies have suggested that PTSD is associated with altered brain activation patterns.[123] Signaling chemicals in the brain, called

Disorder and Smoking: A Systematic Review, 9 Nicotine & Tobacco Res. 1071, 1071–84 (2007); J.M. Gierisch et al., *Tobacco Use Among Iraq- and Afghanistan-Era Veterans: A Qualitative Study of Barriers, Facilitators, and Treatment Preferences*, 9 Preventing Chronic Disease 1 (2012).

117. Frances Debell et al., *A Systematic Review of the Comorbidity Between PTSD and Alcohol Misuse*, 49 Soc. Psychiatry & Psychiatric Epidemiology 1401, 1401–25 (2014); Mathew G. Fetzner et al., *What Is the Association Between Traumatic Life Events and Alcohol Abuse/Dependence in People with and without PTSD? Findings from a Nationally Representative Sample*, 28 Depression & Anxiety 632, 632–38 (2011); D. Kozarić-Kovacić, T. Ljubin, & M. Grappe, *Comorbidity of Posttraumatic Stress Disorder and Alcohol Dependence in Displaced Persons*, 41 Croatian Med. J. 173, 173–78 (2000).

118. Matthew Jakupcak et al., *PTSD Symptom Clusters in Relationship to Alcohol Misuse Among Iraq and Afghanistan War Veterans Seeking Post-Deployment VA Health Care*, 35 Addictive Behaviors 840, 840–43 (2010).

119. Jacqueline M. Hirth, Mahbubur Rahman, & Abbey B. Berenson, *The Association of Posttraumatic Stress Disorder with Fast Food and Soda Consumption and Unhealthy Weight Loss Behaviors Among Young Women*, 20 J. Women's Health 1141, 1141–49 (2011); Marcio Antonio De Assis et al., *Evaluation of Physical Activity Habits in Patients with Posttraumatic Stress Disorder*, 63 Clinics 473, 473–78 (2008).

120. National Academies, Veterans and PTSD, *supra* note 111.

121. Ralph Adolphs, *The Human Amygdala and Emotion*, 5 Neuroscientist 125, 125–37 (1999); Patricia H. Janak & Kay M. Tye, *From Circuits to Behaviour in the Amygdala*, 517 Nature 284, 284–92 (2015); Sherin & Nemeroff, *supra* note 73, at 263–78.

122. Valerie A. Cardenas et al., *Changes in Brain Anatomy During the Course of Posttraumatic Stress Disorder*, 193 Psychiatry Res. 93, 93–100 (2011).

123. J. Douglas Bremner, *Traumatic Stress: Effects on the Brain*, 8 Dialogues Clinical Neuroscience 445, 445–61 (2006).

neurochemicals, can be altered in people with PTSD when compared to those without PTSD. Alterations in these chemicals can lead to an interference in fear conditioning and memory formation, and they can increase arousal responses, startle responses, blood pressure, heartbeat, hypervigilance, impulsiveness, numbness, derealization, dissociation, and memory intrusion responses while also decreasing communication between critical parts of the brain affecting executive functioning and inhibiting anti-anxiety responses.[124]

Hormone dysregulation. Studies suggest that PTSD is associated with chronic hormonal dysregulation.[125] While a physical response to stress is normal and is an important protection mechanism in the face of danger, chronic physiological stress responses can lead to serious harm. Biological models have proposed that for those with PTSD, chronically dysregulated stress hormones throughout the body begin negatively affecting normal body processes.[126]

Neuroimmune system dysfunction. Researchers have also found that nervous system and immune system interactions, referred to as the neuroimmune system, are more likely to be dysfunctional in PTSD sufferers. A Swedish study with over one million people found that those with PTSD were 1.46 times more likely to have an autoimmune disorder, and 2.29 times more likely to have three or more co-occurring autoimmune disorders.[127] Studies have also found that in children exposed to a suicide bombing and civilians exposed to war, those who developed PTSD were more likely to experience increased inflammatory reactions and immune system impairment.[128] When this occurs, there is an increased risk of negative health outcomes and decreased immune function, thus triggering and worsening common diseases.[129]

Epigenetics, telomeres, and intergenerational biology. Research has supported the theory that some of the physiological alterations associated with PTSD occur due to epigenetic, or gene expression, changes within the cell.[130] It has been found

124. Sherin & Nemeroff, *supra* note 73, at 263–78.

125. Bremner, *supra* note 123.

126. Mayo Clinic Staff, *Chronic Stress Puts Your Health at Risk*, Mayo Clinic (Mar. 19, 2019), https://www.mayoclinic.org/healthy-lifestyle/stress-management/in-depth/stress/art-20046037; Shalev, Liberzon, & Marmar, *supra* note 69.

127. Song et al., *supra* note 96, at 2388–2400. Studies suggest that the neuroimmune system-PTSD interaction is a bidirectional interaction in which traumatic events negatively impact the neuroimmune system, which may in turn lead to an increased risk of developing PTSD. *See* Amit Shalev et al., *Long-Term Immune Alterations Accompanying Chronic Posttraumatic Stress Disorder Following Exposure to Suicide Bomb Terror Incidents During Childhood*, 76 Neuropsychobiology 130, 130–35 (2017).

128. Shalev et al., *supra* note 127; Zhewu Wang, Blaine Caughron, & M. Rita I. Young, *Posttraumatic Stress Disorder: An Immunological Disorder?*, 8 Frontiers Psychiatry 1 (2017).

129. Philip Hunter, *The Inflammation Theory of Disease*, 13 EMBO Reps. 968, 968–70 (2012).

130. Marpe Bam et al., *Dysregulated Immune System Networks in War Veterans with PTSD Is an Outcome of Altered miRNA Expression and DNA Methylation*, 6 Sci. Reps. 1 (2016); Tania

that "stress induce[s] epigenetic alterations" that in turn alter the regulation of stress reactions in the body."[131] In a study of veterans, epigenetic changes were found post-deployment in those who developed PTSD when compared to the same veterans pre-deployment.[132] These alterations have been associated with brain chemical and hormonal dysregulation, brain processing modifications, decreased brain growth, dysregulated immune function, and other physiological problems.[133] In a dose-dependent manner, trauma, PTSD, and early-life stressors have also been found to degrade and alter telomeres, or caps that protect the genetic code.[134] Shrinking telomeres have been associated with aging processes, chronic disease, and longevity, and their dysfunction has been linked to cancer.[135] Studies also suggest possible intergenerational effects of PTSD and trauma in biological markers and other indications.[136]

L. Roth, *How Traumatic Experiences Leave Their Signature on the Genome: An Overview of Epigenetic Pathways in PTSD*, 5 Frontiers Psychiatry 93 (2014) (Epigenetic changes are defined as "a class of molecular mechanisms by which environmental influences, including stress, can interact with the genome to have long-term consequences for brain plasticity and behavior.").

131. Roth, *supra* note 130.

132. Jennifer A. Rusiecki et al., *PTSD and DNA Methylation in Select Immune Function Gene Promoter Regions: A Repeated Measures Case-Control Study of U.S. Military Service Members*, 4 Frontiers Psychiatry 1 (2013).

133. P.F. Kuan et al., *An Epigenome-Wide DNA Methylation Study of PTSD and Depression in World Trade Center Responders*, 7 Translational Psychiatry 1 (2017); Bam, *supra* note 130; Fink & Galea, *supra* note 82; Audrey R. Tyrka et al., *Childhood Maltreatment and Telomere Shortening: Preliminary Support for an Effect of Early Stress on Cellular Aging*, 26 Ageing Res. Revs. 37, 37–52 (2016); Andrea Danese & Bruce S. Mcewen, *Adverse Childhood Experiences, Allostasis, Allostatic Load, and Age-Related Disease*, 106 Physiology & Behavior 29, 29–39 (2012); Lawrence H. Price et al., *Telomeres and Early-Life Stress: An Overview*, 73 Biological Psychiatry 15–23 (2013).

134. Irene Tzanetakou et al., *Telomeres and their Role in Aging and Longevity*, 12 Current Vascular Pharmacology 726, 726–34 (2014).

135. *Id.*; Judith Campisi et al., *Cellular Senescence, Cancer and Aging: The Telomere Connection*, 36 Experimental Gerontology 1619, 1619–37 (2001); Price et al., *supra* note 133.

136. Delan Devakumar et al., *The Intergenerational Effects of War on the Health of Children*, 12 BMC Med. 1 (2014); Robert Feil & Mario F. Fraga, *Epigenetics and the Environment: Emerging Patterns and Implications*, 13 Nature Revs. Genetics 97, 97–109 (2012); *Epigenetics & Inheritance*, Genetic Sci. Learning Ctr., https://learn.genetics.utah.edu/content/epigenetics/inheritance/ (last visited Oct. 5, 2019); Carla Kmett Danielson, Benjamin L. Hankin, & Lisa S. Badanes, *Youth Offspring of Mothers with Posttraumatic Stress Disorder Have Altered Stress Reactivity in Response to a Laboratory Stressor*, 53 Psychoneuroendocrinology 170, 170–78 (2015); *see also* Laura Ramo-Fernández et al., *Epigenetic Alterations Associated with War Trauma and Childhood Maltreatment*, 33 Behavioral Scis. & L. 701, 701–21 (2015) (finding that mothers who were pregnant during the 9/11 attacks and subsequently developed PTSD had infants with significantly lower birth weights); Rachel Yehuda et al., *Low Cortisol and Risk for PTSD in Adult Offspring of Holocaust Survivors*, 157 Am. J. Psychiatry 1252, 1252–59 (2000).

B. Militaries Recognize the Importance and Harms of PTSD

Much of the scientific research into PTSD comes directly from the military experience, and, over time—and due in significant part to the activism of veterans of the Vietnam War—PTSD has become recognized as an important disorder generally and also specifically by militaries.[137] Much PTSD research is focused on understanding how war-related violence can harm members of the military.[138] Indeed, one of the world's leading research centers on PTSD is the U.S. National Center for PTSD, established in 1989 within the U.S. Department of Veterans Affairs by congressional mandate. The Center explains how "PTSD is recognized as a major public health problem and a behavioral health problem for military Veterans and Active Duty personnel subject to the traumatic stress of war, dangerous peacekeeping operations, and interpersonal violence."[139] The U.S. Army has recognized the importance of the issue in various ways, including by "embed[ding] [behavioral health] providers close to operational units to increase access to help and decrease stigma some might feel [about] pursuing mental health treatment or counselling."[140] And in response to specific cases involving civilian casualties, the U.S. military has stated that soldiers should be provided stress and grief counseling.[141] Other militaries, including those of France,[142]

137. *See generally* Judith Lewis Herman, Trauma and Recovery (1992).

138. *History of the National Center for PTSD*, U.S. Dep't of Veterans Aff., https://www.ptsd.va.gov/about/work/ncptsd_history.asp (last visited Oct. 5, 2019).

139. *Id.*

140. Terri Moon Cronk, *DoD Observes National PTSD Awareness Day*, U.S. Dep't of Def. (June 27, 2015), https://dod.defense.gov/News/Article/Article/604911/dod-observes-national-ptsd-awareness-day.

141. Memorandum from Commanding Officer, 3d Battalion, 3d Marines to Commanding Officer, Task Force Thunder on Command Investigation for the Death of a Local National That Occurred in the Korengal Valley on 22 March 2005 (Apr. 2, 2005), https://www3.centcom.mil/FOIA_RR_Files/5%20USC%20552(a)(2)(D)Records/CIVCAS%20Investigations/12-0005%20%20CIVCAS%20Investigations%20sub-folder/004._CIVCAS__22_MAR_05_CLEAR.pdf (explaining that, in the context of an investigation into the death of a teenage Afghan boy in an incident involving U.S. Marines, the marines involved would be "afforded the proper opportunity for stress and grief counselling.").

142. *See* Republique Francaise, Ministère des Armées, Dispositif de Prise en Charge de l'ESPT dans les Armées (Apr. 23, 2015), https://www.defense.gouv.fr/fre/sante/dossiers-complementaires/classeur-stress-post-traumatique/dispositif-de-prise-en-charge-de-l-espt-dans-les-armees (summarizing support for French soldiers); Republique Francaise, Décret du 10 Janvier 1992 Déterminant les Règles et Barèmes pour la Classification et L'évaluation des Troubles Psychiques de Guerre, https://www.legifrance.gouv.fr/affichTexte.do?cidTexte=JORFTEXT000000539618 (last visited Apr. 9, 2019) (referring to PTSD as an "injury"). The original text states: "La névrose traumatique de guerre (ou en relation avec des catastrophes naturelles ou tout autre événement exceptionnel à caractère individuel ou collectif) doit être considéré comme une blessure et ne peut être assimilée, d'un point de vue structural, aux états névrotiques au sens classique attribué à ce terme en psychopathologie, qui constituent des maladies." *Id.*

Australia,[143] Canada,[144] and New Zealand,[145] also take steps to respond to the risks and seriousness of PTSD among members of their armed forces.

In recent years, the seriousness with which the U.S. military treats PTSD has been reflected in a push by some within the military to refer to it as an "injury" instead of a "disorder."[146] General Peter Chiarelli, vice chief of staff of the U.S. Army (retired) said: "For a soldier who sees the kinds of things soldiers see and experience on the battlefield today, to tell them what they're experiencing is a disorder does a tremendous disservice. It's not a disorder. It's an injury."[147]

IV. IS IT FEASIBLE TO INCLUDE PTSD AMONG THE TYPES OF CIVILIAN INJURIES CONSIDERED IN A PROPORTIONALITY ANALYSIS?

Two of the most difficult issues in assessing whether mental harms could be included in proportionality assessments include whether PTSD is a sufficiently measurable and foreseeable consequence of a military attack. Central to an assessment of the inclusion of mental harms like PTSD into the understanding of "civilian injury" in proportionality assessments is whether it would be possible for those launching an attack to assess in any way whether such civilian harm is to be expected and what the quantum of such harm may be.

A. Cognizable Injury to Civilians: Is PTSD Measurable?

Civilian injuries must be sufficiently measurable to be taken into account in a proportionality analysis; otherwise it would be impossible for commanders to weigh

143. *See Post-Traumatic Stress Disorder*, Australian Gov't, Dep't of Defence, http://www.defence.gov.au/health/healthportal/PTSD.asp (last visited Oct. 5, 2019); Australian Gov't, Dep't of Defence, Defence Mental Health and Wellbeing Strategy 2018–2023 (2017), http://www.defence.gov.au/Health/_master/HealthUpdates/docs/Defence_Mental_Health_Wellbeing_Strategy_2018-2023.PDF.

144. *Post-Traumatic Stress Disorder*, Nat'l Defence and the Canadian Armed Forces (Jan. 13, 2016), http://www.forces.gc.ca/en/news/article.page?doc=post-traumatic-stress-disorder/hjlbrhp4.

145. Letter from K.R. Short, Air Vice-Marshall, Vice Chief of Defence Force and Elaine Myers-Davies, Acting Head of Veterans' Affairs, to Jonathan Young, MP, Chairperson, Transport and Industrial Relations Committee (Oct. 12, 2016), https://www.parliament.nz/resource/en-NZ/51SCTIR_EVI_51DBHOH_PET68553_1_A535081/7cd4e34412a4aba18d2792643dca723d427b0590 [hereinafter Young Letter].

146. Greg Jaffe, *New Name for PTSD Could Mean Less Stigma*, Wash. Post (May 5, 2012), https://www.washingtonpost.com/world/national-security/new-name-for-ptsd-could-mean-less-stigma/2012/05/05/gIQAlV8M4T_story.html?utm_term=.e07994daee99.

147. *See* Frank Ochberg, *An Injury, Not a Disorder*, 93 Military Rev. 96, 97 (Mar.–Apr. 2013). In New Zealand, Veterans' Affairs and the Defence Force refer to PTSD as a "Service Induced Mental Injury." *See* Young Letter, *supra* note 145.

the civilian harm against the expected military advantage.[148] Commentators have highlighted that an obstacle to including mental harms in proportionality assessments is due to the perceived difficulty in "assess[ing] the magnitude of the expected losses," and that while this is possible for "losses of life, physical injuries and damage, this is not the case for mental injury."[149]

PTSD is complex, individuals can suffer from it in varying ways, and scientific understanding about it continues to develop. Yet PTSD is not amorphous. It is a measurable and identifiable harm: it has specific criteria for diagnosis, and there are a set of commonly employed and validated tools for diagnosing PTSD in individuals and for measuring PTSD symptoms for the purposes of scientific research. As we summarized in section III.A, the extremely harmful consequences of PTSD are widely documented and provide information which could help commanders to weigh such harms, alongside traditionally recognized physical injuries, against a military advantage.

The criteria for PTSD set out in the American Psychiatric Association's *Diagnostic and Statistical Manual of Mental Disorders* (DSM-5) has been widely adopted as reflecting extensive research and expert discussion, and is used by clinicians, researchers, therapists, and insurance agencies.[150] The current DSM-5 criteria were finalized following 14 years of planning and work involving extensive literature reviews, secondary analyses, professional presentations, debates among experts, and rounds of professional and public reviews on proposed criteria.[151] The lengthy process was taken very seriously due to the potential policy and scientific implications.[152]

The gold-standard diagnostic questionnaire, the Clinician-Administered PTSD Scale for DSM-5 (CAPS-5), recommended by the American Psychiatric Association, was developed and validated through years of research.[153] A PTSD

148. *See, e.g.*, ILA Study Group, *supra* note 37, at 29 (noting the importance of measurability); Wilkinson, *supra* note 46; Lieblich, *supra* note 27, at 201–11.

149. ICRC, Principle of Proportionality, *supra* note 43, at 35.

150. *DSM-5: Frequently Asked Questions*, Am. Psychiatric Ass'n, https://www.psychiatry.org/psychiatrists/practice/dsm/feedback-and-questions/frequently-asked-questions (last visited Oct. 5, 2019). Another widely used set of criteria is the World Health Organization's International Classification of Diseases (ICD-11) (2018).

151. Anushka Pai, Alina Suris, & Carol North, *Posttraumatic Stress Disorder in the DSM-5: Controversy, Change, and Conceptual Considerations*, 7 Behavioral Scis. 1 (2017).

152. *Id.*

153. Frank W. Weathers et al., *The Clinician-Administered PTSD Scale for DSM-5 (CAPS-5): Development and Initial Psychometric Evaluation in Military Veterans*, 30 Psych. Assessment 383, 383–95 (2018). The CAPS-5 is a 30-item structured interview that has demonstrated inter-rater reliability, test-retest reliability, and a strong correspondence with diagnosis. Inter-rater reliability indicates that two different clinicians will come to the same conclusion, test-retest reliability means that the same results are reached through many rounds of testing, and a strong correspondence with diagnosis means that those who use the CAPS-5 questionnaire have a high likelihood of finding the correct diagnosis.

diagnosis requires a presentation of a set of specific symptoms, and the fulfillment of specific criteria. The CAPS-5 is administered as an in-person clinical assessment, with questions assessing the frequency and severity of each symptom, as well as the presence of each criterion. Each question is scored, and combined to produce a total score of severity.[154] For PTSD research, researchers often use self-report surveys such as the Harvard Trauma Questionnaire or the Hopkins Symptom Checklist-25.[155] Although these questionnaires and surveys have been predominately used in Northern American and Western European studies, they have been used in numerous scientific studies and validated in a number of cultural contexts.[156]

While these tools are broadly accepted, they have limitations. One of the more important limitations is a consequence of the fact that as scientists learn more, their measurements, criteria, and definitions change. The criteria for PTSD in the DSM-3 is not the same as the criteria for the DSM-5 because understanding about PTSD has deepened and become more specific. Over time, building upon prior findings, researchers have altered measurements and questionnaires. Another limitation is that there is no single questionnaire used to measure PTSD or trauma. This is in part due to the varying levels of interviewer training, interviewee cultural distinctions, contextual differences, questionnaire purpose, and varying research study requirements and measurements needed to appropriately answer the research question. Cross-cultural comparisons can be difficult, and existing tools need careful examination before application in a specific cultural context. Questionnaires assessing the negative mental health impacts of trauma may need to be adapted to reflect how symptoms and changes in functioning manifest across cultures and contexts. Further, surveys and questionnaires are often retrospective or self-reported and thus may be subject to memory distortions or biased

154. *Clinician-Administered PTSD Scale for DSM-5 (CAPS-5)*, U.S. Dep't of Veterans Affairs, https://www.ptsd.va.gov/professional/assessment/adult-int/caps.asp (last visited Oct. 5, 2019).

155. Measures that are widely used and considered valid and reliable include the Harvard Trauma Questionnaire, the General Health Questionnaire, the WHO World Mental Health Composite International Diagnostic Interview (WHO WMH-CIDI), the Hopkins Symptom Checklist-25, the Posttraumatic Diagnostic Scale for PTSD, the PTSD Symptom Scale, and the Mini-International Neuropsychiatric Interview (MINI). *See, e.g.*, *PTSD Assessment Instruments*, Am. Psych. Ass'n, https://www.apa.org/ptsd-guideline/assessment/index.aspx (last visited Oct. 5, 2019) [hereinafter APA, *PTSD Assessment Instruments*].

156. *See* APA, *PTSD Assessment Instruments*, *supra* note 155; *see also* Richard F. Mollica et al., *The Harvard Trauma Questionnaire*, 180 J. Nervous & Mental Disease, 111, 111–16 (1992); Daniel Conybeare et al., *The PTSD Checklist-Civilian Version: Reliability, Validity, and Factor Structure in a Nonclinical Sample*, 68 J. Clinical Psych. 699, 699–713 (2012); Gyan Chandra Kashyap & Shri Kant Singh, *Reliability and Validity of General Health Questionnaire (GHQ-12) for Male Tannery Workers: A Study Carried out in Kanpur, India*, 17 BMC Psychiatry 1 (2017); Scholastic Ashaba et al., *Reliability, Validity, and Factor Structure of the Hopkins Symptom Checklist-25: Population-Based Study of Persons Living with HIV in Rural Uganda*, 22 AIDS & Behavior 1467, 1467–74 (2017).

self-perception. In addition, trauma is complex and the experience of trauma varies from human to human. It can also be difficult to weed out confounding variables, such as socioeconomic status, educational attainment, or community support systems—although there are survey and statistical methods designed to help account for such issues.[157] These potentially confounding variables are of critical importance when considering factors that might influence predicting the likelihood of PTSD, discussed further in the following subsection.

The extent to which PTSD is both assessable and recognizable as a harm according to globally accepted standards has grown markedly in the past 40 years. In the psychology and public health fields, PTSD is defined and frequently studied and measured. The state of the research and understanding of PTSD provide important information to militaries about the existence of PTSD and the harms a sufferer may face, which could be used to guide commanders when assessing and weighting anticipated civilian harm.

B. Causation and Foreseeability: Is PTSD a Reasonably Foreseeable Consequence of Exposure to a Military Attack?

Causation and reasonable foreseeability of civilian harm are core elements of the proportionality rule.[158] It is not the actual effects of an attack that are judged in applying the proportionality rule, but what was foreseeable to a reasonable commander.[159] A commander must take into account the harm that may be expected to occur based on the specific circumstances at the time and in the place, and also on current understanding of weapons effects and the probability of harm, based on the current scientific understanding.[160] The harm must be caused by the attack, that is, be "expected to occur in the ordinary course of events."[161] As Gillard highlights, because proportionality is assessed *ex ante*, "the relationship between causation and foreseeability is extremely close."[162]

Extensive PTSD research demonstrates that PTSD is a reasonably foreseeable consequence of exposure to a traumatic stressor.[163] It is also clear that traumatic

157. Richard J. McNally, Remembering Trauma (2005); Edgar Jones & Simon Wessely, Shell Shock to PTSD: Military Psychiatry from 1900 to the Gulf War (2009).

158. The proportionality rule prohibits attacks which "may be expected [foreseeability element] to cause [causation element] incidental loss. . . ." *See also* Schmitt & Highfill, *supra* note 29, at 83–90; Gillard, *supra* note 29, at 13–20.

159. Schmitt & Highfill, *supra* note 29, at 83–86.

160. *Id.* at 85.

161. Gillard, *supra* note 29, at 14.

162. *Id.*

163. Outside of the armed conflict context, it has also been noted that certain employers, such as those of emergency personnel, have obligations to take steps to manage the risk of

stressors can include many common types of military or armed group actions, including air strikes, armed raids on homes, or shelling or shooting in populated areas or near civilians. Such actions generally involve exposing a person to a potentially traumatic event—an event that involves experiencing or witnessing actual or threatened serious physical injury or death.[164] Populations exposed to armed conflict stressors are at high risk for PTSD, as shown in many studies of civilians and members of the military in conflicts around the world.[165] Studies

PTSD among employees, given the scientific knowledge about PTSD and its causes. *See* A.C. Mcfarlane & R.A. Bryant, *Post-Traumatic Stress Disorder in Occupational Settings: Anticipating and Managing the Risk*, 57 Occupational Med. 404, 404–10 (2007).

164. Am. Psychiatric Ass'n, *supra* note 70. The DSM-5 sets out a number of kinds of circumstances of exposure, including being an in-person witness to an event occurring to someone else, learning of the events occurring to someone close such as a family member, or repeated exposure to details of the events where connected to professional duties. *See also* Robbin H. Ophuis, Branko F. Olij, Suzanne Polinder, & Juanita A. Haagsma, *Prevalence of Post-Traumatic Stress Disorder, Acute Stress Disorder and Depression Following Violence Related Injury Treated at the Emergency Department: A Systematic Review*, 18 BMC Psychiatry 1, 2 (2018).

165. *See, e.g.*, Ruth Pat-Horenczyk et al., *Posttraumatic Symptoms, Functional Impairment, and Coping among Adolescents on Both Sides of the Israeli-Palestinian Conflict: A Cross-Cultural Approach*, 58 Applied Psych. 688, 688–708 (2009) (exposure to conflict-related violence increased the risk for PTSD symptom development); Joop T.V.M. de Jong et al., *Lifetime Events and Posttraumatic Stress Disorder in 4 Postconflict Settings*, 286 J. Am. Med. Ass'n 555, 555–62 (2001) (finding that conflict-related trauma was a risk factor for developing PTSD, and PTSD prevalence was estimated at 37.4 percent in Algeria, 28.4 percent in Cambodia, 15.8 percent in Ethiopia, and 17.8 percent in Gaza); Willem F. Scholte et al., *Mental Health Symptoms Following War and Repression in Eastern Afghanistan*, 292 J. Am. Med. Ass'n 585, 585–93 (2004) (finding a prevalence rate of 20.4 percent for current PTSD following war and repression in Eastern Afghanistan); Barbara Lopes Cardozo, *Mental Health, Social Functioning, and Disability in Postwar Afghanistan*, 292 J. Am. Med. Ass'n 575, 575–84 (2004) (finding 42 percent looking at mental health in postwar Afghanistan); Mary B. Abu-Saba, *War-Related Trauma and Stress Characteristics of American University of Beirut Students*, 12 J. Traumatic Stress 201, 201–207 (1999) (finding 75 percent PTSD among Beirut students who had been exposed to a high number of traumatic war events); Laila Farhood, Hani Dimassi, & Tuija Lehtinen, *Exposure to War-Related Traumatic Events, Prevalence of PTSD, and General Psychiatric Morbidity in a Civilian Population from Southern Lebanon*, 17 J. Transcultural Nursing 333, 333–40 (2006) (finding that in 2006 "97.7%, had experienced, witnessed, or heard of a war-related traumatic event. Current PTSD prevalence was 29.3%."); Touraj Ayazi et al., *What Are the Risk Factors for the Comorbidity of Posttraumatic Stress Disorder and Depression in a War-Affected Population? A Cross-Sectional Community Study in South Sudan*, 12 BMC Psychiatry 1 (2012) (the prevalence of PTSD was 28.9 percent); Murthy & Lakshminarayana, *supra* note 71 (among children living in an area of bombardments, 54 percent suffered from severe PTSD, and 33.5 percent from moderate PTSD); Yuval Neria, Margarita Bravova, & Jessica M. Halper, *Trauma and PTSD among Civilians in the Middle East*, 21 PTSD Res. Q. 1 (2010) (finding a PTSD rate of 20 percent among internally displaced persons in a country experiencing war); F. Hashemian, *Anxiety, Depression, and Posttraumatic Stress in Iranian Survivors of Chemical Warfare*, J. Am. Med. Ass'n 560, 560–66 (2006) (among individuals exposed to both high-intensity warfare and chemical weapons, prevalence rates for lifetime PTSD were 59 percent); Fuaad Mohammed Freh, *PTSD, Depression, and Anxiety Among Young People in Iraq One Decade After the American Invasion*,

of populations exposed to the same kind of traumatic event (for example, a bombing) can provide information about expected PTSD prevalence rates in certain circumstances. However, gaps, inconsistencies, and insufficient specificity in available research make estimating PTSD probability with precision challenging. Scientific PTSD research can also assist in considering the potential scope of the civilian populations which might be considered in the proportionality analysis, but determining how far to extend the assessment raises difficult feasibility questions. In addition, PTSD research provides information about PTSD risk factors (related to the event itself, and also individual susceptibility factors) which could be taken into account in a proportionality analysis, but they tend to be general factors, and some of the factors could not reasonably be known by a commander in advance of an attack.

Trauma exposure can cause, and is a necessary prerequisite to be diagnosed with, PTSD.[166] In the immediate hours or days after trauma exposure, many people (studies have shown approximately 75 percent)[167] will experience some peri-traumatic reactions or post-traumatic stress symptoms, such as physiological arousal, intrusive memories, or disassociation.[168] Such symptoms generally

22 Traumatology 56, 56–62 (2016) (55.8 percent reported PTSD symptoms); Bramsen & Ploeg, *supra* note 85. Compared to the U.S. lifetime risk of 8.7 percent, the 12-month prevalence in U.S. adults is 3.5 percent; 12-month prevalence in Europe clusters around 0.5–1.0 percent. Am. Psychiatric Ass'n, *supra* note 70; Lisa K. Richardson, B. Christopher Frueh, & Ronald Acierno, *Prevalence Estimates of Combat-Related PTSD: A Critical Review*, 44 Aust. N.Z. J. Psychiatry 4–19 (2010); Jessica J. Fulton et al., *The Prevalence of Posttraumatic Stress Disorder in Operation Enduring Freedom/Operation Iraqi Freedom (OEF/OIF) Veterans: A Meta-Analysis*, 31 J. Anxiety Disorders 98, 98–107 (2015) (analyzed nearly five million Operation Enduring Freedom/Operation Iraqi Freedom (OEF/OIF) veterans and estimated that 23 percent had PTSD); Matthew S. Brooks, Sarah B. Laditka, & James N. Laditka, *Long-Term Effects of Military Service on Mental Health among Veterans of the Vietnam War Era*, 173 Military Med. 570, 570–75 (2008); Jonathan D. Green et al., *The Effect of Enemy Combat Tactics on PTSD Prevalence Rates: A Comparison of Operation Iraqi Freedom Deployment Phases in a Sample of Male and Female Veterans*, 8 Psych. Trauma 634, 634–40 (2016).

166. Am. Psychiatric Ass'n, *supra* note 70.

167. Nikolas Aho, Marie Proczkowska Björklund, & Carl Göran Svedin, *Peritraumatic Reactions in Relation to Trauma Exposure and Symptoms of Posttraumatic Stress in High School Students*, 8 Eur. J. Psychotraumatology 1 (2017).

168. *Id.*; Steven R. Lawyer et al., *Predictors of Peritraumatic Reactions and PTSD Following the September 11th Terrorist Attacks*, 69 Psychiatry: Interpersonal & Biological Processes 130, 130–41 (2006); Shalev, Israel, & Marmar, *supra* note 69, at 2462. These symptoms, if they last less than one month, are not PTSD, and would be weighted less in any proportionality analysis. They would likely fall within the "inconvenience, irritation, stress, or fear" category of effects which are specifically excluded in some expert manual definitions of civilian injury, although it should be noted that Additional Protocol I does not explicitly contain the limitations. *See* AP I, *supra* note 21; Schmitt & Highfill, *supra* note 29, at 92 (noting that some expert manuals, specifically the Harvard University Program on Humanitarian Policy and Conflict

diminish significantly within a few weeks,[169] particularly when the traumatic stressor is removed.[170] A subset of people exposed to a traumatic event will develop PTSD.

There is overwhelming scientific evidence that military attacks can be traumatic events which can lead to PTSD among exposed civilians. The risk of PTSD from exposure to an attack which kills or injures, or which presents a risk of serious injury, is clear. We consider this evidence to be so significant that military forces should seriously consider how they could take this risk into account. Yet the complexity of PTSD and the state of current research makes incorporating PTSD into a proportionality assessment in specific cases difficult in practical terms. This subsection concludes by highlighting some of the most challenging areas.

1. Is It Possible to Predict the Likely Prevalence Rate of PTSD from an Attack?

As Schmitt and Highfill highlight, a central factor in determining whether a particular injury can be taken into account in carrying out a proportionality assessment is "consistency of consequence."[171] Scientific research can aid, to an extent, in predicting the likely prevalence rate (or range of rates) of PTSD for different kinds of traumatic experiences in certain defined circumstances. A systematic review of over 2,500 scientific articles found that 37.1 percent of those exposed to intentional trauma develop PTSD.[172] A number of studies of major, sudden attacks, such as a bombing, found that the PTSD prevalence rate during the following year among survivors can be expected to be approximately one-third of the population in or closely proximate to the explosion.[173] Different rates have been found

Research Manual on International Law Applicable to Air and Missile Warfare and the Tallinn Manual on the International Law Applicable to Cyber Warfare exclude "inconvenience, irritation, stress, or fear" from definitions of civilian injury).

169. Steinert et al., *supra* note 86.

170. Neria et al., *supra* note 165.

171. Schmitt & Highfill, *supra* note 29, at 85.

172. Patcho N. Santiago et al., *A Systematic Review of PTSD Prevalence and Trajectories in DSM-5 Defined Trauma Exposed Populations: Intentional and Non-Intentional Traumatic Events*, 8 PLoS ONE 1 (2013).

173. *See, e.g.*, Carol S. North et al., *Psychiatric Disorders Among Survivors of the Oklahoma City Bombing*, 282 J. Am. Med. Ass'n 755, 755–62 (1999) (among survivors of the Oklahoma City bombing, 34.3 percent developed PTSD, and nearly everyone had at least the reexperiencing and hyperarousal symptoms of PTSD); Sandro Galea et al., *Psychological Sequelae of the September 11 Terrorist Attacks in New York City*, 346 New England J. Med. 982, 982–87 (2002) (finding 30 percent PTSD prevalence among those in the Twin Towers at the time of the attacks); Frank G. Njenga et al., *Post-Traumatic Stress After Terrorist Attack: Psychological Reactions Following the US Embassy Bombing in Nairobi*, 185 British J. Psychiatry 328, 328–33 (2004) (finding a prevalence rate of 35 percent); María Paz García-Vera, Jesús Sanz, & Sara Gutiérrez, *A Systematic*

among other kinds of traumatic experiences. For example, studies have found that approximately 50 percent of those sexually assaulted will develop PTSD.[174] Following a nonsexual, interpersonal physical assault, some studies have shown a PTSD rate of 20.9 percent;[175] 31 percent of people following the unexpected and violent death of a loved one;[176] and 6.4 percent over a year after a motor vehicle accident.[177] More finely grained data related to different kinds of common forms of military attack (for example, comparing PTSD rates from experiencing an air strike versus a roadside improvised explosive device) is difficult to find, and more research is necessary. There are also challenges in reconciling prevalence rates from different studies where they use different diagnostic instruments.[178] To date, there is research on general types of traumas, but perhaps not at the level of granularity that may be needed for a commander assessing specific or different types of attacks.

It is notable that the methodologies currently employed by the United States and other militaries to estimate expected incidental civilian harm incorporate elements of doubt and apply risk thresholds.[179] For example, the U.S. military employs the "collateral damage estimation methodology" (CDM), a process for evaluating the likelihood of incidental civilian harm.[180] The CDM is "derived from physics-based computer models, weapons test data, and operational

Review of the Literature on Posttraumatic Stress Disorder in Victims of Terrorist Attacks, 119 Psych. Reps. 328, 328–59 (2016).

174. Kaitlin A. Chivers-Wilson, *Sexual Assault and Posttraumatic Stress Disorder: A Review of the Biological, Psychological and Sociological Factors and Treatments*, 9 McGill J. Med. 111, 111–18 (2006); *see also* Shalev, Liberzon, & Marmar, *supra* note 69 (reporting that "the respective probabilities for men and women are 65% and 46% after rape").

175. Naomi Breslau et al., *Trauma and Posttraumatic Stress Disorder in the Community*, 55 Archives Gen. Psychiatry 626, 626–32 (1998).

176. *Id.*

177. Michelle Heron-Delaney et al., *A Systematic Review of Predictors of Posttraumatic Stress Disorder (PTSD) for Adult Road Traffic Crash Survivors*, 44 Injury 1413, 1413–22 (2013).

178. Ophuis et al., *supra* note 164, at 4.

179. Chairman of the Joint Chiefs of Staff, CJCSI 3160.01, No-Strike and the Collateral Damage Estimation Methodology D-A-7 to D-A-35 (Feb. 13, 2009), https://www.aclu.org/files/dronefoia/dod/drone_dod_3160_01.pdf [hereinafter Joint Chiefs, Estimation Methodology)]. For a detailed analysis of this, *see* Gregory S. McNeal, *Targeted Killing and Accountability*, 102 Geo. L.J. 740, 740–53 (2014) [hereinafter McNeal, *Targeted Killing*]; Gary P. Corn, James H. Dapper, & Winston Williams, *Targeting and the Law of Armed Conflict*, *in* U.S. Military Operations: Law, Policy, and Practice 193–98 (Gary P. Corn et al. eds., 2015).

180. Note that the methodology is not applied in all cases. For example, it does not apply to certain weapons systems, due to "operational practicality." *See* Corn, Dapper, & Williams, *supra* note 179, at 196; Joint Chiefs, Estimation Methodology, *supra* note 179, at D-4.

combat observations."[181] The U.S. military instruction on CDM notes that collateral damage methodology "is not an exact science."[182] It "provides commanders with an understanding of weapons effects, incidental consequences, and mitigation techniques."[183] The CDM is aimed at providing commanders—who will still make the ultimate decision about whether to take a strike, taking into account a number of other factors with varying degrees of certainty[184]—an "easily recognizable measure of operational risk" of harm to civilians.[185] Depending on the situation, it can aim at reducing the risk of civilian harm to a 10 percent or 1 percent "probability of serious/lethal wounds." When assessing the likelihood of injury to civilians, commanders try to predict the likelihood of incidental physical injury and collateral damage to a civilian object (for example, from shrapnel) for a particular attack by computing a "collateral hazard area" within which civilians might be harmed.[186] Civilian harm is discussed in terms of percentage risk and probability.[187] The analysis will vary depending on a number of factors, including the weapon used, the angle of attack, and circumstances on the ground.[188] It is generally challenging to assess the likely specific physical injuries that may result from an attack, as any assessment of the likelihood of physical injury involves uncertainty at several levels: whether civilians will be within the collateral hazard area; if in the collateral hazard area, where the civilian might be (the risk of injury may vary with precise location); and the type of injury (it will ordinarily be very

181. Joint Chiefs, Estimation Methodology, *supra* note 179, at D-2 (noting that the listed sources "contain some degree of inherent error and uncertainty."); McNeal, *Targeted Killing*, *supra* note 179, at 741.

182. Joint Chiefs, Estimation Methodology, *supra* note 179, at D-2. The CDM goes on to state that "the CDM does not predict the actual outcome of weapon employment. The operational environment, weapon's reliability, and fidelity of intelligence data are primary factors that account for a CDE output differing from actual combat employment. Though the CDM follows a rigid process and generates estimated values, neither analysts or commanders should be under the impression that these values in any way constitute ground truth, an exact science, or flawless data. CDM is merely an estimate to assist a commander in the decision making process relying on informed data and sound judgment." *Id.*; *see also* Corn, Dapper, & Williams, *supra* note 179, at 194 ("The science employed in the CDM is not, however, exact or infallible. . . .").

183. Joint Chiefs, Estimation Methodology, *supra* note 179, at D-2.

184. *Id.* at D-A-2.

185. Corn, Dapper, & Williams, *supra* note 179, at 194. Such factors include the "operational objectives, end-state considerations, other LOAC and ROE considerations, target characteristics, risk to friendly forces, and strategic risk." *Id.*

186. McNeal, *Targeted Killing*, *supra* note 179, at 743.

187. Joint Chiefs, Estimation Methodology, *supra* note 179, at D-A-2.

188. McNeal, *Targeted Killing*, *supra* note 179, at 742–43.

difficult to predict if someone will be injured by a shrapnel wound to the leg or to the eye, for example).[189]

Based on the current state of scientific research, at minimum, militaries have some information which can support assessments of likely mental health harms in certain kinds of cases. Because of existing scientific research on likely PTSD rates, even where not highly precise, a commander may be able to incorporate PTSD risk into an overall assessment of the risk of civilian harm. A closer examination by militaries and scientists of specific military actions and scientific research is warranted, and it may produce actionable data about the likely prevalence rate of PTSD associated with different attacks that could assist in the development of guidance on how to reduce the risks of such harms. Indeed, numerous large studies are producing strikingly similar data about the prevalence rate of PTSD following similar types of traumatic experiences.

2. To Which Populations Should the Analysis Extend? How Far beyond the Core of Civilians at Risk of Death or Physical Injury Might Be Considered?

PTSD research has studied a range of impacted populations, including those physically injured during a traumatic event, those who directly experienced the event (for example, survived a collapsing building), those who directly witnessed the event, those who lost a loved one in an event, rescue workers exposed following the immediate attack, and those vicariously exposed (for example, by interviewing survivors, reviewing evidence, or watching footage of an event). For example, victims of terrorist attacks not themselves present at the site of the attack have been found to have a lower PTSD prevalence of "4% in the affected community, 5%–6% among emergency, rescue, and recovery workers, and 17–29% among relatives and friends of the injured or killed victims."[190] A significant reduction in PTSD is seen within the general community and in rescue workers over time, but not as significantly as in victims directly injured or in the relatives of direct victims.[191]

One concern for militaries may be that if all those at risk of PTSD are potentially included in a proportionality analysis, then analysis may be infeasible in practice. The research summarized in this chapter helps in assessing what may be more feasible, by showing that rates of PTSD are highest among those who directly experienced the event or who lost a close family member or friend. For the purposes of a "reasonable commander," it may be most feasible at present to include in a proportionality analysis those already considered at risk of death or

189. ICRC, Principle of Proportionality, *supra* note 43, at 36 (noting the difficulty in assessing the *type* of injury in existing collateral damage estimation methodology). Experts discussed how "even for physical injury, CDE [collateral damage estimation] methodology does not distinguish between the types of injury foreseen." *Id.*

190. García-Vera, Sanz, & Gutiérrez, *supra* note 173.

191. *Id.*

physical injury. In certain cases, it might also be possible to estimate the likely number of witnesses to the attack—for example, a strike on a vehicle in a remote area may have no witnesses, whereas a strike in a busy area of an urban environment in the middle of the working day may be expected to have many. The U.S. military already collects general population density data in areas in which it is active to aid in collateral damage estimates, suggesting that it may be possible in some cases to estimate the number of people likely to be geographically proximate to an event, or to witness the trauma resulting from it.[192]

3. How Can Known Risk Factors for PTSD Assist in Taking the Risk of Its Occurrence into Account?

Various factors are known to increase PTSD risk and could potentially be taken into account by a commander in assessing the risk of PTSD resulting from an attack. Relevant factors include geographic proximity to the event,[193] witnessing trauma directly,[194] exposure to death,[195] being personally attacked,[196] sustaining a physical

192. McNeal, *Targeted Killing*, *supra* note 179, at 743; Joint Chiefs, Estimation Methodology, *supra* note 179, at D-D-1, D-D-2. Separate from proportionality assessments, consideration of mental harms may have a strong bearing on a military's obligation to take precautions in attack by, for example, launching an attack at a different time or place to reduce the number of people in the vicinity even where there is a high degree of certainty they would not be physically injured. It is worth emphasizing that consideration of the populations potentially harmed may not alter the conclusion about whether to take a strike, but it may affect how and when it is conducted.

193. The closer an individual is to a traumatic event, the more likely PTSD is. For example, New York residents living below Canal Street (closer to the Twin Towers) had a PTSD prevalence of 20 percent, and those actually in the buildings or injured had a 30 percent prevalence, compared to 7.5 percent generally in New York City following 9/11. Galea et al., *supra* note 173. In a study following the 2011 Oslo government building bombing, indirectly exposed employees experienced a PTSD prevalence of 4 percent, 3 percent, and 2 percent at 10, 22, and 34 months, while employees present at the site during the time of the bombing experienced a prevalence of 24 percent, 17 percent, and 17 percent at 10, 22, and 34 months post-attack. Marianne Bang Hansen et al., *Prevalence and Course of Symptom-Defined PTSD in Individuals Directly or Indirectly Exposed to Terror: A Longitudinal Study*, 80 Psychiatry 171, 171–83 (2017).

194. Lukoye Atwoli et al., *Trauma and Posttraumatic Stress Disorder in South Africa: Analysis from the South African Stress and Health Study*, 13 BMC Psychiatry 1 (2013); Laura DiGrande et al., *Long-term Posttraumatic Stress Symptoms Among 3,271 Civilian Survivors of the September 11, 2001, Terrorist Attacks on the World Trade Center*, 173 Am. J. Epidemiology 1 (2010); *see also* Gordana Kuterovac-Jagodić, *Posttraumatic Stress Symptoms in Croatian Children Exposed to War: A Prospective Study*, 59 J. Clinical Psych. 9, 9–25 (2002); Priebe et al., *supra* note 84 (finding that the highest relative risks for developing PTSD included the witnessing of murder or death, along with being tortured and nonsexual or sexual assault by a stranger).

195. Shalev, Liberzon, & Marmar, *supra* note 69, at 2462.

196. Rose E. Obilom & Tom D. Thacher, *Posttraumatic Stress Disorder Following Ethnoreligious Conflict in Jos, Nigeria*, 23 J. Interpersonal Violence 1108, 1108–19 (2008).

injury,[197] bodily disfigurement,[198] the sudden or violent death of a loved one,[199] the number of trauma events,[200] sudden violence,[201] and deliberate violence.[202] Some studies specifically on different amounts of military attack exposure can also provide information useful to considering PTSD risk: ongoing and prolonged missile attacks, for example, have been found to increase PTSD risk.[203]

Whether or to what extent PTSD results is not only influenced by the nature of the stressor but also individual factors.[204] For example, females, children, those lacking social support, and those with a prior history of mental disorders or of exposure to trauma are at greater risk of PTSD.[205] Of all populations, children

197. DiGrande et al., *supra* note 194 (finding that sustaining an injury was one factor that predicted PTSD); Galea et al., *supra* note 173; Berna Güloğlu, *Psychiatric Symptoms of Turkish Combat-Injured Non-Professional Veterans*, 7 Eur. J. Psychotraumatology 1 (2016).

198. Shalev, Liberzon, & Marmar, *supra* note 69, at 2462.

199. *Effects of Traumatic Stress after Mass Violence, Terror, or Disaster*, U.S. Dep't of Veterans Aff., https://www.hsdl.org/?view&did=458141 (last visited Nov. 12, 2019) [hereinafter *Effects of Traumatic Stress*]; Betty Pfefferbaum et al., *Posttraumatic Stress Responses in Bereaved Children After the Oklahoma City Bombing*, 38 J. Am. Acad. Child & Adolescent Psychiatry 1372, 1372–79 (1999) (finding that the post-traumatic stress symptoms score was significantly higher in bereaved youths when compared to nonbereaved youths, and those who had lost an immediate family member scored the highest); Betty Pfefferbaum et al., *Posttraumatic Stress Among Young Children After the Death of a Friend or Acquaintance in a Terrorist Bombing*, 51 Psychiatric Servs. 386, 386–88 (2000) (finding that the closer the child was to someone who had died, the more severe the symptoms had manifested).

200. Murthy & Lakshminarayana, *supra* note 71; DiGrande et al., *supra* note 194 (finding that each "addition of an experience of direct exposure resulted in a 2-fold increase in the risk of PTSD").

201. Shalev, Liberzon, & Marmar, *supra* note 69, at 2462 (referring to "unexpected, inescapable, or uncontrollable" traumatic experiences); Royal Coll. of Psychiatrists & the British Psychological Soc'y, Post-Traumatic Stress Disorder: The Management of PTSD in Adults and Children in Primary and Secondary Care 26 (2005).

202. Fact Sheet, Nat'l Ctr. for PTSD, *reprinted in* https://dmh.mo.gov/media/pdf/phases-traumatic-stress-reactions-disaster ("Studies have shown that deliberate violence creates longer lasting mental health effects than natural disasters or accidents. The consequences for individuals and the community are long lasting and survivors often feel that injustice has been done to them. This can lead to anger, frustration, helplessness, fear, and a desire for revenge."); *Effects of Traumatic Stress*, *supra* note 199 (higher rates of PTSD occur following human-caused trauma); Royal Coll. of Psychiatrists & The British Psychological Soc'y, *supra* note 201.

203. Amit Shrira et al., *Older Adults Exposed to Ongoing Versus Intense Time-Limited Missile Attacks: Differences in Symptoms of Posttraumatic Stress Disorder*, 80 Psychiatry 64, 64–78 (2017); Danny Koren et al., *Acute Stress Reactions Among Medical and Non-Medical Personnel in a General Hospital Under Missile Attacks*, 26 Depression & Anxiety 123, 123–28 (2009).

204. Rachel Yehuda, *Post-Traumatic Stress Disorder*, 346 New England J. Med. 108, 110 (2002).

205. Shalev, Liberzon, & Marmar, *supra* note 69, at 2462; H. Javidi & M. Yadollahie, *Post-Traumatic Stress Disorder*, 3 Int'l J. Occupational & Envtl. Med. 1, 6 (2012).

are the most vulnerable to the detrimental effects of trauma exposure. Children who experience trauma tend to have an elevated risk for PTSD and the sequelae of functional and psychological dysfunction in a dose-dependent manner. This population may also be more feasible in certain circumstances in terms of developing risk assessment and implementation policies, because children are often in schools, educational centers, sports facilities, or other gathering places that cater to children. These gathering centers are places that can be taken into consideration by commanders in considering the risk of mental harms to a known vulnerable population.

It may be difficult or impossible for a "reasonable commander" to incorporate various individual risk factors, such as lacking social support or a prior history of mental disorder, into a collateral damage assessment. Prior exposure to trauma can also raise very difficult causation issues, particularly in the armed conflict context where civilians may be exposed to significant numbers of traumatic events from various sources.[206] Yet the fact of a recent prior attack or of ongoing hostilities may even strengthen the need to take the risk of PTSD into account because there is a clear and strong dose-dependent relationship between the number or severity of traumatic experiences and the development and severity of PTSD.[207] The difficulties of causation call not for ignoring mental harms but for population-specific research and context-specific judgments about risk in the circumstances of an attack.

In certain cases, some vulnerabilities might readily be knowable and might be highly relevant in the circumstances—for example, an attack launched against a military target during school hours near a functioning school might expose children, a known vulnerable population, to a traumatic stressor.[208] Commanders should already be at least assessing whether women and children are present or in the vicinity. The question might therefore become not only whether women or

206. *See, e.g.*, Gillard, *supra* note 19 (noting the difficulties of showing that mental harm is caused by a specific attack in the context of "prolonged hostilities"); ICRC, Principle of Proportionality, *supra* note 43, at 36 (noting how some of the experts in the meeting viewed it as "too difficult to identify a causal link between one particular attack and mental harm, which could be caused by general exposure to hostilities"); ILA Study Group, *supra* note 37, at 29 (stating that the "question of proving a causal link between the attack and the mental injury in question also arose within the S[tudy] G[roup]").

207. Olofsson et al., *supra* note 76; B.D. Perry, *The Neurodevelopmental Impact of Violence in Childhood*, *in* Textbook of Child and Adolescent Forensic Psychiatry 221–38 (D. Schetky & E.P. Benedek eds., 2001); *CDC-Kaiser ACE Study*, *supra* note 76. On some of the legal issues related to PTSD and recurrent attacks, *see* Solomon, *supra* note 49.

208. Lieblich, *supra* note 27, at 188; ICRC Customary IHL Study, *supra* note 21, at 36 ("[I]t was suggested that it could be expected that an attack with explosive weapons on a military objective located next to a kindergarten would traumatize children for many years to come, if not for the rest of their lives. If the military advantage sought by the attack is too minor, such mental harm could be excessive either in isolation or in combination with other expected incidental harm.").

children would be killed or physically injured in the attack but also whether they may be likely to witness the attack.[209]

V. CONCLUSION

War-related violence can cause significant physical and mental harms to civilians. The rules of IHL were written to balance military necessity with the humanitarian goal of reducing unnecessary civilian suffering, and the law is clear that attacks must not be launched where they would cause disproportionate civilian loss of life or injury. Yet while the harms of physical injuries are taken into account in proportionality assessments as a matter of course, civilian mental harms are generally ignored. The mental harms that can be caused by being injured in or witnessing an attack can be serious, long-term, and have crushing functional impairments. Armed forces know this well with respect to their own members—significant research and programming exists around the world to study the mental health of soldiers and to respond to the consequences of armed conflict–related trauma exposure. If the purpose of the proportionality rule is to reduce unnecessary civilian suffering, serious mental harms, as a source of significant suffering, should, in principle, be taken into account.

The key challenge is in how to feasibly operationalize consideration of mental harms during the proportionality assessment. PTSD can be measured, and significant scientific research demonstrates that it is a reasonably foreseeable consequence of an armed attack. The complexity of PTSD, limitations and uncertainties in current scientific research, and the array of risk factors make precise predictions about the likely mental health outcomes of an attack difficult. However, scientific research has progressed significantly, and much is known about the causes and consequences of PTSD. The very real implementation challenges should not function as a complete obstacle to considering mental harms in a proportionality assessment in appropriate cases, or to militaries taking steps to assess how they could improve consideration of civilian mental health consequences. Indeed, the proportionality rule itself is inherently challenging, requiring the balancing and weighing of predicted outcomes and benefits and costs that are difficult to measure and compare. Yet militaries have developed methods and tools to do so, and they are familiar with the uncertainties involved in proportionality assessments. For example, the collateral damage estimation methodology employed by the U.S. military to guide commander decision-making involves the application of risk thresholds as to the expected civilian harm. Civilian death and physical injury estimates are difficult, and commanders are constantly making decisions with varying levels of uncertainty. It is also important to highlight that just as a detailed calculation of the full scope of civilian physical injuries does

209. Such an assessment may not affect the overall evaluation of whether the incidental civilian harm is excessive to the anticipated military advantage but may influence when an attack is conducted (and it thus may be a question of taking precautions to minimize civilian harm rather than impacting the overall calculus of proportionality).

not necessarily result in a commander deciding that an attack would be disproportionate if carried out, calculating mental health harms may not change the ultimate decision about a strike. But incorporating the potential risk of serious mental health harms can reveal the larger scale of anticipated harm to civilians in a particular attack and can aid in conducting a more accurate weighing of civilian harm against military advantage.

As an initial step toward improved and fuller accounting of civilian harm, states should bring psychology, public health, military, and legal experts together to assess the current state of scientific knowledge, methods for assessing and predicting civilian harm in military practice generally, and how mental harms might be incorporated into commanders' proportionality assessments. A multidisciplinary expert group could begin to assess the possibilities of foreseeing mental harms from different kinds of specific attacks and factors that might influence the likelihood of mental harm in various situations, and work toward preparing guidance on how mental harms might be incorporated into collateral damage estimation methodologies and weighed in any proportionality analysis. States should also give consideration to what additional expertise commanders should be able to access in order to best assess the risk of mental harms. Already, targeting, weaponeering, legal, and other experts are on hand to support a commander in making decisions; mental health experts may also prove to be beneficial. And, to address critical gaps in current knowledge, states should support new scientific research to understand the mental health effects of different kinds of attacks in varying circumstances.

The devastating impacts of war have long been known, but IHL theory and practice have often ignored mental health. As scientific understandings of the destructive effects of exposure to trauma has evolved, so too should the law and military practice. Millions of civilians suffering from or at risk of serious mental health impacts in war zones deserve more concrete protections.

13

Toward the Special Computer Law of Targeting

"Fully Autonomous" Weapons Systems and the Proportionality Test

MASAHIRO KUROSAKI*

I. INTRODUCTION

The means of warfare in the new millennium took on a new face with the development of emerging military technologies. The advent of unmanned robotic vehicles has opened a new horizon to the remote-controlled and "risk-free" warfare, and the exponential advancement of artificial intelligence (AI) infused with machine learning algorithms is increasingly reducing the role of humans, notably operators and supervisors in the battlespace. Military experts now share the view that "[a]utonomy in unmanned systems will be critical to future conflicts that will be fought and won with technology."[1] Against this background, the issue of fully autonomous weapons systems—also known as "killer robots"—came to the fore with legal and ethical concerns throughout the international community.

Autonomous weapons systems (AWS) are generally understood as systems that, once activated, are capable of deciding a course of action, in particular, selecting and engaging targets, without further human intervention, control, or

* Associate Professor of International Law and the Director of the Study of Law, Security, and Military Operations at the National Defense Academy of the Japanese Ministry of Defense. The author wishes to thank the participants of the 2018 Lieber Workshop led by Claus Kreß, Michael N. Schmitt, and the Lieber Institute of the U.S. Military Academy at West Point for their insightful and constructive feedback on an earlier draft of this chapter. The opinions expressed here are solely those of the author and do not necessarily represent the position of the Japanese government or the Ministry of Defense of Japan.

1. Office of the Sec'y of Def., Dep't of Def., Unmanned Systems Integrated Roadmap FY2013–2038 67 (2013), https://www.defense.gov/Portals/1/Documents/pubs/DO D-USRM-2013.pdf.

Masahiro Kurosaki, *Toward the Special Computer Law of Targeting* In: *Necessity and Proportionality in International Peace and Security Law.* Edited by: Professor Claus Kreß and Captain Robert Lawless, Oxford University Press (2021).
 DOI: 10.1093/oso/9780197537374.003.0014.

oversight.[2] The level of autonomy in these systems is sometimes further classified into three categories: "Human-in-the-Loop," "Human-on-the-Loop," and "Human-out-of-the-Loop,"[3] which could also be referred to as, but not necessarily identical to, "semi-autonomous," "human-supervised," and "fully autonomous" weapons systems.[4] Fully AWS are particularly controversial because, albeit not yet existing, they exclude human involvement entirely in their targeting decision process, which stokes serious concerns about their potential out-of-control attacks. Although some countries manifestly deny or prohibit possession and development of fully AWS,[5] there is no universal agreement as to the precise definition of such systems.[6] The varying use of terms such as human "intervention," "control," and "oversight" in order to indicate the meaning and level of autonomy[7] has been

2. *See, e.g.*, DEP'T OF DEF., DIRECTIVE 3000.09, AUTONOMY IN WEAPON SYSTEMS 13–14 (Nov. 21, 2012, incorporating change 1, May 8, 2017), https://www.esd.whs.mil/portals/54/documents/dd/issuances/dodd/300009p.pdf [hereinafter DoD DIRECTIVE 3000.09]. AWS could be distinguished from automated weapons systems based on criteria such as their predictability. *See, e.g.*, SELECT COMM. ON ARTIFICIAL INTELLIGENCE, HOUSE OF LORDS, REPORT OF SESSION 2017–19, AI IN THE UK: READY, WILLING AND ABLE? 102 (Apr. 16, 2018), https://publications.parliament.uk/pa/ld201719/ldselect/ldai/100/100.pdf [hereinafter AI IN THE UK] ("Knowing the set of rules under which it is operating means that its output is predictable. . . . Although the overall activity of an autonomous unmanned aircraft will be predictable, individual actions may not be.").

3. Human Rights Watch describes these categories as follows:

> Human-*in*-the-Loop Weapons: Robots that can select targets and deliver force only with a human command; Human-*on*-the-Loop Weapons: Robots that can select targets and deliver force under the oversight of a human operator who can override the robots' actions; and Human-*out-of*-the-Loop Weapons: Robots that are capable of selecting targets and delivering force without any human input or interaction.

HUM. RTS. WATCH, LOSING HUMANITY: THE CASE AGAINST KILLER ROBOTS 2 (2012), https://www.hrw.org/sites/default/files/reports/arms1112_ForUpload.pdf [hereinafter LOSING HUMANITY].

4. *See, e.g.*, AI IN THE UK, *supra* note 2, ¶ 336; DoD DIRECTIVE 3000.09, *supra* note 2, at 13–14; LOSING HUMANITY, *supra* note 3, at 2.

5. *See, e.g.*, MINISTRY OF DEFENCE, JOINT DOCTRINE PUBLICATION 0–30.2, UNMANNED AIRCRAFT SYSTEMS ¶ 2.6, https://assets.publishing.service.gov.uk/government/uploads/system/uploads/attachment_data/file/673940/doctrine_uk_uas_jdp_0_30_2.pdf (U.K.) ("[T]he UK does not possess fully autonomous weapon systems and has no intention of developing them. Such systems are not yet in existence and are not likely to be for many years, if at all."); DoD DIRECTIVE 3000.09, *supra* note 2, ¶ 4a ("Autonomous and semi-autonomous weapon systems shall be designed to allow commanders and operators to exercise appropriate levels of human judgment over the use of force.").

6. AI IN THE UK, *supra* note 2, at 101–105.

7. *See, e.g.*, Merel A.C. Ekelhof, *Complications of a Common Language: Why It Is So Hard to Talk About Autonomous Weapons*, 22 J. CONFLICT & SECURITY L. 311 (2017). Given such circumstances, Schuller suggests that it is "helpful to think of autonomy as a spectrum or series of spectrums rather than a singular concept" from a technological viewpoint, and that we

a source of ongoing semantic debate among states in the Group of Governmental Experts on Lethal Autonomous Weapons Systems (LAWS) established by the High Contracting Parties to the Convention on Certain Conventional Weapons (CCW). Meanwhile, an ever-increasing level of autonomy in weapons systems[8] is increasingly giving rise to concerns about the future deployment of fully AWS and has led critics to call for ensuring effective or meaningful human control[9] over, or more radically, a preemptive ban on, those systems as "one of the most alarming military technologies under development today."[10]

In the context of international law, primary concerns about fully AWS lie in their ability to comply with the rules of the law applicable in armed conflict. In particular, heated debates center on the targeting rules under the law of armed conflict (LOAC).[11] The LOAC requires parties to an armed conflict to abide by three essential principles: distinction, proportionality, and precautions in attack. First, parties must distinguish between military targets on the one hand, and civilians and civilian objects on the other hand, and attacks must be directed at the former. Inherently indiscriminate "weapons that are incapable of distinguishing between civilian and military targets" are therefore illegal per se.[12] Second, parties must not engage in disproportionate attacks, that is, attacks "which may be expected to cause incidental loss of civilian life, injury to civilians, damage to civilian objects, or a combination thereof, which would be excessive in relation to the concrete

"should focus on the combination of authorities granted to the computer system that controls the machine while also taking into account the physical capabilities of the AWS." Alan L. Schuller, *At the Crossroads of Control: The Intersection of Artificial Intelligence in Autonomous Weapon Systems with International Humanitarian Law*, 8 HARV. NAT'L SEC. J. 379, 392–97 (2017).

8. *See* VINCENT BOULANIN & MAAIKE VERBRUGGEN, MAPPING THE DEVELOPMENT OF AUTONOMY IN WEAPON SYSTEMS (Nov. 2017), https://www.sipri.org/publications/2017/other-publications/mapping-development-autonomy-weapon-systems.

9. *Towards Limits on Autonomy in Weapon Systems*, INT'L COMM. RED CROSS (Apr. 9, 2018), https://www.icrc.org/en/document/towards-limits-autonomous-weapons; Michael Horowitz & Paul Scharre, *Defining "Meaningful Human Control" Over Autonomous Weapons*, JUST SECURITY (Mar. 19, 2015), https://www.justsecurity.org/21244/defining-meaningful-human-control-autonmous-weapon-systems; Thompson Chengeta, *Defining the Emerging Notion of "Meaningful Human Control" in Weapon Systems*, 49 N.Y.U. J. INT'L L. & POL. 833 (2017).

10. HUM. RTS. WATCH, HEED THE CALL: A MORAL AND LEGAL IMPERATIVE TO BAN KILLER ROBOTS 1 (2018), https://www.hrw.org/sites/default/files/report_pdf/arms0818_web.pdf.

11. *See, e.g.*, Jeffrey S. Thurnher, *The Law That Applies to Autonomous Weapon Systems*, 17 AM. SOC'Y INT'L L. INSIGHTS (Jan. 18, 2013), https://www.asil.org/insights/volume/17/issue/4/law-applies-autonomous-weapon-systems.

12. Legality of the Threat or Use of Nuclear Weapons, Advisory Opinion, 1996 I.C.J. Rep. 226, ¶ 78 (July 8) [hereinafter *Nuclear Weapons* case]; *see also* Protocol Additional to the Geneva Conventions of 12 August 1949, and Relating to the Protection of Victims of International Armed Conflict (Protocol I) art. 51(4)(b), June 8, 1977, 1125 U.N.T.S. 3 [hereinafter AP I].

and direct military advantage anticipated."[13] Third, all feasible precautions must be taken to avoid and minimize harm to civilians and civilian objects.

Compliance with these principles, which are widely recognized as customary international law applicable to international and non-international armed conflicts,[14] would become most contentious if fully AWS were fielded in urban areas. For while certain military operational settings (including, in particular, on the sea or in the air) lack civilians, an urban battlefield is characterized by the presence of military targets and civilians.[15] In such an instance, the principle of proportionality is likely to become crucial in view of risks for civilians which may prove unavoidable even in case of fully AWS with a high-level ability to distinguish military targets from those protected by the LOAC. The principle of proportionality thus comes into play as "the most controversial and arguably the most important"[16] issue in the modern battlespace, even in the context of the use of AWS.

As discussed in the following section, both proponents and opponents of fully AWS have developed their arguments on the observance of the principle of proportionality, revolving around whether machines outperform, or at least verge on outperforming, humans in rule compliance. However, the very defining feature of fully AWS as an independent decision maker raises the following fundamental question in the first place: Regardless of whether such systems outperform humans, why should we focus on the role of humans and compare fully AWS with human soldiers in addressing the issue? Is it because the LOAC regulates the human conduct of hostilities alone on the premise that only humans can achieve humanity in armed conflict and, as such, it constantly demands human control over the means of warfare? If so, why? Is it because human beings, even if prone to errors at times, remain most rational or at least more so than machines in complex battlespaces?

Such a human-centered paradigm in the regulation of fully AWS has thus far been justified in the name of the "principle of human dignity." It mandates the inherent dignity of all human beings to be respected as representing the supreme

13. AP I, *supra* note 12, art. 51(5)(b).

14. *See, e.g.*, 1 INT'L COMM. OF THE RED CROSS, CUSTOMARY INTERNATIONAL HUMANITARIAN LAW: RULES rr. 16–19, at 55–62 (Jean-Marie Henckaerts & Louise Doswald-Beck eds., 2005) [hereinafter CUSTOMARY IHL STUDY]; Brian Egan, Legal Advisor, Dep't of State, International Law, Legal Diplomacy, and the Counter-ISIL Campaign: Some Observations (Apr. 1, 2016), *in* 92 INT'L L. STUD. 235, 242–43 (2016).

15. Kenneth Anderson, Daniel Reisner, & Matthew Waxman, *Adapting the Law of Armed Conflict to Autonomous Weapon Systems*, 90 INT'L L. STUD. 386, 401–402 (2014) ("Distinction is highly unlikely to be an issue in that particular operational environment, however, because the combat environment would be lacking in civilians. . . . As with the principle of distinction, there are operational settings—air-to-air combat over open water, tank warfare in remote uninhabited deserts, ship antimissile defense, undersea anti-submarine operations, for example—in which civilians are not likely to be present and which, in practical terms, do not require weighing military advantage against civilian harms.").

16. MICHAEL NEWTON & LARRY MAY, PROPORTIONALITY IN INTERNATIONAL LAW 2 (2014).

value and ultimate goal for the rule of law. Fully AWS, "as inanimate machines, could comprehend neither the value of individual life nor the significance of its loss."[17] In consequence, to delegate the decision to kill to fully AWS—"death by algorithm"[18] as Christof Heyns put it—is nothing more than to allow machines to treat "a rational being as if it were merely an object."[19] The intrinsic value of its dignity is thus abandoned, which could render fully AWS totally unethical and unlawful in contravention of the principle of human dignity not only as "the very raison d'être of international humanitarian law and human rights law"[20] but also "as a general principle of law necessary for social coexistence, one that informs the content of fundamental legal norms across the domains of domestic, regional, and public international law."[21]

All that said, it is not clear why this principle matters only in the fully AWS context. Why will human victims become considered as being treated as mere objects once fully AWS attack humans, whereas those victims are not considered as such when human soldiers do the same thing by using traditional means of warfare? Primarily due to the lack of consensus about the meaning of "human dignity" and the loose usage of the term,[22] there have been no convincing reasons offered to take such a human-centered paradigm as given for the regulation of fully AWS under the LOAC.[23]

17. Hum. Rts. Watch, Making the Case: The Dangers of Killer Robots and the Need for a Preemptive Ban 23 (Dec. 2016), https://www.hrw.org/sites/default/files/report_pdf/arms1216_web.pdf.

18. Christof Heyns, *Human Rights and the Use of Autonomous Weapons Systems (AWS) During Domestic Law Enforcement*, 38 Hum. Rts. Q. 350, 370 (2016) ("Death by algorithm means that people are treated simply as targets and not as complete and unique human beings, who may, by virtue of that status, meet a different fate.").

19. Aaron M. Johnson & Sidney Axinn, *The Morality of Autonomous Robots*, 12 J. Mil. Ethics 129, 134 (2013).

20. As "the very raison d'être of international humanitarian law," the principle of humanity "is intended to shield human beings from outrages upon their personal dignity, whether such outrages are carried out by unlawfully attacking the body or by humiliating and debasing the honour, the self-respect or the mental well being of a person." Prosecutor v. Furundžija, Case No. IT-95-17/1-T, Judgement, ¶ 185 (Int'l Crim. Trib. for the Former Yugoslavia Trial Chamber Dec. 10, 1998).

21. Thomas Weatherall, Jus Cogens: International Law and Social Contract 43 (2015).

22. *See, e.g.*, Jacob Weinrib, *Human Dignity and Its Critics*, *in* Comparative Constitutional Theory 167 (Gary Jacobsohn & Miguel Schor eds., 2018); Conor O'Mahony, *There Is No Such Thing as a Right to Dignity*, 1 Int'l J. Const. L. 551 (2012).

23. *See* Ariadna Pop, *Autonomous Weapon Systems: A Threat to Human Dignity?*, Humanitarian L. & Pol'y (Apr. 10, 2018), https://blogs.icrc.org/law-and-policy/2018/04/10/autonomous-weapon-systems-a-threat-to-human-dignity ("I fail to see what the relevant argument could look like and have also not found any satisfactory explanation in the literature. . . . [T]hey must make the relevant argument and spell out the specific understanding of human dignity

If fully AWS refer to weapons systems that are not subject to human decisions whatsoever during their attacks, or at least if the link between human decisions and lethal fully-AWS attacks might become "so diluted that we cannot reasonably say a human decided to kill,"[24] could a human-centered approach to the regulation of future fully AWS then nevertheless best contribute to the object and purpose of the LOAC? Or, if there were to exist certain areas where machines could outperform humans in the targeting process, should we rather seek another approach to the international legal regulation dedicated to fully AWS in order to maximize their potential in achieving the LOAC goal to protect the victims of armed conflict?

With those questions in mind, this chapter, in response to the demands of changing times, aims to question the absoluteness of the existing human-centered approach to the proportionality test and to propose an alternative regulatory model dedicated to fully AWS. In doing so, however, it does not take any position on another (much more fictional) issue of armed conflict between future robot belligerents entirely independent of humans.[25] As the term "weapons systems" suggests, it confines itself to fully AWS as a means of human warfare, meaning that *outside* the firing loop they remain subject to the intervention, control, or oversight of human belligerents—in this chapter's setting, it is exclusively humans that design, develop, deploy, activate, abort, and deactivate them.[26] As such, it must be borne in mind that the aim of this chapter is never to deny any role of humans in the overall regulations of fully AWS under the LOAC and other fields of international law.

they presuppose. Otherwise, the use of human dignity is reduced to a rhetoric maneuver, an empty shell, which, depending on the context and purpose of its use, has a very different theoretical underpinning. . . . It also renders the concept vulnerable to manipulation and thereby undermines the credibility of the debate in question. . . . In order to advance the AWS debate it is therefore preferable to refrain from using the concept of human dignity altogether, at least as long as no consensus regarding its proper meaning has emerged and the relevant assumptions remain unarticulated."); *see also* Amanda Sharkey, *Autonomous Weapons Systems, Killer Robots and Human Dignity*, 20 Ethics & Info. Tech. 1, 1 (2018) (concluding as follows: "[T]he risk to human dignity is only one of many reasons for calling for a ban of autonomous weapons and for insisting on the need for meaningful human control of lethal weapons in war; and it is not the most compelling.").

24. Schuller, *supra* note 7, at 396.

25. On this point, *see, e.g.*, Hin-Yan Liu, *Categorization and Legality of Autonomous and Remote Weapons Systems*, 94 Int'l Rev. Red Cross 627, 636–37 (2012).

26. In a semantic discussion on the meaning of "fully autonomous" weapons systems, however, some find the essence of weapons with a human "out of the loop" in that "humans cannot intervene to stop an attack after the weapon has been activated." *See* Advisory Comm. on Issues of Pub. Int'l L., No. 97 AIV / No. 26 CAVV, Autonomous Weapon Systems: The Need for Meaningful Human Control 9 (Oct. 2015) (Neth.).

II. AWS DEBATE ON THE PROPORTIONALITY TEST

The proportionality test requires a set of comparative factors for the ex ante assessment of whether an attack on a military target causes excessive collateral damage. At the time of the attack, the following must be identified and compared: the expected incidental civilian loss and the concrete and direct military advantage anticipated.[27] These variables for the comparison are highly contextual, which necessitates a complex case-by-case analysis.[28] "Neither the human nor the machine is held to a standard of perfection,"[29] but current AWS debate concerns the relative merits of humans and machines in comporting with the standard in a reasonable manner, asking which is more predictable and reliable in performance of those proportionality calculations to minimize civilian casualties.[30] The subject matter is thus largely technological rather than normative.[31]

27. The anticipated military advantage is not limited to strategic gains of an attacker. It "should be seen in relation to the attack as a whole." INT'L COMM. OF THE RED CROSS, COMMENTARY ON THE ADDITIONAL PROTOCOLS OF 8 JUNE 1977 TO THE GENEVA CONVENTIONS OF 12 AUGUST 1949 ¶ 2217, n.15 (Yves Sandoz, Christophe Swinarski, & Bruno Zimmermann eds., 1987) [hereinafter AP COMMENTARY].

28. Any harm expected to befall civilians and civilian objects caused by a direct attack on a military target would be factored into the proportionality assessment as incidental or collateral damage. Yet, identifying those protected civilians and civilian objects could, in the first place, cause considerable difficulties deriving from their complex and contextual definitions. For instance, unlike in situations of international armed conflict, definition of civilians in non-international armed conflict remains unclear (if any, the "continuous combat function" requirement for functional membership of an organized armed group heavily depends on context). As the "revolving door" issue suggests, the same is true of the rule that attacks must not be directed against civilians *unless and for such time as* they directly participate in hostilities. *See* AP I, *supra* note 12, art. 51(3). Further, while Additional Protocol I defines civilian objects as "all objects which are not military objectives," it provides that the notion of military objectives includes "those objects which by their nature, location, purpose or use make an effective contribution to military action and whose total or partial destruction, capture or neutralization, in the circumstances ruling at the time, offers a definite military advantage." *Id.* art. 52(1)(2). Together with the element of "the concrete and direct military advantage anticipated," all of these require context-driven determinations in the proportionality test. *See, e.g.*, INT'L COMM. RED CROSS, INTERPRETIVE GUIDANCE ON THE NOTION OF DIRECT PARTICIPATION IN HOSTILITIES UNDER INTERNATIONAL HUMANITARIAN LAW (2009), http://www.icrc.org/eng/assets/files/other/icrc-002-0990.pdf [hereinafter INTERPRETIVE GUIDANCE].

29. Michael N. Schmitt & Jeffrey S. Thurnher, *"Out of the Loop": Autonomous Weapon Systems and the Law of Armed Conflict*, 4 HARV. NAT'L SEC. J. 231, 257 (2013).

30. *See generally* Schuller, *supra* note 7, at 409–13.

31. *See* Anderson et al., *supra* note 15, at 406 ("In practical terms, autonomous systems might be better able to satisfy the law in some uses and environments than others, but that is not a matter of principle; it is a matter of whether and how far technological capability advances relative to standard."); Eliav Lieblich & Eyal Benvenisti, *The Obligation to Exercise Discretion in Warfare: Why Autonomous Weapons Systems Are Unlawful*, *in* AUTONOMOUS WEAPONS SYSTEMS 245, 246 (Nehal Bhuta, Susanne Beck, Robin Geiß, Hin-Yan Liu, & Claus Kreß eds.,

Opponents of fully AWS argue that those systems would be inferior to a human commander and be unlawful by their very nature because their software and hardware capabilities (involving unpredictability, vulnerability to cyberattacks, etc.) would preclude them from responding in a legally compliant manner to complicated and shifting scenarios.[32] In addition, such systems "lack morality and mortality,"[33] which should serve as psychological restraints in the proportionality assessment.[34] According to the critics, the subjective, context-driven proportionality test "requires more than a balancing of quantitative data, and a robot could not be programmed to duplicate the psychological processes in human judgment that are necessary to assess proportionality."[35] For this reason, any weapons must be subject to meaningful control by humans. Without such control, they would cause "diffusion of moral responsibility and loss of human dignity."[36]

While admitting some unpredictability and vulnerabilities, including the risk of cyber tampering by enemy belligerents,[37] proponents in turn criticize the opponents for ignoring the potential of AWS to more effectively minimize the unlawful targeting of civilians and civilian objects when compared to other lawful

2016) ("In essence, the current debate on AWS is a manifestation of the circular argument between technological optimists and pessimists found in other contexts.").

32. *See, e.g.*, Losing Humanity, *supra* note 3, at 32–34; Jeroen van den Boogaard, *Proportionality and Autonomous Weapons Systems*, 6 J. Int'l Humanitarian Legal Stud. 247, 260–77 (2015). Van den Boogaard claims: "It is my opinion that autonomous weapons systems must be prevented from making decisions on an operational or strategic level without the input of the relevant, human military commander because at that level, the equation must also include other factors to determine the military advantage sought, including both strategic and political factor." *Id.* at 277.

33. Christof Heyns (Special Rapporteur on Extrajudicial, Summary or Arbitrary Executions), *Report of the Special Rapporteur on Extrajudicial, Summary or Arbitrary Executions*, ¶ 94, U.N. Doc. A/HRC/23/47 (Apr. 9, 2013), https://www.ohchr.org/Documents/HRBodies/HRCouncil/RegularSession/Session23/A-HRC-23-47_en.pdf [hereinafter *Report of the Special Rapporteur*].

34. Losing Humanity, *supra* note 3, at 4 ("First, robots would not be restrained by human emotions and the capacity for compassion, which can provide an important check on the killing of civilians.").

35. *Id.* at 33; *see also* Advisory Comm. on Issues of Pub. Int'l L., *supra* note 26 ("It is highly unlikely that autonomous weapons will be able to independently weigh military advantage against collateral damage within the next 10 years, at least not in most situations. This is because the act of assessing an anticipated military advantage is partly subjective and because each assessment is heavily dependent on the context in which the attack is carried out as well as on a whole range of factors that are liable to change rapidly. These are the kinds of situations in which human reasoning is more reliable than artificial intelligence.").

36. *Towards Limits on Autonomy in Weapon Systems*, *supra* note 9.

37. Schmitt & Thurnher, *supra* note 29, at 239.

weapons.[38] As a promising sign of this potential, an effective system of collateral damage estimation, which could be programmed in AWS, has already come into existence to assist military commanders with warranting a lawful attack.[39] Given unexpected and explosive developments in technology, the advocates claim that AWS would likely be able to "exhibit human-like cognitive abilities, enabling them to make decisions in response to complex problems and situations."[40] It might be a long way off, but advocates assert that one cannot rule out the future possibility that sophisticated fully AWS would make subjective and quantitative value assessments of excessiveness of expected collateral damage in relation to anticipated military gains in a manner resulting in enhanced, albeit not perfect, civilian protection.[41]

As these contentions from both sides illustrate, much of the debate on the principle of proportionality in the AWS context has been conducted around the basic question of whether "*humans* are better suited to make such value judgments, which cannot be boiled down to a simple algorithm"[42] or whether future AWS "could be programmed to behave more ethically and far more cautiously on the

38. *See, e.g.*, *id.*; Chris Jenks, *The Gathering Swarm: The Path to Increasingly Autonomous Weapons Systems*, 57 Jurimetrics J. 341 (2017); John Yoo, *Embracing the Machines: Rationalist War and New Weapons Technologies*, 105 Cal. L. Rev. 443 (2017).

39. It is well known that the United States has introduced the proportionality calculation system called "collateral damage estimate methodology" (CDEM/CDM), which assists military commander with the authority to an attack. *See, e.g.*, Schmitt & Thurnher, *supra* note 29, at 254–55; *see also* Geoffrey S. Corn, Victor Hansen, Richard B. Jackson, Chris Jenks, Eric Talbot Jensen, & James A. Schoettler Jr., The Law of Armed Conflict: An Operational Approach 274–75 (2d ed. 2019) ("[CDEM] mandates a process for identifying potential collateral damage in an operation, considering the method of attack (including an analysis of the critical effects radius of the weapon system proposed to be used), mitigating that damage, and where appropriate, seeking designated authority to conduct the attack if collateral damage cannot be avoided. . . . With this information, commanders are prepared to make well-informed decisions in compliance with both the LOAC and ROE."); Chairman of the Joint Chiefs of Staff, CJCSI 3160.01, No-Strike and Collateral Damage Estimation Methodology (Oct. 12, 2012), https://info.publicintelligence.net/CJCS-CollateralDamage.pdf. Further, Margulies analyzes the potential of AI for the development of situational awareness technology (SAT) that "will make target selection and collateral damage estimation more accurate, thereby reducing harm to civilians." It is argued that the SAT serves for a "constant care" to be taken by a reasonable military commander. Peter Margulies, *The Other Side of Autonomous Weapons: Using Artificial Intelligence to Enhance IHL Compliance*, *in* The Impact of Emerging Technologies on the Law of Armed Conflict 147 (Eric Talbot Jensen & Ron Alcala eds., 2019).

40. Schmitt & Thurnher, *supra* note 29, at 242–43.

41. *Id.* at 257; *see also* Schuller, *supra* note 7, at 401; Benjamin Wittes, *Does Human Rights Watch Prefer Disproportionate and Indiscriminate Humans to Discriminating and Proportionate Robots?*, Lawfare (Dec. 1, 2012), https://www.lawfareblog.com/does-human-rights-watch-prefer-disproportionate-and-indiscriminate-humans-discriminating-and.

42. Losing Humanity, *supra* note 3, at 34 (emphasis added).

battlefield than *a human being*."[43] As mentioned in the introduction, the axis of the debate is the existing human-centered structure of the modern LOAC.

III. THE EXISTING HUMAN-CENTERED APPROACH TO THE PROPORTIONALITY TEST

A. The Principle of Humanity and the Normative Shift from State-Centrism to Human-Centrism

The current proportionality test certainly presupposes a personal judgment call by the military official in charge. Yet history has shown that such human-centrism in the LOAC can never been taken for granted. It has been gradually shaped and fostered by, among other things, an array of developments of the principle of humanity, treaty regimes, and international criminal jurisprudence in keeping with the realities of armed conflicts of the time.

The LOAC is a body of rules that aims to protect combatants and noncombatants from unnecessary suffering and to safeguard the fundamental human rights of persons hors de combat and of civilians.[44] To achieve these aims, the guiding principles of military necessity and humanity animate the interpretation and application of the LOAC.[45] While the former derives from economic efficiency in military operations to accomplish their legitimate objective, the latter is driven by psychological emotions of respect for human dignity and honor. Balancing these principles is most vividly evident in the proportionality test,[46] which sets limits on the degree of incidental harm to civilians and civilian objects caused during an attack.[47]

Between the two, the principle of humanity underlines the humanitarian aspect of the LOAC today. Indeed, it brought about the normative shift from classical

43. Jacob Kellenberger, President, Int'l Comm. of the Red Cross, Keynote Address, International Humanitarian Law and New Weapons Technologies, 34th Round Table on Current Issues of International Humanitarian Law, San Remo, 8–10 September 2011, *in* 94 INT'L REV. RED CROSS 809, 812–13 (2012) (emphasis added).

44. *See generally* MINISTRY OF DEF., JSP 383, THE JOINT SERVICE MANUAL OF THE LAW OF ARMED CONFLICT ¶ 1.8 (2004) (U.K.), https://assets.publishing.service.gov.uk/government/uploads/system/uploads/attachment_data/file/27874/JSP3832004Edition.pdf [hereinafter 2004 U.K. MANUAL].

45. *See* OFF. OF THE GEN. COUNS., DEP'T OF DEF., DEPARTMENT OF DEFENSE LAW OF WAR MANUAL ¶ 2.1.2 (June 2005, updated Dec. 2016) https://dod.defense.gov/Portals/1/Documents/pubs/DoD%20Law%20of%20War%20Manual%20-%20June%202015%20Updated%20Dec%202016.pdf?ver=2016-12-13-172036-190 [hereinafter U.S. LAW OF WAR MANUAL].

46. *See* 2004 U.K. MANUAL, *supra* note 44, ¶¶ 2.4.2, 2.6.2; U.S. LAW OF WAR MANUAL, *supra* note 45, ¶ 2.1.2.3.

47. *See, e.g.*, 2004 U.K. MANUAL, *supra* note 44, ¶ 2.4.2.

state-centrism[48] to modern human-centrism[49] in the *jus in bello*, which led to the establishment of today's principle of proportionality to protect civilians. Prior to that, "[c]lassical international law allowed a State which had a just cause for war to apply the maximum degree of force and destruction to bring about a speedy victory."[50] Since then, its humanized framework has been addressed mainly to military commanders on the battlefield.[51] This can be seen in the 1899 and 1907 Hague Conventions on the Laws and Customs of War on Land,[52] the preamble of which—most famously known as the Martens Clause—attests that the principles of humanity is intended to forestall "the arbitrary judgment of military commanders" in unforeseen cases not covered by written international agreements.[53] The Martens

48. *See, e.g.*, 2 LASSA OPPENHEIM, INTERNATIONAL LAW, A TREATISE: WAR AND NEUTRALITY 266–67 (1906) ("Since International Law is a law between States only and exclusively, no rules of International Law can exist to prohibit private individuals from taking up arms, and committing hostilities against the enemy.").

49. *See* THEODOR MERON, THE HUMANIZATION OF INTERNATIONAL LAW 5 (2006).

50. *Id.* at 61. Oppenheim also supports this line of thinking: "As war is a struggle for existence between States, no amount of individual suffering and misery can be regarded; the national existence and independence of the struggling State is a higher consideration than any individual well-being." OPPENHEIM, *supra* note 48, ¶ 58.

51. *See* Kai Ambos, *Command Responsibility and Organisationsherrschaft: Ways of Attributing International Crimes to the "Most Responsible," in* SYSTEM CRIMINALITY IN INTERNATIONAL LAW 127, 133 (André Nollkaemper & Harmen van der Wilt eds., 2009) ("Although [LOAC rules for military commanders] were initially addressed only to state parties, they have always served as conduct rules for individuals and for prosecution of individual violators."); *see also* Mary Ellen O'Connell, *Historical Development and Legal Basis, in* THE HANDBOOK OF INTERNATIONAL HUMANITARIAN LAW 1, ¶ 135 (Dieter Fleck ed., 3d ed. 2013) ("One of the unusual features of humanitarian law is that, unlike most rules of international law, it binds not only the state and its organs of government but also the individual.").

52. *See* 2004 U.K. MANUAL, *supra* note 44, ¶ 2.4.3.

53. Convention (II) with Respect to the Laws and Customs of War on Land pmbl., July 29, 1899, 32 Stat. 1803, T.S. No. 403; Convention (IV) Respecting the Laws and Customs of War on Land pmbl., Oct. 18, 1907, 36 Stat. 2227, T.S. No. 539. The preamble of Convention (IV) reads that "the high contracting Parties clearly do not intend that unforeseen cases should, in the absence of a written undertaking, be left to the arbitrary judgment of military commanders. Until a more complete code of the laws of war has been issued, the high contracting Parties deem it expedient to declare that, in cases not included in the Regulations adopted by them, the inhabitants and the belligerents remain under the protection and the rule of the principles of the law of nations, as they result from the usages established among civilized peoples, from the laws of humanity, and the dictates of the public conscience." It is reproduced in Articles 63, 62, 142, 158 of Geneva Conventions I through IV, Article 1(2) of AP I, and the preamble of the 1980 Conventional Weapons Convention. Convention (I) for the Amelioration of the Condition of the Wounded and Sick in Armed Forces in the Field art. 63, Aug. 12, 1949, 6 U.S.T. 3114, 75 U.N.T.S. 31 [hereinafter GC I]; Convention (II) for the Amelioration of the Condition of the Wounded, Sick, and Shipwrecked Members of Armed Forces at Sea art. 62, Aug. 12, 1949, 6 U.S.T. 3217, 75 U.N.S.T. 85; Convention (III) Relative to the Treatment of Prisoners of War art. 142, Aug. 12, 1949, 6

Clause is generally understood as the first to have enshrined that the principle of humanity protects "the inhabitants and the belligerents."[54]

B. Commander-Centric Treaty Regimes

This commander-centric approach permeates other LOAC treaty regimes. The principle of proportionality, which has been codified in Additional Protocol I (AP I) of 1977,[55] revolves around military commanders for its implementation. AP I establishes the general duties of military commanders primarily to prevent, suppress, and report breaches of the Geneva Conventions and AP I by members of their armed forces and other persons under their control.[56] To help them in doing so, it requires the contracting parties to ensure that legal advisors are available to assist military commanders when necessary.[57]

In the context of the principle of proportionality, the relevant provisions of AP I "must above all be a question of common sense and good faith for military commanders."[58] Moreover, AP I imposes on military commanders with the authority to plan or decide upon an attack the duty to take all feasible precautions to avoid excessive collateral damage.[59] The willful commission of violations of those provisions constitutes grave breaches of AP I subject to universal jurisdiction.[60]

In a similar vein, the 1954 Hague Convention on the Protection of Cultural Property in the Event of Armed Conflict concentrates the power to find "unavoidable military necessity" for withdrawal of immunity of the cultural property concerned only on "the officer commanding a force the equivalent of a division in size or

U.S.T. 3316, 75 U.N.T.S. 135; Convention (IV) Relative to the Protection of Civilian Persons in Time of War art. 158, Aug. 12, 1949, 6 U.S.T. 3516, 75 U.N.T.S. 287; AP I, *supra* note 12, art. 1(2).

54. *See also* Theodor Meron, *The Martens Clause, Principles of Humanity, and Dictates of Public Conscience*, 94 AM. J. INT'L L. 78 (2000).

55. 2004 U.K. MANUAL, *supra* note 44, ¶ 2.6.1. As for its history, *see* NEWTON & MAY, *supra* note 16, at 89–119. The principle of proportionality under AP I is replicated in Article 3(8) of Amended Protocol II to the Convention on Certain Conventional Weapons.

56. AP I, *supra* note 12, art. 87(1). Article 87 of the Protocol further requires military commanders to ensure that members of the armed forces under their command are aware of their obligations under the Conventions and the Protocol, *id.* art. 87(2), and, in cases where they are aware that their subordinates have either committed or are about to commit breaches of those obligations, to prevent those breaches or initiate appropriate disciplinary or penal action, *id.* art. 87(3).

57. AP I, *supra* note 12, art. 82.

58. AP COMMENTARY, *supra* note 27, ¶ 2208.

59. *See* AP I, *supra* note 12, art. 57(1)(2).

60. *See id.* art. 85(3)(b)(c); Rome Statute of the International Criminal Court art. 8(2)(iv), July 17, 1998, 2187 U.N.T.S. 3 [hereinafter Rome Statute].

larger."[61] The United Kingdom makes an interpretative declaration in relation to the Convention and accompanying protocols, highlighting the central role of "military commanders and others responsible for planning, deciding upon, or executing attacks."[62]

C. International Criminal Jurisprudence and the "Reasonable Military Commander" Standard

This treaty-based approach has been further enhanced by international criminal courts and tribunals in an effort to prosecute and punish individuals who commit international crimes. Notably, the proportionality test owes much to the jurisprudence of the International Criminal Tribunal for the Former Yugoslavia (ICTY), although, as can be seen in its controversial Trial Chamber judgment in the *Gotovina* case,[63] the ICTY has not necessarily contributed to clarity of its interpretation and application.[64]

In its *Galić* trial judgment, the ICTY formulated the so-called "reasonable military commander" standard,[65] holding that "[i]n determining whether an attack

61. Convention for the Protection of Cultural Property in the Event of Armed Conflict art. 11(2), May 14, 1954, 249 U.N.T.S. 240 ("Apart from the case provided for in paragraph I of the present Article, immunity shall be withdrawn from cultural property under special protection only in exceptional cases of unavoidable military necessity, and only for such time as that necessity continues. Such necessity can be established only by the officer commanding a force the equivalent of a division in size or larger. Whenever circumstances permit, the opposing Party shall be notified, a reasonable time in advance, of the decision to withdraw immunity.").

62. Interpretive Declaration of United Kingdom of Great Britain and Northern Ireland on 12 September 2017, *in* Declarations and Reservations to the Convention for the Protection of Cultural Property in the Event of Armed Conflict, United Nations Educational, Scientific and Cultural Organization Legal Instruments, http://portal.unesco.org/en/ev.php-URL_ID=13637&URL_DO=DO_TOPIC&URL_SECTION=201.html ("It is the understanding of the United Kingdom that military commanders and others responsible for planning, deciding upon, or executing attacks necessarily have to reach decisions on the basis of their assessment of the information from all sources which is reasonably available to them at the relevant time.").

63. The Trial Chamber adopted the "200-metre" standard in its impact analysis for the proportionality test, which was later rejected by the Appeals Chamber. *See* Prosecutor v. Gotovina, Case No. IT-06-90-T, Judgment (Int'l Crim. Trib. for the Former Yugoslavia Trial Chamber Apr. 15, 2011); Prosecutor v. Ante Gotovina, Case No. IT-06-90-A, Judgment (Int'l Crim. Trib. for the Former Yugoslavia Appeals Chamber Nov. 16 2012); *see also* Marko Milanovic, *The Gotovina Omnishambles*, EJIL: Talk! (Nov. 18, 2012), https://www.ejiltalk.org/the-gotovina-omnishambles; Jens David Ohlin, *Why the Gotovina Appeals Judgment Matters*, EJIL: Talk! (Dec. 21, 2012), https://www.ejiltalk.org/why-the-gotovina-appeals-judgment-matters.

64. *See, e.g.*, Ian Henderson & Kate Reece, *Proportionality Under International Humanitarian Law: The "Reasonable Military Commander" Standard and Reverberating Effects*, 51 Vand. J. Transnat'l L. 835 (2018).

65. *See, e.g.*, Int'l Crim. Trib. for former Yugoslavia, Final Report to the Prosecutor by the Committee Established to Review the NATO Bombing Campaign Against the

was proportionate it is necessary to examine whether a reasonably well-informed person in the circumstances of the actual perpetrator, making reasonable use of the information available to him or her, could have expected excessive civilian casualties to result from the attack."[66] The ICTY found that this standard in the proportionality test was not exclusive to AP I and that it was broadly applicable to both international and non-international armed conflicts as customary international law.[67]

D. The Compatibility of Fully AWS with the Existing Human-Centered Approach

It is hardly surprising that a human-centered approach to the LOAC has hitherto developed through the commander-centric treaty regimes, given that the full spectrum of military operations and activities has been conducted entirely by humans representing each belligerent party in an attributable manner since the beginning of recorded history. Yet, does that necessarily mean that the applicable LOAC rules must remain human-centered in all phases even in the future when fully AWS could be actually fielded by a party to armed conflict?

The crux of the issue is that, while continuously embedded in the conduct of hostilities by human belligerents as a means of warfare,[68] machines could replace humans as an independent decision maker in the specific phase of selecting and engaging targets. Even if there will be no human involvement in the firing loop, will it be appropriate and meaningful to keep applying the human-centered proportionality test requiring a subjective judgement as a matter of "common sense

Federal Republic of Yugoslavia ¶ 50 (June 13, 2000) ("It is unlikely that a human rights lawyer and an experienced combat commander would assign the same relative values to military advantage and to injury to noncombatants. Further, it is unlikely that military commanders with different doctrinal backgrounds and differing degrees of combat experience or national military histories would always agree in close cases. It is suggested that the determination of relative values must be that of the 'reasonable military commander.' Although there will be room for argument in close cases, there will be many cases where reasonable military commanders will agree that the injury to noncombatants or the damage to civilian objects was clearly disproportionate to the military advantage gained.").

66. Prosecutor v. Stanislav Galić, Case No. IT-98-29-T, Judgment & Opinion, ¶ 58 (Int'l Crim. Trib. for the Former Yugoslavia Dec. 5, 2003).

67. The ICTY, in the *Galić* case, noted that "[t]he jurisprudence of the Tribunal has already established that the principle of protection of civilians has evolved into a principle of customary international law applicable to all armed conflicts," *id.* ¶ 19, and, in the *Kupreškić* case, accentuated that "certain fundamental norms still serve to unambiguously outlaw such conduct (wide-spread and indiscriminate attacks against civilians), such as rules pertaining to proportionality," Prosecutor v. Kupreškić, Case No. IT-95-16, Judgment, ¶ 513 (Int'l Crim. Trib. for the Former Yugoslavia Jan. 14, 2000).

68. In contrast, there is also research that addresses the combatant privilege of fully AWS. *See, e.g.*, van den Boogaard, *supra* note 32.

and good faith for military commanders" to a fully-AWS attack? If so, what will be the reason for that? For the purpose of judging the legality of fully AWS, must we stick to such rules even though, as the advocates argue, fully AWS could have the potential to outperform humans in minimizing civilian casualties during attacks? Some claim that "respecting the human right to dignity means that killing capacity cannot be delegated to a machine; rather, the decision to take someone's life must remain with humans."[69] Is this claim based on the principle of human dignity as well as the assumption that only humans can achieve a humanitarian purpose of the LOAC? As pointed out in the introduction, those who contend that "[a] 'human-centred' approach must guide the identification of limits to autonomy in weapon systems and of possible options to address 'autonomous weapon systems of concern' "[70] would need to make a more convincing case for the proper regulation of fully AWS under the LOAC.

As Eric Talbot Jensen rightly asks, the problem to be highlighted here is this: "Is the law regulating armed conflict designed to provide the 'best protections possible' for victims of armed conflict or the 'best protections humanly possible?' "[71] No doubt fully AWS offer an opportunity to go back to the basics or to challenge such human-centered assumptions in the LOAC. Admittedly, some could still question, as a matter of "respecting the human right to dignity," "whether the principles of humanity and the dictates of public conscience allow life and death decisions to be taken by a machine with little or no human control."[72] However, it should be recalled that, as the Martens Clause enunciates, the humanitarian purpose of the LOAC consists in protecting "the inhabitants and belligerents," no more and no less. The ICTY similarly opined that "[t]he basic obligation to spare civilians and civilian objects as much as possible must guide the attacking party when considering the proportionality of an attack."[73]

A human-centered approach is nothing more than the traditional means to achieve that purpose. The reason that the LOAC has perennially focused on the role of experienced "reasonable military commanders" with "common sense

69. Int'l Comm. of the Red Cross, Summary Report of the ICRC Expert Meeting on "Autonomous weapon systems: technical, military, legal and humanitarian aspects," 26–28 March 2014, Geneva 16 (May 9, 2014).

70. *Towards Limits on Autonomy in Weapon Systems*, *supra* note 9.

71. Eric Talbot Jensen, *The Human Nature of International Humanitarian Law*, Humanitarian L. & Pol'y (Aug. 23, 2018), http://blogs.icrc.org/law-and-policy/2018/08/23/human-nature-international-humanitarian-law.

72. Int'l Comm. of the Red Cross, *supra* note 69, at 15.

73. Prosecutor v. Galić, IT-98-29-T, Judgement, ¶ 58 (Int'l Crim. Trib. for the Former Yugoslavia Trial Chamber Dec. 5, 2003). It relies on the ICRC's commentary that "the disproportion between losses and damages caused and the military advantages anticipated raises a delicate problem; in some situations there will be no room for doubt, while in other situations there may be reason for hesitation. In such situations, the interests of the civilian population should prevail." AP Commentary, *supra* note 27, ¶ 1979.

and good faith" is that it has self-evidently been the best approach for protecting civilians and civilian objects during the conduct of hostilities. But now, in the dawn of a new AI era, such a framework might need to be overhauled by reason of the introduction of highly sophisticated fully AWS, provided, of course, that they were to exhibit the potential to provide the "best protections possible." Although worthy of consideration, there seems to be no longer an unquestionable necessity to cling to a human-centered approach in the LOAC on the assumption that the protection of civilians and belligerents is best achieved by humans. Indeed, it remains an open question whether and to what extent machines need to be subject to human control in the targeting decision process[74] insofar as they could exceed humans in accomplishing the purpose of the LOAC.

Admittedly, the existing human-centered proportionality test requiring subjective, "common sense and good faith" calculations could be ill-suited to the case of a fully-AWS attack. Yet this does not necessarily mean that those systems would be unethical and dehumanizing as long as they could nevertheless contribute to the best protection of the victims of armed conflict. On the contrary, subjugating machines to rules for humans—rules devised with human cognitive flaws and emotion tendencies in mind—may rather vitiate the humanitarian potential of fully AWS. Instead, away from the existing commander-centric perspective, a new special approach to the law of targeting dedicated to computer learning algorithms in line with the actual process of machine decision-making might better guide the identification of more proper regulation of fully AWS, whereby its potential for the best protection is maximized. At minimum, and in view of the fact that the existing human-centered paradigm is merely a product of the history of LOAC and does not exist a priori, an alternative approach to adjust to changing times and circumstances should be explored.

IV. A COMPUTER-CENTERED APPROACH TO THE PROPORTIONALITY TEST

A. Principles, Rules, and Standards: What Will Change and What Will Stay the Same?

What then might such a computer-centered approach look like? For the sake of clarity, in what follows, the question will be dealt with in line with the existing principles, rules, and standards in international law.

74. It goes without saying that the question should be dealt with in combination with the scope of the targeting decision-making process, which could refer to "the critical processes (target selection and engagement) that weapons carry out autonomously (the narrow loop) as well as to the wider targeting process in which humans play a decisive role (the wider loop)." The wider loop could cover a series of processes prior to the narrow loop that include formulating objectives, selecting targets and weapons, planning implementation, and anticipating consequences for the civilian population. *See* ADVISORY COMM. ON ISSUES OF PUB. INT'L L., *supra* note 26, at 9.

According to Rüdiger Wolfrum, a legal principle—as distinct from a "metalegal principle" in a philosophical or ethical discourse—is understood as "a binding legal statement which describes obligations of conduct or obligations to achieve an objective."[75] It is of abstract nature, in contrast with a rule that is, albeit still abstract to some degree, more concrete and "ready for direct application" of an obligation.[76] Yet, due to their abstractness, principles are "open to the influence of new developments or legal trends, and thus they are a mechanism for the progressive development of international law."[77] Further, they could "serve as mechanisms to bridge different legal regimes and thus counterbalance the fragmentation of international law."[78] In the same vein, the extant principles of the LOAC continue to form the foundation and driving force for the development of the proposed approach to the proportionality test tailored to fully AWS.[79]

There are no LOAC provisions specifically dealing with AWS or computer decision-making processes. Nevertheless, there is no legal vacuum on the issue by virtue of the Martens Clause[80] to the extent that it matters in the context of armed conflict, meaning that "the principles of international law derived from established custom, from the principles of humanity and from the dictates of public conscience" govern "all forms of warfare and to all kinds of weapons, those of the past, those of the present and those of the future."[81] Besides, the extant customary LOAC principles of distinction, proportionality, and precautions in attack must remain at the core of the proposed approach all the more because this chapter does not deviate from traditional settings of armed conflict in which weapons

75. Rüdiger Wolfrum, *General International Law (Principles, Rules, and Standards)*, ¶ 6, Max Planck Encyclopedia of Public International Law (last updated Dec. 2010), http://opil.ouplaw.com/view/10.1093/law:epil/9780199231690/law-9780199231690-e1408.

76. *Id.* at ¶¶ 6, 65. Not surprisingly, it does not mean that all "rules" of international law are ready for direct application. *See* Yuji Iwasawa, *Domestic Application of International Law*, 378 Recueil des Cours: Collected Courses of The Hague Acad. Int'l L. 9 (2016).

77. Wolfrum, *supra* note 75, ¶ 60.

78. *Id.* ¶ 63.

79. *See, e.g.*, 2004 U.K. Manual, *supra* note 44, ¶ 2.1 ("Despite the codification of much customary law into treaty form during the last one hundred years, four fundamental principles still underlie the law of armed conflict. These are military necessity, humanity, distinction, and proportionality."). Geoffrey S. Corn et al. define the five fundamental LOAC principles as follows: (1) Military necessity as the first principle of authority; (2) Humanity: the first principle of restraint; (3) Distinction: the essential requirement for lawful targeting; (4) Proportionality: the balancing principle; (5) Precautions: the precondition for all combat operations. Corn et al., *supra* note 39, at 46–61.

80. The Martens Clause "has proved to be an effective means of addressing the rapid evolution of military technology." *Nuclear Weapons* case, *supra* note 12, ¶ 78.

81. *Id.* ¶ 86.

are used by human belligerents for the conduct of hostilities causing collateral damage to civilians and civilian objects.[82]

Those three principles are interconnected and overlap in the law of targeting as a subset of the LOAC. While the proportionality test rests on well-established categories of military targets, civilians, and civilian objects, its implementation is ensured by the requirement of constant care and all feasible precautionary measures taken by a party to armed conflict. Hence, in proposing a computer-centered approach to the proportionality test, one must duly account for the well-established principles of distinction and precautions. In particular, the following customary rules deriving from the principle of distinction would remain relevant to the proposed approach:[83] (1) combatants in international armed conflict as well as members of state and dissident armed forces and other organized armed groups in non-international armed conflict are constantly targetable during armed conflict, unless they are hors de combat; (2) civilians are immune from direct attack unless and for such times as they take a direct part in hostilities;[84] (3) attacks must not be directed at civilian objects; (4) civilian objects are all objects other than military objectives, which, in so far as objects are concerned, are defined as

82. *See also* William H. Boothby, The Law of Targeting 563–64 (2012).

83. In contrast, certain LOAC rules about which their customary status is controversial, such as the principle of presumption of civilian character in case of doubt should be dealt with carefully. As to its customary status, *see* Customary IHL Study, *supra* note 14, r. 6 at 23–24, r. 10, at 35–36. Yet, the United States is of the opinion that "[u]nder customary international law, no legal presumption of civilian status exists for persons or objects." U.S. Law of War Manual, *supra* note 45, ¶ 5.4.3.2; *see also* AP I, *supra* note 12, arts. 50(1), 52(3); Protocol on Prohibitions or Restriction on the Use of Mines, Booby-Traps and Other Devices as Amended on 3 May 1996 (Protocol II as Amended on 3 May 1996) Annexed to the Convention on Prohibitions or Restrictions on the Use of Certain Conventional Weapons Which May Be Deemed to Be Excessively Injurious or to Have Indiscriminate Effects art. 3(8)(a), May 3, 1996, 2048 U.N.T.S. 93, 35 I.L.M. 1206 [hereinafter Amended Protocol II].

84. AP I, *supra* note 12, art. 51(3); *see also* GC I, *supra* note 53, art. 3; Protocol Additional to the Geneva Conventions of August 12, 1949, and Relating to the Protection of Victims of Non-international Armed Conflicts (Protocol II) art. 13(3), June 8, 1977, 1125 U.N.T.S. 609. The United States opines that "[a]lthough, as drafted, Article 51(3) of AP I does not reflect customary international law, the United States supports the customary principle on which Article 51(3) is based." U.S. Law of War Manual, *supra* note 45, ¶ 5.8.1.2. Yet it accepts the notion of direct participation of hostilities by civilians—as distinct from that of engagement in hostilities by private persons that comes into play primarily in the context of unlawful/unprivileged belligerency—only in the context of the forfeiture of civilian protection against direct attack. *See id.* ¶¶ 4.18.1, 5.8.1. There is a controversy regarding what it means to be a civilian taking direct part in hostilities and how long that civilian is deprived of protected status from direct attack. *See, e.g.*, Interpretive Guidance, *supra* note 28. It offers three cumulative criteria of threshold of harm, direct causation, and belligerent nexus. *See generally Forum: Direct Participation in Hostilities: Perspectives on the ICRC Interpretive Guidance*, 42 N.Y.U. J. Int'l L. & Pol. 637 (2010). For the views of the United States, *see* U.S. Law of War Manual, *supra* note 45, ¶ 5.8.

"those objects which by their nature, location, purpose or use make an effective contribution to military action and whose total or partial destruction, capture or neutralization, in the circumstances ruling at the time, offers a definite military advantage."[85] Rules on the criteria for comparison in the proposed approach to the proportionality test would also be identical to customary ones enshrined in AP I, namely, "incidental loss of civilian life, injury to civilians, damage to civilian objects, or a combination thereof" on the one hand, and "the concrete and direct military advantage anticipated" on the other hand. The same would go for the feasibility rule in the principle of precautions that hinges on practicability.[86] All these basic principles and rules under the LOAC thus stay the same.

What needs to be changed for the proposed computer-centered approach rather consists in a standard for the proportionality test. A standard is "a reference" to principles and rules of international law, allowing "a wide margin of interpretation."[87] As such, it is not binding in itself, but it functions as "a mechanism to develop international legal regimes progressively without necessarily having to formally amend the relevant international agreements."[88] It could therefore play a significant role in advancing the proposed approach. The principle of proportionality in modern LOAC has developed through the "reasonable military commander" standard. However, it is not intrinsically tied to, or at least not limited to, the judgment of military commanders. It could be subject to adaptation in its application to a given circumstance by way of legal standards reflecting the sophisticated characteristics of fully AWS.

85. It is reflected not only in Article 52(1) and 52(2) of AP I, to which some states like the United States and Israel are not parties, but also CCW Amended Protocol II on Mines, Booby-Traps and Other Devices, Articles 2(6) and 2(7) and CCW Protocol III on Incendiary Weapons Articles 1(3) and (4), to which the United States is a contracting party. Israel is also a party to CCW Amended Protocol II.

86. Protocol on Prohibitions or Restrictions on the Use of Incendiary Weapons (Protocol III) Annexed to the Convention on Prohibitions or Restrictions on the Use of Certain Conventional Weapons Which May Be Deemed to Be Excessively Injurious or to Have Indiscriminate Effects art. 1(5), Oct. 10, 1980, 1342 U.N.T.S. 137; Amended Protocol II, *supra* note 83, art. 3(10); Protocol on Explosive Remnants of War to the Convention on Prohibitions or Restrictions on the Use of Certain Conventional Weapons Which May Be Deemed to Be Excessively Injurious or to Have Indiscriminate Effects (Protocol V) art. 5(1), Nov. 28, 2003, 2399 U.N.T.S. 100 ("'feasible precautions' are those precautions which are practicable or practically possible taking into account all circumstances ruling at the time, including humanitarian and military considerations"); *see also* U.S. Law of War Manual, *supra* note 45, ¶ 5.2.3.

87. Wolfrum, *supra* note 75, ¶ 108.

88. *Id.* ¶ 60; *see also id.* ¶ 124 ("The problem international relations face in respect of international treaties is that they cannot be modified easily since they are static and are not prone to a progressive development of international law. This lacuna is to some extent ameliorated through the development of standards, the possibility of supplementing treaties through meeting of States Parties, and by the development of principles.").

B. Setting New Standards

1. Special Regime to Avoid Cross-fertilization

However, care must be taken in setting a computer-centered proportionality standard. It needs to be done in a way that differs from the human-centered standard.[89] More to the point, to ensure that fully AWS constantly outperform humans in the protection of civilians, notably through discerning with considerable accuracy who is to be protected from direct attack and excessive collateral damage,[90] relevant standards for such systems would have to be relatively stringent. In particular, such standards must be stringent in terms of quantifiable certainty and predictability relative to those that apply to humans, in view of the high-performance ability of AWS.[91] This is especially so given that AWS, unlike human soldiers on the battlefield, could "operate without existential risk to themselves."[92] The LOAC cannot go so far as to strictly demand that human soldiers protect civilians at the sacrifice of their own lives. Machines, however, may be

89. *See* Schmitt & Thurner, *supra* note 29, at 266 ("An autonomous engagement must be conceptualized somewhat differently than one controlled by a human when considering the issue of subjectivity, but it can still meet the requirements of the law.").

90. On this point, it is remarkable that the U.S. Defense Advanced Research Projects Agency (DARPA) is currently developing predictive algorithm that enables machines to determine an adversary's intentions and what the adversary is trying to do. For more details, *see, e.g.*, Ashley Deeks, *Predicting Enemies: Military Use of Predictive Algorithm*, Lawfare (Apr. 10, 2018), https://www.lawfareblog.com/predicting-enemies-military-use-predictive-algorithms.

91. Christof Heyns, *Increasingly Autonomous Weapon Systems: Accountability and Responsibility*, *in* Int'l Comm. of the Red Cross, Autonomous Weapon Systems: Technical, Military, Legal and Humanitarian Aspects 45, 47 (2014) ("[W]hile autonomous weapons systems cannot be required to be perfect, they will in practice be held to standards that are significantly higher than those posed for humans."); Geoffrey S. Corn, *Autonomous Weapons Systems: Managing the Inevitably of "Taking the Man Out of the Loop," in* Autonomous Weapons Systems, *supra* note 31, at 209, 231–32 ("[A]n AWS developed as a substitute for human soldiers engaged in close combat will certainly require a capacity to engage in split-second distinction judgments but not necessarily in sophisticated proportionality balancing. . . . [T]here is no reason to demand more from the autonomous weapon than is demanded of the human soldier. . . . [T]here is no compelling justification for subjecting these systems to a use-of-force regime more restrictive than that imposed on human soldiers.").

92. Robin Geiss, The International-Law Dimension of Autonomous Weapons Systems 17 (Oct. 2015), http://library.fes.de/pdf-files/id/ipa/11673.pdf ("[O]ne can conclude that such systems—if at all—should have to satisfy a much higher standard. . . . [A] legal duty could be established for the developers of autonomous weapons systems to program them in such a way that they use force only in the case of unequivocally aggressive and offensive behavior on the part of enemy combatants/fighters. In situations, by contrast, that are not clear-cut in this respect, such systems would have to refrain from the use of lethal force even if human soldiers in an identical situation would be permitted to reach for their weapons. Because autonomous systems can operate without existential risk to themselves it appears entirely reasonable—at least in scenarios in which such systems encounter human beings directly—to require a significantly longer delay and to hold them to a higher legal standard of protection.").

exposed to the risk of destruction, thereby creating more opportunities for saving innocent civilians.

At the same time, it would also be necessary to ensure that such higher proportionality standards would not negatively affect the existing human-centered standards. Some experts are actually concerned that "the higher certainty-based standard applied to autonomous systems will steadily bleed over into the analysis of decisions and attacks by human actors, changing the foundational standard of objectively reasonable into one based on certainty at the time of decision or, more likely, on actually being correct."[93] As they argue, it eventually "would require commanders to operate with a standard that allows for no errors."[94] In order to eschew this possibility, any computer-centered proportionality standards would need to be systematized as a new special or sui generis regime distinct from the existing general (or another special) human-centered regime on the proportionality principle.

It goes without saying that both proportionality standards would share common foundational principles of military necessity and humanity as well as distinction, proportionality, and precautions.[95] Yet, the proportionality standards for military commanders and fully AWS would have to be separately construed and articulated to avoid confusion between the two. The fundamental difference between humans and machines—notably, that humans have minds of their own and machines merely operate as they are programmed to—must be reflected in the applicable standards.

2. Standardized Learning Algorithms and Accessibility of Big Data

Within such a special computer-centered regime, the rigid regulatory standards for proportionality calculations would be implemented and applied through algorithmic parameters. An algorithm is a step-by-step sequence of unambiguous instructions to solve a problem by using a computer-coded program, which in turn is an operating system to implement specific algorithms. Whereas algorithms with clear applications and more rigorous performance could be a strong point for fully AWS, "some of these algorithms—especially those capable of 'self-learning' and whose 'choices' might be difficult for humans to anticipate or unpack—seem to challenge fundamental and interrelated concepts that underpin international

93. Laurie R. Blank, *New Technologies and the Interplay Between Certainty and Reasonableness, in* Complex Battlespaces: The Law of Armed Conflict and the Dynamics of Modern Warfare 339 (Christopher M. Ford & Winston Williams eds., 2018) [hereinafter Complex Battlespaces].

94. *Id.* at 340.

95. *See, e.g.*, Bruno Simma & Dirk Pulkowski, *Of Planets and the Universe: Self-Contained Regimes in International Law*, 17 Eur. J. Int'l L. 483, 491 (2006); Report of the Study Group of the International Law Commission, Fragmentation of International Law: Difficulties Arising from the Diversification and Expansion of International Law, U.N. Doc. A/CN.4/L.682 (Apr. 13, 2006).

law pertaining to armed conflict and related accountability frameworks."[96] The advent of "Explainable AI" is expected to cut down this problem considerably,[97] but to help further reduce the risk of uncertainty and unpredictability in machine decision-making for the value judgment in the proportionality test,[98] it could be an option to standardize and optimize auditable underlying algorithms through quality assurance by an independent, international certification body composed of AI and data scientists as well as of military and legal experts.

It should also be borne in mind that the performance of fully AWS would depend on the existence of sufficient data for their learning. The more complicated a problem becomes, the more data an algorithm needs to be able to make a decision to solve it.[99] As already noted, the proportionality test concerns the most complex and context-driven problems and situations in the LOAC. That means that, together with future generation computer systems such as quantum computing, "big data"—extremely large data sets—would be vital to the high performance of fully AWS to the extent that they could robustly satisfy such rigid special algorithmic standards.[100] Care must also be taken to avoid human biases in collecting those

96. Dustin A. Lewis, Gabriella Blum, & Naz K. Modirzadeh, War-Algorithm Accountability 10 (2016), http://blogs.harvard.edu/pilac/files/2016/09/War-Algorithm-Accountability-Without-Appendices-August-2016.pdf.

97. DARPA is now developing AI systems' explanatory capabilities on their behavior, which could "list critical factors that influenced the analysis or produce visual displays that pinpoint determinative features from the raw data used to make a decision." For more details, *see, e.g.*, Natalie Salmanowitz, *Explainable AI and the Legality of Autonomous Weapon Systems*, Lawfare (Nov. 21, 2018), https://www.lawfareblog.com/explainable-ai-and-legality-autonomous-weapon-systems.

98. On the issue of human control over AWS, Schuller contends that the critical issue is not about human intervention in the targeting decision-making loop, but "whether designers have granted the machine some combination of tasks that *functionally* delegates the decision to kill from human to machine." Schuller, *supra* note 7, at 393. Using the Boyd Cycle/OODA Loop, he dissects the technological aspect of autonomy and suggests that the predictability of machines by humans to a reasonable certainty in LOAC compliance is the key yardstick against which human control over AWS should be measured. According to Schuller, "If we can reasonably predict compliance, then we maintain control no matter the level or type of our interaction with the machine at the instant of lethal action. But if we cannot reasonably predict whether the machine will comply with IHL, it may be unlawfully autonomous." *Id.* at 409; *see also id.* at 390–413.

99. *See, e.g.*, Jim Baker, *President Trump's Executive Order on Artificial Intelligence*, Lawfare (Feb. 28, 2019), https://www.lawfareblog.com/president-trumps-executive-order-artificial-intelligence ("AI algorithms learn from having access to relevant data. The more data made accessible, the more learning can occur. Exactly how all of this learning happens is complex and messy, and real success is hard to achieve. But the point is that in order to improve our AI systems, we need to provide developers with lawful access to large datasets.").

100. *See, e.g.*, Stuart Russell & Peter Norvig, Artificial Intelligence: A Modern Approach ¶ 1.3.10 (3d ed. 2010).

data sets.[101] Thus, developing and ensuring standardized learning algorithms, unbiased data access, and data-sharing mechanisms at an international level would be imperative for fully AWS to maintain legally compliant responses to complicated and shifting scenarios.

Not surprisingly, however, any attempt to set these regulatory standards must account for the interests in national security secrecy of each state. As the negotiating history of an effort in the U.N. Cyber Group of Government Experts to create an international cybersecurity regime suggests, one could easily imagine that states would be unwilling to share any information closely associated with their operational secrecy. That said, leaving a machine's decision-making process in a black box would never convince the international community of the consistent compliance of a fully-AWS attack with the proportionality test and other relevant LOAC rules. In view of this, one could suggest that pioneering like-minded states initiate a dialogue among themselves to find out what levels of information could be shared and with whom. Another practical option may be for the International Committee of the Red Cross to take an initiative in formulating, implementing, and strengthening the proposed international regulatory standards and mechanisms, including establishing the said quality certification body, to take full advantage not only of its professional experience in the practice of international humanitarian law but also of its neutral, impartial, and independent character.

C. Weapons Review as a Major Accountability Mechanism and a Pivotal Form of Human Control

Finally, mention should be made of who would be accountable for proportionality calculations conducted by fully AWS under a future computer-centered standard. Accountability is one of the most heated issue in AWS debates.[102] Yet, as far as fully AWS are concerned, it seems dubious to what extent the legal framework of individual criminal responsibility would work effectively, given AWS' defining capability of engaging in targeting decision-making free of human involvement.

101. *See* Richard Socher, *AI Isn't Dangerous, But Human Bias Is*, World Economic Forum (Jan. 17, 2019), https://www.weforum.org/agenda/2019/01/ai-isn-t-dangerous-but-human-bias-is ("AI is not sentient but merely a tool and therefore morally neutral . . . . One way that AI can cause harm is when algorithms reflect our human biases in the datasets that organizations collect. The effects of these biases can compound in the AI era, as the algorithms themselves continue to 'learn' from the data. . . . AI bias isn't the result of the technology being flawed. Algorithms don't become biased on their own—they learn that from us. So we have to take responsibility for helping to avoid any negative effects spawned from the AI systems that we've created.").

102. *See, e.g.*, Hum. Rts. Watch, Mind the Gap: The Lack of Accountability for Killer Robots (2015), https://www.hrw.org/sites/default/files/reports/arms0415_ForUpload_0.pdf.

Under current international criminal law, the commission of a war crime generally requires intent (mens rea).[103] Yet, what matters here is that, unlike other weapons systems equipped with computers that are less independent, fully AWS could by definition make decisions that humans did not intend. In such a case, it may be inappropriate to identify human criminal intent.[104] This, however, may not exclude commander responsibility for negligence or culpable failure to prevent LOAC violations by fully AWS in the decision to deploy them,[105] despite the fact that the Rome Statute at least does not foresee such responsibility except in the case of command responsibility for the conduct of subordinates.[106] Unless the existing mental standard for the commission of war crimes is lowered so that, for example, designers and programmers may be liable in cases of a failure to exercise due diligence or even to the point of strict liability, the current criminal

103. *See, e.g.*, Rome Statute, *supra* note 60, art. 30 ("[A] person shall be criminally responsible and liable for punishment for a crime within the jurisdiction of the Court only if the material elements are committed with intent and knowledge.").

104. On the other hand, some research has attempted to reflect more deeply about whether AWS qualify as moral agents to be held accountable for their own violations of LOAC through machine punishment, while separating the issue of criminal responsibility of military commanders for those AWS' violations. *See* Jens David Ohlin, *The Combatant's Stance: Autonomous Weapons on the Battlefield*, 92 Int'l L. Stud 1 (2016).

105. *See* DoD Directive 3000.09, *supra* note 2, at 3 ("Persons who authorize the use of, direct the use of, or operate autonomous and semiautonomous weapon systems must do so with appropriate care and in accordance with the law of war, applicable treaties, weapon system safety rules, and applicable rules of engagement (ROE)."); *see also* Anderson et al., *supra* note 15, at 405–406; Schmitt & Thurnher, *supra* note 29, at 257.

106. Some might further argue that, depending on the circumstances of how the notion of command is formulated, such commanders' responsibility comes into play even in the context of fully AWS by the command responsibility doctrine which is currently meant for the human relationship between superiors and subordinates. *See* Nikolas Stürchler & Michael Siegrist, *A "Compliance-Based" Approach to Autonomous Weapon Systems*, EJIL: Talk! (Dec. 1, 2017), https://www.ejiltalk.org/a-compliance-based-approach-to-autonomous-weapon-systems ("Conceptually, command responsibility does not entail the commander's direct criminal responsibility for crimes committed by his subordinates, but for his or her culpable failure to prevent, suppress or repress crimes committed by persons (i.e. not machines) under his or her command and control. Strictly speaking, therefore, a commander's failure to duly control autonomous weapon systems operating under his command is not a case of command responsibility within the contemporary understanding of this concept, but may constitute a direct violation of the duties of precaution, distinction, proportionality or any other obligation imposed by IHL. This does not exclude that, as the functions of human soldiers are increasingly 'delegated' to autonomous weapon systems, it may become appropriate *de lege ferenda* to extend the commander's supervisory duty, *mutatis mutandis* and *by analogy*, also to autonomous weapon systems operating under his direct command and control."). *See also* Peter Margulies, *Making Autonomous Weapons Accountable: Command Responsibility for Computer-Guided Lethal Force in Armed Conflicts*, *in* Research Handbook on Remote Warfare 405 (Jens David Ohlin ed., 2017).

law framework would not capture alleged LOAC violations "committed" by, or deriving from, fully AWS. To move the issue forward, it is imperative to clarify fully AWS' assigned internal authorities and responsibilities in accordance with their status in relation to a party to armed conflict. As part of this effort, it would be realistic to start with focusing on states' duty to ensure respect for LOAC, notably, by way of strengthening the weapons review mechanism for such systems.[107]

AP I provides that a contracting party is obligated to "determine whether its employment would, in some or all circumstances, be prohibited by this Protocol or by any other rule of international law applicable" to the party "in the study, development, acquisition or adoption of a new weapon, means or method of warfare."[108] The United States and Israel are not state parties to AP I, but both countries have utilized their own weapons review mechanism to ensure compliance with the LOAC,[109] even if they do not believe such an obligation exists as a matter of customary international law.[110]

Since AP I–type weapons reviews are conducted by states prior to the employment of new weapons, they might not in themselves be suited to assessing the legality of an ongoing attack through fully AWS in specific circumstances.[111] But it is worth noting that debriefs and reviews of such attacks by belligerent parties could also be characterized as a proper implementation of the constant care obligation

107. *See* Advisory Comm. on Issues of Pub. Int'l L., *supra* note 26, at 31 ("The duty of care plays a key role in state responsibility. States are obliged to take adequate steps to ensure that the deployment of autonomous weapons does not lead to potential or actual violations of international law. For example, they are obliged to make sure that such weapons are procured from reliable producers, that they are adequately tested prior to use and that commanders receive sufficient training and information on the functioning and risks of autonomous weapons."); Marco Sassóli, *Autonomous Weapons and International Humanitarian Law: Advantages, Open Technical Questions and Legal Issues to be Clarified*, 90 Int'l L. Stud. 308, 324 (2014) ("Based on their Protocol I, Article 36 assessment, States deploying robots must give military commanders and operators clear instructions as to when and under what circumstances the robots may be actually be used. . . . As for the manufacturer, domestic criminal laws often hold criminally responsible those who deliberately, recklessly or negligently construct defective buildings or machines that lead to the loss of human life.").

108. AP I, *supra* note 12, art. 36.

109. *See, e.g.*, U.S. Law of War Manual, *supra* note 45, ¶ 19.20.1.2; Anderson et al., *supra* note 15. In the AWS context, *see also* Michael W. Meier, *Lethal Autonomous Weapons Systems: Is It the End of the World as We Know It . . . Or Will We Be Just Fine?*, *in* Complex Battlespaces, *supra* note 93, at 289.

110. There is a controversy as to the customary status of the weapons review obligation. *See* Natalia Jevglevskaja, *Weapons Review Obligation Under Customary International Law*, 94 Int'l L. Stud. 186 (2018).

111. *See* Schmitt & Thurnher, *supra* note 29, at 276.

in the precautions principle during armed conflict,[112] which is of utmost importance in advancing AWS' machine learning for subsequent deployments, which would strengthen respect for the LOAC. Combined with the future development of the above-mentioned "Explainable AI" that enables states to better assess the reliability of fully AWS as well as their contours and limits,[113] weapons reviews could therefore be the most conceivable and effective mechanism in ensuring state and human control over fully AWS at all phases outside the firing loop.[114] As such, they would be expected to function as the primary accountability and compliance mechanism for the proposed algorithmic regulatory standards. One could see how a human-centered paradigm thus could continue to be relevant in regulating fully AWS, although in a different manner from the existing commander-centric treaty regimes.

V. CONCLUSION

One of the implications of fully AWS as independent decision makers in the targeting process is that a human-centered paradigm should not be considered the only potential means to ensure adherence to the foundational principles underlying the LOAC. Instead, the emergence of technology that makes use of fully AWS possible should in turn lead to a LOAC debate in which an alternative to the human-centered paradigm is not considered taboo. This is all the more true because the "principle of human dignity" does not offer convincing reasons for rejecting upfront any such alternative in international legal discourse. Furthermore, the history of the LOAC tells us that the existing human-centered approach to the proportionality test—the commander-centric approach—although vigorously supported by states and developed in international criminal jurisprudence (especially since the end of World War II), is nothing more than a product of the time. So long as fully AWS exhibit the potential for better contribution to the LOAC goals to protect the victims of armed conflict than human

112. *See, e.g.*, Int'l L. Ass'n Stud. Group on the Conduct of Hostilities in the 21st Century, *The Conduct of Hostilities and International Humanitarian Law: Challenges of 21st Century Warfare*, 93 Int'l L. Stud. 322, 381 (2017) ("The obligation to take constant care is best understood as an obligation of conduct, i.e., a positive and continuous obligation aimed at risk mitigation and harm prevention and the fulfillment of which requires the exercise of due diligence.").

113. *See* Salmanowitz, *supra* note 97.

114. *See also* Anderson et al., *supra* note 15, at 406–407 (Autonomous systems "are subject to the customary law requirements of legal review of weapons."). In addition, the proposition by Nehal Bhuta and Stavros-Evdokimos Pantazopoulos is very insightful in advancing the mechanism of weapons reviews. They argue that behavioral uncertainty problems of AWS can be "productively addressed" through international legal framework pertaining to the risk of environmental harm deriving from (ultra-)hazardous technological activities, combined with the establishment of international group of experts and states. Nehal Bhuta & Stavros-Evdokimos Pantazopoulos, *Autonomy and Uncertainty: Increasingly Autonomous Weapons Systems and the International Legal Regulation of Risk*, *in* Autonomous Weapons Systems, *supra* note 31, at 284.

soldiers, it is worth exploring an alternative computer-centered approach to the law of targeting tailored to the defining characteristics of fully AWS in a manner to maximize their potential as well as to make the law more responsive to the needs of ever-changing battlespaces.

Assuming that machines remain a means of urban warfare implemented by belligerent parties led by and made up of humans, the proposed computer-centered approach should focus on standards for proportionality calculations, while maintaining the well-established principles and rules on distinction, proportionality, and precautions in the law of targeting. In doing so, given the potential high-performance of fully AWS in complex battlespaces and context-driven rule compliance, the proportionality standards in the proposed approach must be more stringent, but without prejudice to the integrity of the existing commander-centric standard wherever a human makes the targeting decision. To that end, any new computer-centered standard would need to take the form of a special legal regime, clearly distinct from the existing human-centered regime under the LOAC. The new standard must also be based on standardized, auditable algorithms in an operational environment in which big data access and sharing mechanisms are ensured at the international level. This is vital to ensure that all fully AWS used by belligerent parties in armed conflict can constantly provide a legally compliant response to complicated and shifting scenarios in the battlespace. Finally, weapons reviews are expected to play a primary role not only as a major accountability mechanism but also as a pivotal form of human control over fully AWS in underpinning the proposed special LOAC regime.

The proposed computer-centered approach to the proportionality test thus questions the absoluteness of the existing human-centered paradigm in the LOAC. However, this does not mean that the proposed approach denies the importance of the role of humans in the regulation of fully AWS. In this regard, it must be highlighted that even this chapter putting forward a proposal toward the special computer law of targeting envisions the involvement of humans at various stages, such as the establishment and application of a quality assurance mechanism for standardized, auditable algorithms by establishing an independent, international certification body, and of a weapons review mechanism to be implemented by all armed conflict parties.

These considerations are submitted as food for thought for ongoing efforts to develop the best interpretive guidance on the regulation of fully AWS under the LOAC. More sober and healthy reflections are needed on the issue, particularly under the circumstances in which such weapons systems have not yet come into existence. Thinkers must move past the realm of science fiction and develop practical and achievable ways of regulating this new technology.

PART FIVE

Jus Post Bellum

14

The Duty to Pay Reparations for the Violation of the Prohibition of the Use of Force in International Relations and the *Jus Post Bellum*

ELISABETH GÜNNEWIG*

I. INTRODUCTION

> [T]he standard of justice depends on the equality of power to compel . . . : the strong do what they have the power to do and the weak accept what they have to accept.[1]

This quote by the Greek historian Thucydides around 500 BC in his work on the Peleponnesian War captured the essence of "law" and "war" in the following centuries. Despite all philosophical theories of *just war*, the practice related to war was best described as a reflection of the "law of the jungle." This is true with respect to the decision to go to war, conduct during the war, as well as the ending of the war and its aftermath. Beginning from the mid-nineteenth century, however,

* This chapter draws on and follows the author's doctoral thesis. *See* Elisabeth Günnewig, *Schadensersatz wegen der Verletzung des Gewaltverbotes als Element eines ius post bellum*, 11 COLOGNE STUD. INT'L PEACE & SECURITY L. (2019). The author wishes to thank Professor Claus Kreß not only for his most valuable comments on an earlier draft of this chapter but also for his invaluable input while supervising the completion of the thesis. The author would also like to express her gratitude to Dr. Wenke Brückner, Mehrnusch Anssari, and Dr. Erin Pobje for their edits and written comments on an initial draft of this chapter.

1. JOHN TORPEY, POLITICS AND THE PAST: ON REPAIRING HISTORICAL INJUSTICES 2 (2003).

Elisabeth Günnewig, *The Duty to Pay Reparations for the Violation of the Prohibition of the Use of Force in International Relations and the* Jus Post Bellum In: *Necessity and Proportionality in International Peace and Security Law.*
Edited by: Professor Claus Kreß and Captain Robert Lawless, Oxford University Press (2021). © Oxford University Press.
DOI: 10.1093/oso/9780197537374.003.0015.

increasingly important steps were taken toward the formulation of modern international peace and security law. This development started with regard to the conduct during war. Subsequently, the right to resort to war itself was progressively curtailed, a development which culminated after the Second World War in the codification of the prohibition of the use of force in international relations in Article 2(4) of the U.N. Charter. As a result, modern international peace and security law rests on two main pillars: the prohibition of the use of force as well as its exceptions (*jus ad bellum* or *jus contra bellum*) and the law of armed conflict governing the conduct of the opposing parties during the hostilities (*jus in bello*). During the twentieth century, both areas of law are covered by important international treaties, all of them largely reflective of customary international law—the former area, after more timid earlier steps, most prominently by the U.N. Charter and the latter by the Hague Conventions[2] as well as the four Geneva Conventions[3] and Additional Protocols.[4]

This current system of international peace and security law is the result of the classic conception of war and peace as two mutually exclusive states of affairs. Throughout history, war and peace have been understood as a dichotomy. As a consequence, different rules of international law were exclusively applied during peace time or exclusively during a state of war.[5] This dichotomy is grounded in the negative concept of peace as the absence of war (*absentia belli*), which was

2. *E.g.*, Convention (IV) Respecting the Laws and Customs of War on Land and Its Annex: Regulations Concerning the Laws and Customs of War on Land, Oct. 18, 1907, 36 Stat. 2227, T.S. No. 539 [hereinafter Convention IV].

3. Geneva Convention for the Amelioration of the Condition of the Wounded and Sick in Armed Forces in the Field, Aug. 12, 1949, 6 U.S.T. 3114, 75 U.N.T.S. 31; Geneva Convention for the Amelioration of the Condition of Wounded, Sick and Shipwrecked Members of Armed Forces at Sea, Aug. 12, 1949, 6 U.S.T. 3217, 75 U.N.T.S. 85; Geneva Convention Relative to the Treatment of Prisoners of War, Aug. 12, 1949, 6 U.S.T. 3316, 75 U.N.T.S. 135; Geneva Convention Relative to the Protection of Civilians Persons in Time of War, Aug. 12, 1949, 6 U.S.T. 3516, 75 U.N.T.S. 287.

4. Protocol Additional to the Geneva Conventions of 12 August 1949, and Relating to the Protection of Victims of International Armed Conflict (Protocol I), June 8, 1977, 1125 U.N.T.S. 3 [hereinafter AP I]; Protocol Additional to the Geneva Conventions of 12 August 1949, and Relating to the Protection of Victims of Non-International Armed Conflict (Protocol II), June 8, 1977, 1125 U.N.T.S. 609; Protocol Additional to the Geneva Conventions of 12 August 1949, and Relating to the Adoption of Additional Distinctive Emblem (Protocol III), Dec. 8, 2005, 2404 U.N.T.S. 261.

5. This classic conception of war and peace as two separate concepts in international law is illustrated by the structure of Oppenheim's authoritative discourse about international law, which analyzes rules of international law in two separate volumes, one for peace and one for war. *See* 1 Lassa Oppenheim, Oppenheim's International Law: Peace (Hersch Lauterpacht ed., 8th ed. 1955); 2 Lassa Oppenheim, Oppenheim's International Law: Disputes, War and Neutrality (Hersch Lauterpacht ed., 8th ed. 1955).

predominant for centuries. However, during the last few decades, legal scholarship as well as international practice have opened up toward a more positive definition of peace which would include the requirement of compliance with certain material standards.[6] Although there is no universal agreement about an exact list of positive elements of peace, the respect for certain fundamental human rights including the guarantee of basic social, economic, and cultural rights is recurring in the literature as the central indicator for a positive peace.[7] Such a concept of positive peace must be understood more as a process than a status, and it tends to overcome the classic dichotomy between war and peace toward the identification of a third phase in connection with an armed conflict—the transitional post-conflict phase. This phase is characterized by posing specific challenges to those stakeholders which, after the end of the actual hostilities, act in order to secure a durable (positive) peace. As a result, calls have been made to complement modern international peace and security law's well-entrenched division between *jus ad bellum* and *jus in bello* with a third pillar: a *jus post bellum*.

The idea of a *jus post bellum*, the roots of which can be traced back to ancient *just war theory*, but has been neglected during the codification efforts of the twentieth century,[8] first resurfaced among moral philosophers at the beginning of the twenty-first century,[9] and was subsequently taken up in legal scholarship.[10] Even though the discussion of a *jus post bellum* as a legal concept has fast gained

6. Statement of the President of the U.N. Security Council, July 20, 2000, U.N. Doc. S/PRST/2000/25; Djacoba Liva Tehindrazanarivelo & Robert Kolb, *Peace, Right to, International Protection*, *in* 8 Max Planck Encyclopedia of Public International Law ¶ 12, at 155 (Rüdiger Wolfrum ed., 2012).

7. *Id.* To exemplify the new approach to understanding peace, *see* the work of the Institute for Economics and Peace. This institute uses more than 23 separate indicators to rank nations according to their peacefulness. The results are published yearly in a comprehensive global peace index. *See, e.g.*, Inst. for Econ. & Peace, Global Peace Index 2018: Measuring Peace in a Complex World, http://visionofhumanity.org/app/uploads/2018/06/Global-Peace-Index-2018-2.pdf (last visited Oct. 11, 2019).

8. Carsten Stahn, Jus Post Bellum: *Mapping the Discipline(s)*, *in* jus post bellum: Towards a Law of Transition from Conflict to Peace 93, 94–95 (Carsten Stahn & Jann Kleffner eds., 2008).

9. *See* Larry May, After War Ends: A Philosophical Perspective (2012); Brian Orend, Jus Post Bellum: *The Perspective of a Just-War Theorist*, 20 Leiden J. Int'l L. 571 (2007); Richard DiMeglio, *The Evolution of the Just War Tradition: Defining* Jus Post Bellum, 186 Mil. L. Rev. 116 (2005); Gary Bass, Jus Post Bellum, 32 Phil. & Pub. Aff. 384 (2004). Michael Walzer, arguably the most prominent representative of the modern just war theorists, picked up this development in his work *Arguing About War* and acknowledged that his treatment of the *jus post bellum* in his previous work had been "much too brief." *See* Michael Walzer, Arguing about War xiii (2004).

10. For the pioneer contributions to the discussion in legal scholarship, *see* Carsten Stahn, "Jus ad Bellum," "Jus in Bello" . . . "Jus Post Bellum"?—*Rethinking the Conception of the Law of Armed Force*, 17 Eur. J. Int'l L. 921 (2006); Stahn, *supra* note 8, at 93–112.

traction,[11] it is still in its very early stages. While the approaches taken to the idea of a *jus post bellum* as a new concept of international law vary greatly, two main camps can be identified. Certain scholars enthusiastically embrace the concept of a *jus post bellum* as a new discipline of international law, culminating in the demand for the codification of this body of law reminiscent of the already mentioned great conventions of the last century.[12] Other voices question the usefulness or even appropriateness of a new branch of international peace and security law. Indeed, these skeptics doubt whether a *jus post bellum* as a legal concept has anything to add to the current framework of international peace and security law.[13]

While this discussion has been conducted at the theoretical level, the concept of a *jus post bellum* has, more or less unnoticed by legal scholarship, already found its way into practice. In 2009, the Eritrea-Ethiopia Claims Commission (EECC), a commission which was set up by the Algiers Agreement in 2000[14] to adjudicate reparation claims between Ethiopia and Eritrea after the 1998–2000 war, decided that Eritrea violated the prohibition of the use of force according to Article 2(4) of the U.N. Charter by invading Ethiopia in May 1998.[15] In laying out its guidelines for determining the amount of compensation Eritrea was required to pay to Ethiopia for its unlawful resort to force, the Commission referred to the concept of *jus post bellum* as a basis for their argument that the award of reparations must not lead to a deterioration of the relations between the former warring parties and must not negatively impact the development of a lasting peace.[16] Without

11. Jens Iverson has done a particularly illustrative account of the increasing discussion about the *jus post bellum* in scholarship by displaying the frequency of use of the term in a diagram. *See* Jens Iverson, *Contrasting the Normative and Historical Foundations of Transitional Justice and* Jus Post Bellum*—Outlining the Matrix of Definitions in Comparative Perspective*, *in* JUS POST BELLUM—MAPPING THE NORMATIVE FOUNDATIONS 100 (Carsten Stahn, Jennifer Easterday, & Jens Iverson eds., 2014).

12. Representative of this extensive demand, *see, e.g.*, Inger Österdahl & Esther van Zadel, *What Will* Jus Post Bellum *Mean? Of New Wine and Old Bottles*, 14 J. CONFLICT & SECURITY L. 184 (2009).

13. Representative of the more critical voices, *see, e.g.*, Eric De Brabandere, *The Responsibility for Post-Conflict Reforms: A Critical Assessment of* Jus Post Bellum *as a Legal Concept*, 43 VAND. J. TRANSNAT'L L. 142 (2010). For a not so much critical, but cautious, voice, *see* Robert Cryer, *Law and the* Jus Post Bellum: *Counseling Caution*, *in* MORALITY, JUS POST BELLUM, AND INTERNATIONAL LAW 232 (Larry May & Andrew T. Forcehimes eds., 2012).

14. Agreement Between the Government of the Federal Republic of Ethiopia and the Government of the State of Eritrea, Dec. 12, 2000, 2138 U.N.T.S. 93.

15. *Jus ad Bellum*, Ethiopia's Claims 1–8 (Eth. v. Eri.), Partial Award, ¶ 10 (Eri. Eth. Claims Comm'n, Dec. 19, 2005). For a text of the decision, *see* LITIGATION WAR—ARBITRATION OF CIVIL INJURY BY THE ERITREA-ETHIOPIA CLAIMS COMMISSION 803–809 (Sean Murphy, Won Kidane, & Thomas Snider eds., 2013).

16. Ethiopia's Damages Claims (Eth. v. Eri.), Final Award, ¶ 315 (Eri. Eth. Claims Comm'n Aug. 17, 2009). For a text of the decision, *see* LITIGATION WAR, *supra* note 15, at 661.

delving any further into the Commission's decision at this point, the mere fact that it made this reference illustrates that at least the commissioners of the EECC saw a practical need to resort to this freshly discussed concept of law in their reparation decision.

This reference by the EECC provided the initial impulse for this chapter. The author agrees with the more cautious voices in the literature insofar as the initial step of the inquiry should be a thorough analysis of the usefulness of this possibly new concept of law. However, this necessary analysis cannot be (at least not exclusively) done in the abstract. Instead, concrete norms or ideas which could be part of a *jus post bellum* must be identified and analyzed in order to see whether there are certain lacunae in the current framework of international peace and security law which could be meaningfully addressed by a *jus post bellum*. As outlined earlier, the EECC apparently came to the conclusion that there is indeed a gap in the current rules of international law governing the award of reparations for a violation of the prohibition of the use of force, and it has addressed this gap by reference to a *jus post bellum*.

This chapter seeks to examine the premise behind the EECC's reasoning. It therefore analyzes whether there is indeed added value in the idea of a *jus post bellum* as a legal concept with regard to the obligation to make reparation for a violation of the *jus ad bellum*. In order to reach a well-founded conclusion, it is necessary to take stock of the current rules of international law pertaining to the duty to pay reparations for an unlawful use of force and to identify specific developments as well as recurring problems which are not covered by the current legal framework, but could be meaningfully addressed by a *jus post bellum*. In this sense, the first section of this chapter will examine the customary international law status of the aggressor state's duty to make reparation for an unlawful resort to force. It will proceed with a closer look at the principle of full reparation, as enshrined in the law of state responsibility, and the deviations thereof in state practice before addressing the unique function a *jus post bellum* principle of proportionality could play in determining the adequate amount of reparations after an armed conflict. The chapter will finish with a nuanced assertion of the usefulness of the *jus post bellum* as a legal concept with regard to the aggressor state's reparations obligation.

II. THE DUTY TO MAKE REPARATION FOR A VIOLATION OF THE *JUS AD BELLUM*

The prohibition of the use of force in international relations, as enshrined in Article 2(4) of the U.N. Charter and in customary international law, is one of the central norms of modern international law.[17] However, in contrast to the law of

17. For the customary international law status of Article 2(4) of the U.N. Charter, *see* YORAM DINSTEIN, WAR, AGGRESSION AND SELF-DEFENCE ¶ 271 (6th ed. 2017). This assessment has been confirmed by the International Court of Justice (ICJ) in its *Case Concerning Military and Paramilitary Activities in and Against Nicaragua* (*Nicaragua* case). Military and Paramilitary Activities in and Against Nicaragua (Nicar. v. U.S.), Judgment, 1986 I.C.J. Rep. 14, ¶¶ 188–90 (June 27).

armed conflict (*jus in bello*), the obligation to make reparation for an unlawful use of force is not codified in international treaty law.[18] Consequently, the identification of rules of customary international law governing the aggressor state's reparation obligation is central to the first part of the present chapter.

A. The Current Law of State Responsibility

As early as 1927, the Permanent Court of International Justice (PCIJ) has recognized in its *Chorzów Factory* judgment the basic principle of international state responsibility—a state's obligation to repair the consequences following from a wrongful act: "It is a principle of international law that the breach of an engagement involves an obligation to make reparation in an adequate form."[19]

During the twentieth century, much effort was put into developing and codifying this basic principle of state responsibility, beginning with the early work by the League of Nations and culminating in the adoption of the Draft Articles on Responsibility of States for Internationally Wrongful Acts by the U.N. International Law Commission (ILC) in August 2001 (ILC Draft Articles).[20] Even though the ILC Draft Articles have not been recommended for transposition in the form of an international treaty, they largely constitute an integral part of international law as they widely reflect customary international law.[21] With regard

18. Andrea Gattini, *The UN Compensation Commission: Old Rules, New Procedures on War Reparations*, 13 Eur. J. Int'l L. 162 (2002). For the treaty provisions with regard to reparations for *jus in bello* violations, *see* Convention IV, *supra* note 2, art. 3; AP I, *supra* note 4, art. 91. In addition, the reparation obligation for *jus in bello* violations is recognized by customary international law. *See* 1 Int'l Comm. of the Red Cross, Customary International Humanitarian Law: Rules r. 150, at 537 (Jean-Marie Henckaerts & Louise Doswald-Beck eds., 2005).

19. Factory at Chorzów (Claim for Indemnity) (Ger. v. Pol.), Jurisdiction, 1928 P.C.I.J. (ser. A) No. 9, at 21 (July 26). The reasoning of the Court is ambiguous as to whether it considers the principle of state responsibility as a general principle of international law or as part of customary international law. In its reasoning concerning the merits of the case, the Court seems to suggest that a rule of customary law has emerged: "The essential principle . . . which seems to be established by international practice and in particular by the decisions of arbitral tribunals is that reparation must, as far as possible, wipe out al1 the consequences of the illegal act and reestablish the situation which would, in all probability, have existed if that act had not been committed." Factory at Chorzów (Claim for Indemnity) (Merits) (Ger. v. Pol.), Merits, 1928 P.C.I.J. (ser. A) No. 17, at 47 (Sept. 13). This way, the PCIJ seems to conceptualize an overlap between international customary law as well as the general principles with regard to state responsibility. *See* Brian Lepard, Customary International Law—A New Theory with Practical Applications 166–67 (2010).

20. Draft Articles on Responsibility of States for Internationally Wrongful Acts art. 16, Rep. of the Int'l L. Comm'n on Its Fifty-Third Sess., U.N. Doc. A/56/10, at 26 (2001) [hereinafter Draft Articles].

21. James Crawford, *State Responsibility*, *in* 9 Max Planck Encyclopedia of Public International Law ¶ 65, at 531 (Rüdiger Wolfrum ed., 2012).

to reparations, Article 31 of the ILC Draft Articles sets out the following basic principle:

> 1. The responsible State is under an obligation to make full reparation for the injury caused by the internationally wrongful act.
> 2. Injury includes any damage, whether material or moral, caused by the internationally wrongful act of a State.[22]

Breaking down this paragraph, four basic elements must be fulfilled in order to trigger a state's obligation to make reparation. There must be an internationally wrongful act, consisting of (1) the breach of an international obligation, (2) attributable to a state, and this act must (3) cause (4) injury or damage. If these requirements are met, the obligation to make reparation follows *ipso jure* as a legal consequence from the commission of the internationally wrongful act without any intermediary legal act, for example, an international treaty, necessary to constitute the responsible state's liability.[23] According to the ILC Draft Articles, the reparation obligation can take different forms which are listed in Article 34, namely, restitution, compensation, and satisfaction. While restitution is generally conceived of as the primary form of reparation,[24] it is not the central aspect with regard to reparations for an unlawful resort to force as examined in this chapter. In this context, the term "reparation" is usually used to describe monetary compensation which the responsible state is obligated to pay to the victim state. If not indicated otherwise, the term "reparation" is used in this sense for the purpose of this chapter as well.

As the rules of state responsibility are purely secondary in nature, they are generally applicable to every breach of a primary international obligation to which the responsible state is bound. Nevertheless, some doubts still persist as to whether the violation of the prohibition of the use of force as enshrined in Article 2(4) of the U.N. Charter *ipso jure* leads to the aggressor state's obligation to make reparation. At times, it has been argued that after an armed conflict there is, if nothing else, a practical necessity to stipulate the relevant reparation provisions in a special treaty.[25] An unlawful use of force would then not give rise to an obligation to pay reparations as enshrined in the ILC Draft Articles, but rather would create the obligation to enter into negotiations about the duty to pay reparations.[26] Others have refined this argument to the effect that the duty to make reparation directly

22. Draft Articles, *supra* note 20, art. 31.

23. Crawford, *supra* note 21, ¶ 23.

24. *Id.* ¶ 28.

25. Markus Eichhorst, Rechtsprobleme der United Nations Compensation Commission 100 (2002).

26. *Id.* at 101.

follows from the unlawful use of force, whereas the determination of the precise amount needs to be specified in a treaty.[27] Still others point out that the real question is not whether the violation of the prohibition of the use of force leads to the international responsibility of the aggressor state, but whether this responsibility specifically entails the duty to pay monetary compensation.[28]

On a more general level, the question has been raised if and to what extent the legal consequences of a wrongful act can be generalized irrespective of the primary norm in question.[29] As we have seen, the ILC Draft Articles provide for a duty to make reparation as a general rule of state responsibility. Therefore, any skepticism with regard to reparations as an *ipso jure* consequence of an unlawful use of force must be grounded in the practice, or rather the lack of practice, with respect specifically to the prohibition of the use of force. In fact, while the prohibition of the use of force and the reparation principle are both firmly entrenched in modern international law, there have only been four instances in which comprehensive reparations programs have been established after an armed conflict, namely, the First World War, the Second World War, the First Gulf War between Iraq and Kuwait and the subsequent intervention of the international community from 1990 to 1991, as well as the already mentioned Ethiopia-Eritrea War from 1998 to 2000. Meanwhile, in the majority of instances of armed violence in international relations, no reparations program was set up. However, the mere reference to the lack of relevant state practice is not sufficient to reach the conclusion that the rules of state responsibility as enshrined in the ILC Draft Articles and in customary international law do not—or at least do not fully—apply in the event of an unlawful use of force. Instead, it must be carefully analyzed whether diverging rules of customary international law have emerged with regard to reparations for *jus ad bellum* violations.

B. State Practice after Armed Conflicts with Regard to Reparations

As rules of customary international law, the rules of state responsibility can be further developed, modified, or abolished by other rules of international law. Since there is no treaty law with regard to reparations for the violation of the *jus*

27. Bernd Eichhorn, Reparation als völkerrechtliche Deliktshaftung—Rechtliche und praktische Probleme unter besonderer Berücksichtigung Deutschlands (1918–1990) 81–82 (1992).

28. Vera Gowlland-Debbas, *Some Remarks on Compensation for War Damages Under* Jus Ad Bellum, *in* The 1998–2000 War Between Eritrea and Ethiopia—An International Legal Perspective 436 (Andrea de Guttry, Harry H.G. Post, & Gabriella Venturini eds., 2009); Luisa Castagnetti, *The Damages Awards of the Eritrea-Ethiopia Claims Commission: War Damages and Reparations for Violation of* Jus Ad Bellum, 19 It. Y.B. Int'l L. 281 (2009).

29. Yumi Nishimura, *Source of the Obligation*, *in* The Law of International Responsibility 367 (James Crawford, Alain Pellet, & Simon Olleson eds., 2010).

ad bellum, a modification of the law of state responsibility requires the emergence of diverging customary international law. This requires diverging state practice accepted as law according to which an unlawful use of force does not—at least not *ipso jure*—lead to the aggressor state's obligation to make reparation for injuries and damages caused.[30]

1. Inaction as Negative State Practice

At first, one must take a closer look at the fact that reparations for the violation of the prohibition of the use of force have only been extracted in limited cases. Generally speaking, inaction can be interpreted as "negative state practice" in determining whether a new rule of customary international law has emerged if this inaction is the manifestation of a corresponding *opinio juris* and not merely the result of practical constraints or political considerations.[31] A closer look at the scarce practice reveals that the hesitance in asserting a right to reparations after an armed conflict is not so much a sign of a lacking *opinio juris* than the manifestation of the lack of enforcement measures to implement the reparation obligation.[32]

This lack of enforcement measures in international law arises twofold in the context of reparations for an unlawful use of force. First, and this is perhaps the more obvious reason, there is no general mechanism in international law to enforce a peaceful settlement of disputes.[33] There is simply no permanent forum in which a victim state can bring possible reparation claims against an aggressor state. As a consequence, the enforcement of reparation claims essentially rests on the consent of the parties to the conflict to establish such a forum. It should not come as a surprise that Article 5 of the Algiers Agreement, in which Eritrea and Ethiopia were able to agree on establishing the EECC in order to adjudicate reparation claims between the two states, is the exception and not the rule in the aftermath of an armed conflict.

Second, there is no mechanism in international law to authoritatively assert whether the prohibition of the use of force has been violated.[34] The identification

30. For the formation of customary law in general, *see* Tullio Treves, *Customary International Law*, *in* 2 Max Planck Encyclopedia of Public International Law ¶ 8, at 939 (Rüdiger Wolfrum ed., 2012).

31. Int'l L. Comm'n, Second Report on Identification of Customary International Law, U.N. Doc. A/CN.4/672, ¶ 42 (May 22, 2014); Int'l L. Comm'n, Third Report on Identification of Customary International Law, U.N. Doc. A/CN.4/682, ¶ 20 (Mar. 27, 2015).

32. Elke Schwager, Ius Bello durante et Bello Confecto—Darstellung am Beispiel von Entschädigungsansprüchen der Opfer von Antipersonenminen 119 (2008); Eichhorst, *supra* note 25, at 95.

33. *Id.* at 118.

34. Yaël Ronen, *Avoid or Compensate? Liability for Incidental Injuries to Civilians Inflicted During Armed Conflict*, 42 Vand. J. Transnat'l L. 206 (2009). There is especially no final authority of the U.N. Security Council with regard to such a determination. *See* Military and

of the aggressor of an armed conflict often is a highly controversial matter; seldom is the responsibility for the outbreak of armed fighting as clear-cut as it was during the Iraqi invasion of Kuwait in 1990, when the U.N. Security Council condemned the Iraqi invasion as a "breach of the peace,"[35] reaffirmed Iraq's liability under international law for damages caused by its unlawful invasion,[36] and established the U.N. Compensation Commission (UNCC) to enforce Iraq's reparation obligations.[37]

However, the lack of enforcement measures alone cannot explain the lack of reparations programs, as the issue of reparations has not even been raised in various cases of armed violence which have been condemned by the United Nations, either through the Security Council or the General Assembly.[38] Three examples, among many, are the Turkish invasion in North Cyprus in 1974,[39] the Israeli invasion in Lebanon in 1982,[40] and the Argentinian armed attack on the Falkland Islands in the same year.[41] In the latter case, the U.N. Security Council even used the same wording—"breach of the peace"—it used eight years later to condemn the Iraqi invasion in Kuwait.[42]

This different approach of the U.N. Security Council to the reparation question, which is reflective of the international community's conduct as a whole, must be viewed in the specific context. After the cessation of hostilities, a lot of issues must be addressed among which the implementation of a reparation program is rarely the first priority. And if it is difficult to reach a consensus between former enemies with regard to the establishment of a reparation mechanism, it is no less of a challenge to reach an agreement among the members of the U.N. Security Council. After all, the establishment of the UNCC took place more or less directly after the end of the Cold War, which provided a singular historical setting for the international community to react in a united way to a threat to international peace and security and to commit itself to establishing the most comprehensive reparations mechanism since the Second World War, which has still not completely finished its work 29 years after the cessation of hostilities.[43]

Paramilitary Activities in and Against Nicaragua (Nicar. v. U.S.), Judgment, 1986 I.C.J. Rep. 14, ¶ 90 (June 27).

35. S.C. Res. 660, pmbl. (Aug. 2, 1990).

36. S.C. Res. 687, ¶ 16 (Apr. 3, 1991).

37. S.C. Res. 692, ¶ 3 (May 20, 1991).

38. Gowlland-Debbas, *supra* note 28, at 437.

39. S.C. Res. 353 ¶¶ 3–6 (July 20, 1974); S.C. Res. 360, ¶ 1 (Aug. 16, 1974).

40. S.C. Res. 508, pmbl. (June 5, 1982); S.C. Res. 509, pmbl. (June 6, 1982).

41. S.C. Res. 502, pmbl. (Apr. 3, 1982).

42. S.C. Res. 660, pmbl. (Aug. 2, 1990).

43. For the status of the UNCC's work, *see* U.N. Compensation Comm'n, https://uncc.ch/home (last visited May 27, 2020). The UNCC finished its claims-processing in 2005 with more than $52.4

Taking these considerations into account, there are convincing arguments to presume that the prevalent inaction of the U.N. Security Council and of the international community as a whole with regard to reparations after an armed conflict is the reflection of practical and political considerations and not of any negative *opinio juris* regarding the duty to make reparation. This appraisal is supported by an analysis of the positive state practice.

2. Analysis of the Positive State Practice

It must be carefully analyzed whether the existing, albeit scarce, positive state practice with regard to reparations after an armed conflict has led to the emergence of customary law diverging from the principle of state responsibility.

After the First World War, the Entente—the victorious Allied Powers—and Germany negotiated the relevant provisions of the German reparations obligation during the Paris Peace Conference, which ended with the signature of the Treaty of Peace between the Allied and Associated Powers and Germany, better known as the Treaty of Versailles.[44] In Article 231(1)—its notorious "War Guilt Clause"—the parties directly linked Germany's obligation to make reparation to its aggression:

> The Allied and Associated Governments affirm and Germany accepts the responsibility of Germany and her allies for causing all the loss and damage to which the Allied and Associated Governments and their nationals have been subjected as a consequence of the war imposed upon them by the aggression of Germany and her allies.[45]

In contrast to former peace treaties, the Treaty of Versailles did not stipulate a specific reparation sum due by Germany for its aggression.[46] Instead, an allied

billion awarded to 1.5 million successful claimants. To date, approximately $49.6 billion have been paid out by the Commission with $2.8 billion outstanding for a claim of the Kuwait Petroleum Corporation for oil production and sales losses as a result of damages to Kuwait's oil field assets. Most recently, $440 million have been made available by the Commission on April 28, 2020.

44. Treaty of Peace Between the Allied and Associated Powers and Germany, June 28, 1919, 1919 U.S.T. LEXIS 42 [hereinafter Treaty of Versailles]. The United States did not ratify the Treaty of Versailles, mainly due to the U.S. Senate's opposition to the participation in the League of Nations, and instead concluded a separate bilateral peace treaty with Germany in 1921. *See* Treaty Concerning the Reestablishment of Peace Between Germany and the United States, Aug. 25, 1921, T.S. No. 658, 1921 U.S.T. LEXIS 15. Article 1 of this treaty obligated Germany to grant the United States all rights and privileges enjoyed by the other members of the Entente who ratified the Treaty of Versailles. Article 2 of the treaty explicitly specified the articles of the Treaty of Versailles to be applied to the United States, including the reparations provisions under Chapter VIII. The peace treaties with the other Central Powers were negotiated during the Paris Peace Negotiations as well and modeled after the Treaty of Versailles. *See* Elyse Garmise, *The Iraqi Claims Process and the Ghost of Versailles*, 67 N.Y.U. L. Rev. 853 (1992).

45. Treaty of Versailles, *supra* note 44, art. 231.

46. Pierre d'Argent, Les Réparations de Guerre en Droit International Public—La Responsabilité Internationale des États à l'Épreuve de la Guerre 50 (2002).

Reparation Commission was established and assigned to determine the amount of compensation Germany had to pay.[47]

After the Second World War, there were several international treaties regulating the reparations obligations of the former Axis Powers, namely, Germany, Japan, Italy, Romania, Hungary, Finland, and Austria. After the end of the war, the Allies quickly entered into negotiations about the conditions of the peace with the European Axis Powers except for Germany. These so-called Paris Negotiations concluded with the signing of the Paris Peace Treaties in February 1947,[48] which exhaustively regulated the reparations obligations of the European Axis Powers by stipulating a fixed reparations sum which they had to pay in kind. Although there was no liability clause comparable to Article 231 of the Treaty of Versailles, the preamble of every treaty linked the state's responsibility to its participation in the war. Accordingly, the preamble of the Italian peace treaty stated:

> Whereas Italy under the Fascist regime became a party to the Tripartite Pact with Germany and Japan, undertook a war of aggression and thereby provoked a state of war with all the Allied and Associated Powers and with other United Nations, and bears her share of responsibility for the war. . . .[49]

The identical preambles of the other peace treaties picked up on this point as well:

> Whereas [Romania, Bulgaria, Hungary, and Finland] having become an ally of Hitlerite Germany and having participated on her side in the war against the Union of Soviet Socialist Republics, the United Kingdom, the United States of America and other United Nations, bears her share of responsibility for this war. . . .[50]

After Japan had declared its capitulation in September 1945, various documents were drawn up to outline the guidelines for extracting reparations. As an example, the Basic Post-Surrender Policy for Japan stated the following with regard to reparations:

> For acts of aggression committed by Japan and for the purpose of equitable reparation of the damage caused by her to the Allied Powers and in the interests of destruction of the Japanese war potential in those industries which could lead to Japan's rearmament for waging war, reparations shall be exacted from Japan

47. Treaty of Versailles, *supra* note 44, art. 233.

48. Treaty of Peace with Italy, Feb. 10, 1947 49 U.N.T.S. 3; Treaty of Peace with Romania, Feb. 10, 1947, 42 U.N.T.S. 3; Treaty of Peace with Hungary, Feb. 10, 1947, 41 U.N.T.S. 135; Treaty of Peace with Bulgaria, Feb. 10, 1947, 41 U.N.T.S. 21; Treaty of Peace with Finland, Feb. 10, 1947, 48 U.N.T.S. 203.

49. Treaty of Peace with Italy, *supra* note 48, pmbl., at 127.

50. *E.g.*, Treaty of Peace with Bulgaria, *supra* note 48, at 50.

> through the transfer of such existing Japanese capital equipment and facilities or such Japanese goods as exist or may in future be produced. . . .[51]

After the Allies had started to deconstruct Japanese industrial plants for the purpose of reparations, they ceased with this policy in May 1950 to strengthen the Japanese economy in the course of the intensifying Cold War.[52] Nevertheless, the Japanese obligation to make reparation found its way into the Peace Treaty of San Francisco, which was signed in September 1951:

> It is recognized that Japan should pay reparations to the Allied Powers for the damage and suffering caused by it during the war. Nevertheless it is also recognized that the resources of Japan are not presently sufficient, if it is to maintain a viable economy, to make complete reparation for all such damage and suffering and at the same time meet its other obligations.[53]

Instead of stipulating a fixed reparations sum, Article 14A(1) obliged Japan to enter into negotiations with the Allied Powers to assist the countries in compensating for the cost of the damage done. The German reparations question was addressed differently in large part due to the fact that there was no German government in place to negotiate the conditions of peace in the aftermath of Germany's complete surrender in May 1945. Instead, the agenda for the German reparations question was set in three major Allied conferences: the Conference of Quebec in September 1944, the Yalta Conference in February 1945, as well as the Potsdam Conference in August 1945. Generally speaking, the Allies came to the conclusion that, first, Germany should make reparation in kind mainly through the dismantling of Germany's key industries, through German labor, as well as confiscation of German assets; and that, second, the reparations regime would be based on the agreed division of Germany into occupation zones.[54] However, the ramifications of the ideological and political division of the international community in East and West soon took precedence over the reparations question. As a result, the practice of unilateral extraction of reparations in kind was ceased, first in the Western Zone and later in the Eastern Zone,[55] and replaced by various multilateral treaties to which the Federal Republic of Germany was a party. The aim of these treaties was, on the one hand, to defer the final settlement of the reparations

51. For the text of this document, *see* Tetsuo Ito, *Japan's Settlement of the Post-World War II Reparations and Claims*, 37 Japanese Annual Int'l L. 40 n.3 (1994).

52. Pierre d'Argent, *Reparations after World War II*, *in* 8 Max Planck Encyclopedia of Public International Law, *supra* note 6, at 893, ¶ 24, at 894; Ito, *supra* note 51, at 50.

53. Treaty of Peace with Japan art. 14(a), Sept. 8, 1951, 136 U.N.T.S. 45.

54. d'Argent, *supra* note 46, at 133; d'Argent, *supra* note 52, ¶ 7, at 894.

55. Rudolf Dolzer, *The Settlement of War-Related Claims: Does International Law Recognize a Victim's Private Right of Action? Lessons after 1945*, 20 Berkeley J. Int'l L. 321 (2002).

question to a comprehensive peace treaty with a unified Germany,[56] and, on the other hand, to ensure adequate compensation for individual victims of Nazi persecution.[57] In the latter context, the Federal Republic of Germany concluded 12 lump-sum agreements in the 1960s to compensate foreign individuals.[58]

This practice did not go unnoticed by the ILC during its codification efforts on state responsibility. In its report on the work of its forty-fifth session, the commission outlined general comments on the compensation provision proposed by the commission in the draft articles, which it adopted at its forty-fifth session in 1993:[59]

> [T]he current text disregard[s] the practice followed since the end of the Second World War, namely the conclusion of bilateral agreements through diplomatic negotiations, under which States undertook to pay compensation for any damages by means of an overall fixed amount to be determined by mutual agreement—a practice which should be encouraged.[60]

The ILC specifically refers in this context to the various lump-sum agreements that Germany entered into after the Second World War and seems to consider the agreement of a fixed reparations sum by treaty as an established practice.

However, this analysis of the practice after the Second World War is incomplete. As outlined earlier, while there have been various agreements and treaties with regard to reparations, the Allied governments unilaterally extracted reparations from Germany and Japan directly after the cessation of hostilities before any treaty could constitute any reparations obligation. And even though there is no liability clause comparable to Article 231 of the Treaty of Versailles, it is obvious that the Allied governments based their practice on the conviction that Germany (and its allies) were obligated to make reparation for the damage caused by initiating or participating in an unlawful war.[61] In the end, it was not necessary to expressly state this link as it has been done in the Treaty of Versailles because the status of the *jus ad bellum* had significantly changed between the two world

56. *See, e.g.*, Agreement on Reparation from Germany, on the Establishment of an Inter-Allied Reparation Agency and on the Restitution of Monetary Gold, Jan. 14, 1946, 555 U.N.T.S. 69; Agreement on German External Debts, Feb. 27, 1953, 333 U.N.T.S. 3.

57. Dolzer, *supra* note 55, at 327.

58. *Id.* at 331.

59. For the wording of the relevant compensation provision, *see* Int'l L. Comm'n, Commentary on Article 8 of the Draft Articles of State Responsibility Provisionally Adopted So Far by the Commission, *reprinted in* [1993] 2 (pt. 2) Y.B. Int'l L. Comm'n 67 (1993).

60. Int'l L. Comm'n, Report of the Work of Its Forty-Fifth Session, U.N. Doc. A/CN.4/457, ¶ 303 (Feb. 15, 1994).

61. d'Argent, *supra* note 52, ¶ 36, at 894.

wars.[62] While the delegates at the Paris Peace Conference, after an at times heated debate, only agreed that Article 231 of the Treaty of Versailles morally (and not legally) condemned Germany for waging an aggressive war,[63] there was no doubt that Germany (and its allies) breached international law by initiating and waging the Second World War.[64] It was not felt at the time that the consequence of this breach of international law—the obligation to make reparation—needed to be expressly stipulated as was done after the First World War.[65] The fact that the Allied governments considered the duty to make reparation as being the immediate legal consequence following from this breach of international law is exemplified by their widespread practice of declaring waivers even before any final agreement about Germany's or Japan's reparations obligation could be achieved.[66] If they had been convinced that an intermediary legal act was necessary to constitutively establish the aggressor state's reparations obligation, there would have been no need to declare such waivers.

The outlined assessment of the reparations practice does not hold up against the continuing state practice either. After the first Gulf War, the U.N. Security Council declared Iraq to be liable under international law in Resolution 687 (1991): "*Reaffirms* that Iraq . . . is liable under international law for any direct loss, damage, including environmental damage and the depletion of natural resources, or injury to foreign Governments, nationals and corporations, as a result of its unlawful invasion and occupation of Kuwait."[67]

However, instead of determining the amount of compensation Iraq was liable to pay, as expected under the reported assessment of the practice in 1994, the U.N. Security Council delegated this task to the UNCC. The wording of the U.N. Security Council resolution, reaffirming Iraq's liability to be "*under international law*," explicitly reflects the member states' *opinio juris* that Iraq's obligation to make reparation for its unlawful use of force already existed under international

62. On the development on the use of force between the end of the First and of the Second World War, *see* Ian Brownlie, International Law and the Use of Force by States 51–111 (1963).

63. d'Argent, *supra* note 46, at 73; Bernard Baruch, The Making of the Reparation and Economic Sections of the Treaty 36 (1920); 2 A History of the Peace Conference of Paris 45 (Harold William Vazeille Temperley ed., 1920–1924); Alan Sharp, The Versailles Settlement—Peacemaking in Paris 1919, at 87 (1991).

64. Brownlie, *supra* note 62, at 66–111; Dinstein, *supra* note 17, ¶ 238; *see also* Claus Kreß, *Introduction: The Crime of Aggression and the International Legal Order*, *in* 1 The Crime of Aggression: A Commentary 3 (Claus Kreß & Stefan Barriga eds., 2017).

65. Eichhorn, *supra* note 27, at 45.

66. d'Argent, *supra* note 52, ¶ 36, at 894.

67. S.C. Res. 687, ¶ 16 (Apr. 3, 1991).

law.[68] The same *opinio juris* is reflected in numerous other Security Council resolutions in which the U.N. Security Council confirmed the aggressor state's liability for the damages caused without going so far as establishing a reparations mechanism under Chapter VII of the U.N. Charter.[69] Interestingly, even the Iraqi delegate at the United Nations did not question the premise for Iraq's reparations obligation under international law, but emphasized that Iraq, too, possessed a right to reparations because of alleged violations of international law by the Allied Forces.[70] Instead of denying a reparations obligation, the harsh criticism by the Iraqi delegation was directed at the U.N. Security Council's authority to establish the UNCC as the competent body to adjudicate reparation claims against Iraq.[71] In short, critics questioned the legal basis for the implementation mechanism, not for the reparations obligation itself. All this reflects the fact that, under the existing law, the U.N. Security Council, in the absence of a permanent enforcement mechanism for reparations, was required to take constitutive legal action in order to establish the UNCC, while the Council could limit itself to declaratorily affirm Iraq's liability for initiating and waging the war, as it existed under customary international law.

A similar observation can be made about the reception of the EECC's work on adjudicating reparations claims between Ethiopia and Eritrea. In contrast to the previous reparations programs, there was no legal act or document which—if only in a declaratory manner—stated one party's responsibility for the outbreak of fighting in May 1998 and its liability for damages caused. Instead, the commissioners interpreted their mandate under Article 5 of the Algiers Agreement

68. Gowlland-Debbas, *supra* note 28, at 439; Eichhorst, *supra* note 25, at 114; Jeremy Craver, *Dispute Resolution or Administrative Tribunal: A Question of Due Process*, *in* The United Nations Compensation Commission 69 (Richard B. Lillich ed., 1995); John Crook, *The United Nations Compensation Commission—A New Structure to Enforce State Responsibility*, 87 Am. J. Int'l L. 146 (1993). For a different appraisal, *see* Hans Wassgren, *The UN Compensation Commission: Lessons of Legitimacy, Responsibility, and War Reparations*, 11 Leiden J. Int'l L. 484 (1998).

69. *See* S.C. Res. 290, ¶ 3 (Dec. 8, 1970) (concerning Portuguese invasion in Angola); S.C. Res. 387, ¶ 4 (Mar. 31, 1976) (concerning the South African aggression against Angola); S.C. Res. 455, ¶ 5 (Nov. 23, 1979) (concerning the South Rhodesian and South African aggression against Zambia); S.C. Res. 487, ¶ 6 (June 19, 1981) (concerning an Israeli strike on an Iraqi nuclear reactor); S.C. Res. 546, ¶ 7 (Jan. 6, 1984) (again concerning a South African aggression against Angola); S.C. Res. 573, ¶ 4 (Oct. 4, 1985) (concerning armed activities of Israel against Tunisia). However, in contrast to Resolution 687 (1991), the Security Council did not act under Chapter VII of the U.N. Charter in any of these instances.

70. U.N. SCOR, 2981st mtg. at 32, U.N. Doc. S/PV.2981 (Apr. 3, 1991).

71. In the words of the Iraqi delegate at the United Nations, "We believe that the Council exceeded its mandate, because it is a political body consisting of members who seek only to advance their own political interests. It is not a judicial body consisting of independent, impartial

to include the authority to determine and to adjudicate *jus ad bellum* violations.[72] While this wide interpretation of the mandate was criticized by legal scholarship,[73] the fundamental premise of this decision—the obligation to make reparation for an unlawful use of force under international law—was not questioned at all.

To conclude, the observation in 1994 as outlined by the ILC has not developed into a consistent practice. Instead, when analyzing the various legal acts governing reparations programs after armed conflicts, a careful distinction must be made between the obligation to pay reparations itself and its implementation. As there is no obligatory enforcement mechanism in international law, legal action is required to facilitate the implementation of the aggressor state's liability, but not to establish such responsibility.[74] The relevant state practice has not crystallized into a rule of customary international law requiring intermediate legal action to establish the aggressor state's reparations obligation in derogation from the law of state responsibility as enshrined in the ILC Draft Articles.[75] This conclusion is supported by the jurisprudence of the International Court of Justice (ICJ), which has ruled in various cases on a state's obligation to pay reparations for violating norms of international peace and security law, although it has yet to award a reparation sum.[76]

judges competent to rule on compensation for those entitled to it in any conflict." U.N. SCOR, 2951st mtg. at 32, U.N. Doc. S/PV.2951 (Oct. 29, 1990).

72. *Jus ad Bellum*, Ethiopia's Claims 1–8 (Eth. v. Eri.), Partial Award, ¶ 5 (Eri. Eth. Claims Comm'n, Dec. 19, 2005).

73. Christine Gray, *The Ethiopia/Eritrea Claims Commission Oversteps Its Boundaries: A Partial Award?*, 17 Eur. J. Int'l L. 704 (2006); Gro Nystuen & Ketjil Tronvoll, *The Eritrean-Ethiopian Peace Agreement: Exploring the Limits of Law*, 26 Nordic J. Hum. Rts. 31 (2008); Christian Ponti, *The Eritrea-Ethiopia Claims Commission on the Threat of Use of Force and Individual Self-Defence*, *in* The 1998–2000 War Between Eritrea and Ethiopia, *supra* note 28, at 267, 269.

74. Eichhorst, *supra* note 25, at 112–14.

75. Schwager, *supra* note 32, at 118; d'Argent, *supra* note 46, at 449–61; Eichhorn, *supra* note 27, at 189; Gattini, *supra* note 18, at 162; G.A. Res. 3314 (XXIX), annex art. 5(2) (Dec. 14, 1974); G.A. Res. 42/22, annex art. 1 (Nov. 18, 1987).

76. In the *Nicaragua* case, the Court had already found the United States to be liable to pay compensation to Nicaragua for its unlawful use of force before Nicaragua withdrew its compensation claims. Military and Paramilitary Activities in and Against Nicaragua (Nicar. v. U.S.), Judgment, 1986 I.C.J. Rep. 14, ¶ 184 (June 27); Military and Paramilitary Activities in and Against Nicaragua (Nicar. v. U.S.), Order, 1991 I.C.J. Rep. 48 (Sept. 26). In addition, the ICJ determined in its Advisory Opinion on the *Legal Consequences of the Construction of a Wall in the Occupied Palestinian Territory* that Israel breached various international obligations, including the prohibition of the acquisition of territory by the use of force, which gave rise to its responsibility including the duty to pay damages. Legal Consequences of the Construction of a Wall in the Occupied Palestinian Territory, Advisory Opinion, 2004 I.C.J. Rep. 136, ¶¶ 115, 117, 142, 143, 152 (July 9). Lastly, in its judgment concerning *Armed Activities on the Territory of the Congo* (*Armed Activities Case*), the ICJ concluded that Uganda violated the prohibition of the use of force as laid down in Article 2(4) of the U.N. Charter by invading the DRC and as a

III. THE PRINCIPLE OF FULL REPARATION

In its *Chorzów Factory* judgment, the PCIJ identified a second fundamental principle on the law of state responsibility: the duty to make full reparation. As the Court stated, "The essential principle contained in the actual notion of an illegal act . . . is that reparation must, as far as possible, wipe out all the consequences of the illegal act and re-establish the situation which would, in all probability, have existed if that act had not been committed."[77] This "essential principle" found its way into Article 31 of the ILC Draft Articles: "The responsible State is under an obligation to make full reparation for the injury caused by the internationally wrongful act."

This principle of full reparation is one of the fundamental principles of state responsibility and works twofold as a limiting factor. On the one hand, it embodies the minimum level of compensation due because only complete reparation of the damages caused can wipe out the consequences of an internationally wrongful act, as envisioned by the PCIJ in its *Chorzów Factory* judgment.[78] On the other hand, it defines the maximum level of reparations to be granted to a victim state.[79]

However, in none of the four cases, in which wide-ranging reparations programs have been established after an armed conflict, has full reparation of the damages and injuries caused by the unlawful use of force been made. Even though the reparations program initiated by the Treaty of Versailles after the First World War has been described as draconian by the German public and been used as an agitating tool by the Nazis in the 1930s,[80] the very provisions of the treaty did not provide for full reparation of the damages caused. While the already mentioned Article 231 demanded German responsibility for "all the loss and damage to which the Allied and Associated Governments and their nationals have been subjected," the following Article 232 limited Germany's obligation to pay reparations to "all damage done to the civilian population as well as damage as defined in annex 1 to the treaty." In doing so, the Allied and Associated governments explicitly acknowledged that Germany's resources were not adequate to make full reparation.[81]

consequence was obligated to make reparation. Armed Activities on the Territory of the Congo (Dem. Rep. Congo v. Uganda), Judgment, 2005 I.C.J. Rep. 168, ¶ 259 (Dec. 19). As the DRC did not bring forward specific reparation claims, the court authorized the parties to negotiate the nature, form, and amount in which Uganda should make reparation but reserved its right to decide on Uganda's reparation obligation in case the parties could not come to an agreement. *Id.* ¶¶ 260, 345.

77. Factory at Chorzów (Claim for Indemnity) (Merits) (Ger. v. Pol.), Merits, 1928 P.C.I.J. (ser. A) No. 17, at 47 (Sept. 13).

78. Stephan Wittich, *Compensation*, *in* 2 Max Planck Encyclopedia of Public International Law, *supra* note 30, at 499, ¶ 16, at 501.

79. *Id.*

80. Jörg Fisch, Reparationen nach dem Zweiten Weltkrieg 28 (1992).

81. 2 A History of the Peace Conference of Paris, *supra* note 63, at 74.

After the Second World War, various actors asserted that they would not demand full compensation for the damages caused from the former Axis Powers. With regard to the German reparations obligation, the Yalta Protocol as well as the Potsdam Declaration only demanded German reparations "to the greatest extent possible."[82] Furthermore, the Peace Treaty of San Francisco explicitly acknowledged in the already cited Article 14A that Japan was not able to make complete reparation. In conformity with this practice, the UNCC's Governing Council limited Iraq's duty to pay compensation mainly to civilian damages.[83] And lastly, the EECC explicitly acknowledged in its final decision that the assigned compensation sums do not reflect full reparation of the damages caused.[84]

In short, as diverse as these conflicts are, there is one overarching theme which stands in stark contrast to one of the fundamental principles of state responsibility: even though the prohibition of the use of force in international relations is one of the central norms of modern international law, the violation of this norm did not lead to the implementation of the principle of full reparation. Instead, two main factors were used to moderate the aggressor state's liability: the severity of its wrongdoing and its economic capabilities.

A. The Gravity of Wrongdoing as a Limiting Factor

In the aforementioned reparations programs, one factor which was repeatedly considered in determining the aggressor state's scope of liability was the severity of its wrongdoing.

1. The Practice of Considering the Severity of the Aggressor's Wrongdoing

After the First World War, the Entente agreed on a special reparations regime to the benefit of Belgium, which was stipulated in Article 232 of the Treaty of Versailles. In contrast to the other members of the Entente, which were limited to reparations for damages of their civilian population according to Article 232 as

82. d'Argent, *supra* note 46, at 133.

83. Governing Council, U.N. Compensation Comm'n, Eligibility for Compensation of Members of the Allied Coalition Armed Forces (Decision No. 11), U.N. Doc. S/AC.26/1992/11 (June 26, 1992). According to this decision, only members of the allied coalition who had been taken as prisoners of war and suffered injuries caused by a violation of international humanitarian law could claim compensation before the UNCC. In addition, the Governing Council stipulated in its decision No. 19 that the costs of the allied coalition forces, including those of military operations against Iraq, were not eligible for compensation. *See* Governing Council, U.N. Compensation Comm'n, Military Costs (Decision No. 19), U.N. Doc. S/AC.26/Dec.19 (Mar. 24, 1994).

84. Eritrea's Damages Claim (Eth. v. Eri.), Final Award, ¶ 2 (Eri. Eth. Claims Comm'n Aug. 17, 2009). For a text of the decision, *see* Litigation War, *supra* note 15, at 567–660.

well as damages as enlisted in Annex I, Belgium was entitled to complete reparation, including its war costs:

> In accordance with Germany's pledges, already given, as to complete restoration for Belgium, Germany undertakes, in addition to the compensation for damage elsewhere in this Part provided for, as a consequence of the violation of the Treaty of 1839, to make reimbursement of all sums which Belgium has borrowed from the Allied and Associated Governments up to November 11, 1918, together with interest at the rate of five per cent (5%) per annum on such sums.[85]

To understand the background of this "Belgian exception," it requires a closer look at the negotiations in Paris. While there was a substantial disagreement whether Germany had violated norms of international law by resorting to armed force, there was a consensus among the delegates, notably including the German representatives, that Germany had violated international law by invading Belgium.[86] In 1839, the Concert of Europe, which Germany was part of, and the Kingdom of Belgium signed a treaty in London, which guaranteed the independence and neutrality of Belgium. Nevertheless, having declared war on France on August 3, 1914, the so-called "Schlieffen-Plan" was put into action by the German military leadership. According to this plan, German forces advanced through Belgium to force a battle with the French troops on France's northern border,[87] a strategic move which intentionally violated Belgium's neutrality which was guaranteed by the Treaty of London. This treaty violation was the legal basis for the Belgian reparation clause in Article 232(3) of the Treaty of Versailles,[88] which granted Belgium a wider scope of reparations than any other nation even though a substantial fraction of the Allied delegates in Paris, especially the French representatives, vehemently demanded complete compensation of their war costs as well.[89] In providing a special reparations regime for Belgium, the Entente seems to have appraised the German aggression against Belgium under violation of Belgium's neutrality as a more severe wrongdoing than Germany's aggression against the other nations. Completing this train of thought, the scope of the German reparations obligation—at least in part—corresponded with the perceived gravity of its wrongdoing according to the Versailles reparations scheme.[90]

A similar observation can be made in relation to the other reparations programs. After the Second World War, reparations were not only extracted from Germany

85. Treaty of Versailles, *supra* note 44, art. 232.

86. D'ARGENT, *supra* note 46, at 75, 80.

87. MICHAEL HOWARD, FIRST WORLD WAR: A VERY SHORT INTRODUCTION 26 (2007).

88. D'ARGENT, *supra* note 46, at 49.

89. SHARP, *supra* note 63, at 79; MARC TRACHTENBERG, REPARATION IN WORLD POLITICS—FRANCE AND EUROPEAN ECONOMIC DIPLOMACY 1916–1923, at 43 (1980).

90. EICHHORN, *supra* note 27, at 110.

and Japan but from the other European Axis Powers as well. Having established in the preambles of the Paris Peace Treaties that the European Axis Powers bore their share of responsibility for participating in the war, the treaties expressly recognized their later withdrawal. In this context, Article 22 of the Romanian Peace Treaty, which is representative of similar provisions in the other treaties, stated:

> [T]aking into consideration that Romania has not only withdrawn from the war against the United Nations, but has declared and, in fact, waged war against Germany, it is agreed that compensation for the above losses will be made by Romania not in full but only in part. . . .[91]

According to this provision, the reduction of Romania's reparations obligation was directly linked to its withdrawal from the war. The exact wording of this provision goes further than a mere stating of Romania's responsibility for damages caused by its (limited) participation in the war. Instead, from the assertion that Romania "has declared and, in fact, waged war against Germany" it is evident that the scope of Romania's liability is directly linked to the assessment of the severity of its wrongdoing,[92] a practice which found its precedent in the determination of the scope of German reparations owed to Belgium after the First World War.

Taking a leap into the new millennium, the gravity of Eritrea's violation of the prohibition of the use of force was one of the main points discussed by the EECC in determining Eritrea's scope of liability. In its *Partial Award on the Jus ad Bellum* issued on December 19, 2005, the Commission determined that Eritrea violated the prohibition of the use of force, as laid down in Article 2(4) of the U.N. Charter, by invading the town of Badme in May 1998:

> [T]he Commission holds that Eritrea violated Article 2, paragraph 4, of the Charter of the United Nations by resorting to armed force to attack and occupy Badme, then under peaceful administration by Ethiopia, as well as other territory in the Tahtay Adiabo and Laelay Adiabo Weredas of Ethiopia, in an attack that began on May 12, 1998. . . . [O]nce the armed attack in the Badme area occurred and Ethiopia decided to act in self-defense, a war resulted that proved impossible to restrict to the areas where that initial attack was made.[93]

In a further decision, in which the Commission outlined the basic guidelines for assessing the scope of Eritrea's liability for this unlawful use of force,[94] it made

91. Treaty of Peace with Romania *supra* note 48, art. 22(1).

92. Eichhorn, *supra* note 27, at 110–11.

93. Ethiopia's Damages Claims (Eth. v. Eri.), Final Award, ¶¶ 16, 19 (Eri. Eth. Claims Comm'n Aug. 17, 2009).

94. Guidance Regarding *Jus ad Bellum* Liability (Decision No. 7) (Eri. Eth. Claims Comm'n July 27, 2007). For a text of the decision, *see* Litigation War, *supra* note 15, at 436–44.

great efforts to differentiate its characterization of Eritrea's unlawful use of force from the preceding violations of the *jus ad bellum* which led to wide ranging reparations programs: "The Commission does not regard its *jus ad bellum* finding as a finding that Eritrea initiated an aggressive war for which it bears the extensive financial responsibility claimed by Ethiopia. At the same time, it does not accept Eritrea's argument that there is no financial responsibility."[95]

It further elaborated:

> It [the Commission] made a specific finding regarding that violation that did not include a finding that Eritrea had waged an aggressive war, had occupied large parts of Ethiopia, or otherwise engaged in the sort of widespread lawlessness that the Security Council identified in the case of the invasion and occupation of Kuwait.[96]

Apparently, the EECC identified two distinct concepts of armed force in the context of reparations: an "armed attack," which later develops into a full-grown war, and an "aggressive war," which has a higher threshold.[97] Even though the Commission did not succeed in systematically deducing and developing this differentiation, which has led to substantial criticism,[98] there are two main conclusions which can be drawn from this decision. First, even though the commissioners emphasized that the Eritrean use of force did not reach the threshold of an "aggressive war," Eritrea was obligated to make reparation for the damages caused to Ethiopia under international law. Second, the intensity of Eritrea's use of force was a factor to be considered in determining the scope of Eritrea's liability, a factor which had already been recognized in the aforementioned decisions after the First and the Second World Wars. The commissioners continued this line of reasoning in their final decision determining Eritrea's scope of liability:

> In a similar vein, the Commission believes that the law of State responsibility must maintain a measure of proportion between the character of a delict and the compensation due. Ethiopia strongly urged this principle in a different setting, in claiming huge moral damages, on the ground that Eritrea had committed egregious delicts meriting massive additional compensation. Eritrea's violation of the *jus ad bellum* in May 1998 as found by the Commission was serious, and had serious consequences. Nevertheless, that violation was different

95. *Id.* ¶ 5.

96. *Id.* ¶ 32.

97. Claus Kreß, *The State Conduct Element*, *in* 1 The Crime of Aggression, *supra* note 64, at 521; Vaios Koutroulis, *The Prohibition of the Use of Force in Arbitrations and Fact-Finding Reports*, *in* The Oxford Handbook of the Use of Force in International Law 618 (Marc Weller ed., 2015). For a similar appraisal, *see* Castagnetti, *supra* note 28, at 286.

98. Dinstein, *supra* note 17, ¶ 547; Litigation War, *supra* note 15, at 118.

> in magnitude and character from the aggressive uses of force marking the onset of the Second World War, the invasion of South Korea in 1950, or Iraq's 1990 invasion and occupation of Kuwait. The Commission believes that determination of compensation must take such factors into account.[99]

The wording of the paragraph remains ambiguous as to whether the commissioners believed that the current law of state responsibility already provided for the possibility to take a "measure of proportion" into account when determining the amount of compensation due or whether this possibility was required *de lege ferenda*. Hence, it was at times argued that these deliberations were of a mere factual nature and the result of evidentiary problems as well as time constraints the EECC faced and therefore could only be considered sui generis.[100]

However, appraising the EECC's remarks as sui generis completely disregards that the correlation between the gravity of the *jus ad bellum* violation and the scope of the responsible state's liability can be traced back to the First and the Second World Wars. In addition, this interpretation of the commissioners' findings does not take into account that they in fact made an explicit reference to the law of state responsibility, while they based other considerations on limited resources or evidentiary challenges. Indeed, with regard to the determination of adequate compensation, the Commission explicitly stated at another point of their decision, "[T]his Commission did not—nor could it—alter the international rules defining the extent of compensable damages that follow from the breach of international law. . . ."[101]

This statement in connection with the considerations above strongly suggests that the Commission referred to the concept of proportionality from a legal standpoint. However, there is no provision in the law of state responsibility, as envisioned by the ILC Draft Articles, to consider the gravity of the responsible state's wrongdoing in assessing the amount of compensation due.

2. The Law of State Responsibility on Considering the Severity of Wrongdoing

As already mentioned, the principle of full reparation is one of the main pillars of the current law of state responsibility. As a consequence, the ILC Draft Articles do not contain a provision that provides for taking account of the character of the violated primary obligation and the gravity of the wrongdoing when assessing the responsible state's reparations obligation. However, during the decades of negotiations within the ILC, the gravity of a state's wrongdoing has actually been

99. Ethiopia's Damages Claims (Eth. v. Eri.), Final Award, ¶ 312 (Eri. Eth. Claims Comm'n Aug. 17, 2009).

100. Romesh Weeramantry, *Eritrea's Damages Claims (Eritrea v. Ethiopia)*, 104 Am. J. Int'l L. 486 (2010).

101. Guidance Regarding *Jus ad Bellum* Liability (Decision No. 7), ¶ 32 (Eri. Eth. Claims Comm'n July 27, 2007).

discussed as a factor in determining the reparations obligation, just from a different point of view: the imposition of punitive damages.

In developing the ILC Draft Articles, there have been varying viewpoints with regard to the imposition of punitive damages.[102] According to Article 45(2) of the 1996 draft, it would have been possible to impose reparations exceeding the compensation of the damages caused under the umbrella of satisfaction: "Satisfaction may take the form of one or more of the following: . . . (c) In cases of gross infringement of the rights of the injured State, damages reflecting the gravity of the infringement."[103]

While it remained disputed whether this provision could be construed as an endorsement of the concept of punitive damages,[104] the 2000 draft explicitly conceptualized this possibility as a consequence flowing from a serious violation of a primary obligation arising under peremptory norms: "A serious breach within the meaning of article 41 may involve, for the responsible State, damages reflecting the gravity of the breach."[105]

However, this provision was met with widespread rejection[106] and as a consequence was not included in the final draft in 2001. Instead, the commentary to the ILC Draft Articles now explicitly states that "[compensation] is not concerned to punish the responsible State, nor does compensation have an expressive or exemplary character. . . . The award of punitive damages is not recognized in international law even in relation to serious breaches of obligations arising under peremptory norms."[107]

Accordingly, there is no provision in the current law of state responsibility to consider the gravity of the infringement as a form of punitive damage.[108] In this respect, there is no friction between the law of state responsibility and the practice with regard to *jus ad bellum* reparations, as there is no discernable practice of punitive damages, arguably in contrast to a widespread public misconception.[109] However, this express rejection of punitive damages still leaves open the question

102. Christian Tams, *Do Serious Breaches Give Rise to Any Specific Obligations of the Responsible State?*, 13 Eur. J. Int'l L. 1161 (2002).

103. Int'l L. Comm'n, Text of the Draft Articles Provisionally Adopted by the Commission on First Reading, art. 45(2)(c), *reprinted in* [1996] 2 (pt. 2) Y.B. Int'l L. Comm'n 63 (1996).

104. *Id.* art. 52, cmt. 8. For the reception of this provision in legal scholarship, *see* Tams, *supra* note 102, at 1166 n.23.

105. Int'l L. Comm'n, Draft Articles Provisionally Adopted by the Drafting Committee on Second Reading, art. 42(1), *reprinted in* [2000] 2 (pt. 2) Y.B. Int'l L. Comm'n 69 (2000).

106. For an appraisal with further references, *see* Tams, *supra* note 102, at 1169 nn.43–44.

107. Draft Articles, *supra* note 20, art. 36, cmt. 4; *id.* ch. III, pt. 2, cmt. 5.

108. Tams, *supra* note 102, at 1170.

109. *See* Friedrich Rosenfeld, *Individual Civil Responsibility for the Crime of Aggression*, 10 J. Int'l Crim. Just. 259 (2012).

of whether the character and gravity of the internationally wrongful act could be employed as a limiting factor in determining the amount of compensation under the law of state responsibility. As the EECC has already identified, a legal concept which embodies the outlined considerations in determining the aggressor state's scope of liability is the concept of proportionality. More precisely, it is possible to encapsulate the identifiable state practice in a rule stating that the full compensation of the damages caused by the unlawful use of force must not be disproportionate to the gravity of the *jus ad bellum* violation. Even though conceptualizing the proportionality between the gravity of the wrongdoing and the scope of liability in this way would not imply an acknowledgment of the concept of punitive damages, the inclusion of this principle in the ILC Draft Articles has been rejected.[110] Specifically with regard to monetary compensation according to Article 34, it has been argued that all questions of proportionality have been sufficiently addressed by limiting the responsible state's obligation to pay compensation to damages causally linked to its wrongdoing.[111]

In conclusion, there is no possibility in the current law of state responsibility to take the proportionality of damages into account when assessing the responsible state's scope of liability. And even though the analysis of the relevant state practice has shown the repeated limitation of the aggressor state's liability in correlation to the gravity of its infringement, there is no sufficient *opinio juris* to discern the crystallization of a rule of customary international law diverging from the law of state responsibility. Only the EECC conceptualized this relation within the principle of proportionality. However, the commissioners misguidedly derived this principle from the law of state responsibility.[112] Moreover, there is no indication that any of the actors after the First or the Second World War engaged in legal considerations when limiting the aggressor states' liability, even though Wladyslaw Czaplinski stated matter of factly in his analysis of the reparation system after the Second World War, "Another point that also has to be considered is the principle of proportionality: an offender cannot be required to pay for all the consequences of an illegal act if indemnity would be excessively disproportionate to the offence."[113]

All in all, in the aftermath of armed conflicts there is a recurring practice of considering the proportionality between the aggressor state's wrongdoing and the amount of compensation being awarded. This development has not led to any increased attention in legal scholarship although this practice runs counter to the principle of full reparation, a fundamental pillar of the law of state responsibility from its very beginning. It was only when the EECC first tried to frame this decades-old practice as a legal concept that criticism was raised.

110. Draft Articles, *supra* note 20, art. 34, cmt. 5.

111. *Id.*

112. Ethiopia's Damages Claims (Eth. v. Eri.), Final Award, ¶ 308 (Eri. Eth. Claims Comm'n Aug. 17, 2009).

113. Wladyslaw Czaplinski, *Concept of War Reparations in International Law and Reparations after World War II*, 14 Pol. Q. Int'l Aff. 70 (2005).

B. The Economic Capacity of the Aggressor State as a Limiting Factor

Apart from considering the gravity of the aggressor state's wrongdoing, a second factor has been repeatedly used in practice to limit the aggressor state's liability: its economic capacity to pay reparations.

1. The Practice of Considering the Aggressor State's Economic Capacity

After the First World War, Article 232 of the Treaty of Versailles expressly raised Germany's limited economic capacity as a reason to reduce its reparations obligation:[114] "The Allied and Associated Governments recognise that the resources of Germany are not adequate, after taking into account permanent diminutions of such resources which will result from other provisions of the present Treaty, to make complete reparation for all such loss and damage."[115]

Despite its central meaning in the Versailles reparations regime, at no point during the Paris peace negotiations did the delegates define their understanding of economic capacity.[116] Interestingly, this was one of the main reasons why the Entente did not impose a fixed reparations sum on Germany as it had been done in previous peace treaties. At the beginning of the negotiations, it was the Entente's initial goal to agree on a fixed sum which would take Germany's economic capacity into account and which should be distributed among the allies according to a yet-to-be-agreed allocation formula.[117] Especially the American delegation favored this approach, as it would have guaranteed a fast processing of the reparations question.[118] However, this approach would have forced the Allies to agree at a very early stage of the negotiation process on a sum acceptable to their respective populations at home as well as the German government, an endeavor which failed as even the Allies among themselves could not come to an agreement.[119] Instead, the Allies decided to delegate the determination of the reparation sum to the allied Reparation Commission. According to the treaty provisions, this Commission was not authorized to consider Germany's limited economic capacity in determining the final reparations sum, as the Entente considered it to be sufficiently addressed by the limitations in Article 232.[120] In retrospect, it is hardly

114. 2 A History of the Peace Conference of Paris, *supra* note 63, at 74.

115. Treaty of Versailles, *supra* note 44, art. 232.

116. Trachtenberg, *supra* note 89, at 72–84.

117. Sharp, *supra* note 63, at 87–93.

118. Baruch, *supra* note 63, at 51, 69.

119. *Id.* at 47.

120. 2 A History of the Peace Conference of Paris, *supra* note 63, at 79; Trachtenberg, *supra* note 89, at 71.

possible to make a definite assessment of the final reparations sum of 132 billion Goldmark, which the Reparation Commission determined in April 1921, as the Commission did not publish any sound reasoning.[121] However, even if the letter of the treaty evidences no will to burden Germany with reparations beyond its economic capacity, and even though Germany in fact only paid a fraction of the sum, the Versailles reparations system is nonetheless oftentimes equated with the draconian punishment of the German people through the extraction of excessive reparations, which disrupted the global economy and contributed to the decay of the Weimar Republic.[122]

In light of this history, it is no surprise that the economic effects of reparation demands took a central role in the considerations after the Second World War. As a consequence, there was no prominent claim for complete reparation as a legal principle. Instead, the Allies agreed to merely claim German reparations "to the greatest extent possible"[123] from the very beginning. In contrast to the representatives in Versailles, the acting stakeholders put great effort into defining the responsible state's economic capability and made these assessments the basis of their reparation policy. In this sense, the Potsdam Agreement stated prominently:

> Payment of reparations should leave enough resources to enable the German people to subsist without external assistance. In working out the economic balance of Germany, the necessary means must be provided to pay for imports approved by the Control Council in Germany. The proceeds of exports from current production and stock shall be available in the first place for payment for such imports.[124]

The connection between the economic capability and the limitation of reparations claims is expressly stipulated in the already mentioned Article 14(a) of the Treaty of San Francisco:

> It is recognized that Japan should pay reparations to the Allied Powers for the damage and suffering caused by it during the war. Nevertheless it is also recognized that the resources of Japan are not presently sufficient, if it is to maintain a viable economy, to make complete reparation for all such damage and suffering and at the same time meet its other obligations.[125]

121. 2 A History of the Peace Conference of Paris, *supra* note 63, at 78.

122. Gabriella Blum, *The Crime and Punishment of States*, 38 Yale J. Int'l L. 88 (2013); Fisch, *supra* note 80, at 28. This assessment of the Versailles reparations regime is still prevalent in German society today despite the fact that Germany did only pay a fraction of the determined reparation sum. For an assessment, *see* Garmise, *supra* note 44, at 859.

123. d'Argent, *supra* note 46, at 133.

124. Dolzer, *supra* note 55, at 315; Eichhorn, *supra* note 27, at 119.

125. Treaty of Peace with Japan, *supra* note 53, art. 14(a).

From the systematic structure of both sentences, it is evident that the signatory states in a first step recognized the right to claim complete reparation for the damages caused which was in a second step waived due to Japan's limited economic capacity. The British delegate, Kenneth Younger, elaborated on this point by stating that the demand for complete reparation would be a "short sighted policy" which would lay the basis for lasting resentment between Japan and the Allies.[126] There is no indication, however, that the Allies based the limitation of their reparation demands on legal considerations. In this sense, Pierre d'Argent concluded his analysis of the reparations system after the Second World War with the following statement: "It is a truism that total war can only result in partial reparations. The World War II reparations do not contradict this elementary truth."[127]

The practice of considering the aggressor's economic capacity in determining adequate reparations can also be identified in the work of the UNCC. This is despite the fact that Iraq had significant financial capabilities immediately after the fighting came to an end due to its enormous wealth in natural resources, especially oil. The latter constitutes a unique set of circumstances in the aftermath of an armed conflict which the U.N. Security Council capitalized on by establishing the U.N. Compensation Fund pursuant to Resolution 692 in 1991.[128] This fund, which was mainly supplied with proceeds generated by the export sales of Iraqi petroleum and petroleum products, was set up to pay out compensation to successful claimants. In determining the percentage of oil proceeds to be allocated to the fund, the U.N. Security Council and U.N. Secretary-General took care to ensure that Iraq had adequate means to pay for imports and debt service despite its reparations obligations.[129]

And lastly, the EECC explicitly acknowledged Eritrea's and—to a lesser degree—Ethiopia's disastrous financial and economic situation after the cessation of hostilities in determining their reparations obligations: "In assessing both Parties' damages claims, the Commission has been mindful of the harsh fact that these countries are among the poorest on earth."[130]

Determining the amount of compensation Eritrea had to pay for violating the prohibition of the use of force and other rules of international law, the Commission elaborated on this point by stating, "The Commission also considered whether an award of compensation should be limited as necessary to ensure that the financial burden imposed on Eritrea would not be so excessive, given Eritrea's economic

126. Ito, *supra* note 51, at 42.

127. d'Argent, *supra* note 52, ¶ 35, at 894.

128. S.C. Res. 692, ¶ 3 (May 20, 1991).

129. Report of the Secretary-General Pursuant to Paragraph 10 of Security Council Resolution 687, U.N. Doc. S/22559 (May 2, 1991).

130. Ethiopia's Damages Claims (Eth. v. Eri.), Final Award, ¶ 18 (Eri. Eth. Claims Comm'n Aug. 17, 2009).

condition and its capacity to pay, as seriously to damage Eritrea's ability to meet its people's basic needs."[131]

In this paragraph, the Commission recognized Eritrea's economic situation by explicitly linking its reparations obligation toward Ethiopia to its human rights obligations toward its own population. For the first time, the EECC thereby undertook to find a legal basis for limiting the responsible state's reparations obligation with regard to its financial capability. In this instance, the EECC explicitly referred to the Common Articles 1(2) of the International Covenant on Civil and Political Rights (ICCPR)[132] and the International Covenant on Economic, Social, and Cultural Rights (ICESCR),[133] which require that "[i]n no case may a people be deprived of its own means of subsistence."

As will be discussed in the next subsection in more detail, the Commission was well aware that the law of state responsibility does not recognize the responsible state's human rights obligations as a factor in determining the amount of compensation owed.[134] Nevertheless, the commissioners saw their reasoning as a continuation of a line of state practice identifiable since the First World War of taking the need of the civilian population into account when determining the scope of reparations: "[T]he prevailing practice of States in the years since the Treaty of Versailles has been to give very significant weight to the needs of the affected population in determining amounts sought as post-war reparations."[135]

According to the EECC's assessment, this practice has led to the continuous acceptance of reparations programs which awarded compensation for far less than the totality of damages caused by the unlawful use of force.[136] But despite the identification of this long-standing practice, the commissioners did not elaborate further on the legal reasoning behind this practice.

2. The Law of State Responsibility on Considering Economic Factors

The EECC's reluctance to outline its legal reasoning apart from the referral to human rights obligations for taking Eritrea's financial capabilities into account might have one simple reason: there is no legal basis in the current law of state responsibility for considering the responsible state's economic capabilities.

131. *Id.* ¶ 313.

132. International Covenant on Civil and Political Rights art. 1(2), *opened for signature* Dec. 19, 1966, 999 U.N.T.S. 171.

133. International Covenant on Economic, Social and Cultural Rights art. 1(2), *opened for signature* Dec. 19, 1966, 993 U.N.T.S. 3.

134. Ethiopia's Damages Claims (Eth. v. Eri.), Final Award, ¶¶ 19, 22 (Eri. Eth. Claims Comm'n Aug. 17, 2009).

135. *Id.* ¶ 21.

136. *Id.* ¶ 314.

In its 1996 Draft Articles, the ILC included the following provision: "In no case [shall] reparation result in depriving the population of a State of its own means of subsistence."[137]

However, this article, which uses nearly identical wording as the Common Articles 1(2) of the ICCPR and ICESCR, was controversial from the very beginning and was not adopted in the final draft. The main point of criticism was that this provision did not adequately recognize the situation of the victim state's population, which could also be severely disadvantaged without adequate compensation.[138] At times, it has been argued that the noncompliance with a reparation obligation due to limited financial capabilities could be recognized as a circumstance precluding wrongfulness according to chapter five of the final ILC Draft Articles. In this case, the aggressor state's reparation obligation would accrue in full, but its noncompliance would be excused upon invocation of a circumstance precluding wrongfulness, namely, necessity according to Article 25.[139]

According to this article, necessity can be invoked if (a) it is the only way to safeguard an essential interest against a grave and imminent peril, and (b) it does not seriously impair an essential interest of the state or states toward which the obligation exists or of the international community as a whole. Irrespective of the contested question whether the concept of necessity can generally be applied to reparations obligations,[140] it does not cover the identified state practice with regard to reparations for an unlawful use of force.

It can be assumed that a reparations obligation exceeding the aggressor state's financial capabilities does indeed impair its means of subsistence and its capability to fulfill its human rights obligations toward its own population, which can be considered an essential interest according to Article 25.[141] In addition, one can make the sound argument that the provision in Article 25(2), which precludes the invocation of necessity if the responsible state contributed to the situation, cannot be applied in situations in which the responsible state would be forced to disregard its human rights obligations.[142]

However, this provision, which has been created as a limited exception to the general rules of state responsibility, must be construed in a narrow sense and

137. Int'l L. Comm'n, *supra* note 103, art. 42(3).

138. *See* Draft Articles, *supra* note 20, art. 42(3), cmt. 8(b).

139. *See id.* art. 27, cmt. 2.

140. For an elaboration on this point, *see* Mathias Forteau, *Reparation in the Event of a Circumstance Precluding Wrongfulness*, *in* The Law of International Responsibility, *supra* note 29, at 879.

141. Sarah Heathcote, *Circumstances Precluding Wrongfulness in the ILC Articles on State Responsibility*, *in* The Law of International Responsibility, *supra* note 29, at 496.

142. Matthias Herdegen, Völkerrecht 468 (17th ed. 2018).

cannot be invoked if essential interests of the victim state are at stake.[143] This will, however, regularly be the case with reparations after armed conflicts as most of the time both sides—the aggressor state and the victim state—have been subjected to vast devastation. Consequently, noncompliance with the reparations obligation would normally impair the victim state's ability to fulfill its own human rights obligations toward its population, which precludes the invocation of necessity under the current law of state responsibility.

An extensive balancing of interests is not possible according to the wording of Article 25(1)(b) and would contradict the rationale of necessity as an exceptional provision.[144] Nevertheless, it is exactly this balancing of interests which the Entente did in Versailles in limiting Germany's reparation obligation to damages of the civilian population; that the Allies had in mind while taking pains to guarantee not to obligate Germany or Japan beyond their capabilities after the Second World War; that the U.N. Security Council recognized while determining Iraq's contributions to the U.N. Compensation Fund; and that the EECC acknowledged in their reasoning for considering the economic realities. Without putting a name to it, there is a long-established practice of considering the proportionality between the award of reparations for an unlawful use of force and the economic and financial impact it has on the aggressor state and its people, a concept which is alien to the law of state responsibility.

Despite the existing practice, a corresponding rule of customary international law has not emerged yet, as only the commissioners of the EECC employed legal considerations and even they did not identify this practice as a manifestation of the principle of proportionality. The decisions of the actors after the other conflicts, based on factual and economic considerations, cannot be characterized as the expression of an *opinio juris*.[145]

C. Interim Conclusion

The analysis of state practice with regard to reparations for an unlawful use of force leads to the following interim result: A rule of customary international law which deviates from the principle of full compensation as enshrined in the law on state responsibility has not crystallized, neither with regard to considering the aggressor state's economic capability nor with regard to considering the gravity of its wrongdoing in resorting to armed force. Still, it is notable that both concepts, which have emerged as a recurring practice in reparations programs after armed conflicts, can systematically be subsumed under the principle of proportionality. However, exactly this principle is alien to the system of state responsibility. This

143. *See* Draft Articles, *supra* note 20, art. 25, cmt. 14.

144. *See id.* art. 25, cmt. 17.

145. Int'l L. Comm'n, Second Report on Identification of Customary International Law, *supra* note 31, ¶ 61.

disconnect between state practice and the current law of state responsibility with regard to the proportionality of reparations leaves a legal void which gives reason to analyze whether it can be meaningfully addressed by a *jus post bellum*.[146]

IV. THE *JUS POST BELLUM* PRINCIPLE OF PROPORTIONALITY AS A MITIGATING FACTOR

In its most basic sense, proportionality means balancing different things.[147] In international law, the principle of proportionality can be found in various disciplines, most notably in both branches of international peace and security law, the *jus in bello*[148] as well as the *jus ad bellum*.[149] Therefore, it can only be considered consistent that the principle of proportionality has been prominently taken up in the current discussion about a *jus post bellum* as well.[150] In this context, it is argued that the principle of proportionality can work as a meta-principle[151] or structural principle[152] which can balance and harmonize the various interests and problems in a post-conflict phase. Exactly this conception of post-conflict proportionality is the *jus post bellum* factor that can uniquely contribute to the conceptualization of the aggressor state's reparations obligation.

In view of the practice of taking the gravity of the aggressor state's wrongdoing into account when determining the reparation sum owed for an unlawful resort to force, skeptical voices could argue that there is no significant added value in a *jus post bellum* principle of proportionality. The necessary balancing between the gravity of the *jus ad bellum* violation and the scope of the reparations obligation could be achieved by situating the aggressor's reparations obligation within the existing *jus ad bellum* regime and by developing a principle of proportionality as part of this regime. This would be in line with the current legal situation under

146. For a different opinion, *see* Eric de Brabandere, *The Concept of* Jus Post Bellum *in International Law: A Normative Critique*, *in* JUS POST BELLUM—MAPPING THE NORMATIVE FOUNDATIONS, *supra* note 11, at 134. De Brabandere determines that the ILC Draft Articles contain "sufficient provisions in this regard," without explaining this assessment any further.

147. Anne Peters, *Verhältnismäßigkeit als globales Verfassungsprinzip*, *in* VERHÄLTNISMÄSSIGKEIT IM VÖLKERRECHT 1 (Björnstjern Baade ed. 2016).

148. Emily Crawford, *Proportionality*, *in* 8 MAX PLANCK ENCYCLOPEDIA OF PUBLIC INTERNATIONAL LAW, *supra* note 6, ¶ 19, at 537.

149. Peters, *supra* note 147, at 2–6.

150. For an important exposition, *see* MICHAEL NEWTON & LARRY MAY, PROPORTIONALITY IN INTERNATIONAL LAW 74–78 (2014); James Gallen, Jus Post Bellum*: An Interpretive Framework*, *in* JUS POST BELLUM—MAPPING THE NORMATIVE FOUNDATIONS, *supra* note 11, at 58, 77–79; Dieter Fleck, Jus Post Bellum *as a Partly Independent Legal Framework*, *in* JUS POST BELLUM—MAPPING THE NORMATIVE FOUNDATIONS, *supra* note 11, at 53.

151. NEWTON & MAY, *supra* note 150, at 77.

152. Peters, *supra* note 147, at 13.

the *jus in bello*.[153] However, even if the *jus ad bellum* principle of proportionality is further developed, taking the aggressor state's economic capacity into account would be as alien to the framework of the *jus ad bellum* as it is to the law of state responsibility.

It is exactly at this intersection between the *jus ad bellum* as the source of the primary obligation, the law of state responsibility as the source of the secondary obligation, and the special challenges in a post-conflict society, where the *jus post bellum* principle of proportionality can play a unique role as a meta-principle to assess the adequate amount of reparations while taking the concrete post-conflict situation into account.[154] Following this line of thought, the application of the *jus post bellum* principle of proportionality would allow the decision makers to work within a sufficiently flexible legal framework, to allow them to consider the aggressor state's human rights obligations,[155] to balance them with the obligations and needs of the victim state, and to thereby harmonize the reparations obligation with other post-conflict challenges such as reconciliation or the rebuilding of devastated societies.[156] Furthermore, conceptualizing the aggressor state's economic capacity as a factor to be considered within the principle of proportionality can refute one of the main points of criticism of the current practice: even though the principle of proportionality gives the decision makers the necessary flexibility to address the concrete post-conflict situation, the amount of reparations due for a violation of the *jus ad bellum* would remain legally definable. This is of paramount importance because according to the analysis at the beginning of this chapter, the obligation to make reparation emerges *ipso jure* from a violation of the *jus ad bellum* without any intermediary legal act under the current rules of customary international law. However, this requires the reparations obligation to be sufficiently definable because otherwise it would necessarily require a legal act, for example, a peace treaty, to set the terms for the specific reparations obligation.[157] In addition, future reparations programs, which will almost certainly have to deal with the same challenges as the ones analyzed, will not have to face the

153. *See supra* note 18.

154. Peters, *supra* note 147, at 5–6.

155. Stahn identified the consideration of an aggressor state's human rights obligations as a principle of a *jus post bellum* in his pioneer work. *See* Stahn, *supra* note 10, at 939; *see also* DiMeglio, *supra* note 9, at 143; Brian Orend, *Justice after War*, 16 ETHICS & INT'L AFF. 48 (2002). Even the ILC's special rapporteur recommended the consideration of human rights obligations in implementing state responsibility. *See* Int'l L. Comm'n, Fourth Report on State Responsibility, U.N. Doc. A/CN.4/444, *reprinted in* [1992] 2 (pt. 1) Y.B. INT'L L. COMM'N 1, ¶¶ 78–83, at 30–32 (1992).

156. For an appraisal of the "principle of rebuilding" as a principle of a *jus post bellum*, *see* MAY, *supra* note 9, at 143–80.

157. For an appraisal, *see* EICHHORST, *supra* note 25, at 105.

same—at times harsh—criticism as the EECC did in trying to address these recurring problems in a legal manner.

Nevertheless, one could still argue that a different and less onerous way to address the identified practical challenges might be to develop a principle of proportionality in the law of state responsibility, especially since there have been discussions during the ILC's work about including such a principle with regard to reparations. In the end, both the UNCC and the EECC have identified the aggressor state's reparations obligation as part of the law of state responsibility, where it could be further developed. The systematic analysis of the reparations programs could lead to a differentiation and development of the law of state responsibility, as particularly the work of the UNCC has done in the past.[158] However, as has been outlined, modifications of the reparations obligation based on a principle of proportionality have been rejected because the majority of the ILC's members considered the question of proportionality to be sufficiently addressed by the different forms of reparations.[159] Especially with regard to compensation, it is argued that considerations of proportionality are sufficiently addressed by limiting the responsible state's obligation to damage suffered as a result of the internationally wrongful act and by excluding damage which is indirect or remote—in short, damage with a sufficient causal link to the wrongdoing[160]—an argument which might be valid in most cases of international law violations but not in cases of *jus ad bellum* violations, which typically lead to wide-ranging devastation which can be causally linked to an unlawful resort to force. However, without being explicitly stated, there is a more fundamental underlying reasoning for the ILC's reluctance to articulate a principle of proportionality as an integral part of the obligation to make reparation: the compensatory or remedial function of reparations which is the basic premise of the principle of full reparation. This fundamental function of reparations under the law of state responsibility was explicitly stated as the reason for the initial reluctance, and ultimately rejection, of including the concept of punitive damages: "[T]he function of article 36 is purely compensatory. . . . It is not concerned to punish the responsible State, nor does compensation have an expressive or exemplary character."[161]

Limiting reparations obligations based on a principle of proportionality would in the end only be the other side of the same coin to the imposition of punitive damages. Developing a principle of proportionality in the law of state

158. Int'l L. Comm'n, Third Report on State Responsibility, *reprinted in* [2000] 2 (pt. 1) Y.B. INT'L L. COMM'N 3, ¶ 156, at 49 (2000). In particular, the UNCC's work on compensation for environmental damage and lost profit found its way into the ILC's Draft Articles. *See* Draft Articles, *supra* note 20, art. 36, cmts. 14, 27.

159. *See* Draft Articles, *supra* note 20, art. 34, cmt. 5.

160. *Id.*

161. Int'l L. Comm'n, *supra* note 103, art. 36, cmt. 4.

responsibility would henceforth require the abandonment or at least modification of one of its fundamental principles. In contrast, developing such a principle of proportionality as part of a *jus post bellum* and applying it to the aggressor state's reparations obligation would not pose the same systematic challenge. After all, an additional function of reparations after an armed conflict has crystallized: their peacebuilding function. As has been shown, every reparations regime has addressed the question of reparations in the context of all the different practical needs and challenges specific to the situation after an armed conflict. Again, the EECC was the first body to acknowledge this practice by arguing that the amount of reparations awarded to Ethiopia for Eritrea's unlawful use of force must not endanger the development of a lasting peace between the former warring parties.[162] It is exactly at this point that the EECC referred—even if only in a footnote—to the *jus post bellum* and acknowledged the peacebuilding function of reparations, which can be traced back to state practice since the First World War.[163] This peacebuilding function of reparations, which is unique to the award of reparations in post-conflict situations, not only justifies the deviation from the principle of full reparation but requires a consideration of the political and financial situation of the aggressor state as well as its human rights obligations when determining the extent of reparations in order to advance the formation of a positive peace as outlined in the introduction to this chapter. In short, it demands the application of the *jus post bellum* principle of proportionality.[164]

V. CONCLUSION

The analysis of state practice has shown a practical need for considering the proportionality of reparations for an unlawful resort to force based on their peacebuilding function, which can best be addressed by a *jus post bellum* principle of proportionality. As can be seen from the various reparations regimes, the principle of full reparation, one of the fundamental premises to the law of state responsibility, is still central to every reparations system after an armed conflict.

162. Ethiopia's Damages Claims (Eth. v. Eri.), Final Award, ¶ 315 (Eri. Eth. Claims Comm'n Aug. 17, 2009).

163. *Id.* ¶ 315 n.86.

164. Following this line of argument, serious thought must be given to applying a *jus post bellum* principle of proportionality to reparations for violations of the *jus in bello* as well. Without having analyzed the treaty provisions as well as customary international law pertaining to reparations for *jus in bello* violations, it can be assumed that the outlined challenges, which are unique to the determination of adequate reparations in post-conflict societies, also arise in the context of *jus in bello* violations. In the end, the identified peacebuilding function of post-conflict reparations, which is the basic premise for the required modification of the principle of full reparation, applies to *jus in bello* reparations as well. In addition, not applying the principle of proportionality to *jus in bello* reparations might undermine the desired effect of applying it in the *jus ad bellum* realm and endanger the overarching goal: the formation of a positive and lasting peace.

However, if this principle is disproportionate to the gravity of the breach of law or if it endangers the consolidation of a lasting peace, the aggressor state's liability must be limited by applying the principle of proportionality. The special set of challenges unique to a *post bellum* society can only be adequately addressed by resorting to the *jus post bellum* principle of proportionality. Coming to a full circle with the introduction to this chapter, there is a systemic gap in the current framework of international peace and security law with regard to reparations for the violation of the prohibition of the use of force. This gap can be filled by a *jus post bellum* principle.

To preemptively address a possible (and certainly justified) skepticism about devising a whole new branch of international peace and security law solely based on the findings of this chapter, a nuanced and more careful approach is favored. The current framework of the law of state responsibility provides the possibility to develop *leges speciales* rules determining the legal consequences of an internationally wrongful act. According to Article 55 of the ILC Draft Articles, the rules on state responsibility do not apply as far as a special set of rules addresses the international responsibility of a state. Consequently, a *jus post bellum* principle of proportionality can be developed and applied to the aggressor state's reparations obligation under Article 55 of the ILC Draft Articles without completely reconceptualizing the obligation to pay reparations for an unlawful resort to force in a separate body of law. This approach provides the possibility to base the aggressor state's reparations obligation on the established and accepted rules of state responsibility while at the same time applying *jus post bellum* rules addressing the special circumstances in a post-conflict society.

INDEX

For the benefit of digital users, indexed terms that span two pages (e.g., 52–53) may, on occasion, appear on only one of those pages.